AF805000

Graphics Programming with PHIGS and PHIGS PLUS

About the Cover

The images on the cover were all created from the same PHIGS program. Each time the image was drawn, different PHIGS and PHIGS PLUS features were used to produce more realistic pictures. The images demonstrate depth cuing, hidden surface removal, lighting, and shading. The first three images (smallest first) use basic wireframe, depth cuing, and hidden surface removal. The fourth image combines hidden surface removal with lighting and "flat shading" where each facet gets a single colour. The fifth image combines hidden surface removal with lighting and "smooth shading," where colours are blended (interpolated) across each facet.

Graphics Programming with PHIGS and PHIGS PLUS

Joseph E. Kasper
David Arns

Addison-Wesley Publishing Company, Inc.
Reading, Massachusetts Menlo Park, California New York
Don Mills, Ontario Wokingham, England Amsterdam Bonn Paris Milan
Madrid Sydney Singapore Tokyo Seoul Taipei Mexico City San Juan

The publisher offers discounts on this book when ordered in quantity for special sales. For more information, please contact:

Corporate & Professional Publishing Group
Addison-Wesley Publishing Company
One Jacob Way
Reading, Massachusetts 01867

Library of Congress Cataloging-in-Publication Data

Kasper, Joseph Edward, 1948–
Graphics programming with Phigs and Phigs Plus / Joseph E. Kasper and David Arns.
p. cm.
Includes bibliographical references and index.
ISBN 0-201-56343-6
1. Computer graphics. I. Arns, David. II. Title.
T385.K357 1993
006.6'6—dc20 92-39579
CIP

Copyright © 1993 by Hewlett-Packard Company

All rights reserved. No part of this publication may be reproduced, stored in a retrieval system, or transmitted, in any form, or by any means, electronic, mechanical, photocopying, recording, or otherwise, without the prior consent of the publisher. Printed in the United States of America. Published simultaneously in Canada.

Figures 4-2, 4-3, 7-4, 7-5, 14-1, B-2, and B-3 have been reproduced with permission from ANSI X3.144-1988. Figures 12-1, 18-3, and Table 17-2 have been reproduced with permission from ISO/IEC 9592-4:1992. Appendix D has been adapted with permission from ISO/IEC 9593-4:1991. Copies of these standards may be purchased from the American National Standards Institute at 11 West 42nd Street, New York, N.Y. 10036.

Cover design by Simone R. Payment

ISBN 0-201-56343-6

Text printed on recycled and acid-free paper.

1 2 3 4 5 6 7 8 9 10 MU 96959493
First Printing: March 1993

Contents

Preface

Chapter 1 What is PHIGS?

Chapter 2 An Introduction to PHIGS

Chapter 3 Controlling PHIGS

Chapter 6 Modelling Transformations

Chapter 7 Viewing and Workstation Transformations

Chapter 8 HLHSR

Chapter 9 Using Attributes

Chapter 10 Primitives and Attributes

Chapter 11 Using Text

Chapter 12 Using Colour

Chapter 13 Name Sets and Filters

Chapter 14 Graphical Input

Chapter 15 Front and Back Facet Processing

Chapter 16 Intrinsic Colour and Data Mapping

Chapter 17 Lighting and Shading

Chapter 18 Depth Cueing

Chapter 19 Colour Mapping

Chapter 20 B–Splines

Chapter 23 Extensions

Chapter 24 Using PHIGS with X Windows

Appendix A PHIGS Lists

Appendix B PHIGS Colour Models

Appendix C Sample Programs

Appendix D PHIGS C Binding Data Types

Bibliography

Index

Figures

Tables

Preface

This book is designed to teach you how to use the routines that are included in an international standard software system called PHIGS, with additional functionality defined by an extension to the standard called PHIGS PLUS.

- PHIGS stands for Programmer's Hierarchical Interactive Graphics System.
- PHIGS PLUS stands for PHIGS Plus Lumiere Und Surfaces.

We list the official standards documents later in this preface.

Prerequisites to This Manual

This manual was written with the following assumptions:

- You have access to a PHIGS implementation such as HP-PHIGS, SUNPHIGS, or DEC-PHIGS on a workstation with a UNIX operating system.
- You are at least passingly familiar with your operating system. This includes a knowledge of what files are, how to move around in the directory structure, and how to use a text editor.
- You know either C or FORTRAN 77, and you know how to compile and run a program.

This manual also assumes that you are familiar with basic computer graphics concepts. If this is not the case, there are many excellent books and courses available to provide this information. See the list in the *Bibliography* at the end of the book.

Documentation Conventions

Unless otherwise noted in the text, this manual uses the following typographical conventions:

plain font	The plain font is used for the bulk of the text.
bold text	Boldface words are new terms being introduced.
`computer font`	A constant-width, computer-like font is used for literal, verbatim input or output, including routine names, parameters being used literally, directory names, file names, and program listings.
italics	Italic type is used in book and journal titles and emphasized words.
⟨*italics_in_brackets*⟩	Italic type within angle brackets is used for subroutine parameters being described conceptually.
SMALL CAPITALS	Small capitals are used for PHIGS functional names (e.g., OPEN WORKSTATION).
⋮	Vertical ellipsis points mean that irrelevant parts of a figure or example have been omitted.
. . .	Horizontal ellipsis indicate that irrevelant parts of an example have been omitted.

Note that when enumerated type values are listed for a parameter, they are placed in parentheses with the FORTRAN value listed first. For example:

> To turn clipping on, specify Clip (`PCLIP`, `PIND_CLIP`).

Some Comments about FORTRAN Comments

The FORTRAN examples developed for this book were written on two different operating systems: HP-UX and Apollo Domain. These two operating systems use different conventions for creating inline comments for FORTRAN. Inline comments are those comments delineated somewhere after column 1 by a special character such as an exclamation mark (as in HP-UX) or a left brace (as in Domain). As usual with ANSI-standard comments (denoted by a "`C`" in column 1), the whole line is ignored by the compiler, and thus cannot contain a program statement. The following example shows an ANSI standard comment and an inline comment:

```
C Await event variables
      real      TimeOut          { Timeout value for await event
```

Inline comments are so useful and space-saving that they are used in the example programs in order to avoid doubling the programs' size. Keep in mind, though, that if you plan on porting these examples to your own system, you may have to convert the comments to an appropriate form, convert them to ANSI-standard form, or remove them altogether.

The Standards Documents

This manual was based on the following standards documents. While it is not necessary to have copies of these documents to use PHIGS, we recommend that you obtain the first two since they are the final word on the standard. When we refer in this book to the PHIGS standard, we are referring to the first document. The PHIGS PLUS standard refers to the second.

- *International Standard for Information Processing Systems—Computer Graphics—Programmer's Hierarchical Interactive Graphics System (PHIGS)* American National Standard ISO/IEC 9592–1, X3.144–1988.
- *International Standard for Information Processing Systems—Computer Graphics—Programmer's Hierarchical Interactive Graphics System (PHIGS)*, Part 4 Plus Lumiere und Surfaces, PHIGS PLUS ISO/IEC 9592–4:1992(E).
- *International Standard for Information Systems Computer Graphics—Programmer's Hierarchical Interactive Graphics System (PHIGS) FORTRAN Binding*, ISO/IEC 9593–1:1989(E).

- *International Standard for Information Systems Computer Graphics—Programmer's Hierarchical Interactive Graphics System (PHIGS) C Binding*, ISO/IEC 9593–4:1991(E).

For more information on these documents contact one of the following:

- International Organization for Standardization (Case postale 56, CH–1211 Geneve 20, Switzerland)
- American National Standards Institute (ANSI) (1430 Broadway, New York NY 10018)
- British Standards Institution (BSI) (2 Park Street, London W1A 2BS)

Language Bindings, Fragments, and Pseudo-Code

The PHIGS and PHIGS PLUS standards are written in a language-independent manner. To make PHIGS and PHIGS PLUS usable, there must be a standard for expressing the language-independent features in language-dependent ways. The **language binding** documents perform this function. They provide a language-dependent layer that obeys the particular conventions of that programming language.

As of this writing, the basic PHIGS C and FORTRAN language bindings are fully approved by both ISO and ANSI. All of the basic PHIGS programs in this manual use the final versions of the C and FORTRAN bindings. Most of these programs are available free of charge as described at the beginning of Chapter 2.

We were faced with a dilemma when writing the PHIGS PLUS sections of the book: We wanted to provide real programming examples but the PHIGS PLUS C and FORTRAN bindings were still in review and had not been finalized. We decided to do the following:

- We used program fragments to illustrate PHIGS PLUS features and used the latest version of the C binding (March 1992) for the fragments. We expect that the March 1992 version of the C binding will be very close to the final version.
- For PHIGS PLUS, we decided not to describe the FORTRAN binding at all. We decided that one moving target was enough!

We recommend that you treat the PHIGS PLUS program fragments in this book as **pseudo-code**. They give a good indication of how to use the various features, but you should check your own implementation for the exact syntax.

Appendix D, *C Binding Data Types*, contains all of the C binding data types defined for the basic PHIGS standard. We did not include the PHIGS PLUS data types in that appendix since they are not finalized. However, we define individual PHIGS PLUS data types as they come up in the manual. In all cases we use the March 1992 version of the PHIGS PLUS C binding.

For More Information on PHIGS

For a complete understanding of PHIGS, we recommend that you obtain the following books.

Howard, T., Hewitt, W., Hubbold, R., Wyrwas, K. (1991). *A Practical Introduction to PHIGS and PHIGS PLUS*, Reading MA: Addison-Wesley. Besides providing an overview of PHIGS and PHIGS PLUS, this book has an excellent PHIGS bibliography and glossary.

Gaskins, T. (1992). *PHIGS Programming Manual*, Sebastopol, CA: O'Reilly and Associates. This book is "required reading" if you are programming with the PEX Sample Implementation (PEX-SI). Besides dealing with using PHIGS with the X Window system, the book also covers the features of PHIGS and PHIGS PLUS that are common to all PHIGS implementations.

Kosko, L. (1992). *PHIGS Reference Manual*, Sebastopol, CA: O'Reilly and Associates. This is the companion reference manual for the *PHIGS Programming Manual*. You can use it as an excellent reference for all basic PHIGS routines. The PHIGS PLUS routines use the version of the PHIGS PLUS C binding that was used for PEX-SI.

Acknowledgements

It is with great pleasure that we take this oportunity to thank the people who helped us plan and develop this book. First of all, thanks to thank Tom Gross and Tom Morrissey for helping us develop an outline for the book. Thanks also to Griff Hamlin and Bill Wernsing for their reviews of the early versions of the book and for their advice on the types of programming examples to include. We would also like to thank Linda Cain, Dave Larson, Kent Montgomery, Ken Shrum, and John Waitz for their reviews and for their willingness to leap in and review chapters on a moment's notice.

The three reviewers who had the most influence on this book were Jan Hardenbergh, Jim Michener, and Jane Sczechowski. Besides reviewing many chapters, they were always available for advice and encouragement.

We would also like to thank Anita Reiner, Roz Hoffman, and Kirk Birrell for their support over the last two years. Thanks to Pam Sullivan for taking all of the photos that were used in the book. And thanks to Kristen Cassereau, whose excellent copy edit helped to tie the book together. Thanks to Ted Ricks for being the person to get us involved with the HP Press in the first place. And thanks to Mimi, Seth, Margaret, Kathy, and Matthew for being so patient and supportive during the last two years. Thanks also to Karl Dahlen, Dick Morrison, and Rick Schuetz for their support and advice.

We would also like to thank the following engineers for their help with program examples and for reviewing earlier versions of this book: Terry Crane, Richard Ellis, Jim Hall, Cathy Hevish, Mehrdad Khademi, Derek Larsson, Lynn Miller, Peter Nelson, Bob Spector, Tom Woycik, and Steve Wright.

Joe Kasper
Dave Arns

Chapter 1

What Is PHIGS?

PHIGS (Programmer's Hierarchical Interactive Graphics System) is a computer graphics standard that has been approved by the American National Standards Institute (ANSI) and the International Standards Organization (ISO). PHIGS allows a graphics application developer to do the following:

- Create, display, modify, store, and retrieve device-independent graphics
- Support high-performance, dynamic applications
- Support interactive definition and modification of graphics data
- Develop 2D and 3D graphics applications

PHIGS PLUS (PHIGS Plus Lumiere Und Surfaces) extends PHIGS to offer advanced graphics capabilities. PHIGS PLUS is being developed by ISO. PHIGS PLUS allows an application developer to:

- Operate on additional primitives, such as curved (B-spline) surfaces, quadrilateral mesh, and triangle strip, in addition to the flat areas that PHIGS allows.
- Create images giving the impression of lighting effects and gradual shade changes, in addition to the flat constant colours that PHIGS allows.

Refer to the *Preface* for a list of the documents that make up the PHIGS and PHIGS PLUS standards.

Figure 1–1 shows how the major components of PHIGS relate to an application program and to each other. The figure shows how data moves around in PHIGS.

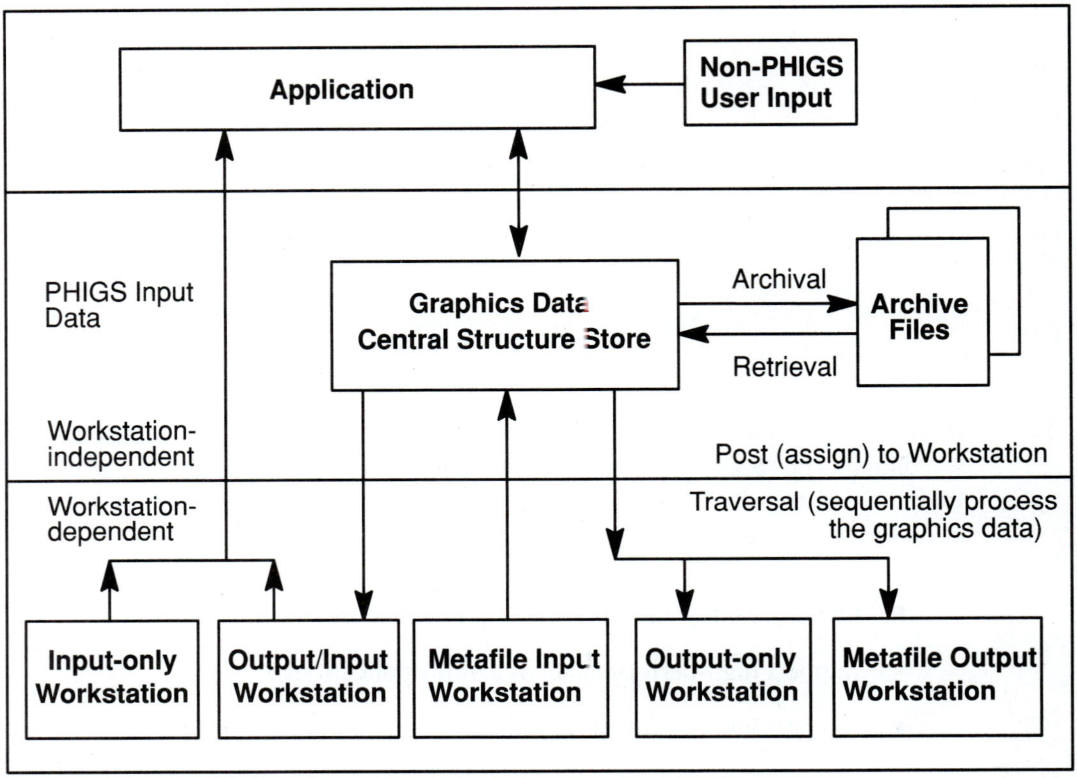

Figure 1–1. PHIGS Data Flow

We briefly describe each of the major components here and include references to appropriate chapters for more information.

A **workstation**, in the context of PHIGS, is an abstract collection of graphics capabilities that provides the logical interface to control the actual graphics hardware and software. For output, the PHIGS abstract "display surface" is implemented via a connection to an output device, for example, an X window for displaying an image, or a metafile for storing or printing an image. For input, the workstation has zero or more abstract "logical input devices" that are implemented via connections to physical input devices such as keyboards, graphics tablets, and window system pointers. Chapter 3, *Controlling PHIGS*, describes the five categories of workstations. Input routines are described in Chapter 14, *Graphical Input*.

PHIGS organizes graphical data into units called **structures**. Each structure is identified by a unique, application-supplied name. A structure contains a list of elements that define a geometric model. The application program creates structures for its use and inserts structure elements such as line primitives and attributes (for example, line colour) into it. See Chapter 3, *Controlling PHIGS*, and Chapter 5, *Using Structures*.

PHIGS stores structures in the **central structure store** (**CSS**). The structures in the CSS can be displayed and rendered by any workstation of the appropriate category opened by the (same) application program. Structures can be saved between executions of an application program by writing them to an archive file and later retrieving them. Structures can also be examined by an application to determine their contents and edited to change their contents.

Before you can display a structure on a workstation, you must associate the structure with the workstation using a mechanism called **posting**. See Chapter 4, *Posting Structures and Controlling Picture Changes*.

After you post a structure, PHIGS displays it by performing a top–down processing, or **traversal**, through the structure. During traversal PHIGS sequentially processes each structure element that it encounters (for example, a *polyline* primitive element or a *set line colour index* attribute element).

In PHIGS, features are described as being **workstation-dependent** or **workstation-independent**. A feature is workstation-dependent if it has an effect that may vary from workstation to workstation. For example, line drawing is workstation-independent since all output workstations can display a line. However, whether the line can be drawn with some choice as to its width is workstation-dependent: Some hardware can display lines of only a single width, but other hardware is more capable.

Given this exceedingly brief introduction to PHIGS, let's start learning more about it by looking at some real programs in the next chapter.

Chapter 2

An Introduction to PHIGS

This chapter presents two programs. The first is a simple program named `hello_world` that quickly shows you how to write a PHIGS program. The program is presented in both C and FORTRAN. The second program is a progressive example based on a simple charting application using the C programming language. The pieces of code, added one at a time, are listed in this chapter so you can see what code causes what changes in the graphics image. There is a FORTRAN version of the full program in Appendix C.

The examples in this chapter are presented in small, bite-sized pieces that are quickly entered into your computer. You are encouraged to enter, compile, and run these programs as you read the manual. When you see how the programs work, modify them as you desire to see how each part contributes to the whole.

In this chapter we very briefly introduce a number of PHIGS routines and concepts. We present the routines in a general fashion to give a brief overview of their use. Throughout the rest of the book we show the exact syntax to use for the FORTRAN binding and the C binding.

Online Examples

The source code for most of the examples in this book is available free of charge through the Internet by using anonymous FTP from `ftp.uu.net`. The programs are located in the following file:

```
/published/books/kasper-arns.grfxprogphigs.tar.Z
```

You may need to have your system administrator perform the anonymous FTP. Note that the file name `kasper-arns.grfxprogphigs.tar.Z` exceeds 14 characters in length. If your system does not have long-file-name capability, the file is truncated to 14 characters in length during the FTP `get` operation. If this happens, rename the file to any name you want (for example, `gpPHIGS.tar.Z`). However, be sure to include the `.Z` extension, otherwise the uncompress command will not work. Place the file in your directory and execute the following commands (assuming you renamed the file to `gpPHIGS.tar.Z`):

```
uncompress gpPHIGS.tar.Z
tar -xvf gpPHIGS.tar
```

The `tar` command builds a directory called `GrfxProgPHIGS` and places the source code files for all programs in subdirectories under this directory. Consult the included README file for descriptions of the programs.

Why Graphics?

Table 2–1 contains 100 voltage readings between the values of 0 and 1 volt, taken over time, 100 readings per second. As quickly as you can, determine if the general trend is steady, rising, or falling. Are there any periodic motions exhibited? If so, how many cycles?

Table 2–1. Table of Time and Voltage Data

.00	.05	.25	.12	.50	.34	.75	.67
.01	.12	.26	.14	.51	.28	.76	.57
.02	.12	.27	.22	.52	.33	.77	.61
.03	.14	.28	.22	.53	.31	.78	.58
.04	.18	.29	.29	.54	.34	.79	.48
.05	.16	.30	.30	.55	.34	.80	.51
.06	.14	.31	.35	.56	.41	.81	.50
.07	.04	.32	.36	.57	.44	.82	.42
.08	.05	.33	.33	.58	.43	.83	.53
.09	.03	.34	.29	.59	.54	.84	.48
.10	.03	.35	.31	.60	.58	.85	.58
.11	.08	.36	.23	.61	.58	.86	.65
.12	.07	.37	.16	.62	.47	.87	.69
.13	.13	.38	.17	.63	.49	.88	.69
.14	.17	.39	.18	.64	.42	.89	.76
.15	.20	.40	.23	.65	.42	.90	.66
.16	.28	.41	.26	.66	.36	.91	.74
.17	.30	.42	.28	.67	.41	.92	.65
.18	.22	.43	.38	.68	.42	.93	.59
.19	.25	.44	.45	.69	.42	.94	.55
.20	.17	.45	.40	.70	.41	.95	.54
.21	.21	.46	.48	.71	.49	.96	.53
.22	.14	.47	.40	.72	.52	.97	.55
.23	.10	.48	.37	.73	.62	.98	.56
.24	.15	.49	.38	.74	.65	.99	.60

Unless you are unusually perceptive, it probably took you several seconds to answer each of the questions preceding the table.

Now, take a look at the graph in Figure 2–1. It shows exactly the same data, but it is much easier to read. With the graph, it is obvious that the general trend is rising. It is also obvious that there are some periodic motions exhibited by the data—seven cycles, to be exact.

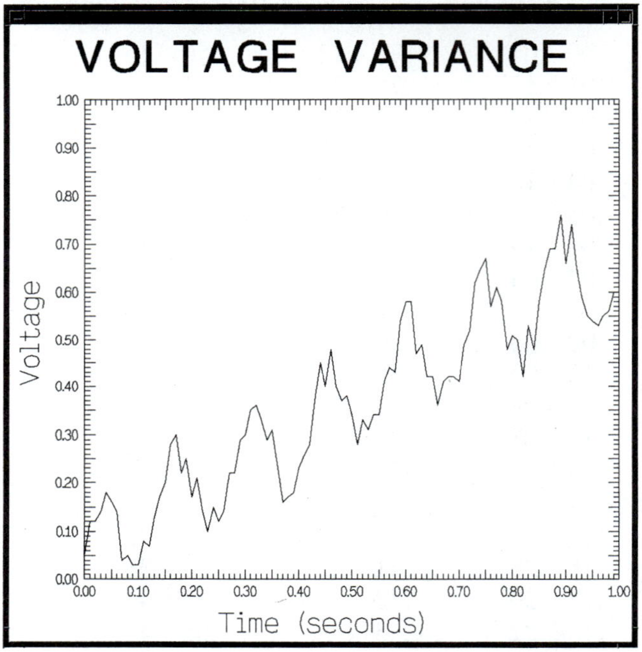

Figure 2–1. "Voltage Variance" Data Represented Graphically

This readability and understandability at a glance is what computer graphics is all about. Later in this chapter we will develop the PHIGS program that created this plot. In a step-by-step fashion, all the concepts and tools needed will be explained. However, before developing this graph program, we will take a detour to introduce some fundamental concepts, illustrating those concepts with a simple program named `hello_world`.

Preparation

There are two concepts that must be understood before PHIGS programming can make sense: **workstation** and **structure**.

A workstation, in the context of PHIGS, is an abstract collection of hardware and software with graphics capabilities. It provides the logical interface through which the application program controls the graphics hardware. In this chapter, we will deal with the concept of workstation as little as possible: only enough to run a simple program. For detailed information on the concepts relating to the PHIGS workstations, see Chapter 3, *Controlling PHIGS*.

Within the context of a PHIGS program, all the **primitives** (the building blocks describing a model), along with their **attributes** (their current characteristics), are contained in structures. A structure, in this context, is one piece of a hierarchical collection of elements that creates a certain graphical output. That is, it contains a geometric model of the objects to be drawn. Structures can reference, or execute, other structures in this hierarchical arrangement to build complex, yet easily understandable, models. Such a reference is shown in Figure 2–2.

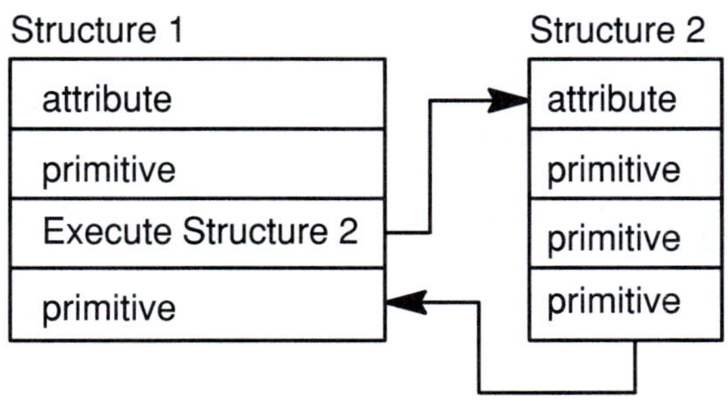

Figure 2–2. Structure Reference

In PHIGS all structures that can be displayed are stored in the central structure store, or CSS. In this introductory chapter, our simple examples will contain only a single structure. Later chapters discuss structures in greater detail.

The Basic PHIGS Routines

Before you can write a program to use PHIGS, you'll need to know about a few fundamental routines. These are described—rather sketchily—here; for detailed information on the routines and their parameters, see Chapter 3.

Opening and Closing PHIGS

```
popen_phigs(stderr, 0);                 /* open PHIGS */
...
pclose_phigs();                         /* close PHIGS */
```

The lowest-level operations that can be done in PHIGS are those of opening and closing the PHIGS environment. Opening PHIGS must be done before almost anything else can take place. The routines that accomplish these two operations are OPEN PHIGS and CLOSE PHIGS.

The OPEN PHIGS routine takes two input parameters:

- The first, ⟨*error_file*⟩, is an integer specifying an output stream. Any error messages are printed via this stream.
- The second, ⟨*buffer_size*⟩, specifies the size, in bytes, of the PHIGS buffer area.

The CLOSE PHIGS routine takes no parameters.

Opening and Closing a Workstation

```
Pint    workstation_id = 1;           /* workstation identifier    */
Pint    connection_id;                /* connection identifier     */
Pint    workstation_type = POIDDX;    /* implementation-dependent */
...
/* open workstation */
popen_ws(workstation_id, connection_id, workstation_type);
...
pclose_ws(workstation_id);           /* close workstation */
```

To render an image using PHIGS, a workstation must be opened; that is, the application must tell PHIGS what display device to use. Specifically, the OPEN WORKSTATION routine, which takes three parameters, does the following:

- The first parameter, ⟨*workstation_id*⟩, associates a user-specified identifier with the workstation so that later calls to PHIGS can easily identify the workstation.

- The second parameter, ⟨*connection_id*⟩, makes a connection to the physical graphics devices with which I/O is to take place.

- The third parameter, ⟨*workstation_type*⟩, specifies certain operating characteristics of the workstation.

When an application is through using a graphics device, the corresponding workstation should be closed. The CLOSE WORKSTATION routine takes a single input parameter, namely the workstation identifier passed to OPEN WORKSTATION when the workstation was opened. The identifier parameter is needed because PHIGS allows multiple workstations to be opened simultaneously, so CLOSE WORKSTATION must be told on which one to operate.

Opening and Closing Structures

```
Pint    structure_id = 1;               /* structure ID    */
...
popen_struct(structure_id);             /* open structure */
...
pclose_struct();                        /* close structure */
```

Structures contain geometric models of the objects to be drawn. In order to put primitives describing a model into a structure, applications usually "open" the structure. (Later chapters will describe other methods for getting primitives into structures, like retrieval from an archive file.)

The OPEN STRUCTURE routine takes a single input parameter, a structure ID (integer) that distinguishes the desired structure from other structures in the CSS.

The CLOSE STRUCTURE routine takes no parameters. (Because PHIGS only allows one structure to be opened at a time, CLOSE STRUCTURE need not be told on which structure to operate.)

Posting an Image to the Workstation

```
Pfloat   display_priority = 1.0;
...
ppost_struct(workstation_id, structure_id, display_priority);
```

Posting a structure is the process of declaring it part of the image to be displayed. Posted structures can be seen on the image. Nonposted structures cannot be seen unless they are referenced, directly or indirectly, by a posted structure.

The POST STRUCTURE routine takes three input parameters:

- A ⟨*workstation_id*⟩ that identifies the workstation on which the structure will be displayed
- A ⟨*structure_id*⟩ that identifies the structure for display
- A ⟨*display_priority*⟩ for this structure compared to other structures displayed on the same workstation

Displaying the Image

```
pupd_ws(workstation_id, PFLAG_PERFORM); /* update workstation */
```

PHIGS displays an image by *traversing*, or stepping through, the structures posted to the workstation. There are several ways to cause PHIGS to display the currently posted structures. Making the displayed image correct, or "up to date", is a rather complicated topic and we defer the discussion until Chapter 4, *Posting Structures and Controlling Picture Changes*. The method we will use here is the UPDATE WORKSTATION routine.

UPDATE WORKSTATION instructs PHIGS to execute all deferred actions on the workstation. This routine allows the application program to specify whether the display should also be redrawn (retraversed). The UPDATE WORKSTATION routine takes two input parameters:

- A ⟨*workstation_id*⟩ identifies which workstation to update.
- A ⟨*regeneration_flag*⟩ allows the application to choose between PERFORMing and POSTPONing certain actions described in Chapter 4. In this chapter we will always use the PERFORM option.

Writing a Real Program

Before we get into the progressive example, let's "get our feet wet" by writing a simple program that draws two primitives—a text string and a fill area (a polygon). This will give you a chance to practice compiling, linking, and running a PHIGS program. The program is named `hello_world`. The output is shown in Figure 2–3.

Figure 2–3. Output from hello_world Program

The hello_world program can be written in pseudo-code as follows:

```
Identify include files
Define parameters
OPEN PHIGS (ErrorFile, BufferSize)
OPEN WORKSTATION (WorkID, ConnectionID, WorkstationType)
OPEN STRUCTURE (StructID)
  SET INTERIOR STYLE (Hollow)
  FILL AREA PRIMITIVE (FourPoints, PointList)
  SET TEXT CHARACTER HEIGHT (0.04)
  TEXT (0.3X, 0.5Y, 'Hello World')
CLOSE STRUCTURE
POST STRUCTURE (WorkID, StructID, Priority 1.0)
UPDATE WORKSTATION (WorkID, PerformTheUpdate)
SET CHOICE MODE (WorkID, Device2, RequestMode, NoEcho)
REQUEST CHOICE (WorkID, Device2, ChoiceStatus, ReturnedChoiceValue)
CLOSE WORKSTATION (WorkID)
CLOSE PHIGS
```

Hello World Using the C Binding

The C binding version of the hello_wcrld program follows:

```
#include <phigs.h>                 /* get PHIGS definitions for C */
#include <stdio.h>                 /* get standard I/O definitions */

main()                                    /* file "hello_world.c" */
{
    Pint    WorkstnID = 1;          /* workstation identifier   */
    Pint    ConnID;                 /* connection identifier    */
    Pint    WorkstnType = POIDDX;   /* implementation-dependent */
    Pint    StructureID = 1;        /* structure ID             */
    static Ppoint3 SquarePts[4] = {
        0.25, 0.25, 0.0,
        0.75, 0.25, 0.0,
        0.75, 0.75, 0.0,
        0.25, 0.75, 0.0};
    static Ppoint_list3 Square = {4, SquarePts};
    static Ppoint TextLocation = {0.3, 0.5};
    Pin_status  ChoiceStatus;       /* returned from "preq_choice" */
```

```
    Pint        ChoiceNum;          /* choice value */

    popen_phigs(stderr, 0);           /* open PHIGS */
    pescape_u4("/dev/screen/phigs_window", &ConnID);
    popen_ws(WorkstnID, ConnID, WorkstnType); /* open workstation */
    /*---- define the structure ------------------------------------*/
    popen_struct(StructureID);      /* open structure */
    pset_int_style(PSTYLE_HOLLOW); /* set interior style */
    pfill_area3(&Square);           /* fill area3 primitive */
    pset_char_ht(0.04);             /* set character height */
    ptext(&TextLocation, "Hello World");/* text primitive */
    pclose_struct();                /* close structure */
    /*---- display the structure -----------------------------------*/
    ppost_struct(WorkstnID, StructureID, 1.0);  /* post structure */
    pupd_ws(WorkstnID, PFLAG_PERFORM);        /* update workstation */
    /*---- make keyboard a choice device ----------------------------*/
    pset_choice_mode(WorkstnID, 2, POP_REQ, PSWITCH_NO_ECHO);
    preq_choice(WorkstnID, 2, &ChoiceStatus, &ChoiceNum);
    /*---- That's all, folks! --------------------------------------*/
    pclose_ws(WorkstnID);           /* close workstation */
    pclose_phigs();                 /* close PHIGS */
}
```

Hello World Using the FORTRAN Binding

The FORTRAN binding version of the `hello_world` program follows:

```
      program hello_world  { program "hello_world.ftn"
C This program draws a text string and a fill area.
C It waits for the user to press a key to exit.
%include '/sys/ins/phigs.ins.ftn'
      integer*4 WorkID      { workstation id
      integer*4 ConnectID  { connection id
      integer*4 StrucID    { structure ID
      real      FAX(4), FAY(4), FAZ(4)   { points for fill area
      integer*4 ChoiceStatus, ChoiceNum  { choice status and value
      parameter (StrucID=1)
      data FAX /0.25, 0.75, 0.75, 0.25/
      data FAY /0.25, 0.25, 0.75, 0.75/
      data FAZ /0.0,  0.0,  0.0,  0.0/

      call popph(1, 0)                  { open PHIGS
      call popwk(WorkID, 1, POIDSX)     { open workstation
```

```
C Define the structure
      call popst(StrucID)              { open structure
      call pfa3(4,FAX,FAY,FAZ)         { fill area3 primitive
      call pschh(0.04)                 { set character height
      call ptx(0.3, 0.5,'Hello World') { text
      call pclst                       { close the structure
C Display the structure
      call ppost(WorkID, StrucID, 1.0) { post structure
      call puwk(WorkID,PPERFO)         { update workstation
C Wait for user input
      call pschm(WorkID, 2, PREQU, PNECHO)              { set choice mode
      call prqch(WorkID, 2, ChoiceStatus, ChoiceNum) { request choice
C That's all, folks!
      call pclwk(WorkID)         { close the workstation
      call pclph                 { close PHIGS
      stop                       { stop processing
      end                        { end of main program
```

Note that the `hello_world` program is used again in Chapter 5, *Using Structures*. That version, named `inquire_structs`, adds features to show how to inquire the contents of a structure element. The program is also used in Chapter 12, *Using Colour*, to show how to set colour values.

Some Implementation-dependent Aspects of the Programs

There will always be a certain number of implementation-dependent aspects to every PHIGS program. This is largely due to the differing capabilities of different vendors' hardware. While the PHIGS standard specifies that a certain number of criteria *must* be met for a full PHIGS implementation, there is fair-sized list of things that a PHIGS vendor can make decisions about whether and how to implement. Appendix D of the PHIGS standard lists what PHIGS calls the "allowable differences." A PHIGS implementation should specify how it implements the features listed in that appendix.

There is also the issue of just getting a program to run on different systems. There will be different techniques for loading or linking the PHIGS software with your application program and the various include files may be in different locations on different systems. If you will be running the programs in this book on your own system, we recommend that you first obtain some sample PHIGS programs that run on your system and read your implementation documentation for details on how to run the programs. Next, get the `hello_world` program running on your system. Then you can use the resulting program as a base for adding new features as you read additional chapters.

Also keep in mind that the actual C or FORTRAN bindings used by your implementation may be different from the ones presented in this book. Use your own implementation documentation as the final source for the correct syntax. See "Language Bindings, Fragments, and Pseudo-code" in the *Preface*.

This section describes some of the implementation-dependent aspects of the programs presented in this book. The C binding programs in this chapter were written on HP-PHIGS on HP-UX. Most of the FORTRAN binding programs were written on HP-PHIGS on Apollo Domain/OS.

Include Files

```
#include <phigs.h>                /* get PHIGS definitions for C */
#include <stdio.h>                /* get standard I/O definitions */

%include '/sys/ins/phigs.ins.ftn'  ! get PHIGS definitions for FORTRAN
```

Every implementation has one (or more) include file that defines the PHIGS constants and routines. The name (or names) of the include file and its actual location on the system will vary. For example, HP-PHIGS on HP-UX requires two include files, while HP-PHIGS on Domain only requires one. In addition, the form of the compiler directive that reads the file may be compiler-dependent.

Opening PHIGS

```
popen_phigs(stderr, 0);              /* errors go to "stderr" */
```

The first parameter to the OPEN PHIGS routine identifies the stream that will be used for error output. Usually a value of 1 is sufficient to direct error output to standard out (to the same screen or window from which the program was executed), but you should check your implementation documentation to make sure. The second parameter identifies the size, in bytes, of the PHIGS buffer area. HP-PHIGS ignores this value, so we use a value of 0.

The Connection ID in the OPEN WORKSTATION Routine

```
Pint    WorkstnID = 1;          /* workstation identifier   */
Pint    ConnID;                 /* connection identifier    */
```

```
Pint    WorkstnType = POIDDX;    /* implementation-dependent */
...
 pescape_u4("/dev/screen/phigs_window", &ConnID);
 popen_ws(WorkstnID, ConnID, WorkstnType);
```

There is an implementation-dependent routine early in the C binding programs—the `pescape_u4` routine is specific to HP-PHIGS. It is an escape routine that allows the application to get a connection identifier for an X window (the FORTRAN version of the escape is `pue400`). The application can then pass the connection ID to the OPEN WORKSTATION routine.

Each implementation deals a little differently with opening a workstation. In particular, the third parameter to the OPEN WORKSTATION routine varies from one implementation to the next. For example, the `POIDDX` token often used in this book basically means open an input–output, double-buffered workstation in an X window. The other token often used is `POIDSX`, which uses single buffering instead of double buffering. Check your implementation documentation for the correct tokens to use for your programs.

A Few More Words about Hello World

This section describes some general aspects of the program that apply to many other programs in this book as well as to many programs that you will write yourself.

Using the Default View Table Entry 0

This program uses the default view—entry 0 in the workstation view table. If PHIGS does not encounter a *set view index* structure element, it uses the default view index 0.

The default view places the viewing reference coordinate system coincident with the **world coordinate** (**WC**) origin. This displays objects that have world coordinate values in a rectangular solid between 0.0 and 1.0 in x, y, and z. Since the fill area primitive lies between 0.25 and 0.75 in x and y, and has $z = 0.0$, the primitive fits within the rectangular solid.

Allow the Operator to Signal When to Exit the Program

```
Pin_status   ChoiceStatus;          /* returned from "preq_choice" */
Pint         ChoiceNum;             /* choice value */
...
/*---- make keyboard a choice device ---------------------------*/
pset_choice_mode(WorkstnID, 2, POP_REQ, PSWITCH_NO_ECHO);
preq_choice(WorkstnID, 2, &ChoiceStatus, &ChoiceNum);
```

Although the reader of this book is likely to be both the application writer ("user" of PHIGS) and the **operator** ("user" of an interactive PHIGS program), in the larger context these will be different people. In this book we call the person who interacts with a PHIGS application program an operator. Part of your job as an application programmer is to try and anticipate what the operator will want to do and what kind of behavior the operator will expect from the program. One thing that the operator will expect is that the program will provide a smooth way to exit when he or she is through using it.

One problem with writing short example programs is how to exit gracefully from a program that displays graphical output. For many of the programs in this book we use PHIGS input routines to wait for an action from the operator. We open an OUTIN workstation so we will have access to the various input devices at PHIGS' disposal (see Chapter 14, *Graphical Input*). Then we put choice device 2 in Request mode and call REQUEST CHOICE. The REQUEST CHOICE routine causes PHIGS to stop and wait for the user to satisfy the request. On HP-PHIGS, choice device 2 corresponds to input from the keyboard. In this case, the user puts the cursor in the display window and presses any key. The REQUEST CHOICE routine returns the value of the key that was pressed. You probably already noted that in this sample program we ignore the value of the key. We chose the "no echo" mode so that PHIGS will not display a prompt to the user. Prompts are implementation-dependent.

The implementation of choice devices may be different on your system. Check your implementation documentation for details. You may want to substitute another choice device or a completely different input device such as a locator or pick device. If you don't want to use an OUTIN workstation at all, then you can devise another way to exit the program. Check the sample programs that come with your implementation software for some appropriate ways to exit a program.

Now that you have been introduced to the basic procedure for writing and executing a graphics program using PHIGS, we'll move on to the progressive example.

The Progressive Example

As its name implies, every successive iteration of the progressive example program adds another concept to the program, which gets progressively more complex. This example creates the "voltage vs. time" plot given at the beginning of the chapter. Seeing that the progressive example is an *example*, we have sacrificed efficiency in some places in order to enhance understandability and make the point clearer.

This chapter uses the C binding version of the progressive example. There is a FORTRAN version of the entire program in Appendix C.

The progressive example programs use a two-dimensional Cartesian coordinate system. "*x*" indicates the left-to-right distance, with values increasing as you go toward the right, and "*y*" indicates the down-to-up distance, with values increasing as you go up. Also, the programs expect to read the *x* and *y* data from a file called "`data`." The file is part of the online examples described at the beginning of this chapter. Copy it into your working directory. Or, if the file is not available on your system, create it as an ASCII file, one number-pair per line, using the numbers from Table 2–1 at the beginning of this chapter.

One of the most important characteristics of PHIGS is that it is not an "immediate-mode" graphics system. That means, for example, that when a POLYLINE call is encountered, the polyline is *not* immediately drawn; its definition is simply placed in the central structure store as part of the geometric model of the image you are defining. Later, you render that model by "updating the workstation," which reads the description posted from the CSS and actually draws it. So, in the context of a PHIGS program, "drawing a line" usually means "calling the routine that places an element in the open structure in the centralized structure store that, when traversed, causes a line to be drawn." This is an important point, but since it is so tedious to say it in the latter form, it is referred to many times as simply "drawing a line."

Defining Lines

To define lines, PHIGS offers the POLYLINE routine. This routine creates a structure element that, when traversed, renders a user-specifiable number of connected straight lines. We will use the 2D routine to draw the curve described by our data. There is also a 3D polyline routine, but we will save that for another chapter.

The POLYLINE routine takes as input a list of 2D points. The parameters are defined differently for the PHIGS C and FORTRAN bindings. In FORTRAN you specify a count of points, a list of *x* values, and a separate list of *y* values (using two separate arrays). For the C binding, the *x* and *y* values are contained in a single array, and the count of points and the pointer to the array are placed in a C structure and passed as a single parameter.

The following program reads the *xy* data from the file, then plots the data. Type it in, noting how one POLYLINE routine is used to draw the multiple lines in the data curve:

```
#include <phigs.h>                          /* get PHIGS definitions for C */
#include <stdio.h>                          /* get standard I/O definitions */

main()                                        /* file "Lines.c" */
{
    int          WorkstnID = 1;               /* workstation identifier */
    int          ConnID;                      /* connection identifier */
    int          WorkstnType = POIDDX;        /* implementation-dependent */
    int          TheCurve = 1;                /* structure ID  */
    Ppoint       LinePts[100];                /* points for the polyline */
    Ppoint_list  LineData;                    /* data for the polyline */
    FILE         *datafile, *fopen();         /* file pointer */
    int          I;                           /* loop control variable */

  /*=== read data file into the structure array ==================*/
  datafile = fopen("data", "r"); /* open data file (2 numbers/line) */
  while (fscanf(datafile, "%f%f", &LinePts[I].x, &LinePts[I].y) != EOF)
     I++;
  fclose(datafile);
  LineData.num_points = I;
  LineData.points = LinePts;
  /*=== set up PHIGS to plot data ============================*/
  popen_phigs(stderr, 0);              /* errors go to "stderr" */
  pescape_u4("/dev/screen/phigs_window", &ConnID);
  popen_ws(WorkstnID, ConnID, WorkstnType);
  popen_struct(TheCurve);
  ppolyline(&LineData);
  pclose_struct();
  /*=== post the image and close up shop ======================*/
  ppost_struct(WorkstnID, TheCurve, 1.0);
  pupd_ws(WorkstnID, PFLAG_PERFORM);   /* (regeneration flag) */
  pclose_ws(WorkstnID);
  pclose_phigs();
}
```

Compile and run the program. Figure 2–4 shows the output of the program.

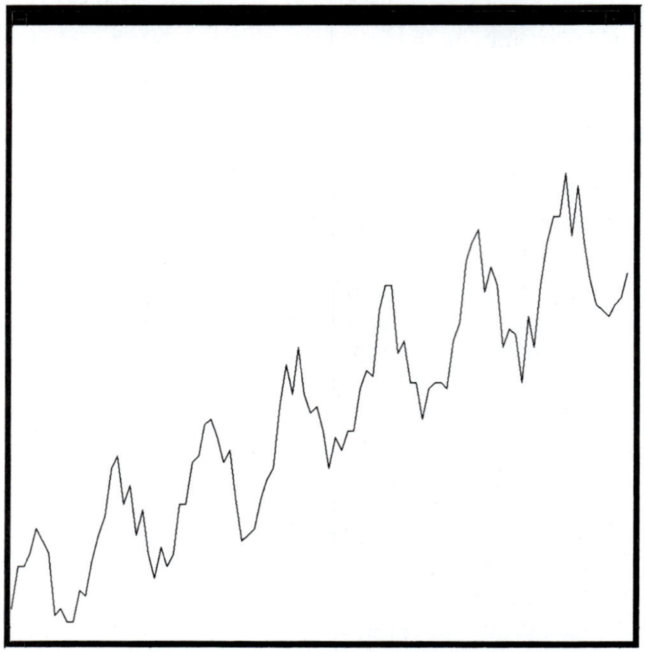

Figure 2–4. Progressive Example: Lines

Not bad, but it certainly needs work! The curve is there, but what does it mean? The missing parts—those parts that tell the reader what the graph means—are the subject of the following sections of this chapter. Included are topics such as the viewport, clipping, and text labels.

Trouble Shooting: If your program flashes the output briefly and then exits, copy the code from the `hello_world` example to wait for operator input into this example before the call to `pclose_ws`.

Defining a View Window

If you'll refer back to Figure 2–1 at the beginning of the chapter, you'll notice that the area in which the actual data curve is plotted is not the entire plotting surface. It is a subset of the plotting surface, with textual information around the outside. Part of creating a program whose display is like that of Figure 2–1 is to place the data curve more precisely on the viewing area. But how do you tell PHIGS that you want the data curve to be restricted to "that spot right there"? The answer is by specifying a *virtual plotting surface* called a **projection viewport** in PHIGS.

In this example, we position the virtual plotting surface as follows:

- The left side is 12% from the left edge of the physical plotting surface.
- The right side is 2% from the right edge of the physical plotting surface.
- The bottom is 10% up from the bottom of the physical plotting surface.
- The top is 12% down from the top of the physical plotting surface.

Figure 2–5 shows the positioning. This leaves room for text on the top, left side, and bottom of the display. Compare this illustration to Figure 2–1.

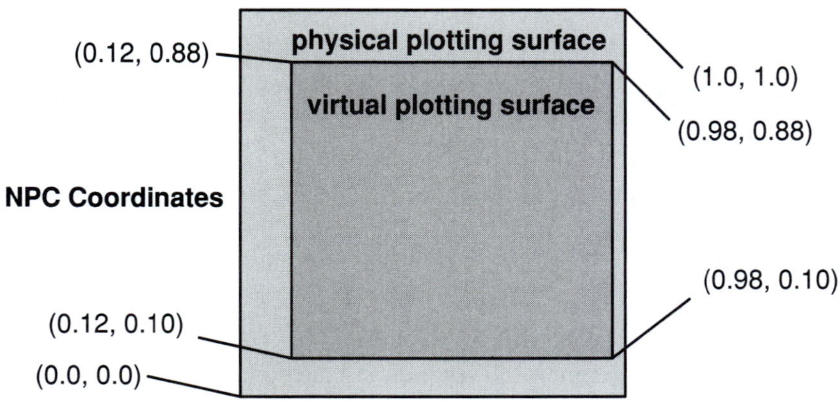

Figure 2–5. Positioning the Virtual Plotting Surface within the Physical Plotting Surface

For the purposes of this chapter we will address points on the physical plotting surface using **normalized projection coordinates** (**NPCs**) in the range of [0, 1], inclusive (see Chapter 6, *Modelling Transformations*, for details on NPCs). This means that our choice of virtual plotting surface (our projection viewport) will have the following values (see Figure 2–5):

- Lower x limit of 0.12 (12%)
- Upper x limit of 0.98 (100% –2%)
- Lower y limit of 0.10 (10%)
- Upper y limit of 0.88 (100% –12%)

Just as we may wish to select a virtual plotting surface having bounds different from those of the physical plotting surface, we may also wish to select a virtual data space having limits different from the real limits of our data. This virtual data space is called a **view window**. In our example, the time data ranges from 0 seconds to .99 seconds, and the voltage ranges from .03 volts to .76 volts (see Table 2–1). For esthetic purposes (when we eventually put tic marks and labels on the edges) we will choose our virtual data limits to be 0 to 1 seconds and 0 to 1 volts. Because we will be displaying seconds horizontally and volts vertically, we choose a view window from 0–1 (seconds) in x and 0–1 (volts) in y. These x and y ranges define the extent of the whole world, at least as far as our program's data points are concerned. Thus, these coordinates are called world coordinates (WCs). Of course, if our data had significantly different minimum and maximum values, we would choose a different view window.

All this is fine, but we still haven't answered the question of exact placement that we raised in the first paragraph! The answer: Make it so that the left, bottom, right, and top edges of the view window are logically at the same place as the left, bottom, right, and top edges of the projection viewport. With this rule, one can take a data point (of x seconds and y volts in our example) and determine its x and y NPCs using simple proportions. By the way, the rule works equally well for points outside as well as inside the view window.

Note that the view window and projection viewport are fundamentally different even though the values in this example are close to each other. The 0–1 x range of the view window is interpreted as "the lower limit is 0.0 seconds and the upper limit is 1.0 seconds," whereas the 0–1 x range in NPCs is interpreted as "the full width of the NPC space." That is, the former is understood as seconds (data values), and the latter is understood as fractions of a unit cube of NPC space.

A Plan of Attack

In our sample program, three steps are needed to inform PHIGS about using our particular rule to map our data for display:

1. we use a utility routine to convert our view window and projection viewport to a coordinate transformation matrix, which
2. we store in a "view" representation, which we finally
3. select for use via a structure element.

The next few sections will go over these three steps in more detail.

Using a Utility Routine to Obtain the View Mapping Matrix

The EVALUATE VIEW MAPPING MATRIX routine creates a **view mapping matrix** from the parameters passed to it. This is the utility routine we spoke of Step 1 in the previous section. In general, the routine allows you to specify an axis-aligned window rectangle in **view reference coordinate** (**VRC**) space and to specify an axis-aligned viewport rectangle in NPC space. The 2D routine produces a 3×3 matrix that is a representation of the scaling and translation needed to map the window to the viewport. See Chapter 7, *Viewing and Workstation Transformations*, for a complete description of the view mapping matrix. In our example, view reference coordinates are the same as world coordinates.

The EVALUATE VIEW MAPPING MATRIX routine takes two input parameters and two output parameters:

- ⟨*window_limits*⟩ is a four-element real array, passed to the routine, that specifies the limits of the window. The array element order is window–left, window–right, window–bottom, window–top. The values are expressed in VRCs.
- ⟨*viewport_limits*⟩ is a four-element real array passed to the routine. The array's values, expressed in NPCs, are ordered x_{min}, x_{max}, y_{min}, and y_{max}.
- ⟨*error*⟩ is an integer that is returned with the error code of any error that occurred in the routine. If no error occurred, ⟨*error*⟩ returns 0.
- ⟨*view_mapping_matrix*⟩ is a 3×3 real array that is returned containing the view mapping matrix derived from the input parameter values. This matrix can be sent to SET VIEW REPRESENTATION, as described previously.

Storing the Mapping Matrix in a View Representation

The view mapping matrix is part of what PHIGS considers a **view**. The view is a collection of information that controls how the geometry of graphics primitives is transformed for display on the screen. PHIGS allows you to control three different aspects of the view (that is, what you see on the display) independently. They are

- The orientation. This deals with whether the image appears "tipped" on the screen. For our two-dimensional graph example, we don't want the orientation to be non-standard—we want seconds to be horizontal and volts to be vertical—so we'll specify the parameters accordingly.
- The geometric mapping. This deals with scaling and shifting the view window to coincide with the projection viewport.
- The clipping. This deals with cutting off any graphical output that "hangs off the edge" of the projection viewport (or some other rectangle of interest) .

These three aspects are specified via the 2D version of the SET VIEW REPRESENTATION routine (there is also a 3D version; see Chapter 7 for details).

The SET VIEW REPRESENTATION routine takes six input parameters:

- ⟨*workstation_id*⟩ is the integer workstation identifier uniquely representing the specific workstation opened by the OPEN WORKSTATION routine.
- ⟨*view_index*⟩ is an integer assigned to identify this particular view.
- ⟨*orientation_matrix*⟩ is a 3×3 real array that specifies the orientation of the view. In our progressive example, we don't want the orientation to be anything fancy, so we'll just pass the identity matrix; this invokes a "normal" view.
- ⟨*mapping_matrix*⟩ is another 3×3 real array, as returned from EVALUATE VIEW MAPPING MATRIX. This matrix specifies what portion of the image is visible, and where it should be displayed.
- ⟨*clip_limits*⟩ is a four-element real array that specifies the clip limits in normalized projection coordinates (NPCs). Put simply, NPCs are the 0–1 coordinates in which the projection viewport is defined (see Chapter 7 for more detail). The order of array elements is x_{min}, x_{max}, y_{min}, and y_{max}. In our example, we will use either the projection viewport or 0, 1, 0, 1 depending on content.

- ⟨*clip_indicator*⟩ is an integer through which you turn clipping on and off. **Clipping** is the process of suppressing graphical data that extends outside the ⟨*clip_limits*⟩. To turn clipping on, specify clip (`PCLIP`, `PIND_CLIP`); to turn clipping off, specify no clip (`PNCLIP`, `PIND_NO_CLIP`).

So, before we can call SET VIEW REPRESENTATION to define our view, we must define a view mapping matrix and a clip limits array. These operations are described in the next few sections.

Don't be taken unawares by the fact that a 2D routine takes 3×3 matrices and a 3D routine takes 4×4 matrices! See Chapter 6 for more information.

Selecting the View Representation via a Structure Element

The SET VIEW REPRESENTATION routine does not cause the newly defined view to take effect; it merely associates a view representation (derived from the orientation matrix, the view mapping matrix, and the clip limits) with an integer view index. You cause a particular view to be used by placing a SET VIEW INDEX element into a structure (remember, PHIGS is not an immediate-mode system; many things are specified via elements that are created and placed into the CSS).

The SET VIEW INDEX routine takes a single input parameter: ⟨*view_index*⟩ is the integer associated with the desired view.

You have the option of setting the view representation before creating the structure element, or vice versa. We recommend that you set the view representation first.

Implementing It Thus Far

Because defining a view window and a projection viewport is a very useful action, let's put the actual code into a subroutine so it can be easily copied to other programs later. Put the following subroutine at the end of your program.

```
/*************************************************************************/
DefineView(WorkstnID, ViewIndex, Wxmin, Wxmax, Wymin, Wymax,
  Vxmin, Vxmax, Vymin, Vymax, ClipAtViewport)
int     WorkstnID;                          /* workstation identifier */
```

```
int     ViewIndex;                          /* the view being defined */
float   Wxmin, Wxmax, Wymin, Wymax;         /* view window limits */
float   Vxmin, Vxmax, Vymin, Vymax;         /* projection viewport limits */
int     ClipAtViewport;                     /* window (or display surface?) */
{
    Pview_map   Mapping;                    /* window-onto-viewport mapping */
    Pint        ErrorReturn;                /* error-return variable */
    Pview_rep   ViewRep;                    /* complete description of view */
    int         I, J;                       /* loop control variables */

    /*--- define the view orientation matrix as identity ------------------*/
    for (I = 0; I < 3; I++)
        for (J = 0; J < 3; J++)
            ViewRep.ori_matrix[I][J] = (I == J);
    /*--- define view mapping matrix ---------------------------------------*/
    Mapping.win.x_min = Wxmin;                      /* \                     */
    Mapping.win.x_max = Wxmax;                      /*  \ put individual values */
    Mapping.win.y_min = Wymin;                      /*  / into the structure    */
    Mapping.win.y_max = Wymax;                      /* /                     */
    Mapping.proj_vp.x_min = Vxmin;                  /* \                     */
    Mapping.proj_vp.x_max = Vxmax;                  /*  \ put individual values */
    Mapping.proj_vp.y_min = Vymin;                  /*  / into the structure    */
    Mapping.proj_vp.y_max = Vymax;                  /* /                     */
    peval_view_map_matrix(&Mapping, &ErrorReturn, ViewRep.map_matrix);
    if (ErrorReturn != 0) {                         /* did we get an error? */
        printf("%s %d %s %s\n", "Error", ErrorReturn, "occurred during",
          "call to Evaluate View Mapping Matrix.");
        exit(1);
    }
    /*--- define the clip limits -------------------------------------------*/
    if (ClipAtViewport)
        ViewRep.clip_limit = Mapping.proj_vp;   /* clip at viewport */
    else {
        ViewRep.clip_limit.x_min = 0.0;         /* \                 */
        ViewRep.clip_limit.x_max = 1.0;         /*  \ clip at edges of */
        ViewRep.clip_limit.y_min = 0.0;         /*  / display surface  */
        ViewRep.clip_limit.y_max = 1.0;         /* /                 */
    }
    /*--- define clip indicator --------------------------------------------*/
    ViewRep.xy_clip = PIND_CLIP;
    /*--- set the view representation --------------------------------------*/
    pset_view_rep(WorkstnID, ViewIndex, &ViewRep);
}
```

Notice that five things are passed into this subroutine: the workstation ID, the index of the view being defined, the window limits, the viewport limits, and a logical value that specifies whether the clipping is to be applied at the projection viewport edges or at the display edges.

Now, since we want a rectangle around the projection viewport, place the following subroutine after the `DefineView` subroutine just listed.

```
/******************************************************************************/
DefineRectangle(Xmin, Xmax, Ymin, Ymax)
float   Xmin, Xmax, Ymin, Ymax;                      /* rectangle's limits */
{
    Ppoint_list Rectangle;
    Ppoint      Corners[5];

    Rectangle.num_points = 5;
    Corners[0].x = Xmin, Corners[0].y = Ymin;    /* lower left corner */
    Corners[1].x = Xmax, Corners[1].y = Ymin;    /* lower right corner */
    Corners[2].x = Xmax, Corners[2].y = Ymax;    /* upper right corner */
    Corners[3].x = Xmin, Corners[3].y = Ymax;    /* upper left corner */
    Corners[4].x = Xmin, Corners[4].y = Ymin;    /* lower left corner */
    Rectangle.points = Corners;
    ppolyline(&Rectangle);
}
```

Once the subroutines have been entered, put in the following lines immediately before the OPEN STRUCTURE line.

```
DefineView(WorkstnID, 1,                /* mapping for view index 1: */
  0.0,  1.0,  0.0,  1.0,                /*   window: 0-1, 0-1 */
  0.12, 0.98, 0.10, 0.88,               /*   viewport: in a subset */
  FALSE);                               /*   don't clip at view window */
```

This statement says, "For the workstation designated by the value of `WorkstnID`, define view #1 such that data points with world coordinates of seconds in the range of 0–1 and voltage in the range of 0–1 should be mapped to a viewport of 12%–98% of the display surface in x and 10%–88% of the display surface in y." We're saying that we *don't* want clipping at the edges of the projection viewport, because different points might be entered (via the input file) and we are making a stylistic choice that it is OK to see the graph go outside the box (if necessary).

Now, immediately after the OPEN STRUCTURE line, include these lines:

```
pset_view_ind(1);
DefineRectangle(0.0, 1.0, 0.0, 1.0);
```

Now, recompile and run your program. Figure 2–6 shows the output of the program.

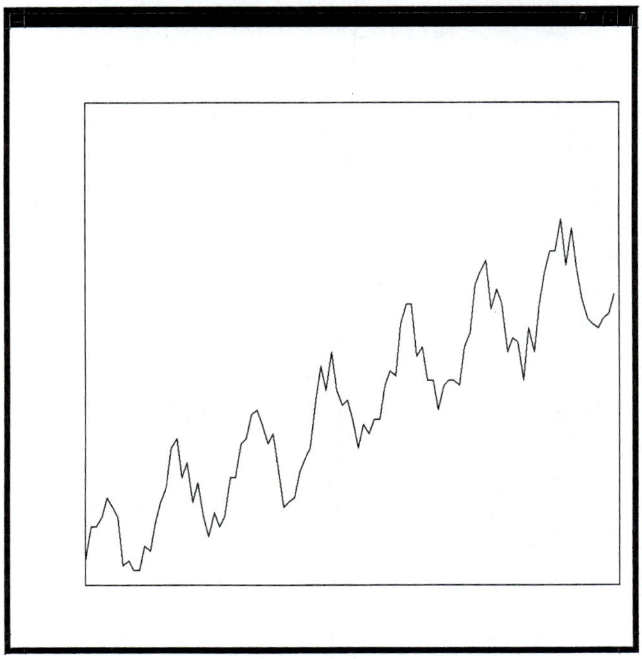

Figure 2–6. Progressive Example: Viewport and Window Defined

It's now beginning to look like it's supposed to! The guts of the program are working correctly; now it's just a matter of making the plot "reader-friendly", or understandable at a glance. This includes such items as textual labels and tic marks. These topics are discussed next.

Textual Labels

The next concept to learn about is plotting labels: How do you put textual information on the plot? Chapter 11, *Using Text*, discusses text in great detail, but we can use enough of the routines here to get the job done. There are several attributes of text drawn on a plot:

- What font is being used?
- How big are the characters?
- How is the label justified, both horizontally and vertically? That is, what part of the label rests at the user-specified location?
- How is the label oriented?

The next several sections deal with the attributes needed for the progressive example.

Bear in mind that in the following discussions, the words "character" and "text" imply different things and are *not* interchangeable. **Character** implies a single member of a set of glyphs or symbols, and **text** implies a set of characters taken as a unit—a "string" of characters. Being aware of this difference will help you understand the concepts being discussed; for example, SET CHARACTER HEIGHT sets the height of the individual characters, whereas SET TEXT ALIGNMENT sets the alignment of an entire block of characters, regardless of how many characters it contains.

Text Font

The SET TEXT FONT routine creates a structure element that, when traversed, sets the text font attribute. It takes a single integer argument, an integer font ID.

PHIGS defines a default font as font 1 and defines an additional font 2. Implementations may add additional fonts as negative values. If you specify a font number that does not exist on your system, PHIGS uses font 1. This example uses two implementation-dependent fonts: –4 is a bold sans serif font, and –2 is a simplex sans serif font. If your implementation does not have fonts –4 or –2, PHIGS uses the default font 1. The program will still run correctly; the text on your output will just look different from the diagrams in this book. And of course, if your implementation has different fonts defined as –2 and –4, the text will also look different.

Character Size

Two of the routines for specifying the size of characters are SET CHARACTER HEIGHT and SET CHARACTER EXPANSION FACTOR.

The SET CHARACTER HEIGHT routine takes a single input parameter, a real number that specifies the character height from bottom to top.

The SET CHARACTER EXPANSION FACTOR routine takes a single input parameter, a real number that specifies the desired multiplier with which to change the default character width. For example, 0.5 would make the characters half as wide as normal; 3.0 would make them three times as wide; 1.25 would make them 25% wider; etc. "As wide as normal" means, in this context, that the character has the width defined by the current height of the character and the default aspect ratio (the width:height ratio) of the character, as defined in the active font.

Text Location

In our example, the main title of the plot "VOLTAGE VARIANCE," the title of the *x*-axis "Time (seconds)," and the title of the *y*-axis, "Voltage," are *global* labels; their positions and content do not vary with, say, number of readings or voltage read. In contrast, the tic labels, which specify curve-related information, could vary with the curve if we generalize the program to deal with arbitrary ranges of data points.

In order to place these labels where we want them, we should place the global labels while an easily calculated view is in effect. This is very easy, because we can use SET VIEW REPRESENTATION (discussed previously) to define as many views as we want. We already set up View #1 to a subset of the display space, so let's set up a View #2 that uses simpler values; e.g., 0–1 in both x and y. Thus, centering the main title at the top of the image, for example, would be as easy as putting text at $x = 0.5$, $y = 1.0$. The x- and y-axes labels are just as easy: They should be centered on their respective sides of the display space.

For the labels that are data-dependent, their locations should be defined after the data-dependent viewing is effected.

Text Alignment

The SET TEXT ALIGNMENT routine specifies where, on the text itself, is the point that will be specified in the TEXT routine. Another way to think about this concept is illustrated by the questions: "If I draw some text at (0, 0), which part of the text is at (0, 0)? How do I right-justify text? Or center it?"

The SET TEXT ALIGNMENT routine solves the problem. The routine takes two input parameters. The first specifies horizontal justification, and its value can be normal, left, center, or right. The second specifies vertical justification, and its value can be normal, top, cap, half, base, or bottom. Figure 2–7 shows how these values relate to text characters.

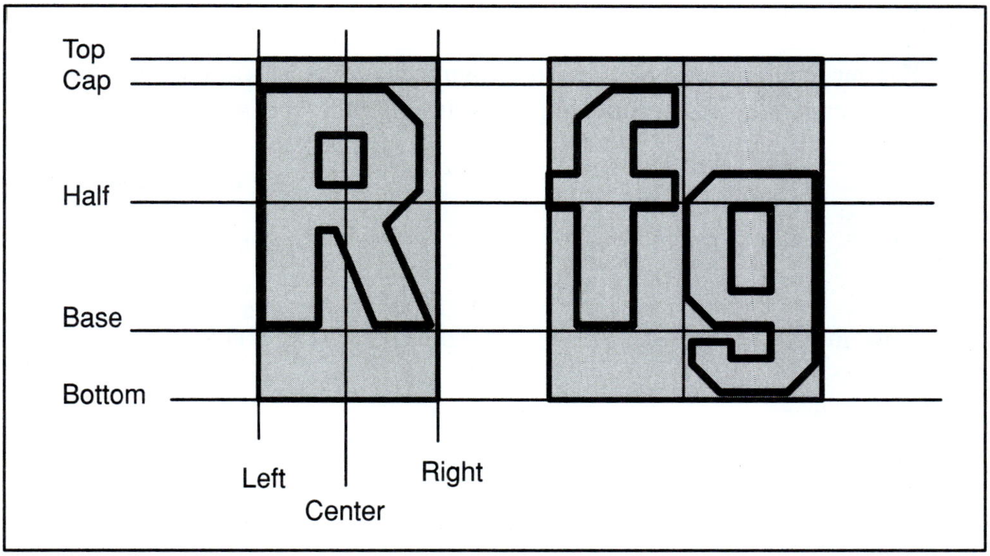

Figure 2–7. Text Alignment

For our progressive example, the main title of the plot should be horizontally justified with center (PACENT, PHOR_CTR) and vertically justified with top (PATOP, PVERT_TOP); i.e., the top center of the label should be at (0.5, 1.0).

Creating the Two Labels

First we will define another view with these easily manipulated values. Insert these statements right after the first call to `DefineView`, and right before the call to OPEN STRUCTURE:

```
DefineView(WorkstnID, 2,              /* mapping for view index 2: */
  0.0,  1.0,  0.0,  1.0,              /*   window: 0-1, 0-1 */
  0.0,  1.0,  0.0,  1.0,              /*   viewport: 0-1, 0-1 */
  TRUE);                              /*   clip at view window */
```

(These values actually create a view identical to the PHIGS default view (view index 0). See Chapter 7 for more information on the default view.)

For our program we'll need two text alignment variables, `CenterTop` and `CenterBottom`, for reference. Add the following lines just after the `LineData` variable:

```
static Ptext_align  CenterTop =      /* alignment for the main title */
            {PHOR_CTR, PVERT_TOP};
static Ptext_align  CenterBottom =   /* alignment for the x-axis title */
            {PHOR_CTR, PVERT_BOTTOM};
```

Now, insert these statements right after the OPEN STRUCTURE call:

```
/*=== create the labels ================================================*/
pset_view_ind(2);
/*--- do main title ----------------------------------------------------*/
pset_text_font(BoldSansSerif);
pset_text_align(&CenterTop);
pset_char_ht(0.05);
Point.x = 0.5, Point.y = 1.0;
ptext(&Point, "VOLTAGE VARIANCE");
```

Similar to the main title, the *x*-axis title is a horizontal label and should be justified with "center" and "bottom." Insert these statements right after the ones for labelling the main title:

```
/*--- do the x-axis title ----------------------------------------------*/
pset_text_font(SimplexSansSerif);
pset_text_align(&CenterBottom);
```

```
pset_char_ht(0.03);
Point.x = 0.5, Point.y = 0.0;
ptext(&Point, "Time (seconds)");
```

And finally, the text for the *y*-axis. We want the *y*-axis text to print vertically, so we will use the SET CHARACTER UP VECTOR routine to point the text in the right direction. This is discussed next.

Text Orientation

Use the SET CHARACTER UP VECTOR routine to orient your text in a given direction. This routine take two input arguments that together specify a **character up vector**. This vector defines the direction of the normally vertical components of characters. (The phrase "normally vertical" was used in the previous sentence because after calling SET CHARACTER UP VECTOR, the normally vertical parts of characters may not be truly vertical anymore.)

For example, take the uppercase letter "L." It has one normally horizontal component and one normally vertical component. For the default character orientation, the character up vector—the vector that defines the direction of the normally vertical part—is (0.0, 1.0). That is, to go the direction that this up vector defines, go 0 units to the right and 1 unit up: It is indeed vertical.

To rotate a label 90° to the left, the up vector would have to point straight to the left, or (–1.0, 0.0). So, let's define a vector variable called `ToTheLeft` initialized to point left. Insert the following line just after the `CenterTop` and `CenterBottom` variables.

```
static Pvec ToTheLeft = {-1.0, 0.0};/* sent to "pset_char_up_vec" */
```

Now, insert these statements right after the ones for labelling the *x*-axis:

```
/*--- do the y-axis title -------------------------------------------*/
pset_char_up_vec(&ToTheLeft);
pset_text_align(&CenterTop);
Point.x = 0.0, Point.y = 0.5;
ptext(&Point, "Voltage");
```

The text alignment must be center/top because the definitions of top, bottom, left, and right are relative to the *label*, not to the display surface.

As a checkpoint to see if you have inserted the new lines in the correct places, compare the following listing to your current program:

```
#include <phigs.h>                              /* get PHIGS definitions for C */
#include <stdio.h>                              /* get standard I/O definitions */
#define  FALSE                    0             /* boolean false is integer 0 */
#define  TRUE                     1             /* boolean true is integer 1 */
#define  SimplexSansSerif        -2             /* sent to "pset_text_font" */
#define  BoldSansSerif           -4             /* sent to "pset_text_font" */

main()                                          /* file "CharLbls.c" */
{
    int          WorkstnID = 1;                 /* workstation identifier */
    int          ConnID;                        /* connection identifier */
    int          WorkstnType = POIDDX;          /* out/in, direct, dbl bfr, Xwindow */
    int          TheCurve = 1;                  /* structure ID (chosen by user) */
    Ppoint       LinePts[100];                  /* points for the polyline */
    Ppoint_list LineData;                       /* data for the polyline */
    static Ptext_align  CenterTop =             /* alignment for the main title */
                 {PHOR_CTR, PVERT_TOP};
    static Ptext_align  CenterBottom =          /* alignment for the x-axis title */
                 {PHOR_CTR, PVERT_BOTTOM};
    static Pvec ToTheLeft = {-1.0, 0.0};/* sent to "pset_char_up_vec" */
    Ppoint       Point;                         /* one point (for various purposes) */
    FILE         *datafile, *fopen();           /* file pointer */
    int          I;                             /* loop control variable */

    /*=== read data file into the structure array ==========================*/
    datafile = fopen("data", "r");         /* open data file (2 numbers/line) */
    while (fscanf(datafile, "%f%f", &LinePts[I].x, &LinePts[I].y) != EOF)
        I++;
    fclose(datafile);
    LineData.num_points = I;
    LineData.points = LinePts;
    /*=== set up PHIGS to plot data =====================================*/
    popen_phigs(stderr, 0);                     /* errors go to "stderr" */
    pescape_u4("/dev/screen/phigs_window", &ConnID);
    popen_ws(WorkstnID, ConnID, WorkstnType);
    DefineView(WorkstnID, 1,                    /* mapping for view index 1: */
      0.0,  1.0,  0.0,  1.0,                    /*   window: 0-1, 0-1 */
      0.12, 0.98, 0.10, 0.88,                   /*   viewport: in a subset */
      FALSE);                                   /*   don't clip at view window */
```

```
    DefineView(WorkstnID, 2,                /* mapping for view index 2: */
      0.0,  1.0,  0.0,  1.0,                /*   window: 0-1, 0-1 */
      0.0,  1.0,  0.0,  1.0,                /*   viewport: 0-1, 0-1 */
      TRUE);                                /*   clip at view window */
    popen_struct(TheCurve);
    /*=== create the labels ================================================*/
    pset_view_ind(2);
    /*--- do main title ----------------------------------------------------*/
    pset_text_font(BoldSansSerif);
    pset_text_align(&CenterTop);
    pset_char_ht(0.05);
    Point.x = 0.5, Point.y = 1.0;
    ptext(&Point, "VOLTAGE VARIANCE");
    /*--- do the x-axis title ----------------------------------------------*/
    pset_text_font(SimplexSansSerif);
    pset_text_align(&CenterBottom);
    pset_char_ht(0.03);
    Point.x = 0.5, Point.y = 0.0;
    ptext(&Point, "Time (seconds)");
    /*--- do the y-axis title ----------------------------------------------*/
    pset_char_up_vec(&ToTheLeft);
    pset_text_align(&CenterTop);
    Point.x = 0.0, Point.y = 0.5;
    ptext(&Point, "Voltage");
    /*=== graph the data ===================================================*/
    pset_view_ind(1);
    DefineRectangle(0.0, 1.0, 0.0, 1.0);
    ppolyline(&LineData);
    pclose_struct();
    /*=== post the image and close up shop ================================*/
    ppost_struct(WorkstnID, TheCurve, 1.0);
    pupd_ws(WorkstnID, PFLAG_PERFORM);  /* (regeneration flag) */
    pclose_ws(WorkstnID);
    pclose_phigs();
}
/****************************************************************************/
DefineView( ... )
/****************************************************************************/
DefineRectangle( ... )
```

When you recompile and run your program, the output should look like the image in Figure 2–8.

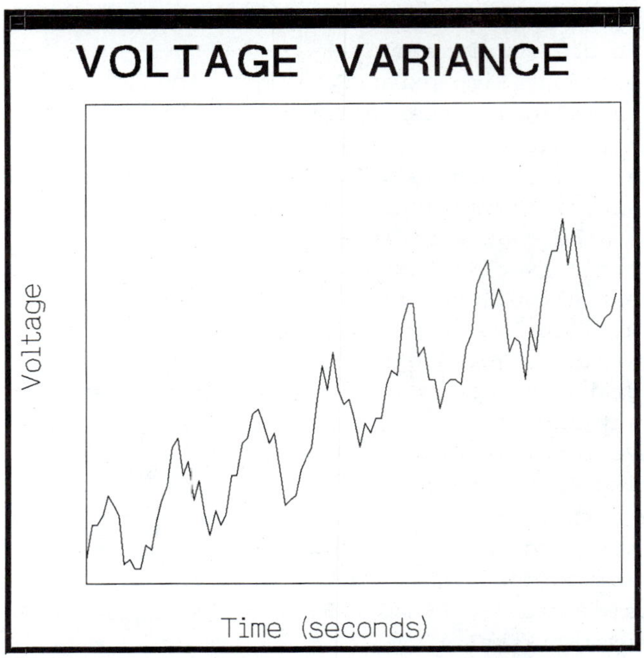

Figure 2–8. Progressive Example: Textual Labels

Next, the items bound to the viewport need to be drawn. These include the tic marks and the tic labels. The next sections discuss this.

Tic Marks

Tic marks are small lines that indicate intermediate points on an axis. They can be on any axis and usually indicate numbers with nice "round" values. We pointed out earlier that for esthetic reasons we chose our virtual data limits as 0.0–1.0 in both directions, rather than 0.00–0.99 and 0.03–0.74, which are the actual limits of the data. Round numbers are much more well behaved when making tic marks and their labels.

Another characteristic of tic marks is that there are usually two sizes of them used simultaneously, sometimes three, and maybe even more. The longer the tic mark is, the larger the division it indicates. A good example is a one-foot ruler. The major divisions are the inches; they have long, readily apparent tic marks. The half-inch tic marks are shorter, the quarter-inch tics are shorter yet, and the eighth-inch tics are still shorter.

All tic mark arrangements are not powers of two, despite the one-foot ruler example. Contrast a meter stick: the most fundamental division divides it (by ten) into decimeters. The decimeters are divided (by ten) into centimeters. These are usually grouped into two groups of five millimeters. The point is: The number of tic marks, and their grouping, can be whatever your application demands; there is no "correct" way to draw tic marks, although there are certain guidelines to help readability:

- Don't have too many tic marks. The eye can get confused trying to distinguish between tics that are extremely close together.
- Don't have too few tic marks. The eye is not very good at interpolating accurately over long distances.
- Place the tic marks on nice, round numbers. It's easier to count by multiples of 0.1 than of 0.095.
- Place major tics (the longer ones) on nice, round multiples of the small tics; e.g., a major tic every ten minor tics is probably better than one every eleven minor tics.
- It is often good to have tic marks on all edges of a graph, so a straight edge can be placed across the plot to ensure a datum is where you thought it was.

Our application requires tics from 0.00 through 1.00 by intervals of 0.01 on both axes. We want them on all four edges of the graph, for the reason mentioned in the last bulleted sentence.

There are seven things one needs to know when drawing tic marks. They are as follows:

- Which kind of axis will get the tics? That is, will they be labelling the x-axis or the y-axis?
- Where are the tics supposed to go? Assuming tics along an x-axis, should the tic marks be along the $y = 0$ line? At $y = 10$? In our example, the latter would all be invisible. We need to have them on the $y = 0.0$ and $y = 1.0$ lines.
- Where is the smallest-valued tic; i.e., where do you start drawing tics?
- Where is the largest-valued tic; i.e., where do you stop drawing tics?
- What is the delta? In other words, how far apart are the tics?
- How long should the tic marks themselves be?
- How often should there be a major tic? Every second one? Every tenth?

PHIGS does not have any procedures that create tics directly. However, the following routine can be used to generate tic marks. Because of the relatively large number of lines of code for each set of tic marks, it is more convenient to put the code into its own routine, as opposed to having inline code do similar things multiple times.

Insert the following subroutine at the end of the program.

```
/***************************************************************************/
DefineTics(Axis, Location, Start, End, Delta, Size, Major)
char    Axis;                               /* which axis are the tics for? */
float   Location;                           /* where is this line of tics? */
float   Start;                              /* where do the tics start? */
float   End;                                /* where do they end? */
float   Delta;                              /* draw a tic every how often? */
float   Size;                               /* how big should the tics be? */
int     Major;                             /* how often does a major tic occur? */
{
    int         TicNumber = 0;              /* which tic are we on? */
    Ppoint_list Tic;                        /* polyline data */
    Ppoint      TicPoints[2];               /* both ends of a tic mark */
    float       CurrentX, CurrentY;         /* loop control variables */
    float       Length;                     /* length of current tic mark */
```

```
    if ((Axis == 'x') || (Axis == 'X')) {
        for (CurrentX = Start; CurrentX <= End; CurrentX+=Delta,TicNumber++) {
            Length = Size * (1 + (TicNumber % Major == 0));
            Tic.num_points = 2;
            TicPoints[0].x = CurrentX;          /* x: bottom of tic mark */
            TicPoints[0].y = Location - Length; /* y: bottom of tic mark */
            TicPoints[1].x = CurrentX;          /* x: top of tic mark */
            TicPoints[1].y = Location + Length; /* y: top of tic mark */
            Tic.points = TicPoints;
            ppolyline(&Tic);
        }
    }
    else if ((Axis == 'y') || (Axis == 'Y')) {
        for (CurrentY = Start; CurrentY <= End; CurrentY+=Delta,TicNumber++) {
            Length = Size * (1 + (TicNumber % Major == 0));
            Tic.num_points = 2;
            TicPoints[0].x = Location - Length; /* x: bottom of tic mark */
            TicPoints[0].y = CurrentY;          /* y: bottom of tic mark */
            TicPoints[1].x = Location + Length; /* x: top of tic mark */
            TicPoints[1].y = CurrentY;          /* y: top of tic mark */
            Tic.points = TicPoints;
            ppolyline(&Tic);
        }
    }
}
```

Then, to actually define the tics, insert these five lines immediately after the curve-drawing code (between the POLYLINE and CLOSE STRUCTURE statements).

```
/*--- define the tic marks -------------------------------------------*/
DefineTics('X', 0.0, 0.0, 1.0, 0.01, 0.01, 5);
DefineTics('X', 1.0, 0.0, 1.0, 0.01, 0.01, 5);
DefineTics('Y', 0.0, 0.0, 1.0, 0.01, 0.01, 5);
DefineTics('Y', 1.0, 0.0, 1.0, 0.01, 0.01, 5);
```

Again compile and run the program. Figure 2–9 shows the output of the program.

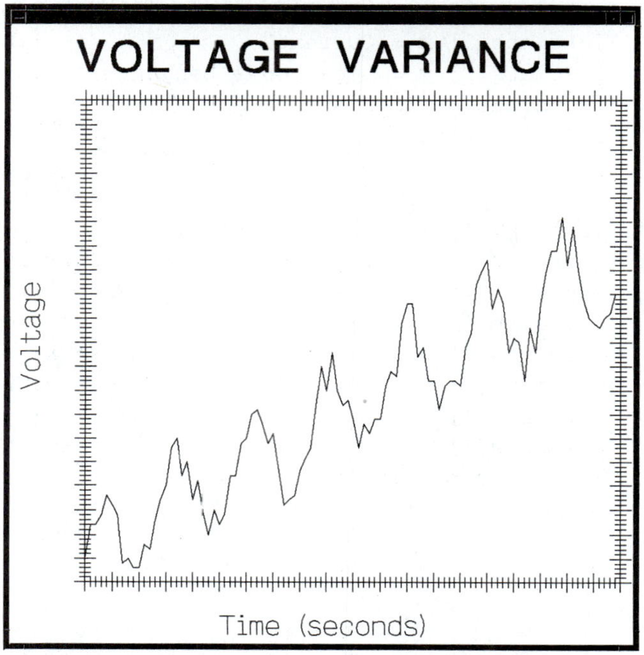

Figure 2–9. Progressive Example: Tic Marks on the Axes

Obviously, something is amiss. The tic marks extend *outside* the viewport as well as inside. This should be changed; it looks rather sloppy. The tic marks should be clipped at the viewport boundaries. It is evident that they were not.

The problem is that when we defined the view for the data-relative drawing (View #1), we set the clip limits equal to the whole display space, because we chose to be able to plot outside the viewport. But now we need a data-relative view that *does* clip at the viewport. Were we too smart for our own good when we defined View #1 *not* to clip at the projection viewport boundaries? No, not really. We'll still need a data-dependent view without clipping at the viewport (for the tic labels); now, we simply see that we'll also need a data-dependent view *with* clipping at the viewport (for the tic marks themselves). All the parameters for this new view, #3, would be the same as for View #1, except the last one; we *do* want clipping at the viewport boundaries this time. Thus, we see that we need three views in total:

- View #1: The viewport with its associated scaling and clip limits, in order to plot the curve and the tic labels
- View #2: The viewport that covers the whole display space and scales it from 0–1 in both directions, in order to place the global labels easily
- View #3: The viewport with its associated world coordinates, but *with* the clip limits imposed at the edges of the projection viewport, in order to clip the tic marks at the edge of the projection viewport

Add these lines right before the OPEN STRUCTURE call:

```
DefineView(WorkstnID, 3,             /* mapping for view index 3: */
  0.0,  1.0,  0.0,  1.0,             /*   window: 0-1, 0-1 */
  0.12, 0.98, 0.10, 0.88,            /*   viewport: in a subset */
  TRUE);                             /*   clip at view window */
```

And add the following line right before the calls to `DefineTics`:

```
pset_view_ind(3);
```

Now, after you recompile your program, the image should look like that in Figure 2–10.

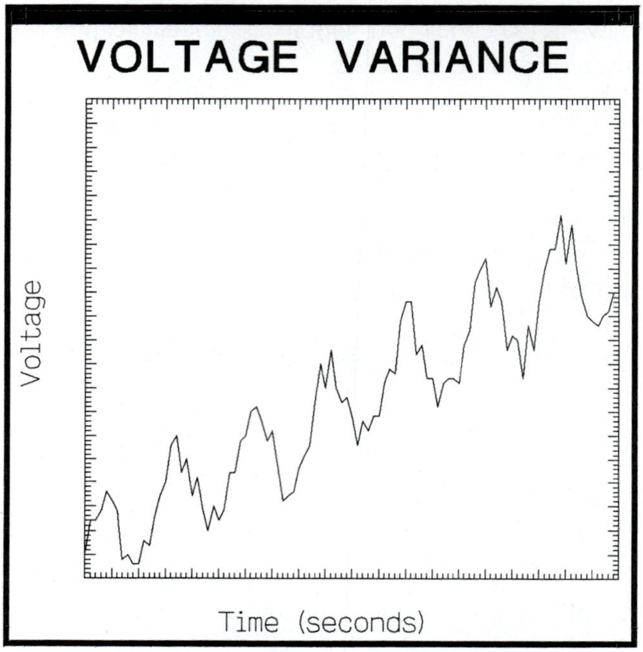

Figure 2–10. Progressive Example: Clipped Tic Marks

There is one final step to our progressive example: drawing the labels that indicate the tics' values. The next section deals with this.

Tic Labels

The **tic labels** should be rather straightforward; we covered almost all the necessary concepts when we did the other labels. Note that View #1 must be in effect in order for the tic labels to show up.

When View #1 is in effect, the characters' heights and widths will need to be redefined. After that, drawing the labels is a simple matter of a `while` loop. Insert this declaration line into your program immediately before the loop control variable declaration:

```
char         Strng[10];                /* temporary variable */
```

And insert these lines with the other text-alignment variable declarations:

```
static Ptext_align  RightHalf =      /* alignment for the y-axis tics */
             {PHOR_RIGHT, PVERT_HALF};
static Pvec StraightUp = {0.0, 1.0};/* sent to "pset_char_up_vec" */
```

. . . and put these lines right after the calls to `DefineTics`:

```
/*--- label the X tic marks ---------------------------------------------*/
pset_view_ind(1);
pset_char_up_vec(StraightUp);
pset_char_ht(0.02);
pset_char_expan(0.7);
pset_text_align(&CenterTop);
for (I = 0; I <= 100; I+=10) {
    Point.x = I * 0.01, Point.y = -0.005;
    sprintf(Strng, "%3.2f", I * 0.01);
    ptext(&Point, Strng);
}
/*--- label the Y tic marks ---------------------------------------------*/
pset_text_align(&RightHalf);
for (I = 0; I <= 100; I+=10) {
    Point.x = 0.0, Point.y = I * 0.01;
    sprintf(Strng, "%3.2f ", I * 0.01);
    ptext(&Point, Strng);
}
pclose_struct();
/*=== post the image and close up shop ==================================*/
```

Now, compile and run the program one more time. The final version of the output from the progressive example appears as in Figure 2–11.

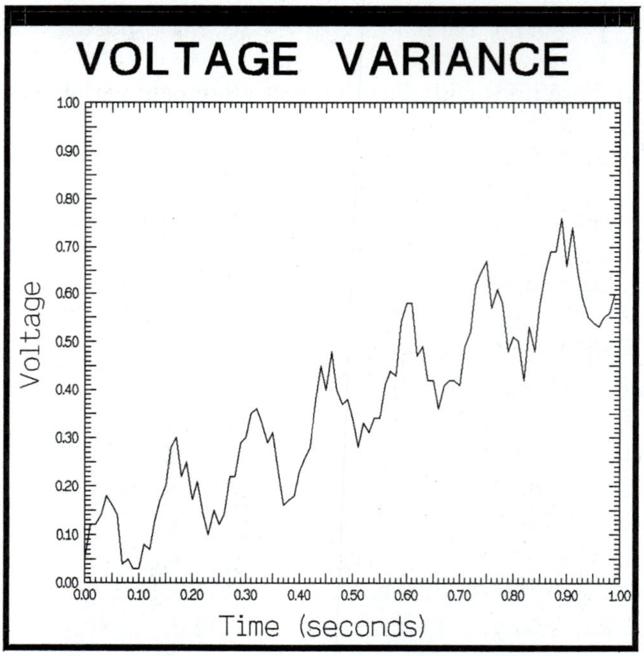

Figure 2–11. Progressive Example: Final Version

The Whole Progressive Example Program

Here is a listing of the final version of the progressive example program. It should be the same as the program you have been building throughout the chapter.

```
#include <phigs.h>                            /* get PHIGS definitions for C */
#include <stdio.h>                            /* get standard I/O definitions */
#define  FALSE                 0              /* boolean false is integer 0 */
#define  TRUE                  1              /* boolean true is integer 1 */
#define  SimplexSansSerif      -2             /* sent to "pset_text_font" */
#define  BoldSansSerif         -4             /* sent to "pset_text_font" */

main()                                        /* file "TicLabels.c" */
{
    int         WorkstnID = 1;                /* workstation identifier */
    int         ConnID;                       /* connection identifier */
    int         WorkstnType = POIDDX;         /* out/in, direct, dbl bfr, Xwindow */
    int         TheCurve = 1;                 /* structure ID (chosen by user) */
    Ppoint      LinePts[100];                 /* points for the polyline */
    Ppoint_list LineData;                     /* data for the polyline */
    static Ptext_align  CenterTop =           /* alignment for the main title */
                {PHOR_CTR, PVERT_TOP};
    static Ptext_align  CenterBottom =        /* alignment for the x-axis title */
                {PHOR_CTR, PVERT_BOTTOM};
    static Ptext_align  RightHalf =           /* alignment for the y-axis tics */
                {PHOR_RIGHT, PVERT_HALF};
    static Pvec ToTheLeft = {-1.0, 0.0};/* sent to "pset_char_up_vec" */
    static Pvec StraightUp = {0.0, 1.0};/* sent to "pset_char_up_vec" */
    Ppoint      Point;                        /* one point (for various purposes) */
    FILE        *datafile, *fopen();          /* file pointer */
    char        Strng[10];                    /* temporary variable */
    int         I;                            /* loop control variable */

    /*=== read data file into the structure array ==========================*/
    datafile = fopen("data", "r");       /* open data file (2 numbers/line) */
    while (fscanf(datafile, "%f%f", &LinePts[I].x, &LinePts[I].y) != EOF)
        I++;
    fclose(datafile);
    LineData.num_points = I;
    LineData.points = LinePts;
    /*=== set up PHIGS to plot data ====================================*/
    popen_phigs(stderr, 0);                   /* errors go to "stderr" */
```

```
pescape_u4("/dev/screen/phigs_window", &ConnID);
popen_ws(WorkstnID, ConnID, WorkstnType);
DefineView(WorkstnID, 1,              /* mapping for view index 1: */
  0.0,  1.0,  0.0,  1.0,              /*   window: 0-1, 0-1 */
  0.12, 0.98, 0.10, 0.88,             /*   viewport: in a subset */
  FALSE);                             /*   don't clip at view window */
DefineView(WorkstnID, 2,              /* mapping for view index 2: */
  0.0,  1.0,  0.0,  1.0,              /*   window: 0-1, 0-1 */
  0.0,  1.0,  0.0,  1.0,              /*   viewport: 0-1, 0-1 */
  TRUE);                              /*   clip at view window */
DefineView(WorkstnID, 3,              /* mapping for view index 3: */
  0.0,  1.0,  0.0,  1.0,              /*   window: 0-1, 0-1 */
  0.12, 0.98, 0.10, 0.88,             /*   viewport: in a subset */
  TRUE);                              /*   clip at view window */
popen_struct(TheCurve);
/*=== create the labels ================================================*/
pset_view_ind(2);
/*--- do main title ----------------------------------------------------*/
pset_text_font(BoldSansSerif);
pset_text_align(&CenterTop);
pset_char_ht(0.05);
Point.x = 0.5, Point.y = 1.0;
ptext(&Point, "VOLTAGE VARIANCE");
/*--- do the x-axis title ----------------------------------------------*/
pset_text_font(SimplexSansSerif);
pset_text_align(&CenterBottom);
pset_char_ht(0.03);
Point.x = 0.5, Point.y = 0.0;
ptext(&Point, "Time (seconds)");
/*--- do the y-axis title ----------------------------------------------*/
pset_char_up_vec(&ToTheLeft);
pset_text_align(&CenterTop);
Point.x = 0.0, Point.y = 0.5;
ptext(&Point, "Voltage");
/*=== graph the data ===================================================*/
pset_view_ind(1);
DefineRectangle(0.0, 1.0, 0.0, 1.0);
ppolyline(&LineData);
/*--- define the tic marks ---------------------------------------------*/
pset_view_ind(3);
DefineTics('X', 0.0, 0.0, 1.0, 0.01, 0.01, 5);
DefineTics('X', 1.0, 0.0, 1.0, 0.01, 0.01, 5);
DefineTics('Y', 0.0, 0.0, 1.0, 0.01, 0.01, 5);
```

```
    DefineTics('Y', 1.0, 0.0, 1.0, 0.01, 0.01, 5);
    /*--- label the X tic marks -------------------------------------------*/
    pset_view_ind(1);
    pset_char_up_vec(StraightUp);
    pset_char_ht(0.02);
    pset_char_expan(0.7);
    pset_text_align(&CenterTop);
    for (I = 0; I <= 100; I+=10) {
        Point.x = I * 0.01, Point.y = -0.005;
        sprintf(Strng, "%3.2f", I * 0.01);
        ptext(&Point, Strng);
    }
    /*--- label the Y tic marks -------------------------------------------*/
    pset_text_align(&RightHalf);
    for (I = 0; I <= 100; I+=10) {
        Point.x = 0.0, Point.y = I * 0.01;
        sprintf(Strng, "%3.2f ", I * 0.01);
        ptext(&Point, Strng);
    }
    pclose_struct();
    /*=== post the image and close up shop ===============================*/
    ppost_struct(WorkstnID, TheCurve, 1.0);
    pupd_ws(WorkstnID, PFLAG_PERFORM);  /* (regeneration flag) */
    pclose_ws(WorkstnID);
    pclose_phigs();
}
/**************************************************************************/
DefineView(WorkstnID, ViewIndex, Wxmin, Wxmax, Wymin, Wymax,
  Vxmin, Vxmax, Vymin, Vymax, ClipAtViewport)
int     WorkstnID;                      /* workstation identifier */
int     ViewIndex;                      /* the view being defined */
float   Wxmin, Wxmax, Wymin, Wymax;     /* view window limits */
float   Vxmin, Vxmax, Vymin, Vymax;     /* projection viewport limits */
int     ClipAtViewport;                 /* window (or display surface?) */
{
    Pview_map   Mapping;                /* window-onto-viewport mapping */
    Pint        ErrorReturn;            /* error return variable */
    Pview_rep   ViewRep;                /* complete description of view */
    int         I, J;                   /* loop control variables */

    /*--- define the view orientation matrix as identity ------------------*/
    for (I = 0; I < 3; I++)
        for (J = 0; J < 3; J++)
```

```
            ViewRep.ori_matrix[I][J] = (I == J);
    /*--- define view mapping matrix ------------------------------------------*/
    Mapping.win.x_min = Wxmin;                        /* \                       */
    Mapping.win.x_max = Wxmax;                        /*  \ put individual values */
    Mapping.win.y_min = Wymin;                        /*  / into the structure    */
    Mapping.win.y_max = Wymax;                        /* /                       */
    Mapping.proj_vp.x_min = Vxmin;                    /* \                       */
    Mapping.proj_vp.x_max = Vxmax;                    /*  \ put individual values */
    Mapping.proj_vp.y_min = Vymin;                    /*  / into the structure    */
    Mapping.proj_vp.y_max = Vymax;                    /* /                       */
    peval_view_map_matrix(&Mapping, &ErrorReturn, ViewRep.map_matrix);
    if (ErrorReturn != 0) {                           /* did we get an error? */
        printf("%s %d %s %s\n", "Error", ErrorReturn, "occurred during",
          "call to Evaluate View Mapping Matrix.");
        exit(1);
    }
    /*--- define the clip limits ----------------------------------------------*/
    if (ClipAtViewport)
        ViewRep.clip_limit = Mapping.proj_vp;   /* clip at viewport */
    else {
        ViewRep.clip_limit.x_min = 0.0;           /* \                  */
        ViewRep.clip_limit.x_max = 1.0;           /*  \ clip at edges of */
        ViewRep.clip_limit.y_min = 0.0;           /*  / display surface  */
        ViewRep.clip_limit.y_max = 1.0;           /* /                  */
    }
    /*--- define clip indicator -----------------------------------------------*/
    ViewRep.xy_clip = PIND_CLIP;
    /*--- set the view representation -----------------------------------------*/
    pset_view_rep(WorkstnID, ViewIndex, &ViewRep);
}
/*****************************************************************************/
DefineRectangle(Xmin, Xmax, Ymin, Ymax)
float   Xmin, Xmax, Ymin, Ymax;                    /* rectangle's limits */
{
    Ppoint_list Rectangle;
    Ppoint      Corners[5];

    Rectangle.num_points = 5;
    Corners[0].x = Xmin, Corners[0].y = Ymin;   /* lower left corner */
    Corners[1].x = Xmax, Corners[1].y = Ymin;   /* lower right corner */
    Corners[2].x = Xmax, Corners[2].y = Ymax;   /* upper right corner */
    Corners[3].x = Xmin, Corners[3].y = Ymax;   /* upper left corner */
    Corners[4].x = Xmin, Corners[4].y = Ymin;   /* lower left corner */
```

```
    Rectangle.points = Corners;
    ppolyline(&Rectangle);
}
/**************************************************************************/
DefineTics(Axis, Location, Start, End, Delta, Size, Major)
char    Axis;                               /* which axis are the tics for? */
float   Location;                           /* where is this line of tics? */
float   Start;                              /* where do the tics start? */
float   End;                                /* where do they end? */
float   Delta;                              /* draw a tic every how often? */
float   Size;                               /* how big should the tics be? */
int     Major;                             /* how often does a major tic occur? */
{
    int         TicNumber = 0;              /* which tic are we on? */
    Ppoint_list Tic;                        /* polyline data */
    Ppoint      TicPoints[2];               /* both ends of a tic mark */
    float       CurrentX, CurrentY;         /* loop control variables */
    float       Length;                     /* length of current tic mark */
    if ((Axis == 'x') || (Axis == 'X')) {
        for (CurrentX = Start; CurrentX <= End; CurrentX+=Delta,TicNumber++) {
            Length = Size * (1 + (TicNumber % Major == 0));
            Tic.num_points = 2;
            TicPoints[0].x = CurrentX;          /* x: bottom of tic mark */
            TicPoints[0].y = Location - Length; /* y: bottom of tic mark */
            TicPoints[1].x = CurrentX;          /* x: top of tic mark */
            TicPoints[1].y = Location + Length; /* y: top of tic mark */
            Tic.points = TicPoints;
            ppolyline(&Tic);
        }
    }
    else if ((Axis == 'y') || (Axis == 'Y')) {
        for (CurrentY = Start; CurrentY <= End; CurrentY+=Delta,TicNumber++) {
            Length = Size * (1 + (TicNumber % Major == 0));
            Tic.num_points = 2;
            TicPoints[0].x = Location - Length; /* x: bottom of tic mark */
            TicPoints[0].y = CurrentY;          /* y: bottom of tic mark */
            TicPoints[1].x = Location + Length; /* x: top of tic mark */
            TicPoints[1].y = CurrentY;          /* y: top of tic mark */
            Tic.points = TicPoints;
            ppolyline(&Tic);
        }
    }
}
```

Chapter 3

Controlling PHIGS

This chapter describes the following topics:

- Opening and closing the PHIGS package
- The PHIGS workstation
- Opening and closing structures and the central structure store (CSS)
- Operating states
- Error handling

You will notice that in this chapter we begin using the following formats for the routines:

- For the FORTRAN binding we show the calling syntax. This shows the way to include a routine in your program. For example:

  `call popph(`*error_file*, *buffer_size*`)`

- For the C binding we show the function prototype. This shows how to declare the parameters for the routine. For example:

  ```
  popen_phigs(
  const char *error_file,
  size_t     buffer_size
  );
  ```

We invoke "literary license" and refer to the two formats as the **calling signatures** in order to save space. See Appendix D for the definition of the various C binding data types.

Also note that whenever we give the FORTRAN and C binding values for enumerated types, we put the values in parentheses and list the FORTRAN value first. For example, the values for error-handling state off are (`POFF`, `PERR_OFF`).

Opening and Closing PHIGS

Before virtually anything else can be done with PHIGS, it must be opened, or "turned on." This is accomplished through the OPEN PHIGS routine. The following shows the calling signatures for OPEN PHIGS:

```
call popph(error_file, buffer_size)
```

```
popen_phigs(
   const char     *error_file,
   size_t          buffer_size
);
```

where:

> ⟨*error_file*⟩ identifies the stream to which error messages are sent. The value you supply is implementation-dependent. Usually a value of 1 is sufficient to direct error output to standard out.
>
> ⟨*buffer_size*⟩ is an integer that specifies the size, in bytes, of the PHIGS buffer area. This value is implementation-dependent. Some implementations choose to ignore it.

As you might guess, you can't open PHIGS unless it is closed.

Once you have opened PHIGS, in order to close it, use the CLOSE PHIGS routine:

```
call pclph
```

```
pclose_phigs(
   void
);
```

CLOSE PHIGS requires no parameters for operation. Before you call this routine all workstations, structures, and archive files must be closed. PHIGS can be reopened after it is closed.

Description Tables and State Lists

There are two conceptual groupings of data used by PHIGS: **description tables** and **state lists**. Description tables contain default values, capabilities, and characteristics and cannot be modified by the application. State lists contain the current values set by the application (or defaults that are being used). Table 3–1 lists the different kinds of tables and state lists.

Table 3–1. Description Tables and State Lists

Type	Contents	Names
Description Tables	Initial values and system limits. Not modifiable by the application but can be inquired.	PHIGS description table Workstation description tables (one for each workstation type)
State Lists	Current application–dependent values. An application modifies state list values either directly or indirectly. All state list values can be inquired.	PHIGS state list Workstation state list (one for each open workstation) Structure state list (one for each structure in the CSS) Traversal state list Error state list

The PHIGS Description Table

When you open PHIGS, it makes available a **PHIGS description table** (**PDT**), which is a list of capabilities that relate to the PHIGS system in general. Included are items such as the list of available workstation types, the default linetype, and the default height for text. You can interrogate these values through inquiry routines, but you cannot change any of the values. See the "Inquiring the PHIGS Description Table" section in Chapter 22, *Programming with PHIGS* for more information. Also refer to Appendix A for a list of routines that inquire the PHIGS description table.

The PHIGS State List

When you open PHIGS, it also sets up a **PHIGS state list** (**PSL**) and initializes it with default values. This is a list of the current values of PHIGS-level state variables that can be changed at will by the application program. In it are such things as the set of currently open workstations, the name of the open structure (if any), the current element pointer, the edit mode, and so forth. All of these things, and many others in the PSL, can be changed and inquired by the application program by calling the appropriate PHIGS routines. Refer to Appendix A for a list of routines that inquire values from the PHIGS state list.

The rest of the description tables and state lists are described in sections treating the functions related to them. For example, the workstation description table and PHIGS state list are described in this chapter in the next section, "The PHIGS Workstation."

Refer to Clause 6 in the PHIGS standard for a complete list of all the values in the various description tables and state lists.

The PHIGS Workstation

A workstation, in the context of PHIGS, is an abstract collection of graphics capabilities that provides the logical interface to control the actual graphics hardware and software. For output, the PHIGS abstract display surface is implemented via a connection to an output device, for example, an X window for displaying an image, or a metafile for storing or printing an image. For input, the workstation has zero or more abstract "logical input devices" that are implemented via connections to physical input devices such as keyboards, graphics tablets, and window system pointers.

Each PHIGS implementation has a limited variety of actual graphics equipment that it can control. In addition, a single set of equipment can be used to implement PHIGS functions in, perhaps, a few different ways (for example, double-buffered versus single-buffered). The **workstation type** in PHIGS is used to differentiate among the following:

- Among the different classes of graphics equipment an implementation can control
- Among the significantly different modes of use of one set of equipment

Refer to Chapter 1, *What Is PHIGS?*, for a description of the terms "workstation-dependent" and "workstation-independent."

The Workstation Category

As mentioned, a workstation is a combination of a display surface and zero or more logical input devices. To describe the combinations that can constitute a valid workstation, PHIGS defines the concept of a **workstation category**. Each type of workstation is of one of the following categories:

OUTPUT Has a display surface but no logical input devices. One example would be a pen plotter. Also, if you just want to display output on a terminal screen and don't expect input from the operator, you could use the terminal screen as an output workstation.

INPUT Has no display surface and has one or more logical input devices. For example, a digitizing tablet.

OUTIN (from OUTput/INput) Has a display surface and one or more logical input devices. This is our common conception of a workstation with one or more input devices such as a mouse and keyboard.

MO (from Metafile Output) Writes graphics image information to an external file called a **metafile**. The metafile can be used for information storage and exchange with other graphics libraries.

MI (from Metafile Input) Reads information from a metafile into PHIGS data structures.

One important purpose of the workstation category is to define which operations are valid for a particular workstation. For example, if you attempt to do any input operations on a workstation that is of category OUTPUT, you will receive error messages indicating that the workstation is of the wrong category.

The workstation category is also relevant when choosing a workstation type for opening a workstation. You can select the workstation type based on the operations you wish to perform once the workstation is open.

Different PHIGS implementations support different numbers of workstation categories. The list of categories that an implementation supports is stored in the workstation description tables (more on this later). You can use the INQUIRE WORKSTATION CATEGORY routine to inquire the available categories. Refer to your implementation documentation for specifics on each workstation category.

Opening and Closing a Workstation

The calling signatures for the OPEN WORKSTATION and CLOSE WORKSTATION routines are as follows:

```
call popwk(workstation_id, connection_id, workstation_type)
```

```
popen_ws(
   Pint          workstation_id,
   const void    *connection_id,
   Pint          workstation_type
);
```

and

```
call pclwk(workstation_id)
```

```
pclose_ws(
   Pint          workstation_id
);
```

where:

⟨*workstation_id*⟩ is an integer, specified by the application program, that will identify this particular workstation for all subsequent operations pertaining to it until the workstation is closed.

⟨*connection_id*⟩ is the "connection identifier," which is an implementation-specific means of defining the connection between the logical workstation and the actual device.

⟨*workstation_type*⟩ is an implementation-specific integer that specifies the desired general input/output capabilities and characteristics of the workstation being opened. Legal values are implementation-dependent and are defined in the PHIGS "include" file.

Note that the ⟨*workstation_type*⟩ used by OPEN WORKSTATION represents a *generic* workstation type. There is also such a thing as a *specific* workstation type; this is covered in the next section.

Workstation Types and Workstation Description Tables

Workstation types are either generic or specific; generic workstation types exist even before any workstations are open, and a specific workstation type is created whenever a workstation is opened. You pass a generic type to PHIGS when you call OPEN WORKSTATION. As mentioned earlier, the names of the generic types are listed in the PHIGS "include" file.

There exists for each workstation type a **workstation description table** (**WDT**) that defines characteristics about the workstation type which generally do not change. Each WDT is identified by its associated workstation type. The following are some of the values in a workstation description table:

- Workstation category
- Device coordinate units
- Maximum display space size
- The number of predefined view table entries
- Default values for each view table entry
- The number of available linetypes
- A list of the available linetypes

When you invoke OPEN WORKSTATION, PHIGS performs the following steps:

4. Opens a workstation and assigns it a new "specific workstation type."
5. Creates a workstation description table for the new specific workstation type. PHIGS obtains many of the values from the generic WDT.

Note that the words "specific" and "generic" apply to *workstation types*, not to workstations!

A generic WDT has default values that never change. A generic WDT in some cases has undefined entries because those entries cannot be known until a connection is made to a physical device for that workstation type. For example, a generic workstation that displays in an X window will probably not have a defined value for the "display space size" entry because an X window could be of *any* size; there is no way of knowing how big the display space will ultimately be until the workstation is actually opened to a window. Once the workstation is opened, its specific workstation type will have a display space size in its WDT. This value may change if the user resizes the window, but at any given time there will be a value.

One of the reasons for making a distinction between generic and specific workstation types is to allow the application to make decisions about which workstation type to select for a particular graphics session. The entire list of generic workstation types can be inquired. Also, for each type, every value in the corresponding workstation description table can be inquired. By inquiring these values you can determine which workstation type you want to use and also make decisions about how your application will operate while using that workstation type.

Generally, the WDTs of generic workstation types are inquired before a workstation is opened, and the WDTs of specific workstation types are inquired afterwards. It is usually better to inquire values pertaining to the specific workstation type, as those are more accurate for the device. See the "Device-Independent Programming" section in Chapter 22.

See Appendix A for a list of routines that inquire the workstation description table.

The Workstation State List

In addition to the workstation description table, there is a collection of information called the **workstation state list (WSL)**. When a workstation is opened, PHIGS defines a WSL for the workstation and initializes it with default values, many of which are copied from the WDT.

As its name implies, the WSL represents the current state of the various workstation attributes that can be modified by the application program. In other words, this state list represents dynamic data for a given workstation at a specific point in time, in contrast to the information in the WDT, which is largely static. The WSL contains information such as the current definitions of the viewing transformation matrices, clip limits and their indicators, update states, and workstation attribute table definitions. The following is a list of some of the values in the WSL:

- A list of structures posted to the workstation
- The state of visual representation (correct, deferred, or simulated)
- The number of entries in the polyline bundle table
- Current values for each entry in the polyline bundle table
- The number of view table entries

- Current and requested values for each view table entry
- Values for input device state (set and realized values)

Current and Requested Values

There are "current" and "requested" entries for some kinds of information in the WSL, such as view table data. Requested entries contain values most recently set by the application (or defaults). Current entries contain values (requested at some time by the application, or defaults) that are potentially in use for mapping input location data from device coordinates to modelling coordinates and for mapping output coordinate data when image regeneration is deferred (see Chapter 4, *Posting Structures and Controlling Picture Changes*, and Chapter 14, *Graphical Input*).

Current entries are frequently the same as requested entries. When you inquire this kind of information, you get both current and requested values.

Set and Realized Values

There are "set" and "realized" values in some WSL entries, such as a logical input device's state. Set values are the values requested by the application. PHIGS may or may not be able to actually use those values. Realized values are the values that PHIGS will actually use. When you inquire the values, you can specify that you want either the set or the realized values returned.

Structures and the Central Structure Store

PHIGS organizes graphical data into units called structures. Each structure is identified by a unique, application-supplied structure name. A structure contains a list of structure elements that define a geometric model.

The following lists the structure elements:

Output primitive — Describes the indivisible, displayable components of a picture, such as polylines, fill areas, and text.

Attribute — Contains values that determine how a primitive is displayed (for example, text height or line colour). There are four types of attribute elements: geometric, nongeometric, viewing, and identification.

Modelling transformation	Defines how output primitives are positioned in relationship to world coordinates. The structure element contains either a 4×4 or a 3×3 transformation matrix.
Modelling clip element	Allows the application to clip primitives at the modelling stage, before the viewing transformation. This is useful for seeing into a model that would otherwise be obscured by an opaque cover.
Execute structure element	References (executes) another structure. Similar to a subroutine call in a program. This feature allows you to build a description of a large, complex model from a collection of simple pieces.
Label element	Marks a point in a structure. It contains an integer marker that allows you to associate groups of elements within a structure. This allows for convenient interactive editing of structures (for example, delete all of the elements between two labels).
Application data element	Offers a way to store non–PHIGS-related data within a structure (for example, a part number).
Generalized structure element	Allows an implementation to create its own specialized structure elements.

Structure elements are always inside structures; they cannot exist outside of structures.

Central Structure Store

The PHIGS standard defines a central structure store (CSS) that contains structures that can be traversed and rendered by any workstation opened by the (same) application program. Structures can be saved between executions of an application program by writing them to an archive file.

One implication of this display list functionality is that the creation and manipulation of the data in the CSS are completely independent of its display; that is, you can define models, change them, and remove them—all without ever displaying them. Of course, there would be little reason for defining a model if it weren't going to be output somewhere *eventually*.

Structures can be related to each other in a hierarchy known as a **structure network**. You can have many structure networks in the CSS. See Chapter 5, *Using Structures*, for more information on structures.

The Operating States

The operation of PHIGS is organized according to the values of four state variables. Each of these variables can have the state "open"—meaning that the variable is logically associated with the application and available for modification—or "closed"—meaning that the variable is logically unassociated with the application and therefore unavailable for modification. The four state variables and possible values are as follows:

- System state
  - PHIGS is open (`PPHOP`, `PSYS_ST_PHOP`).
  - PHIGS is closed (`PPHCL`, `PSYS_ST_PHCL`).
- Workstation state
  - At least one workstation is open (`PWSOP`, `PWS_ST_WSOP`).
  - No workstations are open (`PWSCL`, `PWS_ST_WSCL`).
- Structure state
  - A structure is open (`PSTOP`, `PSTRUCT_ST_STOP`).
  - No structure is open (`PSTCL`, `PSTRUCT_ST_STCL`).
- Archive state
  - At least one structure archive file is open (`PAROP`, `PST_AROP`).
  - No structure archive files are open (`PARCL`, `PST_ARCL`).

This list shows the FORTRAN and C binding values. When we refer to state values throughout this book, we use the standard PHIGS four letter notation. This is the FORTRAN notation without the leading "`P`." For example, `PHOP` stands for "PHIGS is open."

At any specific time, PHIGS is in a particular operating state defined by the current values of the four state variables. This "overall" state is important in determining which routines can subsequently be called.

Any desired (and legal) combination of the four states can be expressed according to the standard PHIGS convention by listing them in the previously mentioned order, separated by commas, and surrounded by parentheses. For example, before anything PHIGS-related at all happens in a program, the state is `(PHCL,WSCL,STCL,ARCL)`; everything is in a closed state. Then, after OPEN PHIGS is successfully called, the state is `(PHOP,WSCL,STCL,ARCL)`. Figure 3–1 shows the relationship between the open states.

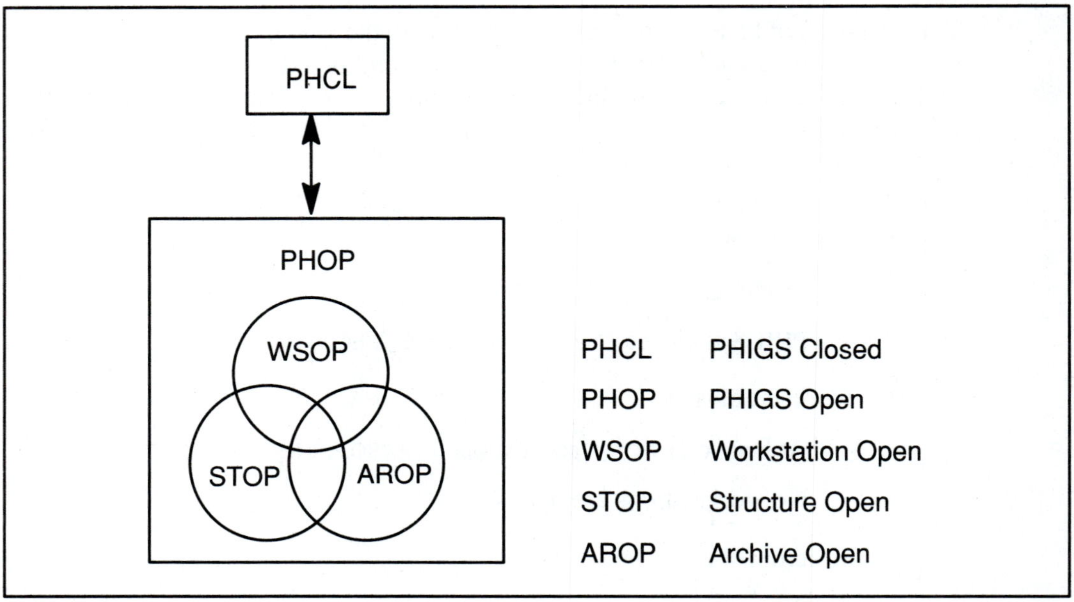

Figure 3–1. PHIGS Operating States

Every routine in PHIGS requires the application to be in one (of perhaps several) specific operating state when the routine is called. In many cases, one or more of the state variables is irrelevant; the value of that particular state variable can be either open or closed. In these cases, the irrelevant state variable value is denoted by an asterisk. One example of this is the POLYLINE routine: Its state requirements are `(PHOP,*,STOP,*)`. This means that PHIGS must be open, a workstation may or may not be open, a structure must be open, and an archive may or may not be open.

Error Handling

For most PHIGS routines, several error situations can occur, any one of which causes the ERROR HANDLING routine to be called. The ERROR HANDLING routine is an interface between PHIGS and your application program. There is a default error-handling routine, of course. However, most implementations allow you to replace this default routine with a customized error-handling routine of your own. You may also want your error routine to set a flag in some application-defined data area, so that the application can take appropriate action upon return from the PHIGS routine that detected the error.

There are three different situations in which PHIGS can detect errors:

Situation A:	An error is detected in one of the PHIGS routines.
Situation B:	An error is detected in routines called from PHIGS, such as driver or system calls.
Situation C:	An error is detected in other areas of the application program

In addition, there are three different classes of errors that can occur:

Class I:	Errors result in a precisely defined reaction.
Class II:	Errors result in an attempt to save the results of previous operations.
Class III:	Errors cause unpredictable results, including the loss of data.

As you might expect, with three situations in which errors can occur and three different classes of errors, there are several error-handling options that can be derived from the various combinations. These are discussed next.

Actions Caused by Error Conditions

The most common case first: All errors that are explicitly listed as part of the definition of PHIGS routines are Class I errors. For example, if you attempt to post a structure before opening a workstation, PHIGS responds with error message number 3:

```
Ignoring function, function requires state (PHOP,WSOP,*,*)
```

When a Class I error occurs, either Situation A or Situation B can result:

- The error is detected within PHIGS itself (Situation A), or
- A routine that was called from PHIGS has returned control, with the appropriate error information, to the corresponding PHIGS routine (Situation B).

In either of these Class I cases, PHIGS calls the ERROR HANDLING routine. If a PHIGS routine is called when multiple error conditions exist, at least one error is reported.

If errors are detected outside PHIGS—that is, detected by the application program—(Situation C), one of two outcomes results. Either:

- The application program regains control over the program execution, or
- Program execution will be terminated abnormally.

If an error occurs and your application can regain control over program execution the latter case, the results are unpredictable—it is a Class III error—and in the worst case, all graphical information produced thus far by the application can be lost. However, if the program regains control, it may attempt to close PHIGS in the normal manner or at least attempt an emergency closure by calling EMERGENCY CLOSE PHIGS. Similarly, if the error occurs in a routine that was called by PHIGS (for example, an operating system routine), and control is not returned to PHIGS properly, the results are likewise unpredictable.

Most error conditions are considered Class I errors. They fall into Situation A (they are detected within PHIGS). The exceptions are "900" errors, which usually fall into Situation B.

The Error-Handling Process

Upon entry to every PHIGS routine, several tests are automatically performed. Whenever an error is detected by PHIGS, the following sequence of events takes place:

- The error state (part of the PHIGS state) is set to on.
- The ERROR HANDLING routine is called with appropriate parameters.
- Upon return from ERROR HANDLING, the error state is set to off.
- The built-in error response is executed (in most cases, the routine detecting the error becomes a no-op; occasionally, this requires some extra clean-up).

Figures 3–2 and 3–3 show an approximation of the PHIGS error-handling process. As shown in Figure 3–3, the ERROR HANDLING routine—the default routine provided by PHIGS—merely calls the ERROR LOGGING routine. ERROR LOGGING then does the following:

- Writes the error message and PHIGS routine identification on the error file (identified in the OPEN PHIGS routine)
- Returns to the routine that called ERROR LOGGING

It is beneficial to the user that the error processing takes place in two stages as it allows the application to supply its own error-handling routine and still have access to services provided by the ERROR LOGGING routine. This is illustrated in the upcoming example program.

Error State List

PHIGS maintains an **error state list** that stores the following information:

- The error state (on or off).
- The error-handling mode (on or off).
- The error file ID.
- If an input queue overflow has occurred, the identification of (any one of the) logical input devices that caused the overflow. This includes the workstation ID, input class, and logical device number (see Chapter 14 for information on logical input devices).

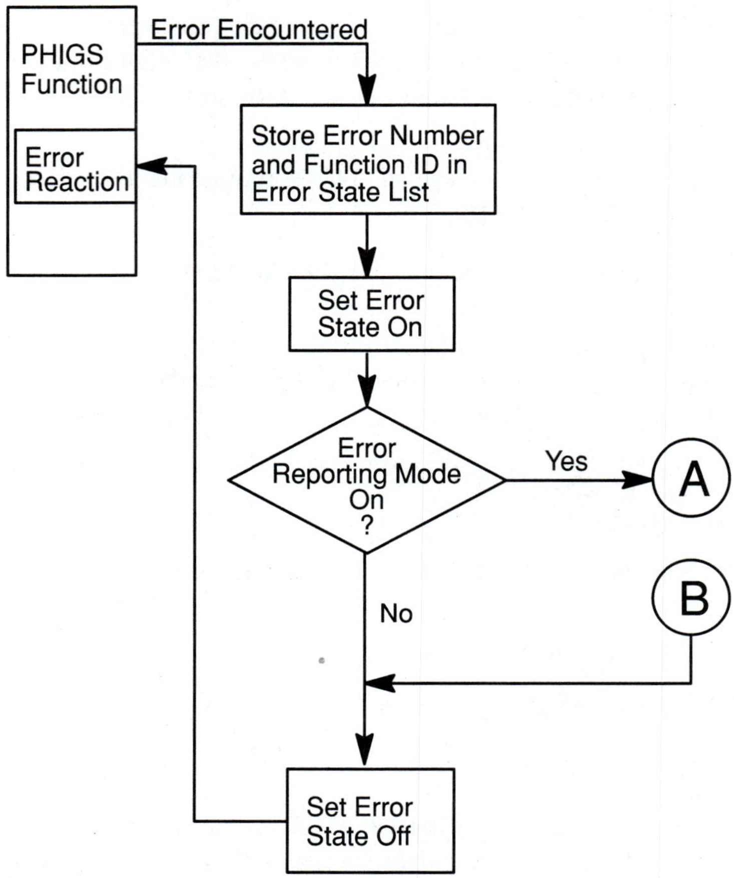

Figure 3–2. PHIGS Error Handling

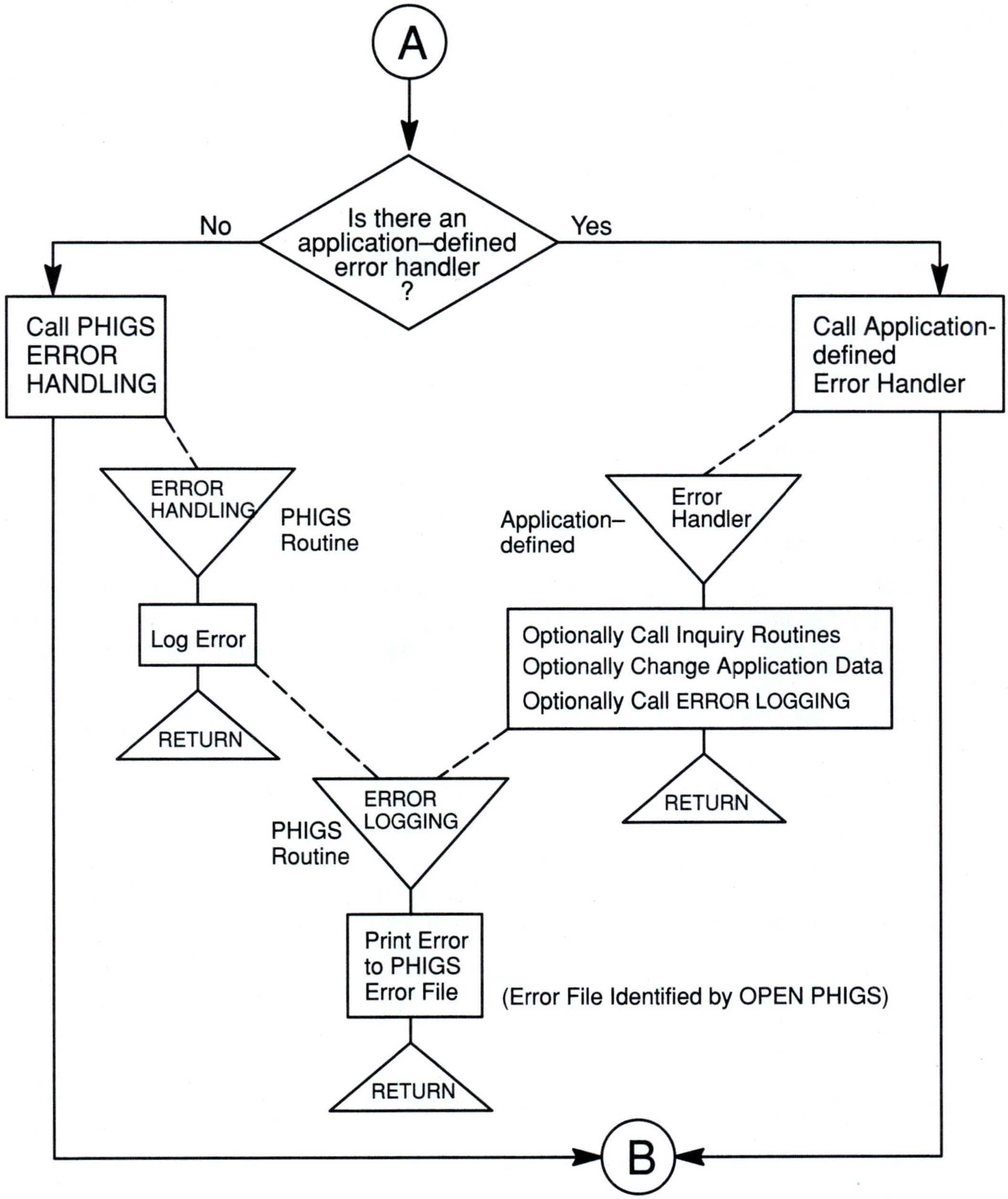

Figure 3–3. PHIGS Error Handling (continued)

The Error-handling Routines

The following standard routines relate to error handling:

- EMERGENCY CLOSE PHIGS
- SET ERROR HANDLING MODE
- INQUIRE ERROR HANDLING MODE
- ERROR LOGGING
- ERROR HANDLING

These routines are discussed in detail in the following sections.

Emergency Close

The EMERGENCY CLOSE PHIGS routine can be called directly from your application. You would typically use this routine if you caught an error in your application program and you realized that the best thing to do is exit PHIGS as quickly and as gracefully as possible.

```
call peclph
```

```
pemegency_close_phigs(
   void
);
```

The EMERGENCY CLOSE PHIGS routine attempts to save as much of the graphical information as possible. The following actions are performed (if possible):

- Close structure (if open)
- Close all open archive files
- Update all open workstations to make all pending values current
- Close all open workstations
- Close PHIGS

PHIGS may automatically call this routine if it detects an unrecoverable system error.

Note that the PHIGS standard says that you can call EMERGENCY CLOSE PHIGS from an application-defined error handler. However, a subsequent return from the error handler may have unpredictable results. For example, if the EMERGENCY CLOSE PHIGS routine destroys the error state list, when PHIGS attempts to set the error state to off or tries to execute an error reaction (see Figure 3–2), the routines may not execute correctly. Our advice is that you should never expect your program to live after calling EMERGENCY CLOSE PHIGS.

Set/Inquire Error Handling Mode

The SET ERROR HANDLING MODE routine disables/enables the call to ERROR HANDLING when an error is encountered. The INQUIRE ERROR HANDLING MODE routine returns the current value. The default value is on, which enables error handling.

```
call pserhm(state)
```

```
pset_err_hand_mode(
    Perr_mode        state
);
```

and

```
call pqerhm(error_indicator, state)
```

```
pinq_err_hand_mode(
    Pint             *error_indicator,
    Perr_mode        *state
);
```

where:

⟨*state*⟩ is an integer, specifying the state of error handling. The value is either off (`POFF, PERR_OFF`) or on (`PON, PERR_ON`).

⟨*error_indicator*⟩ is an integer that indicates which error, if any, was detected by the inquiry routine.

Error Logging

The ERROR LOGGING routine writes the appropriate error message and the PHIGS routine identifier in the error file. The calling signatures for the routine are as follows:

```
call perlog(error_num, routine_id, error_file)
```

```
perr_log(
   Pint            error_num,
   Pint            routine_id,
   const char      *error_file
);
```

where:

⟨*error_num*⟩ is an integer that tells which error was detected.

⟨*routine_id*⟩ in an integer that identifies the PHIGS routine that initiated the error-handling process.

⟨*error_file*⟩ indicates the stream to which the error-message text is to be written (the same one that was given to OPEN PHIGS). For FORTRAN this parameter is an integer, but for C it is a "`const char *`" which is the name of a file.

Creating Your Own Error Handler

There may be times when you want to have PHIGS call your own error-handling routine. For example, you may want PHIGS to handle most error conditions and call your own error handler for special cases only.

Most implementations allow the application to identify its own error handler. For the FORTRAN binding, the standard method for implementations to allow this type of extension to PHIGS is to provide an escape routine. For the C binding, you can use the `pset_err_hand` routine. Check your implementation documentation for details.

If you define your own error-handling routine, it must be able to receive the same three parameters as described for ERROR LOGGING.

Any error-handling routine you write can use the PHIGS inquiry routines to access the set of PHIGS state variables (the various state lists and description tables). These are available only for reading; no modification of PHIGS state is possible during error handling. Specifically, only PHIGS inquiry routines, ERROR LOGGING, and EMERGENCY CLOSE PHIGS can be called by your error-handling routine. Inquiry routines return error indicators through their parameter lists, so the error handling cannot recur.

The PHIGS Error-handling Routine

An error-handling routine—be it the default one or a user-defined one—is called by the PHIGS system whenever an error is encountered (assuming the error-handling mode is on). Therefore, definition of the following routine is not to indicate when you should call the ERROR HANDLING routine; it is called automatically. This definition shows you the parameter information you'll need to know when you are writing your own error-handling routine for PHIGS to call when errors occur.

`call perhnd(`*error_num*, *routine_id*, *error_file*)

```
perr_hand(
   Pint             error_num,
   Pint             routine_id,
   const char       *error_file
);
```

where the parameter definitions are the same as those of ERROR LOGGING.

An Error-handling Example

As described above, PHIGS has its own error-handling routines; these are in effect until you specify otherwise.

The next example illustrates several of the error-handling concepts just discussed. An error is deliberately made three times. The first time, the PHIGS default error-handling is used. The next time, the error-handling mode has been turned off, so nothing happens. The last time, the error-handling hook has been taken over by the user program.

This example runs on HP-PHIGS and uses the escape routine SET ERROR HANDLING FUNCTION (`pue700`) that is part of the HP-PHIGS implementation. Refer to your implementation documentation for information on escape routines used to call application-defined error handlers.

```
      program Error                     { program "Error.ftn"
%include '/sys/ins/phigs.ins.ftn'
      integer*4  BufferLength           { PHIGS buffer size
      integer*4     WorkstnID               { workstation identifier
      parameter  (BufferLength=0, WorkstnID=1)
      integer*4     ConnID                  { connection identifier
      parameter  (ConnID=1)
```

```
      integer*4     WorkstnType         { workstation type
      parameter (WorkstnType=POIDDX){ implementation-dependent
      integer*4     ErrorRtn            { error-return variable
      integer*4     OldHandler          { storage for addresses
      external MyErrorHandler       { forward reference

      call popph(1, BufferLength)
      call popwk(WorkstnID, ConnID, WorkstnType)
      {--- make an error with the standard error-handler in effect -----------
      print *, "--- Default error-handler in effect ------------------"
      call pswkw(WorkstnID, 0.0, 0.0, 0.0, 0.0)    { set workstation window
      {--- turn off error handling completely --------------------------------
      print *, "--- Error-handling mode off -----------------------"
      call pserhm(POFF)             { set error-handling mode: off
      call pswkw(WorkstnID, 0.0, 0.0, 0.0, 0.0)    { set workstation window

      {--- install custom error-handler and make error again -----------------
      print *, "--- Custom error-handler in effect -------------------"
      call pserhm(PON)              { set error-handling mode: on
C Replace error handler
      call pue700(MyErrorHandler, ErrorRtn, OldHandler)
      if (ErrorRtn .ne. 0) then
          print *, "Error", ErrorRtn, "from pue700; terminating."
          call peclph               { emergency close PHIGS!
      end if
      call pswkw(WorkstnID, 0.0, 0.0, 0.0, 0.0)    { set workstation window
      call pclwk(WorkstnID)         { close workstation
      call pclph                    { close PHIGS
      stop                          { stop processing
      end                           { end of program
{*****************************************************************+*****
      subroutine MyErrorHandler(ErrorNo, FuncID, ErrorFile)
      integer*4     ErrorNo             { which error happened?
      integer*4     FuncID              { which routine had the error?
      integer*4     ErrorFile           { print error messages where?

      print *,"MyErrorHandler: Error", ErrorNo, " occurred in ",
     +  "routine", FuncID
      print *,"My own call to the ERROR LOGGING routine (perlog):"
      call perlog(ErrorNo, FuncID, ErrorFile)
      return
      end
```

The first time, the program prints the following messages:

```
--- Default error-handler in effect ------------------
Error in PSWKW. Ignoring function, invalid window;
XMIN ≥ XMAX, YMIN ≥ YMAX, ZMIN > ZMAX, UMIN ≥ UMAX, or, VMIN ≥ VMAX
```

The second time, when error handling is turned off, this is all that is printed:

```
--- Error handling-mode off -----------------------
```

The last time—the time when error handling is done by the user's routine—the following is printed:

```
--- Custom error-handler in effect -------------------
MyErrorHandler: Error 151 occurred in routine 87
My own call to the ERROR LOGGING routine (perlog):
Error in PSWKW. Ignoring function, invalid window;
XMIN ≥ XMAX, YMIN ≥ YMAX, ZMIN > ZMAX, UMIN ≥ UMAX, or, VMIN ≥ VMAX
```

Of course, your error–handling routine can print anything you wish.

Chapter 4

Posting Structures and Controlling Picture Changes

This chapter describes how to begin connecting the various pieces of PHIGS together to display an image on the screen. It describes how to create a model and display it on the screen, and then how to update the picture when needed. Displaying and updating center around the following topics:

- Posting structures to the workstation for display
- Controlling picture changes

Before we begin we must give a brief explanation of structure networks and traversal. These topics are described in detail in Chapter 5, *Using Structures*, but we can't get very far discussing posting and updating without at least a brief introduction.

Structure Networks

In PHIGS it is permissible to put all the structure elements for a model into a single structure. However, this can result in a structure of an unwieldly size. More commonly, a model is subdivided into reasonably sized portions (usually a subjective choice), and each portion is put into a separate structure. The separate structures are assembled into a single model for display purposes by placing references (called *execute structure* elements) into one (or more) of the structures.

This brings up the concept of a **structure network**: Given a structure, the corresponding structure network is the set of all structures, including the given structure, all structures referenced by that structure (if any), and so on. Recursively: The structure network includes the given structure and all structures referenced by a structure in the structure network.

Figure 4–1 shows two structures. These are two structure networks: The structure network for B is just B itself. The structure network for A is {A, B}.

Incidentally, circular structure references are not allowed in PHIGS: A structure is not allowed to refer to itself, nor may it refer to a structure in whose structure network it lies.

The structure with which we start in figuring a structure network is called the **root** of that network. In Figure 4–1, Structure A is the root of the structure network containing both A and B; at the same time, B is the root of the structure network containing only B.

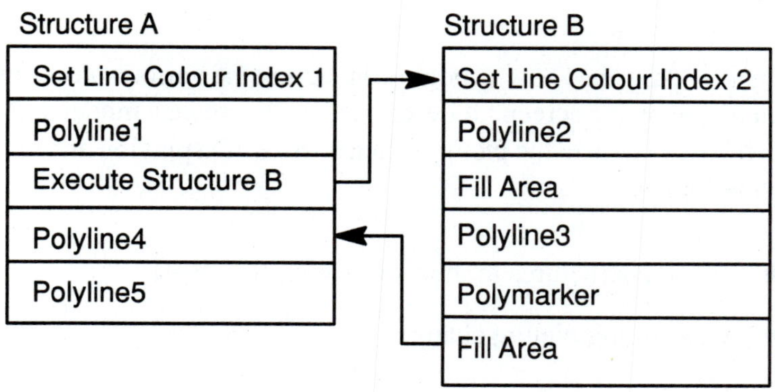

Figure 4–1. Traversal through Two Structures

Traversal

When you instruct PHIGS to display a structure, it performs a top–down processing, or traversal, through the structure's network. During traversal PHIGS sequentially processes each structure element that it encounters (for example, a *polyline* primitive element or a *set line colour index* element). To quote the PHIGS standard, traversal is "the process of stepping through a structure network, elaborating each structure element by generating an output primitive or changing the state lists."

If PHIGS encounters an execute structure element during structure traversal, it executes the referenced structure (and any of its *execute structure* elements) and then returns to finish executing the original structure.

Figure 4–1 shows the traversal path on an element-by-element basis through two structures. Notice that after PHIGS finishes traversing structure B, it resumes the execution of structure A.

Refer to Chapter 5 for more information on structure networks. Refer to Chapter 9, *Using Attributes*, for an explanation of how attributes like colour are set (and inherited) during traversal.

Traversal State List

The **traversal state list** (TSL) is a collection of state data that represents the dynamic workstation-independent parameters of the PHIGS system during traversal of a structure network; that is, it exists only during a single traversal and vanishes when the traversal is complete. When traversal begins, the TSL values are set to the default values defined in the PHIGS description table (PDT). Since traversal is an automatic operation, during which the application program never gets control, the application program cannot inquire the traversal state list.

The application cannot inquire the defaults for the TSL entries, because for most of them there is no need—they are specified as part of the standard.

Creating and Displaying an Image

Now that we have briefly described structure networks and traversal, we can begin with the main topic of this chapter: how to create an image, display it on the screen, and update the picture at the correct time.

There are four basic steps involved in using PHIGS to create an image on the display:

1. *Set up desired values in the workstation state list (WSL).* This includes any viewing parameters required by your application, such as the view orientation matrix, the view mapping matrix, clip limits, etc. Also included is the setting of the workstation attributes: desired modification and deferral modes and update states. This latter subject is rather complex, and most of this chapter is devoted to its discussion.

2. *Create the necessary structures.* As mentioned earlier in this chapter, structures are lists of elements, and elements are the building blocks for creating geometric models of the scene you want to display.

3. *Post the structures you want to see.* "Posting" a structure network means specifying that it is to be part of the displayed image. Then later, when the structure network is traversed, the output primitive elements in the posted structure networks are traversed, and they contribute to the final image. Output primitive elements in structures that are not part of any posted structure network do not contribute to the final image. In other words, there may be more models in the CSS than are drawn at any given time.

4. *Cause a traversal.* One way to make the display up-to-date is to call a routine that actually causes traversal of posted structures in the CSS, interpreting their contents and rendering the appropriate output on the display. Your application might use REDRAW ALL STRUCTURES or UPDATE WORKSTATION. Or, if you set the deferral modes appropriately (using the SET DISPLAY UPDATE STATE routine), traversal can take place automatically.

When you create an image for the first time, you must at least do Step 2, and, in most cases, Steps 3 and 4 as well. With appropriate data, you can use the default viewing parameters and attribute tables, and thus skip Step 1. However, Step 2's default is "no structures," and Step 3's default is "nothing posted"; thus, these two are not optional if you want a visible image to appear.

Regarding Step 4, the default deferral mode is workstation dependent. If the default is ASAP (update as soon as possible), then no action is needed. However, if the default deferral mode is WAIT (wait until the application requests an update), then you must call an update routine in order for a visible image to appear.

Posting

At some point after you have partially or completely defined your model within structure networks, you will probably want to display it on a workstation. Use the POST STRUCTURE routine to tell PHIGS which structure network(s) to display. Multiple structures can be posted by making multiple calls to POST STRUCTURE. If you have a complex set of structures, at different times you might want to display different structure networks. Referring back to Figure 4–1, at different times you might want to display just B and at other times the structure network {A, B}. In general, if you want to display a given structure network, post the root of the network.

The verb "to post" can be thought of in terms of the workstation's screen being a bulletin board, and each structure network being drawn on a transparent sheet of plastic. Posting a single structure network corresponds to putting it on an empty bulletin board. Posting multiple networks, each with its own priority, corresponds to sorting the sheets into priority and putting them all on the bulletin board. Priority is described near the end of this section.

The opposite operation of posting a structure to a workstation is, predictably, unposting it from a workstation. Unposting a structure, accomplished with UNPOST STRUCTURE, is simply the dissociation of a structure and its network from a workstation. UNPOST ALL STRUCTURES performs just the action its names implies—it unposts all of the posted structures from the workstation.

The calling signatures for the POST STRUCTURE, UNPOST STRUCTURE, and UNPOST ALL STRUCTURES routines are as follows:

```
call ppost(workstation_id, structure_id, priority)
```

```
ppost_struct(
    Pint            workstation_id,
    Pint            structure_id,
    Pfloat          priority
);
```

and

```
call pupost(workstation_id, structure_id)
```

```
punpost_struct(
    Pint            workstation_id,
    Pint            structure_id
);
```

and

```
call pupast(workstation_id)
```

```
punpost_all_structs(
    Pint            workstation_id
);
```

Use the ⟨*priority*⟩ parameter to indicate the relative importance of a posted structure network in relation to other structure networks that may be displayed on the same workstation. If multiple structures are simultaneously posted for display to the same location on the display surface, PHIGS will ensure that the higher-priority structure network is not obscured by a lower-priority network. If two structures have exactly the same priority, an implicit priority based on the sequence of posting is used, whereby the most recently posted structure network has the higher priority.

If multiple networks are rendered to the same area of the display, the structure network with the highest priority ends up "on top of the pile" visually since conceptually, it is drawn last. Note that hidden line, hidden surface removal (HLHSR) can override the priority. (See Chapter 8 for a more lengthy discussion of HLHSR.)

Controlling Picture Changes

This section describes how to control the process of updating the picture. The picture needs to be updated when the geometric model defined by the posted structure networks and/or the workstation attributes defined by the workstation state list (WSL) are modified. You can control the following aspects of display updating:

- Control whether or not the display surface reflects the actual state of the graphics data and the WSL.
- Control the timing of display modification to gain certain visual effects and to use the capabilities of a workstation more efficiently.
- Simulate display changes using quick update methods.

The picture currently displayed on a workstation may no longer be "correct" (may need updating) if you perform one of the following operations:

- You might create, delete, or modify a structure in a posted structure network. This would change the contents of the image.
- You might post previously unposted structures, unpost previously posted structures, or change the priority of posted structures. In this case, new parts of the image would appear, or old parts would disappear.
- You might change one or more parameters in the WSL. For example, if you've defined a camera model (a view), you might change what you're looking at or where you're looking from; you'd see the image from a different perspective.

In any of these cases you would have to either call an update routine (REDRAW ALL STRUCTURES or UPDATE WORKSTATION) or set the *display update state* so that the change appears automatically. But just what happens when you call an update routine? And what is a display update state?

PHIGS allows the application program to decide when to make the picture correct. It is not always desirable to make the picture correct immediately, because the correction may involve redrawing the entire picture; this can take a long time for some pictures. PHIGS gives you the following options:

- Update the picture immediately whenever one of the above changes occurs.
- Only update the picture when the application calls REDRAW ALL STRUCTURES or UPDATE WORKSTATION.
- Simulate the correct picture without the time-consuming complete redraw, and only update the picture as in the previous bullet.

These options are the subject of the rest of this chapter.

In PHIGS, there is a very important difference between the phrase "the image is changed" and the phrase "the image is to be changed." Just because an image is *to be* changed doesn't mean that this change happens right away. The image change may be delayed until a "more convenient" time. Also, not all PHIGS implementations have the same pattern of delaying changes. Therefore, the image on the screen may or may not be the same as what your application would think.

The State of Visual Representation

Because image status is likely to be important to many applications, PHIGS provides a way for the application to inquire the **state of visual representation** (**SVR**) of a workstation. If the displayed image is out of date, then inquiring the SVR indicates "not correct." Then, when the pending changes are actually reflected in the image, the image is no longer out of date. At this point, inquiring its SVR indicates "correct."

The advantages of being able to delay an update are discussed later in this chapter, under "Updating Images."

The workstation state list contains an entry called the *state of visual representation.* The *state of visual representation* entry describes the relationship between the current state of the image and the "correct" image, according to the CSS and the workstation state. Because it is a status flag, it cannot be set by the user— it can only be interrogated. It has one of the following values:

CORRECT	The displayed image agrees completely with the definition given by the CSS and the workstation state list.
DEFERRED	At least one image change necessary to make the image current has been deferred (postponed).
SIMULATED	At least one image change necessary to make the image current has been simulated by a quick update method, and no changes have been deferred.

To determine the state of visual representation, refer to the description of the INQUIRE DISPLAY UPDATE STATE routine later in this section.

Update Routines

There are three routines that allow you to update the display image:

- REDRAW ALL STRUCTURES
- UPDATE WORKSTATION
- SET DISPLAY UPDATE STATE

We introduce the term **regeneration** here. A regeneration includes the following:

- Clear the display (if it is not empty).
- Effect all changes that are pending in the workstation state list. The three kinds of changes that can be pending are those made to views, the workstation transformation, and the hidden surface removal mode.
- Traverse the posted structures networks.
- Set the *state of visual representation* entry in the workstation state list to CORRECT.

REDRAW ALL STRUCTURES

The REDRAW ALL STRUCTURES routine forces a redisplay of the image. This routine instructs PHIGS to execute all deferred actions and redraw the image by traversing the posted structure networks. The calling signatures for REDRAW ALL STRUCTURES are as follows:

```
call prst(workstation_id, control_flag)
```

```
predraw_all_stucts(
    Pint            workstation_id,
    Pctrl_flag      control_flag
);
```

where:

⟨*workstation_id*⟩ is the workstation identifier passed to OPEN WORKSTATION.

⟨*control_flag*⟩ allows you to clear the display conditionally. This parameter takes one of the following values:

- **Conditionally** clear (`PCONDI, PFLAG_COND`). Clear the display only if the surface is not empty.
- **Always** clear the display (`PALWAY, PFLAG_ALWAYS`).

The default action is that PHIGS always clears the display before redrawing. When you use the conditional option, the routine checks the *display surface empty* entry in the workstation state list before clearing the display. This option is most useful on a hardcopy output device where "clearing" would correspond to ejecting a page. On most screen workstations, the time saved is very small. When using the option on a hardcopy output device, you may wish to have an accurate count of the pages ejected (use Always) or you may wish to conserve paper (use Conditionally).

Note that another way to clear the display is to call UNPOST ALL STRUCTURES and then cause a regeneration.

While REDRAW ALL STRUCTURES guarantees an updated picture, it is usually more efficient to force a regeneration using UPDATE WORKSTATION (described next). This is because UPDATE WORKSTATION allows the implementation to take any shortcuts that it can. REDRAW ALL STRUCTURES will never be faster than UPDATE WORKSTATION.

UPDATE WORKSTATION

UPDATE WORKSTATION instructs PHIGS to execute all deferred actions on the workstation and conditionally redraw the image. The calling signatures for the UPDATE WORKSTATION routine are as follows:

```
call puwk(workstation_id, regeneration_flag)
```

```
pupd_ws(
   Pint            workstation_id,
   Pregen_flag     regeneration_flag
);
```

where:

⟨*workstation_id*⟩ is the workstation identifier passed to OPEN WORKSTATION.

⟨*regeneration_flag*⟩ allows the application program to specify whether the display should also be redrawn (retraversed). This parameter takes one of the following values:

- **Postpone** (`PPOSTP, PFLAG_POSTPONE`). Postpone the visual update. Do not redraw the display.
- **Perform** (`PPERFO, PFLAG_PERFORM`). Perform the update based on the value of the *state of visual representation* entry in the workstation state list. Cause a regeneration the display if the value is DEFERRED or SIMULATED.

The state of visual representation is described earlier in this chapter.

SET DISPLAY UPDATE STATE

The SET DISPLAY UPDATE STATE sets the deferral and modification modes on a workstation. For example, you can set the deferral mode so that every time a structure element is added or deleted during an editing session, the display is updated visually. You can also set the deferral mode so that editing changes will not be displayed until the application program makes a call to REDRAW ALL STRUCTURES or UPDATE WORKSTATION. The calling signatures for the SET DISPLAY UPDATE STATE routine are as follows:

```
call psdus(workstation_id, deferral_mode, modification_mode)
```

```
pset_disp_upd_st(
   Pint            workstation_id,
   Pdefer_mode     deferral_mode,
   Pmod_mode       modification_mode
);
```

where:

⟨*workstation_id*⟩ is the workstation identifier passed to OPEN WORKSTATION.

⟨*deferral_mode*⟩ and ⟨*modification_mode*⟩ are described later in this chapter, under "Updating Images."

Inquiring the Display Update State

Use INQUIRE DISPLAY UPDATE STATE to inquire the current display update state. The routine expects a workstation ID and returns the current deferral mode, the modification mode, whether or not the display surface is empty, and the current state of visual representation (CORRECT, DEFERRED, or SIMULATED).

Use INQUIRE DEFAULT DISPLAY UPDATE STATE to inquire the default display update state for a workstation type. The routine expects a workstation type identifier and returns the default deferral and modification modes.

Ways to Change the Image

An image displayed on the display surface is defined by the current values in the workstation state list and the elements contained in the posted structures. Any changes made to the contents of the posted structure networks or to the workstation state may require the image to change. The image is guaranteed to be correct—to depict the state of the posted structures accurately—only when the *state of visual representation* value of the workstation has the value CORRECT.

PHIGS defines many different reasons that the current image might be "out of date" with respect to the correct image:

- Workstation state list changes:
  - A view representation changed.
  - A polyline bundle representation changed.
  - A polymarker bundle representation changed.
  - A text bundle representation changed.
  - An interior bundle representation changed.
  - An edge bundle representation changed.

  - A colour representation changed.
  - A pattern table representation changed.
  - The workstation transformation changed.
  - The highlighting filter changed.
  - The invisibility filter changed.
  - The HLHSR mode changed.
  - A depth cueing representation changed.
  - A colour mapping representation changed.
- Central structure store changes:
  - A structure's content changed.
  - A structure was posted.
  - A structure was unposted.
  - A structure was deleted.
  - A structure identifier changed.

An implementation may have other ways of changing the image. For example, some implementations define a workstation highlight table and provide extension routines to allow the application to define entries in the table. In this case, changing an entry in the table would be considered a change in the workstation state list.

Dynamic Modifications

For each of the categories listed in the previous section, there is a flag in the workstation description table that indicates whether or not dynamic modifications are supported. Each of these "dynamic modification flags" has one of the three following values:

IMM (immediate) — All changes to the image can be executed immediately. Today very few workstations have IMM capabilities, except for colour representation changes.

IRG (implicit regeneration) — Some changes can be performed only by completely regenerating the image, while others can be accomplished without regenerating the image. For example, unposting a structure network usually requires a regeneration to get rid of its contribution to the picture. However, if the structure network either is empty or has no primitives, it is not contributing to the picture, and regeneration is not necessary.

CBS (can be simulated)

In some cases, changing the image in the correct way can only be accomplished by completely regenerating the image. But there is a simpler and faster—albeit less accurate—method. In these cases, a **quick update method** is provided to indicate to the operator what the real change would be without taking the time to completely regenerate the image. A completely correct effect still requires regenerating the image. As with IRG, it may be possible that some changes can be accomplished correctly immediately if the state of the picture allows it. For example, a deleted primitive being drawn in the background colour to "erase it" would result in a correct image if the primitive is by itself. However, if the primitive overlaps other primitives, redrawing it in the background colour would cause an incorrect image.

Use the following routines to inquire the dynamic modification flags:

- INQUIRE DYNAMICS OF WORKSTATION ATTRIBUTES
- INQUIRE DYNAMICS OF STRUCTURES

The above routines tell you whether or not a workstation supports dynamic image-changing for each of the categories of picture changes. You can use this information to customize your application's behavior in response to a workstation's image-changing capabilities.

Updating Images

In order to take advantage of the capabilities of your workstation and to meet the requirements of your application, you can choose any one of several strategies for updating the image. For example:

- You can control the timing of image modification to gain certain visual effects and to use the capabilities of a workstation more efficiently.

- You can control how closely the displayed image reflects the actual state of the CSS and the workstation tables. This is possible because display changes can be postponed until later or simulated by using a quick update method.

  Be aware, though, that quick update methods vary from workstation to workstation within different implementations, but worse, even within a single implementation. Don't count on portability if you use quick update methods.

The workstation state list contains two entries: the *deferral mode* and the *modification mode*. Both entries are set by SET DISPLAY UPDATE STATE. These entries are described next.

The Deferral Mode

The **deferral mode** determines when the image is brought into agreement with the correct image. The possible values of the deferral mode are as follows:

ASAP (as soon as possible)
: PHIGS initiates whatever actions are necessary to update the image before returning control to the application program. Note that although these actions are *initiated* before control is returned to the calling context, they are not always *completed* before control is returned, because of delays caused by factors outside the control of PHIGS. The value of the modification mode is ignored, and the *state of visual representation* entry in the workstation state list is always CORRECT.

BNIG (before next interaction globally)
BNIL (before next interaction locally)
: These two modes allow the application to make sure the image is correct while an input interaction is in progress. BNIG ensures that the image is correct while an interaction with any PHIGS logical input device is in progress on any workstation. BNIL is similar but only considers the input devices on the workstation on which BNIL is in effect. An interaction is considered underway when an input request is pending or when an input device is in Event or Sample mode. If no interactions are taking place, BNIG and BNIL operate like ASTI. See Chapter 14, *Graphical Input*, for more details on input requests.

ASTI (at some time)

PHIGS can choose any convenient time to update the image so it is visually correct. Whenever it chooses to make it correct, the *state of visual representation* entry is set to CORRECT. At other times it acts like WAIT.

WAIT (when the application requests it)

The image is made correct via UPDATE WORKSTATION or REDRAW ALL STRUCTURES. Between the times these routines are called, only those image changes that can be done using the method specified by the modification mode can occur.

Check your implementation documentation for details on the various deferral modes, including which value is used as the default.

Note that for ASAP, BNIG, and ASTI, the implementation automatically regenerates at certain times. For WAIT, the implementation never automatically regenerates at any time. However, the application program can force a regeneration *at any time* using UPDATE WORKSTATION or REDRAW ALL STRUCTURES.

The Modification Mode

The **modification mode** specifies the method to use for image changes between the times that the image is made actually "correct," according to the CSS and the workstation tables. The possible values of the modification mode are as follows:

NIVE (no immediate visual effects)

Do not make image changes between the times the image is made correct. No changes occur. Note that depending on the implementation, some colour table and colour mapping changes may not be deterrable. Also note that some implementations automatically regenerate in response to window system events (i.e., expose, stretch) even when in WAIT/NIVE (although the PHIGS standard says the old image should be redisplayed).

UWOR (update without regeneration)

All image changes that can be correctly made immediately, without simulation or regenerating the image, are performed. For example, an unfilled polygon (not overlapping any other primitives) could be filled immediately: The image would be correct, and a complete image regeneration is not required. On the other hand, a polygon that is reduced in size could not be updated without regeneration; a regeneration would be necessary to remove its old rendering. Image changes made in this mode include, but are not restricted to, picture changes whose *dynamic modification flag* entries in the workstation description table are IMM. No simulations nor regenerations are performed.

UQUM (use quick update methods)

All picture changes that can be correctly realized immediately, without using regeneration (like UWOR, above), together with those that can be simulated, are performed when the modification mode is UQUM. This includes, but is not restricted to, picture changes whose *dynamic modification flag* entries in the workstation description table are IMM or CBS. No regenerations are performed.

The modification mode applies between regenerations when the deferral mode is anything but ASAP. In ASAP mode the picture is always correct.

Operations That Are Simulated in UQUM Mode

Check your implementation documentation to see which operations are simulated in quick update mode (UQUM). The following is a sample list:

- All primitive insertion and deletion
- Insertion or deletion of EXECUTE STRUCTURE elements
- Insertion or deletion of attributes
- SET INDIVIDUAL ASF
- COPY STRUCTURE
- DELETE BETWEEN LABELS and DELETE ELEMENT RANGE
- POST or UNPOST STRUCTURE
- SET COLOUR REPRESENTATION

Simulations of insertions are frequently done on raster display devices by drawing the relevant part of the picture "on top" of the current image. Simulations of deletions are frequently done on raster display devices by drawing the relevant parts in the background colour "on top" of the current image. The latter process can leave "holes" in other primitives.

Operations That Are Deferred in UQUM Mode

Again, check your implementation documentation for an accurate list of deferred operations. The following is a sample list:

- Insertion or deletion of local or global transformations
- Add or delete names to or from the current name set
- Change to a bundle table entry
- DELETE STRUCTURE
- DELETE STRUCTURE NETWORK
- SET VIEW REPRESENTATION
- SET VIEW INDEX
- SET WORKSTATION WINDOW
- SET WORKSTATION VIEWPORT
- DELETE ALL STRUCTURES

Summary of Deferral and Modification Modes

The following items give some advice about useful combinations of deferral and modification modes:

- Commonly used deferral modes are ASAP and WAIT.
- Commonly used modification modes are NIVE and UQUM.
- The default update state is implementation-dependent. For example, some systems use WAIT/NIVE as the default. Others use ASAP.
- In ASAP mode, all changes that affect the visual display are performed immediately. ASAP deferral mode overrides the modification mode.
- In WAIT mode, the following two combinations are commonly used:
    1. NIVE: Defer changes that affect the visual display until the application program calls REDRAW ALL STRUCTURES, calls UPDATE WORKSTATION, or changes the deferral mode.
    2. UQUM: Perform operations that can be done correctly without regeneration. Use quick update methods to simulate changes that affect the visual display until the application program calls REDRAW ALL STRUCTURES, calls UPDATE WORKSTATION, or changes the deferral mode.
- ASAP is useful for debugging. WAIT/NIVE is useful when you are trying to show one frame at a time, for example, for viewing dynamic pictures on a double-buffered workstation. WAIT/UQUM is useful for interactive picture editing (see the example at the end of this chapter).

Flow Diagram for Deferral and Modification Modes

The PHIGS standard presents two diagrams that describe the flow of control for events that are significant in the context of controlling picture changes. We have reproduced the information in Figures 4–2 and 4–3 with slight modifications to fit the artwork on the page.

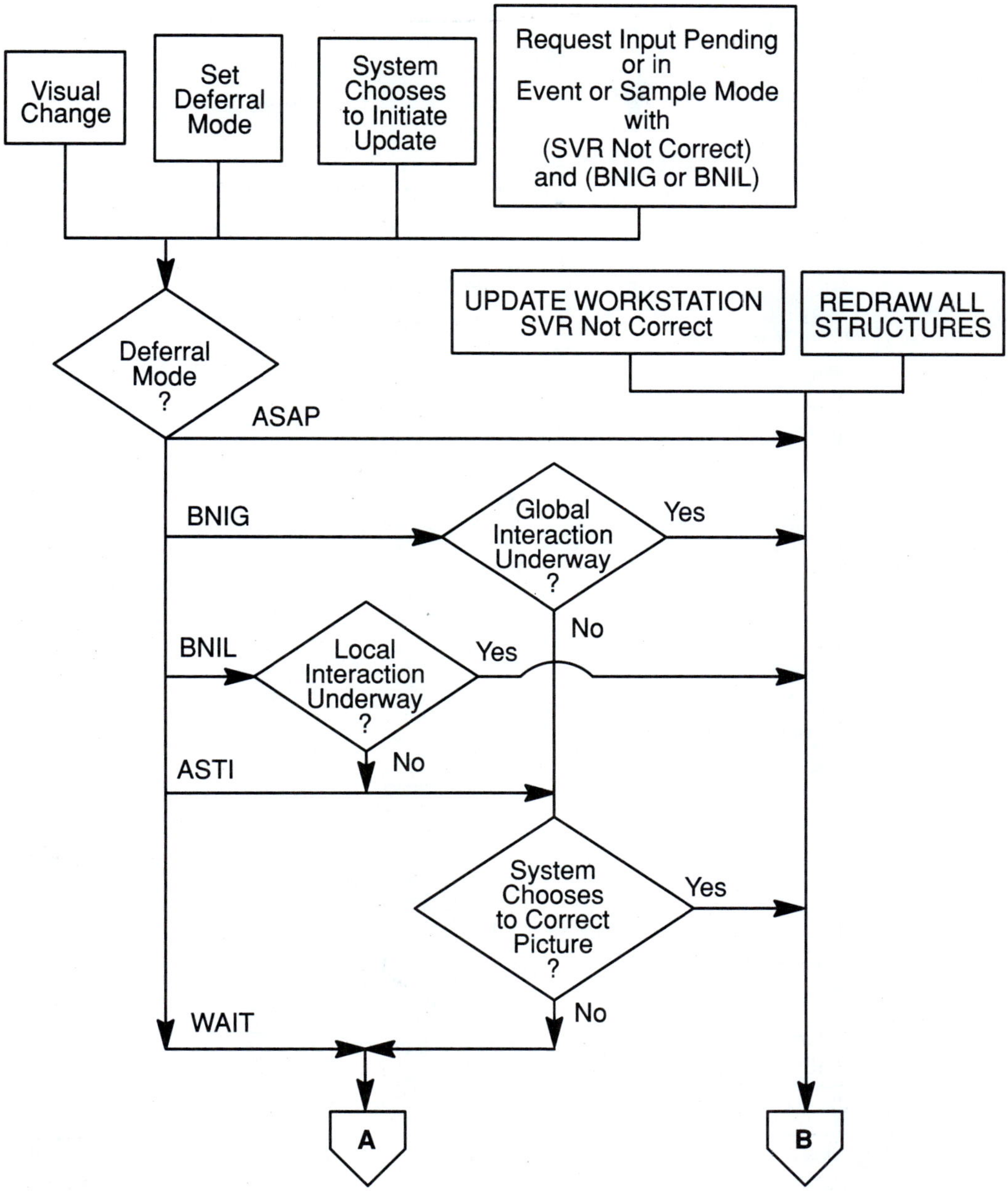

Figure 4–2. Display Update/1: Is Correct Picture Required?

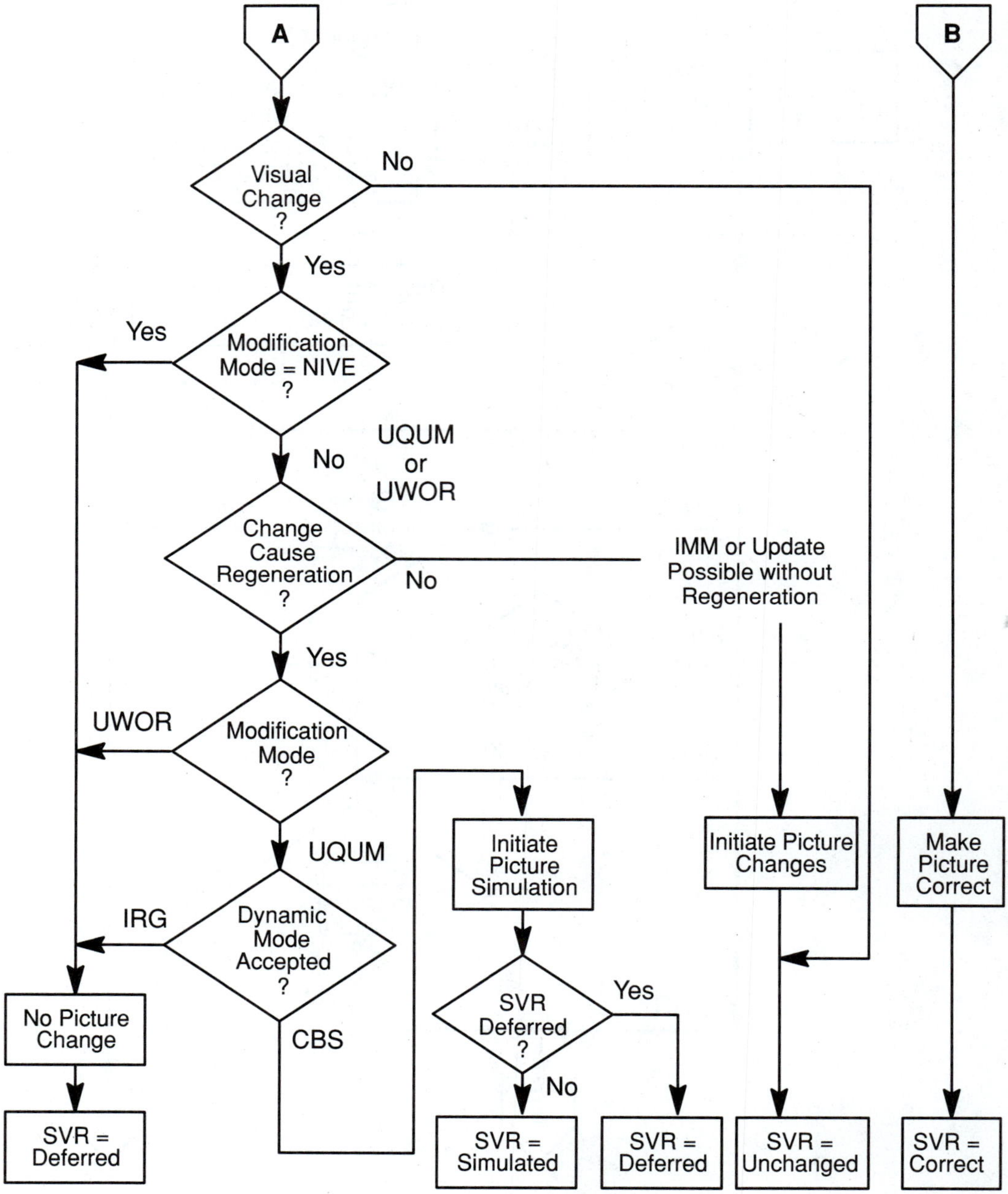

Figure 4–3. Display Update/2: Check Modification Mode

Quick Update Example

The example in this section shows how to use the WAIT/UQUM modes for interactive picture editing. In this example we have a horizontal line and a fill area primitive. We interactively move the line across the screen, past the fill area. This is done by editing the structure that contains the line and repeatedly replacing the local transformation matrix.

Instead of redrawing the entire picture each time we move the line, we use quick update methods to erase the line and redraw it in the new position. In order to erase the line, PHIGS redraws it in the background colour. This has the effect of generating a "swath" of background-coloured lines across the fill area as the line moves across it. However, this is more desirable than completely redrawing the image each time we move the line. Although it would not take a long time to redraw this simple scene, the repeated screen flashes can be distracting. After we have finished moving the line, we call REDRAW ALL STRUCTURES to force a regeneration and make the picture correct.

Figure 4–4 shows an approximation of the images created by the program. This program uses two features that we haven't covered yet: structure editing and modelling transformations. Structure editing is covered in Chapter 5. Transformations are discussed in Chapter 6, *Modelling Transformations.*

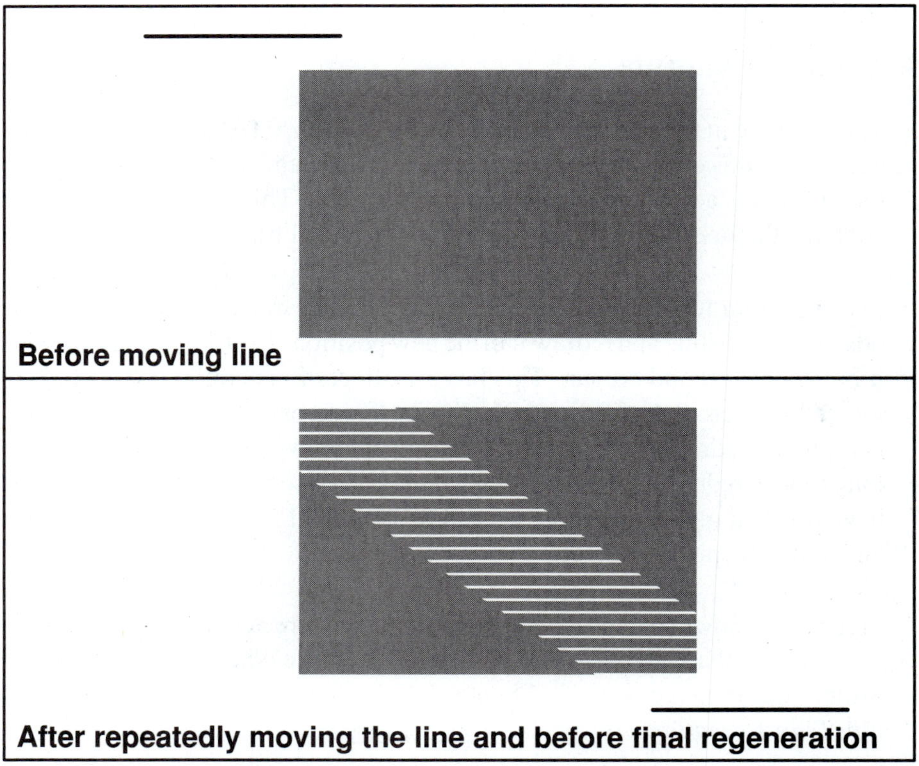

Figure 4–4. Using Quick Update Methods in the move_line Program

```
      program move_line
C  Description: Demonstrates how to use quick update methods to simulate
C               moving a line across the screen.
C    Deferral mode = PWAITD
C    Make the picture correct when the application program calls REDRAW
C    ALL STRUCTURES or UPDATE WORKSTATION.  Between calls to these
C    routines, the modification mode determines which picture changes
C    will occur.
C    Modification mode = PUQUM
C    Use Quick Update Methods. PHIGS immediately performs all picture
C    changes that it can make correctly without using regeneration,
C    together with changes that it can simulate.
%include '/sys/ins/phigs.ins.ftn'          { implementation-dependent
      integer*4   ConnectID                { communication channel ID
```

```
integer*4    BufferLength                { buffer length
integer*4    ErrorOut                    { stream for error output
integer*4    WorkID                      { workstation ID
parameter    (ConnectID=1, BufferLength=0, ErrorOut=1, WorkID=1)
integer*4    WorkType                    { workstation type
parameter    (WorkType=0)                { implementation-dependent
integer*4    Structure1                  { structure ID
parameter    (Structure1=1)
integer*4    ElementPointer              { for structure edit
integer*4    errind                      { error indicator
real*4       dx, dy                      { for x and y translation
real*4       Matrix1(3,3), Matrix2(3,3){ transformation matrices
real         Line1X(2), Line1Y(2)        { points for line primitive
data         Line1X /0.1, 0.4/
data         Line1Y /0.8, 0.8/
real         FAreaX(4), FAreaY(4)        { points for fill area
data         FAreaX /0.25, 0.75, 0.75, 0.25/
data         FAreaY /0.25, 0.25, 0.75, 0.75/
real         Red(3)                      { for the line colour
data         Red/ 1.0, 0.0, 0.0 /
integer*4    ColorIndex                  { for workstation colour table

call popph(ErrorOut, BufferLength)       { open PHIGS
call popwk(WorkID, ConnectID, WorkType) { open workstation
ColorIndex=2                             { entry 2 in wrkst colour table
call pscr(WorkID, ColorIndex, 3, Red) { set colour representation

call ptr(0.0, 0.0, errind, Matrix1)      { create an identity matrix

call popst(Structure1)                   { open structure
call psis(PSOLID)                        { set interior style
call pfa(4,FAreaX,FAreaY)                { 2D fill area primitive
call pslmt(Matrix1, PCREPL)              { Insert local xform for
                                         { structure editing later.
call psplci(2)                           { set line colour index
call ppl(2,Line1X, Line1Y)               { 2D polyline
call pclst                               { close structure
call ppost(WorkID, Structure1, 1.0)      { post structure
call puwk(WorkID, PPERFO)                { update workstation
call psdus(WorkID, PWAITD, PUQUM)        { set display update state
call psedm (PREPLC)                      { set edit mode to replace
dx=0.0
dy=-0.01
```

```
      ElementPointer=3              { element 3 is the local xform element
C The set local transform element is replaced 60 times,
C each time with a slightly different matrix.
      call popst(Structure1)                 { open structure
      call psep(ElementPointer)              { set element pointer
      DO 10 i = 1, 60
        call ptr(dx, dy, errind, Matrix2)    { create translation matrix
        call pslmt(Matrix2, PCREPL)          { set local transform
        dy=dy-0.01                           { change x and y values
        dx=dx+0.01                           { line moves down and to right
10    CONTINUE                               { end do loop
      call pclst                             { close structure
      READ *
      call prst(WorkID, PALWAY)              { redraw all structures
      READ *
      call pupost(WorkID, Structure1)        { unpost structure
      call pclwk(WorkID)                     { close workstation
      call pclph                             { close PHIGS
      stop
      end
```

Chapter 5

Using Structures

This chapter describes the following aspects of PHIGS structures:

- Definition
- Hierarchy
- Editing
- Archiving

Structure Definition

In PHIGS, a structure is a representation of part or all of a geometric model. This model can be rendered, modified, archived to a file, and retrieved from a file. The fundamental unit of data within a structure is called a **structure element**, or simply, **element**. A structure element is a fundamental building block for a geometric model (for example, a line or colour). Refer to Chapter 3, *Controlling PHIGS*, for a list that summarizes the types of structure elements. Refer to Appendix A for a list of structure elements.

A structure exists if and only if the PHIGS' CSS has knowledge of the structure's unique identifying number. Perhaps the most common method of telling the CSS about a new structure is to open a nonexistent one, thus creating it.

You can compare opening a structure to opening a bottle so that liquid can be put into it or taken out of it. This is done with the OPEN STRUCTURE routine:

```
call popst(struct_id)
```

```
popen_stuct(
   Pint             struct_id
);
```

where:

⟨*struct_id*⟩ identifies the structure.

Of course, if OPEN STRUCTURE is called with ⟨*struct_id*⟩ specifying an already-existing structure, that existing structure is opened for editing or modification as you would expect.

Only one structure can be open at any one time; if you attempt to open Structure B while Structure A is still open, an error is reported, and Structure A remains open. Because of this "only one structure open at a time" restriction, the CLOSE STRUCTURE routine doesn't need any parameters at all; there is at most one structure that can be closed:

```
call pclst
```

```
pclose_struct(
   void
);
```

If you call CLOSE STRUCTURE when no structure is open, an error is reported, and no further action is taken.

Although opening a nonexistent structure is the most common way of creating a new structure, there are other ways also. A structure can be created in any one of the following ways:

- When a nonexistent structure is opened (covered above)
- When a reference to a nonexistent structure is inserted into an existing structure in the CSS (an *execute structure* element)
- When the structure is posted for display on a workstation
- When the structure is referenced in a routine that changes the structure identifier

- When a structure not existing in the CSS is retrieved from an archive
- When a nonexistent structure is "emptied"

As a point of comparison, the following list identifies times when structures *are not* created:

- Attempting to copy all elements from a nonexistent structure into the currently open structure does not lead to any action.
- Unposting, deleting, or emptying a nonexistent structure does not cause any action to be taken.

The Structure State List

When you create a structure, PHIGS creates a **structure state list** (**SSL**). This is a short list containing the following three items:

- The structure identifier
- A list of workstations to which the structure has been posted
- A list of its structure elements (there may be none)

Each structure has a corresponding SSL that exists until the structure is deleted from the CSS.

Traversing a Structure Network

As described at the beginning of Chapter 3, there is a structure network for each structure. PHIGS stores the structures in the CSS and infers the extent of the structure network from the presence of *execute structure* elements. Use the EXECUTE STRUCTURE routine to create an *execute structure* element.

Graphical output on a workstation is produced by traversing a structure network identified for display on that workstation and interpreting the structure elements. Traversing, in this context, is the process of "stepping through" a structure network, operating as appropriate upon each structure element encountered, be that generating an output primitive, changing an attribute, referencing another structure, and so forth.

This "referencing" process is very much like subroutine-calling in a programming language: processing steps through a series of commands sequentially until a reference to another series of commands is encountered, at which time the following happens:

1. Execution of the calling program is temporarily suspended,
2. The called subroutine is executed,
3. When the called subroutine is finished, control returns to the calling program, which continues from where it left off.

This is similar to what happens during traversal of structure references. Specifically, in the context of PHIGS, the structure elements of the structure network are executed sequentially, but when an *execute structure* element is encountered during the traversal, the effect is as if the following actions occur:

1. Traversal of the current structure is suspended,
2. The current state of the PHIGS traversal state list is saved (for restoration when the referenced structure has completed traversal),
3. Global and local modelling transformations are initialized for the referenced structure,
4. The referenced structure network is completely traversed (note that the referenced structure may modify the state inherited from the referencing structure),
5. The PHIGS traversal state list values (including the local and global modelling matrices) saved in Step 2 are restored.
6. Traversal of the current structure is resumed.

This means that:

- At structure traversal time, a structure may inherit the attributes of those structures to which it is subordinate in the network.
- At structure traversal time, a structure's attribute settings may affect the display of only those structures subordinate to it in the network.

Recall that the traversal state list (TSL) is the current attribute state as defined when traversed elements modify the default state.

Of course, the "referenced structure" in Step 4 could reference yet other structures, and the referencing process would occur recursively.

Structure Hierarchy

The basic organization of structure networks is hierarchical. In a hierarchical system, objects are usually organized in logical or spatial groups, but no such restrictions are imposed by PHIGS. This allows you to group objects in the manner most convenient to your application. Figure 5–1 illustrates structure hierarchy.

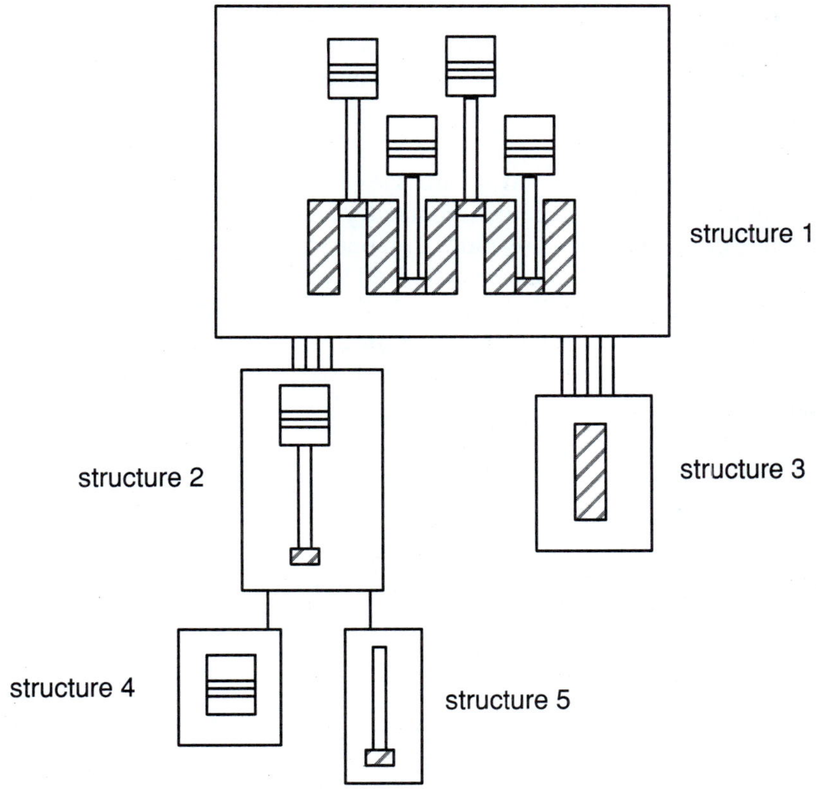

Figure 5–1. Building Geometric Components into a Whole

The hierarchical model presented in Figure 5–1 uses three basic structures (structures 3, 4, and 5). Structure 3 is referenced five times by structure 1. Structures 4 and 5 are combined to create structure 2, which is referenced four times by structure 1.

At the beginning of each traversal of a referenced structure, there is an identity local transformation matrix and an inherited global transformation matrix. This is a powerful feature that allows you to attach component parts in the correct locations, as shown in Figure 5–1. Transformation matrices are described in the next chapter.

In Figure 5–1, if you rotate structure 1, all of the referenced structures rotate with it. If you make a change to structure 3, the change is reflected in all references to it in structure 1 (whether or not this change is displayed immediately depends on the display update state). Also, each time you reference structure 3, you can apply a different attribute, such as colour.

This referencing, or reusing, of structures is also known as **instancing**. An instance of a structure is uniquely identified by the entire path from a posted structure (a structure assigned for display on a workstation) to a single execute structure element. For a discussion of both, see the section entitled "Incremental Spatial Search" later in this chapter.

Figure 5–1 shows a straightforward use of structure hierarchy. The path is easily followed from the top–down. More complicated hierarchical structures are also possible because a structure can be instanced by more than one structure. Figure 5–2 shows a more complicated model where two structures are instanced by more than one higher-level structure. Here, the structures are represented by circles labelled with the structure identifiers, and structure references are shown by arrows, which point to the invoked structures. (Two arrows from one circle to another represent the presence of two execute structure elements referring to the instanced structure.)

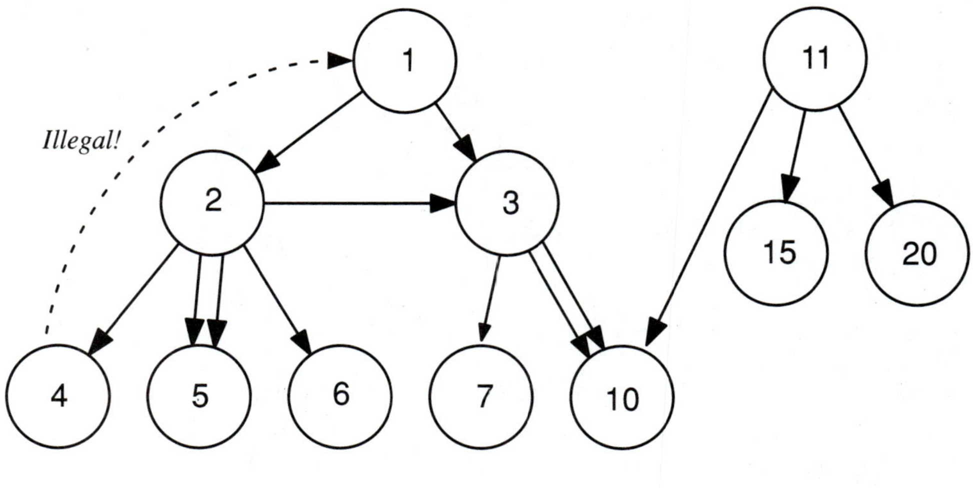

Figure 5–2. Example Structure Networks

When the invocation of one structure causes the invocation of another, either directly or indirectly, the structures are related. For example, some of the relationships in Figure 5–2 are as follows:

- Structure 2 is the parent of structures 3, 4, 5, and 6; structure 11 is the parent of structures 10, 15, and 20.
- Structures 2 and 3 are children of structure 1; structures 10, 15, and 20 are children of structure 11.
- Structures 1 and 2 are ancestors of structures 3, 4, 5, 6, 7, and 10.
- Structures 7 and 10 are descendants of structures 1, 2 and 3. Structure 10 is also a descendant of structure 11.

Editing Structure Networks

The concept of a structure network is a powerful and versatile tool for developing geometric models. But even for all its good points, a structure network would quickly become restrictive if it weren't for the ability to define a structure and then change it dynamically. An example of this was shown at the end of the previous chapter.

PHIGS allows an application to access and modify each individual structure element within a structure. There are editing routines available to accomplish all of the following tasks:

- Select an element within a specified structure
- Insert new structure elements
- Replace structure elements with new structure elements
- Copy structure elements from one structure to another
- Delete structure elements
- Interrogate the content of structure elements

A structure consists of zero or more elements, arranged linearly. Element positions are implicitly numbered 0–*n*, where element position 0 is before the first element, element position 1 is the first element, and element position *n* is the last element. This implicit numbering is always maintained in a consecutive, ascending order with one number per structure element; this means that a structure element's position is not fixed and may change as elements are inserted into or deleted from a structure.

Opening a Structure for Editing

An application opens a structure for editing with the OPEN STRUCTURE routine. If the structure does not exist in the CSS, a structure will be created. If you need to know which structure, if any, is currently open, use the INQUIRE OPEN STRUCTURE routine. Structure editing can continue until the structure is closed; which occurs when the CLOSE STRUCTURE routine is invoked.

Setting the Element Pointer

All the time a structure is open, an element pointer, which points to the current element, exists. The initial value of the element pointer following an OPEN STRUCTURE is the last element in the structure (if the structure is not empty), or 0 (if it is empty). After opening the structure, the application may set the element pointer anywhere in the range 0–*n*, where 0 refers to the beginning of the structure (i.e., before the first element) and *n* refers to the last element in the structure. By calling the INQUIRE ELEMENT POINTER routine, you can interrogate PHIGS to determine the value of the element pointer.

If you want to set the element pointer to a particular location—for example, when preparing to replace one structure element with another—you can do so. PHIGS provides several routines for manipulating the element pointer as described below.

Absolute Positioning

An application can set the element pointer to an absolute position with the routine SET ELEMENT POINTER:

```
call psep(ele_pos)
```

```
pset_elem_ptr(
    Pint            ele_pos
);
```

where:

> ⟨*ele_pos*⟩ is an integer specifying the desired position of the element pointer in the currently open structure. A range limit of 0–*n* is imposed, where *n* is the position of the last existent element in the open structure. If you attempt to set the element pointer to a value less than 0, it is set to 0; if you attempt to set the element pointer to a value greater than *n*, it is set to *n*.

If you call this routine when no structure is open, PHIGS reports an error.

Relative Positioning

An application can set the element pointer relative to its current position with the routine OFFSET ELEMENT POINTER:

```
call posep(offset)
```

```
poffset_elem_ptr(
   Pint             offset
);
```

where:

> ⟨*offset*⟩ is the delta, an integer specifying the number of positions to move the pointer from its current location. If the offset value is negative, the element pointer will move toward position 0; if positive, it will move toward the final element in the structure. As above, any attempt to set the pointer beyond the structure's bounds (elements 0–*n*) will leave the element pointer at the bound it would have exceeded.

If you call this routine when no structure is open, PHIGS reports an error.

Figure 5–3 shows the effects of the SET ELEMENT POINTER and OFFSET ELEMENT POINTER routines. The arrow indicates the position of the element pointer.

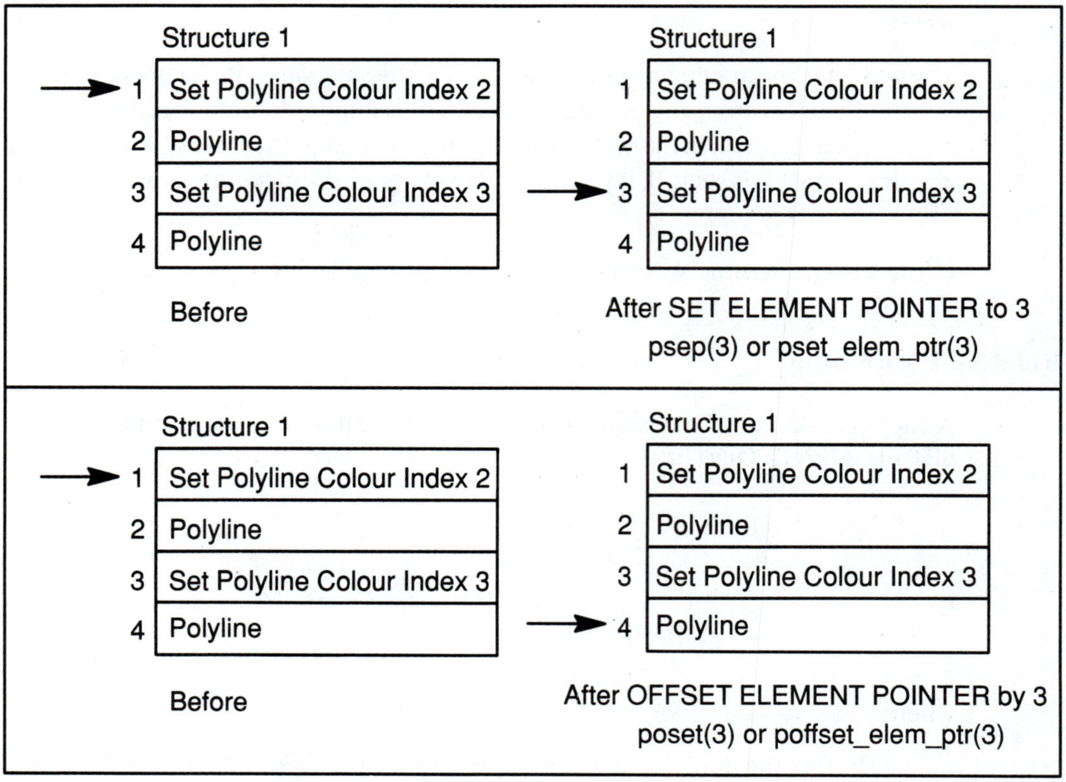

Figure 5–3. Moving the Element Pointer

Positioning the Pointer at a Label

An application can also set the element pointer to a special kind of structure element whose sole purpose in a structure is to mark a location. Using the routine SET ELEMENT POINTER AT LABEL, you can position the element pointer at one of these labels:

```
call pseplb(label)
```

```
pset_elem_ptr_label(
   Pint            label
);
```

where:

⟨*label*⟩ is an integer specifying the label to which you want the element pointer set.

If you call this routine when no structure is open, PHIGS reports an error.

When attempting to set the element pointer to a label, PHIGS searches the open structure in a forward direction, from the element following the current element's position, to the first occurrence of the label sought. If the label cannot be found at a position following the element pointer's starting position, error 205 is reported. The search does not wrap around to the first element if the end of the structure is reached before the label is found.

Of course, setting the element pointer to a label position cannot happen until a label has been put into the structure. To do this, use the LABEL routine:

```
call plb(label)
```

```
plabel(
    Pint                label
);
```

where:

⟨*label*⟩ is an integer specifying the numeric label.

Labels need not be unique within a structure; for example, you can put a label—say, label 25—into a structure, move the element pointer, and insert *another* label 25 into the same structure (or a different structure, for that matter). You can have as many occurrences as desired of a particular label value within a structure (or the CSS), and as long as your application keeps them straight, PHIGS is satisfied. Of course, this is a self-limiting practice, in that the more instances of a particular label number you have at a time, the more difficult it can become to keep them all straight. At some point, a practical maximum will probably be reached, and it becomes easier to have different labels than to keep track of yet more elements with the same label.

Note that you don't have to offset the element pointer between multiple calls to SET ELEMENT POINTER AT LABEL when searching for the same label. PHIGS searches for the label in an element *following* the current position.

Figure 5–4 shows the effect of moving the element pointer to a label structure element. Since PHIGS positions the element pointer at the end of a newly opened structure, you may need to set the element pointer to 0 before you use SET ELEMENT POINTER AT LABEL.

Note that some implementations also allow the application to use pick IDs in structure navigation. This is done by providing escape routines that "set element pointer at pick ID." Pick IDs are described in Chapter 14, *Graphical Input*.

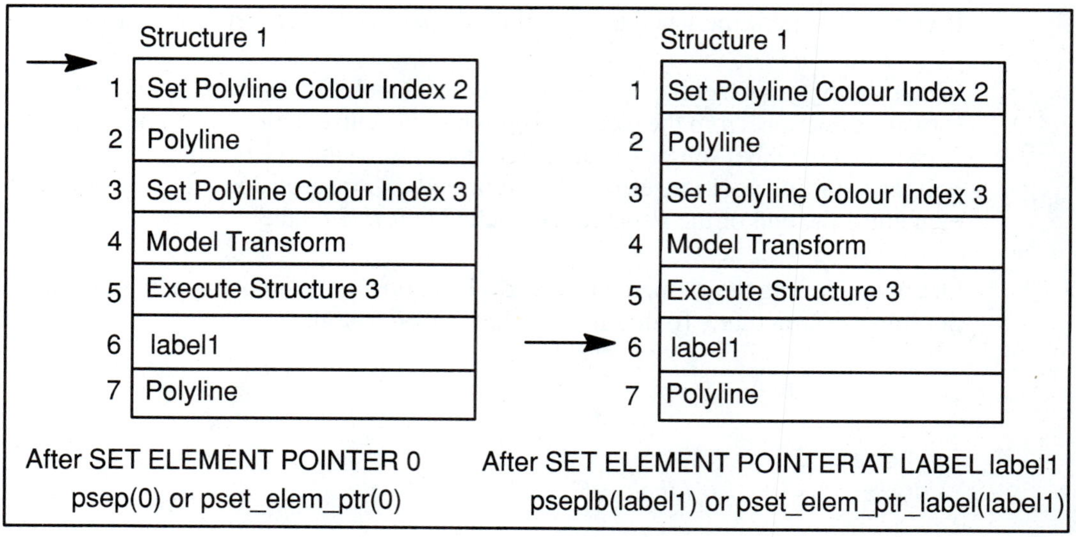

Figure 5–4. Moving the Element Pointer to a Label

Interrogating the Element Pointer

All of the above routines *set* the element pointer. This is fine, but you might also want to find out what the current value of the element pointer is, i.e., "Where am I now?" This is the function of the INQUIRE ELEMENT POINTER routine:

```
call pqep(error, ele_pos)
```

```
pinq_elem_ptr(
    Pint            *error,
    Pint            *ele_pos
);
```

where:

⟨*error*⟩ is an error-return indicator; if its value is zero, ⟨*ele_pos*⟩ is valid.

⟨*ele_pos*⟩ is the current value of the element pointer; i.e., the integer specifying the entry in the ascending list of contiguous numbers associated with the elements in the open structure.

You might consider adapting the practice of writing modular editing code to inquire the current element pointer at the beginning of your module and restore it at the end. Of course, restoring it might be tricky if you have inserted or deleted elements numbered lower than the initial element pointer.

Editing Operations

Adding Elements

When a structure is open, the application program can insert new elements into the structure or replace existing structure elements using the routines that define structure elements (e.g., TEXT, LABEL, SET POLYLINE INDEX, or EXECUTE STRUCTURE). At any time (assuming both PHIGS and a structure are open), you can put new structure elements into a structure. What *else* happens when you put new elements into a structure depends on the edit mode.

The Edit Mode

The edit mode defines whether the new element, whatever that may be, replaces the element pointed to by the element pointer, or is *added* after the element pointed to by the element pointer, moving all subsequent elements down one position to make room. As previously stated, when you open a structure, PHIGS initially sets the element pointer to point to the last element in the structure (or to 0 if the structure is empty).

Insert Mode versus Replace Mode

In either case, after the new element is put into the structure, the element pointer points to the new element (see Figure 5–5). Note that since the element pointer doesn't change after an element replacement, it must be explicitly moved if you want to replace several consecutive elements. Otherwise, you would replace the same element repeatedly, overwriting all but the last new element. Of course, you might *want* to replace the same element repeatedly, as we did in the quick update example at the end of the previous chapter.

If you want to replace a range of several elements, it might be better to delete that range and then add the replacements, staying in insert mode all the while.

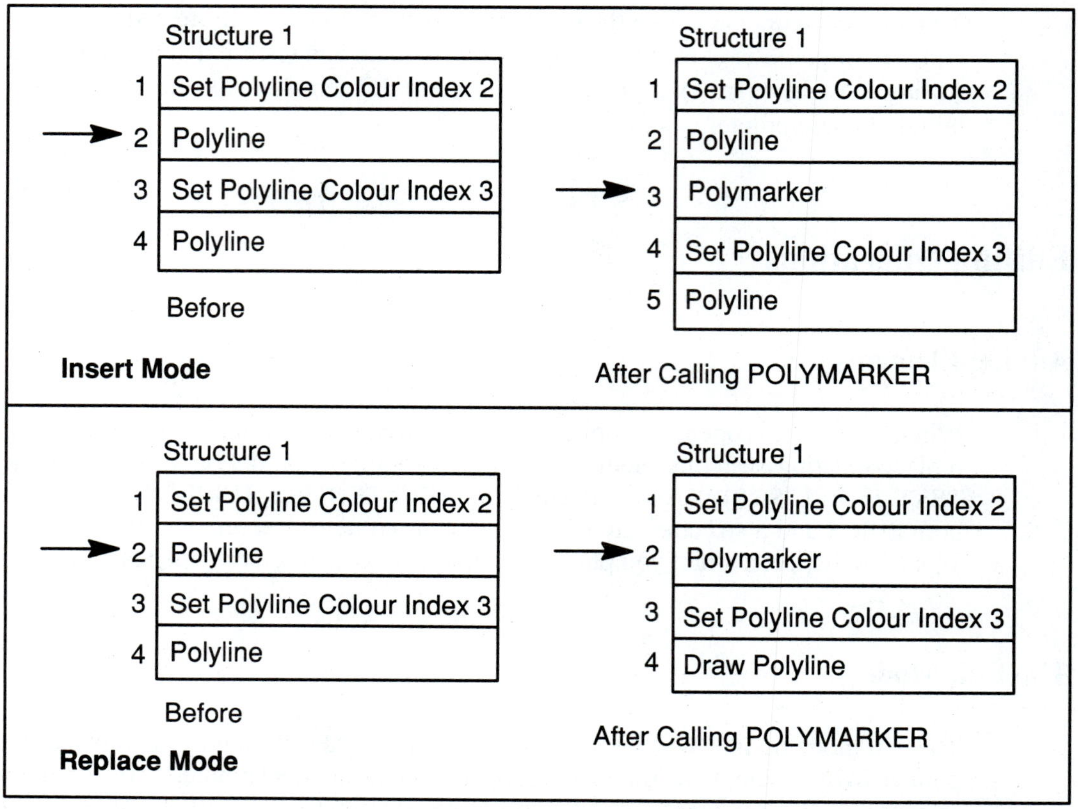

Figure 5–5. Insert and Replace Mode

If the element pointer points at element 0, putting an element into the structure will create a new first element, regardless of the edit mode. Note that the element pointer may be pointing to element 0 because the structure is empty or because the element pointer was set there.

The edit mode is defined by SET EDIT MODE as follows:

```
call psedm(mode)
```

```
pset_edit_mode(
   Pedit_mode          mode
);
```

where:

⟨*mode*⟩ is an integer specifying the desired edit mode. It can take on one of two values: insert (PINSRT, PEDIT_INSERT) or replace (PREPLC, PEDIT_REPLACE). The default is insert.

The edit mode remains as you set it until it is explicitly changed by another invocation of SET EDIT MODE. This is true even if structures are opened and closed.

Copying Elements between Structures

Use COPY ALL ELEMENTS FROM STRUCTURE to copy elements from one structure into another:

```
call pcelst (struct_id)
```

```
pcopy_all_elems_struct(
   Pint              struct_id
);
```

where:

⟨*struct_id*⟩ is the integer specifying the source structure; that is, the structure from which the elements are to be copied. The destination structure is always the open structure. If the structure indicated by ⟨*struct_id*⟩ does not exist, no action takes place and no error is reported. Otherwise, the elements from the referenced structure are inserted into the current structure, starting at the location following the current element pointer.

This operation always *inserts* the copied elements regardless of the current edit mode. The element pointer is left pointing to the last element copied.

You might use this routine to optimize the insertion of some elements that you want in multiple places. But you should consider whether EXECUTE STRUCTURE might better suit your needs. As a rule of thumb, you might use EXECUTE STRUCTURE for primitives you want in multiple places. Then use COPY ALL ELEMENTS FROM STRUCTURE for attribute and transform elements that you want in multiple places or for elements where you wish to edit each copy independently.

Deleting Elements

When you delete elements from a structure, any remaining elements following the deleted ones move up to new element positions (so there are no "holes"), and the structure becomes shorter.

PHIGS provides four different routines for deleting elements:

- The DELETE ELEMENT routine deletes the current element; i.e., the element at which the element pointer is currently pointing. If the element pointer is at 0, nothing happens.
- Consecutive elements may be deleted as a group with the DELETE ELEMENT RANGE routine. This routine deletes all the elements between and including two specified element positions.
- To delete a group of elements delimited by labels, use the DELETE ELEMENTS BETWEEN LABELS routine. This routine will delete all elements between the specified labels. The label elements themselves are not deleted.
- Finally, to delete all elements from a structure, call the EMPTY STRUCTURE routine. This routine only deletes the contents of the structure and has no effect on references to it (for a discussion of structure references, see the "Manipulation of Structures in the CSS" section later in this chapter). Upon completion of this routine, an empty structure will always exist; i.e., if the structure didn't exist before, it will be created.

Following any delete operation on an open structure, the element pointer is positioned at the element immediately preceding the element (or group of elements) that was deleted. Note that this may be element 0, if the first element was deleted.

Note that the first three of these routines operate only on the open structure; the fourth works on any structure, whether open or not. The routines are defined as follows:

DELETE ELEMENT:

```
call pdel
```

Delete the current element.

```
pdel_elem(
   void
);
```

DELETE ELEMENT RANGE:

```
call pdelra(ele_pos1, ele_pos2)

pdel_elem_range(
   Pint          ele_pos1,
   Pint          ele_pos2
);
```

Delete the position-specified range. Does delete the elements specified by ⟨*ele_pos1*⟩ and ⟨*ele_pos2*⟩.

DELETE ELEMENTS BETWEEN LABELS:

```
call pdellb(label1, label2)

pdel_elems_labels(
   Pint          label1,
   Pint          label2
);
```

Delete the label-specified range. Does not delete the elements specified by ⟨*label1*⟩ and ⟨*label2*⟩.

EMPTY STRUCTURE:

```
call pemst(struct_id)

pempty_struct(
   Pint          struct_id
);
```

Delete all elements in the structure.

where:

⟨*ele_pos1*⟩ and ⟨*ele_pos2*⟩ specify the inclusive range of elements to delete. All structure elements between and including the lower element position and the higher element position are deleted. After deletion, the element pointer is set to the element immediately preceding the deleted elements. If an element position value is less than 1, PHIGS uses a value of 0. If an element position value is greater than the number of elements in the open structure, PHIGS uses a value pointing to the last element in the structure.

⟨*label1*⟩ and ⟨*label2*⟩ specify the exclusive range of elements to delete. That is, elements between ⟨*label1*⟩ and ⟨*label2*⟩, *not* including the labels themselves, will be deleted. PHIGS searches for the first label starting at the element following the current element pointer position, then searches for the second label starting with the element following the first label. If either of the specified labels is not found before the end of the open structure, error 206 is reported and the deletion is not performed.

⟨*struct_id*⟩ specifies the structure to be emptied of it's contents.

The DELETE ELEMENT routine doesn't need a parameter specifying an element to delete; it deletes the current element. If you want to delete an element in the open structure other than the current element, you could call DELETE ELEMENT RANGE with ⟨*ele_pos1*⟩ equal to ⟨*ele_pos2*⟩.

Manipulation of Structures in the CSS

Similar to how you can manipulate elements in a structure, you can also manipulate the structures themselves in the CSS.

Deleting a Structure

An application can delete a structure by calling the DELETE STRUCTURE routine. This routine deletes the specified structure as well as all *execute structure* elements referencing it that are contained in any other structures. Its calling signatures are as follows:

```
call pdst (struct_id)
```

```
pdel_struct(
    Pint            struct_id
);
```

where:

⟨*struct_id*⟩ is the integer identifier of the structure to be deleted.

The DELETE STRUCTURE routine will work regardless of whether or not the specified structure is the open structure; however, if the target structure is the open structure, the operation of the routine is not obvious. First, the simple case: If the specified structure is not open, the following actions occur:

1. The specified structure is deleted; its contents are erased, and its ⟨*struct_id*⟩ is again considered unused.
2. All *execute structure* elements in the CSS that reference the specified structure are deleted. Their respective structures are collapsed to fill the vacancies.

3. The structure is unposted from all workstations to which it had been posted.

Now, the more difficult case: If the specified structure is open, it is as if the following actions occur (in this order):

1. The structure is closed.
2. The structure is deleted; all actions listed above for deletion of a closed structure are executed.
3. The structure is reopened. Because of its deletion in Step 2, it doesn't exist, so opening it actually creates an empty open structure.

The fundamental difference between deleting a closed structure and deleting an open structure is this: If you delete a closed structure, all traces of it disappear; if you delete an open structure, the structure remains after the deletion, albeit empty. Deleting the open structure is a more thorough operation than that of EMPTY STRUCTURE, because it also deletes all references and unposts the structure, which EMPTY STRUCTURE does not do.

If the deleted structure is referenced by an element in the currently open structure, and if the element pointer is positioned after the *execute structure* element to be deleted, the element pointer is updated so that it still refers to the same element after the structure is collapsed to fill the vacancy. If the element pointer is pointing directly at an *execute structure* element that will be deleted, the element pointer will be positioned at the preceding element after the structure deletion operation.

Deleting a Structure Network

If you need to delete an entire structure network, PHIGS provides a routine to do so. The DELETE STRUCTURE NETWORK routine will delete the specified structure and all structures in the structure network originating with the specified structure. In other words, it deletes a specified structure and all of its descendants, but not any of its ancestors. The calling signatures of the DELETE STRUCTURE NETWORK routine follow:

```
call pdsn(struct_id, ref_handling_flag)
```

```
pdel_struct_net(
   Pint            struct_id,
   Pref_flag       ref_handling_flag
);
```

where:

⟨*struct_id*⟩ is the integer identifier of the root structure of the network to delete.

⟨*ref_handling_flag*⟩ is a flag that specifies how to treat any structures in the affected network that are referenced by structures *outside* the affected network. There are two possible values:

- **Delete** (`PDELE, PFLAG_DEL`). Tells PHIGS to delete all structures in the specified network regardless of whether or not structures outside the network reference any of the structures in the network.
- **Keep** (`PKEEP, PFLAG_KEEP`). Tells PHIGS to delete only the structures in the specified network that are *not* referenced by structures outside the deleted network. In other words, "Delete the structures unless someone else needs them too."

For each structure deleted, it is first unposted if necessary, then the structure, as well as all *execute structure* elements referring to it, are deleted.

Clearing the CSS Completely

In the event that you want to delete *all* structures from the CSS regardless of ancestral relationships, use the DELETE ALL STRUCTURES routine.

```
call pdas
```

```
pdel_all_structs(
   void
);
```

This routine executes the DELETE STRUCTURE routine for all structures defined in the CSS. If a structure is open at the time DELETE ALL STRUCTURES is executed, the open structure is emptied and unposted (if posted), but not deleted.

Changing Structure Identifiers

Sometimes there is a need to change the name—the **structure identifier**—of a particular structure. Suppose, for example, that you have a structure network in your CSS that defines a car. For simplicity, let's use the structure network illustrated in Figure 5–6.

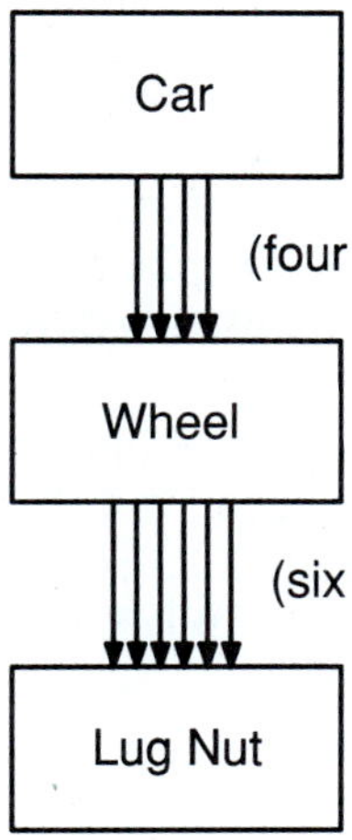

Figure 5–6. Simple "Car" Structure Network

Suppose that you need to change the structure identifier of the Lug Nut structure in Figure 5–6 from 4 to 8. You could use the CHANGE STRUCTURE IDENTIFIER routine:

`call pcstid(`*old_struct_id, new_struct_id*`)`

```
pchange_struct_id(
   Pint           old_struct_id,
   Pint           new_struct_id
);
```

where:

> ⟨*old_struct_id*⟩ is the integer identifier of the structure whose identifier you want to replace; i.e., the "before" number.
>
> ⟨*new_struct_id*⟩ is the integer value that will become the new identifier of the affected structure; i.e., the "after" number.

When you change structure identifiers, if ⟨*old_struct_id*⟩ was not referenced anywhere nor posted, it will not exist after the operation; otherwise, it will exist. When you change structure identifiers, if ⟨*new_struct_id*⟩ already exists, its contents are overwritten by the contents of the structure indicated by ⟨*old_struct_id*⟩. If ⟨*old_struct_id*⟩ is equal to ⟨*new_struct_id*⟩, two things can happen, depending on whether or not the indicated structure exists. If it does, no action is taken; if it doesn't, an empty structure with the specified identifier is created. One way or the other, ⟨*new_struct_id*⟩ will always exist after this call.

In our example, ⟨*old_struct_id*⟩ would be 4, and ⟨*new_struct_id*⟩ would be 8. However, after this operation is done, all the Wheel structures will still reference structure 4 (which will still exist, although empty), not realizing that the Lug Nut structure identifier has been changed to 8. In our example, there are only six places that the Lug Nut structure is referenced, but in a large database, there might be thousands of references to a particular structure.

In order to solve this problem, PHIGS introduces the next routine, CHANGE STRUCTURE REFERENCES. You can follow a call to CHANGE STRUCTURE IDENTIFIER with a call to CHANGE STRUCTURE REFERENCES. You can also combine the two operations in one call with CHANGE STRUCTURE IDENTIFIER AND REFERENCES.

Changing Structure References

The CHANGE STRUCTURE IDENTIFIER routine has a companion routine, CHANGE STRUCTURE REFERENCES, that changes all the references to a given structure identifier to refer to a different structure identifier:

```
call pcstrf(old_struct_id, new_struct_id)
```

```
pchange_struct_refs(
   Pint          old_struct_id,
   Pint          new_struct_id
);
```

where:

> ⟨*old_struct_id*⟩ is the structure identifier to be replaced in all the *execute structure* elements in the CSS.
>
> ⟨*new_struct_id*⟩ is the structure identifier to replace ⟨*old_struct_id*⟩ in all the *execute structure* elements in the CSS.

In our example, the six *execute structure* element references to structure 4 (the old Lug Nut structure identifier) would be changed to refer to structure 8 (the new Lug Nut structure identifier). These six changes to the elements in the Wheel structure would make the structure network functional once again.

If there are references to ⟨*old_struct_id*⟩ but ⟨*new_struct_id*⟩ does not exist, PHIGS creates an empty structure named ⟨*new_struct_id*⟩. If ⟨*old_struct_id*⟩ is equal to ⟨*new_struct_id*⟩, no action is taken. On all workstations where the new structure is posted, it remains posted with unchanged priority, and the old structure, if posted there, is unposted. On all workstations where the old structure is posted and the new one is not, the new structure is posted with the priority of the old structure, and the old structure is unposted. If the old structure does not exist, or if there are no references to the old structure identifier, no action is taken.

Changing Identifier and References at the Same Time

The CHANGE STRUCTURE IDENTIFIER AND REFERENCES routine combines the features of CHANGE STRUCTURE IDENTIFIER and CHANGE STRUCTURE REFERENCES into a single call.

```
call pcstir(old_struct_id, new_struct_id)
```

```
pchange_struct_id_refs(
   Pint            old_struct_id,
   Pint            new_struct_id
);
```

where ⟨*old_struct_id*⟩ and ⟨*new_struct_id*⟩ are as defined for the CHANGE STRUCTURE IDENTIFIER and CHANGE STRUCTURE REFERENCES routines.

This routine, and the two related routines, can (but don't necessarily) change the arrangement (topology) of an existing structure network. If any part of a posted structure network is modified by calling any of these routines, visual changes will probably result, subject to the display update state.

CSS Search and Inquiry

PHIGS provides functionality for interrogating the CSS by means of inquiry routines. The following routines fall into that category (details for all but the first two routine follow this list):

- INQUIRE OPEN STRUCTURE returns the open structure's identifier.
- INQUIRE STRUCTURE STATUS returns whether or not the specified structure exists. If the structure exists, the routine also returns whether or not the structure is empty.
- INQUIRE STRUCTURE IDENTIFIERS returns a list of all structures currently defined in the CSS.
- ELEMENT SEARCH allows you to search for the next element in a particular structure that matches given criteria.
- INCREMENTAL SPATIAL SEARCH and INCREMENTAL SPATIAL SEARCH3 search a particular structure network for the next graphical output structure element that matches a given criteria.
- The following routines allow the full details of a specified structure element to be determined:
  - INQUIRE CURRENT ELEMENT TYPE AND SIZE
  - INQUIRE ELEMENT TYPE AND SIZE
  - INQUIRE CURRENT ELEMENT CONTENT
  - INQUIRE ELEMENT CONTENT

Inquiring Structure Identifiers

In an interactive application, there may be an unknown number of structures defined by the user. In such a case, the application should have some way of getting a list of all structures currently defined in the CSS, regardless of their number or identifiers (which need not be consecutive). For this purpose, the INQUIRE STRUCTURE IDENTIFIERS routine is supported.

This routine can be useful if your application has a modular design. Since the PHIGS structure name space is common across all modules of an application, separately written code can depend on PHIGS to keep track of which structures exist, which avoids naming collisions in the application.

```
call pqsid(n, error, number, strid)
```

```
pinq_struct_ids(
    Pint            num_elems_appl_list,
    Pint            start_ind,
    Pint            *error,
    Pint_list       *struct_ids,
    Pint            *num_elems_impl_list
);
```

where:

FORTRAN binding parameters:

> ⟨*n*⟩ is the list element requested. PHIGS returns the *n*th element from the list with element 1 being the first element.
>
> ⟨*error*⟩ is the error-return indicator.
>
> ⟨*number*⟩ is the number of existing structure identifiers.
>
> ⟨*strid*⟩ is the *n*th structure identifier.

C binding parameters:

> ⟨*num_elems_appl_list*⟩ is the number of list elements that will fit into the ⟨*struct_ids*⟩ parameter allocated by the application. If you set this to zero, the routine will return just the number of actual structure identifiers.
>
> ⟨*start_ind*⟩ is an index into the actual list of structure identifiers with index 0 as the first element of both the actual and returned lists. This input parameter indicates the item in the actual list that should be copied into index 0 of the returned list.
>
> ⟨*error*⟩ is the error indicator.
>
> ⟨*struct_ids*⟩ is the returned list of structure identifiers.
>
> ⟨*num_elems_impl_list*⟩ is the total number of actual structure identifiers.

For the FORTRAN binding, INQUIRE STRUCTURE IDENTIFIERS returns one element from the list of structures contained in the CSS. If you want to examine the entire list of structures currently defined in the CSS, do the following:

1. Call INQUIRE STRUCTURE IDENTIFIERS once, with *n* equal to 0, to find out how many items are in the list of structures.

2. Call the routine ⟨*number*⟩ times, passing it values from 1 to *number*, to determine all of the supported values.

For the C binding, INQUIRE STRUCTURE IDENTIFIERS returns the (sub)list starting with ⟨*start_ind*⟩ and ending with this number:

min(⟨*num_elems_impl_list*⟩ + ⟨*start_ind*⟩ –1, ⟨*num_elems_appl_list*⟩ –1), inclusive, numbering from 0.

Searching for an Element

The ELEMENT SEARCH routine searches the specified structure for the closest element (in a specified direction) matching the search criteria.

The search criteria are based on element type. Two parameters specify a set of types to be included and a set to be excluded. An element is selected ("found") if the type of that element is in an inclusion set and is *not* in an exclusion set. The element type `PEALL` is a shorthand for all possible element types. If an element type is specified in both the inclusion set and the exclusion set, it is excluded.

```
 call pels (struct_id, start_loc, direction, incl_set_size, incl_set, excl_set_size,
+ excl_set, error, status, found_loc)
```

```
pelem_search(
    Pint                    struct_id,
    Pint                    start_loc,
    Psearch_dir             direction,
    const Pelem_type_list   *incl_set,
    const Pelem_type_list   *excl_set,
    Pint                    *error,
    Psearch_status          *status,
    Pint                    *found_loc
);
```

where:

⟨*struct_id*⟩ is the structure identifier.

⟨*start_loc*⟩ is an integer that specifies the element pointer of the first position to be tested. If ⟨*start_loc*⟩ is less than 0, the search begins at element 0; if ⟨*start_loc*⟩ is greater than the number of elements in the structure, the search begins at the last element in the structure.

⟨*direction*⟩ is a token that indicates the search direction. Valid values are forward (`PFWD, PDIR_FORWARD`) and backward (`PBWD, PDIR_BACKWARD`).

⟨*incl_set_size*⟩ is an integer specifying the number of elements in the inclusion set array ⟨*incl_set*⟩. This parameter is required only by the FORTRAN binding.

⟨*incl_set*⟩ is an integer array that specifies the element inclusion set. Refer to the element type list in Appendix A for the complete list of tokens.

⟨*excl_set_size*⟩ is an integer specifying the number of elements in the exclusion set array ⟨*excl_set*⟩. This parameter is required only by the FORTRAN binding.

⟨*excl_set*⟩ is an integer array that specifies the element exclusion set. The valid values are the same as for ⟨*incl_set*⟩.

⟨*error*⟩ is the error indicator.

⟨*status*⟩ is an integer status indicator that indicates whether the search

- Failed (`PFAIL, PSEARCH_STATUS_FAILURE`)

  or

- Succeeded (`PSUCC, PSEARCH_STATUS_SUCCESS`)

⟨*found_loc*⟩ specifies where the sought element was found. This assumes, of course, that ⟨*status*⟩ came back "succeeded." If ⟨*status*⟩ came back "failed," the value of ⟨*found_loc*⟩ is undefined.

The search begins at the specified element and proceeds in the specified direction. Searching is terminated when a suitable element is found or the limit of the structure is reached.

If the search is successful, the status indicator returns the "succeeded" value, and the found element position parameter is set at the matching element.

Incremental Spatial Search

The INCREMENTAL SPATIAL SEARCH 3 and INCREMENTAL SPATIAL SEARCH routines allow you to search a particular structure network for the next graphical output structure element that matches given criteria. The criteria contain three main components:

- The structure element must be within the specified structure network. It must occur "after" (in a depth-first ordering) the start point of the search. You can also specify a "ceiling" value that limits the search (stop at the end of a particular structure other than the root of the network).

- The output primitive must be within a specified distance of a specified world coordinate reference point.
- The name set associated with the primitive must be *accepted* by each of zero or more specified so-called normal filters and *rejected* by each of zero or more so-called inverted filters. Inclusion and exclusion filters are described in Chapter 13, *Name Sets and Filters*.

If the search is successful, the routine returns the path to the element. The path consists of a list of (structure ID, element position) pairs. There is more than one pair in the list if the element is found in a descendant of the topmost structure of the structure network. In that case, the first pair would contain the identifier of the topmost structure in the specified network, and the element position would identify an *execute structure* element referring to the structure that contains the second pair.

The length of the list is determined by how far down in the structure network the "found element" is. For example, in Figure 5–7, if the search located the *polymarker* element in structure 2, there would be two pairs in the list: (structure 1, element 3), (structure 2, element 5).

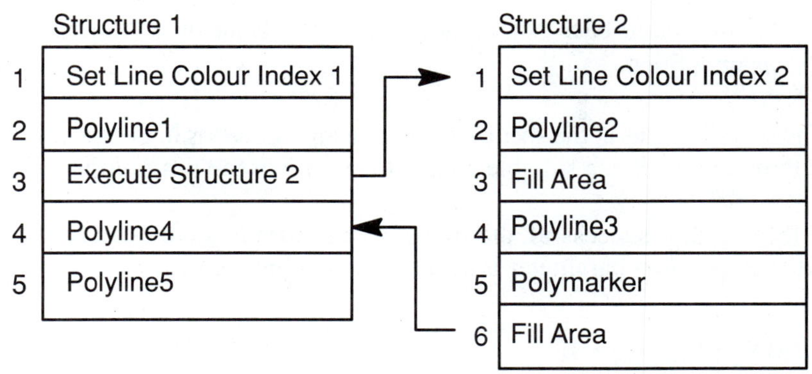

Figure 5–7. A Simple Structure Network

PHIGS performs the search by traversing the structure network (without sending anything to the workstation for display). PHIGS starts just after the point in a depth-first traversal indicated by ⟨*start_path*⟩. If an element is found that matches the name set criteria, then PHIGS checks to determine whether or not the element is within the specified distance to the reference point.

The term "incremental" is part of the name because you can use the path to the "found element" as the start of another search. (It is for this reason that the first element tested by a search is just after the element position indicated by the start path.) In this way you can make multiple calls to the routine and find all of the elements that match a certain criterion. For example, you could find "all of the polylines" within a certain area and then perform an action on all of them such as move them all, rotate them all, or delete them all. (To do this you would have to test the type of the matched primitive yourself, using INQUIRE ELEMENT TYPE AND SIZE.)

Refer to *A Practical Introduction to PHIGS and PHIGS PLUS* and *PHIGS Programming Manual* for more information on incremental spatial search.

Inquiring the Type and Contents of a Structure Element

So far, we have been talking exclusively about the *general* aspects of structure elements; e.g., they exist in structures, they can be added/moved/copied/deleted, they are implicitly numbered, and so forth. But we have yet to say anything about the *specific* aspects of elements. For example, there are many different kinds of elements: How do you know what kind of element is at the current position? What's in it?

These questions can be answered by the following four routines:

- INQUIRE CURRENT ELEMENT TYPE AND SIZE
- INQUIRE CURRENT ELEMENT CONTENT
- INQUIRE ELEMENT TYPE AND SIZE
- INQUIRE ELEMENT CONTENT

The two "current" routines supply information about the current element, requiring that a structure be open, whereas the other two supply information about any element in any structure, whether open or not. The "noncurrent" routines require a ⟨*struct_id*⟩ and an ⟨*ele_pos*⟩ to specify which element in which structure is being inquired about.

Since the two sets of routines are so similar, we only describe the "current" routines here.

The calling signatures for INQUIRE CURRENT ELEMENT TYPE AND SIZE are as follows:

```
call pqcets(error, ele_type, int_size, real_size, str_size)
```

```
pinq_cur_elem_type_size(
   Pint              *error,
   Pelem_type        *ele_type,
   size_t            *elem_size
);
```

where:

⟨*error*⟩ is an integer error indicator. If the value returned is zero, no error occurred; if the value returned is nonzero, the type of error is indicated by the value.

⟨*ele_type*⟩ is an integer that is set to indicate the type of element it is; i.e., what routine created this element. The mnemonic tokens are listed in Appendix A.

Note that the type of all generalized structure elements (GSEs) is returned as `PEGSE` or `PELEM_GSE`, depending on the binding. Likewise, the type of all generalized drawing primitives (GDPs) is returned as `PEGDP` or `PELEM_GDP`, and all GDP3s as `PEGDP3` or `PELEM_GDP3`. Their contents must be examined to determine exactly which GSE or GDP it is.

⟨*elem_size*⟩ is the size of the element's contents, in bytes. This parameter is used only by the C binding.

⟨*int_size*⟩, ⟨*real_size*⟩, and ⟨*str_size*⟩ are all returned integers that are the array sizes required to hold the data in the element being interrogated (⟨*str_size*⟩ is the number of 80-byte strings required to contain the data). These parameters are used only by the FORTRAN binding. The sizes depend both on the type of element and, for elements (like POLYLINE) that can take variable-sized data arrays, on the amount of data associated with the element. These size parameters can be passed to the INQUIRE CURRENT ELEMENT CONTENT routine, shown next.

The INQUIRE CURRENT ELEMENT CONTENT routine allows the application to examine any kind of structure element. The calling signatures of the routine are as follows:

```
 call pqceco(int_dim, real_dim, str_dim, error, int_size, int_array, real_size,
+ real_array, str_size, str_len, str_array)
```

```
pinq_cur_elem_content(
   Pstore              store,
   Pint                *error,
   Pelem_data          **elem_data
);
```

where:

> ⟨*store*⟩ is a handle to a store object for the C binding. The store is created by CREATE STORE, and this store contains memory that is managed by PHIGS. The actual data for the ⟨*elem_data*⟩ parameter is in the store's memory, but must be accessed via the *⟨*elem_data*⟩ pointer.
>
> *⟨*elem_data*⟩ is set to a pointer to the element contents as defined for the C binding.
>
> ⟨*int_dim*⟩, ⟨*real_dim*⟩, and ⟨*str_dim*⟩ are the allocated sizes of the arrays ⟨*int_array*⟩, ⟨*real_array*⟩, and ⟨*str_array*⟩, respectively, for the FORTRAN binding. These arrays must be large enough to contain all the data that INQUIRE CURRENT ELEMENT CONTENT wants to return. The routine calculates the size required, based on the current element's type and size, and then compares the ⟨*..._dim*⟩ values with the ⟨*..._size*⟩ values, and if any of the ⟨*..._size*⟩ values is larger than the corresponding ⟨*..._dim* ⟩ value, nothing is copied into the corresponding array, and an error is returned.
>
> ⟨*error*⟩ is an integer error indicator. If the value returned is zero, no error occurred; if the value returned is nonzero, the type of error is indicated by the value.
>
> ⟨*int_size*⟩ is an integer containing the actual returned size of ⟨*int_array*⟩, expressed in integer-sized units; ⟨*real_size*⟩ is an integer containing the actual returned size of ⟨*real_array*⟩, expressed in real-sized units; and ⟨*str_size*⟩ is an integer containing the actual number of strings (whose lengths are indicated by the corresponding elements in the ⟨*str_len*⟩ array) in ⟨*str_array*⟩. Note that the required array sizes are returned through ⟨*int_size*⟩, ⟨*real_size*⟩, and ⟨*str_size*⟩ even if the array sizes were not large enough.

Once you have the information in the respective arrays, you can interpret it as appropriate for the element type (returned from INQUIRE CURRENT ELEMENT TYPE AND SIZE).

For the FORTRAN binding, PHIGS returns the contents of a structure element as a list of integers, reals, and strings. Depending on the element type, there may be only one or two fields containing data. For example, suppose the element type is `PEPL`, a polyline. A polyline element's contents are defined as follows:

int_size	= 1
int_array(1)	= the number of points in the polyline
real_size	= (2 * *int_array*(1)) i.e., for each point in the polyline, there are two reals: the *x* and the *y* values.
real_array	= the polyline data. Elements 1 through *int_array*(1) contain the *x* components of the polyline; elements *int_array*(1) + 1 through (2 * *int_array*(1)) contain the *y* components of the polyline.
str_size	= 0

All other values and arrays are undefined for the polyline primitive element. The application must know in advance what type of data is present for a given structure element (whether there are integers, reals, and/or strings). For the standard elements, PHIGS specifies the data. Refer to your implementation documentation for a list of the contents of structure elements that are supported.

For the C binding, PHIGS returns the data in the `Pelem_data` data type (see the definition in Appendix D). Again, the application must know the format of the data in advance.

Using Structure Contents Inquiry Routines

Use the following procedure to examine the contents of a structure element:

1. Inquire the element type and size using either INQUIRE CURRENT ELEMENT TYPE AND SIZE or INQUIRE ELEMENT TYPE AND SIZE. If you are examining the current element, then you must make sure the correct structure is open and the element pointer is positioned as desired.

   C Binding:

   ```
   popen_struct(StructureID);
   pset_elem_ptr(CurrentElement);
   pinq_cur_elem_type_size(&Error, &ElementType, &ElementSize);
   ```

FORTRAN Binding:

```
 call popst(StructureID)              ! open structure
 call psep(CurrentElement)            ! set element pointer
 call pqcets(Error, ElementType,      ! inquire element type, size
+      IntSize, RealSize, StringSize)
```

2. Use INQUIRE CURRENT ELEMENT CONTENT or INQUIRE ELEMENT CONTENT to inquire the contents. For the C binding, this involves first using the CREATE STORE routine to allocate storage memory for the information.

```
Pstore      Store;                   /* storage area */
Pint        Error;                    /* error-return variable */
Pelem_data  *ElementDataPtr;             /* the data */

pcreate_store(&Error, &Store);        /* allocate storage memory */

pinq_cur_elem_content(Store, &Error, &ElementDataPtr);
```

For the FORTRAN binding, the INQUIRE CURRENT ELEMENT TYPE AND SIZE routine returns the size needed for the real, integer, and string arrays. Pass these values to INQUIRE CURRENT ELEMENT CONTENT or INQUIRE ELEMENT CONTENT to inquire the contents. In this example, the arrays that will receive the data are all defined as 100-element arrays, and any strings returned can be up to 100 characters long.

```
 integer*4          Error
 integer*4          IntSize, RealSize, StrSize
 integer*4          Ints(100)
 real               Reals(100)
 integer*4          StrLen(100)
 character*100      Strings(100)

 call pqceco(100, 100, 100,    ! inq. current element content
+  Error, IntSize, Ints, RealSize, Reals, StrSize, StrLen,
+  Strings)
```

3. Use the element type information from INQUIRE CURRENT ELEMENT TYPE AND SIZE or INQUIRE ELEMENT TYPE AND SIZE to determine how to examine the data. Refer to the `inquire_structure` example program in Appendix C for information on how to do this.

For all of the above fragments, it is good programming practice to examine the returned error indicator before you proceed. If the value is not equal to 0, then you can take appropriate action. For example, the following fragments merely call EMERGENCY CLOSE PHIGS:

C Binding:

```
if (Error) {
  printf("Error %d in pinq_cur_elem_type_size; terminating.", Error);
  pemergency_close_phigs();
    }
```

FORTRAN Binding:

```
if (Error .ne. 0) then
    print *, "Error", Error, " in pqceco, terminating."
    call peclph        ! emergency close PHIGS
endif
```

Structure Element Inquiry Example

The following fragment is taken from the C binding version of the `inquire_structure` program found in Appendix C. The fragment performs the following tasks (the points of interest in the program are numbered to correspond to the tasks):

1. Opens a structure and uses INQUIRE ELEMENT POINTER to determine how many elements are in the structure. This action takes advantage of the fact that when you first open a structure, PHIGS sets the element pointer to the last element in the structure.

2. Next it loops through the entire structure and inquires the current element type and size of each structure element. It uses SET ELEMENT POINTER to move the element pointer to the next element. The program uses INQUIRE CURRENT ELEMENT CONTENT AND SIZE to examine the type and size of the element.

3. If the element is a *set interior style* element, the program replaces the element with another *set interior style* element that sets the interior style to solid. (Assumption: The edit mode is Replace.)

4. Then it calls a function named `GetInfo` to inquire the contents of the structure element. The `GetInfo` function uses the INQUIRE CURRENT ELEMENT CONTENT routine. Refer to Appendix C for a full listing of the program in both C and FORTRAN.

```
1 popen_struct(StructureID);
  pinq_elem_ptr(&Error, &ElementPos);
  if (Error) {
      printf("Error %d in pinq_elem_ptr; terminating.", Error);
      pemergency_close_phigs();
  }
  printf("Number of elements in structure: %d\n", ElementPos);

  NumElements = ElementPos;
2  for (CurrentElement = 1; CurrentElement <= NumElements;
       CurrentElement++){
      pset_elem_ptr(CurrentElement);
      pinq_cur_elem_type_size(&Error, &ElementType, &ElementSize);
    if (Error) {
      printf("Error %d in pinq_cur_elem_type_size; terminating.",
           Error);
           pemergency_close_phigs();
      }
      printf("----------------------------------------------\n");
      printf("Element type: %d (%s)\n", ElementType,
        ElementNames[ElementType]);
      if (ElementType == PELEM_INT_STYLE)
3          pset_int_style(PSTYLE_SOLID);
4     GetInfo(ElementType);
      }
```

Inquiring Structure Network Information

The relationship of a structure to other structures within the CSS can be determined by INQUIRE PATHS TO ANCESTORS and INQUIRE PATHS TO DESCENDANTS. The former returns paths that reference the specified structure, while the latter returns paths that are referenced by a particular structure. Paths are returned as a list of element references. The path order and path depth can be specified to determine the portion of each path returned. Path depth determines the maximum number of element references returned in any one path or portion of a path.

There are cousins to these routines which operate on archive file contents: RETRIEVE PATHS TO ANCESTORS and RETRIEVE PATHS TO DESCENDANTS.

Adding Application Data to a Structure

The APPLICATION DATA routine allows you to add application-specific data to a structure. The data stored in the structure element is not interpreted or otherwise used by PHIGS. This provides a way for the application to store useful data (useful to the application rather than to PHIGS) with the geometric model.

The calling signatures for the routine are as follows:

```
call pap(ldr, datrec)
```

```
pappl_data(
   const Pdata          *data
);
```

where:

> ⟨*data*⟩ is the application data for the C binding. See Appendix D for the definition of `Pdata`.
>
> ⟨*ldr*⟩ is the dimension of the data record for the FORTRAN binding. This parameter specifies the number of 80-byte blocks required to store the application data.
>
> ⟨*datrec*⟩ is the data record for the FORTRAN binding. You may use your own scheme to pack data into ⟨*datrec*⟩, or you can use the two routines defined by the FORTRAN binding: PACK DATA RECORD and UNPACK DATA RECORD. Use PACK DATA RECORD to pack a variety of integers, floating-point numbers, and strings into the data record before sending it to the APPLICATION DATA routine. Use UNPACK DATA RECORD to unpack the data from the data record when the element is inquired.

A simple use of an application data element would be to store information such as a part number within a structure. A more sophisticated use would be to allow access to an application-specific database at a particular place. For example, you may have another database running alongside the PHIGS package. You can use an application data element to contain a pointer or a "key" for accessing information in the other database.

Alternatively, the entire database could be implemented using PHIGS application data elements for its storage mechanism.

Structure Archival and Retrieval

In order to store the contents of your CSS in a file, PHIGS provides functionality for creating archive files, and then storing the contents of the CSS in them for subsequent retrieval. PHIGS also provides the ability to delete structures from an archive file.

There are a lot of archiving routines. We only describe a few of the routines in this chapter. See your implementation documentation for more information. Also refer to *A Practical Introduction to PHIGS and PHIGS PLUS* and *PHIGS Programming Manual* for more information on structure archiving (see the *Preface* for information on these books).

The following routines initiate and terminate access to archive files:

- OPEN ARCHIVE FILE
- CLOSE ARCHIVE FILE

If your application needs to know whether or not an archive file is currently open, use the INQUIRE ARCHIVE STATE VALUE routine. This routine returns an integer equal to `PARCL` or `PST_ARCL` if no archive files are open, or `PAROP` or `PST_AROP` if one or more archive files is open. Then if you need to know how many archive files are open, or what they are, you can use INQUIRE ARCHIVE FILES.

The PHIGS standard suggests a method for storing information in archive files—**clear text encoding**. Clear text encoding allows applications running on different PHIGS implementations to exchange information since the contents of the CSS are stored in English-language symbols. However, it is up to the implementation to decide on whether to use clear text encoding or to use another format. For example, several implementations use the PEX binary archive file format. Some implementations support a binary encoding that can't be exchanged between implementations but is very quick for storage and retrieval using a single implementation. Refer to your implementation documentation for information on the type of files created for archiving. It may describe a utility program for converting a nonexchangeable file format to and from clear text encoding. Refer to the PHIGS standard for a description of clear text encoding.

Conflict Resolution

The ability to store structures in an archive file and then retrieve them later brings up an interesting problem: What happens if you try to archive a structure in a file that already contains a copy of that structure (i.e., a structure with the same identifier)? Does the new one overwrite the file copy? Or does the presence of the structure in the file negate the need to archive it? Does it represent a programming error? The opposite problem may also occur: What happens if you try to retrieve a structure from a file, but a copy of that structure already exists in the CSS? Such situations are called **conflicts**, and PHIGS' taking a specified action in response to a conflict is called **conflict resolution**.

There are two conflict resolution flags: One, for the first situation just mentioned, is called the *archival conflict resolution flag*, and the other, for the second situation, is called the *retrieval conflict resolution flag*. Each of these conflict resolution flags specifies the action to take when a conflict occurs. The two flags are set by the SET CONFLICT RESOLUTION routine:

```
call pscnrs (arch_conf_res_flag, retr_conf_res_flag)

pset_conf_res(
   Pconf_res             arch_conf_res_flag,
   Pconf_res             retr_conf_res_flag
);
```

where both ⟨*arch_conf_res_flag*⟩ and ⟨*retr_conf_res_flag*⟩ may have any of the following three values:

- **Maintain** (PCRMNT, PRES_MAINTAIN) causes the archival or retrieval operation to write structures into the archive or CSS only if they do not already exist, thereby maintaining existing structures.
- **Abandon** (PCRABA, PRES_ABANDON) causes the entire archival or retrieval operation to be abandoned in the event of such conflict, leaving the archive and CSS as they were before the operation started. An error is generated to notify the user that such a conflict occurred.
- **Update** (PCRUPD, PRES_UPD) allows structures to be overwritten. This permits newer versions of structures to overwrite obsolete ones.

Refer to the summary of conflict resolution in Figure 5–8 at the end of this chapter.

There is also an inquiry for determining the current conflict resolution flags; it is called INQUIRE CONFLICT RESOLUTION.

Archiving/Retrieving Structures

Your application can store all the CSS structures in an archive file with ARCHIVE ALL STRUCTURES. Its calling signatures are as follows:

```
call parast (arch_file_id)
```

```
par_all_structs(
   Pint              arch_file_id
);
```

where:

> ⟨*arch_file_id*⟩ is an integer that identifies the archive file to be written to. This value was assigned by the application when the archive file was opened.

All CSS structures will be archived if any of the following is true:

- The archive file is empty.
- None of the structures existing in the archive file exists in the CSS.
- The archival conflict resolution flag is Update.

Similar to the routine that archives structures in an archive file, PHIGS supports a corresponding routine that conditionally retrieves all structures from an archive file: RETRIEVE ALL STRUCTURES.

```
call prast (arch_file_id)
```

```
pret_all_structs(
   Pint              arch_file_id
);
```

where ⟨*arch_file_id*⟩ is defined as it is for its archive counterpart.

This routine uses the same conditions described previously to determine whether or not to retrieve all of the structures in the CSS.

Retrieving Structure Identifiers from an Archive

In addition to the routines listed above, there is a routine to inquire information about the contents of an archive file. The RETRIEVE STRUCTURE IDENTIFIERS routine returns the identifiers of structures in an open archive file.

```
call prsid(arch_file_id, buf_size, n, struct_ids)
```

```
pret_struct_ids(
   Pint                     arch_file_id,
   Pint                     num_elems_in_appl_list,
   Pint                     start_ind,
   Pint_list                *struct_ids,
   Pint                     *num_elems_in_impl_list
);
```

where:

FORTRAN binding parameters:

⟨*arch_file_id*⟩ is the identifier of a currently open archive file.

⟨*buf_size*⟩ is the size of the buffer allocated for the archive file's list of structure identifiers. If you specify a size that is not large enough for the requested information, PHIGS generates error 2001. In this case, the value of ⟨*n*⟩ and ⟨*struct_ids*⟩ may be incorrect.

⟨*n*⟩ is the number of structure identifiers in the list.

⟨*struct_ids*⟩ is the list of structure identifiers in the specified open archive file.

C binding parameters:

⟨*arch_file_id*⟩ is the identifier of a currently open archive file.

⟨*num_elems_in_appl_list*⟩ is the length of the returned list. This input parameter indicates the number of list elements which will fit into the returned list. If this is set to zero, you can determine the number of actual structure identifiers.

⟨*start_ind*⟩ is an index into the actual list of structure identifiers with index 0 as the first element of both the actual and returned lists. This input parameter indicates the item in the actual list that should be copied into index 0 of the returned list.

⟨*struct_ids*⟩ is the returned list of structure identifiers.

⟨*num_elems_in_impl_list*⟩ is the total number of actual structure identifiers.

Use this routine similarly to the way you use INQUIRE STRUCTURE IDENTIFIERS as explained earlier in this chapter.

Summary of Archiving Routines

The following is the complete list of PHIGS structure archiving routines. The routines covered in this Chapter are identified in the list. Refer to your implementation documentation for information on routines that we have not covered.

- The following routines initiate and terminate access to archive files:
  - OPEN ARCHIVE FILE
  - CLOSE ARCHIVE FILE
- Several archive files can be open at the same time. INQUIRE PHIGS FACILITIES returns (among other things) the maximum number of archive files that may be open at the same time.
- The following routines store structures in an archive file:
  - ARCHIVE STRUCTURES
  - ARCHIVE STRUCTURE NETWORKS
  - ARCHIVE ALL STRUCTURES (described in chapter)
- The following routines retrieve structures from an archive file:
  - RETRIEVE STRUCTURES
  - RETRIEVE STRUCTURE NETWORKS
  - RETRIEVE ALL STRUCTURES (described in chapter)
- The following routines delete structures from an archive file:
  - DELETE STRUCTURES FROM ARCHIVE
  - DELETE STRUCTURE NETWORKS FROM ARCHIVE
  - DELETE ALL STRUCTURES FROM ARCHIVE
- The following routines retrieve information about structures in an archive file:
  - INQUIRE ARCHIVE FILES returns the names of currently opened archive files

- RETRIEVE STRUCTURE IDENTIFIERS (described in chapter)
- INQUIRE ARCHIVE STATE VALUE returns the PHIGS archive state (open or closed).
- RETRIEVE PATHS TO ANCESTORS
- RETRIEVE PATHS TO DESCENDANTS

- The following routines deal with the protection of data in the archive and in the CSS:
  - SET CONFLICT RESOLUTION (described in chapter)
  - INQUIRE CONFLICT RESOLUTION (described in chapter)
  - INQUIRE ALL CONFLICTING STRUCTURES compares the list of structure identifiers in the CSS with the structure identifiers in a specified archive file and returns the identifiers that occur in both.
  - INQUIRE CONFLICTING STRUCTURES IN NETWORK compares the list of structure identifiers in a particular structure network in the CSS with the structure identifiers in a specified archive file and returns the identifiers that occur in both.

Summary of Conflict Resolution

The "sentences" in Figure 5–8 explain all six archival and retrieval functions and the three states of the two conflict flags.

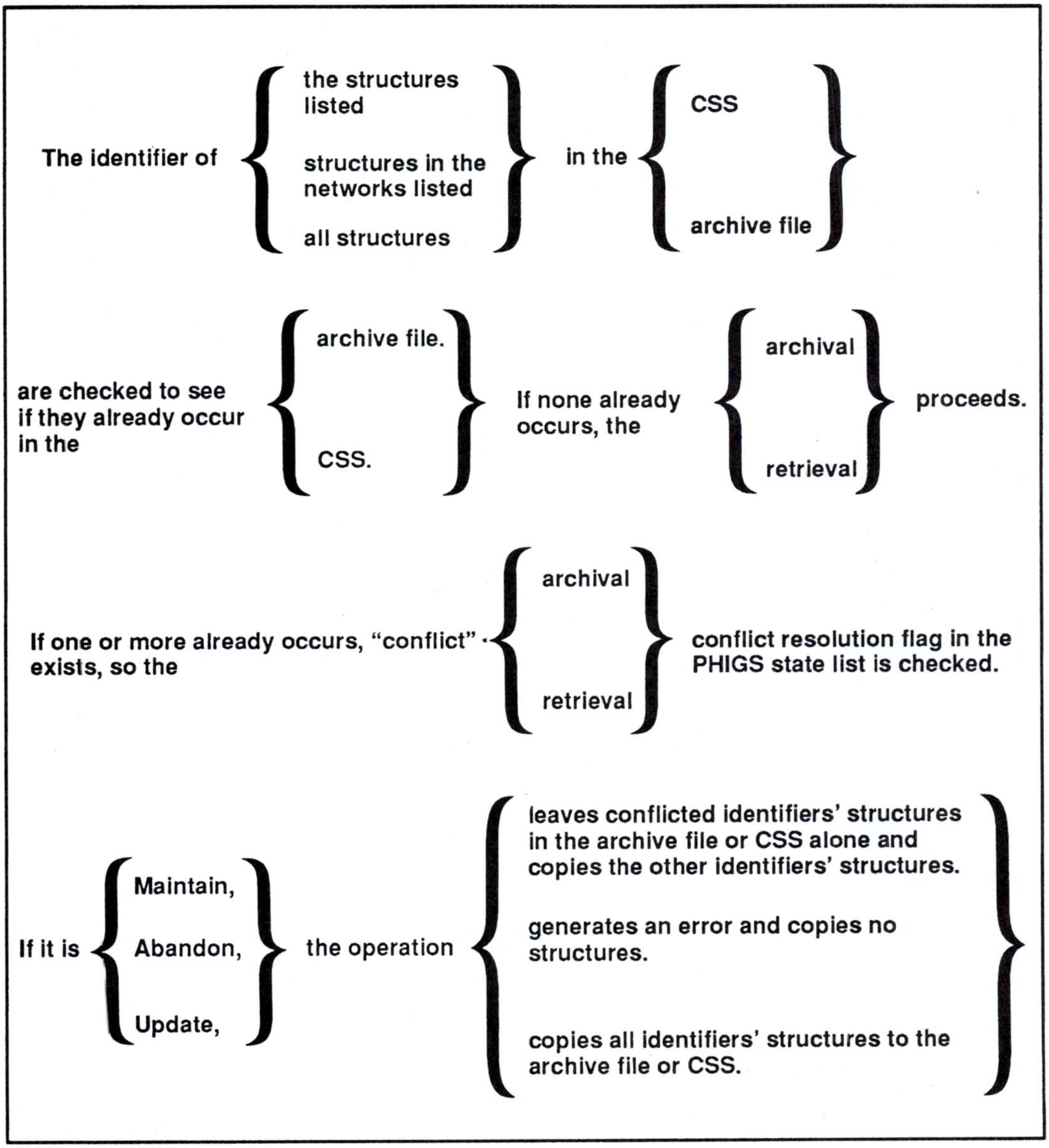

Figure 5–8. Conflict Resolution

Chapter 6

Modelling Transformations

PHIGS defines a multi-stage transformation pipeline through which primitives pass during traversal. Modelling transformations are its first stage. In PHIGS, you can create a geometric model from separate parts, each of which can be defined within its own **modelling coordinate** (**MC**) system. The single parts are positioned relative to each other by defining a modelling transformation for each part. PHIGS uses these transformations to combine all of the modelling coordinate systems into a single common world coordinate system.

This chapter describes the transformation pipeline and the five coordinate systems that PHIGS uses in the pipeline. Then it goes on to describe the first two stages of the pipeline.

The Transformation Pipeline

The process of translating a geometric model to a picture consists of several sequential and logically independent steps. These steps make up the **transformation pipeline** as illustrated in Figure 6–1.

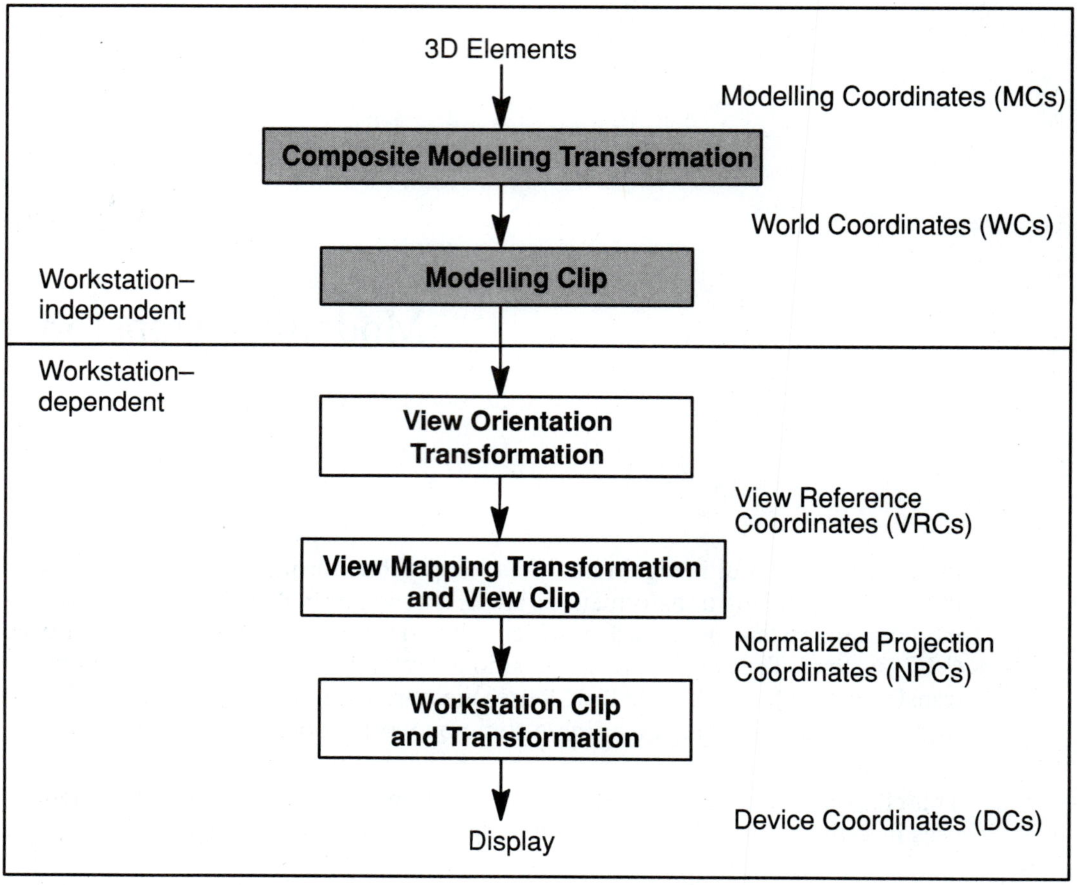

Figure 6–1. The Transformation Pipeline

Primitives pass through the transformation pipeline at traversal time. Each primitive goes through five stages and a total of five different coordinate systems before being displayed.

While the transformations are "conceptually" performed one at a time, the implementation usually optimizes part or all of the process. The most common optimization is to concatenate matrices.

There are 2D and 3D versions of most of the PHIGS routines that deal with positions (for example, primitive structure element routines) and with transformations (described in this chapter and the next). Keep in mind that PHIGS is a 3D system. The 2D primitive routines are merely "shorthand" versions of the 3D routines with $z = 0$. The 2D transformation routines (which take a 3×3 homogeneous matrix) are merely shorthand versions of the 3D transformation routines (which take 4×4 matrices), with the third row and third column containing all zeroes, except for a 1 (one) on the main diagonal.

Coordinate Systems

This section describes the five coordinate systems used by the PHIGS graphics pipeline. All five coordinate systems are right-handed, Cartesian coordinate systems. Figure 6–2 shows two right-handed Cartesian coordinate systems. In that illustration, positive z is pointing out of the page.

Modelling Coordinates (MCs)

Modelling coordinates are coordinates based on the mathematical model that you are rendering; they are for your convenience in making the geometrical model. For example, if you want to draw a picture of a car, you might have the car defined in "car coordinates" (for example, –10 to +10 feet in x, –4 to +4 feet in y, and 0 to 5 feet in z). Then, the wheel's modelling coordinates might be –2 to +2 feet in x, y, and z, and the modelling coordinates of the wheel's lug nut might be 0 to 1 inch in x, y, and z.

Figure 6–2 illustrates two separate structures, each defined in its own modelling coordinate system.

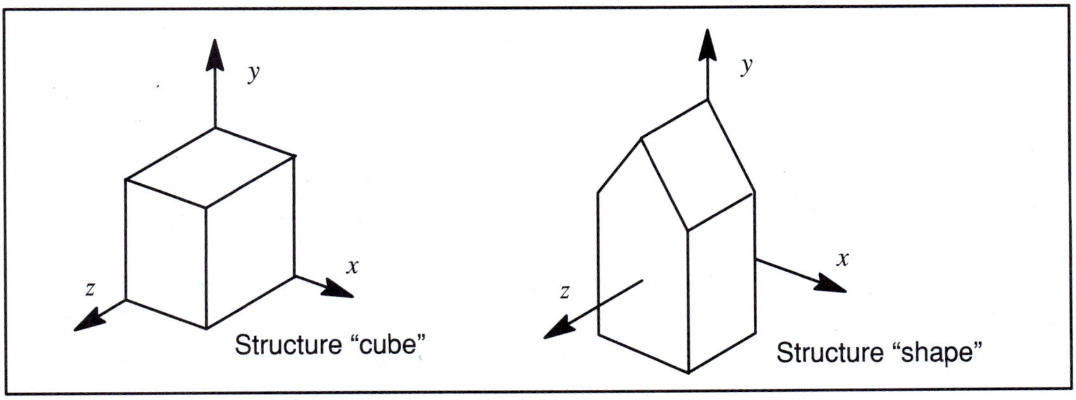

Figure 6–2. Separate Modelling Coordinate Systems

Modelling coordinates are transformed by modelling transformations, such as translation, scaling, and rotation, into the next coordinate system: world coordinates.

World Coordinates (WCs)

The world coordinate system is the coordinate system in which the entire geometric model, "everything in the world" (at least in the context of your drawing), is represented. That is, the WC system exists so you have a common coordinate system in which to represent "the big picture." Without a common frame of reference, there would be no way of determining the position of one point relative to any other.

After all the various geometrical models go through the various modelling transformations, they end up in the common coordinate system: world coordinates. Like modelling coordinates, world coordinates axes are labelled *xyz*.

As you place structures within the world coordinate system you can apply scaling, rotation, and translation operations to them. Figure 6–3 shows the two structures from Figure 6–2 combined in the world coordinate system. Notice that the cube is scaled and translated. The shape is rotated and translated.

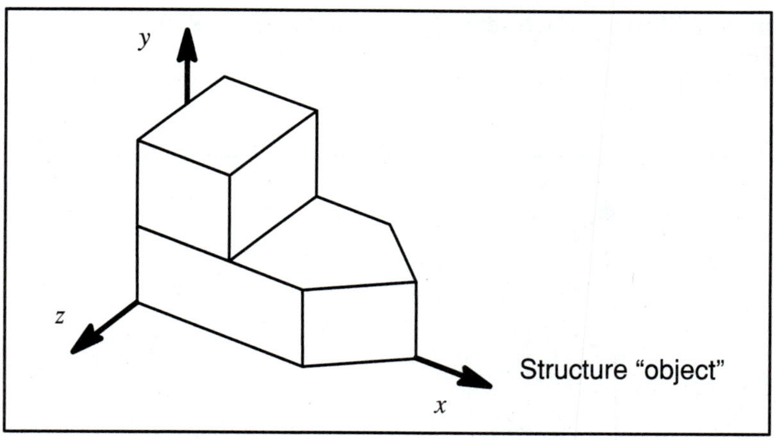

Figure 6–3. An Object in the World Coordinate System

From WCs, a **view orientation transformation** takes the scene and transforms it into a coordinate system called **view reference coordinates**.

View Reference Coordinates (VRCs)

Since world coordinates are static relative to the definition of the model, you need another coordinate system to define how the model is viewed. The purpose of the view reference coordinate system is to select the direction from which the geometric model will be viewed.

As mentioned, the view orientation transformation converts points expressed in WCs into another coordinate system called view reference coordinates. The VRC system is a user-specifiable, three-dimensional, Cartesian coordinate system in which the parameters for the view mapping transformation are specified.

PHIGS defines the three axes in VRC space as *u*, *v*, and *n*; for this reason, VRC space is also called UVN space. The VRC coordinate system is defined in Chapter 7, *Viewing and Workstation Transformations*, in the section entitled "View Orientation Transformation."

Typically, the specific transformations used for the WC–to–VRC conversion are only rotation and translation; no scaling is done at this point. Because of this, you can think of the VRC coordinate system in terms of a camera. The VRC coordinate system represents the position of the camera (see Figure 6–4). You can position the camera anywhere in world coordinate space.

Continuing this analogy, we think of the VRC *n*-axis as pointing out the back of the camera and the *v*-axis as pointing out its top. This lets you orient the camera to point in any direction.

An alternative analogy is that the VRC is like a handle you can fasten any which way to the object you want to view. You then "hold" this handle up right in front of you to look at the object. This is illustrated in Figure 6–5, which shows three separate view orientations, each with its own VRC system.

The camera analogy is sometimes called **viewer-centered**, and the handle analogy is sometimes called **object-centered**. We describe how to define both types of view in Chapter 7.

A handy way to "position the camera" or "attach the handle" is to use the EVALUATE VIEW ORIENTATION MATRIX 3 routine. This routine, described in Chapter 7, returns a 4 × 4 floating-point matrix that you put in a view representation as the view orientation matrix.

In the camera analogy, the origin of the VRC system is the center of the camera. In the handle analogy, the origin is typically on or near the object being viewed.

VRCs are translated into normalized projection coordinates via the view mapping matrix, which is described in the next section.

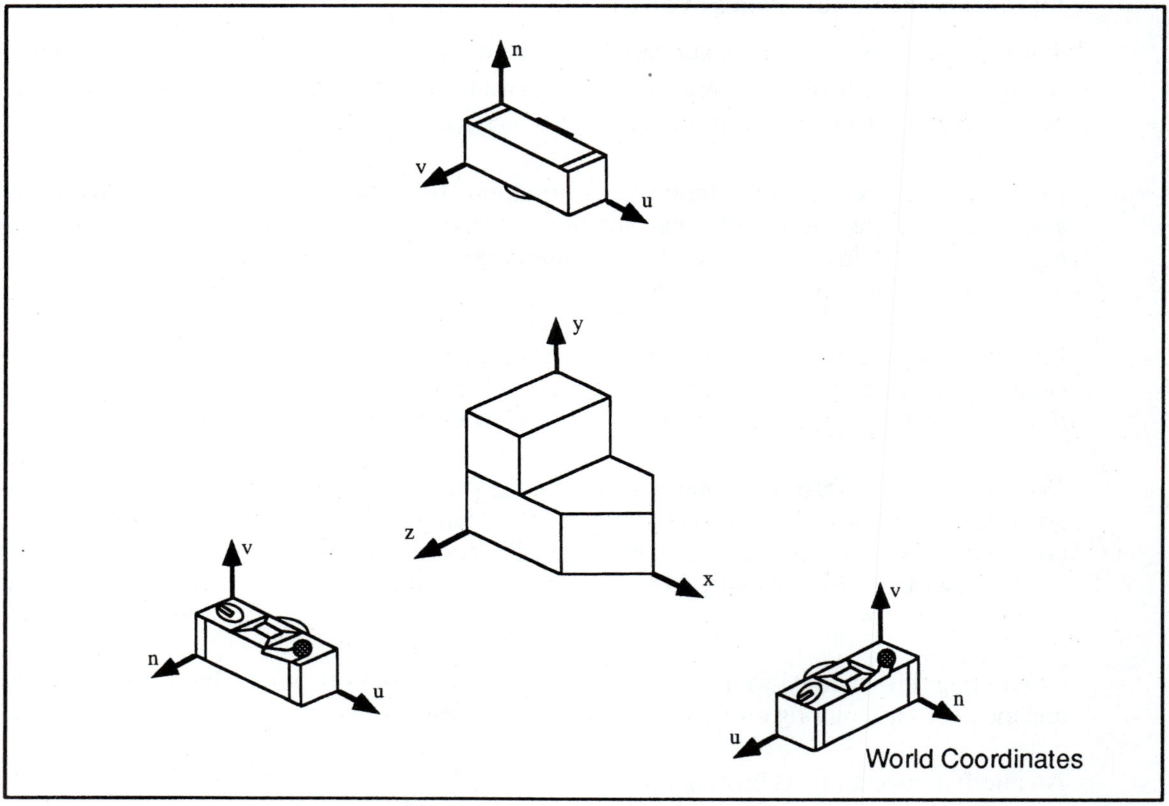

Figure 6–4. Creating Three Different VRC Systems (Viewer-Centered Views)

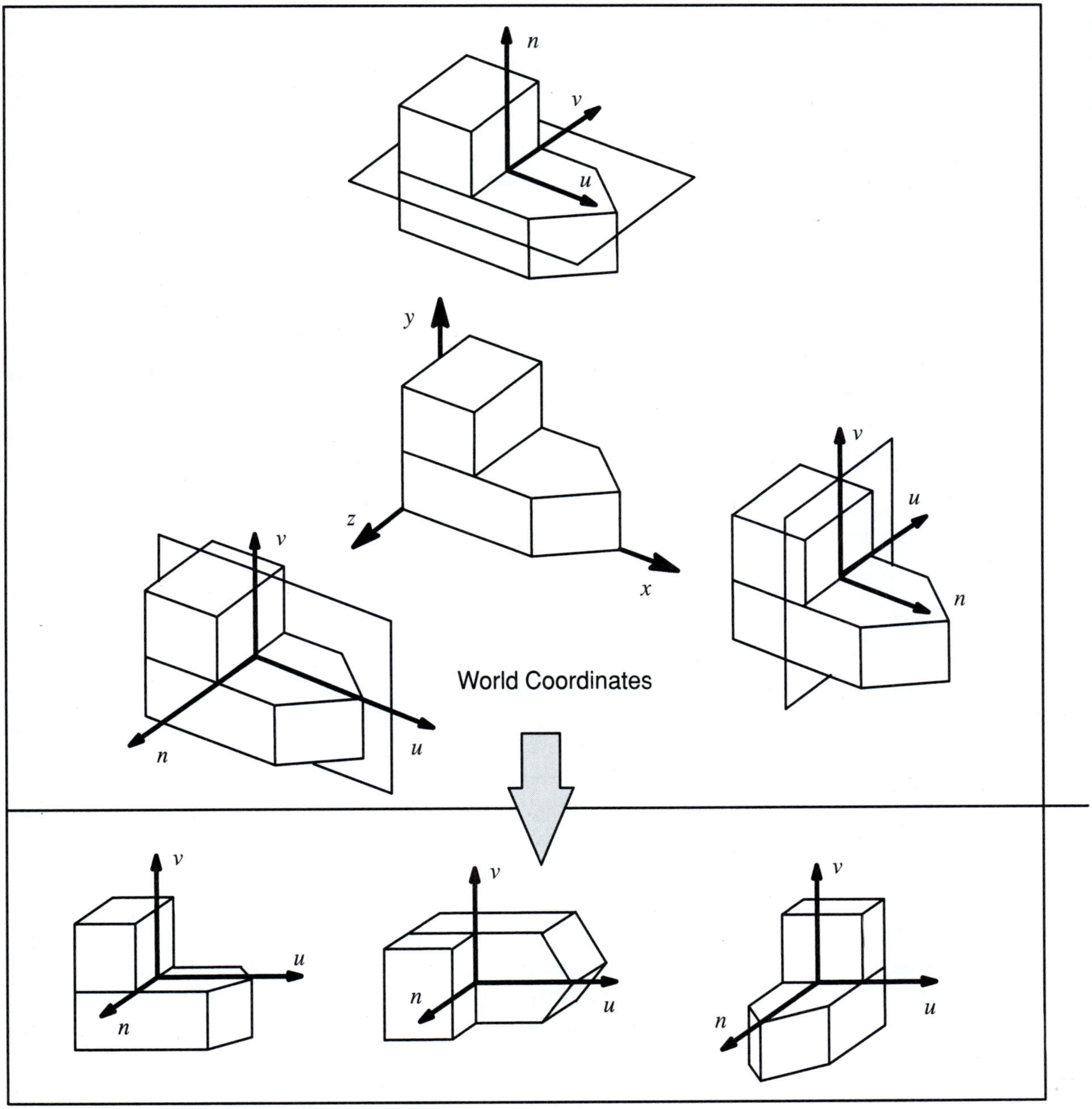

Figure 6–5. Three Different VRC Coordinate Systems (Object-Centered Views)

Normalized Projection Coordinates (NPCs)

A matrix in the view representation called the view mapping matrix transforms points from VRCs into normalized projection coordinates. (You can use the EVALUATE VIEW MAPPING MATRIX 3 routine to create matrices for this purpose.) The NPC coordinate system is a device-independent, three-dimensional, Cartesian coordinate system. As the name implies, NPCs are normalized (that is, they range from 0.0 to 1.0). NPC space is where all the views are combined into a single picture.

The purpose of the view mapping matrix when combined with the clip limits entries in a view representation is to put boundaries on what is being viewed in VRC space. The view orientation matrix helps to define *how* we view the geometric model. The view mapping matrix defines *how much* of the otherwise infinitely sized world coordinate system we will view. In constructing a view mapping matrix, one takes into account the "front," "back," and "sides" of what PHIGS calls the **view volume** in VRCs. One also considers where to place this bounded model in NPC space. Figure 6–6 show three views mapped into the NPC system.

NPCs are translated into device coordinates by the workstation transformation.

Device Coordinates (DCs)

Device coordinates are an abstraction of the coordinates used by the device. PHIGS considers logical device coordinates as three-dimensional space. The DC origin is the lower left, rear corner of the rectangular solid of DC space. You can use INQUIRE DISPLAY SPACE SIZE or INQUIRE DISPLAY SPACE SIZE 3 to find out the actual size available to the PHIGS display. The actual units may vary from one implementation to the next. For example, if the program is displaying in an X window, the routine could return the size of the window in pixel values. Refer to your implementation documentation for details.

The workstation transformation describes which portion of the combination of views in NPC space will be mapped to the display. It also identifies the portion of the display that will be used. Figure 6–7 shows a sample mapping from the entire unit cube in NPC space to device coordinate space for two different-sized X windows. Notice that the available range of *x* and *y* device coordinates depends on the size of the X window.

In Figure 6–7 the white background of the line drawings (as opposed to the dark gray area surrounding it) is intended to show, in device coordinates, the edges of the regions occupied by views in NPCs.

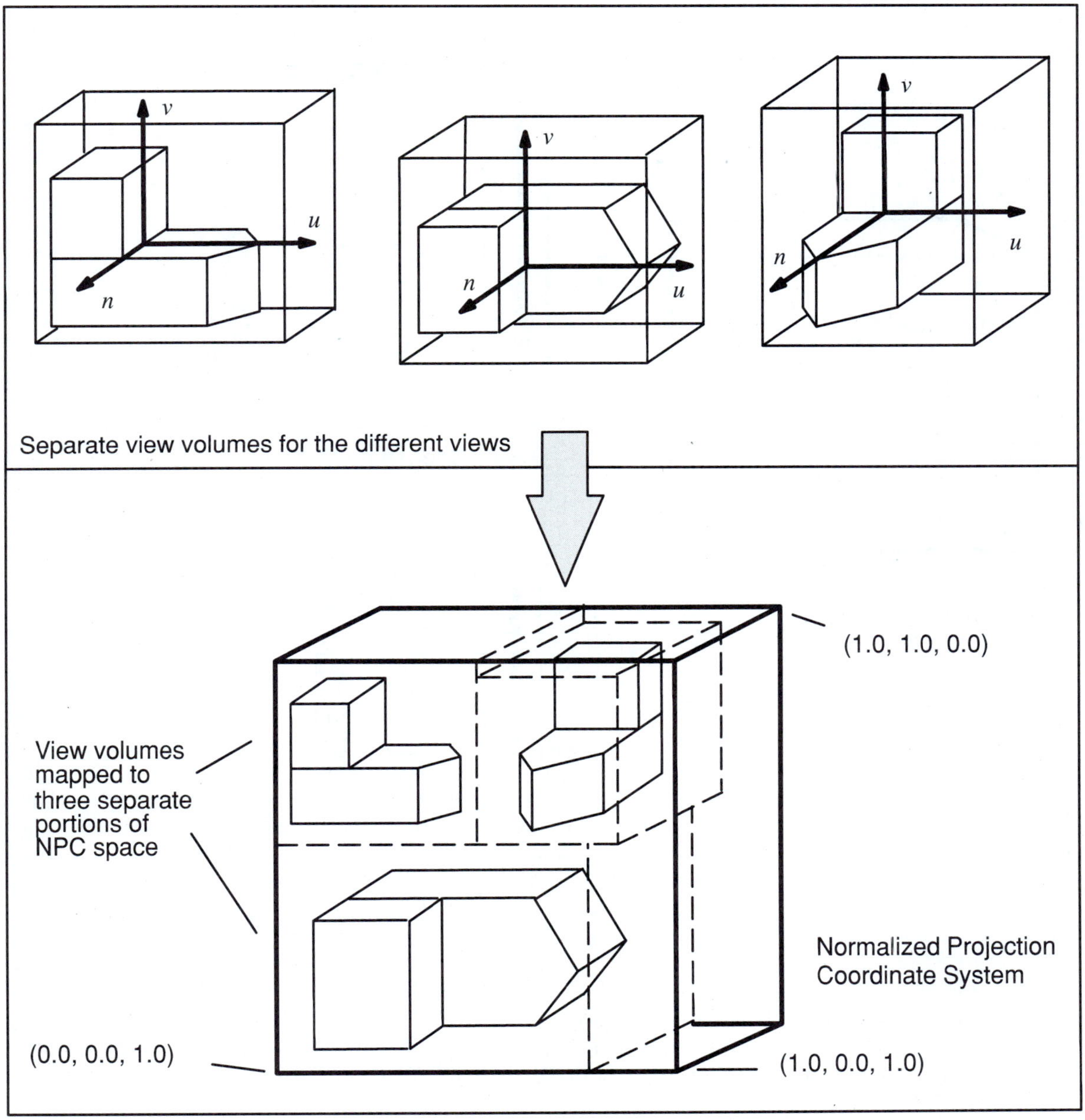

Figure 6–6. Composing the Three Views in the NPC System

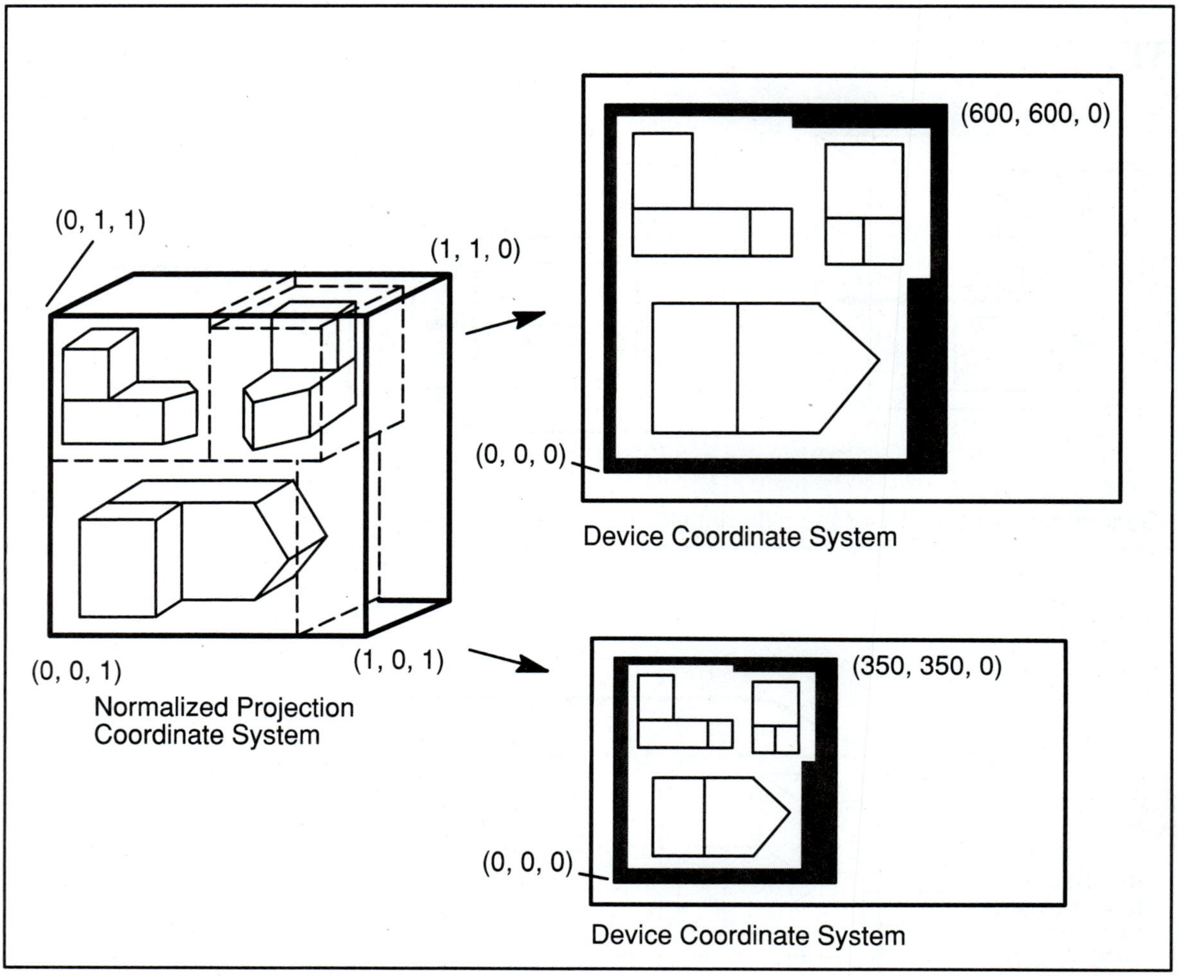

Figure 6–7. Workstation Window-to-Viewport Mappings for Different-sized Windows

The workstation viewport is the portion of display space that is being rendered to. In the two examples in Figure 6–7, the workstation viewport is denoted by the outside of the dark gray areas. You can change the position and size of the workstation viewport, although they must remain within the maximum device limits. Refer to "Workstation Transformations" in Chapter 7, for more information.

This ends our brief walk through the PHIGS coordinate systems. We go on to consider modelling transformations in the rest of this chapter and leave viewing to the next chapter.

What Are Modelling Transformations Used For?

Let's look at an example that uses modelling transformations. We'll create a simple bicycle and "roll it" across the screen in an animation. Figure 6–8 shows three frames of the animation. (In the third frame the bicycle is starting to exit the viewing area.) This example uses a number of routines described later in the chapter. We hope to give you an idea of the routines' usefulness before you begin reading about them. The complete program is in Appendix C.

Figure 6–8. A Simple Bicycle Using Structure Hierarchy and Modelling Transformations

If we just wanted to draw a simple set of objects like the bicycle in Figure 6–8, it would be easy simply to draw the lines and fill area primitives right where you see them. However, let's assume a few things about the drawing:

- Let's assume that in real life two different engineers are working on the project. One designs wheels and the other designs bicycle frames. Each part gets designed in its own "modelling coordinate space," and the parts get combined later.
- Let's also assume that the wheel designer only creates one wheel. We want to place two copies of the wheel in the proper locations.
- We want to be able to make the wheels turn independently on the bicycle.
- We want to be able to move the bicycle across the screen while the wheels are turning.

All of these requirements are easily met if we use structure hierarchy and modelling transformations.

The bicycle frame is created using a single fill area set primitive:

```
Pint         Bike = 1, Wheel = 2, Frame = 3; /* structure IDs */
static Ppoint FramePoints[] = {
          -0.95,-1.03, -0.87,-1.05, -0.60,-0.33,  /* fork */
          -0.05,-1.05,  1.00,-1.05,  0.55, 0.00,  /* rear triangle */
           0.50,-0.10,  0.85,-0.95,  0.08,-0.95, 0.60, 0.10,
           0.70, 0.10,  0.73, 0.15,  0.70, 0.20,  /* seat */
           0.37, 0.20,  0.34, 0.15,  0.51, 0.13,
          -0.01,-0.92, -0.56,-0.20, -0.52,-0.10,  /* front triangle */
           0.40,-0.10,  0.44, 0.00, -0.51, 0.00,
          -0.45, 0.15, -0.10, 0.15, -0.10, 0.20,  /* handlebars */
          -0.50, 0.20};
static Ppoint_list FrameData = {26, FramePoints};
...
popen_struct(Frame);
pfill_area(&FrameData);
...
```

The wheels consist of a polyline primitive drawn in a circle (polylines connecting 30 points around a circle). Spokes connect the points on the circle.

```
#define  Spokes         30        /* number of spokes, sides on rim */
#define  dTheta         (2*M_PI/Spokes) /* angle between spokes */
...
Ppoint      SpokeData[2], RimData[Spokes + 1];
Ppoint_list Spoke, Rim;
int         I;                          /* loop control variable */
float       Theta;                      /* temporary variable */
...
popen_struct(Wheel);
Rim.points = RimData;
for (I = 0; I <= Spokes; I++) {
    Theta = I * dTheta;                /* calculate required angle */
    Rim.points[I].x = cos(Theta);   /* x = r*cos(Theta) where r = 1 */
    Rim.points[I].y = sin(Theta);   /* y = r*sin(Theta) where r = 1 */
}
Rim.num_points = Spokes + 1;
ppolyline(&Rim);
Spoke.num_points = 2;
Spoke.points = SpokeData;
for (I = 0; I < Spokes; I++) {
    Theta = I * dTheta;                /* calculate required angle */
    Spoke.points[0].x = 0.0;           /* \  Start defining each */
    Spoke.points[0].y = 0.0;           /*  \ spoke from the center */
    Spoke.points[1].x = cos(Theta);    /*  / and proceed */
    Spoke.points[1].y = sin(Theta);    /* /  rimward. */
    ppolyline(&Spoke);
}
pclose_struct();
```

We put the bicycle together as follows:

1. Put the wheels on the frame. Do this within the frame's MC system.

2. Place the frame in a scene so we can look at it and then later move the bicycle across the scene.

In order to put the wheels on the frame, we need to reference the `Wheel` structure twice. We use an EXECUTE STRUCTURE routine for this task. This is where the modelling transformations come into play. We need a way to tell PHIGS, "Scale the wheel to the right size and put it in this location." So, here is the new `Frame` structure:

```
static Ppoint LocalOrigin = {0.0, 0.0};  /* for rotation/scaling */
static Pvec TransF = {-0.9, -1.0};       /* front wheel translation */
static Pvec TransR = { 0.9, -1.0};       /* rear wheel translation */
static Pvec Scale = {0.5, 0.5};          /* reduce to half size */
Pmatrix     Matrix[3][3];                /* temporary matrix */
Pint        Error;                       /* error-return variable */
...
/*--- define the "Frame" structure ---------------------------------*/
popen_struct(Frame);
pfill_area(&FrameData);
pbuild_tran_matrix(&LocalOrigin, &TransF, 0.0, &Scale,
                   &Error, Matrix);
pset_local_tran(Matrix, PTYPE_REPLACE);
pexec_struct(Wheel);
pbuild_tran_matrix(&LocalOrigin, &TransR, 0.0, &Scale,
                   &Error, Matrix);
pset_local_tran(Matrix, PTYPE_REPLACE);
pexec_struct(Wheel);
pclose_struct();
```

First we draw the frame using a fill area. Then we use the BUILD TRANSFORMATION MATRIX to create a modelling transformation matrix that will position the wheel. BUILD TRANSFORMATION MATRIX is a utility routine that does not create a structure element. We pass the new matrix to the SET LOCAL TRANSFORMATION routine to actually put the matrix in the structure (this routine does create a structure element). We create two separate *set local transformation* elements, once for each instance of the wheel.

Now that we have the bicycle, we need to put it some place where we can manipulate the bicycle as a unit. We create a `Bike` structure for this purpose. Before we call EXECUTE STRUCTURE, we need to set the local transformation matrix for the scene so the bicycle will be scaled down and placed in the proper position. Here is the `Bike` structure:

```
/*--- define the "Bike" structure ----------------------------------*/
popen_struct(Bike);
pset_char_ht(0.04);
TempLoc.x = 0.1, TempLoc.y = 0.8;
ptext(&TempLoc, "Joe's Bike Shop");
TempScale.delta_x = TempScale.delta_y = 0.25;
pscale(&TempScale, &Error, Scaling);
TempTrans.delta_x = TempTrans.delta_y = 0.6;
ptranslate(&TempTrans, &Error, Translation);
pcompose_matrix(Translation, Scaling, &Error, Matrix);
pset_local_tran(Matrix, PTYPE_REPLACE);
pexec_struct(Frame);
pclose_struct();
```

In the `Frame` structure we used one utility routine to build a matrix that performed scaling, rotation, and translation. This time we want to create a matrix that performs only scaling and translation, so we build the matrices separately and then concatenate them. Again, since these are only utility routines that don't create structure elements, we pass the final matrix to the SET LOCAL TRANSFORMATION routine to actually put the matrix in the structure. Notice that we put the text into the structure before the *set local transformation* element. This ensures that the text will not be affected by any of the modelling transformations that occur later on in the hierarchy.

Figure 6–9 shows a diagram of the final structure network:

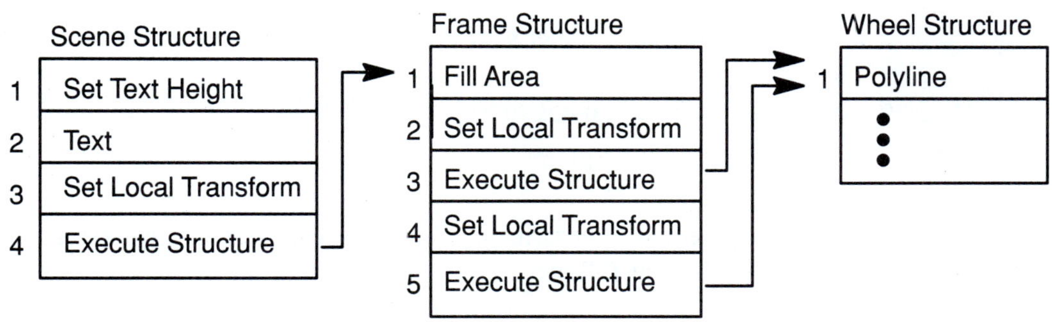

Figure 6–9. Structure Network for the Bicycle Program

Each time traversal returns to the calling structure, PHIGS resets the modelling transformation matrix that was in place before the execute structure element was invoked. This means that the local transformations in the `Frame` structure affect the `Wheel` structure, but they do not affect the `Scene` structure. There are also a global and a composite transformation in effect, but for this simple example we can skip their explanation.

Rotating the Wheels and Moving the Bicycle

Now that we have the structure network set up, it is a simple matter to display the bicycle and to create an animation sequence. The following routines post the `Scene` structure to the workstation and tell PHIGS to display the structure network:

```
ppost_struct(WorkstnID, Bike, 1.0);
...
pupd_ws(WorkstnID, PFLAG_PERFORM);
```

In order to create the animation sequence, we need to do the following:

- The deferral and modification modes should be WAIT and NIVE, respectively. This tells PHIGS not to make any visual updates until we call UPDATE WORKSTATION or REDRAW ALL STRUCTURES. By doing this we can edit both the `Scene` structure and the `Frame` structure and not have the display updated until we are done with all the edits. Our implementation uses NIVE/WAIT as the default. Even so, our program will be more portable if we make fewer assumptions about the implementation, so we include the following:

  ```
  pset_disp_upd_st(WorkID, PDEFER_WAIT, PMODE_NIVE);
  ```

- Set the structure edit mode to Replace as follows:

  ```
  pset_edit_mode(PEDIT_REPLACE);
  ```

- Now we can edit the two structures and replace the transformation matrices. We can do this in a loop as follows:

  a. Edit the `Bike` structure and replace the local transform with one that has a change in the *x* translation value.

  b. Edit the `Frame` structure and replace both transformation matrices with matrices that have a slightly different rotation value.

  c. Update the workstation to display the changes, go back into the loop and do it again.

The following fragment of the program shows the animation loop:

```
#define  dX          -0.003          /* speed of moving bike */
#define  deg         *M_PI/180.      /* convert degrees to radians */
...
float       WheelAngle;              /* current rotation of wheels */
float       Xpos;                    /* current position of bike */
Ppoint      TempLoc;                         /* for text only */
Pvec        TempScale;                       /* for text only */
Pvec        TempTrans;                       /* for text only */
/*--- transformation matrix variables ------------------------------*/
Pmatrix  Translation[3][3],Scaling[3][3];/* transformation matrices */
Pmatrix     Matrix[3][3];                    /* temporary matrix */
...
Xpos = 1.4;                                 /* first location for bike */
WheelAngle = 0.0;                           /* first angle for wheels */
for (Xpos = 1.4; Xpos > -0.36; Xpos += dX) {
/*--- first, open "Bike" structure and move the frame ----------*/
    popen_struct(Bike);
    pset_elem_ptr(3);                       /* bike xform is element #3 */
    TempTrans.delta_x = Xpos, TempTrans.delta_y = 0.6;
    ptranslate(&TempTrans, &Error, Translation);
    pcompose_matrix(Translation, Scaling, &Error, Matrix);
    pset_local_tran(Matrix, PTYPE_REPLACE);
    pclose_struct();
    /*--- next, open the "Frame" structure and rotate the wheels ---*/
    popen_struct(Frame);
    pbuild_tran_matrix(&LocalOrigin, &TransR, WheelAngle deg, &Scale,
      &Error, Matrix);
    pset_elem_ptr(2);                       /* fr. wheel xform is ele 2 */
    pset_local_tran(Matrix, PTYPE_REPLACE);
    pbuild_tran_matrix(&LocalOrigin, &TransF, WheelAngle deg, &Scale,
      &Error, Matrix);
    pset_elem_ptr(4);                       /* bk. wheel xform is ele 4 */
    pset_local_tran(Matrix, PTYPE_REPLACE);
    WheelAngle -= dX * 3000/(2 * M_PI);     /* increment wheel angle */
    pclose_struct();
    pupd_ws(WorkstnID, PFLAG_PERFORM);
   }
```

The entire program is listed in Appendix C.

In this simple example we know the location of structure elements within the structure; so it is safe to "hardwire" the values for setting the element pointer. Figure 6–9 shows the element numbers. However, in a more complex model it would better to design an algorithm to ensure that you were editing the correct element. The following methods show one way to do this:

- When you create the structure, use the LABEL routine to insert labels into the structure before each element that you want to change.
- When you edit the structure, use the SET ELEMENT POINTER AT LABEL routine to find the correct label.
- Having found the label, increment the element pointer by 1 to get to the correct element (use OFFSET ELEMENT POINTER).
- Then replace the structure element with a new one.

These methods work even if the structure changes in length, where the elements to be replaced move around. Another method that works only when the elements are stationary is to use INQUIRE ELEMENT POINTER while constructing the structure.

How Modelling Transformations Work

In the geometric model, all objects are defined in terms of their own convenient modelling coordinates (MCs). When PHIGS renders the model, each object's definition is converted such that it is expressed in a common coordinate system called world coordinates (WCs). This conversion takes place by means of a **composite modelling transformation** (**CMT**). The composite modelling transformation is a 4×4 matrix. Figures 6–10 and 6–11 show how PHIGS maps modelling coordinates for 2D and 3D primitives in FORTRAN and C, respectively. The CMT is a "composite" in that is the product of a **global modelling transformation** (**GMT**) and a **local modelling transformation** (**LMT**).

The application is responsible for placing the object in the common world coordinate system. There are two approaches to doing this that are worthy of mention at this point. Both approaches have their relative strengths and both can be accomplished using PHIGS.

One way, which we call **absolute modelling**, proceeds by saying: "The primitives in this model are in "this part" of modelling coordinates and I want them to be in "this other part" of world coordinates. The matrix to accomplish what I want is [. . .]."

The other way, which we call **relative modelling**, proceeds by saying "The primitives in this fragment of the model fit geometrically into this other (preceding) fragment of the model via this transformation [. . .]. For example, the bicycle example earlier in this chapter used relative modelling to fit each wheel to the frame. Relative modelling assumes that the fragment of the model being fitted *to* is displayed correctly. It only concerns itself with fitting the next fragment to the previous fragment.

Note that there is no functional difference between absolute modelling and modelling that is relative to world coordinates. Both accomplish the function "put this part of modelling coordinates in that part of world coordinates." Understanding this is key to answering the question "Is it possible to program using only relative modelling? Can one avoid infinite regress?" The answer is yes. Because PHIGS traversal starts out with an identity CMT, the first transformation structure element of an application using only relative modelling is relative to world coordinates. So, that structure element's transformation anchors the rest of the (relative) model in WCs, and there is no infinite regress.

Relative modelling is good for situations in which a model fragment is intended both to be displayed as part of an assembly and to be displayed by itself.

Absolute modelling is useful in situations where world fragments that are not geometrically related are composed in a single presentation.

Although the bicycle example earlier in this chapter used only relative modelling, it us quite reasonable for an application to use both absolute and relative modelling. In fact, some of the situations in which one might use absolute modelling can use viewing transformations instead (as we did in the progressive example in Chapter 2). For more information on viewing, see Chapter 7.

PHIGS has two kinds of structure elements that affect modelling coordinates. The *set global transformation* structure element is useful for absolute modelling. The *set local modelling transformation* structure element is useful for relative modelling. Both kinds of structure elements contain a 4×4 homogeneous transformation matrix (there is a 3×3 shorthand for 2D transformations) and, for LMTs, a rule for combining the matrix with the existing LMT (the "composition type").

$$\begin{bmatrix} WC_x \\ WC_y \\ WC_z \\ WC_w \end{bmatrix} = \begin{bmatrix} C_{1,1} & C_{1,2} & C_{1,3} & C_{1,4} \\ C_{2,1} & C_{2,2} & C_{2,3} & C_{2,4} \\ C_{3,1} & C_{3,2} & C_{3,3} & C_{3,4} \\ C_{4,1} & C_{4,2} & C_{4,3} & C_{4,4} \end{bmatrix} \times \begin{bmatrix} MC_x \\ MC_y \\ MC_z \\ 1 \end{bmatrix}$$

Figure 6–10. Composite Modelling Transformation in FORTRAN

$$\begin{bmatrix} WC_x \\ WC_y \\ WC_z \\ WC_w \end{bmatrix} = \begin{bmatrix} C_{0,0} & C_{0,1} & C_{0,2} & C_{0,3} \\ C_{1,0} & C_{1,1} & C_{1,2} & C_{1,3} \\ C_{2,0} & C_{2,1} & C_{2,2} & C_{2,3} \\ C_{3,0} & C_{3,1} & C_{3,2} & C_{3,3} \end{bmatrix} \times \begin{bmatrix} MC_x \\ MC_y \\ MC_z \\ 1 \end{bmatrix}$$

Figure 6–11. Composite Modelling Transformation in C

When building the CMT, PHIGS calculates it from the matrix multiplication of two other parts:

- The local modelling transformation, which is defined within the current structure. For ease of reference, let's call this transformation *L*.
- The global modelling transformation, which is the composite modelling transformation initially inherited from the parent structure. Let's call this transformation *G*.

The composite modelling transformation is computed as follows:

$$C = G \times L$$

Note that from these definitions, a CMT has a recursive definition: A CMT is the product of an LMT and a GMT, where the GMT is the CMT for the parent structure. This is not a mistake if we provide a starting point for the recursion. That starting point is this: The topmost structure of a posted structure network has an identity matrix as its initial GMT. Thus, every structure (including the topmost one) inherits a GMT and applies an LMT to create its CMT. If that structure references another structure, the CMT of the referencing structure becomes the GMT of the referenced structure. At this point, the referenced structure can apply its own LMT and the process recurs. Thus, every structure has its own idea of what the GMT is, and every structure's idea may be different.

Figures 6–12, 6–13, and 6–14 show how the CMT, LMT, and GMT are modified during structure traversal. In order to illustrate the concept, we invented a new term called the **transformation state stack**. This would be a subset of the **traversal state list stack** that PHIGS uses to keep track of attribute inheritance during structure traversal.

In the following figures, no matter what changes are made to "state $i + 1$", PHIGS will restore "state i" when it returns to the parent structure. This reinforces the five steps we learned about structure traversal in the previous chapter. When PHIGS encounters an *execute structure* element, it performs the following six steps:

1. Traversal of the current structure is suspended,
2. The current state of the PHIGS traversal state list is saved (for restoration when the referenced structure has completed traversal),
3. Global and local modelling transformations are initialized for the referenced structure,
4. The referenced structure network is completely traversed (note that the referenced structure may modify the state inherited from the referencing structure),
5. The saved PHIGS traversal state list values (including the local and global modelling matrices) saved in Step 2 are restored,
6. Traversal of the current structure is resumed.

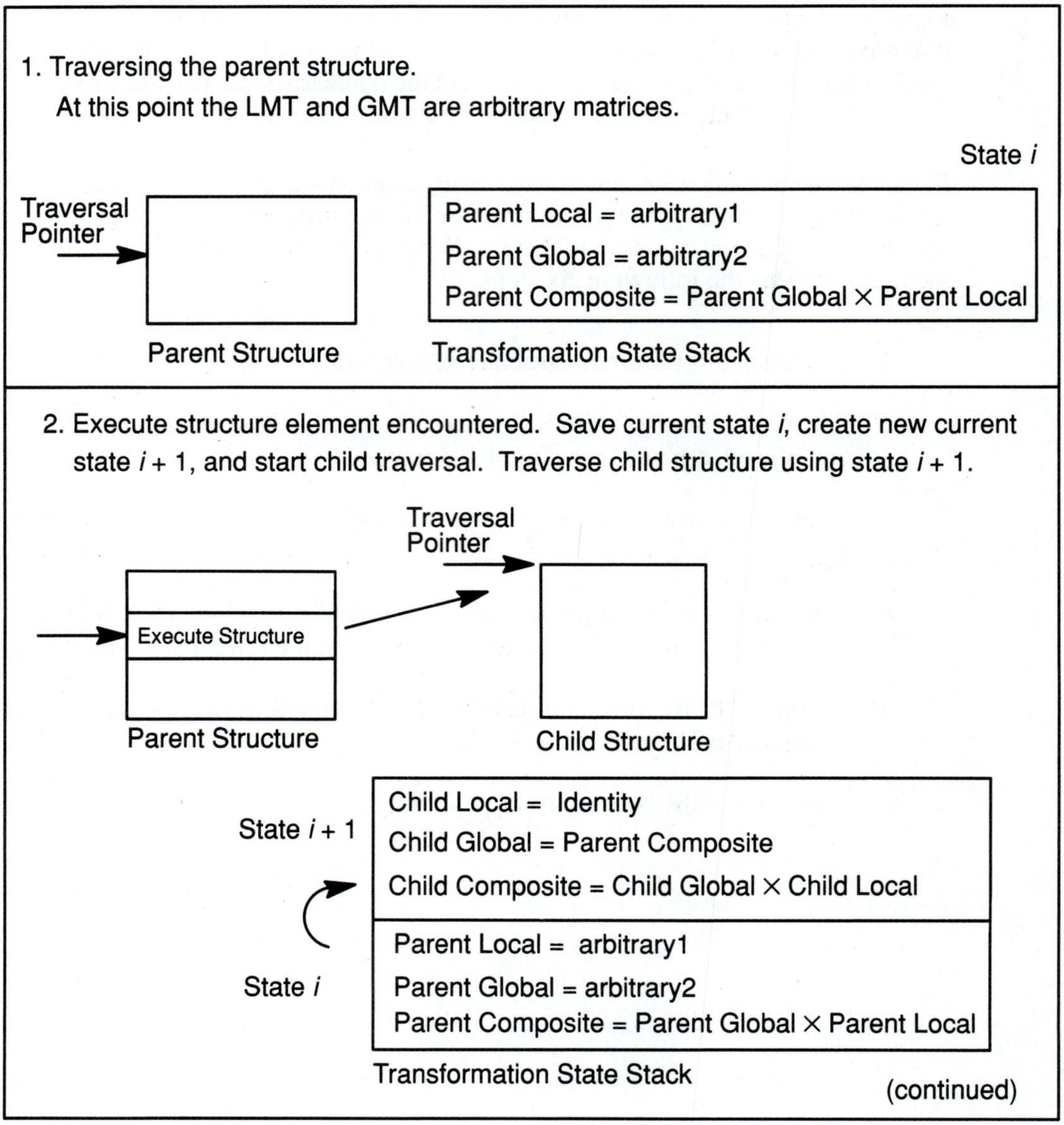

Figure 6–12. Structure Traversal and the Transformation State

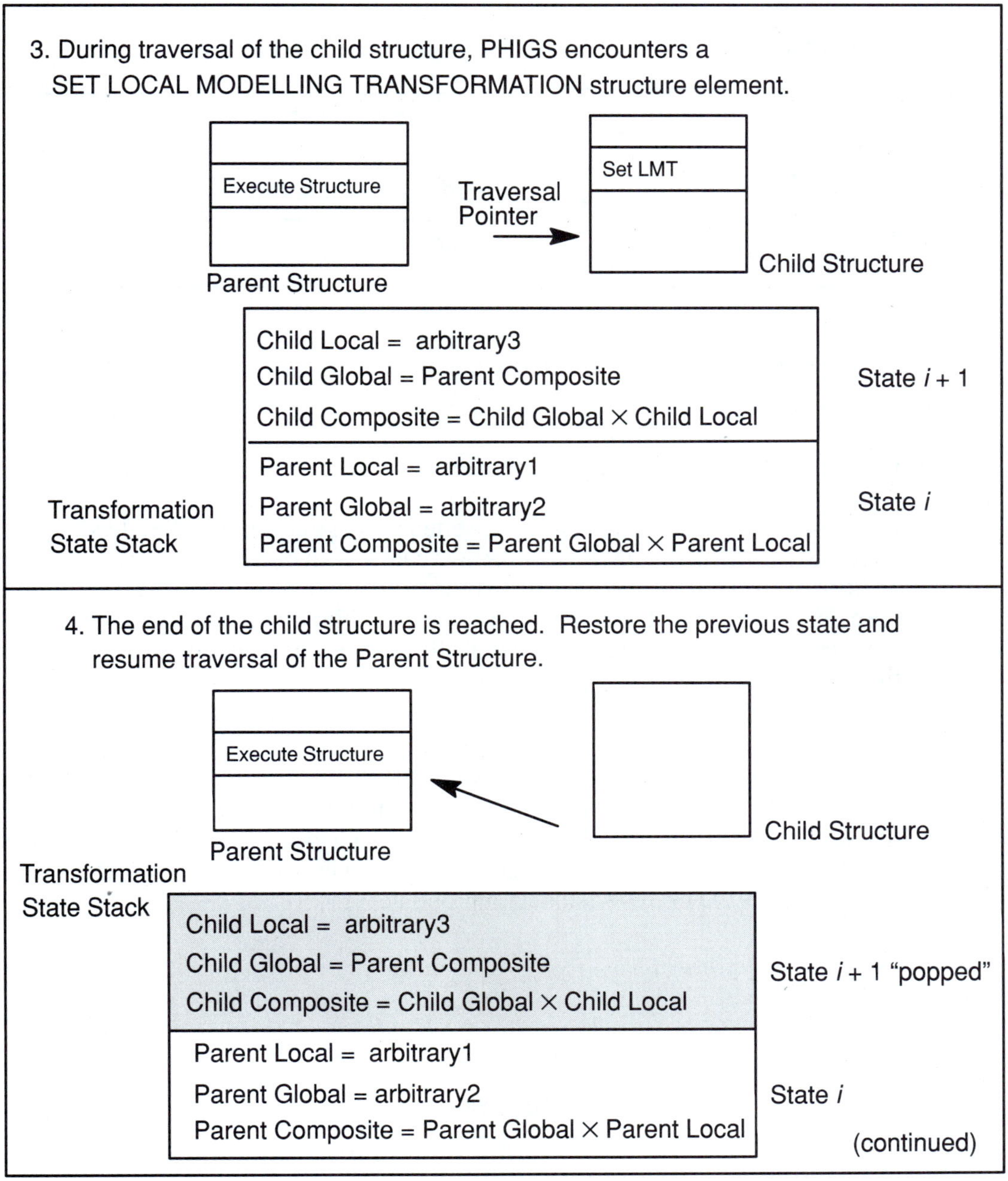

Figure 6–13. Structure Traversal and the Transformation State (continued)

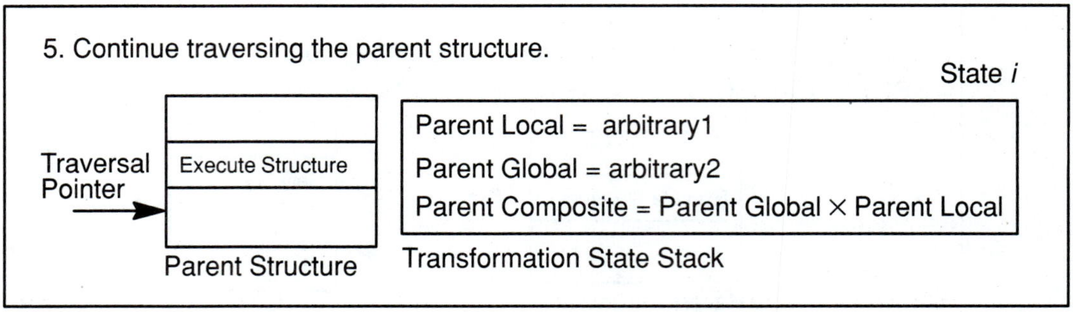

Figure 6–14. Structure Traversal and the Transformation State (continued)

Setting the Local Modelling Transformation

Local modelling transformations are inserted into a structure with SET LOCAL TRANSFORMATION and SET LOCAL TRANSFORMATION 3, both of which require two parameters. In addition to the transformation matrix itself, these routines require a parameter that specifies the composition type. The composition type is merely a flag that instructs PHIGS how to compose the LMT. The LMT can be dynamically modified or replaced within a structure as many times as you require.

The LMT for a structure is initially the identity matrix, so if you don't define an LMT for a particular structure, no harm is done—when the GMT is multiplied by the LMT to create the CMT, the CMT is identical to the GMT, since multiplying a transformation matrix by an identity matrix doesn't change anything. When you want to define an LMT to be something other than the identity matrix, use SET LOCAL TRANSFORMATION or SET LOCAL TRANSFORMATION 3, the 2D or 3D version as appropriate:

```
call pslmt(xform, comp_type)
```

```
pset_local_tran(
   Pmatrix            xform,
   Pcompose_type      comp_type
);
```

or

```
call pslmt3(xform, comp_type)
```

```
pset_local_tran3(
   Pmatrix3          xform,
   Pcompose_type     comp_type
);
```

where:

> ⟨*xform*⟩ is a 3×3 (for 2D) or 4×4 (for 3D) floating-point transformation matrix that describes the desired local transformation.
>
> ⟨*comp_type*⟩ is an integer that specifies how the transformation matrix ⟨*xform*⟩ is to affect the composite transformation matrix. PHIGS defines the mnemonic constants to specify the possible values (see below); you are encouraged to use these instead of integer constants to make your program more readable.

The transformation matrix (let's call it *T*) is passed into the appropriate SET LOCAL TRANSFORMATION routine and is incorporated into the LMT (and therefore the CMT) as follows, depending on the composition type:

Composition Type = Replace (`PCREPL`, `PTYPE_REPLACE`)

$$\text{LMT} \leftarrow \text{T}$$
$$\text{CMT} \leftarrow \text{GMT} \times \text{LMT}$$

Composition Type = Preconcatenate (`PCPRE`, `PTYPE_PRECONCAT`)

$$\text{LMT} \leftarrow \text{LMT} \times \text{T}$$
$$\text{CMT} \leftarrow \text{GMT} \times \text{LMT}$$

Composition Type = Postconcatenate (`PCPOST`, `PTYPE_POSTCONCAT`)

$$\text{LMT} \leftarrow \text{T} \times \text{LMT}$$
$$\text{CMT} \leftarrow \text{GMT} \times \text{LMT}$$

The SET GLOBAL TRANSFORMATION and SET GLOBAL TRANSFORMATION 3 routines can be used to replace the global modelling transformation. Unlike the local versions, the two global versions have only one parameter since the composition type by definition is Replace.

```
call psgmt(xform)
```

```
pset_global_tran(
   Pmatrix          xform
);
```

or

```
call psgmt3(xform)

pset_global_tran3(
   Pmatrix3          xform
);
```

where:

> ⟨*xform*⟩ is a 3×3 (for 2D) or 4×4 (for 3D) floating-point transformation matrix that describes the desired global transformation.

For these two SET GLOBAL TRANSFORMATION routines, there is no composition-type parameter required, because for global transformations, the composition type is always Replace. Note also that the CMT is formed by always preconcatenating the GMT with the LMT.

One example of why one might want the GMT to be changed is this: Suppose you have a structure deep in the hierarchy, and it is supposed to go in a known place, regardless of the contents of the rest of the hierarchy, but you still want its attributes to be controlled by the rest of the hierarchy. One example of this is a line graph—multiple lines in different colours and styles, and an arbitrary scaling, but its legend, using matching line colours and styles, in a constant location.

During structure traversal, modifications to the local and global transformations only have effect within the structure in which they are encountered and, therefore, also within child structures—those referenced by that structure. Remember, what PHIGS calls "global" transformation matrices are not really global in the usual sense of the word. The "global" transformation matrices are actually "relatively global" or "locally global"; the global transformation matrix is just the *inherited* transformation matrix. This is why each structure can have its own unique version of the "global" transformation matrix. This is also why when a structure changes the GMT, only it and descendant structures are affected; the "global" changes do not affect parent and ancestor structures.

Modelling Utility Functions

Now that we've discussed the set local and global transformation routines, we've seen how to pass transformation matrices to PHIGS. But now that we know about these routines, one might now think, "Well, where do I get the matrices to pass to them?" To answer such a question, this section of the chapter deals with the PHIGS-supplied utility routines with which you can create, concatenate, and modify transformation matrices.

Throughout this section, as well as the 3D section that follows, realize that in PHIGS, points are considered *column* vectors, not *row* vectors, as is done in some other graphics systems; thus, matrices are transposed from their usual representations. Also, PHIGS represents matrix operations backward from the usual manner.

Matrices for 2D Transformations

In two dimensions, the general form of the transformation of a point [x, y] is this:

$$\begin{bmatrix} x' \\ y' \\ 1 \end{bmatrix} = \begin{bmatrix} a & c & e \\ b & d & f \\ g & h & 1 \end{bmatrix} \times \begin{bmatrix} x \\ y \\ 1 \end{bmatrix}$$

The transformation matrix that needs to be defined is the preceding 3×3 "array", where the values of a, b, c, d, e, and f are defined as appropriate for the operation desired, and the third row exists solely to make the matrix multiplications work correctly. The values of g and h are always zero for 2D applications. See Foley, J., and Van Dam, A. (1990). *Computer Graphics; Principles and Practices*, 2nd edition, Reading, MA: Addison-Wesley, for a discussion of homogeneous coordinates.

There are three main operations that can be done on 2D graphical data:

- **Translation**, or relocating an object. This operation utilizes elements e and f in the transformation matrix.
- **Scaling**, or resizing an object. This operation utilizes elements a and d.
- **Rotation**, or reorienting an object. This operation utilizes elements a, b, c, and d, and the values may be calculated using the sine and cosine functions.

For each of these operations, there is a corresponding PHIGS routine that defines a transformation matrix to do the desired operation. For each routine, the appropriate parameters are passed, and the resultant transformation matrix is passed back (if no errors occurred). If any error occurred, the error indicator is returned with the nonzero value that indicates which error took place.

Each routine starts with an identity matrix and then modifies it as necessary for the transformation matrix being constructed. Thus, the matrices will be returned with 1s (ones) on the main diagonal unless those elements are overwritten in the process of constructing the desired matrix.

The transformation routines are described next.

2D Translation

As previously noted, translation is the moving of a point or an object from one position to another. A translated object maintains the same orientation and size in MCs as before the translation.

The calling signatures for TRANSLATE are as follows:

```
call ptr(tx, ty, error, xform)
```

```
ptranslate(
   const Pvec          *trans_vec,
   Pint                *error,
   Pmatrix             xform
);
```

where:

⟨*trans_vec*⟩ is a 2D vector whose values indicate the amount of translation along the corresponding axis.

⟨*tx*⟩ and ⟨*ty*⟩ are floating-point expressions whose values indicate the amount of translation along the corresponding axis.

⟨*error*⟩ is an integer variable, through which any error condition is returned. If ⟨*error*⟩ is zero, no error occurred; if nonzero, the value indicates which error occurred.

⟨*xform*⟩ is the returned 3 × 3 floating-point transformation matrix that expresses the requested translation. ⟨*xform*⟩ is of the form:

$$\begin{bmatrix} 1 & 0 & t_x \\ 0 & 1 & t_y \\ 0 & 0 & 1 \end{bmatrix}$$

Since all PHIGS coordinate systems are right-handed, a positive x value indicates movement to the right in MC space; a negative value indicates movement to the left. For y values, a positive value indicates movement up; a negative value indicates movement down. Of course, directions could change after subsequent modelling transformations or a viewing transformation. A zero value indicates no movement at all in the corresponding direction.

Translation is illustrated in the following diagram, where the primed coordinate system is the one used before the translation took effect, and the unprimed coordinate system is the one used after the translation is in effect.

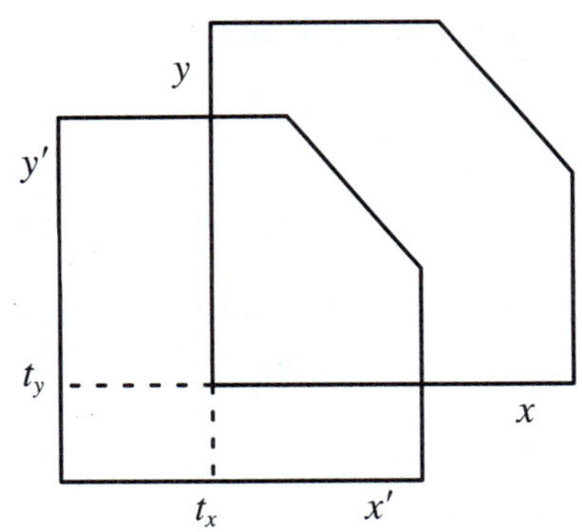

Since all possible values of the input x and y values can make valid translation matrices, the only PHIGS error that could possibly occur is if PHIGS is in the wrong state; i.e., not in the state `(PHOP,*,*,*)`. Of course, you could still make non-PHIGS errors, like the application allocating insufficient memory for ⟨*xform*⟩, passing integers for the x and/or y values, etc.

2D Scaling

Scaling is the process of enlarging or shrinking a point or an object about the origin. A scaled object remains in the same orientation as before the scaling. Since "center of scaling" (the reference point for scaling any object) is always the origin, the object is always considered not to have moved during the operation although, for an object not centered on the origin, it will appear to move with respect to its *own* center.

The calling signatures for SCALE are

```
call psc(sx, sy, error, xform)
```

```
pscale(
   const Pvec          *scale_vec,
   Pint                *error,
   Pmatrix             xform
);
```

where:

⟨*scale_vec*⟩ is a 2D scaling vector that indicates the amount of scaling along the x- and y-axes.

⟨*sx*⟩ and ⟨*sy*⟩ are floating-point scaling factors that indicate the amount of scaling along the corresponding axis.

⟨*error*⟩ is an integer variable, through which any error condition is returned. If ⟨*error*⟩ is zero, no error occurred; if nonzero, the value indicates which error occurred.

⟨*xform*⟩ is the returned 3×3 floating-point transformation matrix that expresses the requested scaling, based on the x and y values of the scale vector. ⟨*xform*⟩ is of the form:

$$\begin{bmatrix} s_x & 0 & 0 \\ 0 & s_y & 0 \\ 0 & 0 & 1 \end{bmatrix}$$

Magnitudes greater than 1.0 for the x and y scale values cause an increase in size; magnitudes equal to 1.0 cause no change in size; and magnitudes less than 1.0 cause a decrease in size. Positive values cause size change only, while negative values cause a mirror-image reflection along the corresponding axis in addition to the size change determined by the magnitude.

Scaling is illustrated in the following diagram, where the "before" image is the original data, and the "after" image is the data after a scaling by 0.5 in both x and y.

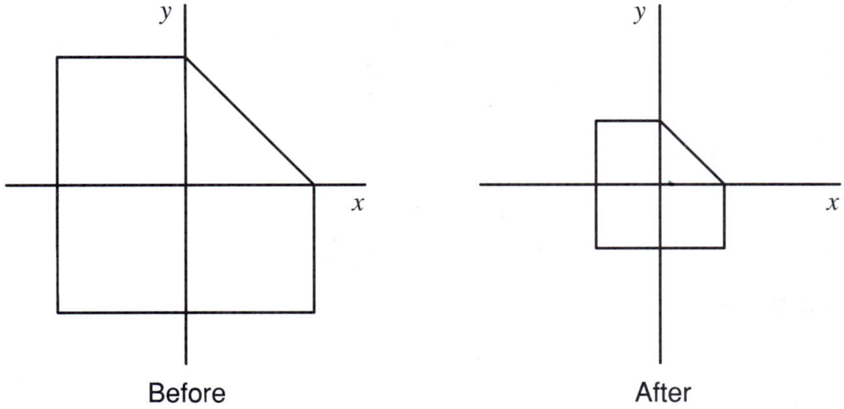

SCALE is like TRANSLATE in that all possible values of the input *x* and *y* values can make valid scaling matrices, and the only PHIGS error that could occur is if PHIGS is not in the `(PHOP,*,*,*)` state.

2D Rotation

Rotation is the process of rotating a point or object around the origin. During this process, the size remains fixed, but the orientation changes. Since the center of rotation is always the origin, the object is always considered not to have moved during the operation although, for an object not centered on the origin, it will appear to move with respect to its *own* center.

The calling signatures for ROTATE are

```
call pro(theta, error, xform)
```

```
protate(
   const Pfloat        theta,
   Pint                *error,
   Pmatrix             xform
);
```

where:

⟨*theta*⟩ is the rotational displacement desired. The angle is expressed in radians, and a positive value indicates a counterclockwise rotation.

⟨*error*⟩ is an integer variable, through which any error condition is returned. If ⟨*error*⟩ is zero, no error occurred; if nonzero, the value indicates which error occurred.

⟨*xform*⟩ is the returned 3 × 3 floating-point transformation matrix that expresses the requested rotation, based on the value of ⟨*theta*⟩. ⟨*xform*⟩ is of the form:

$$\begin{bmatrix} \cos(\theta) & -\sin(\theta) & 0 \\ \sin(\theta) & \cos(\theta) & 0 \\ 0 & 0 & 1 \end{bmatrix}$$

Rotation is illustrated in the following diagram, where the "before" image is the original data, and the "after" image is the data after a rotation of π/6 radians (30°).

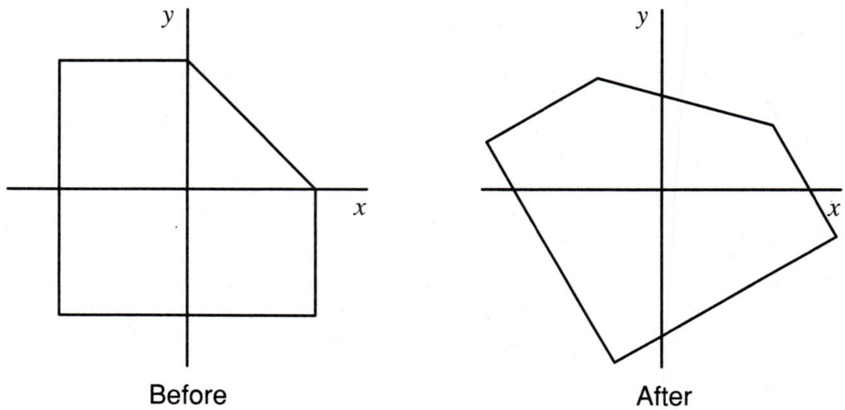

ROTATE is like SCALE and TRANSLATE in that all possible values of ⟨*theta*⟩ can make valid rotation matrices, and the only PHIGS error that could occur is if PHIGS is in the wrong state; i.e., not in the state `(PHOP,*,*,*)`.

Other 2D Matrix Operations

There are several utility functions for composing, combining, and applying transformation matrices. Several of the following routines are shortcuts for calling other routines one at a time and combining the results by hand.

Multiplying 2D Matrices

PHIGS supports a standard matrix multiplication routine called COMPOSE MATRIX:

`call pcom(`*left_matrix*, *right_matrix*, *error*, *result_matrix*)

```
pcompose_matrix(
   Pmatrix           left_matrix,
   Pmatrix           right_matrix,
   Pint              *error,
   Pmatrix           result_matrix
);
```

where:

⟨*left_matrix*⟩ and ⟨*right_matrix*⟩ are 3 × 3 floating-point arrays.

⟨*error*⟩ is an integer variable through which any error condition is returned. If ⟨*error*⟩ is zero, no error occurred; if nonzero, the value indicates which error occurred.

⟨*result_matrix*⟩ is a 3 × 3 floating-point array that is the matrix product of ⟨*left_matrix*⟩ × ⟨*right_matrix*⟩.

Transforming a 2D Point

Once you have the desired transformation matrix, you can apply that transformation to a point and, thus, to entire objects. The routine to do this is called TRANSFORM POINT:

```
call ptp(xin, yin, xform, error, xout, yout)
```

```
ptran_point(
   const Ppoint      *point,
   Pmatrix           xform,
   Pint              *error,
   Ppoint            result
);
```

where:

⟨*point*⟩ contains the point to be transformed for the C binding.

⟨*xin*⟩ and ⟨*yin*⟩ specify the location of the point to be transformed for the FORTRAN binding.

⟨*xform*⟩ is the 3 × 3 floating-point matrix that expresses the desired transformation. Depending on the values in the matrix, the source and destination coordinate systems could be whatever coordinate systems your application requires.

⟨*error*⟩ is an integer variable, through which any error condition is returned. If ⟨*error*⟩ is zero, no error occurred; if nonzero, the value indicates which error occurred.

⟨*result*⟩ is the point after having been transformed by ⟨*xform*⟩.

⟨*xout*⟩ and ⟨*yout*⟩ specify the location of the point after having been transformed by ⟨*xform*⟩.

Using Combined 2D Transformations

As shortcuts to defining and combining transformations one at a time, PHIGS offers the BUILD TRANSFORMATION MATRIX and COMPOSE TRANSFORMATION MATRIX routines.

The BUILD TRANSFORMATION MATRIX routine creates a transformation matrix that includes a scaling, a rotation, and a translation (in that order), and it returns a single matrix that expresses all of these transformations. Note that this matrix utility allows an arbitrary origin rather than assuming (0, 0, 0).

```
call pbltm(xo, yo, tx, ty, theta, sx, sy, error, xform)
```

```
pbuild_tran_matrix(
   const Ppoint      *point,
   const Pvec        *shift_vec,
   Pfloat            theta,
   const Pvec        *scale_vec,
   Pint              *error,
   Pmatrix           xform
);
```

where:

⟨*point*⟩ specifies the "local origin" for the C binding.

⟨*xo*⟩ and ⟨*yo*⟩ specify the "local origin" for the FORTRAN binding.

⟨*shift_vec*⟩ specifies the translation vector for the C binding.

⟨*tx*⟩ and ⟨*ty*⟩ specify the translation vector for the FORTRAN binding.

⟨*theta*⟩ expresses the rotation angle, expressed in radians. If ⟨*theta*⟩ is positive, it indicates a counterclockwise rotation.

⟨*scale_vec*⟩ specifies the scale factors in the respective dimensions for the C binding.

⟨*sx*⟩ and ⟨*sy*⟩ specify the scale factors in the respective dimensions for the FORTRAN binding.

⟨*error*⟩ is an integer variable, through which any error condition is returned. If ⟨*error*⟩ is zero, no error occurred; if nonzero, the value indicates which error occurred.

⟨*xform*⟩ is the resultant 3×3 floating-point matrix, expressing a scaling about the fixed point, a rotation about the fixed point, and finally an *xy* displacement.

The local origin is the fixed point around which to do the scaling and rotation.

The rules for what scale values cause what changes are those described earlier in this section.

Note that since scalings and rotations can only operate centered on the origin, PHIGS internally translates the fixed point to the *real* origin, does the scaling and rotation, and then translates back to the fixed point, effectively scaling and rotating about the specified fixed point. Then, the final translation is done. Of course, these conceptual steps are combined into a single transformation, so there is no performance penalty for the "extra" steps.

These multiple operations are illustrated in the following diagram, where the "before" image is the original data, and the "after" image is the data after a scaling by 0.5, rotation of $\pi/6$ radians or 30° (both of which take place about the object's upper left corner), and a translation toward the southeast.

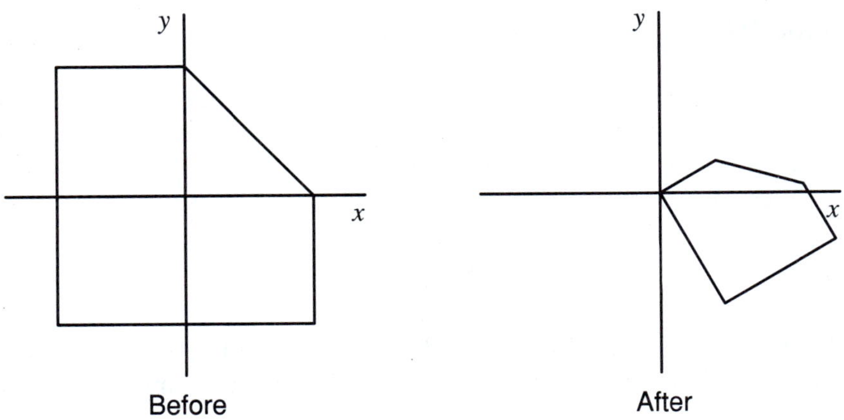

After the transformation matrix is returned from BUILD TRANSFORMATION MATRIX, you can combine that matrix with another (via COMPOSE MATRIX). Or you can combine the matrix creation with the matrix multiplication into one step by using the COMPOSE TRANSFORMATION MATRIX routine:

call pcotm(*xform_in*, *xo*, *yo*, *tx*, *ty*, *theta*, *sx*, *sy*, *error*, *xform_out*)

```
pcompose_tran_matrix(
   Pmatrix          xform_in,
   const Ppoint     *point,
   const Pvec       *shift_vec,
   Pfloat           theta,
   const Pvec       *scale_vec,
   Pint             *error,
   Pmatrix          xform_out
);
```

where:

> ⟨*xform_in*⟩ is a 3×3 floating-point transformation matrix to be combined with the matrix created using the point, shift vector, and scale vector.
>
> ⟨*point*⟩, ⟨*shift_vec*⟩, ⟨*scale_vec*⟩, ⟨*xo*⟩, ⟨*yo*⟩, ⟨*tx*⟩ , ⟨*ty*⟩, ⟨*sx*⟩, ⟨*sy*⟩, ⟨*theta*⟩, and ⟨*error*⟩ are the same as described for the BUILD TRANSFORMATION MATRIX routine.
>
> ⟨*xform_out*⟩ is a 3×3 floating-point transformation matrix that is the matrix product of ⟨*xform_in*⟩ and the matrix created using the point, shift vector, angle, and scale vector.

Matrices for 3D Transformations

In three dimensions, the general form of the transformation of a point $[x, y, z]$ is this:

$$\begin{bmatrix} x' \\ y' \\ z' \\ 1 \end{bmatrix} = \begin{bmatrix} a & d & g & l \\ b & e & h & m \\ c & f & i & n \\ p & q & r & s \end{bmatrix} \times \begin{bmatrix} x \\ y \\ z \\ 1 \end{bmatrix}$$

The transformation matrix that needs to be defined is this 4×4 group, where the values of the elements are defined as appropriate for the operation desired.

Similar to 2D operations, there are three main operations that can be done on 3D graphical data:

- Translation. This operation utilizes elements l, m, and n in the 4×4 matrix.

- Scaling. This operation utilizes elements *a*, *e*, and *i*.
- Rotation. This operation utilizes elements *a* through *i*, and the values may be calculated using the sine and cosine functions.

Although there are these similarities, there is also a significant difference between 2D and 3D rotation. With 2D rotation, there is only one axis available about which to rotate (the *z*-axis). (Recall that PHIGS is a 3D system, and 2D routines are really a shorthand version of the 3D routine with $z = 0.0$.) With 3D rotation, there are three different axes to choose from. Depending on which axis is chosen, the resultant matrix differs accordingly.

Like the corresponding 2D versions, for each of these 3D operations there is a PHIGS routine that defines a transformation matrix to do the desired operation. For each routine, the appropriate parameters are passed, and the resultant transformation matrix is passed back. Also passed back is an error indicator, which indicates if any error took place, and if so, which one. The routines are described next.

3D Translation

A 3D translation is the moving of a point or an object from one position to another position in 3D space. The translated object remains the same size and orientation as before the translation.

The calling signatures for TRANSLATE 3 are

```
call ptr3(tx, ty, tz, error, xform)
```

```
ptranslate3(
    const Pvec3          *trans_vec,
    Pint                 *error,
    Pmatrix3             xform
);
```

where:

⟨*trans_vec*⟩ is a 3D vector whose values indicate the amount of translation along the corresponding axis.

⟨*tx*⟩, ⟨*ty*⟩, and ⟨*tz*⟩ are floating-point expressions whose values indicate the amount of translation along the corresponding axis.

⟨*error*⟩ is an integer variable, through which any error condition is returned. If ⟨*error*⟩ is zero, no error occurred; if nonzero, the value indicates which error occurred.

⟨*xform*⟩ is the 4 × 4 floating-point transformation matrix that expresses the requested translation, based on the *x*, *y*, and *z* values of the translation vector. ⟨*xform*⟩ is of the form:

$$\begin{bmatrix} 1 & 0 & 0 & t_x \\ 0 & 1 & 0 & t_y \\ 0 & 0 & 1 & t_z \\ 0 & 0 & 0 & 1 \end{bmatrix}$$

Since all PHIGS coordinate systems are right-handed, a positive *x* value indicates movement to the right; a negative value indicates movement to the left. For *y* values, a positive value indicates movement up; a negative value indicates movement down. For *z* values, a positive value indicates movement toward you; a negative value indicates movement away from you. These directions are appropriate if you are viewing from t_z toward the origin in MCs. A zero value indicates no movement at all in the corresponding direction.

Translation is illustrated in the following diagram, where the primed coordinate system is the one used before the translation took effect, and the unprimed coordinate system is the one used after the translation is in effect.

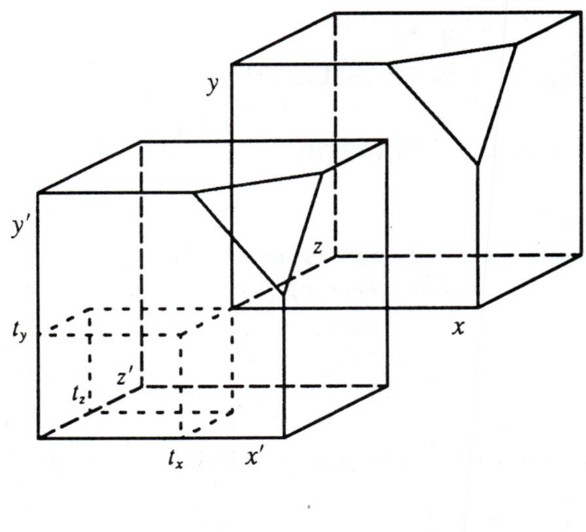

Since all possible values of the input *x*, *y*, and *z* values can make valid translation matrices, the only PHIGS error that could possibly occur is if PHIGS is not in the `(PHOP,*,*,*)` state.

3D Scaling

Scaling is the process of enlarging or shrinking a point or an object about the origin. A scaled object remains in the same orientation as before the scaling. Since "center of scaling" (the reference point for scaling any object) is always the origin, the object is always considered not to have moved during the operation although, for an object not centered on the origin, it will appear to move with respect to its *own* center.

The calling signatures for SCALE 3 are

```
call psc3(sx, sy, sz, error, xform)
```

```
pscale3(
    const Pvec3          *scale_vec,
    Pint                 *error,
    Pmatrix3             xform
);
```

where:

⟨*scale_vec*⟩ is the 3D scaling vector, that indicates the amount of scaling along the *x*-, *y*-, and *z*-axes.

⟨*sx*⟩, ⟨*sy*⟩, and ⟨*sz*⟩ are floating-point scaling factors that indicate the amount of scaling along the corresponding axis.

⟨*error*⟩ is an integer variable through which any error condition is returned. If ⟨*error*⟩ is zero, no error occurred; if nonzero, the value indicates which error occurred.

⟨*xform*⟩ is the 4×4 floating-point transformation matrix that expresses the requested scaling, based on the *x*, *y*, and *z* values of the scale vector. ⟨*xform*⟩ is of the form:

$$\begin{bmatrix} s_x & 0 & 0 & 0 \\ 0 & s_y & 0 & 0 \\ 0 & 0 & s_z & 0 \\ 0 & 0 & 0 & 1 \end{bmatrix}$$

Magnitudes greater than 1.0 for the *x*, *y*, and *z* values cause an increase in size; magnitudes equal to 1.0 cause no change in size; and magnitudes less than 1.0 cause a decrease in size. Positive values cause size change only, while negative values cause a mirror-image reflection along the corresponding axis in addition to the size change determined by the magnitude.

Scaling is illustrated in the following diagram, where the "before" image is the original data, and the "after" image is the data after an *x* scaling by –0.6, a *y* scaling by –1, and a *z* scaling by –0.25. The negative values merely cause a mirror-image flip in addition to the scaling caused by the magnitude of the number.

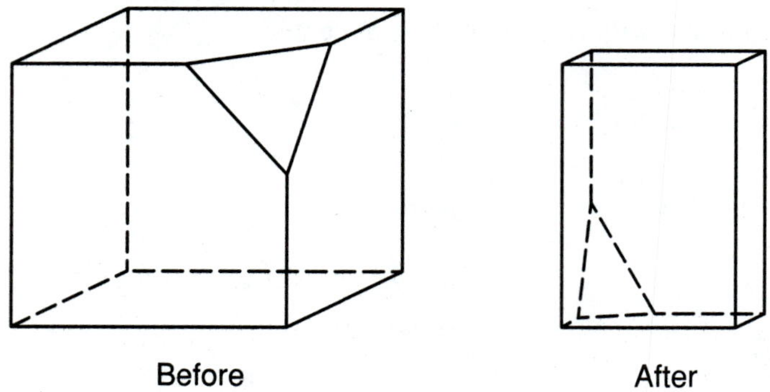

SCALE 3 is like TRANSLATE 3 in that all possible values of the input *x*, *y*, and *z* values can make valid scaling matrices, and the only PHIGS error that could occur is if PHIGS is in the wrong state; i.e., not in the state `(PHOP,*,*,*)`.

3D Rotation

Rotation is the process of rotating a point or object around the origin. During this process, the size remains fixed, but the orientation changes. Since the center of rotation is always the origin, the object is always considered not to have moved during the operation although, for an object not centered on the origin, it will appear to move with respect to its *own* center.

There are three 3D rotation matrix routines, one for each axis:

```
call prox(theta, error, xform)                ROTATE X
```

```
protate_x(
   const Pfloat        theta,
   Pint                *error,
   Pmatrix3            xform
);
```

and

`call proy(`*theta, error, xform*`)` ROTATE Y

```
protate_y(
   const Pfloat        theta,
   Pint                *error,
   Pmatrix3            xform
);
```

and

`call proz(`*theta, error, xform*`)` ROTATE Z

```
protate_z(
   const Pfloat        theta,
   Pint                *error,
   Pmatrix3            xform
);
```

where:

⟨*theta*⟩ is the rotational displacement desired. The angle is expressed in radians, and a positive value indicates a counterclockwise rotation.

⟨*error*⟩ is an integer variable through which any error condition is returned. If ⟨*error*⟩ is zero, no error occurred; if nonzero, the value indicates which error occurred.

⟨*xform*⟩ is the 4×4 floating-point transformation matrix that expresses the requested rotation, based on the value of ⟨*theta*⟩. ⟨*xform*⟩ is of one of the following three forms, depending on which axis the rotation was with respect to:

$$\text{For x}: \begin{bmatrix} 1 & 0 & 0 & 0 \\ 0 & \cos(\theta) & -\sin(\theta) & 0 \\ 0 & \sin(\theta) & \cos(\theta) & 0 \\ 0 & 0 & 0 & 1 \end{bmatrix}$$

$$\text{For y}: \begin{bmatrix} \cos(\theta) & 0 & \sin(\theta) & 0 \\ 0 & 1 & 0 & 0 \\ -\sin(\theta) & 0 & \cos(\theta) & 0 \\ 0 & 0 & 0 & 1 \end{bmatrix}$$

$$\text{For z}: \begin{bmatrix} \cos(\theta) & -\sin(\theta) & 0 & 0 \\ \sin(\theta) & \cos(\theta) & 0 & 0 \\ 0 & 0 & 1 & 0 \\ 0 & 0 & 0 & 1 \end{bmatrix}$$

Note that the trigonometric functions (arranged in a square within the matrix) are not signed the same in each case. For the x and z rotations, the negative value on the $\sin(t)$ is in the upper right corner of its square, but for the y rotation, the negative value is in the lower left corner. Also note that for rotation about the *whatever* axis, the trigonometric functions appear in the *other two* axes' positions. That is, for rotation about the x-axis, the trigonometric functions appear only in the y and z rows/columns. This is also similar for the y and z rotations.

With rotation matrices about the three main axes, you can cause rotations about arbitrary axes. For example, if you want to rotate an object about the $x = y$ line, you could rotate the object $-\pi/4$ radians (–45°) about the z-axis to get the desired rotation axis on one of the main three axes, do the desired rotation, and then rotate $\pi/4$ radians (45°) about z to put the object back into its previous orientation.

Rotation is illustrated in the following diagram, where the "before" image is the original data, and the "after" image is the data after a rotation of π radians (180°) about the x-axis, followed by $\pi/2$ radians (90°) about the y-axis.

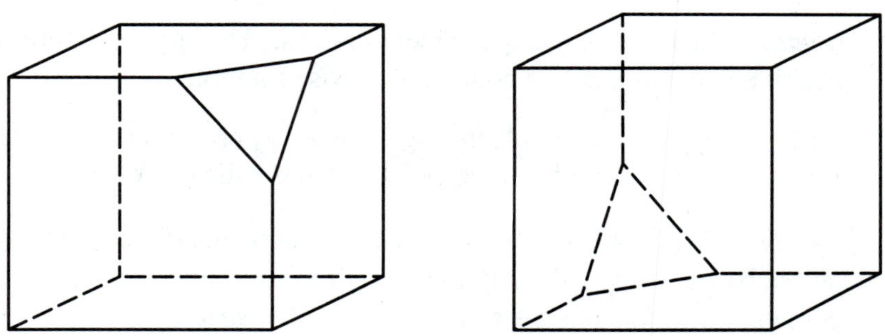

Before　　　　　　　　After

ROTATE X, ROTATE Y, and ROTATE Z are like SCALE 3 and TRANSLATE 3 in that all possible values of ⟨*theta*⟩ can make valid rotation matrices, and the only PHIGS error that could occur is if PHIGS is in the wrong state; i.e., not in the state `(PHOP,*,*,*)`.

Other 3D Matrix Operations

As in 2D, there are several 3D utility functions for composing, combining, and applying transformation matrices. Several of the following routines are shortcuts for calling other routines one at a time and combining the results by hand.

Multiplying 3D Matrices

PHIGS supports a standard matrix multiplication routine called COMPOSE MATRIX 3:

```
call pcom3(left_matrix, right_matrix, error, result_matrix)
```

```
pcompose_matrix3(
   Pmatrix3            left_matrix,
   Pmatrix3            right_matrix,
   Pint                *error,
   Pmatrix3            result_matrix
);
```

where:

⟨*left_matrix*⟩ and ⟨*right_matrix*⟩ are 4×4 floating-point arrays.

⟨*error*⟩ is an integer variable through which any error condition is returned. If ⟨*error*⟩ is zero, no error occurred; if nonzero, the value indicates which error occurred.

⟨*result_matrix*⟩ is a 4×4 floating-point array that is the matrix product of ⟨*left_matrix*⟩ × ⟨*right_matrix*⟩.

Transforming a Point

Once you have the desired transformation matrix, you can apply that transformation to a 3D point and, thus, to entire objects. The routine to do this is called TRANSFORM POINT 3:

```
call ptp3(xin, yin, zin, xform, error, xout, yout, zout)
```

```
ptran_point3(
   const Ppoint3     *point,
   Pmatrix3          xform,
   Pint              *error,
   Ppoint3           result
);
```

where:

⟨*point*⟩ contains the point to be transformed for the C binding.

⟨*xin*⟩, ⟨*yin*⟩, and ⟨*zin*⟩ specify the location of the point to be transformed for the FORTRAN binding.

⟨*xform*⟩ is the 4×4 floating-point matrix that expresses the desired transformation.

⟨*error*⟩ is an integer variable through which any error condition is returned. If ⟨*error*⟩ is zero, no error occurred; if nonzero, the value indicates which error occurred.

⟨*result*⟩ is the point after having been transformed by ⟨*xform*⟩.

⟨*xout*⟩, ⟨*yout*⟩, and ⟨*zout*⟩ specify the location of the point after having been transformed by ⟨*xform*⟩.

This routine is useful when you need to translate a point between coordinate systems. Say, for example, a user indicates a position on the display, and you want its location in modelling coordinates. However, REQUEST LOCATOR returns coordinates only in world coordinates. You could use TRANSFORM POINT 3 to convert the point to MCs.

Using Combined 3D Transformations

As shortcuts to defining and combining transformations one at a time, PHIGS offers the following two routines. The first, called BUILD TRANSFORMATION MATRIX 3, creates a transformation matrix that includes a scaling, a rotation about *x*, a rotation about *y*, a rotation about *z*, and a translation (in that order), and it returns a single matrix that expresses all of these transformations.

Note that this matrix utility allows an arbitrary origin rather than assuming (0, 0, 0).

```
call pbltm3(xo, yo, zo, tx, ty, tz, x_theta, y_theta, z_theta, sx, sy, sz, error, xform)
```

```
pbuild_tran_matrix3(
    const Ppoint3     *point,
    const Pvec3       *shift_vec,
    Pfloat            x_theta,
    Pfloat            y_theta,
    Pfloat            z_theta,
    const Pvec3       *scale_vec,
    Pint              *error,
    Pmatrix3          xform
);
```

where:

⟨*point*⟩ specifies the "local origin" for the C binding.

⟨*xo*⟩, ⟨*yo*⟩, and ⟨*zo*⟩ specify the "local origin" for the FORTRAN binding.

⟨*shift_vec*⟩ specifies the translation vector for the C binding.

⟨*tx*⟩, ⟨*ty*⟩, and ⟨*ty*⟩ specify the translation vector for the FORTRAN binding.

⟨ *x_theta*⟩, ⟨*y_theta*⟩, and ⟨*z_theta*⟩ express the rotation angles about the respective axes, expressed in radians. If any of the angles is positive, it indicates a counterclockwise rotation about the corresponding axes.

⟨*scale_vec*⟩ is the 3D scaling vector, for the C binding, that indicates the amount of scaling along the *x*-, *y*-, and *z*-axes.

⟨*sx*⟩, ⟨*sy*⟩, and ⟨*sz*⟩ specify the scale factors in the respective dimensions for the FORTRAN binding.

⟨*error*⟩ is an integer variable through which any error condition is returned. If ⟨*error*⟩ is zero, no error occurred; if nonzero, the value indicates which error occurred.

⟨*xform*⟩ is the resultant 4×4 floating-point matrix, expressing a scaling about the fixed point, *x*, *y*, and *z* rotations about the fixed point, and finally an *xyz* displacement.

The local origin is the fixed point around which to do the scaling and rotation.

The rules for what scale values cause what changes are described earlier in this section.

Note that since scalings and rotations can only operate centered on the origin, PHIGS translates the "fixed point" to the real origin, does the scaling and rotations, and then translates back to the fixed point, effectively scaling and rotating about the fixed point. Then, the final translation is done. Of course, these conceptual steps are combined into a single transformation, so there is no performance penalty for the "extra" steps.

After the transformation matrix is returned from BUILD TRANSFORMATION MATRIX 3, you can combine that matrix with another (via COMPOSE MATRIX 3). Or you can combine the matrix creation with the matrix multiplication into one step by using the COMPOSE TRANSFORMATION MATRIX 3 routine:

```
 call pcotm3 (xform_in, xo, yo, zo, tx, ty, tz, x_theta, y_theta, z_theta, sx, sy, sz,
+ error, xform_out)
```

```
pcompose_tran_matrix3(
   Pmatrix3          xform_in,
   const Ppoint3     *point,
   const Pvec3       *shift_vec,
   Pfloat            x_theta,
   Pfloat            y_theta,
   Pfloat            z_theta,
   const Pvec3       *scale_vec,
   Pint              *error,
   Pmatrix3          xform_out
);
```

where:

⟨*xform_in*⟩ is a 4 × 4 floating-point transformation matrix to be combined with the matrix created using the next dozen parameters.

⟨*point*⟩, ⟨*shift_vec*⟩, ⟨*scale_vec*⟩, ⟨*xo*⟩, ⟨*yo*⟩, ⟨*zo*⟩, ⟨*tx*⟩, ⟨*ty*⟩, ⟨*tz* ⟩, ⟨*sx*⟩, ⟨*sy*⟩, ⟨*sz*⟩, ⟨*x_theta*⟩, ⟨*y_theta*⟩, ⟨*z_theta*⟩, and ⟨*error*⟩ are the same as described for the BUILD TRANSFORMATION MATRIX 3 routine.

⟨*xform_out*⟩ is a 4 × 4 floating-point transformation matrix that is the matrix product of ⟨*xform_in*⟩ and the matrix created using the point, shift vector, angles, and scale vector.

Be aware that the order of rotations about *x*, *y*, and *z* is significant. If your application requires rotations in a different order, you will have to do the operation in multiple steps. For example, suppose you need a rotation about *z*, then *x*, then *y*. COMPOSE TRANSFORMATION MATRIX 3 will not be able to do this, at least not in a single step. Assuming you need rotations of 15° about *z*, then 30° about *x*, then 45° about *y* (and that `rad()` is a user-defined degrees-to-radians function), you could do it this way:

```
...
call pcotm3(Mat1, ..., rad(30.), rad(45.), 0., ..., Mat2)
call pcotm3(Mat2, ...,  0.,  0., rad(15.), ..., Mat3)
...
```

At first glance, it looks as if the two statements are in the wrong order, but they are not: Since COMPOSE TRANSFORMATION MATRIX 3 only does *pre*concatenation, the 30° rotation and the 45° rotation are preconcatenated to the matrix contained in `Mat1`, then the 15° rotation is preconcatenated to that. Thus, in the resulting matrix, the 15° rotation is indeed done first.

Similar approaches can be used if you need transformations done in any other order than the one supported by COMPOSE TRANSFORMATION MATRIX 3; for example, a translation before a scaling, a rotation before a scaling, or a translation before a rotation.

Example: Using 2D Transformation and Rotation Matrices

This example program creates a `Shape` structure containing a 2D fill area primitive and positions two instances of the shape in a second structure called `Scene`. The first instance uses the identity matrix. The second instance is rotated by 90° ($\pi/2$ radians) and then translated by 0.5 in the x direction and 0.5 in the y direction.

This program creates two separate matrices and concatenates them to form a modelling transformation matrix. The order of matrix multiplication is important for the desired result. The program uses the order illustrated at the top of Figure 6–15.

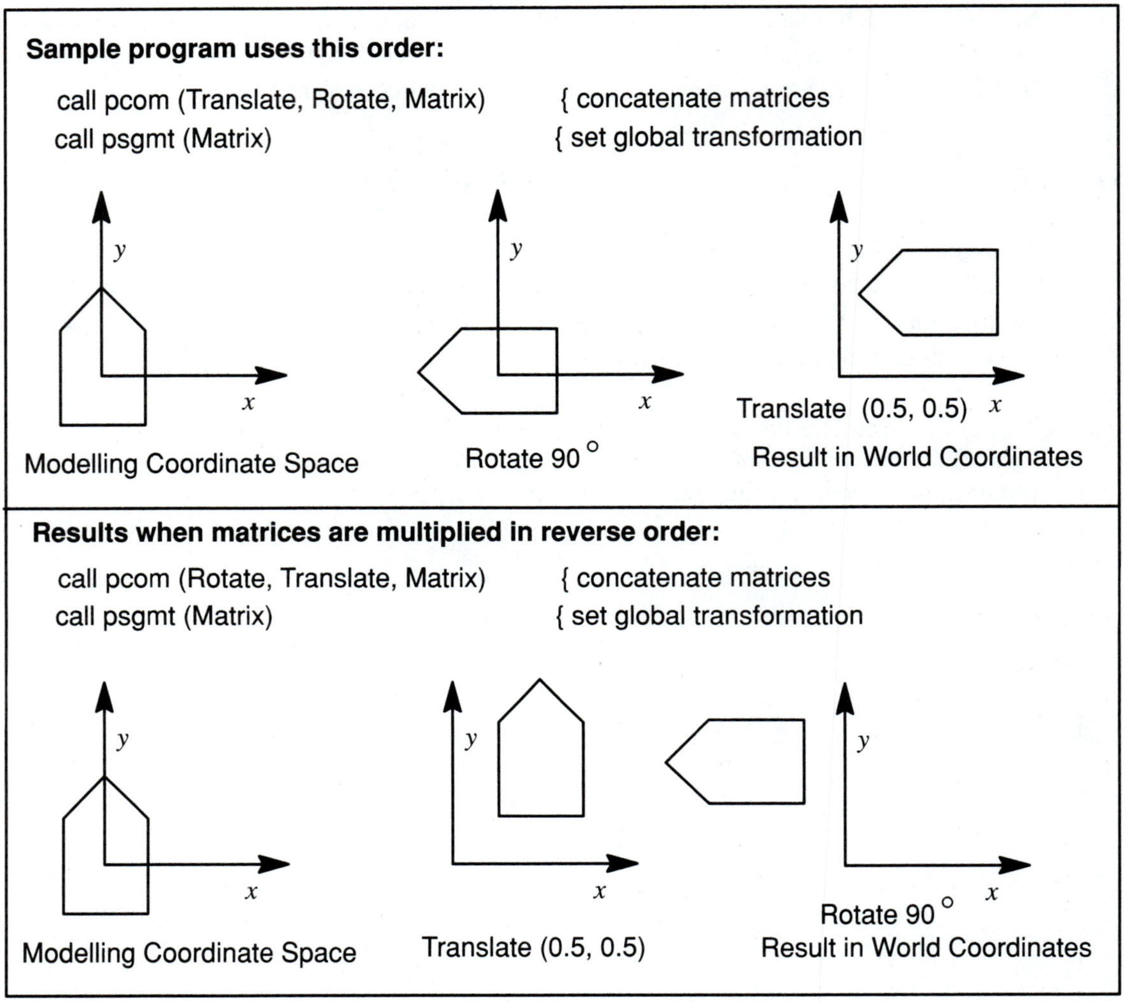

Figure 6–15. Different Results Depending on Matrix Multiplication Order

The complete listing follows:

```
          PROGRAM transform
C   Description:
C    This program demonstrates how to modify the
C    global modelling matrix.
C
```

```
%include '/sys/ins/phigs.ins.ftn'
      integer*4 WorkID                    { workstation ID
      parameter (WorkID=1)
      integer*4 ChoiceStatus, ChoiceNum  { choice status and value
      integer*4 ixa(2), Shape, Scene, i, j
      parameter (Shape = 1, Scene = 2)
      real Line1X(2), Line1Y(2), Line2X(2), Line2Y(2)
      real X, PI, Angle
      real BoxX( 5 ),BoxY( 5 )
      parameter (PI = 3.1415926)
      real Rotate(3,3),Translate(3,3)
      real Matrix(3,3), Identity(3,3)
      integer*4 errind
      real orient(4,4), map(4,4)
      real window(4)
      real vp_lim(6), clip(6)
      real White(3), Red(3), Green(3), Blue(3)
      data window /-1.0, 1.0, -1.0, 1.0/
      data vp_lim /0.0, 1.0, 0.0, 1.0, 0.0, 1.0/
      data clip /0.0, 1.0, 0.0, 1.0, 0.0, 1.0/
      data BoxX /0.0, 0.2, 0.2, -0.2, -0.2/
      data BoxY /0.35, 0.15, -0.25, -0.25, 0.15/
      data Line1X,Line1Y /-0.8, 0.8, 0.0, 0.0/
      data Line2X,Line2Y /0.0, 0.0, 0.8, -0.8/
      data White / 1.0, 1.0, 1.0 /
      data Red   / 1.0, 0.0, 0.0 /
      data Green / 0.0, 1.0, 0.0 /
      data Blue  / 0.0, 0.0, 1.0 /
C Load the identity matrix into Identity
      Identity(1,1)=1.0
      Identity(2,1)=0.0         { This is the 3 x 3 identity matrix:
      Identity(3,1)=0.0                 { 1.0  0.0  0.0
      Identity(1,2)=0.0                 { 0.0  1.0  0.0
      Identity(2,2)=1.0                 { 0.0  0.0  1.0
      Identity(3,2)=0.0
      Identity(1,3)=0.0
      Identity(2,3)=0.0
      Identity(3,3)=1.0
C Load a 2D translation matrix into Translate
      Translate(1,1)=1.0        { This is the translation matrix:
      Translate(2,1)=0.0                { 1.0  0.0  0.5
      Translate(3,1)=0.0                { 0.0  1.0  0.5
      Translate(1,2)=0.0                { 0.0  0.0  1.0
```

```
      Translate(2,2)=1.0
      Translate(3,2)=0.0        { Array is loaded as follows:
      Translate(1,3)=0.5               { 1,1  1,2  1,3
      Translate(2,3)=0.5               { 2,1  2,2  2,3
      Translate(3,3)=1.0               { 3,1  3,2  3,3

      call popph(1, 0)                  { open PHIGS
      call popwk(WorkID, 1, POIDSX)     { open workstation
      call pscr(WorkID, 0, 3, White)    {set colour representation
      call pscr(WorkID, 1, 3, Red)      {to define colours
      call pscr(WorkID, 2, 3, Green)
      call pscr(WorkID, 3, 3, Blue)
C Define Workstation View Table Entry '1'
      call pevom3(0.0, 0.0, 0.0, 0.0, 0.0, 1.0, 0.0, 1.0, 0.0,
     +            errind, orient)
      call pevmm3(window, vp_lim, PPARL, 0.0, 0.0, 1.0,
     +            0.0, -1.0, 0.0, errind, map)
      call psvwr3(WorkID, 1, orient, map, clip, PCLIP, PCLIP, PCLIP)
C Create the Shape structure
      call popst(Shape)                 {open structure
      ixa(1)=5
      call pfas(1,ixa,BoxX,BoxY)        {create the shape
      call pclst                        {close structure
C Create the Scene structure
      call popst(Scene)                 {open structure
      call psvwi(1)                     {insert view index
      call psedfg(PON)                  {turn edges on
      call psedci(1)                    {edge colour red
      call pexst(Shape)                 {execute structure
      call psis(PSOLID)                 {solid fill
      call psici(1)                     {red fill
      call psedci(2)                    {edge colour green
      Angle=PI/2
      call pro(Angle, ERRIND, Rotate)   {Build a 2D rotation matrix
C Concatenate the two matrices
      call pcom(Translate, Rotate, errind, Matrix)
      call psgmt(Matrix)                {set global transform
      call pexst(Shape)                 {execute structure
      call psgmt(Identity)          {reset global transform to identity
      call psplci(3)                    {line colour
      call pschh(0.05)                  {text height
      call pstxci(3)                    {text colour green
      call ppl(2,Line1X,Line1Y)         {2D Polylines to show x- and
```

```
       call ppl(2,Line2X,Line2Y)        {y-axes.
       call ptx(0.7,-0.1,'X Axis')      { Text
       call ptx(0.05,-0.8,'Y Axis')     { Text
       call pclst                       {close structure
C Display the structure
       call ppost(WorkID, Scene, 1.0)   {post structure
       call puwk(WorkID,PPERFO)         {update workstation
C Wait for user input
       call pschm(WorkID, 2, PREQU, PNECHO)           { set choice mode
       call prqch(WorkID, 2, ChoiceStatus, ChoiceNum) { request choice
       call pupost(WorkID , Scene)      {close and exit
       call pclwk(WorkID)
       call pclph
       STOP
       END
```

Model Clipping

Model clipping (also called **sectioning**) is defined in Section 4.7.2 of the PHIGS standard as follows: "PHIGS provides a modelling clip which may optionally be applied to primitives before viewing transformations are applied. Modelling clip limits may be specified to define a complex volume within the world coordinate system." Model clipping is useful for "sectioning" operations that show a cross section of a design..

Model clipping, as its name implies, is a clipping operation that is done while still in modelling space. All portions of the geometric model that reside in the **acceptance region** are rendered in the usual fashion. Conversely, all portions of the geometric model that reside in the **rejection region** are discarded—not rendered. Both the acceptance region and rejection region are volumes of space, either finite or infinite in extent.

Acceptance and rejection regions are created by combining a number of **half-spaces**. A half-space is defined by specifying, in modelling coordinates, the space on one side or the other of a given plane. For example, "clip everything to the right of $x = 5$" specifies a half-space in which all parts of the model that have an x value greater than 5 are not passed through the pipeline. You can combine multiple half-spaces to create a model-clipping volume that clips, for example, everything that has an x value less than 2 or greater than 5, a y value less than -10 or greater than 10, and a z value less than 2.5 or greater than 4.5. Thus, everything inside the rectangular volume is rendered, and everything outside is not. Also, if you desire the opposite effect, you can invert the volume, such that everything inside the rectangular volume is ignored, and everything outside is rendered.

The following routines pertain to model clipping:

- INQUIRE MODELLING CLIPPING FACILITIES
- SET MODELLING CLIPPING VOLUME
- SET MODELLING CLIPPING VOLUME 3
- SET MODELLING CLIPPING INDICATOR
- RESTORE MODELLING CLIPPING VOLUME

Refer to *A Practical Introduction to PHIGS and PHIGS PLUS* and *PHIGS Programming Manual* for information on model clipping (see the *Preface* for information on these books).

Chapter 7

Viewing and Workstation Transformations

This chapter describes the viewing and workstation stages of the PHIGS transformation pipeline.

2D and 3D Transformation Routines

There are 2D and 3D versions of most of the PHIGS routines that deal with viewing and workstation transformations. Keep in mind that PHIGS is a 3D system. The 2D primitive routines are merely "shorthand" versions of the 3D routines with $z = 0$. The 2D transformation routines (which take a 3×3 homogeneous matrix) are merely shorthand versions of the 3D transformation routines (which take 4×4 matrices) with the third row and third column containing all zeroes, except for a 1 (one) on the main diagonal.

Viewing Transformations

In Chapter 6 we compared PHIGS viewing operations to a camera. This "synthetic" camera takes perspective or parallel images. Some viewing parameters determine the position and orientation of the camera. Still other viewing parameters determine the portion of the image clipped out for display. The synthetic camera also has "depth of field" adjustments that clip objects that are too close or too far away.

There are two stages for the viewing transformations. Figure 7–1 highlights both stages.

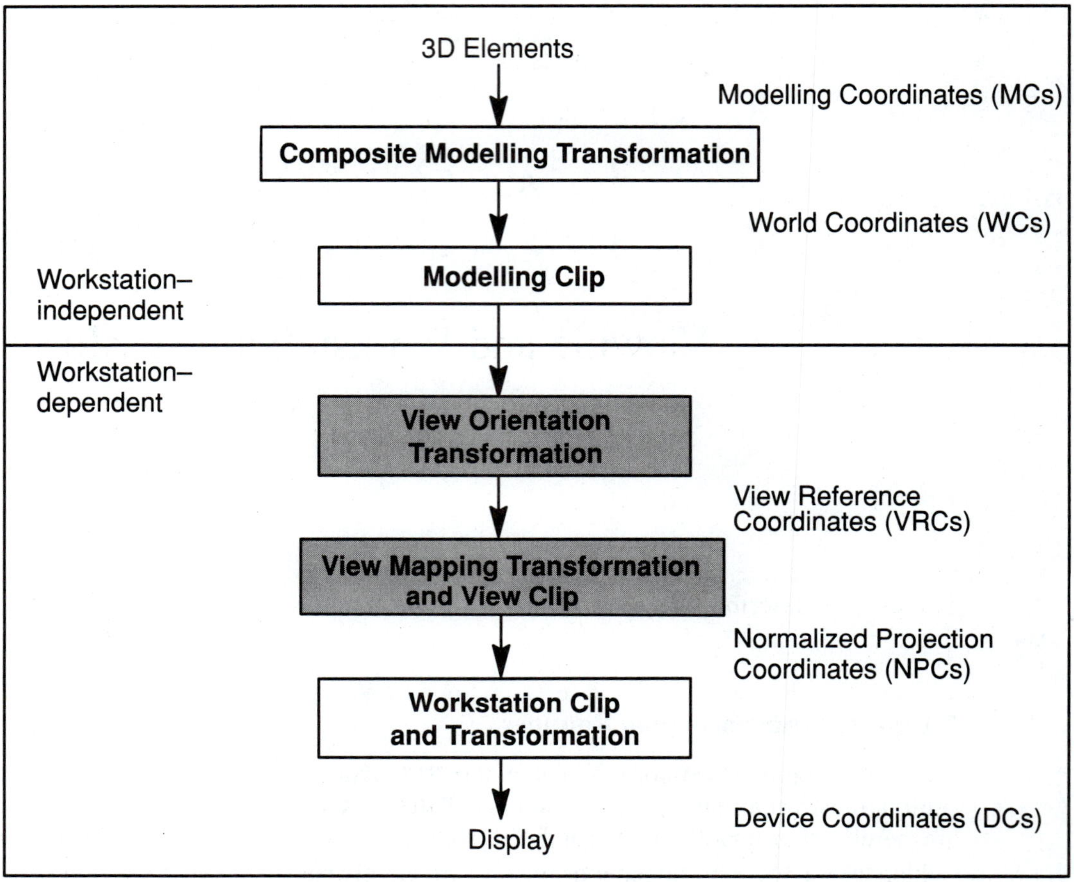

Figure 7–1. The Transformation Pipeline

View Orientation Transformation

The view orientation transformation converts world coordinate points into another coordinate system called vew reference coordinates (VRCs). The main purpose of the VRC space is to orient how the world coordinate model will be viewed. This is where you "position" the synthetic camera discussed earlier.

An easy way to introduce the VRC coordinate system is first to describe two common viewing models: viewer-centered views and object-centered views.

There are two typical ways of orienting a view.

- In a **viewer-centered view** you define the VRC in terms of where you are looking from. For example, this type of view can be useful when there are several objects in a scene and the user wants to be able to stay in one place and look around at the different objects. It is also useful when you want to "fly around" a scene.
- In an **object-centered view** you define the VRC in terms of what you are looking at. For example, this type of view is useful when there is only one object in the scene and the viewer wants to look at the object from different angles.

We compared these two types of views briefly in the previous chapter. Now we will see how to define them. Figure 7–2 shows examples of both viewing models.

In a viewer-centered view you typically define the origin of the VRC space as your eyepoint and then choose a vector that indicates the direction in which you are looking (**gaze direction**) and a second vector that defines which way is up (**view up vector**). Using an EVALUATE VIEW ORIENTATION MATRIX utility routine, you supply the following information in world coordinates:

- The view reference point (a WC point that defines the origin of the VRC).
- The negative of the gaze direction (expressed as an *xyz* direction vector in WC). This negative is called the **view plane normal**.
- A view up vector (also expressed as an *xyz* direction vector in WC).

PHIGS uses this information to define a VRC system as follows:

- PHIGS defines a plane that contains the view reference point and that is perpendicular to the view plane normal. This plane is at $n = 0$ and is called the **view reference plane**.
- PHIGS projects the view up vector onto the view reference plane (see Figure 7–3). Note that because the view up vector is *projected* onto the view reference plane, the point that specifies the view up vector cannot be on the n-axis; if it were, the projection would degenerate to a point and the v-axis would be undefined.
- PHIGS determines the u-axis by the v-axis, the n-axis, and the handedness of the UVN coordinate system. In a right-handed system, if u, v, and n are unit vectors, then $u = v \times n$ (cross product).

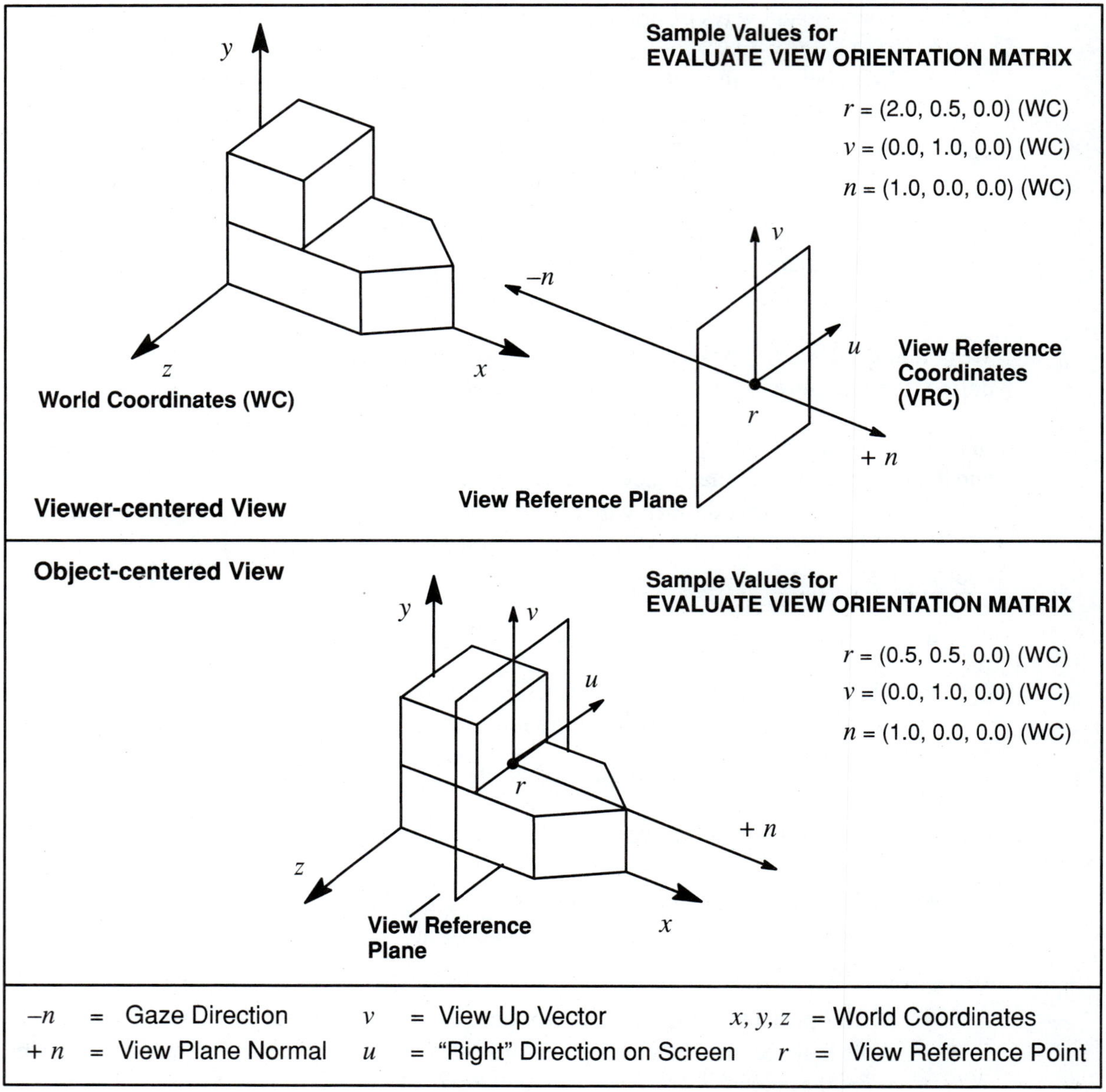

Figure 7–2. Viewer-centered and Object-centered Views

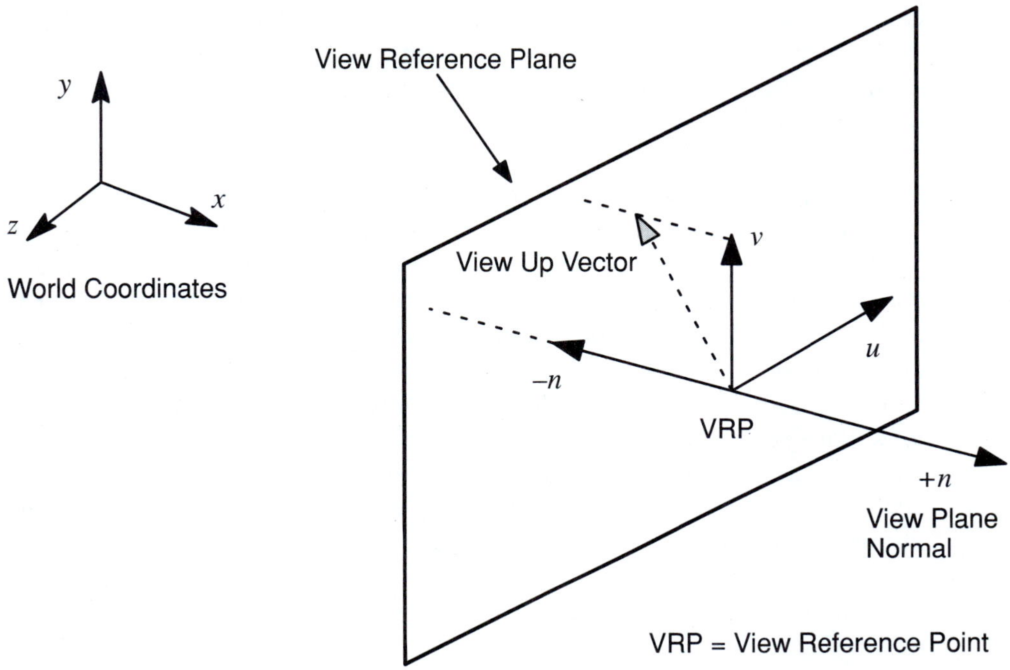

Figure 7–3. The View Reference Coordinate System

In an object-centered view you typically define a point on the object as the view reference point (see Figure 7–2). Then you define a view plane normal to point out from the object along the axis in which you wish to view the object. The up vector is again used to define which way is up as you look at the object.

Note that the major difference between viewer-centered and object-centered views is whether the view reference point and the view reference plane are at your eyepoint or on the object you are viewing. This difference is possible because the only part of the VRC space to be used later is the view reference plane. This plane, along with the VRC *v*- axis, provides an orientation of the object within world coordinates. In reality, you don't have to use one of the two models described above to define the VRC space. You can use whatever model is convenient for your application as long as you end up with a view reference plane and an up vector.

A key point to notice about the VRC space is that it is typically defined using only rotations and translations to move from the WC origin to the VRC origin. This means that the model has not been distorted in any way (no scaling or perspective has been done). One way for an application to follow this typical pattern of use is to use the EVALUATE VIEW ORIENTATION MATRIX utility routine to determine matrices for use as a view orientation transformation. This makes the VRC space a convenient place for the implementation to perform lighting calculations (more on this later).

Figure 7–2 shows two possible VRC coordinate systems that would yield the same picture. The difference between the two systems is related to what types of viewing operations you want to perform during the PHIGS session. In the bottom illustration you could "fly around" the object by changing the view plane normal. In the top illustration, changing the view plane normal would allow you to look "someplace else" in the scene, assuming that there were other objects of interest in the scene. Both of these scenarios would work as long as you didn't attempt to look straight up or straight down. In this case looking straight up would mean that the view plane normal would equal the view up vectors, so PHIGS would not be able to calculate an orientation matrix. If you wanted to look straight up or straight down, you would simply need to change the view up vector as well. See Appendix E of the PHIGS standard for more information on viewer-centered and object-centered views.

The following fragments show how to define the view orientation used in the bottom illustration in Figure 7–2.

C Binding:

```
Pint          Error;                    /* error indicator */
Pmatrix3      ViewOriMatrix;            /* for "peval_view_ori_matrix3" */
static Ppoint3      ViewRefPt4 = {0.5, 0.5, 0.0};
static Pvec3        ViewNormVec4 = {1.0, 0.0, 0.0};
static Pvec3        ViewUpVec4 = {0.0, 1.0, 0.0};
...
peval_view_ori_matrix3(&ViewRefPt4, &ViewNormVec4, &ViewUpVec4,
                       &Error, ViewOriMatrix);
```

FORTRAN Binding:

```
integer*4    ERRIND              { error indicator
real         vwrx, vwry, vwrz    { view reference point
real         vpnx, vpny, vpnz    { view plane normal
real         vupx, vupy, vupz    { view up vector

real*4 Orientation(4,4)          { view orientation matrix
...
```

```
      vwrx = 0.5              { view reference point
      vwry = 0.5
      vwrz = 0.0
      vpnx = 1.0              { view plane normal
      vpny = 0.0
      vpnz = 0.0
      vupx = 0.0              { view up vector
      vupy = 1.0
      vupz = 0.0
      call pevom3(vwrx, vwry, vwrz, vpnx, vpny, vpnz,
     +            vupx, vupy, vupz, ERRIND, Orientation)
```

View Mapping Transformation

The view orientation matrix (the transformation from WCs to VRCs) has oriented our view, but at this point our view stretches infinitely in all directions. The next step is to define a volume which contains (in VRCs) what we really want to look at. This is called the **view volume**. At the same time we will describe the next coordinate space, in normalized projection coordinates (NPCs). NPC space ranges from 0.0 to 1.0 in all three directions. All views on a workstation are mapped into NPC space. What is seen on the display is some portion of NPC space. So, to arrange several views on your display, arrange them in NPC space. To bound our view in VRC space and map it into NPC space, we use one of the EVALUATE VIEW MAPPING MATRIX routines (described later) to define the view mapping transformation.

Clipping Planes

The first step is to bound the volume (in VRC space) we are going to be looking at. To do this we need to define the following three planes:

- **Front plane** and **back plane** (representing the front and back of the volume to be viewed).
- **View plane**—this can be anywhere between the front and back planes. In an object-centered view it often slices through the object.

All three of these planes are parallel to the view reference plane defined by the view orientation matrix. They are therefore simply defined as (signed) distances from the view reference plane along the *n*-axis.

Defining the View Window

The definition of the clipping planes has bounded the volume in front and back, but the sides still need to be defined. This is done by defining the view window, the area on the view plane which is to be viewed. We define the view window by providing minimum and maximum u and v values in VRC space. Point (u_{min}, u_{max}) defines the lower left-hand corner of the area to be viewed. Point (u_{max}, v_{max}) defines the upper right-hand corner.

Let's take a look at two pictures that contain all of the values we are discussing. Figure 7–4 shows a typical perspective view volume, and Figure 7–5 shows a typical parallel view volume. (These illustrations are adaptations of the figures from the PHIGS standard.) We will describe parallel and perspective viewing in the next section.

Perspective and Parallel Projections

The projection type is also selected during the view mapping transformation. You may select either a perspective or a parallel projection.

Parallel projection is used to represent the metric properties of an object (such as distances, sizes, and angles) at the expense of realism. For example, receding parallel lines remain parallel. Although this gives a somewhat distorted appearance to the drawing for the casual viewer, parallel projections are well suited for working drawings because they make it easy to judge metric properties.

Perspective projection gives a realistic representation of an object as seen from an observer at a specific position. An object appears smaller the greater its distance is from the observer. Parallel lines converge at a vanishing point (for example, railroad tracks give the appearance of converging in the distance).

Perspective projections are often used for presentation purposes and for advertising. They do not usually make good working drawings, because it is difficult to judge metric properties.

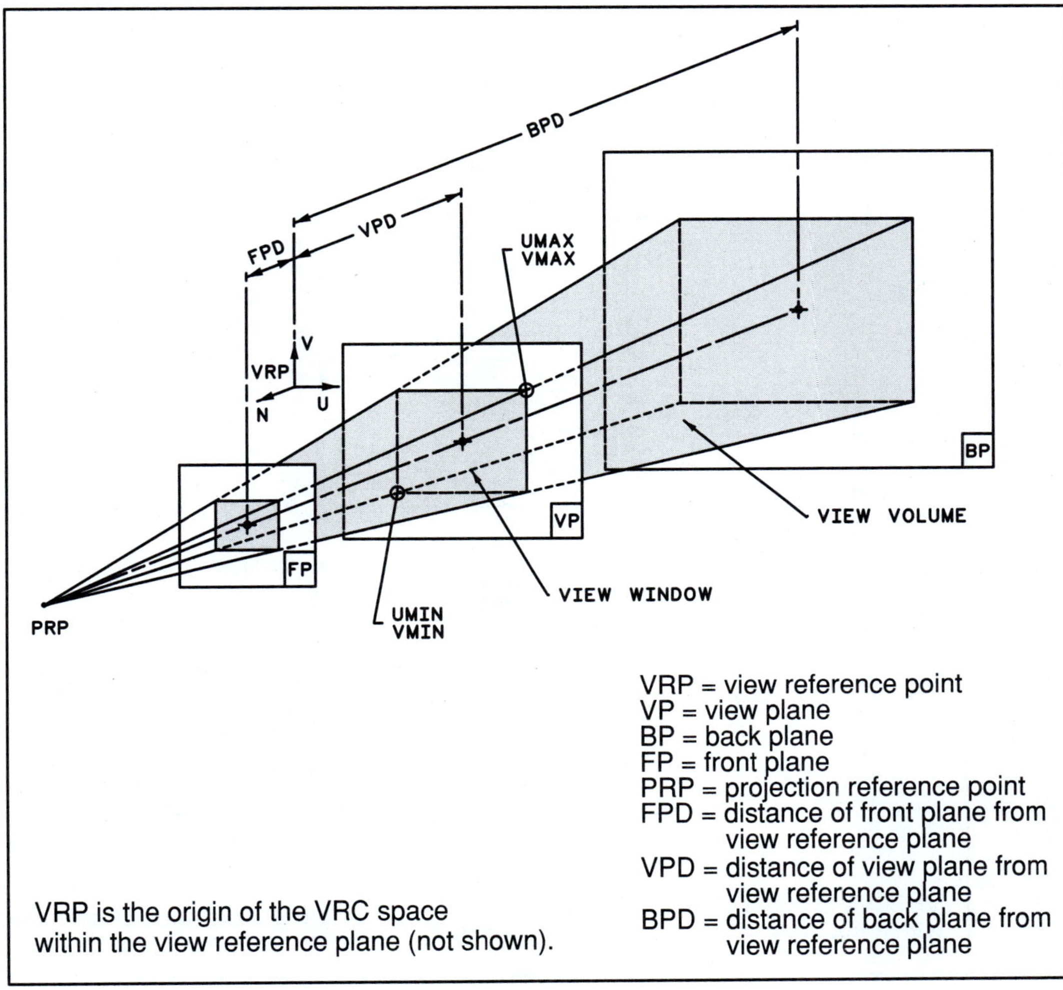

Figure 7–4. Perspective Projection View Volume

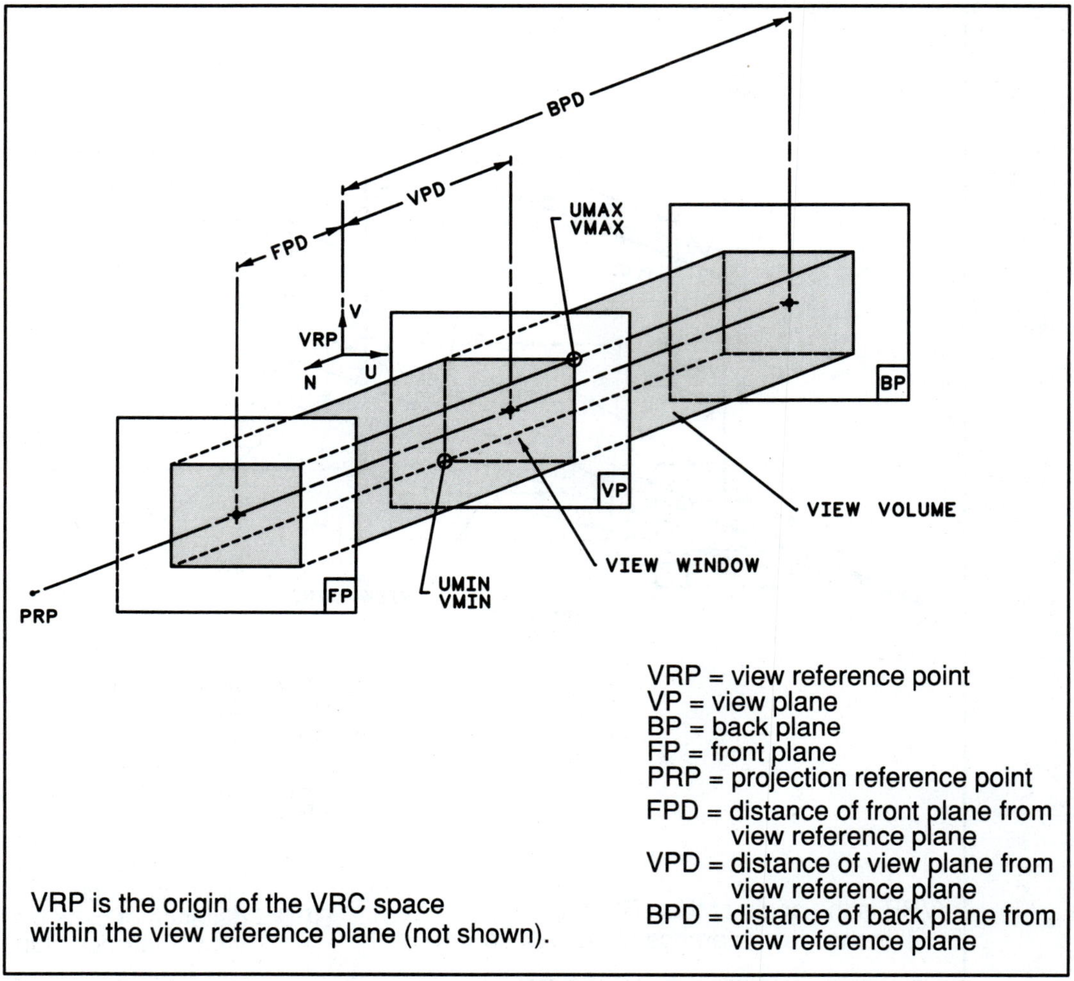

Figure 7–5. Parallel Projection View Volume

Projection Reference Point

When you use the viewing utility routines to define a view, each view needs a projection reference point. This represents the eyepoint, where the object is being viewed from. If parallel projection is selected, imagine a single vector between the projection reference point and the midpoint of the view window. This vector is surrounded by parallel vectors passing through the view window (see Figure 7–5). In the case of perspective projection, all vectors passing through the view window pass through the projection reference point (and are therefore not parallel to one another); see Figure 7–4.

Where the projection vectors pass through the front and back planes, a front plane window and back plane window are defined. This volume, defined by the front plane window, view plane window, and back plane window, is the volume that will be viewed. If the projection is parallel, it is a parallelpiped; if the projection is perspective, it is a rectangular cone.

Now That the View Volume Is Defined

At this point the model to be viewed is fully bounded, and oriented relative to the viewer, within VRC space. This is when **facet culling**, if enabled, is applied (see Chapter 15, *Front and Back Facet Processing*). This is the first time it is possible to distinguish which facets face toward the viewer and which face away. If the viewer wants to ignore (cull) those facets facing either toward or away from him or her, they are removed now. This saves unnecessary calculations on unwanted facets further down the pipeline.

This is also when lighting calculations can be performed. Since PHIGS' lighting calculations include reflection, which depends on the relative position of the light, facet, and viewer, this is the first time that lighting can be calculated. More importantly, the calculations cannot be delayed until a later stage, because VRC space is the last space in which the model is guaranteed not to be distorted.

Mapping the View Volume to NPC Space

As mentioned before, the final step in the view mapping transformation is to map the volume in VRCs to NPCs. This is done by defining minimum and maximum x, y, and z values in NPC space to which the volume will be mapped. Since NPC space ranges from 0.0 to 1.0 in all directions, this means that all values must be in the range [0.0, 1.0], inclusive. Additionally, all the minimum values must be truly less than their corresponding maximum values.

The VRC view volume is fit into this NPC volume, called the projection viewport. The projection viewport has the same orientation as the VRC space, as follows:

- Up is positive *y* in NPCs.
- The front plane maps to the maximum *z* value given.
- The back plane maps to the minimum *z* value given.

Refer to Figures 6–4 and 6–5 in Chapter 6 for illustrations of how a VRC system maps into NPC space.

The dimensions do not need to stay proportionally the same as you move from VRC to NPC space. This is called **anisotropic mapping**. Other than the application of perspective projection, this is the first place in the pipeline where the object can be distorted as it is viewed. Hence, as mentioned, lighting calculations are performed before this mapping.

At this point the *only* aspects of the view orientation matrix (WCs to VRCs) that are used in defining the view mapping matrix (VRCs to NPCs) are the view reference plane and the direction of the *n*-axis. It is not necessary, for example, to define the view plane to be the same as the view reference plane, nor is it necessary to define the projection reference point to be the same as the view reference point. The real purpose of the view orientation matrix is truly just to orient the view. The methods we described earlier to do this (making the view reference point equal to the eyepoint, or placing the view reference point on the object being viewed) are merely examples of ways you could end up with the view reference plane and its normal.

Also note that the projection reference point and the center of the view are typically defined on the *n*-axis, but they do not have to be. Likewise, the center of the view window and the projection reference point do not even have to share the same *u* and *v* coordinates; if they don't, it will have the effect of skewing the view, another case where the model can be distorted (see "Additional Viewing Topics," later in this chapter).

The Viewing Utility Routines

The previous sections gave an overview of how PHIGS uses the viewing utility routines to create a view orientation matrix and a view mapping matrix. This section describes the actual calling signatures for the routines.

Evaluate View Orientation Matrix

The EVALUATE VIEW ORIENTATION MATRIX routines define the transformation from WCs to VRCs. They take several parameters, including the view reference point, the view up vector, and the view plane normal. They return the resulting view orientation matrix. To actually apply this matrix to the definition of a view, you pass the view orientation matrix to one of the SET VIEW REPRESENTATION routines (described in a later section).

The calling signatures for the two EVALUATE VIEW ORIENTATION MATRIX routines are

```
call pevom(view_ref_x, view_ref_y, view_up_x, view_up_y, error, view_orient_matrix)
```

```
peval_view_ori_matrix(
    const Ppoint      *view_ref_point,
    const Pvec        *view_up_vector,
    Pint              *error,
    Pmatrix           view_orient_matrix
);
```

and

```
 call pevom3(view_ref_x, view_ref_y, view_ref_z, view_plane_norm_x,
+ view_plane_norm_y, view_plane_norm_z, view_up_x, view_up_y,
+ view_up_z, error, view_orient_matrix)
```

```
peval_view_ori_matrix3(
    const Ppoint3     *view_ref_point,
    const Pvec3       *view_plane_normal,
    const Pvec3       *view_up_vector,
    Pint              *error,
    Pmatrix3          view_orient_matrix
);
```

where:

⟨*view_ref_point*⟩ specifies the view reference point for the C binding. This is the origin of the VRC coordinate system, expressed in WCs.

⟨*view_ref_x*⟩, ⟨*view_ref_y*⟩, and ⟨*view_ref_z*⟩ are real values that specify the location of the view reference point for the FORTRAN binding.

⟨*view_plane_normal*⟩ specifies the view plane normal for the C binding. These values are expressed in WCs and specify the 3D orientation of the viewing plane in which the view reference point resides. In other words, by specifying the normal to the viewing plane, it defines a direction vector that is the *n*-axis of UVN space. For 2D, the view plane normal is implicitly parallel to the world coordinate +*z*-axis.

⟨*view_plane_norm_x*⟩, ⟨*view_plane_norm_y*⟩, and ⟨*view_plane_norm_z*⟩ are real values that specify the view plane normal for the FORTRAN binding.

⟨*view_up_vector*⟩ specifies the view up vector for the C binding. This is the local "up" direction, expressed in WCs.

⟨*view_up_x*⟩, ⟨*view_up_y*⟩, and ⟨*view_up_z*⟩ are real values that define a 2D or 3D direction vector for the FORTRAN binding.

⟨*error*⟩ is an integer that contains the error code of any error that occurred during the execution of the routine. If no error occurred, ⟨*error*⟩ is zero.

⟨*view_orient_matrix*⟩ is a real array containing the orientation matrix derived from the input parameters. EVALUATE VIEW ORIENTATION MATRIX returns a 3×3 array, and EVALUATE VIEW ORIENTATION MATRIX 3 returns a 4×4 array. This matrix is typically used in one of the view representation setting routines.

Evaluate View Mapping Matrix

The EVALUATE VIEW MAPPING MATRIX routines define the transformation from VRCs to NPCs by defining the mapping of the view volume (specified as a region of interest in VRC space) into the projection viewport (a subset of the 0.0 to 1.0 NPC space). Note that the mapping is anisotropic; i.e., one unit in u is not necessarily equal to one unit in v in Figure 7–6.

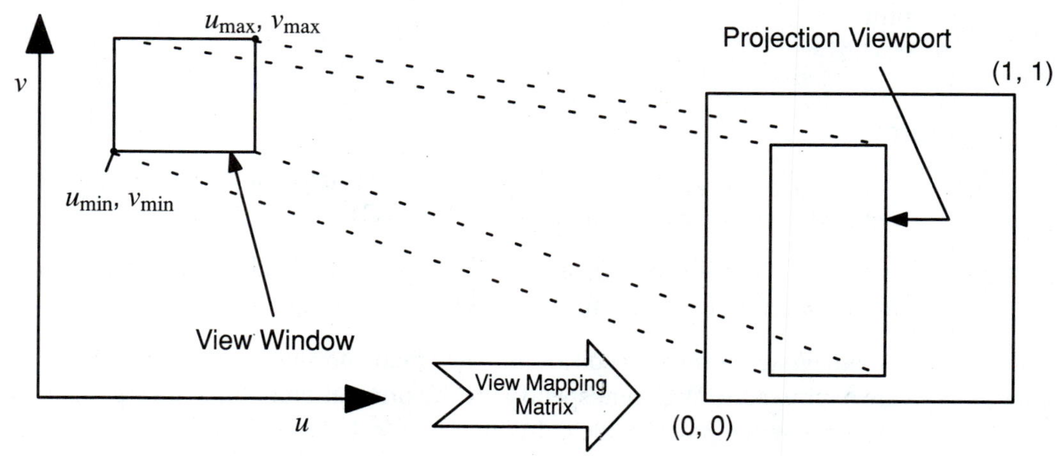

Figure 7–6. Mapping the View Window into the Projection Viewport

Note that Figure 7–6 represents a 2D view; however, similar things happen in the third dimension.

The calling signatures of the 2D and 3D EVALUATE VIEW MAPPING MATRIX routines follow. Since the signatures are very different for the FORTRAN and C bindings, we present them separately.

C Binding:

```
peval_view_map_matrix(
   const Pview_map  *mapping,
   Pint             *error,
   Pmatrix          view_map_matrix
);
```

and

```
peval_view_map_matrix3(
   const Pview_map3 *mapping3,
   Pint             *error,
   Pmatrix3         view_map_matrix
);
```

where:

⟨*mapping*⟩ specifies the view window limits (u_{min}, u_{max}, v_{min}, v_{max}) in VRCs and the 2D projection viewport limits (x_{min}, x_{max}, y_{min}, y_{max}) in NPCs.

⟨*mapping3*⟩ specifies the following aspects of the 3D view mapping matrix:

- View window limits (u_{min}, u_{max}, v_{min}, v_{max}). Values are expressed in VRCs.
- Projection viewport limits (x_{min}, x_{max}, y_{min}, y_{max}, z_{min}, z_{max}). The projection viewport limits define a rectangular volume in NPC space into which the view volume is anisotropically mapped.
- Projection type: either parallel projection (`PTYPE_PARAL`) or perspective projection (`PTYPE_PERSPECT`).
- Projection reference point (in VRCs). For perspective projections, the projection reference point is the same as the eyepoint; for parallel projections, these values specify the direction of the gaze relative to the center of the view window.
- View plane distance, front plane distance, and back plane distance (distances in VRCs along the *n*-axis from the view reference plane). The front and back planes are clipping planes, and the view plane is the plane being "looked at." The view plane contains the view window.

⟨*error*⟩ is the error code of any error that occurred in the routine. If no error occurred, ⟨*error*⟩ is zero.

⟨*view_map_matrix*⟩ is an array returned containing the view mapping matrix describing the transformation from VRCs to NPCs. For the 2D routine the matrix is 3×3; for the 3D routine, it is 4×4. This matrix is typically used in one of the view representation setting routines.

FORTRAN Binding:

```
call pevmm(window_limits, proj_viewpt_limits, error, view_map_matrix)
```

and

```
call pevmm3(window_limits, proj_viewpt_limits, proj_type, proj_ref_x,
+ proj_ref_y, proj_ref_z, view_pln_dist, back_pln_dist, front_pln_dist,
+ error, view_map_matrix)
```

where:

⟨*window_limits*⟩ is a four-element real array specifying the limits of the view window in VRCs. The array contains four elements for both the 2D and 3D cases.

⟨*proj_viewpt_limits*⟩ is a real array that specifies the limits of the projection viewport in NPCs. The parameter contains four elements for `pevmm` and six elements for `pevmm3`.

⟨*proj_type*⟩ is an integer specifying the projection type: either parallel (`PPARL`) or perspective (`PPERS`).

⟨*proj_ref_x*⟩, ⟨*proj_ref_y*⟩, and ⟨*proj_ref_z*⟩ are real values that specify the position of the projection reference point for the FORTRAN binding.

⟨*view_pln_dist*⟩, ⟨*back_pln_dist*⟩, and ⟨*front_pln_dist*⟩ are real values that specify the signed distance from the view reference plane to the view plane, back plane, and front plane, respectively.

⟨*error*⟩ is an integer returned with the error code of any error that occurred in the routine. If no error occurred, ⟨*error*⟩ is zero.

⟨*view_map_matrix*⟩ is a real array returned containing the view mapping matrix derived from the input parameter values. For 2d the matrix is is 3×3; for 3D it is 4×4. This matrix is typically used in one of the view representation setting routines.

The 2D routine makes the following assumptions:

- Front plane distance = 1.0
- Back plane distance and view plane distance = 0.0
- $z_{min} = z_{max} = 0$

- Projection type = parallel
- Projection reference point = $[(u_{min} + u_{max})/2, (v_{min} + v_{max})/2, 1.0]$

Using the Workstation View Table

Calling the view matrix evaluating routines described in the previous chapter does not define a view as far as PHIGS is concerned. These are just utility routines that do some work for the application programmer. Once you have the orientation and mapping matrices for a view, you need to use one of the SET VIEW REPRESENTATION routines to store the values within an entry in the workstation view table.

Multiple view definitions are stored in the workstation view table. The application program uses an integer "view index" to reference these view definitions. The application uses the view index to set and inquire view table entries. It also uses the view index directly from the model via the *set view index* element in the CSS. When this element is traversed, PHIGS reads the corresponding view table entry and sets up the view for the geometry to follow in the traversal.

The view representation definition not only includes the view orientation matrix and the view mapping matrix, but it also allows the application to set clipping limits in all directions in NPC space and to indicate if this clipping should be applied. For example, if the front clipping indicator is set to no clip, the region of NPC space in which visible data may appear is unlimited in the positive z-direction. Note that PHIGS always applies a workstation clip (to avoid drawing outside the display surface).

Defining an Entry in the Workstation View Table

The SET VIEW REPRESENTATION routines take view orientation and view mapping matrices, derives the internal values needed for viewing, and associate the view with a user-specified view index. This view index can later be sent to SET VIEW INDEX to actually select the view.

The calling signatures of the 2D and 3D SET VIEW REPRESENTATION routines are presented next. As before, we present the FORTRAN and C bindings separately.

C Binding:

```
pset_view_rep(
    Pint                workstation_id,
    Pint                view_index,
    const Pview_rep     *view_rep
);
```

and

```
pset_view_rep3(
    Pint                workstation_id,
    Pint                view_index,
    const Pview_rep3    *view_rep3
);
```

where:

⟨*workstation_id*⟩ is the integer workstation identifier passed to OPEN WORKSTATION.

⟨*view_index*⟩ is an integer specifying which view table entry you wish to associate with this view definition. This entry is later accessed through a *set view index* element.

⟨*view_rep*⟩ is the 2D view representation. This parameter specifies the following aspects of the 2D view:

- View orientation matrix (3 × 3 matrix derived from EVALUATE VIEW ORIENTATION MATRIX)
- View mapping matrix (3 × 3 matrix derived from EVALUATE VIEW MAPPING MATRIX)
- View clip limits (x_{min}, x_{max}, y_{min}, y_{max} in NPCs)
- XY clip indicator (`PIND_NO_CLIP`, or `PIND_CLIP`)

⟨*view_rep3*⟩ is the 3D view representation. This parameter specifies the following aspects of the 3D view:

- View orientation matrix (4 × 4 matrix derived from EVALUATE VIEW ORIENTATION MATRIX 3)
- View mapping matrix (4 × 4 matrix derived from EVALUATE VIEW MAPPING MATRIX 3)

- View clip limits (x_{min}, x_{max}, y_{min}, y_{max}, z_{min}, z_{max} in NPCs)
- XY, front, and back clip indicators (`PIND_NO_CLIP`, or `PIND_CLIP`)

These view orientation and view mapping matrices may be defined by the appropriate viewing utility routine (described earlier), or you can calculate them yourself if desired.

FORTRAN Binding:

```
  call psvwr(workstation_id, view_index, view_orient_matrix,
+ view_map_matrix, view_clip_limits, xy_clip)
```

and

```
  call psvwr3(workstation_id, view_index, view_orient_matrix,
+ view_map_matrix, view_clip_limits, xy_clip, back_clip, front_clip)
```

where:

⟨*workstation_id*⟩ is the integer workstation identifier passed to OPEN WORKSTATION.

⟨*view_index*⟩ is an integer specifying which view table entry you wish to associate with this view definition.

⟨*view_orient_matrix*⟩ is a transformation matrix whose dimensions are 3×3 for the 2D version and 4×4 for the 3D version. The matrix can be derived from EVALUATE VIEW ORIENTATION MATRIX.

⟨*view_map_matrix*⟩, like ⟨*view_orient_matrix*⟩, is a transformation matrix whose dimensions are 3×3 for the 2D version and 4×4 for the 3D version. The matrix can be derived from EVALUATE VIEW MAPPING MATRIX.

⟨*view_clip_limits*⟩ is a real array with four elements for `psvwr` (x_{min}, x_{max}, y_{min}, y_{max}) and six elements for `psvwr3` (x_{min}, x_{max}, y_{min}, y_{max}, z_{min}, z_{max}). Values are expressed in NPCs.

⟨*xy_clip*⟩, ⟨*back_clip*⟩, and ⟨*front_clip*⟩ are integers that specify whether to turn clipping on (`PCLIP`) or off (`PNCLIP`) at the indicated edges and planes.

Selecting an Entry from the Workstation View Table

SET VIEW INDEX creates a structure element called a *set view index* element in the current open structure and assigns it the specified view index. At traversal time, *set view index* elements determine the view index attribute associated with primitive structure elements. If PHIGS does not encounter any *set view index* structure elements, it uses the default view index 0.

Since a *set view index* element is an attribute element, you can use it the same way that you use other attribute elements. You can change the current view within a structure or substructure. The rules of traversal-time attribute binding apply to view index elements just as they apply to other attribute elements. However, performance can be affected if you force PHIGS to change views often within a structure. It is usually advisable to put your *set view index* elements near the top of a structure or keep them all in a "scene" structure that controls the different views (see the "Multiple-Views" example later in this chapter).

Default Viewing Parameters

The workstation view table contains a special entry (index 0) that is predefined and cannot be modified. During traversal, PHIGS automatically uses entry 0 if it does not encounter any set view index structure elements. Table 7–1 lists the information contained in view table entry 0.

Table 7–1. Values Stored in Workstation View Table Entry 0

Entry Name	**Data Type**	**Value**
View orientation matrix	4 × 4 × R	Identity matrix = 1, 0, 0, 0 0, 1, 0, 0 0, 0, 1, 0 0, 0, 0, 1
View mapping matrix	4 × 4 × R	Identity matrix
View clipping limits	6 × R	0, 1, 0, 1, 0, 1
xy clipping limits	E	`PCLIP, PIND_CLIP`
Back clipping limits	E	`PCLIP, PIND_CLIP`
Front clipping limits	E	`PCLIP, PIND_CLIP`
R = real, E = enumerated type (4-byte integer)		

The default view table entry (index 0) places the viewing reference coordinate system (VRC) coincident with the world coordinate system. View table entry 0 maps the cube $[0, 1] \times [0, 1] \times [0, 1]$ in VRC to the cube $[0, 1] \times [0, 1] \times [0, 1]$ in normalized projection coordinate space.

The number of modifiable views varies between implementations. The predefined values in these views can also vary. Use the following routines to determine the number of predefined view table entries and the values in each entry:

- INQUIRE VIEW FACILITIES returns the number of predefined view indices.
- INQUIRE PREDEFINED VIEW REPRESENTATION returns the predefined values for a particular entry in the workstation view table.

PHIGS also supports the following additional view inquiry routines:

- INQUIRE LIST OF VIEW INDICES returns the list of defined view indices. The list is ordered by view transformation input priority, starting with the highest priority view.
- INQUIRE VIEW REPRESENTATION returns the values stored in a particular view table entry.

Deferral of View Modifications

You can set the display update state so that calls to SET VIEW REPRESENTATION have a deferred effect. This is useful because under some circumstances a complete regeneration may be time-consuming and could be distracting to the user. For example, consider an application where the user is interacting with the display and moving or deleting primitives. In this case you might not want the entire display to be updated every time an object is deleted. It would be useful to instruct PHIGS to use quick update methods to move or delete the primitives and then update the entire display at a later time. In this case you could set the display update state to (WAIT, UQUM) which means "don't regenerate the display until the application requests it and use quick update methods whenever possible." Under these circumstances PHIGS may be able to delete a primitive from the screen by redrawing it in the background colour.

In order to allow the operator to interact multiple times with the picture while quick update operations are being performed, it is necessary for the view transformation and workstation transformation to remain constant. The reason for this is that PHIGS maps operator locator input from device coordinates to world coordinates using the inverses of the workstation transformation and of one of the active views. Because locator input is mapped through these inverse transformations, a consistent interaction requires repeated use of the same transformations that generated the picture.

This is accomplished through the use of *current* and *requested* entries in the workstation state list. Each entry in the view table in the workstation state list contains the following values:

- A list of current viewing parameters
- A list of requested viewing parameters
- A *viewing transformation update state* entry

When an application program calls SET VIEW REPRESENTATION, PHIGS sets the requested viewing parameters and sets the *viewing transformation update state* entry to Pending (`PPEND`, `PUPD_PEND`). The current viewing parameters continue to hold their previous values. The next time the workstation is updated (via UPDATE WORKSTATION or REDRAW ALL STRUCTURES), PHIGS sets the current values to the requested values and sets the *viewing transformation update state* entry to Notpending (`PNPEND`, `PUPD_NOT_PEND`).

If the deferral mode in the display update state is ASAP, PHIGS performs an update immediately upon setting a view representation (see SET DISPLAY UPDATE STATE in Chapter 4, *Posting Structures and Controlling Picture Changes*). Since an update copies the requested viewing parameters to the current ones, you may see that the requested and current viewing parameters are always the same in ASAP.

Note that the above statements are true for OUTPUT, OUTIN, and MO workstations. Since INPUT workstations do not display data, PHIGS allows a new view representation to go into effect immediately.

Use INQUIRE VIEW REPRESENTATION to inquire the view transformation update state for a particular view table entry.

Single-View Example

Let's take a look at the viewing parameters for a simple example. Figure 7–7 shows a view of an object that appears repeatedly in this book. We call it the "cube-with-the-corner-cut-off." It is a simple object made up of seven fill area set primitives and three text primitives. The program that creates the object is called `SingleView`.

Figure 7–7. Initial Output from SingleView

As just mentioned, the object created in this example is used a lot in this book. In Chapter 18, *Depth Cueing*, we show how to make the 3D wireframe image more realistic. In Chapter 15, *Front and Back Facet Processing*, we discuss how to remove the portions (facets) that are facing away from the observer. In Chapter 17, *Lighting and Shading*, we show how to shine lights on the object and how to interpolate colours across its surface.

We create the object centered around the modelling coordinate origin and then map it directly to world coordinates with no scaling, rotation, or transformation matrices, so that it maintains the same simple orientation. Figure 7–8 shows the coordinates for the front face of the object.

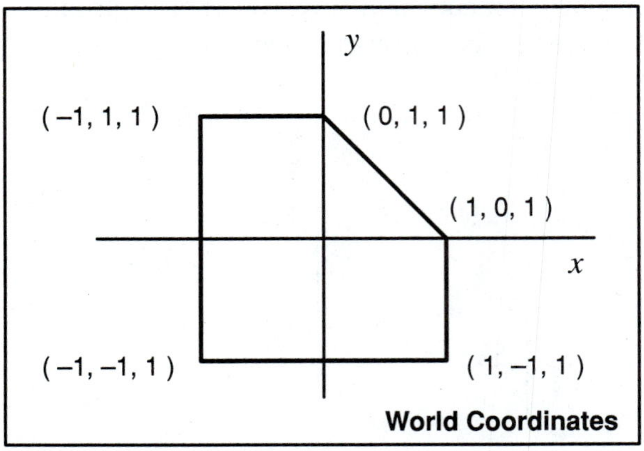

Figure 7–8. Front Face of Cube-with-the-corner-cut-off

This example uses the object-centered view paradigm. The following parameters are used to create the view orientation matrix for the object:

- View reference point = (0.0, 0.0, 0.0)
- View plane normal = (0.4, 0.3, 1.0)
- View up vector = (0.0, 1.0, 0.0)

The following parameters create the view mapping matrix for the object:

- Front plane distance = 5.0
- Back plane distance = –5.0
- View plane distance = 0.0 (coincident with the view reference plane)
- Projection reference point = (0.0, 0.0, 10.0)

- Projection type = perspective
- Window limits (on VRC view plane)
  - $u_{min} = -1.75$
  - $u_{max} = 1.75$
  - $v_{min} = -1.75$
  - $v_{max} = 1.75$
- Projection viewport limits (NPC)
  - $x_{min} = 0.0$
  - $x_{max} = 1.0$
  - $y_{min} = 0.0$
  - $y_{max} = 1.0$
  - $z_{min} = 0.0$
  - $z_{max} = 1.0$

Front and back plane distances of 5.0 and –5.0, respectively, ensure that the entire object will fit into the view volume even when we begin spinning the object around the origin later on in the program.

We use view plane values ranging from –1.75 to +1.75 to ensure that the entire object will be within the view (the object ranges from –1.0 to +1.0 in WCs). If we make the values closer to –1.0 and 1.0, the object will appear larger in the view. If we use increasingly larger values, the object will appear smaller.

Using projection viewport limits of 0.0 to 1.0 in all directions tells PHIGS that the view should occupy the entire NPC space. Later in this chapter we will see how to arrange, or tile, several views into NPC space.

This program has the following additional features:

- It uses a simple structure network. The object is created in a structure named `BuildCube` and instanced (using an *execute structure* element) from a structure named `Scene`. The following fragment from the C binding shows the `Scene` structure with added comments:

```
popen_struct(Scene);                          /* open structure */
pset_view_ind(1);                             /* set view index */
pset_local_tran3(Transform, PTYPE_REPLACE);
pexec_struct(Cube);                           /* execute structure */
pclose_struct()                               /* close structure */;
```

The SET LOCAL TRANSFORMATION routine is a place holder that will be used later when we edit the structure. The first time through, the `Transform` matrix contains the identity matrix.

- After displaying the object an initial time, the program opens the `Scene` structure for editing. Within a loop, the program repeatedly replaces the local transformation matrix, each time with a slightly greater rotation angle. After each edit, the program calls the REDRAW ALL STRUCTURES routine to redraw the image with the new transformation matrix applied. In this object-centered example, the object itself is rotated while the view remains stationary.
- The program also shows how to place 3D text anywhere in modelling coordinates. We will defer discussion of that topic until we discuss 3D text in Chapter 11, *Using Text*.

SingleView.c

The following is the complete C binding version of the `SingleView` program. See Appendix C for the FORTRAN version.

```
#include <phigs.h>              /* get PHIGS definitions for C */
#include <stdio.h>              /* get standard I/O definitions */
#include <math.h>               /* compile with library "-lm" */

#define  deg  *M_PI/180.        /* convert degrees to radians */

main()                                /* file "SingleView.c" */
{
    Pint        WorkstnID = 1;        /* workstation identifier */
    Pint        ConnID;               /* connection identifier */
    Pint        WorkstnType = POIDDX; /* implementation dependent */
    Pint        Scene = 1, Cube = 2;  /* structure IDs */
    float       Angle;                /* rotation angle */
    Pint        Error;                /* error indicator */
    int         I, J;                 /* loop control variables */
```

```
/*--- viewing parameters -------------------------------------------*/
    static Pview_map3   ViewMapping = { /* sent to
                                         "peval_view_map_matrix3" */
    {-1.75, 1.75, -1.75, 1.75},        /* window limits */
    {0.0, 1.0, 0.0, 1.0, 0.0, 1.0},    /* projection viewport limits */
    PTYPE_PERSPECT,                     /* perspective projection */
    {0.0, 0.0, 10.0},                   /* projection reference point */
    0.0, -5.0, 5.0};              /* view/back/front plane distances */
    static Ppoint3      ViewRefPt = {0.0, 0.0, 0.0};
    static Pvec3        ViewNormVec = {0.4, 0.3, 1.0};
    static Pvec3        ViewUpVec = {0.0, 1.0, 0.0};
    Pmatrix3       ViewMapMatrix;  /* from "peval_view_map_matrix3" */
    Pmatrix3       ViewOriMatrix;  /* from "peval_view_ori_matrix3" */
    static Plimit3 ClipLimits = {0.0, 1.0, 0.0, 1.0, 0.0, 1.0};
    Pview_rep3     ViewRep;
    Pmatrix3       Xmatrix, Ymatrix, Transform;

    popen_phigs(stderr, 0);              /* errors go to "stderr" */
    pescape_u4("/dev/screen/phigs_window", &ConnID);
    popen_ws(WorkstnID, ConnID, WorkstnType);
    peval_view_map_matrix3(&ViewMapping, &Error, ViewMapMatrix);
    if (Error) {
        fprintf(stderr, "Error %d in peval_view_map_matrix3;
                terminating.\n",
          Error);
        exit(1);
    }
    peval_view_ori_matrix3(&ViewRefPt, &ViewNormVec, &ViewUpVec,
      &Error, ViewOriMatrix);
    if (Error) {
        fprintf(stderr, "Error %d in peval_view_map_matrix3;
                terminating.\n",
          Error);
        exit(1);
    }
    for (I = 0; I < 4; I++)
        for (J = 0; J < 4; J++)
            ViewRep.ori_matrix[I][J] = ViewOriMatrix[I][J],
            ViewRep.map_matrix[I][J] = ViewMapMatrix[I][J];
    ViewRep.clip_limit = ClipLimits;
    ViewRep.xy_clip = ViewRep.back_clip =
    ViewRep.front_clip = PIND_CLIP;
    pset_view_rep3(WorkstnID, 1, &ViewRep);
```

```
    BuildCube(Cube);
/* create an identity matrix */
    protate_x(0.0, &Error, Transform);

    popen_struct(Scene);
    pset_view_ind(1);
    pset_local_tran3(Transform, PTYPE_REPLACE);
    pexec_struct(Cube);
    pclose_struct();
    ppost_struct(WorkstnID, Scene, 1.0);
    pupd_ws(WorkstnID, PFLAG_PERFORM);
    protate_x(0.0, &Error, Xmatrix);     /* create identity matrices */
    protate_x(0.0, &Error, Ymatrix);
    protate_x(0.0, &Error, Transform);
    pset_edit_mode(PEDIT_REPLACE);
    popen_struct(Scene);
    for (I = 0; I <= 360; I++) {
        Angle = I deg;
        protate_y(Angle, &Error, Ymatrix);
        protate_x(Angle, &Error, Xmatrix);
        pcompose_matrix3(Xmatrix, Ymatrix, &Error, Transform);
        pset_elem_ptr(2);              /* set element pointer to 2 */
        pset_local_tran3(Transform, PTYPE_REPLACE);
        predraw_all_structs(WorkstnID, PFLAG_ALWAYS);
    }
    pclose_struct();
    punpost_all_structs(WorkstnID);
    pclose_ws(WorkstnID);
    pclose_phigs();
}
/*********************************************************************/
BuildCube(StructID)
int     StructID;                 /* structure ID for cube structure */
{
    static Ppoint3 TopPoints[5]     = {-1,1,-1, -1,1,1,
                                        0,1,1, 1,1,0, 1,1,-1};
    static Ppoint_list3 Top         = {5, TopPoints};
    static Ppoint3 BottomPoints[4] = {-1,-1,1, -1,-1,-1,
                                        1,-1,-1, 1,-1,1};
    static Ppoint_list3 Bottom      = {4, BottomPoints};
    static Ppoint3 RightPoints[5]   = {1,-1,-1, 1,1,-1,
                                       1,1,0, 1,0,1, 1,-1,1};
    static Ppoint_list3 Right       = {5, RightPoints};
```

```
    static Ppoint3 LeftPoints[4]    = {-1,-1,1, -1,1,1,
                                        -1,1,-1, -1,-1,-1};
    static Ppoint_list3 Left        = {4, LeftPoints};
    static Ppoint3 FrontPoints[5]   = {1,-1,1, 1,0,1,
                                        0,1,1, -1,1,1, -1,-1,1};
    static Ppoint_list3 Front       = {5, FrontPoints};
    static Ppoint3 BackPoints[4]    = {-1,-1,-1, -1,1,-1,
                                         1,1,-1, 1,-1,-1};
    static Ppoint_list3 Back        = {4, BackPoints};
    static Ppoint3 CornerPoints[3] = {1,0,1, 1,1,0, 0,1,1};
    static Ppoint_list3 Corner      = {3, CornerPoints};
    static Ppoint_list3 CubePoints[7];
    Ppoint_list_list3   Cube;
    /*--- text locations and orientations -------------------------*/
    static Ppoint3      TopTextPos = {-0.75, 1.0, 0.0};
    static Pvec3        TopTextOri[2] = {1,0,0,  0,0,-1};
    static Ppoint3      RightTextPos = {1.0, -0.75, 0.75};
    static Pvec3        RightTextOri[2] = {0,0,-1,  0,1,0};
    static Ppoint3      FrontTextPos = {-0.75, -0.75, 1.0};
    static Pvec3        FrontTextOri[2] = {1,0,0,  0,1,0};
    int                 I;              /* loop control variable */

    CubePoints[0] = Top;        CubePoints[1] = Bottom;
    CubePoints[2] = Right;      CubePoints[3] = Left;
    CubePoints[4] = Front;      CubePoints[5] = Back;
    CubePoints[6] = Corner;
    popen_struct(StructID);
    Cube.num_point_lists = 1;
    for (I = 0; I < 7; I++) {
        Cube.point_lists = &(CubePoints[I]);
        pfill_area_set3(&Cube);
    }
    pset_char_ht(0.4);
    pset_char_expan(0.7);
    ptext3(&TopTextPos, TopTextOri, "Top");
    ptext3(&RightTextPos, RightTextOri, "Right");
    ptext3(&FrontTextPos, FrontTextOri, "Front");
    pclose_struct();
}
```

Multiple-Views Example

The program presented in this section displays four separate views of the cube-with-the-corner-cut-off. Figure 7–9 shows the output of the program.

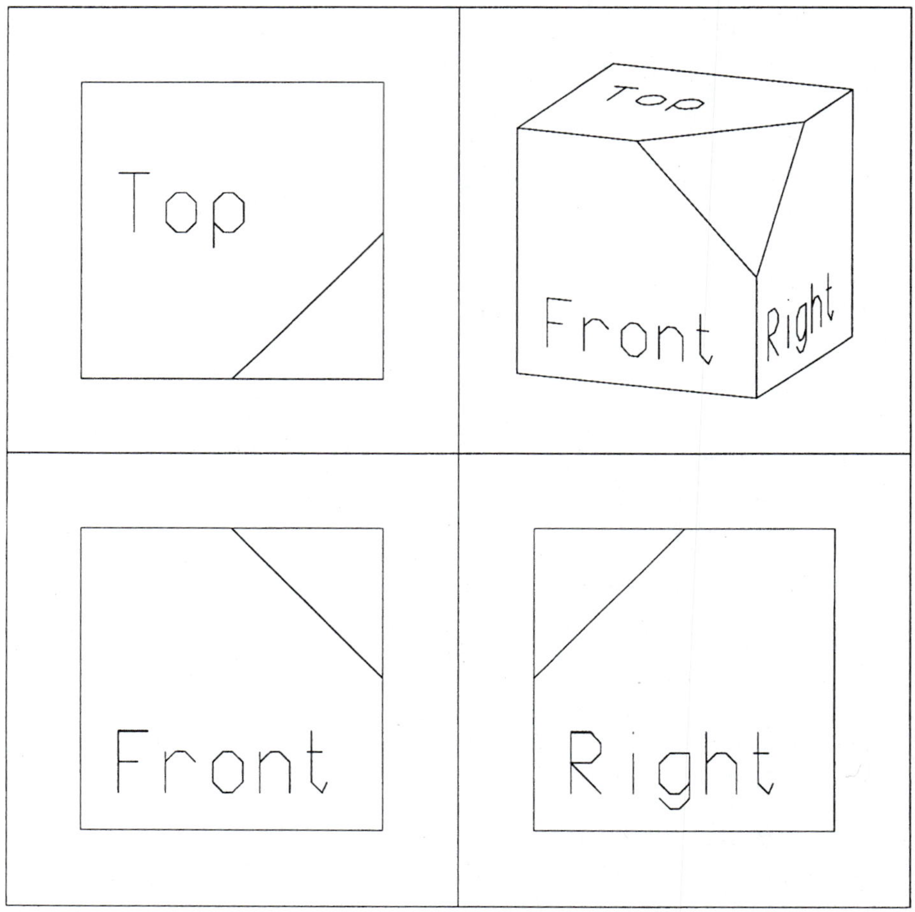

Figure 7–9. Output of four_views Program

Figure 7–9 is the output from the FORTRAN version of the program. That version uses facet culling to remove back-facing portions (facets) and draws lines in View 0 to simulate view borders.

We present two fragments of the program here: one using the C binding and one using the FORTRAN binding. The complete programs are listed in Appendix C.

The fragment defines view table entry 3 (the bottom left view in Figure 7–9). It also creates a `Scene` structure where it instances the object (`Cube` structure) four times, each time with a different view index element. Finally, the fragment posts the `Scene` structure to the workstation and calls UPDATE WORKSTATION to display the object in all four views.

C Binding Fragment from four_views Program

```
/*--- viewing parameters for View 3 ------------------------------------*/
static Pview_map3   ViewMapping3 = {/* sent to "peval_view_map_matrix3" */
  {-1.25, 1.25, -1.25, 1.25},        /* window limits */
  {0.0, 0.5, 0.0, 0.5, 0.0, 1.0},    /* projection viewport limits */
  PTYPE_PARAL,                        /* parallel projection */
  {0.0, 0.0, 10.0},                   /* projection reference point */
  0.0, -2.5, 2.5};                    /* view/back/front plane distances */
static Ppoint3      ViewRefPt3 = {0.0, 0.0, 0.0};
static Pvec3        ViewNormVec3 = {0.0, 0.0, 0.5};
static Pvec3        ViewUpVec3 = {0.0, 1.0, 0.0};
static Plimit3      ClipLimits3 = {0.0, 0.5, 0.0, 0.5, 0.0, 1.0};
Pview_rep3          ViewRep3;
...
/*--- set up View 3 (lower left) ---------------------------------------*/
peval_view_map_matrix3(&ViewMapping3, &Error, ViewMapMatrix);
CheckError(Error, "peval_view_map_matrix3");
peval_view_ori_matrix3(&ViewRefPt3, &ViewNormVec3, &ViewUpVec3, &Error,
  ViewOriMatrix);                                  /*  +---+---+  */
CheckError(Error, "peval_view_ori_matrix3");       /*  |   |   |  */
CopyMatrix(ViewOriMatrix, ViewRep3.ori_matrix);    /*  +---+---+  */
CopyMatrix(ViewMapMatrix, ViewRep3.map_matrix);    /*  | X |   |  */
ViewRep3.clip_limit = ClipLimits3;                 /*  +---+---+  */
ViewRep3.xy_clip = ViewRep3.back_clip = ViewRep3.front_clip = PIND_CLIP;
pset_view_rep3(WorkstnID, 3, &ViewRep3);
...
/*--- draw all four views ---------------------------------------------*/
BuildCube(Cube);
popen_struct(Scene);
pset_view_ind(1);   pexec_struct(Cube);
pset_view_ind(2);   pexec_struct(Cube);
pset_view_ind(3);   pexec_struct(Cube);
pset_view_ind(4);   pexec_struct(Cube);
```

```
pclose_struct();
ppost_struct(WorkstnID, Scene, 1.0);
pupd_ws(WorkstnID, PFLAG_PERFORM);
```

FORTRAN Binding Fragment from four_views Program

Notice that the FORTRAN binding version simulates view borders around the four views by drawing lines in the default View 0. This is the image shown in Figure 7–9. This is a common way to draw view borders with standard PHIGS, since PHIGS has no provisions for view borders.

```
C Viewing variables
      real       vwrx, vwry, vwrz  { view reference point (WC)
      real       vpnx, vpny, vpnz  { view plane normal    (WC)
      real       vupx, vupy, vupz  { view up vector       (WC)
      real       wdw_lim(4)        { window limits        (VRC)
      real       vp_lim(6)         { viewport limits      (NPC)
      real       clip_lim(6)       { clip limits          (NPC)
      real       pjrx, pjry, pjrz  { projection reference point (VRC)
      real       vpld              { view plane distance  (VRC)
      real       bpld              { back plane distance  (VRC)
      real       fpld              { front plane distance (VRC)
C View orientation and view mapping matrices
      real*4 Orientation(4,4), Mapping(4,4)
      ...
C The following values are used in all four views:
      pjrx  = 0.0           { projection reference point (VRC)
      pjry  = 0.0
      pjrz  = 10.0
      vpld  =  0.0          { view plane distance (VRC)
      bpld  = -2.5          { back plane distance (VRC)
      fpld  =  2.5          { front plane distance (VRC)
      ...
C *** Define Workstation View Table Entry '3' ***
      vwrx = 0.0            { view reference point (WC)
      vwry = 0.0
      vwrz = 0.0
      vpnx = 0.0            { view plane normal (WC)
      vpny = 0.0
      vpnz = 0.5
      vupx = 0.0            { view up vector (WC)
      vupy = 1.0
      vupz = 0.0
```

```
      wdw_lim(1)   = -1.5    { window limits (VRC)
      wdw_lim(2)   =  1.5
      wdw_lim(3)   = -1.5
      wdw_lim(4)   =  1.5
                               { relative position of View 3
      vp_lim(1)    =  0.0      {      ______________
      vp_lim(2)    =  0.5      {     |       |       |
      vp_lim(3)    =  0.0      {     |       |       |
      vp_lim(4)    =  0.5      {     |       |       |
      vp_lim(5)    =  0.0      {     |---------------|
      vp_lim(6)    =  1.0      {     |       |       |
C                              {     |   X   |       |
      clip_lim(1) =  0.0       {     |_______|_______|
      clip_lim(2) =  0.5
      clip_lim(3) =  0.0
      clip_lim(4) =  0.5
      clip_lim(5) =  0.0
      clip_lim(6) =  1.0
      call pevom3(vwrx, vwry, vwrz, vpnx, vpny, vpnz,
     +            vupx, vupy, vupz, ERRIND, Orientation)
      call pevmm3(wdw_lim, vp_lim, PPARL, pjrx, pjry, pjrz,
     +            vpld, bpld, fpld, ERRIND, Mapping)
      call psvwr3(WorkID, 3, Orientation, Mapping, clip_lim,
     +            PCLIP, PCLIP, PCLIP)
      ...
C ***************************************************************
      call BuildCube(Cube)

      call popst(Scene)        { open structure
      LineX(1)=0.0             { Since PHIGS does not have facilities
      LineY(1)=1.0             { for defining view borders,
      LineX(2)=0.0             { this code draws 2D lines in
      LineY(2)=0.0             { View 0 to simulate view borders.
      LineX(3)=1.0             { These lines work for this example
      LineY(3)=0.0             { because we have split up the available
      LineX(4)=1.0             { NPC area into four equal viewports.
      LineY(4)=1.0
      LineX(5)=0.0
      LineY(5)=1.0
      call ppl(5, LineX, LineY)
      LineX(1)=0.0
      LineY(1)=0.5
      LineX(2)=1.0
```

```
LineY(2)=0.5
call ppl(2, LineX, LineY)
LineX(1)=0.5
LineY(1)=1.0
LineX(2)=0.5
LineY(2)=0.0
call ppl(2, LineX, LineY)
call psvwi(1)                    { set view index
call pexst(Cube)                 { execute structure
call psvwi(2)                    { set view index
call pexst(Cube)                 { execute structure
call psvwi(3)                    { set view index
call pexst(Cube)                 { execute structure
call psvwi(4)                    { set view index
call pexst(Cube)                 { execute structure
call pclst                       { close structure

call ppost(WorkID, Scene, 1.0)   { post structure Scene
call puwk(WorkID, PPERFO)        { update workstation
```

The FORTRAN binding program turns on "facet culling mode" using the SET FACET CULLING MODE routine. This is done so that portions (facets) of the object that face away from the viewer are not drawn, particularly in View 1. This is done in the `BuildCube` subroutine (not shown in this fragment—see Appendix C).

Pilot's-Eye View Example

The example program described in this section shows how to "encapsulate" the complexities of PHIGS' viewing into a single subroutine. As such, you simply pass in parameters specifying what you're looking at, where you're looking from, the up vector, the field of view and the projection type, and this "black box" routine does the rest.

The routine describes a camera model as follows:

- "What you're looking at" is the subject's location,
- "Where you're looking from" is the camera's location,
- The "up vector" is the camera's tilt (both left/right and down/up),
- The "field of view" is the "length" of the lens (the "zoomedness"),
- The "projection type" specifies parallel or perspective projection (physical cameras are only capable of perspective).

The program illustrates the various camera capabilities. With a scene consisting of several wireframe geometric objects on a section of a plane, the "camera" executes the following moves:

1. Moving around and above the scene; the scene rotates 360° about a vertical axis, then almost 90° up and down. This is done by changing the camera's position while leaving the "looked-at" point the same.
2. Flying "into" the scene; again, this is accomplished by moving the camera to a location above the "floor" of the scene (so the objects "surround" you), while leaving the "looked-at" point the same.
3. Looking up; this "camera tilt" is accomplished by changing the point at which the camera is looking, while leaving the camera position unchanged.
4. Doing a close-up, then a wide-angle view, of the cone/ellipsoid juncture; this happens because the field of view is reduced (causing the close-up) and then increased dramatically (causing the wide-angle effect). At its extreme (135° wide), the wide-angle effect is so pronounced, it simulates a "fisheye" lens.

5. Flying around, between, and finally away from, the objects in the scene. Following a complex path derived from combinations of sines and cosines, an "airplane" path is generated. At each point along the path, the point looked at is the "next" point, and the camera position is the "current" point. Or, in other words, what is the looked-at point during one iteration becomes the camera location during the next iteration, and a new looked-at point is calculated. In this way, a smooth flight path is created.

   Also, based on the *x* and *y* rates of change, the horizontal acceleration determines the up vector, thus simulating the plane banking as it turns.

Figure 7–10 shows a frame from the flying sequence as the "pilot" flies around in the scene.

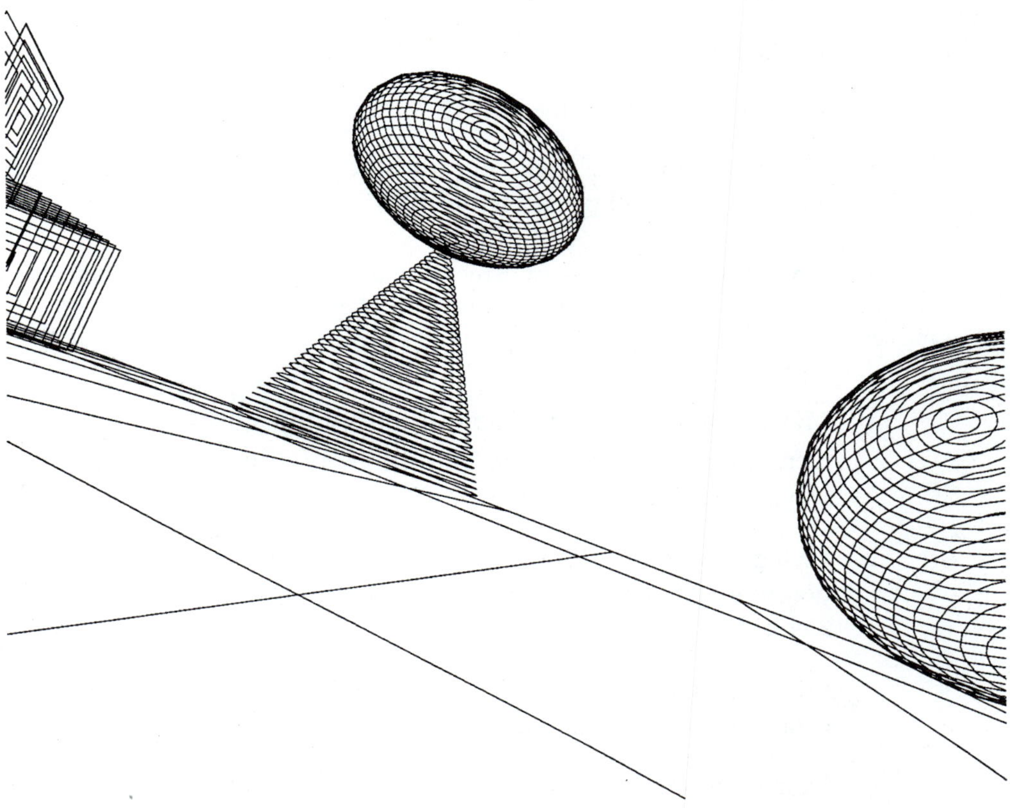

Figure 7–10. Scene from the Pilot's-Eye Program

An All-Purpose Viewing Subroutine

The following fragment presents the "all-purpose" viewing subroutine. Each time the routine is called, it builds an orientation matrix (using `peval_view_ori_matrix3`) and mapping matrix (using `peval_view_map_matrix3`) and then uses the two matrices to set an entry in the workstation view table (using `pset_view_rep3`).

```
/****************************************************************************/
DefineCameraView(WorkstnID, ViewNo, PRPx, PRPy, PRPz, VRPx, VRPy, VRPz,
  FieldOfView, ProjType, VUPx, VUPy, VUPz)
int             WorkstnID, ViewNo;        /* workstn id, view to be defined */
float           PRPx, PRPy, PRPz;         /* proj. ref. pt. (point looked from) */
float           VRPx, VRPy, VRPz;         /* view ref pt. (point looked at) */
float           FieldOfView;              /* "zoomedness" in degrees */
Pproj_type      ProjType;                 /* parallel or perspective? */
float           VUPx, VUPy, VUPz;         /* view up vector */
{
    Pview_map3  MapStruct;                /* structure for view mapping info */
    Ppoint3     ViewRefPt;                /* view reference point */
    Pvec3       ViewNrmVc, ViewUpVec;     /* view normal/up vectors */
    Pmatrix3    Mapping;                  /* view mapping matrix */
    Pmatrix3    Orientation;              /* view orientation matrix */
    float       Distance;                 /* distance from PRP to VRP */
    float       Wndw;                     /* window limits */
    Pview_rep3  ViewRep;                  /* view representation */
    int         Error;                    /* error-return variable */
    int         I, J;                     /* loop control variables */

    ViewRefPt.x = VRPx, ViewRefPt.y = VRPy, ViewRefPt.z = VRPz;
    ViewNrmVc.delta_x = PRPx - VRPx;     /* \  View plane normal determined   */
    ViewNrmVc.delta_y = PRPy - VRPy;     /*  > by projection reference point */
    ViewNrmVc.delta_z = PRPz - VRPz;     /* /  and view reference point.     */
    ViewUpVec.delta_x = VUPx, ViewUpVec.delta_y = VUPy,
      ViewUpVec.delta_z = VUPz;
    peval_view_ori_matrix3(&ViewRefPt, &ViewNrmVc, &ViewUpVec, &Error,
      Orientation);
    if (Error != 0){
        printf("Error %d in peval_view_ori_matrix3; terminating.\n", Error);
        exit(1);
    }
    Distance = sqrt((PRPx-VRPx)*(PRPx-VRPx) + (PRPy-VRPy)*(PRPy-VRPy) +
      (PRPz-VRPz)*(PRPz-VRPz));
    Wndw = Distance * tan(FieldOfView deg/2);    /* FOV controls window size */
```

```
    MapStruct.win.x_min =                   /* \                             */
      MapStruct.win.y_min = -Wndw;          /*  \ This assumes a square window */
    MapStruct.win.x_max =                   /*  / (aspect ratio = 1.00).      */
      MapStruct.win.y_max = Wndw;           /* /                             */
    MapStruct.proj_vp.x_min = MapStruct.proj_vp.y_min =
      MapStruct.proj_vp.z_min = 0.0;
    MapStruct.proj_vp.x_max = MapStruct.proj_vp.y_max =
      MapStruct.proj_vp.z_max = 1.0;
    MapStruct.proj_type = ProjType;
    MapStruct.proj_ref_point.x = 0.0, MapStruct.proj_ref_point.y = 0.0,
      MapStruct.proj_ref_point.z = Distance;
    MapStruct.view_plane = 0.0;
    MapStruct.back_plane = -1E3 * Distance;      /* virtually infinite */
    MapStruct.front_plane = Distance - 0.01;     /* right in front of eye point */
    peval_view_map_matrix3(&MapStruct, &Error, Mapping);
    if (Error != 0){
        printf("Error %d in peval_view_map_matrix3; terminating.\n", Error);
        exit(1);
    }
    for (I = 0; I < 4; I++)
        for (J = 0; J < 4; J++) {
            ViewRep.ori_matrix[I][J] = Orientation[I][J];
            ViewRep.map_matrix[I][J] = Mapping[I][J];
        }
    ViewRep.clip_limit.x_min = 0.0;
    ViewRep.clip_limit.x_max = 1.0;
    ViewRep.clip_limit.y_min = 0.0;
    ViewRep.clip_limit.y_max = 1.0;
    ViewRep.clip_limit.z_min = 0.0;
    ViewRep.clip_limit.z_max = 1.0;
    ViewRep.xy_clip = ViewRep.back_clip = ViewRep.front_clip = PIND_CLIP;
    pset_view_rep3(WorkstnID, ViewNo, &ViewRep);
}
```

Repeatedly Modify One View Table Entry

This program uses entry 1 in the workstation view table and continually modifies the entry as the program progresses. The following fragment shows how view table entry 1 is selected near the top of the main `SceneID` structure:

```
popen_struct(SceneID);
pset_view_ind(1);
pexec_struct(PlaneID);
```

Set the Display Update State

The program sets the display update state to ASAP to ensure that changes in the view table are reflected immediately:

```
pset_disp_upd_st(WorkstnID, PDEFER_ASAP, PMODE_NIVE);
```

Using the DefineCameraView Routine

The following fragment shows one of the loops that use the `DefineCameraView` routine. This loop flies "over" the scene by changing the camera's position while leaving the looked-at point the same.

```
/*---- look down on the scene from above ---------------------------*/
pset_disp_upd_st(WorkstnID, PDEFER_ASAP, PMODE_NIVE);
for (I = 80; I >= 4; I--) {
    PolarToRectangular(25.0, -90 deg, I deg, &X, &Y, &Z);
    DefineCameraView(WorkstnID, 1,   /* workstation ID, view number */
      X + CenterX, Y + CenterY, Z,   /* PRP (point looked from) */
      5.0, 5.0, 0.0,                 /* VRP (point looked at) */
      30.0, PTYPE_PERSPECT,          /* field of view, proj. type */
      0.0, 0.0, 1.0);                /* up vector */
}
for (I = 4; I <= 90; I += 2) {
    PolarToRectangular(25.0, -90 deg, I deg, &X, &Y, &Z);
    DefineCameraView(WorkstnID, 1,   /* workstation ID, view number */
      X + CenterX, Y + CenterY, Z,   /* PRP (point looked from) */
      5.0, 5.0, 0.0,                 /* VRP (point looked at) */
      30.0, PTYPE_PERSPECT,          /* field of view, proj. type */
      0.0, 0.0, 1.0);                /* up vector */
}
```

Figure 7–11 shows two frames that use the loop to fly over the scene.

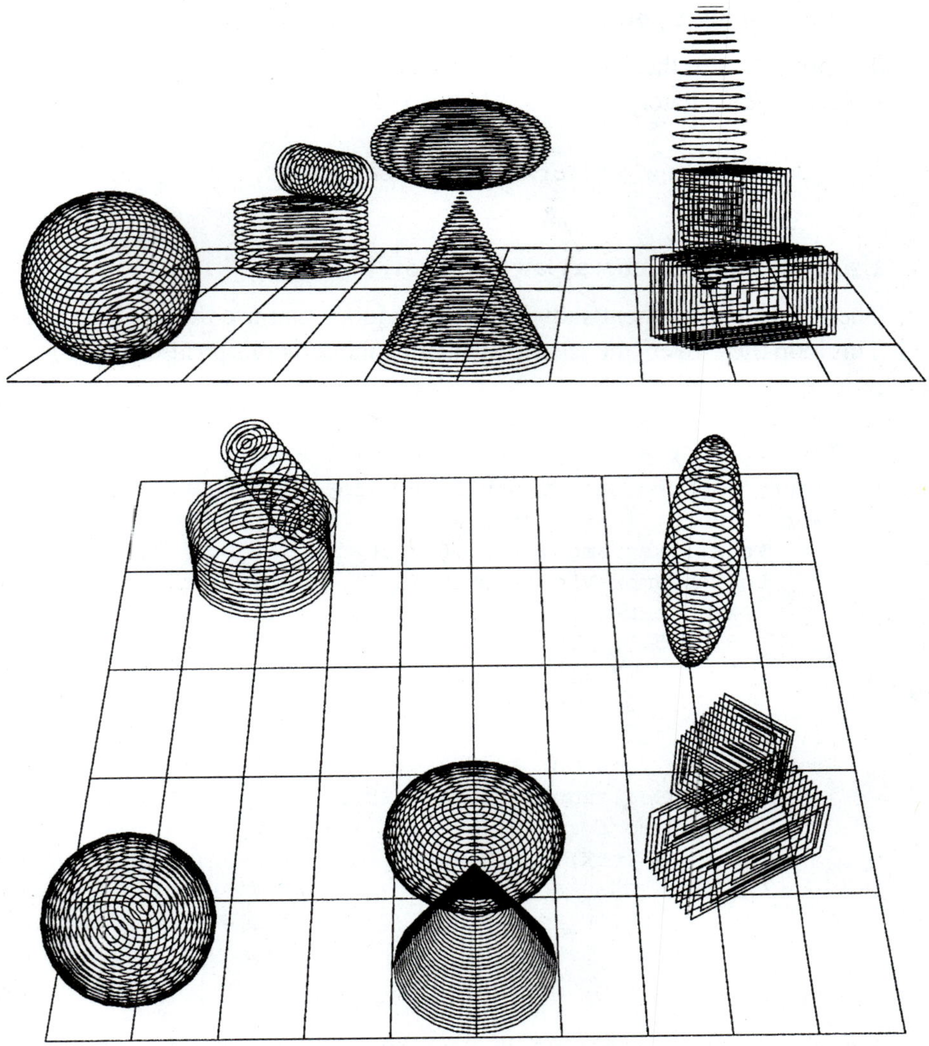

Figure 7–11. Flying over the Scene

Appendix C presents the entire program in both FORTRAN and C.

Additional Viewing Topics

The information in this section is related to the section entitled "View Mapping Transformation" earlier in this chapter. We moved it to the end of the viewing section to simplify the description of how to create a view mapping matrix.

Changing a Perspective View

When you look at an object up close, it looks larger—it subtends a greater angular distance when measured from your eye—than when you look at it from a distance; it apparently "shrinks" as your distance from it increases. The amount of shrink is very orderly: It is directly proportional to the distance. In the following diagram, an observer is looking at an object y units high from a distance of z units. The trigonometric identity (if you're interested; you don't need to know this) $\tan(\theta) = opposite\_side/adjacent\_side$, stated another way, says that $\theta = \arctan(opp/adj)$. From the vantage point in the diagram below, $\arctan(y/z) = \theta$.

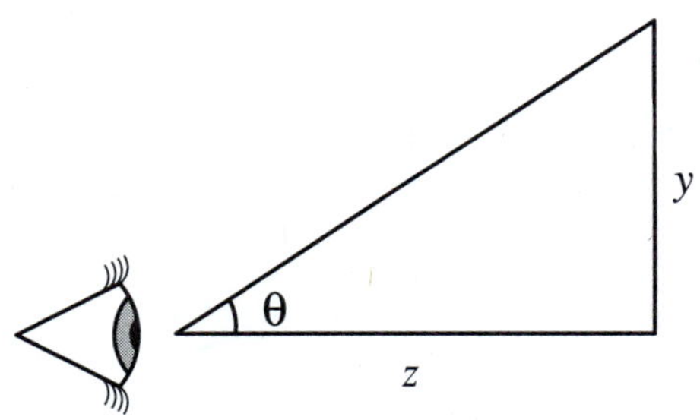

Now, if the observer moves to twice his or her distance from the object:

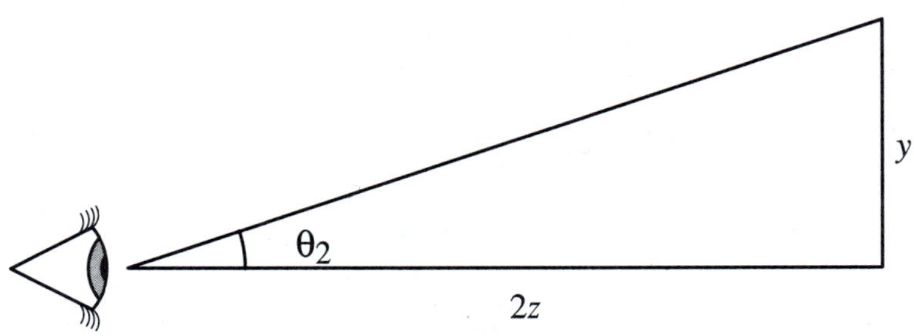

From this new vantage point, $\arctan(y/2z) = \theta_2$. Since y is being divided by twice as much as before, it looks half as high, and $\theta_2 < \theta$. This is the crux of the perspective rule: If height is inversely proportional to the distance, perspective can be obtained by merely dividing the x and y values by the corresponding z value. You, the user, do not have to do this division; it is a function of PHIGS. Perspective occurs in those views where it has been requested (via the EVALUATE VIEW MAPPING MATRIX 3 routine).

Moving the Projection Reference Point

Note that the **projection reference point (PRP)** is *not* necessarily on the n-axis, nor is it necessarily in the n-direction from the center of the view window. It is, however, on the $+n$ side of the view window. Because the PRP does not need to be on the n-axis nor precisely in the n-direction from the center of the view window, this allows useful things to be done, for example, a parallel projection with skew, or stereo imagery—two perspective images with skew.

This "skewability" is illustrated in Figure 7–12. The diagram represents a side view of the UVN space; n goes to your left, v goes up, and u comes out of the page at you.

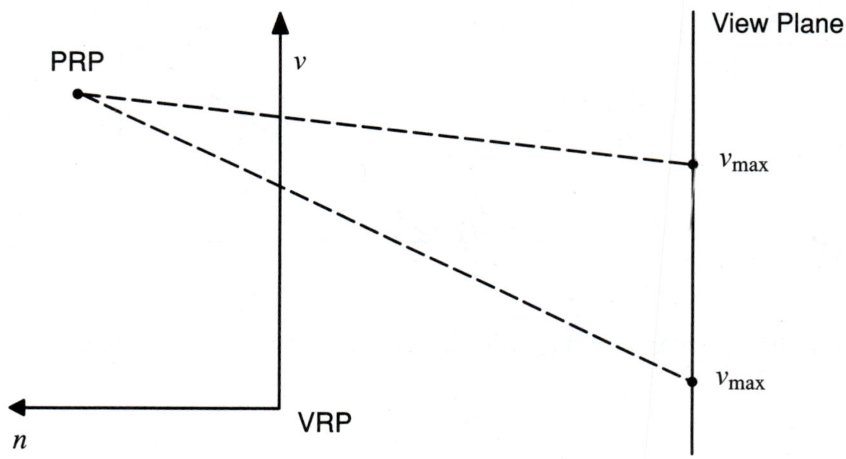

Figure 7–12. Off-axis PRP and View Window

There are several points of note in Figure 7–12:

- The dotted lines are projectors for a perspective view.
- In the illustration the view reference point (VRP) is *not* the "point being looked at," nor is the projection reference point (PRP) on the n-axis, but is off to one side.

- The view plane distance—the distance in n between the VRP and the view plane—is not at $n = 0$ (in this illustration). It has a negative value (in this case) because it is on the negative side of the n-axis.
- The view window is not centered about $v = 0$ (and it need not be centered about $u = 0$ either).

When you put the PRP on the perpendicular line that passes through the center of the view window, you are creating an **orthographic projection**. When you move the PRP off the perpendicular line, you are creating what is known as an **oblique projection**. An oblique projection shows the exact shape of one face of an object and is well suited for displaying objects with detail primarily on one face (for example, a radio). Receding parallel lines are parallel but give the illusion of divergence. Another common application of oblique projections is the "plan oblique" projection used to illustrate exterior and interior building layouts.

Workstation Transformations

The workstation transformation is the final stage in the transformation pipeline (see Figure 7–13). It describes how the workstation window (a portion of NPC space) is mapped onto the workstation viewport (a portion of the display surface). Its main purpose then, is to define how much of the sum of all the oriented views will be displayed.

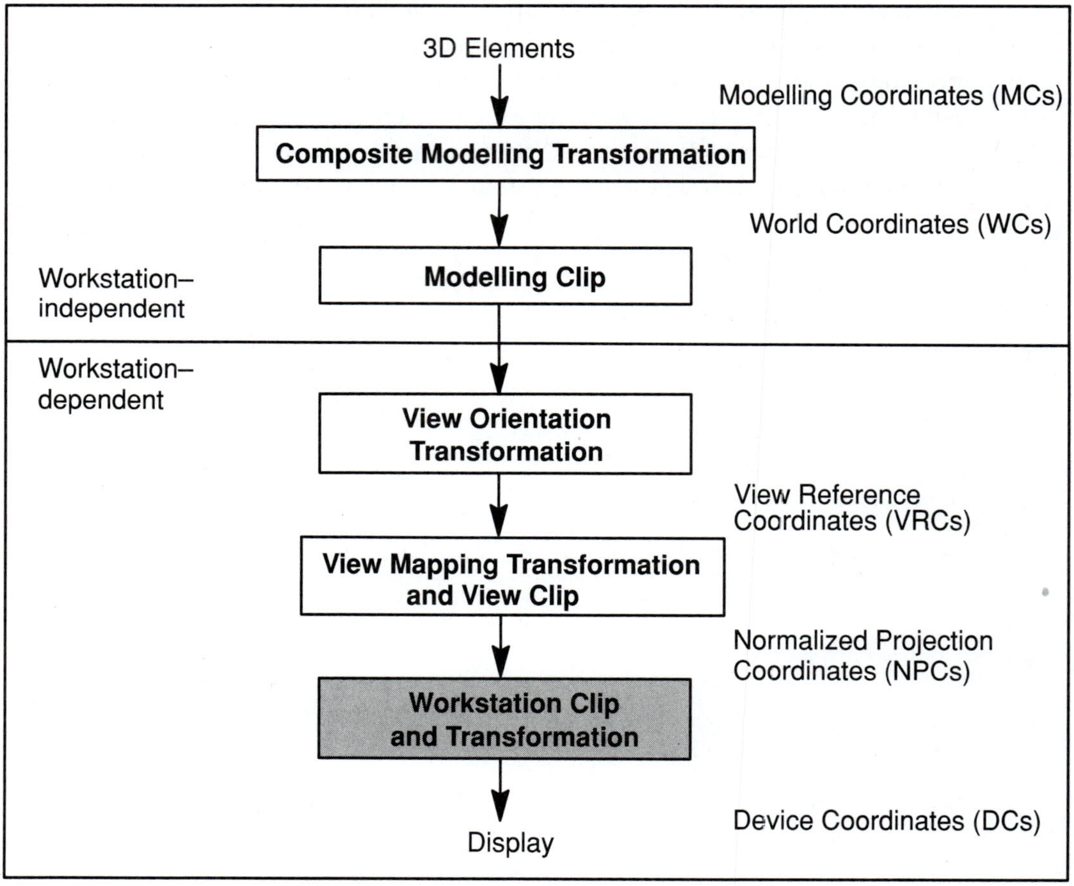

Figure 7–13. The Transformation Pipeline

A workstation transformation is specified by defining the limits of a volume within NPC space (the workstation window) within the range $[0, 1] \times [0, 1] \times [0, 1]$ that is to be mapped onto a specified volume of DC space (the workstation viewport). Workstation window volume and workstation viewport volume limits specify rectangular boxes parallel to the coordinate axes in NPC and DC coordinate space. The rectangular boxes include their boundaries. The workstation transformation can be specified at any time after the workstation has been opened.

The default operation is to map the entire NPC $[0, 1] \times [0, 1] \times [0, 1]$ space onto the largest square portion of the maximum available display space. PHIGS positions this square area in the bottom left-hand corner of the available display space. The ratio of height to width is maintained from NPCs to DCs. PHIGS fits the largest possible picture maintaining the NPC ratio into the viewport. Figure 7–14 shows the default mapping in an X window whose device coordinate limits are 800 in x and 600 in y. Since PHIGS must maintain the height to width ratio, the maximum x device coordinates used is 600.

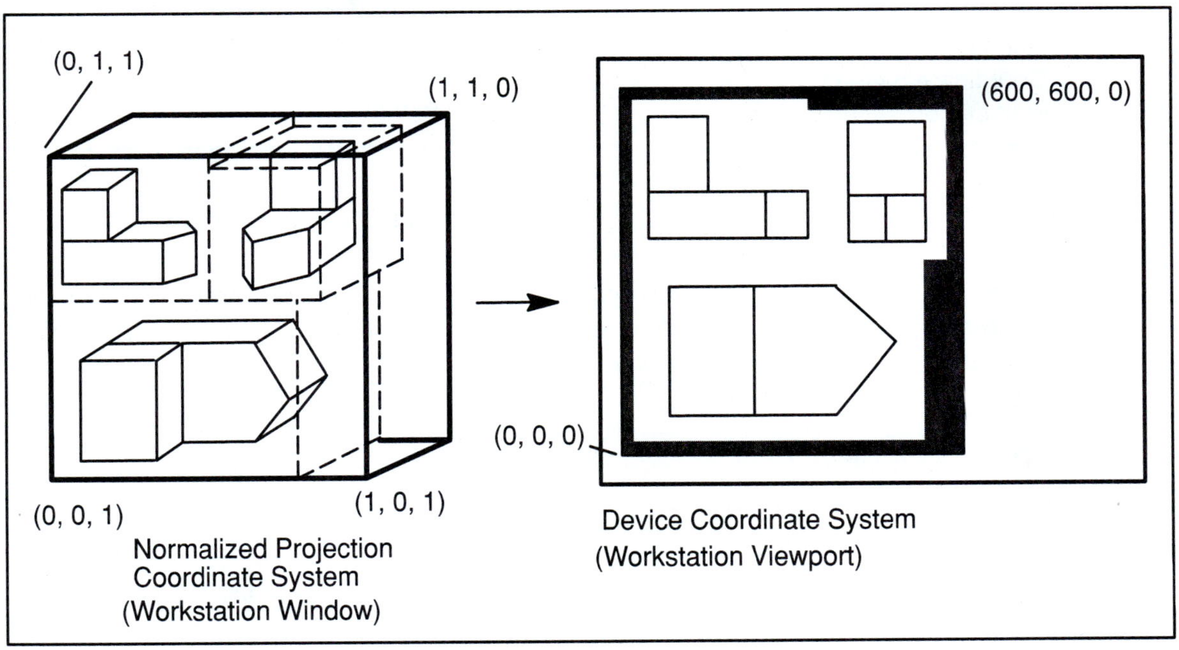

Figure 7–14. Default Window-to-Viewport Mapping with Sample Device Coordinates

You can use the SET WORKSTATION VIEWPORT routine to reposition the workstation viewport within the available display space. For example, Figure 7–15 shows the workstation viewport centered in the available display space.

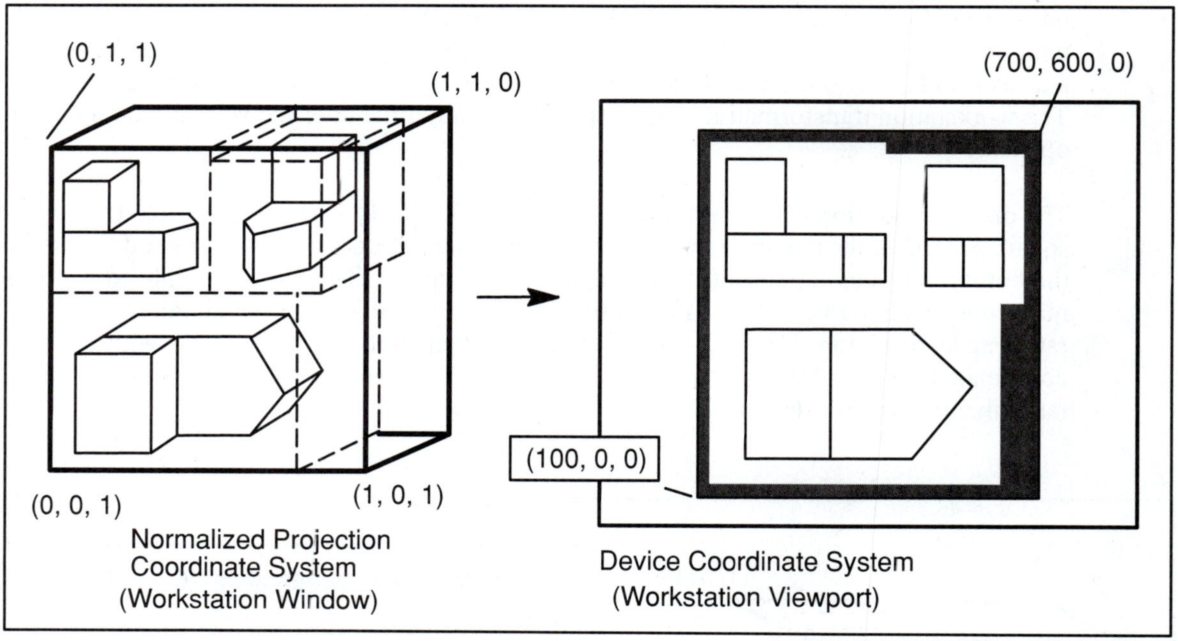

Figure 7–15. Centering the Workstation Viewport within the Available Display Space

In Figures 7–14 and 7–15, the white background of the line drawings (as opposed to the dark gray area surrounding it) is intended to show, in device coordinates, the edges of the regions occupied by the views in NPCs.

Device Coordinates

The device coordinate system maps onto the display space as follows:

- The DC origin is at the bottom left corner of the display space farthest back from the observer.
- *x*, *y*, and *z* increase, respectively, to the right, upward, and toward the observer.

A workstation viewport is a subset of the available display space, always clipped to, onto which an image is drawn. Figure 7–16 shows a workstation viewport mapped into a portion of the available display space in order to give you a sense of where the DC origin is with respect to the image.

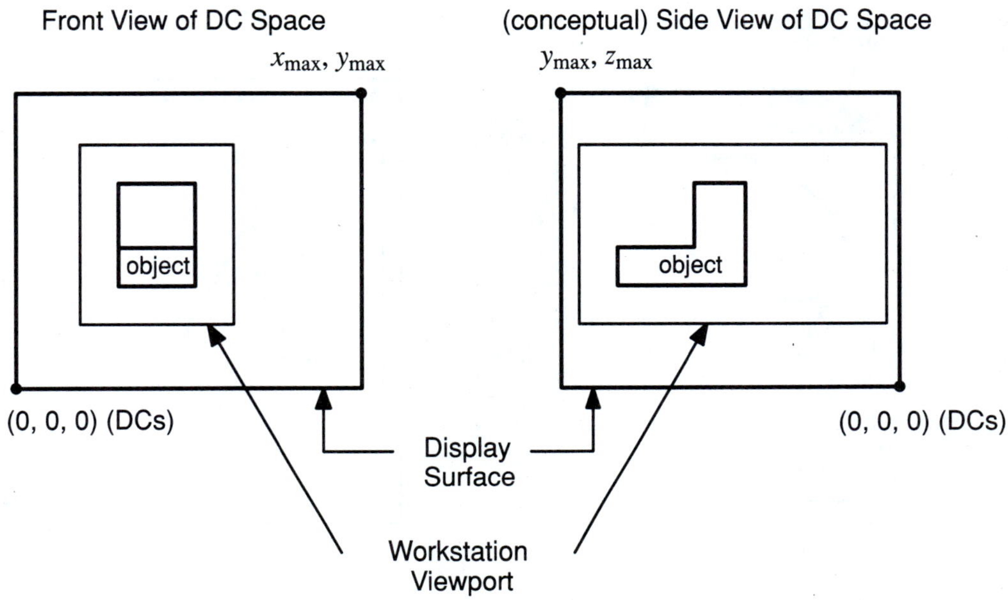

Figure 7–16. The Workstation Viewport and Device Coordinates

Changing the Workstation Window and Workstation Viewport

The following are some reasons for changing the workstation window and workstation viewport:

- Reposition and/or resize the workstation viewport on the display surface as shown in Figure 7–15.
- Display a portion of the NPC space in the workstation viewport. For example, you could zoom in on an object by assigning a small portion of the NPC space to the default viewport (see Figure 7–17).
- Make use of the maximum available *z*-extent, in order to get the best Z-buffer resolution for 3D applications.

Changing either the workstation window or the workstation viewport causes a change in the workstation transformation.

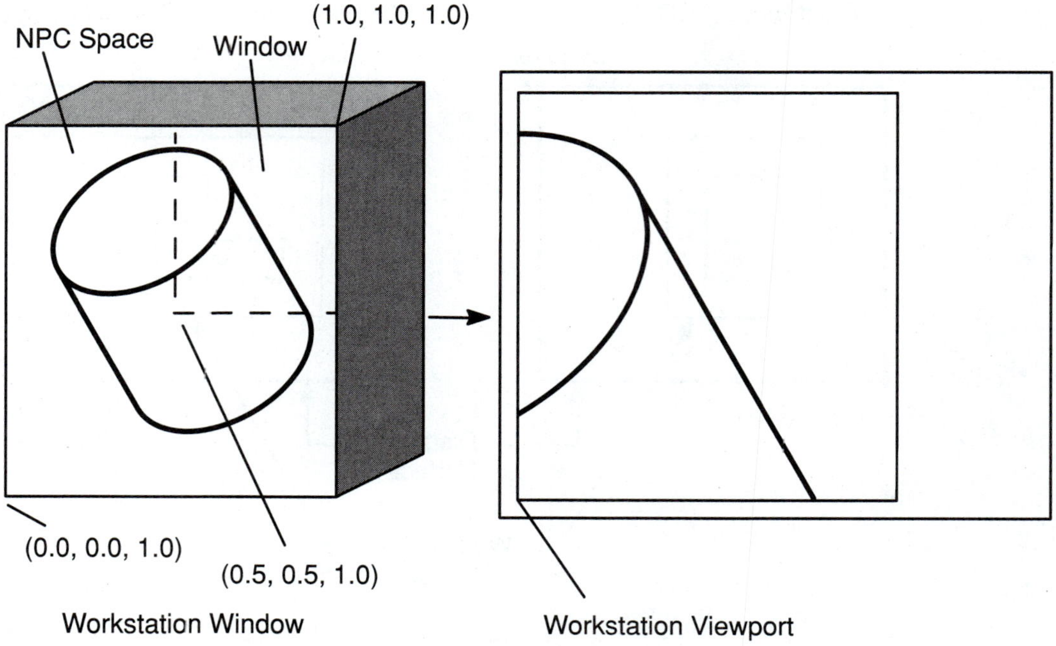

Figure 7–17. Changing the Workstation Window

Using the SET WORKSTATION WINDOW Routine

The workstation window identifies the portion of NPC space that the application wants to display. The default is to display all NPC space. Use the SET WORKSTATION WINDOW and SET WORKSTATION WINDOW 3 routines to specify a portion of NPC space. PHIGS maintains the height-to-width ratio when mapping the workstation window isotropically into the workstation viewport (it is an isotropic mapping).

A workstation window is specified in NPCs. Figure 7–18 shows how workstation windows and projection viewports interact.

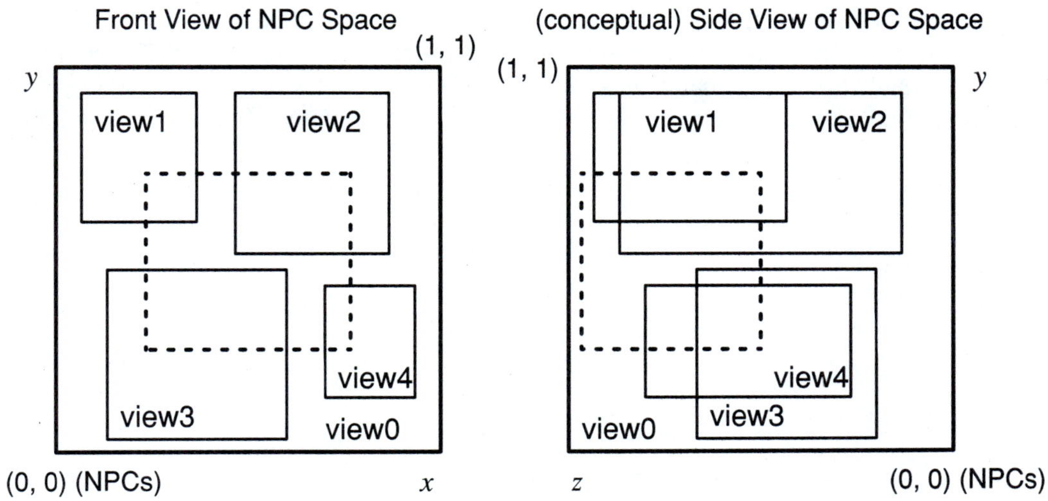

Figure 7–18. Interaction between Projection Viewports and Workstation Window

In Figure 7–18:

- The outlines with solid edges are views (projection viewports). The outline with dashed edges is the workstation window. Note that the views and the workstation window all *have depth.*
- Views are defined within NPC space, and they need not be contained in the workstation window. Thus, you can set up multiple-view layouts simultaneously in different regions of the NPC space and use the workstation window to select desired views.
- Projection viewports may or may not be clipped versions of the VRC view volumes.
- The workstation window is always a clipped version of NPC space. However, it can cover the entire NPC space, essentially clipping nothing.
- View mapping can be anisotropic, but the workstation transformation is always isotropic (at least in x and y; the z dimension is not necessarily transformed isotropically).

Like the SET WORKSTATION VIEWPORT routines, the 2D and 3D SET WORKSTATION WINDOW routines are not implemented in a parallel manner for the FORTRAN binding: The 2D version uses individual values, while the 3D version uses an array containing the values. The C binding versions *are* implemented in a parallel manner. Their calling signatures are

```
call pswkw(workstation_id, xmin, xmax, ymin, ymax)
```

```
pset_ws_win(
    Pint                workstation_id,
    const Plimit        *ws_win_limits
);
```

and

```
call pswkw3(workstation_id, window_limits)
```

```
pset_ws_win3(
    Pint                workstation_id,
    const Plimit3       *ws_win_limits3
);
```

where:

⟨*workstation_id*⟩ is the integer workstation identifier passed to OPEN WORKSTATION.

⟨*ws_win_limits*⟩ and ⟨*ws_win_limits3*⟩ are the 2D and 3D versions of the workstation window limits for the C binding, expressed in NPCs.

⟨*xmin*⟩, ⟨*xmax*⟩, ⟨*ymin* ⟩, and ⟨*ymax*⟩ are real values specifying the workstation window limits for the FORTRAN binding, in NPCs.

⟨*window_limits*⟩ is a six-element real array specifying the workstation window limits for the FORTRAN binding, in NPCs.

For both bindings, the array elements for the workstation window limits are arranged in the order x_{min}, x_{max}, y_{min}, y_{max}, z_{min}, and z_{max}.

Example

Figure 7–17 shows the results of changing the workstation window. In this example a smaller portion of NPC space is mapped to the default workstation viewport, which results in a zoom effect. Notice that the aspect ratio is maintained (a square area of the window is mapped to the default square viewport). The following code shows how to change the workstation window:

```
integer   WorkID                    {workstation ID
real      wkwn(6)                   {window coordinates
data      wkwn / 0.5, 1.0, 0.5, 1.0, 0.0, 0.0 /
...
call pswkw3(WorkID, wkwn)           {set workstation window 3
call prst(WorkID, PALWAY)           {redraw all structures
```

Using the SET WORKSTATION VIEWPORT Routine

The SET WORKSTATION VIEWPORT and SET WORKSTATION VIEWPORT 3 routines specify the location and size of a 2D or 3D viewport, respectively. (Technically, the 2D version also sets a 3D viewport, but it just leaves the *z* values unchanged.) A viewport is a subset of the display space, always clipped to, onto which an image is drawn.

The 2D and 3D versions of the SET WORKSTATION VIEWPORT routines are not implemented in a parallel manner for the FORTRAN binding: The 2D version uses individual values for the minimum and maximum, while the 3D version uses an array containing the values. The C binding versions *are* implemented in a parallel manner. Their calling signatures are

call pswkv(*workstation_id*, *xmin*, *xmax*, *ymin*, *ymax*)

```
pset_ws_vp(
    Pint              workstation_id,
    const Plimit      *ws_vp_limits
);
```

and

call pswkv3(*workstation_id*, *viewport_limits*)

```
pset_ws_vp3(
    Pint              workstation_id,
    const Plimit3     *ws_vp_limits3
);
```

where:

⟨*workstation_id*⟩ is the integer workstation identifier passed to OPEN WORKSTATION.

⟨*ws_vp_limits*⟩ and ⟨*ws_vp_limits3*⟩ are the 2D and 3D versions of the viewport limits for the C binding, expressed in DCs.

⟨*xmin*⟩, ⟨*xmax*⟩, ⟨*ymin*⟩, and ⟨*ymax*⟩ are real values specifying the viewport limits for the 2D FORTRAN binding version, expressed in DCs.

⟨*viewport_limits*⟩ is a six-element real array specifying the viewport limits for the 3D FORTRAN binding version, expressed in DCs.

For both bindings, the array elements for the viewport limits are arranged in the order x_{min}, x_{max}, y_{min}, y_{max}, z_{min}, and z_{max}.

You can change the position and size of the workstation viewport, although they must remain within the maximum device limits. Use INQUIRE DISPLAY SPACE SIZE and INQUIRE DISPLAY SPACE SIZE 3 to determine the maximum DC space available to your application. Typically, this WDT value is fixed over the lifetime of the workstation. Check your implementation documentation to see if and how the display space is affected by window resizing.

To ensure equal scaling on each axis, the default workstation transformation maps the workstation window onto the largest parallelpiped that can fit within the workstation viewport such that:

- The aspect ratio (ratio of height to width) in x and y is preserved.
- The lower left front corner of the workstation window closest to 0.0 in z is mapped to the lower left front corner of the workstation viewport farthest from the observer.
- The z-extent of the workstation window is mapped to the entire z-extent of the workstation viewport.

Figure 7–19 shows the results of repositioning the workstation viewport.

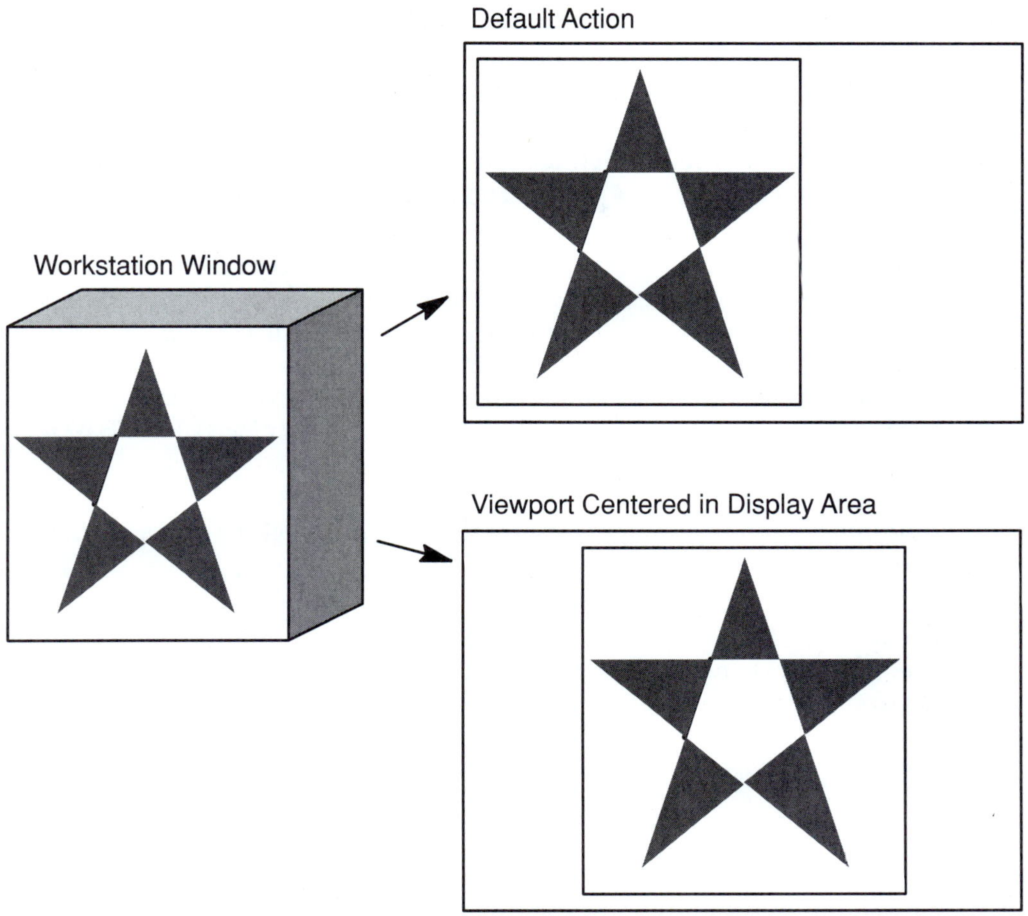

Figure 7–19. Changing the Workstation Viewport

Deferring the Visual Effect of the Workstation Transformation

As with the viewing representation, PHIGS maintains current and requested values for the workstation window and workstation viewport. This is done because it would be confusing to maintain an image with multiple definitions of the workstation window or workstation viewport. See "Deferral of View Modifications" earlier in this chapter for more information.

The SET WORKSTATION WINDOW and SET WORKSTATION VIEWPORT routines set only the *requested workstation window* and *requested workstation viewport* entries in the workstation state list. The *current workstation window* and *current workstation viewport* entries continue to hold the previously set transformation parameters. The current values are set to the requested values when the display is updated (when the existing picture is cleared and a new one is drawn). You can update the workstation by calling either UPDATE WORKSTATION or REDRAW ALL STRUCTURES.

Note that if the display update state is set to ASAP, the workstation transformation is updated immediately (see Chapter 4).

Use INQUIRE WORKSTATION TRANSFORMATION and INQUIRE WORKSTATION TRANSFORMATION 3 to retrieve the current and requested values for the workstation window and the workstation viewport.

Chapter 8

HLHSR

Hidden line/hidden surface removal (**HLHSR**) allows the application to create realistic-looking 3D scenes where objects closer to the observer are drawn "in front of" objects farther away. Portions of the farther-away objects may be invisible because they are obscured by other primitives when observed from the projection reference point or along the projection direction.

When HLHSR is not in effect, objects are drawn as PHIGS encounters the primitive elements in the structure hierarchy. This can result in confusing 3D scenes unless the application programmer carefully arranges the primitives in the CSS. In other words, if you want an object to appear in front of another object, you may have to ensure that the object is drawn last.

Note that you can use the PHIGS PLUS facet culling feature to achieve the effect of hidden surface removal for simple convex objects without using HLHSR. In this case, you would still have to make sure that the closest objects are drawn last.

PHIGS decided to provide a standard mechanism for accessing HLHSR capabilities, while not standardizing the underlying HLHSR methods. This gives implementations a lot of latitude when deciding how (or whether or not) to implement the feature. This means that you should be careful if you write programs that will be portable across different PHIGS implementations. For example, some implementations only implement hidden *surface* removal. In that case, lines and text primitives would not get the HLHSR treatment.

HLHSR is also workstation-dependent, meaning that the feature may be supported only on certain workstation types in the same implementation. For example, the implementation may choose to support HLHSR only on devices that have specialized hardware that can handle the enormous amounts of calculations required when rendering a 3D scene with HLHSR.

Using HLHSR

PHIGS supports two ways of controlling HLHSR:

- A workstation attribute called an **HLHSR mode**. This allows the application to select HLHSR features outside of traversal on a workstation basis.
- An **HLHSR identifier** that allows the application to control HLHSR features during structure traversal.

Using the HLHSR Mode

The calling signatures for the SET HLHSR MODE routine are as follows:

```
call pshrm(workstation_id, hlhsr_mode)
```

```
pset_hlhsr_mode(
    Pint          workstation_id,
    Pint          hlhsr_mode
);
```

where:

⟨*workstation_id*⟩ is the workstation identifier passed to OPEN WORKSTATION.

⟨*hlhsr_mode*⟩ specifies the implementation-dependent HLHSR mode value.

Notice that standard enumerated type values are not defined for the ⟨*hlhsr_mode*⟩ parameter. PHIGS expects the implementation to define its own values. One implementation may use the value to simply turn HLHSR on or off. Another implementation may use the mode value to switch between different HLHSR methods.

The SET HLHSR MODE routine sets the *requested HLHSR mode* entry in the workstation state list.

Using HLHSR Identifiers

The calling signatures for the SET HLHSR IDENTIFIER routine are as follows:

```
call pshrid(hlhsr_id)
```

```
pset_hlhsr_id(
   Pint          hlhsr_id
);
```

where:

⟨*hlhsr_id*⟩ specifies the implementation-dependent HLHSR ID value.

Here again, the implementation decides how to use the ID value. One implementation may simply use a value of 1 to turn the HLHSR mode on and a value of 0 to turn it off during traversal. Another implementation may use the identifier value to switch between different HLHSR methods during traversal.

When PHIGS encounters a *set HLHSR identifier* structure element during traversal, it sets the *current HLHSR identifier* entry in the traversal sate list.

HLHSR Inquiry Routines

INQUIRE HLHSR MODE returns the current and requested HLHSR mode values in the workstation state list and indicates whether or not a change is pending.

INQUIRE HLHSR IDENTIFIERS FACILITIES returns the number of HLHSR identifiers that are supported and the *n*th element in the list of identifiers.

INQUIRE HLHSR MODE FACILITIES returns the number of available HLHSR modes and the *n*th element in the list of available modes.

Determining When the HLHSR Mode Takes Effect

Whether or not the HLHSR mode takes effect immediately depends on the modification and deferral modes; see Chapter 4, *Posting Structures and Controlling Picture Changes.*

Name Sets, Visibility, and HLHSR

Elements of a structure that are "invisible" due to settings of the workstation's invisibility filters and the state of the name set during traversal do not obscure other primitives. See Chapter 13, *Name Sets and Filters*, for a description of invisibility filters.

Some Words on Z-Buffering

Many implementations use a feature called **Z-buffering** to implement HLHSR. A Z-buffer stores *z* values (depth values in device coordinates) for each point in the displayed bitmap. When an image is being rendered, each drawing pixel is added one at a time. At each pixel, the *z* value is compared with the existing value in the Z-buffer. The existing value represents either a background or a previously drawn primitive. If the *z* value for the new primitive is greater than the existing value, then the new value replaces the existing value. In most cases, this corresponds to the understanding that objects closer to the viewer should obscure objects farther away.

The following characteristics of the Z-buffer algorithm should be taken into account:

- When using the Z-buffer hidden surface removal with perspective views, the Z-resolution tends to bunch up toward the hither plane. Thus, to maximize the Z resolution available for an object, you should closely match the front and back planes to the object's size.
- If two adjacent facets share a common edge, but do not share the same vertices along that edge, the edge could be made up of pixels from either facet on a random basis. If the facet edges are different colours, this gives a ragged appearance along the shared edges of the facets. The ragged edges can be eliminated by inserting extra vertices along the edges so that each vertex is shared by both adjacent facets. For example, in Figure 8–1, facet A would have an additional vertex at point 2; facet B would have an additional vertex at point 1; and facet C would have an additional vertex at point 3.

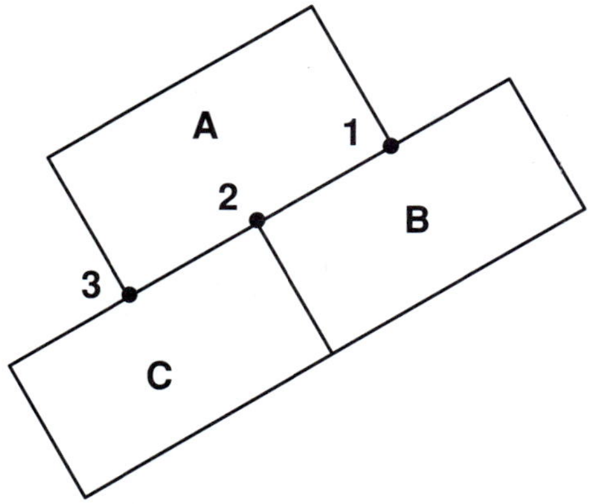

Figure 8–1. Adding Extra Vertices for Smoother Edges

- If two adjacent facets share the same vertices along their common edge, the values in the Z-buffer along that edge are identical for both facets. Since the Z-buffer algorithm draws a new pixel when its *z* value is equal to the value in the Z-buffer, the visible edge is the edge of the last facet rendered. An anomaly occurs when the back-facing cull is off: If the back-facing facet is rendered last and its colours at the edge are different than that of the front-facing facet, then the back-facing edge is visible.

Chapter 9

Using Attributes

The PHIGS standard divides attributes into two main groups: primitive attributes and workstation attributes.

Primitive attributes create structure elements in the CSS. These attributes are bound to the primitive when it is created at structure traversal time. There are geometric and nongeometric primitive attributes (more about this later).

Workstation attributes are set on a workstation basis and can be changed dynamically. This means that they can be changed without having to edit the posted structure network. Workstation attributes include the nongeometric attributes that are workstation-dependent (for example, linetype and linewidth scale factor). Workstation attributes cannot be changed during traversal. They can only be changed in between traversals. Workstation attributes are described in this Chapter in the sections entitled "Bundled Attributes" and "Workstation Attribute Tables."

Primitive attributes are part of the definition of the model. Workstation attributes are applied to the model based on the workstation's display capabilities (for example, whether the workstation can display lines of varying widths).

All primitives are classed as being members of one or more of the following attribute sets: polyline, polymarker, text, interior, and edge. Each primitive is affected by all attributes in one or more of the attribute sets. This makes it easy to determine which attributes affect a particular primitive. For example, the line colour attribute applies to line primitives such as polylines and B-spline curves, but it never applies to text primitives.

Primitive Attribute Types

Each primitive has a set of modifiable attributes that determine how the primitive is displayed at traversal time. There are four types of primitive attributes: **geometric**, **nongeometric**, **viewing**, and **identification**.

Primitive attribute specification routines create structure elements in the CSS. During traversal, these structure elements set corresponding elements in the traversal state list. The traversal state list is described at the beginning of Chapter 4, *Posting Structures and Controlling Picture Changes*.

There is a separate routine for each primitive attribute (except for the ASFs described later in this chapter). The separate routines allow you to specify attribute values one at a time. In addition, you can set related groups of nongeometric attribute values using attribute bundles.

Geometric Attributes

Geometric attributes affect the shape and size of the entire primitive. Table 9–1 lists the geometric attributes.

Table 9–1. Geometric Attributes

Text character height Text character up vector Text text path Text alignment	Annotation text character height Annotation text character up vector Annotation text text path Annotation text alignment
Pattern reference point Pattern width vector Pattern size	Pattern reference vector Pattern height vector

Geometric attributes can only be set individually and do not have corresponding elements in the workstation bundle tables (described later in this section). These attributes are described in Chapter 11, *Using Text*, and Chapter 10, *Primitives and Attributes*, along with the appropriate primitive.

NonGeometric Attributes

Nongeometric attributes affect a primitive's appearance (for example, text font or text colour) or the shape and size of component parts of the primitive (for example, marker size scale factor for polymarkers). These attributes may be specified individually or through an attribute bundle table. Table 9–2 lists the nongeometric attributes.

Table 9–2. NonGeometric Attributes

Linetype	Interior colour (front and back)
Linewidth scale factor	Edge flag
Polyline colour	Edgetype
Marker type	Edgewidth scale factor
Marker size scale factor	Edge colour
Polymarker colour	Data mapping method (front and back)
Text font	Polyline shading method
Text precision	Interior reflectance equation (front and back)
Character expansion factor	Interior shading method (front and back)
Text character spacing	Reflectance properties (front and back)
Text colour	Curve approximation criteria
Annotation text style	Surface approximation criteria
Interior style (front and back)	Trimming curve approximation criteria
Interior stye index (front and back)	Parametric surface characteristics

Note that geometric attributes are transformed during modelling transformations and nongeometric attributes are not.

Except for text attributes (see Chapter 11) and parametric curve and surface attributes (see Chapter 20, *B-Splines*), all of these attributes are described in Chapter 10 along with the primitives that they affect.

Viewing Attributes

Viewing attributes select viewing and HLHSR (hidden line/hidden surface removal) parameters for the workstation-dependent sections of the transformation pipeline. In addition, we have included a number of attributes defined by PHIGS PLUS in this category.

The following lists the viewing attributes:

- HLHSR identifier (see Chapter 8)
- View index (see Chapter 7)
- Colour mapping index (see Chapter 19)
- Depth cue index (see Chapter 18)
- Facet culling mode (see Chapter 15)
- Facet distinguishing mode (see Chapter 15)
- Light source state (see Chapter 17)
- Set reflectance model (see Chapter 17)
- Set rendering colour model (see Chapter 17)

Identification Attributes

Identification attributes determine the visibility, pickability (the ability to be selected interactively by the user), and highlighting of primitives. There are two attributes of this type: name set (see Chapter 13, *Name Sets and Filters*) and pick identifier (see Chapter 14, *Graphical Input*).

Attributes and Aspects

The PHIGS standard uses the concepts of attributes and aspects to describe how an application program controls the appearance of output primitives. You can think of an aspect as a particular property associated with a primitive (for example, colour or linetype). PHIGS determines the aspects of a primitive based on the attributes supplied by the application program. At traversal time, the logic of how the attributes combine determines the aspects of a primitive.

Geometric aspects are controlled by the corresponding attributes. For example, the text character height attribute controls the aspect of text character height.

For nongeometric aspects, the mapping between a particular aspect and its controlling attribute is determined by an **aspect source flag (ASF)**. The aspect source flag tells PHIGS whether to use an attribute from a workstation attribute bundle or from an individual attribute element. Aspect source flags and attribute bundle tables are described in the following section.

Defining Attributes

There are two methods for defining attribute data:

- Change one attribute at a time within the structure. This method is known as **individual attribute selection**.
- Select a group (or bundle) of attributes. This method is known as **bundled attribute selection**. PHIGS has bundles for polyline, polymarker, text, interior, and edge attributes as well as for the data mapping method, reflectance properties, and parametric surface properties attributes.

You can use a combination of both methods. This allows you to switch between different sets of attributes.

All attributes can be set individually. However, only nongeometric attributes can be set through attribute bundles. For example, if you look at the parameters for the SET TEXT REPRESENTATION routine, you will notice that there is no entry for text character height. This is because text character height is a geometric attribute and can only be set by the individual attribute routine SET CHARACTER HEIGHT.

Individual Attributes

Individual attribute elements are structure elements that set one attribute value at a time. During traversal, these attribute-setting structure elements set corresponding elements in the traversal state list. These values are bound to the corresponding primitive during structure traversal. A primitive's attributes cannot be changed after display unless you edit the structure, delete or replace the attribute structure element, or update the picture (via quick update methods or regeneration).

For example, SET POLYLINE COLOUR INDEX creates a structure element that controls the colour of subsequently rendered polylines. The following fragment inserts three attribute-setting structure elements into structure 1 which set the polyline colour index, the text colour index, and the text height. Polyline colour and text colour are nongeometric attributes, and text height is a geometric attribute.

```
real LineX(2), LineY(2)
data LineX /0.1, 0.8/
data LineY /0.1, 0.1/

call popst(1)                     ! open structure
call psplci(3)                    ! set line colour index
call pstxci(2)                    ! set text colour index
call pschh(0.10)                  ! set text height
call ppl(2, LineX, LineY)         ! polyline
call ptx(0.1, 0.2, 'Polyline')    ! text
call pclst                        ! close structure
```

Bundled Attributes

Attribute bundle tables exist on each workstation for the following:

- Edges
- Interiors
- Polylines
- Polymarkers
- Text
- Data mapping method

- Reflectance properties
- Parametric surface properties

Attribute bundle tables are stored in the workstation state list, which makes them independent of the structures in the CSS. Each open workstation has its own state list and thus its own set of attribute bundle tables. Predefined table entries are contained in the workstation description table and are used as initial values.

Each attribute bundle table is an array or "set" of bundled attributes. For example, Table 9–3 shows sample values for entries in the workstation polymarker bundle table. Notice that colours can be expressed either as an index into the workstation colour table or as direct colour values from a colour model such as the RGB or HSV colour models (see Chapter 12 for a description of colour models).

Table 9–3. Sample Values in the Workstation Polymarker Bundle Table

Entry	Marker Type	Marker Size Scale Factor	Polymarker Colour
1	Cross	1.0	Workstation colour table index 1
2	Asterisk	1.5	RGB colour values (1.0, 1.0, 1.0)
3	Cross	2.0	Workstation colour table index 5
⋮			
n	Circle	2.5	HSV colour values (1.0, 0.0, 0.0)

Note that the colour definitions used in Table 9–3 use the PHIGS PLUS method of allowing either an index into the workstation colour table or a direct colour value from a specific colour model. This is referred to as *general colour* and is described in Chapter 12.

Bundled attributes allow the application to describe a set of useful attributes and to access easily those attributes independently of the structure hierarchy. Since attribute bundles are stored independently of structures, you don't have to be concerned about the current set of inherited characteristics each time you render a primitive. This also frees your application from the need to continually and explicitly define attributes.

You can use attribute bundles to take advantage of features available on a particular workstation. For example, use INQUIRE COLOUR FACILITIES to determine whether the workstation supports colour, and then set up attributes accordingly. Different workstations have different capabilities, so not all attribute values are valid on all workstations.

Because it is possible to set bundles differently on different workstations (for example, some workstations do not support colour), the values of their components are restricted to valid values for that workstation. However, such restrictions are not imposed on individual attributes, because individual attributes are defined as part of the model in the CSS (and the CSS is independent of workstation restrictions). The display of a primitive with a value of an individually specified attribute that is invalid on a particular workstation is defined to take place using the traversal default values for that individual attribute. For example, if you use a colour index greater than 1 on a workstation that supports only two colours, PHIGS automatically uses colour index 1.

Defining Attribute Bundle Tables

The following routines define or modify entries in the attribute bundle tables:

- SET EDGE REPRESENTATION
- SET EDGE REPRESENTATION PLUS
- SET INTERIOR REPRESENTATION
- SET INTERIOR REPRESENTATION PLUS
- SET POLYLINE REPRESENTATION
- SET POLYLINE REPRESENTATION PLUS
- SET POLYMARKER REPRESENTATION
- SET POLYMARKER REPRESENTATION PLUS
- SET TEXT REPRESENTATION
- SET TEXT REPRESENTATION PLUS
- SET DATA MAPPING REPRESENTATION
- SET REFLECTANCE REPRESENTATION
- SET PARAMETRIC SURFACE REPRESENTATION

Notice that there are two routines to modify entries in several bundle tables. The "PLUS" routines allow you to set the additional bundle table fields defined for PHIGS PLUS. For example, there is only one edge bundle table. The SET EDGE REPRESENTATION PLUS routine allows you to define all of the fields set by the SET EDGE REPRESENTATION routine with the additional option of specifying edge colour as a general colour (either indexed or direct colour values).

Similarly, use one of the following routines to determine the current representation of an entry in a bundle table:

- INQUIRE ⟨*bundle table name*⟩ REPRESENTATION
- INQUIRE ⟨*bundle table name*⟩ REPRESENTATION PLUS

The number of entries in an attribute bundle table is implementation-dependent. Refer to "Inquiring the Workstation Description Table" in Chapter 22, *Programming with PHIGS*, for a description of the routines that inquire the number of entries in the attribute table.

Selecting an Entry from an Attribute Bundle Table

Recall that each workstation bundle table contains multiple bundles of attributes. You use an index into the table to indicate which bundle is currently active.

Use a SET ⟨*bundle table name*⟩ INDEX routine to create a structure element that selects an entry from the attribute bundle. The following routines select an entry from the appropriate bundle table:

- SET EDGE INDEX
- SET INTERIOR INDEX
- SET BACK INTERIOR INDEX
- SET POLYLINE INDEX
- SET POLYMARKER INDEX
- SET TEXT INDEX
- SET DATA MAPPING INDEX

- SET BACK DATA MAPPING INDEX
- SET REFLECTANCE INDEX
- SET BACK REFLECTANCE INDEX
- SET PARAMETRIC SURFACE INDEX

See Chapter 15 for information on how PHIGS uses "back" routines.

Switching between Individual and Bundled Attributes

You use an aspect source flag (ASF) to switch between individual and bundled attribute settings. There is an ASF for each of those nongeometric primitive attributes that can also be set via bundles. The ASF specifies whether to use the current individual attribute or to use the corresponding value from the currently selected bundle.

The SET INDIVIDUAL ASF routine creates a structure element that selects an aspect source flag for a particular primitive attribute. The calling signatures for the SET INDIVIDUAL ASF routine are as follows:

```
call psiasf(attribute_id, asf_value)
```

```
pset_indiv_asf(
    Paspect        attribute_id,
    Pasf           asf_value
);
```

where:

> ⟨*attribute_id*⟩ identifies the attribute value. Tables 9–4 and 9–5 list the possible values for ⟨*attribute_id*⟩.
>
> ⟨*asf_value*⟩ specifies the aspect source flag value. This parameter can take one of the following values:
>
> – **bundled** (PBUNDL, PASF_BUNDLED)
>
> – **individual** (PINDIV, PASF_INDIV)

The following C and FORTRAN fragments create structure elements that set the ASF for polyline colour to its bundled value:

```
pset_indiv_asf(PASPECT_LINE_COLR_IND, PASF_BUNDLED); /*C binding */

call psiasf(PPLCI, PBUNDL)                         ! FORTRAN binding
```

Remember that selecting bundled is not enough—you must also use a SET ⟨*bundle table name*⟩ INDEX routine to select an entry from the appropriate bundle table.

Default ASF Values

Whether the default ASF values are individual or bundled is implementation-dependent.

Summary of Bundled Attribute Selection

When PHIGS displays a primitive, it determines the values for nongeometric aspects of the primitive as follows:

- If the ASF for an aspect is individual (`PINDIV`, `PASF_INDIV`), PHIGS uses the corresponding individually specified attribute.
- If the ASF for an aspect is bundled (`PBUNDL`, `PASF_BUNDLED`), PHIGS uses the corresponding component of the workstation attribute bundle, pointed to by the bundle index (set by a SET ⟨*bundle table name*⟩ INDEX routine).

Each workstation attribute bundle table has a set of default values that are defined by PHIGS when the application opens a workstation. These values can be inquired by the application (see "Inquiry and Attributes" later in this chapter). If you select a bundle table entry that your application has not yet defined, PHIGS uses the default values for the entry.

Tables 9–4 and 9–5 list the ASF values for standard PHIGS and PHIGS PLUS.

Note that the colour identifiers in Table 9–5 allow you to specify colour either as an index into the workstation colour table or as direct colour values (for example, (1.0, 0.0, 0.0) in the RGB colour model specifies red). The colour identifiers in Table 9–4 only allow for indices into the workstation colour table.

Table 9–4. Aspect Source Flag Identifiers (Standard PHIGS)

FORTRAN	C Binding Value	Description
PLN	PASPECT_LINETYPE	Linetype
PLWSC	PASPECT_LINEWIDTH	Linewidth scale factor
PPLCI	PASPECT_LINE_COLR_IND	Polyline colour index
PMK	PASPECT_MARKER_TYPE	Marker type
PMKSC	PASPECT_MARKER_SIZE	Marker size scale factor
PPMCI	PASPECT_MARKER_COLR_IND	Polymarker colour index
PTXFN	PASPECT_TEXT_FONT	Text font
PTXPR	PASPECT_TEXT_PREC	Text precision
PCHXP	PASPECT_CHAR_EXPAN	Character expansion factor
PCHSP	PASPECT_CHAR_SPACE	Text character spacing
PTXCI	PASPECT_TEXT_COLR_IND	Text colour index
PIS	PASPECT_INT_STYLE	Interior style
PISI	PASPECT_INT_STYLE_IND	Interior stye index
PICI	PASPECT_INT_COLR_IND	Interior colour index
PEDFG	PASPECT_EDGE_FLAG	Edge flag
PEDT	PASPECT_EDGETYPE	Edgetype
PEWSC	PASPECT_EDGEWIDTH	Edgewidth scale factor

Table 9–5. Aspect Source Flag Identifiers (Standard PHIGS PLUS)

FORTRAN	C Binding Value	Description
PPLCOL	PASPECT_LINE_COLR	Line colour
PPMCOL	PASPECT_MARKER_COLR	Marker colour
PTXCOL	PASPECT_TEXT_COLR	Text colour
PINCOL	PASPECT_INT_COLR	Interior colour
PEDCOL	PASPECT_EDGE_COLR	Edge colour
PPSHMD	PASPECT_LINE_SHAD_METHOD	Polyline shading method
PISHMD	PASPECT_INT_SHAD_METHOD	Interior shading method
PDMPMD	PASPECT_DATA_MAP_METHOD	Data mapping method
PREFPR	PASPECT_REFL_PROPS	Reflectance properties
PREFCH	PASPECT_REFL_MODEL	Reflectance model
PBINSY	PASPECT_BACK_INT_STYLE	Back interior style
PBINSI	PASPECT_BACK_INT_STYLE_IND	Back interior style index
PBICOL	PASPECT_BACK_INT_COLR	Back interior colour
PBISHM	PASPECT_BACK_INT_SHAD_METHOD	Back interior shading method
PBDMPM	PASPECT_BACK_DATA_MAP_METHOD	Back data mapping method
PBREFP	PASPECT_BACK_REFL_PROPS	Back reflectance properties
PBREFC	PASPECT_BACK_REFL_MODEL	Back reflectance model
PCAPCR	PASPECT_CURVE_APPROX_CRIT	Curve approximation criteria
PSAPCR	PASPECT_SURF_APPROX_CRIT	Surface approximation criteria
PPASUC	PASPECT_PARAM_SURF_CHARS	Parametric surface characteristics

Use the following procedure to define and use an entry in an attribute bundle table:

1. Define an entry in the appropriate attribute bundle table using a SET ⟨*bundle table name*⟩ REPRESENTATION routine (or use a default entry).

2. Use a SET ⟨*bundle table name*⟩ INDEX routine to create a structure element that selects an entry from the attribute bundle table.

3. Set the ASF value to bundled for each attribute that will take its value from the currently selected attribute bundle (use SET INDIVIDUAL ASF).

Example

The following program uses both individual and bundled attribute values. Numbers inserted into the program identify the sequence of events. This example illustrates the points where ASF values allow you to select individual fields from an entry in an attribute bundle table.

1. Define an entry in the polymarker attribute bundle table. The program defines entry number 2 in the workstation polymarker bundle table as follows: marker type 4 (circle), scale 4.0, and workstation colour table index 1.

2. Set the individual attribute value for marker type to a cross (`PPLUS`).

3. Set the individual attribute value for marker scale factor to 2.0.

   We assume that the default ASF value is individual for all attributes. We will also use the default individual attribute values for polymarker colour index (1), so there is no need to call SET POLYMARKER COLOUR INDEX.

4. Draw the first set of markers. This primitive uses the current individual attribute values because bundles are not used until the specific ASF values are changed from individual to bundled.

5. Create a structure element that selects entry 2 in the polymarker attribute bundle table (entry 1 is the default).

6. Set the ASFs for marker type and size to bundled.

7. Draw the second set of markers. This primitive uses the type and size from entry 2 in the polymarker attribute bundle table.

8. Set the ASF for polymarker type back to individual so that the effective polymarker type will come from the current individual value (cross).

9 Draw the third set of markers. This primitive uses the current individual attribute for marker type and the current bundled values for size.

```
        program markers
C  description: Demonstrate individual and bundled attributes
C               using polymarker primitives.
%include '/sys/ins/phigs.ins.ftn'          { implementation-dependent

      integer*4   ConnectID                { communication channel ID
      integer*4   BufferLength             { memory buffer length
      integer*4   ErrorOut                 { stream for error output
      integer*4   WorkID                   { workstation ID
      parameter   (ConnectID=1, BufferLength=0, ErrorOut=1, WorkID=1)
      integer*4   WorkType                 { workstation type
      parameter   (WorkType=0)             { implementation-dependent
      integer*4   PolyMarkers              { structure ID
      parameter   (PolyMarkers=1)
      real        ScaleFactor              { polymarker scale factor
      integer*4   BundleIndex              { for polymarker bundle table
      integer*4   ColourID              { index into workstation colour table
      parameter   (BundleIndex=2, ColourID=2)
      real MarkerX(4), Marker1Y(4)         { Define coordinates for
      real Marker2Y(4),Marker3Y(4)         { drawing markers.
      data MarkerX  /0.2, 0.4, 0.6, 0.8/
      data Marker1Y /0.7, 0.7, 0.7, 0.7/
      data Marker2Y /0.5, 0.5, 0.5, 0.5/
      data Marker3Y /0.3, 0.3, 0.3, 0.3/

      call popph( ErrorOut, BufferLength)      { open PHIGS
      call popwk( WorkID, ConnectID, WorkType) { open workstation
      ScaleFactor=4.0                          { scale factor for bundle
1     call pspmr(WorkID, BundleIndex, POMARK,  { define an attribute bundle
     +           ScaleFactor, ColourID)

      call popst(PolyMarkers)              { open structure
2     call psmk(PPLUS)                     { set marker type
      ScaleFactor=2.0                      { scale factor for individual
3     call psmksc(ScaleFactor)             { set marker scale factor
4     call ppm(4,MarkerX,Marker1Y)         { draw first set of markers

5     call pspmi(BundleIndex)              { use polymarker bundle 1
6     call psiasf(PMK, PBUNDL)             { use bundled marker type
      call psiasf(PMKSC, PBUNDL)           { use bundled marker size
7     call ppm(4,MarkerX,Marker2Y)         { draw a second set of markers

8     call psiasf(PMK, PINDIV)      { switch back to individual marker type
9     call ppm(4,MarkerX,Marker3Y)         { draw a third set cf markers
      call pclst                           { close structure

      call ppost(WorkID, PolyMarkers, 1.0)  { post structure
      call puwk(WorkID, PPERFO)            { update workstation
      READ *                               { wait for user to press RETURN
```

```
call pupost(WorkID, PolyMarkers)        { unpost structure
call pclwk(WorkID)                      { close workstation
call pclph                              { close PHIGS
stop
end
```

Figure 9–1 shows an approximation of the output of the program, along with a description of which attributes apply to each set of primitives.

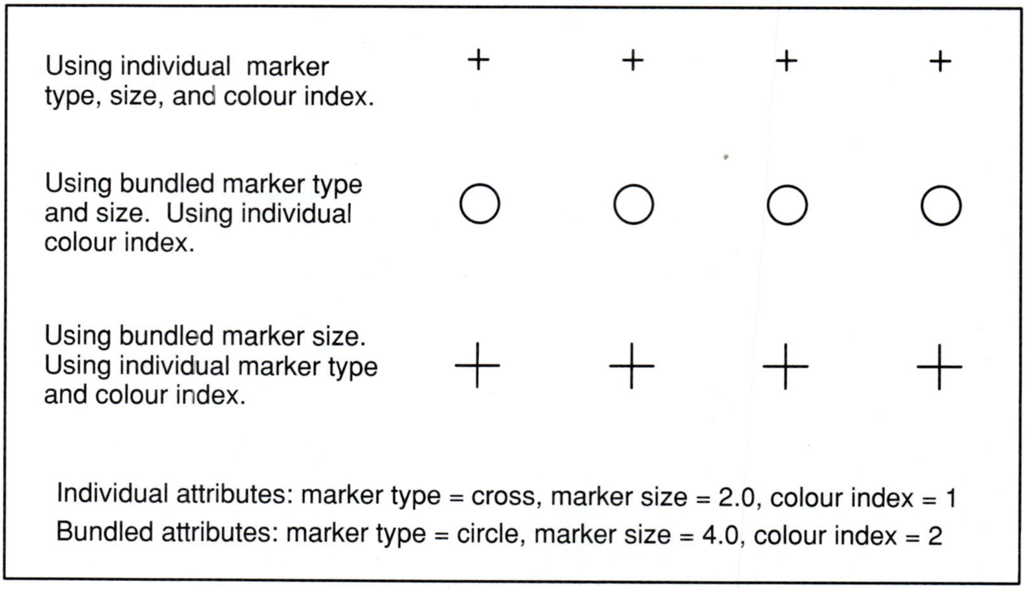

Figure 9–1. Bundled and Individual Polymarker Attributes

Workstation Attribute Tables

Attribute bundles are examples of the workstation attribute tables stored within each workstation description table. The following lists all of the standard workstation attribute tables:

- Polyline bundle table
- Polymarker bundle table

- Text bundle table
- Interior bundle table
- Edge bundle table
- Reflectance bundle table
- Parametric surface bundle table
- Data mapping bundle table
- Colour table
- Pattern table
- View table
- Depth cueing table
- Light source table
- Colour mapping table

Implementations may define additional workstation attribute tables as needed.

Note that the last six tables in the list are not bundle tables and therefore do not have associated individual attributes or ASFs. An entry from each of these tables is always active. The active entry is selected through a corresponding SET ⟨*attribute table*⟩ INDEX element.

All entries in the workstation attribute tables have predefined values. PHIGS places the predefined values in the workstation description table when the application opens a workstation. The current workstation attributes are stored in the workstation state list. You can use a predefined value or define the values of a specific entry. To define a value, use one of the SET ⟨*attribute*⟩ REPRESENTATION routines, where ⟨*attribute*⟩ can be one of the attribute values previously listed.

Recall that several attribute bundles (polyline, polymarker, text, interior, and edge) also have an additional "PLUS" routine that allows you to set the additional PHIGS PLUS values within the tables. For example, SET POLYLINE REPRESENTATION and SET POLYLINE REPRESENTATION PLUS both define entries in the polyline bundle table.

To select an entry of an attribute table, use one of the SET ⟨*attribute*⟩ INDEX routines, where ⟨*attribute*⟩ can be any of the attributes in the previous bulleted list except for colour and pattern. The colour values in the workstation colour table are referenced whenever you provide an indexed colour parameter. Entries in the workstation pattern table are selected by a "set interior style index" attribute.

Inquiry and Attributes

In general, any value that can be set by an application program can also be inquired. This section describes how to inquire attribute values.

Individual Attribute Inquiries

Individual attribute routines create structure elements that modify the workstation state list at traversal time. Use the following routines to inquire the values of a structure element:

- INQUIRE CURRENT ELEMENT CONTENT
- INQUIRE CURRENT ELEMENT TYPE AND SIZE
- INQUIRE ELEMENT CONTENT
- INQUIRE ELEMENT TYPE AND SIZE

Refer to Chapter 5, *Using Structures*, for information on structure inquiry.

Workstation Attribute Table Inquiries

The current values for the workstation attribute tables are stored in the workstation state list. When you open each workstation, PHIGS predefines its workstation state list values from the corresponding workstation description table values.

Workstation state list values can be changed by the application while a workstation is open. The following routines return values from the workstation state list:

- INQUIRE ⟨*attribute*⟩ REPRESENTATION routines return the values associated with a particular entry in an attribute table.

- INQUIRE LIST OF ⟨*attribute*⟩ INDICES routines return the number of defined entries in a workstation attribute table and the *n*th element from the list of defined entries.

Workstation description table values typically do not change over the lifetime of a workstation. The following routines return values from the workstation description table:

- INQUIRE PREDEFINED ⟨*attribute*⟩ REPRESENTATION routines return the predefined values associated with a particular entry in an attribute table. Note that these values are equivalent to the values in the workstation state list until the application explicitly sets the attribute table's values differently.
- INQUIRE ⟨*attribute*⟩ FACILITIES routines return information on the availability and capabilities of certain attributes on a particular workstation type. For example, INQUIRE POLYLINE FACILITIES returns the available linetypes, linewidths, and the number of predefined entries polyline bundle table for a given workstation type.

Refer to Appendix A for a list of attribute inquiry routines.

How Large Is a Workstation Attribute Table?

The number of entries in a given workstation attribute table is implementation-dependent. PHIGS provides the following two routines to allow the application to determine the size of the tables:

- INQUIRE WORKSTATION STATE TABLE LENGTHS
- INQUIRE WORKSTATION STATE TABLE LENGTHS PLUS

Refer to the description of these routines in the section entitled "Inquiring the Workstation Description Table" in Chapter 22.

Attributes and Structure Hierarchy

PHIGS applies attributes to primitives at traversal time. When a structure is traversed, the current attribute settings determine the appearance of its primitives. This "traversal time attribute binding" has two main benefits:

- Subordinate (child) structures inherit the attributes of parent structures. This allows you to execute or reference the same structure several different times and apply a different set of attributes each time.
- You can dynamically change primitive attributes through structure editing.

When a traversal returns from executing a referenced structure, attribute values revert to the values in effect at the time the *execute structure* element was encountered. This means that the part of the structure network potentially affected by an attribute element is the remainder of the structure in which the element occurs and any descendants of the remainder of that structure.

Figure 9–2 shows the traversal path through three structures. Notice that when traversal returns to the calling structure, the attributes in effect before the execute structure call are restored. This example assumes that the ASF for polyline colour index is set to individual. Sample values are used in the workstation colour table entries 0 through 4. The application can set values in the workstation colour table using the SET COLOUR REPRESENTATION routine.

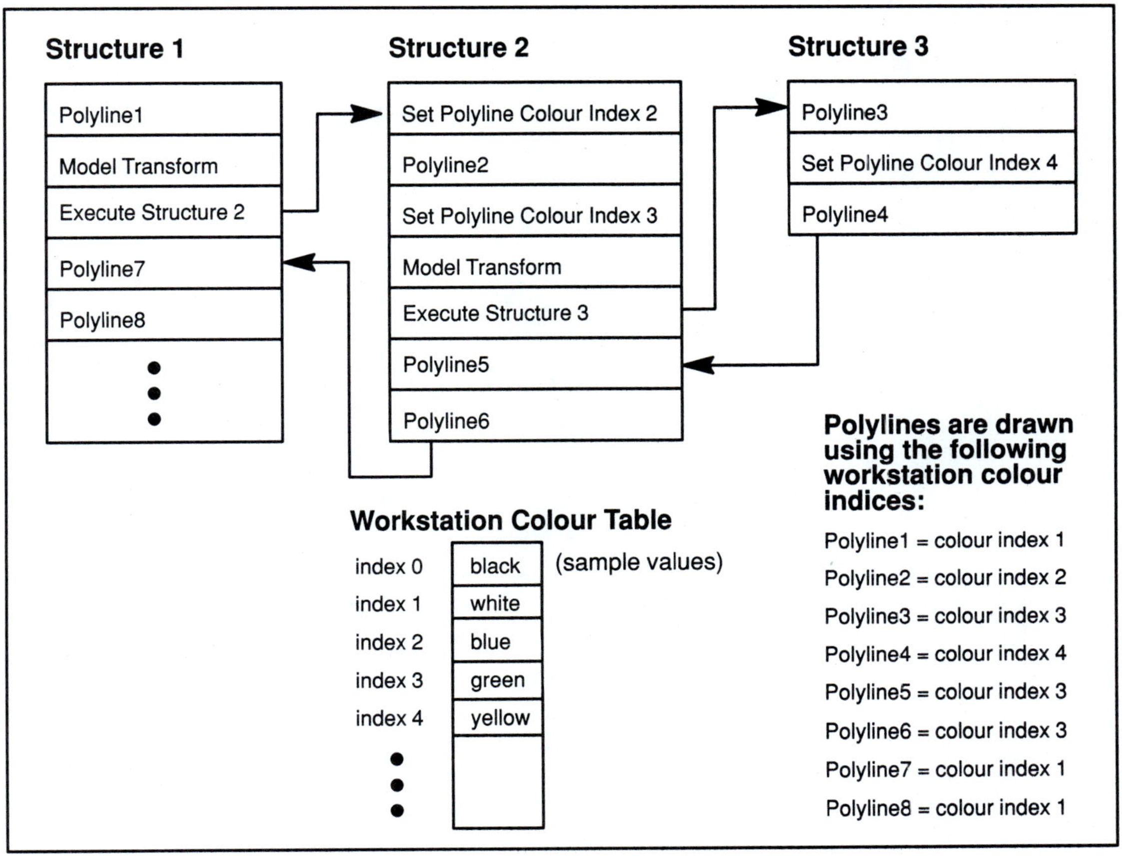

Figure 9–2. Attributes and Structure Hierarchy

Chapter 10

Primitives and Attributes

Primitive routines define objects in the modelling coordinate system. These routines generate structure elements that produce graphical output at structure traversal time. Each time the application program calls an output primitive routine, PHIGS inserts one primitive element into the current open structure.

PHIGS supports the following output primitives:

Polyline	A set of connected lines defined by a point sequence.
Polyline set 3 with colour	A set of unconnected polylines that optionally includes vertex colour values.
Polymarker	A set of markers used to identify positions in modelling coordinate space.
Text	A character string transformed as part of the model.
Annotation text	A character string always drawn parallel to the display surface.
Cell array	A colour grid. Each cell within the grid can be assigned a separate colour.
Fill area	A single planar polygonal area that may be filled in a variety of styles. Edging is not provided for this primitive.

Fill area set A set of independent, coplanar polygonal areas that may be filled in a variety of styles. Edge control is limited to on or off for the entire primitive.

Fill area set with data A set of independent, coplanar polygonal areas that may be filled in a variety of styles. Additional data provides for the following:

- Facet data including facet colour, facet normal, or application–specific facet data
- Vertex data including vertex colours, vertex normals, or application–specific vertex data
- Edge flags for control over individual edges

Set of fill area sets with data A set of independent, non–coplanar polygonal areas as defined by the fill area set with data primitive. The data format allows each vertex to be specified only once, even if several of the facets share it.

Quadrilateral mesh with data A multiplanar, connected quadrilateral mesh primitive that allows specification of facet and vertex data.

Triangle strip with data A multiplanar connection of three–sided facets that allows specification of facet and vertex data.

Triangle set with data A multiplanar set of triangular facets that allows specification of facet and vertex data.

Non–uniform B–spline curve and **non–uniform B–spline curve with colour**
A non–uniform B–spline curve defined by a list of knots and a list of control points. The "with colour" version allows you to supply a "colour spline" for colour interpolation.

Non–uniform B–spline surface and **Non–uniform B–spline surface with data**
A non–uniform B–spline surface defined by a list of knots and a list of control points. The surface *u* and *v* spline orders are implementation–dependent. The surface can optionally be trimmed by any number of curves. The "with data" version allows you to specify a colour spline for colour interpolation or a "data spline" for interpolation of application–dependent data along the surface.

Generalized drawing primitives

The PHIGS standard allows an implementation to define additional output primitives. PHIGS provides a mechanism called generalized drawing primitives (GDPs) to allow the implementation to present the new primitives in a standard format. Circles, arcs, and ellipses are examples of GDPs.

This chapter describes all of these primitives except for text and annotation text (see Chapter 11, *Using Text*) and non–uniform B–spline curves and surfaces (see Chapter 20, *B–Splines*).

The actual appearance of an output primitive on a display device is determined by the value, at structure traversal time, of the following:

- The workstation attributes and primitive attributes
- The modelling, viewing, and workstation transformations

Line Primitives

PHIGS supports the following line primitives:

- Polyline and polyline 3
- Polyline set 3 with colour
- Non–uniform B–spline curve

In addition, some generalized drawing primitives such as circular arcs and elliptical arcs are also considered line primitives and therefore use line attributes (this is implementation–dependent).

Simple Polylines

POLYLINE and POLYLINE 3 each inserts a primitive element into the current open structure, which creates a series of connected line segments. The primitive is called a *polyline* because it can consist of multiple connected lines. At structure traversal time, PHIGS displays the polyline under the interpretation of the polyline attributes. The calling signatures for the POLYLINE routine are as follows:

```
call ppl(n, x, y)
```

```
ppolyline(
    const Ppoint_list        *point_list
);
```

The calling signatures for the POLYLINE 3 routine are as follows:

```
call ppl3(n, x, y, z)
```

```
ppolyline3(
    const Ppoint_list3 *point_list
);
```

where:

⟨*point_list*⟩ is the array of points in MCs for the C binding.

⟨*n*⟩ is the number of points in the polyline for the FORTRAN binding.

⟨*x*⟩, ⟨*y*⟩, and ⟨*z*⟩ are the coordinates of the vertices of the polyline for the FORTRAN binding, expressed in MCs.

The following C program uses the 2D polyline routine to create the design in Figure 10–1:

```
#include <phigs.h>                /* get PHIGS definitions for C */
#include <stdio.h>                /* get standard I/O definitions */
#include <math.h>
#define  deg    *M_PI/180.        /* convert degrees to radians */

main()                                   /* file "Polyline.c" */
{
    Pint         WorkstnID = 1;          /* workstation identifier */
    Pint         ConnID;                 /* connection identifier */
    Pint         WorkstnType = POIDDX;   /* implementation-dependent */
    Pint         TheStructure = 1;   /* structure ID (chosen by user) */
    Ppoint    PentagonPts[100]; /* for the xy values of the polyline */
    Ppcint_list Pentagon;                /* for the polyline */
    float        Theta = 0, Radius = 0;  /* temporary variables */
    int          I;                      /* loop control variable */

    popen_phigs(stderr, 0);              /* errors go to "stderr" */
    pescape_u4("/dev/screen/phigs_window", &ConnID);
```

```
    popen_ws(WorkstnID, ConnID, WorkstnType);
    popen_struct(TheStructure);
    for (I = 0; I < 100; I++) {          /* for each point... */
        PentagonPts[I].x = (Radius * cos(Theta) + 1) * 0.5;
        PentagonPts[I].y = (Radius * sin(Theta) + 1) * 0.5;
        Theta += 73 deg;                 /* roughly pentagonal */
        Radius += 0.01;                  /* enlarge it slightly */
    }
    Pentagon.num_points = 100;
    Pentagon.points = PentagonPts;
    ppolyline(&Pentagon);                /* polyline with 100 points */
    pclose_struct();
    ppost_struct(WorkstnID, TheStructure, 1.0);
    pupd_ws(WorkstnID, PFLAG_PERFORM);   /* (regeneration flag) */
    pclose_ws(WorkstnID);
    pclose_phigs();
}
```

The following is a FORTRAN binding version of the same program:

```
include 'phigs.f1.h'        ! get the PHIGS aliases
program Polyline            ! program "Polyline.f"
include 'phigs.f2.h'        ! get the PHIGS constants

integer*4  WorkstnID        ! workstation identifier
parameter (WorkstnID=1)     ! value chosen by the user
integer*4  ConnID           ! connection identifier
integer*4  WorkstnType      ! workstation type
parameter (WorkstnType=POIDDX) ! implementation-dependent
integer*4  TheCurve         ! display list structure root
parameter (TheCurve=1)      ! value chosen by the user
real  X(100), Y(100)        ! points for polyline
integer*4  I                ! loop control variable

real  rad, deg              ! type the statement function
rad(deg)=  ((deg)*3.14159265358979/180.) ! convert degrees to radians
integer*4 fdopen         ! to get file descriptor

call popph(fdopen(fnum(7), 'w'//char(0)), 0)     ! open PHIGS
call pue004('/dev/screen/phigs_window', ConnID) ! get connection ID
call popwk(WorkstnID, ConnID, WorkstnType)      ! open workstation
call popst(TheCurve)                        ! open display list structure
Theta=0.                                    ! direction
```

```
Radius=0.                                  ! distance from center
do I=1, 100                                ! for each point...
   X(I)=(Radius*cos(Theta)+1)*.5           ! \  convert polar coords.
   Y(I)=(Radius*sin(Theta)+1)*.5           ! /  to rectangular coords.
   Theta=Theta+rad(73.)                    ! roughly pentagonal
   Radius=Radius+0.01                      ! enlarge it slightly
end do
call ppl(100, X, Y)                        ! polyline with 100 points
call pclst                                 ! close display list structure
call ppost(WorkstnID, TheCurve, 1.0)       ! mark structure for display
call puwk(WorkstnID, PPERFO)               ! update the workstation
call pclwk(WorkstnID)                      ! close workstation
call pclph                                 ! close PHIGS
stop                                       ! stop processing
end                                        ! end of program
```

Figure 10–1 shows the output of the program:

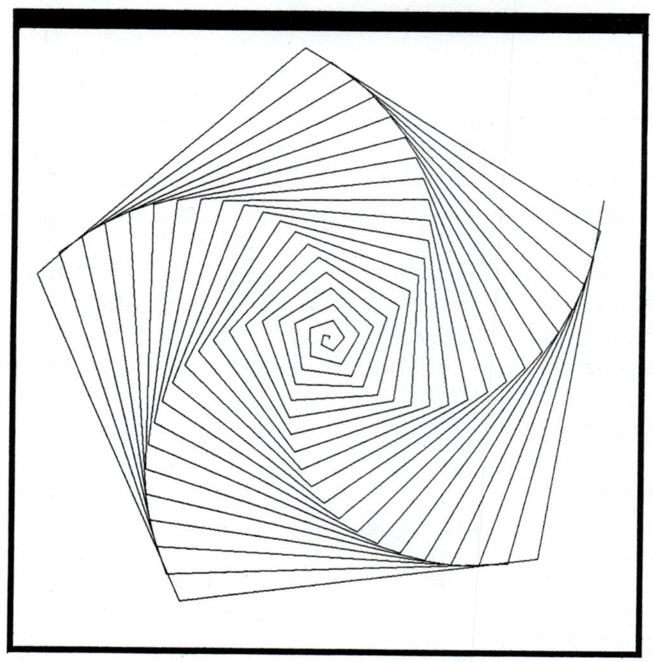

Figure 10–1. Polyline

Polyline Set 3 with Colour

A polyline set is comprised of a number of unconnected 3D polylines. At traversal time, a set of connected lines is generated starting from the first vertex coordinate of each sequence and ending at the last vertex for each set.

Figure 10–2 shows a polyline set made up of four polylines. The first is a box. The last three are straight lines within the box, each having different *y* values. Each polyline in the set is numbered. *z* values are omitted to make the illustration easier to read. Assume $z = 0.0$.

Polyline	Vertex	x	y
1	1	0.2	0.2
	2	0.8	0.2
	3	0.8	0.8
	4	0.2	0.8
	5	0.2	0.2
2	6	0.3	0.7
	7	0.7	0.7
3	8	0.3	0.5
	9	0.7	0.5
4	10	0.3	0.3
	11	0.7	0.3

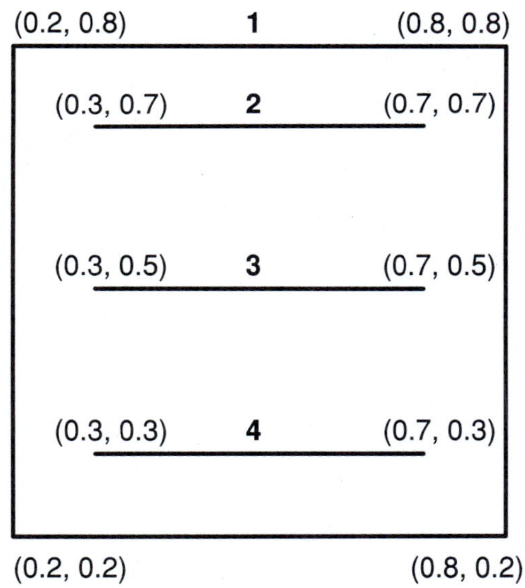

Figure 10–2. Four Polylines in a Polyline Set (assume z = 0.0)

Use the POLYLINE SET 3 WITH COLOUR routine to create a polyline set 3 with colour primitive. The C binding calling signature for the routine is as follows:

```
ppolyline_set3_colr(
   Pint                 colr_type,      /* colour type              */
   const Pvertex3_set   *vertex_data    /* list of vertex lists     */
);
```

where:

⟨*colr_type*⟩ indicates the colour type for vertex colour values. If the application supplies vertex colour information, this parameter indicates whether the colour information is in the form of a list of indices into the workstation colour table or a list of colour values in one of the supported colour types. Possible values are as follows (see Chapter 12 for more information on these colour values):

- PCOLR_INDIRECT. Application supplies indices into the workstation colour table.
- PCOLR_RGB. Application supplies direct RGB colour values.
- PCOLR_CIELUV. Application supplies direct CIELUV colour values.
- PCOLR_HSV. Application supplies direct HSV colour values.
- PCOLR_HLS. Application supplies direct HLS colour values.

⟨*vertex_data*⟩ contains the vertex data. PHIGS defines the Pvertex3_set data type as follows:

```
Pvertex3_set
  typedef struct {
    Pint            num_lists;     /* number of vertex lists */
    Pvertex3_list  *vertices;      /* list of vertex lists   */
}Pvertex3_set;
```

where:

num_lists is the number of polylines in the polyline set. For example, there are four polylines in Figure 10–2.

vertices is the list of vertex lists. The Pvertex3_list data type is defined as:

```
Pvertex3_list
typedef struct {
  Pint       num_vertices;          /* number of vertices   */
  Pint    num_data_per_vertex;      /* # data values/vertex */
  Ppoint3    *vertex_points;        /* vertex point list    */
  Pcolrv_ptr vertex_colrvs;         /* vertex colour list   */
  Pvec3      *vertex_norms;         /* vertex normal list   */
  Pfloat     *vertex_data;          /* vertex data lists    */
}Pvertex3_list;
```

where:

`num_vertices` is the number of vertices in the polyline.

`vertex_points` is the list of *x*, and *y*, and *z* values of the vertices in MCs.

`vertex_colrvs` is a list of values that apply to the corresponding vertex points. Depending on the value of ⟨*colr_type*⟩, this parameter is either a list of indices into the workstation colour table, or a list of direct colour values.

If you are not supplying vertex colour values, set `vertex_colrvs.colr_inds` to NULL.

The polyline set 3 with colour primitive only uses the vertex points and vertex colour portions of the data pointed to by `*vertices`. The additional fields are used by other "with data" primitives described later in this chapter.

In order to use vertex colour interpolation, you must set the polyline shading method to colour, using SET POLYLINE SHADING METHOD. See Chapter 17, *Lighting and Shading*.

Polyline Set 3 with Colour Example

The following fragment defines a polyline set 3 with colour primitive similar to the one shown in Figure 10–3. While the illustration is in black and white, the fragment defines the primitive with vertex colours (red, white, and blue points on the triangles).

```
#define Red            1.0, 0.0, 0.0    /* RGB for red */
#define White          1.0, 1.0, 1.0    /* RGB for white */
#define Blue           0.0, 0.0, 1.0    /* RGB for blue */
    ...
    Pvertex3_set       Triangles;
    Pvertex3_list      TriangleData[25];
    Prgb               TriangleColours[4] = {Red, White, Blue, Red};
    Ppoint3            XYZdata[25][4];
    ...
    Triangles.num_lists = 25;
    Triangles.vertices = TriangleData;
    for (I = 0; I < 25; I++) {
        TriangleData[I].num_vertices = 4;
        for (J = 0; J < 4; J++) {
            XYZdata[I][J].x = ...;
```

```
            XYZdata[I][J].y = ...;
            XYZdata[I][J].z = ...;
        }
        TriangleData[I].vertex_points = &(XYZdata[I][0]);
        TriangleData[I].vertex_colrvs.colr_reps.rgb = TriangleColours;
        TriangleData[I].vertex_norms = NULL;
        TriangleData[I].vertex_data = NULL;
    }
    ppolyline_set3_colr(PCOLR_RGB, &Triangles);
```

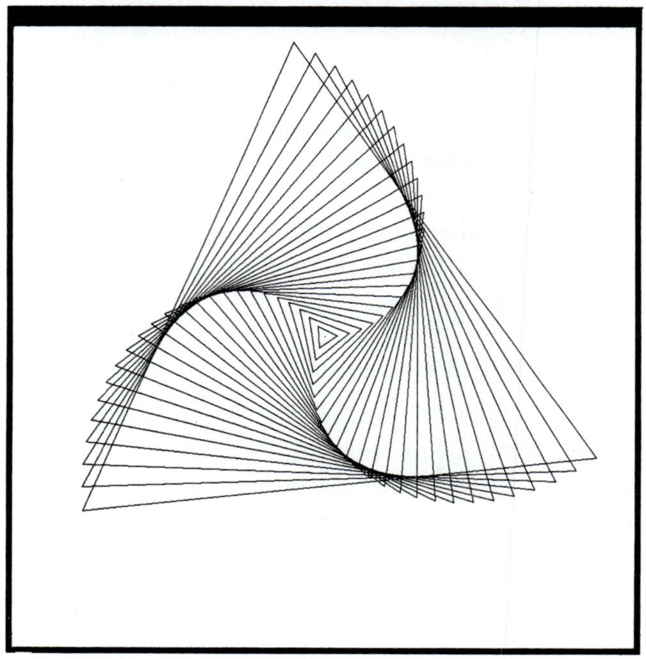

Figure 10–3. Polyline Set 3 with Data

Line Attributes

PHIGS supports the following nongeometric attributes for line primitives:

- Linetype
- Linewidth scale factor
- Polyline colour specification
- Polyline shading method
- Curve approximation criteria

In addition, viewing and identification attributes also apply (see Chapter 9). There are no geometric attributes for line primitives.

Line attributes apply to the following primitives:

- Polylines
- Polyline sets
- Non–uniform B–spline curves
- Some GDPs, such as circular arcs and elliptical arcs (implementation–dependent)

Curve approximation criteria types only apply to curved linear primitives. They do not apply to polylines or polyline set primitives.

Individual Line Attributes

This section describes the individual line attributes. Refer to Chapter 9 for a comparison of individual and bundled attributes.

Linetype

SET LINETYPE creates a structure element that selects the pattern with which lines are drawn. PHIGS uses this value when the *current linetype ASF* entry in the traversal state list is set to individual.

PHIGS defines four linetypes (see Table 10–1). Implementations can add their own linetypes using negative identifiers.

Table 10–1. Linetypes

FORTRAN Name	C Binding Name	Description
`PLSOLID`	`PLINE_SOLID`	Solid
`PLDASH`	`PLINE_DASH`	Dashed
`PLDOT`	`PLINE_DOT`	Dotted
`PLDASD`	`PLINE_DASH_DOT`	Dashed–dotted

Linewidth Scale Factor

SET LINEWIDTH SCALE FACTOR creates a structure element that sets the multiplier used to calculate the linewidth. PHIGS uses this value when the *current linewidth scale factor ASF* entry in the traversal state list is set to individual.

PHIGS multiplies the workstation–dependent nominal linewidth by the linewidth scale factor and then maps this value to the nearest available linewidth. When the linewidth scale factor is less than or equal to 0.0, PHIGS uses the minimum linewidth available on the workstation (that is, it displays the thinnest displayable line).

Linewidths are workstation–dependent. If a workstation is unable to display variable linewidths, PHIGS uses the nominal linewidth.

Polyline Colour Specification

The following routines set the individual polyline colour attribute:

- SET POLYLINE COLOUR INDEX
- SET POLYLINE COLOUR

Both of these routines create structure elements. See Chapter 12, *Using Colour*, for a comparison of the routines and for information on how PHIGS uses the corresponding ASF values.

Polyline Shading Method

SET POLYLINE SHADING METHOD creates a structure element that sets the polyline shading method for the following primitives:

- Polyline set 3 with data
- Non–uniform B–spline curve with colour

PHIGS uses this value when the *current polyline shading method ASF* entry in the traversal state list is set to individual. The polyline shading method allows colour interpolation between vertex colours. Note that vertex colour interpolation works independently of lighting (see Chapter 17).

Curve Approximation Criteria

SET CURVE APPROXIMATION CRITERIA creates a structure element that sets the curve approximation criteria type for the following primitives:

- Non–uniform B–spline curves
- Some GDPs, such as circular arcs and elliptical arcs (implementation–dependent)

Curves are typically drawn as segments. The curve approximation controls how short these segments are, and therefore how smooth the curve looks (see Chapter 20). PHIGS uses this value when the *current curve approximation criteria ASF* entry in the traversal state list is set to individual.

Bundled Line Attributes

There are two routines for setting values in the workstation polyline bundle table:

- SET POLYLINE REPRESENTATION defines an entry in the polyline attribute bundle table. Each entry consists of the following:
  - An index value that identifies the entry in the bundle table
  - Linetype
  - Polyline colour index

- Linewidth scale factor

- SET POLYLINE REPRESENTATION PLUS can also be used to define an entry in the polyline attribute bundle table. This routine allows you to set additional values as defined for PHIGS PLUS. Each entry consists of the following:
  - An index value that identifies the entry in the bundle table
  - Linetype
  - Linewidth scale factor
  - Polyline colour type (indexed or direct)
  - For indexed colour, an index into the workstation colour table
  - For direct colour, colour values from a specified colour model
  - Polyline shading method
  - Curve approximation criteria

SET POLYLINE INDEX creates a structure element that selects an entry from the polyline bundle table.

Use the SET INDIVIDUAL ASF routine to specify whether nongeometric line attributes should be taken from individual attribute values or from the currently selected entry of the polyline bundle table.

Markers

The PHIGS standard does not provide a dot or point primitive. Instead, the **polymarker** primitive is defined as a generalization of the point concept. Typical uses of markers are marking the data points on a graph and as reference points.

POLYMARKER and POLYMARKER 3 each inserts a primitive element into the current open structure that creates a set of markers. At structure traversal time, a series of marker glyphs is displayed under the interpretation of the polymarker attributes.

A marker has only one geometric characteristic (its position) and has three nongeometric attributes affecting its type, scaling, and colour. Markers are centered on their positions, which are specified in modelling coordinates. The exact appearance of the marker glyph is manifested only on the display surface, and not in world coordinate space. Only the position of the marker, not the marker glyph, is affected by the transformation pipeline. This means that if you rotate the view, the marker may change position on the screen, but it will not appear rotated or skewed.

If the marker position is outside the viewport clipping region, the marker is not displayed. If the position is inside the viewport clipping region and part of the marker is outside the clipping region, the results are implementation–dependent.

The calling signatures for the POLYMARKER routine are as follows:

```
call ppm(n, x, y)
```

```
ppolymarker(
    const Ppoint_list      *point_list
);
```

The calling signatures for the POLYMARKER 3 routine are as follows:

```
call ppm3(n, x, y, z)
```

```
ppolymarker3(
    const Ppoint_list3     *point_list
);
```

where:

⟨*point_list*⟩ is the array of polymarker positions in MCs for the C binding.

⟨*n*⟩ is the number of polymarkers for the FORTRAN binding.

⟨*x*⟩, ⟨*y*⟩, and ⟨*z*⟩ are the polymarker positions for the FORTRAN binding (in MCs).

Polymarker Attributes

PHIGS supports the following nongeometric attributes for marker primitives:

- Marker type
- Marker size scale factor

- Marker colour specification

In addition, viewing and identification attributes also apply (see Chapter 9).

Individual Polymarker Attributes

This section describes the individual polymarker attributes. Refer to Chapter 9 for a comparison of individual and bundled attributes.

Marker Type

SET MARKER TYPE creates a structure element that specifies the marker type. PHIGS uses this value when the *current marker type ASF* entry in the traversal state list is set to individual. Table 10–2 lists the five standard marker types. The default value is implementation–dependent.

Table 10–2. Marker Types

FORTRAN Name	C Binding Name	Description
PPOINT	PMARKER_DOT	Single pixel (.)
PPLUS	PMARKER_PLUS	Plus sign (+)
PAST	PMARKER_ASTERISK	Asterisk (*)
POMARK	PMARKER_CIRCLE	Circle (o)
PXMARK	PMARKER_CROSS	Diagonal cross (X)

Marker Size Scale Factor

The SET MARKER SCALE FACTOR routine creates a structure element that specifies the multiplier used to size markers. PHIGS uses this value when the *current marker size scale factor ASF* entry in the traversal state list is set to individual.

PHIGS multiplies the workstation–dependent nominal polymarker scale factor by the specified polymarker scale factor and then maps this value to the nearest available scale factor.

The default scale factor is 1.0. Values less than 1.0 result in a scale factor of 1.0. Scaling has no effect on marker type PPOINT/PMARKER_DOT (one pixel).

Marker Colour Specification

There are two routines to set the individual polymarker colour attribute:

- SET POLYMARKER COLOUR INDEX
- SET POLYMARKER COLOUR

Both of these routines create structure elements. SeeChapter 12 for a comparison of the two routines and for information on how PHIGS uses the corresponding ASF values.

Bundled Polymarker Attributes

There are two routines to set values in the workstation polymarker bundle table:

- SET POLYMARKER REPRESENTATION defines an entry in the polymarker attribute bundle table. Each entry consists of the following:
  - An index value that identifies the entry in the bundle table
  - Marker type
  - Marker size scale factor
  - Polymarker colour index
- SET POLYMARKER REPRESENTATION PLUS also defines an entry in the polymarker attribute bundle table. This routine allows you to set additional values as defined for PHIGS PLUS. Each entry consists of the following:
  - An index value that identifies the entry in the bundle table
  - Marker type
  - Marker size scale factor
  - Polymarker colour type (indexed or direct)
  - For indexed colour, an index into the workstation colour table
  - For direct colour, colour values from a specified colour model

SET POLYMARKER INDEX creates a structure element that selects an entry from the polymarker bundle table.

Use the SET INDIVIDUAL ASF routine to specify whether attributes should be taken from individual attribute values or from the currently selected entry of the polymarker bundle table.

Polymarker Example

The following C program uses the polymarker primitive and several of its attributes:

```
#include <phigs.h>                    /* get PHIGS definitions for C */
#include <stdio.h>                    /* get standard I/O definitions */
main()                                /* file "Polymarker.c" */
{
    Pint         WorkstnID = 1;       /* workstation identifier */
    Pint         ConnID;              /* connection identifier */
    Pint         WorkstnType = POIDDX; /* implementation-dependent */
    Pint         TheStructure = 1;     /* structure ID  */
    static float dY[] = {              /* oscillation about Y values */
                 0.0, -0.05, 0.07, 0.0};
    static Ppoint MarkerPts[4] = {    /* XYs for each set of markers */
       0.1, 0.0,  0.4, 0.0,  0.6, 0.0,  0.9, 0.0};      /* Ys change */
    Ppoint_list MarkerData;            /* whole marker set */
    int          I, J;                 /* loop control variables */
    popen_phigs(stderr, 0);            /* errors go to "stderr" */
    pescape_u4("/dev/screen/phigs_window", &ConnID);
    popen_ws(WorkstnID, ConnID, WorkstnType);
    popen_struct(TheStructure);
    pset_marker_size(10.0);
    MarkerData.num_points = 4;         /* same every time... */
    for (I = PMARKER_DOT; I <= PMARKER_CROSS; I++) {
        for (J = 0; J < 4; J++)        /* define line's Y values */
            MarkerPts[J].y = I * 0.2 - 0.1 + dY[J];
        pset_marker_type(I);
        MarkerData.points = MarkerPts;
        ppolymarker(&MarkerData);
        ppolyline(&MarkerData);       /* polyline joins like markers */
    }
    pclose_struct();
    ppost_struct(WorkstnID, TheStructure, 1.0);
    pupd_ws(WorkstnID, PFLAG_PERFORM);    /* (regeneration flag) */
    pclose_ws(WorkstnID);
    pclose_phigs();
}
```

Figure 10–4 shows the output of the program.

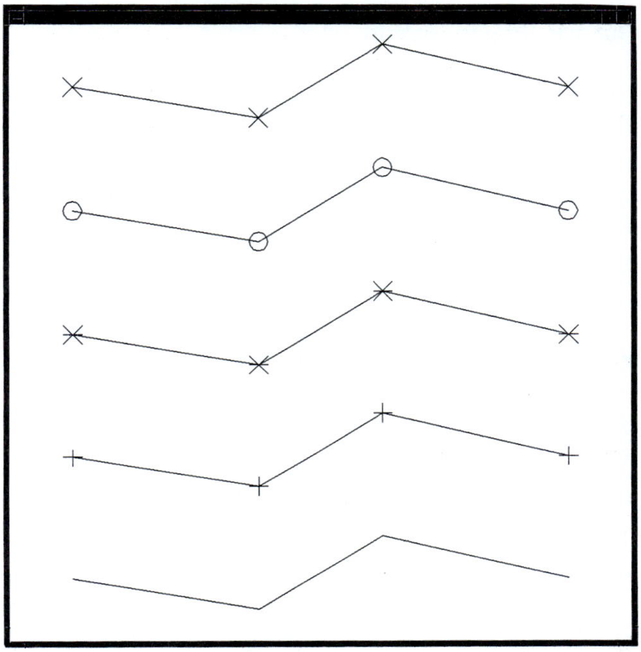

Figure 10–4. Polymarkers

Area–defining Primitives

PHIGS defines the following area–defining primitives:

- Fill area
- Fill area set
- Fill area set with data
- Set of fill area sets with data
- Cell array, cell array plus

- Triangle set with data
- Triangle strip with data
- Quadrilateral mesh with data
- Parametric surfaces (non–uniform B–spline surface and non–uniform B–spline surface with data)

All of these primitives are described in this chapter, except for the parametric surfaces (see Chapter 20). We describe the primitives first and then describe all of the attributes that apply to area–defining primitives at the end of the chapter.

The Optional Data of the "with Data" Primitives

A number of primitives in this chapter are defined as "with data," meaning that besides other attributes that apply to area–defining primitives, they also allow additional attribute data in the primitive definition. The following list summarizes the features and shows where to look for more information:

- Each area–defining primitive is made up of one or more **facets**. Chapter 15, *Front and Back Facet Processing*, describes facets in detail. Figure 10–5 shows several examples of primitives with facets.

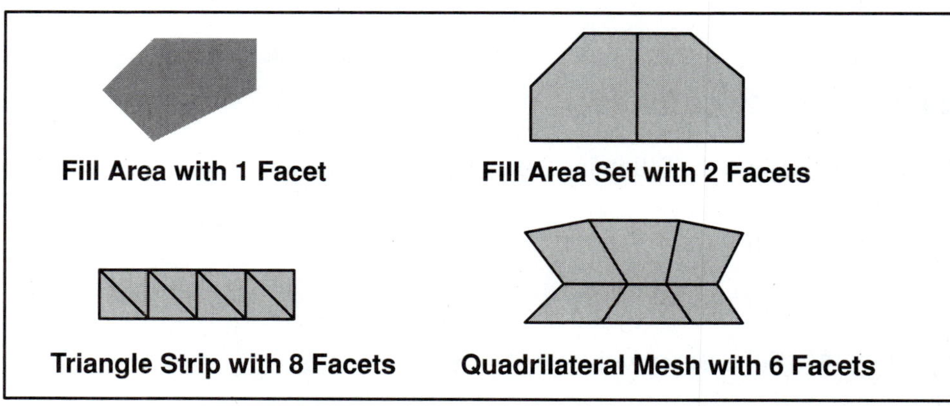

Figure 10–5. Examples of Primitives with Facets

- The **data mapping method** allows an application to specify the source of intrinsic colour. **Intrinsic colour** is the colour associated with a primitive that is independent of lighting, depth cueing, and colour mapping (see Chapter 16, *Intrinsic Colour and Data Mapping*). The source of the intrinsic colour can be one of the following:

  – Interior colour

  – Facet colour

  – Application–supplied facet data

  – Vertex colour

  – Application–supplied vertex data

  Temperature and pressure values are examples of application–supplied data.

- **Edge flags** allow you to turn individual edges on and off. You specify edge flags in an integer array that corresponds to the list of vertices in the point list. Each edge flag is applied to the edge following each vertex. Values can be either off or on. See "Edge Attributes" in the "Individual Attributes for Area–defining Primitives" section later in this chapter.

- The **facet normal** defines the direction the facet is facing. This can spare PHIGS from having to calculate the direction, thus saving time. Facet normals are useful for facet culling (see Chapter 15) and for lighting calculations (see Chapter 17).

- The **vertex normal** defines the direction of the facet at a particular vertex. It is used only for lighting calculations. Vertex normals can make a surface consisting of multiple facets appear smooth when lighting is applied (see Chapter 17). Vertex normals do not have to match the facet normal and, in fact, are not very useful if they *do* match.

- **Facet colours** give you the option of applying a colour specification to all the facets in each area–defining primitive (see Chapter 17). Colour specification can be in the form of either an index into the workstation colour table (indirect colour) or direct colour values.

- **Vertex colour** specification allows you to interpolate colours across polygonal areas (see Chapter 17). Colour specification can be in the form of either an index into the workstation colour table (indirect colour) or direct colour values.

Figure 10–6 shows a single facet for a "with data" primitive with facet and vertex normals. Each facet can also have associated colour and application–specific data such as pressure or temperature. Likewise, each vertex can have associated colour and application–specific data.

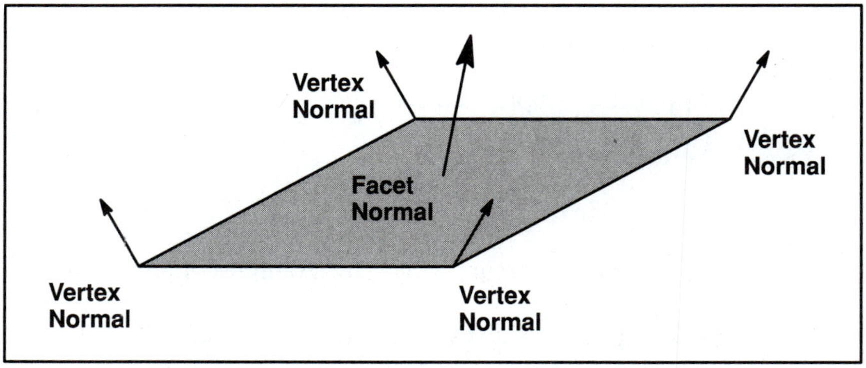

Figure 10–6. Fill Area Set with Data Facet and Vertex Information

Front and Back Facets

Each facet of an area–defining primitive has two sides: front and back. When viewing the facet, the eye sees either the front face or the back face. If back–facing attributes are enabled (using a face–distinguishing mode), the back–facing facets can be rendered differently to let the viewer know that he or she is seeing the back. Another option is to cull (ignore) facets based on their direction. This can speed up rendering by reducing the number of primitives that are drawn.

The application identifies the front face of fill area primitives as follows:

- For fill area and fill area set primitives, the application indirectly specifies the front face by the order of vertex points.
- For the "with data" primitives, the application has the option of supplying a facet normal that indicates the front face of the primitive. If the application does not supply a facet normal, then the order of points indirectly specifies the front face.

As you can see from this description, front and back are relative to the definition of the primitive, not to the position of the viewer. Refer to Chapter 15 for the details of how PHIGS determines the front face from the order of points.

Fill Area and Fill Area Set

This section describes the following primitives:

- Fill area
- Fill area set
- Fill area set with data
- Set of fill area sets with data

Fill area boundaries may cross. The interior of the fill area is defined as follows: The set of all points such that a ray starting at one point and going in any direction to infinity crosses the fill area boundary an odd number of times (see Figure 10–7). If the ray passes through a vertex tangentially, the intersecting count is not affected.

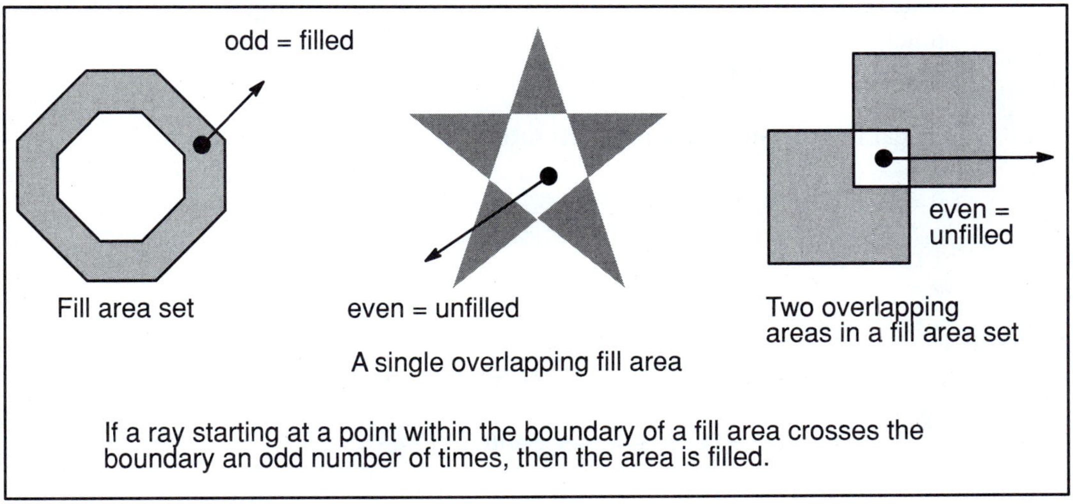

Figure 10–7. Determining whether an Area Is Filled

An area with less than three vertices is considered degenerate. PHIGS stores the element in the CSS, but it has no visual effect at traversal time.

Fill Area versus Fill Area Set

The following lists the differences between fill area and fill area set primitives:

- A fill area primitive represents a *single* enclosed area described by a sequence of vertices which, when connected by straight lines, form the boundary of the area. No edge control is provided for fill area primitives. This means there is no visual difference between the boundary and the interior. The star in Figure 10–7 is a single fill area primitive with five vertices (one at each point of the star).
- The fill area set primitives allow the application to define *multiple* coplanar areas. That is, you can define multiple areas, but they must all be on the same plane. Refer to the two fill area set primitives in Figure 10–7. Another important feature of fill area set primitives is that they allow edge control. For fill area set primitives, edges are either all on or all off. The "with data" primitives allow individual edge control.

Fill Area Primitives

FILL AREA and FILL AREA 3 each inserts a primitive element into the open structure that creates a polygonal area. A fill area primitive represents a single enclosed area described by a sequence of vertices which, when connected by straight lines, form the boundary of the area. No edge control is provided.

The calling signatures for the FILL AREA routine are as follows:

```
call pfa(num_pts, x_values, y_values)
```

```
pfill_area(
   const Ppoint_list      *point_list
);
```

The calling signatures for the FILL AREA 3 routine are as follows:

```
call pfa3(num_pts, x_values, y_values, z_values)
```

```
pfill_area3(
   const Ppoint_list3     *point_list
);
```

where:

⟨*point_list*⟩ is the array of boundary points in MCs for the C binding.

⟨*num_pts*⟩ is the number of boundary points in the fill area for the FORTRAN binding.

⟨*x_values*⟩, ⟨*y_values*⟩, and ⟨*z_values*⟩ are the coordinates of the vertices of the fill area for the FORTRAN binding, expressed in MCs.

Fill Area Attributes

The following attributes apply to fill area primitives:

- Interior style (front and back)
- Interior style index (front and back)
- Interior colour (front and back)
- Pattern attributes
- Interior shading method (front and back)
- Rendering colour model (front and back)
- Interior reflectance model (front and back)
- Interior reflectance properties (front and back)
- Viewing and identification attributes (see Chapter 9).

See "Individual Attributes for Area–defining Primitives," later in this chapter.

Fill Area Example

The following program creates two fill area primitives. One is a simple polygon, and the other is self–intersecting. PHIGS automatically closes a fill area so the first and last points specified need not be identical.

C Binding:

```
#include <phigs.h>                  /* get PHIGS definitions for C */
#include <stdio.h>                  /* get standard I/O definitions */

main()                                    /* file "FillArea.c" */
{
    Pint        WorkstnID = 1;          /* workstation identifier */
    Pint        ConnID;                 /* connection identifier */
    Pint        WorkstnType = POIDDX;   /* implementation dependent */
    Pint        TheStructure = 1;   /* structure ID (chosen by user) */
    static Ppoint Obj1Pts[5] =            /* points for filled area */
               {0.1, 0.1,  0.4, 0.1,  0.4, 0.5,  0.3, 0.6,  0.1, 0.6};
    static Ppoint_list Obj1Data = {5, Obj1Pts};
    static Ppoint Obj2Pts[8] =          /* points for filled area */
                {0.6, 0.4,  0.8, 0.4,  0.8, 0.8,  0.7, 0.8,  0.7, 0.7,
                 0.9, 0.7,  0.9, 0.9,  0.6, 0.9};
    static Ppoint_list Obj2Data = {8, Obj2Pts};

    popen_phigs(stderr, 0);               /* errors go to "stderr" */
    pescape_u4("/dev/screen/phigs_window", &ConnID);
    popen_ws(WorkstnID, ConnID, WorkstnType);
    popen_struct(TheStructure);
    pset_int_style(PSTYLE_SOLID);         /* set interior style */
    pfill_area(&Obj1Data);
    pfill_area(&Obj2Data);
    pclose_struct();
    ppost_struct(WorkstnID, TheStructure, 1.0);
    pupd_ws(WorkstnID, PFLAG_PERFORM);  /* (regeneration flag) */
    pclose_ws(WorkstnID);
    pclose_phigs();
}
```

FORTRAN Binding:

```
include 'phigs.f1.h'        ! get the PHIGS aliases
program FillArea            ! program "FillArea.f"
include 'phigs.f2.h'        ! get the PHIGS constants

integer*4  WorkstnID        ! workstation identifier
parameter (WorkstnID=1)     ! value chosen by the user
integer*4  ConnID           ! connection identifier
integer*4  WorkstnType            ! workstation type
parameter (WorkstnType=POIDDX)    ! implementation-dependent
integer*4  TheStructure           ! display list structure root
parameter (TheStructure=1)        ! value chosen by the user
real X1(5), Y1(5), X2(8), Y2(8) ! points for polygons
data X1 /.1, .4, .4, .3, .1/          ! \
data Y1 /.1, .1, .5, .6, .6/          !  \ define both
data X2 /.6, .8, .8, .7, .7, .9, .9, .6/ !  / polygons' data
data Y2 /.4, .4, .8, .8, .7, .7, .9, .9/ ! /
integer*4 fdopen                  ! to get file descriptor

call popph(fdopen(fnum(7), 'w'//char(0)), 0)     ! open PHIGS
call pue004('/dev/screen/phigs_window', ConnID) ! get connection ID
call popwk(WorkstnID, ConnID, WorkstnType)       ! open workstation
call popst(TheStructure)    ! open display list structure
call psis(PSOLID)           ! set interior style
call pfa(5, X1, Y1)         ! polygon 1 (simple)
call pfa(8, X2, Y2)         ! polygon 2 (self-intersecting)
call pclst          ! close display list structure
call ppost(WorkstnID, TheStructure, 1.) ! mark structure for display
call puwk(WorkstnID, PPERFO)            ! update the workstation
call pclwk(WorkstnID)                   ! close workstation
call pclph                  ! close PHIGS
stop                        ! stop processing
end                         ! end of program
```

Figure 10–8 shows the output of the program.

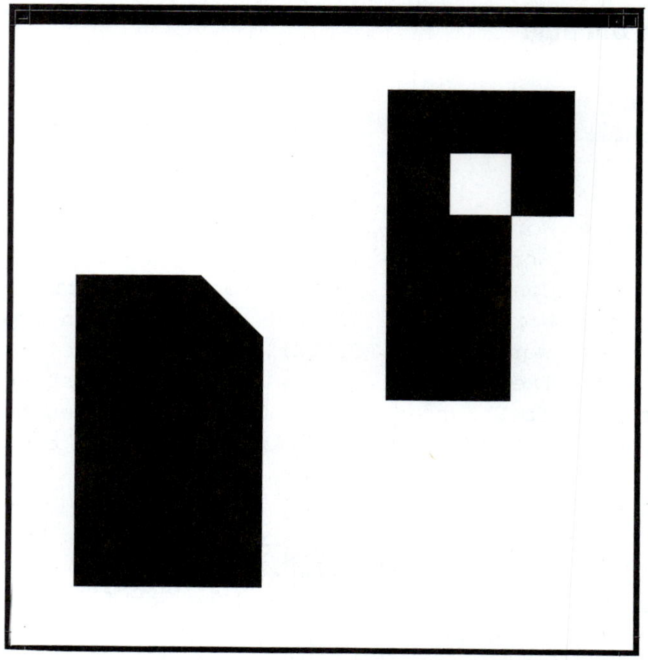

Figure 10–8. Fill Area

Fill Area Set Primitives

FILL AREA SET and FILL AREA SET 3 each inserts a primitive element into the current open structure that creates a set of fill areas. The fill area set primitives differ from the fill area primitives in that multiple coplanar areas can be defined and the boundaries can be made to be distinguishable from the interior. Use fill area set primitives for the following:

- When edge control is needed
- To create multiple coplanar areas that must be treated as a single entity

All subareas must lie on the same plane. PHIGS automatically closes each subarea, so the first and last points of each subarea need not be specified as the same.

PHIGS renders the interiors of all the subareas in a fill area set with a single style. Edges are either distinguishable (on) or not distinguishable (off) for the entire primitive.

The calling signatures for the FILL AREA SET routine are as follows:

```
pfas (num_areas, final_vertices, x_values, y_values)
```

```
pfill_area_set(
   const Ppoint_list_list      *point_list
);
```

The calling signatures for the FILL AREA SET 3 routine are as follows:

```
pfas3 (num_areas, final_vertices, x_values, y_values, z_values)
```

```
pfill_area_set3(
   const Ppoint_list_list3     *point_list
);
```

where:

> ⟨*point_list*⟩ is the "list of point lists" for the C binding in MCs. Each point list includes the *x*, *y* (and *z* for 3D) coordinates of each vertex in that fill area. The maximum number of points allowed is implementation–dependent.
>
> ⟨*num_areas*⟩ is the number of fill areas for the FORTRAN binding.
>
> ⟨*final_vertices*⟩ is an array of integers that specifies the index into ⟨*x_values*⟩, ⟨*y_values*⟩, and ⟨*z_values*⟩ of the last vertex of each fill area in the set for the FORTRAN binding.
>
> ⟨*x_values*⟩, ⟨*y_values*⟩, and ⟨*z_values*⟩ are the lists of *x*, *y*, and *z* values of the vertices in MCs for the FORTRAN binding.

Each fill area is completely defined consecutively.

For the FORTRAN binding, the ⟨*final_vertices*⟩ parameter allows you to identify the end of each fill area in the set. For example, the outside fill area in Figure 10–9 has four vertices (PHIGS automatically closes the fill area). In this case, the first element in the ⟨*final_vertices*⟩ array is 4. The table in Figure 10–9 shows the vertices that belong to each fill area in the set. So, to specify the three fill areas, the ⟨*final_vertices*⟩ array must have three elements: 4, 8, and 12.

Vertex	x	y
1	0.1	0.2
2	0.9	0.2
3	0.9	0.8
4	0.1	0.8
5	0.2	0.3
6	0.4	0.3
7	0.4	0.7
8	0.2	0.7
9	0.6	0.3
10	0.8	0.3
11	0.8	0.7
12	0.6	0.7

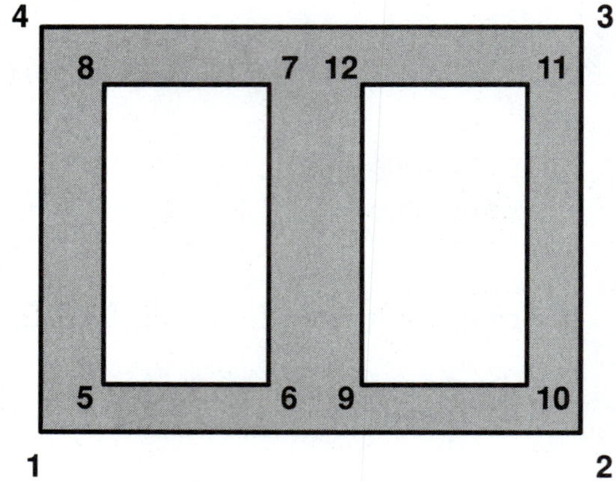

For FORTRAN binding, the final_vertices array contains 4, 8, and 12.

Figure 10–9. Fill Area Set

Fill Area Set Attributes

The same attributes apply to fill area set primitives as for fill area primitives with the addition of edge attributes (see "Individual Attributes for Area–defining Primitives", later in this Chapter).

Fill Area Set Example

The following C binding program draws the 2D fill area set illustrated in Figure 10–9. The fill area set is made up of three fill areas representing a polygon with two holes. Refer to the description in Figure 10–7 of what portions of a fill area set primitive get filled.

```
#include <phigs.h>                         /* get PHIGS definitions for C */
#include <stdio.h>                         /* get standard I/O definitions */

main()                                     /* file "FillAreaSet.c" */
{
    Pint          WorkstnID = 1;           /* workstation identifier */
```

```
    Pint        ConnID;               /* connection identifier */
    Pint        WorkstnType = POIDDX;   /* implementation-dependent */
    Pint        TheStructure = 1;  /* structure ID (chosen by user) */
    static Ppoint OutlinePts[4] =
                {{0.1, 0.2}, {0.9, 0.2}, {0.9, 0.8}, {0.1, 0.8}};
    static Ppoint_list OutlineData = {4, OutlinePts};
    static Ppoint Hole1Pts[4] =
                {{0.2, 0.3}, {0.4, 0.3}, {0.4, 0.7}, {0.2, 0.7}};
    static Ppoint_list Hole1Data = {4, Hole1Pts};
    static Ppoint Hole2Pts[4] =
                {{0.6, 0.3}, {0.8, 0.3}, {0.8, 0.7}, {0.6, 0.7}};
    static Ppoint_list Hole2Data = {4, Hole2Pts};
    static Ppoint_list BlockPts[3] =
                {4, OutlinePts, 4, Hole1Pts, 4, Hole2Pts};
    static Ppoint_list_list BlockData =
                {3, BlockPts};

    popen_phigs(stderr, 0);          /* errors go to "stderr" */
    pescape_u4("/dev/screen/phigs_window", &ConnID);
    popen_ws(WorkstnID, ConnID, WorkstnType);
    popen_struct(TheStructure);
    pset_int_style(PSTYLE_SOLID);  /* set interior style */
    pset_edge_flag(PEDGE_ON);      /* set edge flag */
    pfill_area_set(&BlockData);
    pclose_struct();
    ppost_struct(WorkstnID, TheStructure, 1.0);
    pupd_ws(WorkstnID, PFLAG_PERFORM);  /* (regeneration flag) */
    pclose_ws(WorkstnID);
    pclose_phigs();
}
```

Here is the FORTRAN binding version of the same program (see Figure 10–9):

```
include 'phigs.f1.h'             ! get the PHIGS aliases
program FillAreaSet              ! program "FillAreaSet.f"
include 'phigs.f2.h'             ! get the PHIGS constants

integer*4  WorkstnID             ! workstation identifier
parameter (WorkstnID=1)          ! value chosen by the user
integer*4  ConnID                ! connection identifier
integer*4  WorkstnType           ! workstation type
parameter (WorkstnType=POIDDX)   ! implementation-dependent
integer*4  TheStructure          ! display list structure root
```

```
parameter (TheStructure=1)       ! value chosen by the user
real X(12), Y(12)                ! arrays for filled areas
data X /.1,.9,.9,.1, .2,.4,.4,.2, .6,.8,.8,.6/  ! x values
data Y /.2,.2,.8,.8, .3,.3,.7,.7, .3,.3,.7,.7/  ! y values
integer*4 FinalVerts(3)          ! last vtx in each polygon
data FinalVerts /4, 8, 12/
integer*4 fdopen                 ! to get file descriptor

call popph(fdopen(fnum(7), 'w'//char(0)), 0)  ! open PHIGS
call pue004('/dev/screen/phigs_window', ConnID) ! get connection ID
call popwk(WorkstnID, ConnID, WorkstnType)! open workstation
call popst(TheStructure)         ! open display list structure
call psis(PSOLID)                ! set interior style
call psedfg(PON)                 ! set edge flag
call pfas(3, FinalVerts, X, Y)   ! fill area set
call pclst                       ! close display list structure
call ppost(WorkstnID, TheStructure, 1.) ! mark structure for display
call puwk(WorkstnID, PPERFO)     ! update the workstation
call pclwk(WorkstnID)            ! close workstation
call pclph                       ! close PHIGS
stop                             ! stop processing
end                              ! end of program
```

Fill Area Set 3 with Data Primitives

The FILL AREA SET WITH DATA and FILL AREA SET 3 WITH DATA routines insert primitive elements into the current open structure which create a "fill area set with data" and a " fill area set 3 with data" primitive, respectively. These primitives are similar to the fill area set primitive with the addition of the following optional data:

- Edge flags to allow for displaying individual edges
- Facet colours, facet normals, and application–specific facet data
- Vertex colours, vertex normals, and application–specific vertex data

The C binding calling signature for FILL AREA SET 3 WITH DATA follows. The 2D version is identical, except that ⟨*vertex_data*⟩ uses the 2D data type `Pvertex_set`.

```
pfill_area_set3_data (
   Pint                    colr_type,    /* colour type             */
   const Pfacet            *facet_data,  /* facet data              */
   const Pedge_flag_set    *edge_flags,  /* list of edge flag lists */
   const Pvertex3_set      *vertex_data  /* list of vertex lists    */
);
```

where:

> ⟨*colr_type*⟩ specifies the type of colour data for facet and vertex colours. The colour type can be indirect (use an index into the workstation colour table), or specify a colour model to use for direct colour specification. Possible values follow (see Chapter 12 for information on these colour types):
>
> - `PCOLR_INDIRECT`. Application supplies indices into the workstation colour table.
> - `PCOLR_RGB`. Application supplies direct RGB colour values.
> - `PCOLR_CIELUV`. Application supplies direct CIELUV colour values.
> - `PCOLR_HSV`. Application supplies direct HSV colour values.
> - `PCOLR_HLS`. Application supplies direct HLS colour values.
>
> ⟨*facet_data*⟩, ⟨*edge_flags*⟩, and ⟨*vertex_data*⟩ contain the corresponding facet, edge, and vertex data. If you are not supplying facet, or edge data, set the corresponding parameter(s) to NULL. You must supply vertex data. Pointers within ⟨*vertex_data*⟩ can be set to NULL but some points are required.

Note that all vertices in the primitive must contain the same optional data. That is, all vertices must include the same types of data. This rule also applies to facets and edges. For example, if one facet has a facet normal, then all facets in the primitive must have facet normals.

The following fragment defines a 2D square with the upper two vertices red, the lower left one white, and the lower right one blue:

```
#define Red         1.0, 0.0, 0.0           /* RGB for red */
#define White       1.0, 1.0, 1.0           /* RGB for white */
#define Blue        0.0, 0.0, 1.0           /* RGB for blue */
    ...
    Pint            ColourType = PCOLR_RGB;     /* direct RGB */
    Pvertex_set     Square;
```

```
Pvertex_list        SquareVerts;
Ppoint              SquarePoints[4] = {
         {-1.0, -1.0},  {1.0, -1.0},  {1.0, 1.0},  {1.0, -1.0}};
Prgb                SquareColours[4] = {
         {White}, {Blue}, {Red}, {Red}};
...
SquareVerts.num_vertices = 4;
SquareVerts.vertex_points = SquarePoints;
SquareVerts.vertex_colrvs.colr_reps.rgb = SquareColours;
SquareVerts.vertex_norms = SquareVerts.vertex_data = NULL;
Square.num_lists = 1;
Square.vertices = &SquareVerts;
pfill_area_set_data(&Square);
...
```

Set of Fill Area Sets 3 with Data Primitives

The following routines create 2D and 3D "set of fill area sets" primitive elements:

- SET OF FILL AREA SETS WITH DATA
- SET OF FILL AREA SETS 3 WITH DATA

These are the only fill area primitives that can contain non–coplanar facets. They are also the only fill area primitives that allow the fill areas to be defined by indexing into a single list of vertices. For these reasons, they are often used to represent solid objects that share vertices between multiple edges.

The C binding calling signature for SET OF FILL AREA SETS 3 WITH DATA is shown next. The 2D version is identical, except that ⟨*vertex_list*⟩ uses the 2D data type `Pvertex_list`.

```
pset_of_fill_area_sets3_data (
  Pint                          colr_type,    /* colour type          */
  const Pset_of_fill_area_sets_data *set_data,  /* fill area
                                                        set data  */
  const Pvertex3_list     *vertex_list,   /* vertex list          */
  const Pcontour_set      *contours       /* list of contour sets */
);
```

where:

⟨*colr_type*⟩ is the same as for FILL AREA SET 3 WITH DATA.

⟨*set_data*⟩ contains the data for all the sets of fill area sets defined as follows:

```
Pset_of_fill_area_sets_data
typedef struct {
  Pint           num_sets;    /* number of fill area sets    */
  Pint           num_data_per_facet; /* number of data values
                                        per facet             */
  Pcolrv_ptr     facet_colrvs; /* list of facet colours      */
  Pvec3          *facet_norms; /* list of facet normals      */
  Pfloat         *facet_data;  /* list of facet data lists   */
  Pedge_flag_set *edge_flags;  /* list of edge flag sets     */
} Pset_of_fill_area_sets_data;
```

⟨*vertex_list*⟩ is the list of vertex lists. See the POLYLINE SET 3 WITH COLOUR routine earlier in this chapter for a description of the `Pvertex3_list` data type.

⟨*contours*⟩ is a list of contour sets as defined below:

```
Pcontour_set
typedef struct {
  Pint           num_lists;     /* number of contour lists   */
  Pint_list      *contours;     /* list of contour lists     */}
 Pcontour_set;
```

See Appendix D for a definition of `Pint_list`.

There are additional area–defining primitives beyond the "fill area" primitives. Triangle strip and quadrilateral mesh primitives are described later in this chapter. B–spline surfaces are described in Chapter 20.

Generalized Drawing Primitives

The PHIGS standard allows an implementation to define additional output primitives. PHIGS provides a mechanism called generalized drawing primitives (GDPs) to allow the implementation to present the new primitives in a standard format. The following are examples of GDPs:

- Circle
- Circular arc

- Ellipse
- Elliptical arc
- 2D polyline set

The way that you specify a GDP is implementation–dependent. For example, a circle could be defined in a number of different ways, including a center point and radius, a center point and a peripheral point, or three peripheral points. See Chapter 23, *Extensions*.

Cell Arrays

The PHIGS standard defines a **cell array** as a colour grid. Each cell within the grid can be assigned a separate colour.

A cell is a planar element, analogous to a fill area. The cell array primitive behaves like any other primitive with respect to such parameters as viewing operations, structure editing operations, and clipping.

Cell array primitives are defined by specifying the corners of their extent (a rectangle for 2D and a parallelogram for 3D) in modelling coordinates. You supply an array of either colour indices or direct colour values as part of the primitive definition.

The Cell Array Routines

CELL ARRAY creates a structure element that draws a 2D colour grid. The routine expects two modelling coordinate points (p and q), the number of cells along each axis, and an array of colour indices. The modelling coordinate points represent the opposite corners of a 2D rectangle with sides parallel to the modelling coordinate x– and y–axes. PHIGS divides the rectangle into the appropriate number of cells as specified by the number of requested cells along each axis (see Figure 10–10).

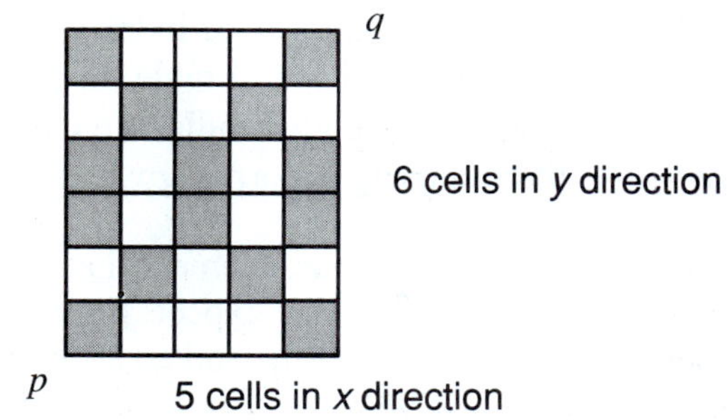

Figure 10–10. 2D Cell Array

The calling signatures for the CELL ARRAY routine are as follows:

```
call pca (px, py, qx, qy, dim_x, dim_y, isc, isr, dx, dy, colour_index_array)
```

```
pcell_array(
    const Prect        *cell_reactangle,
    const Ppat_rep     *colr_array
);
```

where:

⟨*cell_rectangle*⟩ specifies the points *p* and *q* for the C binding.

⟨*colr_array*⟩ is the colour index array for the C binding. This parameter contains the dimensions of the colour array as well as the colour array values.

The remainder of the parameters are for the FORTRAN binding:

⟨*px*⟩, ⟨*px*⟩, ⟨*qx*⟩, and ⟨*qy*⟩ are the *x* and *y* coordinates of the points *p* and *q* as previously described.

⟨*dim_x*⟩ and ⟨*dim_y*⟩ are the *x* and *y* dimensions of the colour index array.

⟨*isc*⟩ and ⟨*isr*⟩ are the indices of the start column and start row, respectively. These parameters allow you to specify any portion of the colour index array for the cell array primitive.

⟨*dx*⟩ and ⟨*dy*⟩ are the number of columns and the number of rows from the colour index array that will be used for the cell array primitive.

⟨*colour_index_array*⟩ is the colour index array. This is a two–dimensional array of indices into the workstation colour table. If a specified entry does not exist, PHIGS uses entry 1. PHIGS maps the colour indices into the two–dimensional cell array primitive on a row–wise basis starting at corner (*px*, *py*) and proceeding to corner *q*, etc.

CELL ARRAY 3 creates a structure element that draws a (planar) colour grid in 3D modelling coordinate space. The routine expects three modelling coordinate points (*p*, *q*, and *r*), the number of cells along each axis, and an array of colour indices. The modelling coordinate points represent two sides of a 3D parallelogram (see Figure 10–11). This allows you to position the grid anywhere in 3D modelling coordinate space. The lines *pq* and *pr* represent two edges of the cell array 3 primitive. *pq* represents the width and *pr* represents the height. Unlike the 2D cell array, the point *q* is not diagonally opposite point *p*.

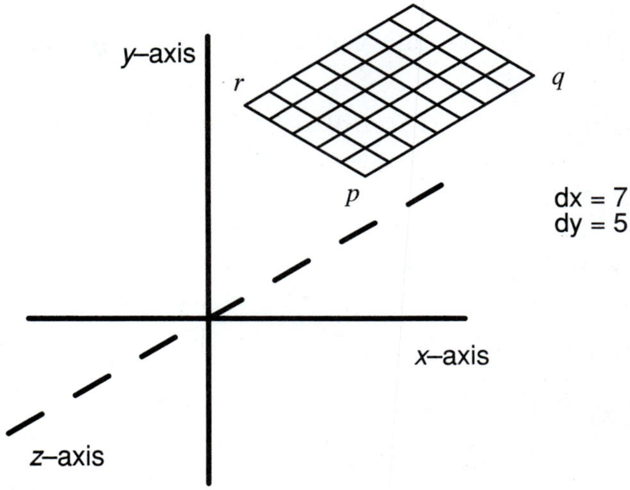

Figure 10–11. 3D Cell Array

CELL ARRAY 3 PLUS is similar to CELL ARRAY 3 except that it allows for general colour specification (either indexed or direct colour values). The direct colour specification gives you much greater flexibility since you do not have to rely on the colours assigned to the workstation colour table.

Cell Array Attributes

Other than the colour array that is supplied as part of the cell array definition, the only attributes that apply to the cell array primitive are lighting, modelling transformations, hierarchical pick, view index, and name sets.

Note that the cell array is not really an area–defining primitive. Area–defining primitives have interior and (sometimes) edge attributes. Cell array primitives have neither.

2D Cell Array Example

This fragment draws the 2D cell array pictured in Figure 10–10. It assumes that a value of black is in entry 2 of the workstation colour table, and a value of white is in entry 3.

```
      integer*4 ColourArray(5,6)
      integer*4 DimensionX, DimensionY
      parameter (DimensionX=5, DimensionY=6)
      integer*4 StartColIndex, StartRowIndex
      parameter (StartColIndex=1, StartRowIndex=1)
      integer*4 NumCols, NumRows
      parameter (NumCols=5, NumRows=6)
      real      Px, Py, Qx, Qy
      parameter (Px=0.1, Py=0.1, Qx=0.8, Qy=0.8)
      data      ColourArray /2, 3, 3, 3, 2,
     +                       3, 2, 3, 2, 3,
     +                       2, 3, 2, 3, 2,
     +                       2, 3, 2, 3, 2,
     +                       3, 2, 3, 2, 3,
     +                       2, 3, 3, 3, 2/
      ...
      call pca(Px, Py, Px, Qy, DimensionX, DimensionY,
     + StartColIndex, StartRowIndex, NumCols, NumRows, ColourArray)
```

Quadrilateral Mesh with Data Primitive

The **quadrilateral mesh with data** primitive is a multiplanar, connected, four–sided polygon primitive. It allows specification of facet and vertex colours, normals, and application–specific data, as well as edge flags for turning individual edges on or off. You can specify colour either as indices into the workstation colour table or as direct colour values.

Rendering performance improves when using quadrilateral mesh primitives over a single fill area primitive approach. The performance improvement is partly due to the fact that each mesh point is transformed only once during structure traversal (that is, polygons share vertices with one another). In contrast, if you use separate fill area primitives to represent mesh patches (quads), each corner where two primitives meet is transformed twice. In the extreme case where four primitives meet at one point, each point must be transformed four times.

Quadrilateral mesh primitives use the following nongeometric attributes:

- Data mapping method (front and back)
- Interior style (front and back)
- Interior style index (front and back)
- Interior colour (front and back)
- Pattern attributes
- Edge attributes
- Interior shading method (front and back)
- Rendering colour model
- Interior reflectance model (front and back)
- Interior reflectance properties (front and back)
- Viewing and identification attributes (see Chapter 9).

These attributes are described later in this chapter.

QUADRILATERAL MESH 3 WITH DATA inserts a primitive element into the current open structure that creates a quadrilateral mesh 3 with data primitive. The C binding calling signature for the routine follows. The 2D version is identical, except that ⟨*vertex_data*⟩ uses the 2D data type `Pvertex_array`.

```
pquad_mesh3_data (
    Pint                    colr_type,     /* colour type           */
    const Pfacet_array      *facet_data,   /* array of facet data   */
    const Pedge_flag_array  *edge_flags,   /* array of edge flags   */
    const Pvertex3_array    *vertex_data   /* array of vertex data  */
);
```

where:

⟨*colr_type*⟩ specifies the type of colour data for facet and vertex colours. The colour type can be indirect (use an index into the workstation colour table), or specify a colour model to use for direct colour specification. See FILL AREA SET 3 WITH DATA earlier in this chapter for a list of possible values.

⟨*facet_data*⟩ is an array of facet data. Set to NULL if not used.

⟨*edge_flags*⟩ is the list of edge flags. Set to NULL if not used.

⟨*vertex_data*⟩ is the vertex data. The `Pvertex3_array` data type is defined as follows:

```
Pvertex3_array
typedef struct {
  Pint_size    dims;         /* vertex array dimensions (m,n)  */
  Pint         num_data_per_vertex;  /* number of data values
                                        per vertex             */
  Ppoint3      *vertex_points;  /* array of vertex points     */
  Pcolrv_ptr   vertex_colrvs;   /* array of vertex colours    */
  Pvec3        *vertex_norms; /* array of vertex normals      */
  Pfloat       *vertex_data;  /* array of vertex data lists   */
} Pvertex3_array;
```

PHIGS uses the `dims` field of the ⟨*vertex_data*⟩ parameter to determine the number of quadrilaterals in the mesh. The dimensions define $(m-1) \times (n-1)$ connected quadrilaterals. Figure 10–12 shows the values of ⟨*m*⟩ and ⟨*n*⟩ for a quadrilateral mesh with 12 vertices and 2×3 quadrilaterals.

Load the `vertex_colrvs`, `vertex_norms`, and `vertex_data` arrays in the same order as `vertex_points`. The data type allows for general colour specification (indirect or direct). Chapter 12 describes general colour. Chapter 17 discusses vertex normals. Chapter 16 describes application–specific data that would be supplied to ⟨*vertex_data*⟩. Set these pointers to NULL if not used.

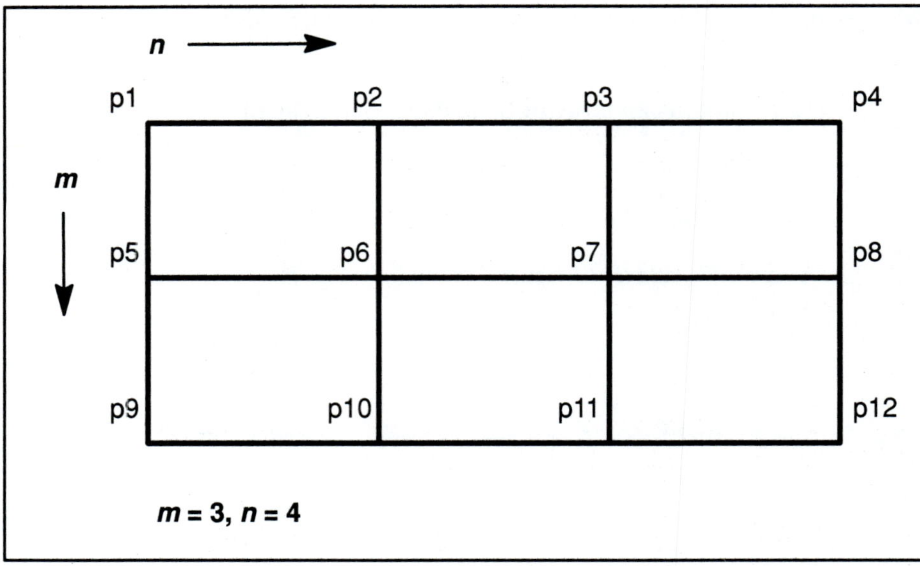

Figure 10–12. Quadrilateral Mesh with 12 Vertices

Quadrilateral Mesh Example

In this example, we create the quadrilateral mesh primitive shown in Figure 10–13. The mesh has 30 vertices and 2 × 9 quadrilaterals. This translates to $m = 3$ and $n = 10$.

```
#define Red      1.0, 0.0, 0.0    /* RGB for red */
#define Yellow   1.0, 1.0, 0.0    /* RGB for yellow */
...
Pedge_flag          EdgeDataFlags[] = {PEDGE_ON, PEDGE_ON, PEDGE_ON,
                    /* ((n-1)x(m-1)+(m-1)+(n-1) times) */  PEDGE_ON};
Pedge_flag_array    EdgeData = {47, EdgeDataFlags};
Ppoint              VertexPoints[30] = {
                     {0.0, 2.0}, {1.0, 2.0}, {2.0, 2.0}, {3.0, 2.0},
                     {4.0, 2.0}, {5.0, 2.0}, {6.0, 2.0}, {7.0, 2.0},
                     {8.0, 2.0}, {9.0, 2.0},
                     {0.0, 1.0}, {1.0, 1.0}, {2.0, 1.0}, {3.0, 1.0},
                     {4.0, 1.0}, {5.0, 1.0}, {6.0, 1.0}, {7.0, 1.0},
                     {8.0, 1.0}, {9.0, 1.0},
                     {0.0, 0.0}, {1.0, 0.0}, {2.0, 0.0}, {3.0, 0.0},
                     {4.0, 0.0}, {5.0, 0.0}, {6.0, 0.0}, {7.0, 0.0},
```

```
                        {8.0, 0.0}, {9.0, 0.0}};
Pcolrv_ptr              vertex_colr;
Prgb                    VertexColours[30] = {
                        Red, Red, Red, Red, Red, Red, Red, Red, Red, Red,
                        Yellow, Yellow, Yellow, Yellow, Yellow, Yellow,
                        Yellow, Yellow, Yellow, Yellow,
                        Red, Red, Red, Red, Red, Red, Red, Red, Red, Red};
Pint_size               Dimensions = {3, 10}; /* m=3 n=10 */
Pvertex_array           VertexData = {Dimensions, 0, VertexPoints,
                        vertex_colr, NULL, NULL};
...
vertex_colr.colr_reps.rgb = VertexColours;
pquad_mesh_data(PCOLR_RGB, NULL, &EdgeData, &VertexData);
```

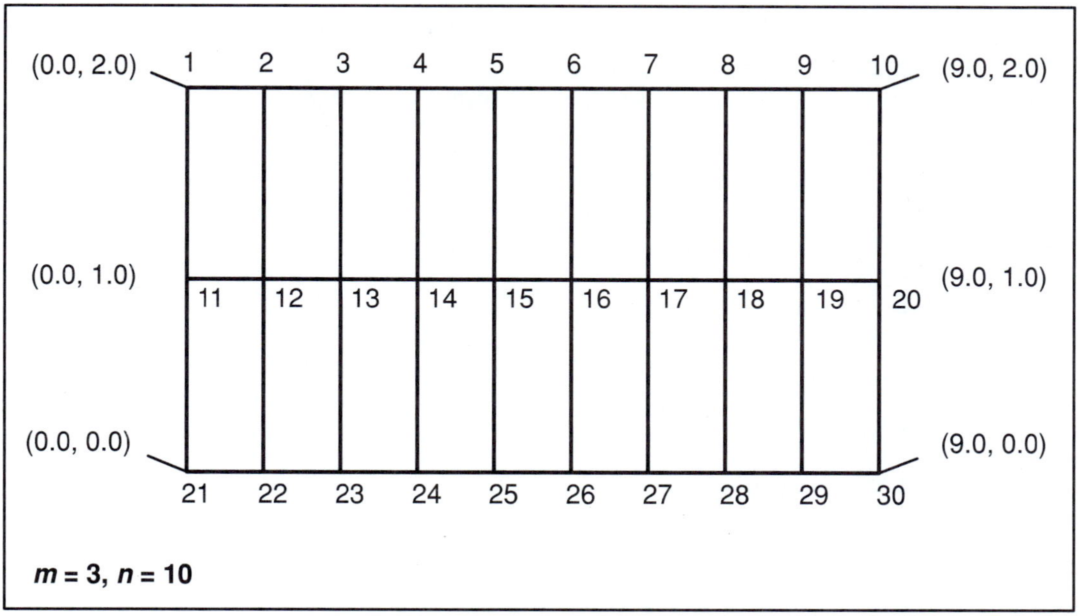

Figure 10–13. Quadrilateral Mesh with 30 Vertices

When using the indirect colour type for vertex colours, store one colour index per vertex. When using vertex normals, load the vertex normal array the same way that you load the vertex coordinate arrays.

The fragment for this example shows how to use individual edge flags. This also requires that you use the SET EDGE FLAG routine to tell PHIGS to use edge flags where indicated. However, since all the edges are on in this example, it would be sufficient to just use SET EDGE FLAG to turn on "all edges," and use `PEDGE_NONE` in the quadrilateral mesh primitive. See "Edge Attributes" in the "Individual Attributes for Area–defining Primitives" section later in this chapter.

Triangle Strip with Data Primitive

The **triangle strip** primitive is a multiplanar, connected, area–defining primitive that allows specification of facet and vertex colours, normals, and application–specific data. You can specify colour either as indices into the workstation colour table or as direct colour values.

Using triangle strip primitives improves rendering performance over a single fill area primitive approach. Refer to the description on performance at the beginning of the "Quadrilateral Mesh with Data Primitive" section earlier in this chapter.

Triangle strip primitives use the same nongeometric attributes as quadrilateral mesh:

- Data mapping method (front and back)
- Interior style (front and back)
- Interior style index (front and back)
- Interior colour (front and back)
- Pattern attributes
- Edge attributes
- Interior shading method (front and back)
- Rendering colour model
- Interior reflectance model (front and back)
- Interior reflectance properties (front and back)
- Viewing and identification attributes (see Chapter 9)

TRIANGLE STRIP 3 WITH DATA inserts a primitive element into the current open structure that creates a "triangle strip 3 with data" primitive. The C binding calling signature is shown here. The calling signature for `ptri_strip_data` is the same except that ⟨*vertex_data*⟩ uses the 2D data type `Pvertex_list`.

```
ptri_strip3_data (
  Pint                 colr_type,    /* colour type          */
  const Pfacet_list    *facet_data,  /* list of facet data   */
  const Pedge_flag_list *edge_flags, /* list of edge flags   */
  const Pvertex3_list  *vertex_data  /* list of vertex data  */
);
```

where:

⟨*colr_type*⟩ specifies the type of colour data for facet and vertex colours. The colour type can be indirect (use an index into the workstation colour table), or specify a colour model to use for direct colour specification. See FILL AREA SET 3 WITH DATA earlier in this chapter for a list of possible values.

⟨*facet_data*⟩ is the facet data. Set to NULL if not used.

⟨*edge_flags*⟩ is the list of edge flags. Set to NULL if not used.

⟨*vertex_data*⟩ is the vertex data. The `Pvertex3_list` data type is defined as follows:

```
Pvertex3_list
typedef struct {
  Pint       num_vertices;          /* number of vertices     */
  Pint       num_data_per_vertex;   /* # data values/vertex */
  Ppoint3    *vertex_points;        /* vertex point list      */
  Pcolrv_ptr vertex_colrvs;       /* vertex colour list     */
  Pvec3      *vertex_norms;       /* vertex normal list     */
  Pfloat     *vertex_data;        /* vertex data lists      */
}Pvertex3_list;
```

The `num_vertices` field specifies the number of vertices in the triangle strip. PHIGS forms $(n-2)$ triangles from n vertices. Figure 10–14 shows the vertices needed to create six triangles. It also shows the correct way to order the vertices.

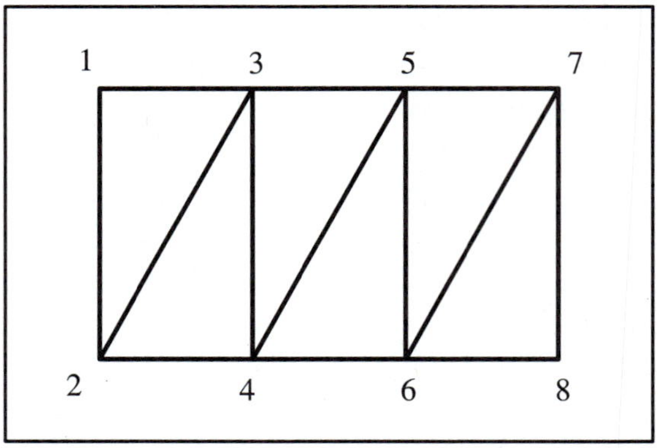

Figure 10–14. Triangle Strip with Eight Vertices

Triangle Strip Example

This section describes how to create the triangle strip shown in Figure 10–15. The primitive has 20 vertices, which create 18 triangles.

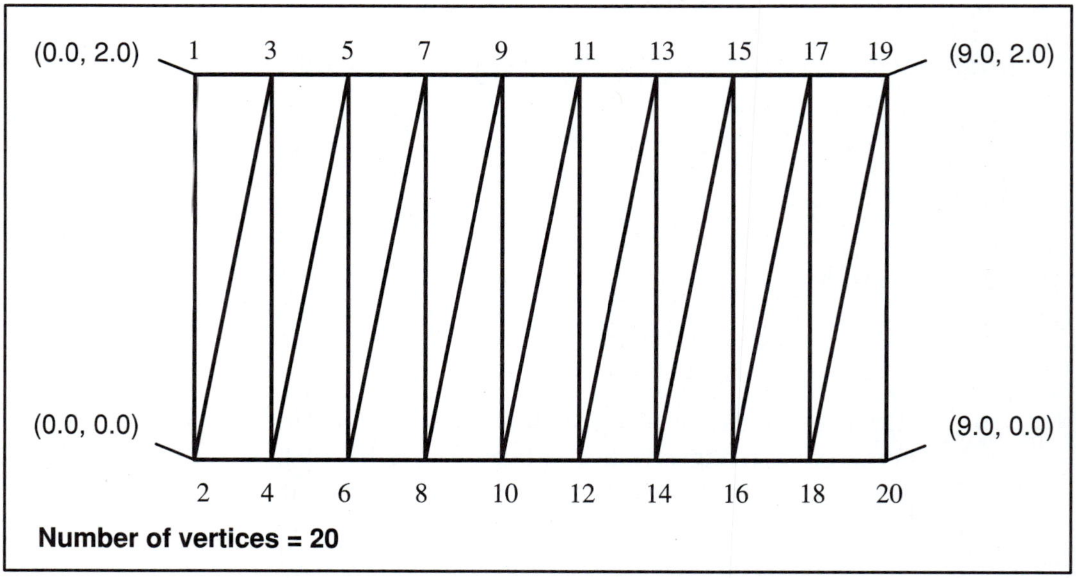

Figure 10–15. Triangle Strip with 20 Vertices

```
#define Red     1.0, 0.0, 0.0   /* RGB for red */
#define Yellow  1.0, 1.0, 0.0   /* RGB for yellow */
...
Pedge_flag          EdgeDataFlags[] = {PEDGE_ON, PEDGE_ON, PEDGE_ON,
                    /* (2n-3 times) */  PEDGE_ON, PEDGE_ON, PEDGE_ON};
Pedge_flag_list     EdgeData = {37, EdgeDataFlags};
Ppoint              VertexPoints[20] = {
                     {0.0, 2.0}, {0.0, 0.0}, {1.0, 2.0}, {1.0, 0.0},
                     {2.0, 2.0}, {2.0, 0.0}, {3.0, 2.0}, {3.0, 0.0},
                     {4.0, 2.0}, {4.0, 0.0}, {5.0, 2.0}, {5.0, 0.0},
                     {6.0, 2.0}, {6.0, 0.0}, {7.0, 2.0}, {7.0, 0.0},
                     {8.0, 2.0}, {8.0, 0.0}, {9.0, 2.0}, {9.0, 0.0}};
Prgb                VertexColours[20] = {
                    Red, Yellow, Red, Yellow, Red, Yellow, Red, Yellow,
                    Red, Yellow, Red, Yellow, Red, Yellow, Red, Yellow,
                    Red, Yellow, Red, Yellow};
Pcolrv_ptr          VertexColr;
Pvertex_list        VertexData = {20, 0, VertexPoints, VertexColr,
                     NULL, NULL};
...
VertexColr.colr_reps.rgb = VertexColours;
ptri_strip_data(PCOLR_RGB, NULL, &EdgeData, &VertexData);
```

This fragment shows how to use individual edge flags. It also requires that you use the SET EDGE FLAG routine to tell PHIGS to use edge flags where indicated. However, since all the edges are on in this example, it would be sufficient to just use SET EDGE FLAG to turn on "all edges" and set the `EdgeFlag` parameter to NULL as we did with the FacetData parameter. See "Edge Attributes" in the "Individual Attributes for Area–defining Primitives" section later in this chapter.

Triangle Set with Data Primitive

The TRIANGLE SET 3 WITH DATA and TRIANGLE SET WITH DATA routines allow for the creation of a set of triangles that do not necessarily have to be connected.

As with the "set of fill area sets with data" primitive, this primitive is often used to represent solid objects that share vertices between multiple edges. You specify the data for each vertex just once in the vertex data list, and you can use the vertices in the list zero, one, or more times.

This primitive uses the same attributes as the triangle strip primitive.

The calling signature for the TRIANGLE SET 3 WITH DATA follows. The calling signature for `ptri_set_data` is the same, except that ⟨*vertex_list*⟩ uses the 2D data type `Pvertex_list`.

```
ptri_set3_data (
  Pint                          colr_type,      /* colour type          */
  const Ptri_set_data           *set_data,      /* triangle set data    */
  const Pvertex3_list           *vertex_list,   /* list of vertex data  */
  const Pvertex_ind_triplet *vertex_inds /* list of triangle
                                                   vertex indices     */
);
```

where:

⟨*colr_type*⟩ specifies the type of colour data for facet and vertex colours. See FILL AREA SET 3 WITH DATA earlier in this chapter for a list of possible values.

⟨*set_data*⟩ is the triangle set data. PHIGS defines `Ptri_set_data` as follows:

```
Ptri_set_data
typedef struct {
  Pint          num_sets;          /* number of triangle sets */
  Pint          num_data_per_facet; /* number of data values
                                       per facet             */
  Pcolrv_ptr    facet_colrvs;       /* list of facet colours */
  Pvec3         *facet_norms;       /* list of facet normals */
  Pfloat        *facet_data;,   /* list of facet data lists  */
  Pedge_flag_triplet *edge_flags;   /* list of triangle
                                       edge flags            */
} Ptri_set_data;
```

⟨*vertex_list*⟩ is the vertex data. The `Pvertex3_list` data type is defined earlier for the triangle strip primitive.

⟨*vertex_inds*⟩ selects vertices from the ⟨*vertex_list*⟩ parameter. To select the first vertex in the vertex data list, specify an index value of 1. To specify the second vertex in the list, specify an index of 2, and so on. Specify the vertices in groups of three. Each triple defines a triangle.

Individual Attributes for Area–defining Primitives

This section describes the attributes that apply to area–defining primitives. The following is the list of area–defining primitives:

- Fill area
- Fill area set; fill area set with data; set of fill area sets with data
- Triangle strip with data; triangle set with data
- Quadrilateral mesh with data
- Non–uniform B–spline surface; non–uniform B–spline surface with data
- Some GDPs, such as circle and ellipse (implementation-dependent)

PHIGS supports the following nongeometric attributes for area–defining primitives. The "front and back" flags in the list below indicate that the corresponding attribute can be individually set for facets' fronts and backs.

- Data mapping method (front and back)
- Interior style (front and back)
- Interior style index (front and back)
- Interior colour (front and back)
- Pattern attributes including the following:
  - Pattern size
  - Pattern reference point
  - Pattern reference point vectors
- Edge attributes including the following:
  - Edgetype
  - Edgewidth scale factor

  - Edge colour
  - Edge visibility flags

- Interior shading method (front and back)
- Rendering colour model
- Interior reflectance model (front and back)
- Interior reflectance properties (front and back)
- Surface approximation criteria
- Viewing and identification attributes (see Chapter 9).

Not all of the attributes apply to all area–defining primitives.

In order for the attributes described in this section to take effect, the corresponding ASF value must be set to individual. Use the SET INDIVIDUAL ASF routine to specify whether attributes should be taken from individual attribute values or from the currently selected entry of the interior edge bundle table.

In order for the separate attributes for back–facing interiors to be applied, use the SET FACE DISTINGUISHING MODE routine to turn on the face–distinguishing mode (see Chapter 15).

Data Mapping Method

Data mapping is used for determining the source of intrinsic colour for the "with data" area–defining primitives (see Chapter 16).

SET DATA MAPPING METHOD and SET BACK DATA MAPPING METHOD create structure elements that set the data mapping method. PHIGS uses these values when the *current data mapping method ASF* or *current back data mapping method ASF* entry in the traversal state list is set to individual.

Interior Style

SET INTERIOR STYLE and SET BACK INTERIOR STYLE create structure elements that specify the interior style for front– and back–facing facets, respectively. PHIGS uses these values when the *current interior style ASF* or *current back interior style ASF* entry in the traversal state list is set to individual. The routine takes one of the following values:

Solid (`PSOLID, PSTYLE_SOLID`)
: Fill the interior using the currently selected interior colour.

Pattern (`PPATTR, PSTYLE_PAT`)
: Fill the interior of the fill area primitives using the interior colour and the currently selected interior style index. For this interior style, the "interior style index" identifies an entry into the workstation pattern table.

Hatch (`PHATCH, PSTYLE_HATCH`)
: Fill the interior of the fill area primitives using the interior colour and the currently selected interior style index. For this interior style, the "interior style index" identifies an entry in a list of implementation–dependent hatch indices.

Hollow (`PHOLLO, PSTYLE_HOLLOW`)
: No filling, but draw the bounding line using the currently selected intrinsic colour. The default intrinsic colour is the currently selected interior colour. You can select a different source of intrinsic colour (see Chapter 16). You see through a hollow primitive to whatever is behind it. The bounding lines include boundaries created by clipping.

Empty (`PISEMP, PSTYLE_EMPTY`)
: No filling. Fill area primitives using this value are invisible. Other area–defining primitives using this value are only visible if their edges are enabled.

Use SET INTERIOR STYLE INDEX or SET BACK INTERIOR STYLE INDEX to select an entry either from a list of implementation–dependent hatch indices or from the workstation pattern table. PHIGS uses these values when the *current interior style index ASF* entry or the *current back interior style index ASF* entry in the traversal state list is set to individual.

Interior Patterns

A *pattern* is a user–defined, two–dimensional pixel pattern selected from the pattern table in the workstation state list (WSL). The pixel pattern is typically rectangular, but it may also be a parallelogram.

There are several steps required to use a patterned interior style:

- Define the desired pattern and pass it to PHIGS via the SET PATTERN REPRESENTATION routine. This equates a pattern with its index in the pattern table in the WSL.
- At some point before defining the area to be filled with a pattern, select a patterned interior with SET INTERIOR STYLE. Then, select the desired pattern with the SET INTERIOR STYLE INDEX routine. At this point, the current interior style index in the PHIGS traversal state list refers to an entry in the pattern table.
- Execute an area–defining primitive. It will be filled with the pattern you have selected.

Use the following routines to define a pattern and put it in the pattern table:

- SET PATTERN REPRESENTATION
- SET PATTERN REPRESENTATION PLUS

SET PATTERN REPRESENTATION PLUS is similar to SET PATTERN REPRESENTATION except that it allows for general colour specification (either indexed or direct colour values). The direct colour specification gives you greater flexibility since you do not have to rely on the colours assigned to the workstation colour table.

Refer to *PHIGS Programming Manual* for a description of how to create entries in the workstation pattern table. See the *Preface* for more information on the book.

Interior Colour Specification

The following routines set the individual front and back interior colour attributes:

- SET INTERIOR COLOUR INDEX
- SET INTERIOR COLOUR
- SET BACK INTERIOR COLOUR

All of these routines create structure elements. See Chapter 12 for a comparison of the three routines and for information on how PHIGS uses the corresponding ASF values.

Edge Attributes

The following describe how edges apply to area–defining primitives:

- Edges do not apply to fill area or fill area 3 primitives.
- Edges are either all on or all off for the following primitives:
  - Fill area set
  - Non–uniform B–spline surface; non–uniform B–spline surface with data
- The following "with data" primitives allow control over individual edges:
  - Fill area set with data; set of fill area sets with data
  - Triangle strip with data; triangle set with data
  - Quadrilateral mesh with data

PHIGS draws edges on top of the interior. Conceptually, edges and interiors are separate. In practice, however, they may overlap. The parts of edges that are clipped are not visible.

In order for edges to be visible, the following conditions must be met:

- The edge flag must be on (see SET EDGE FLAG).
- The edge colour must be an appropriate colour different from the fill area colours and the background colour.
- The ASF values for edge flag and edge colour index must be set to either individual or bundled, depending on whether you want PHIGS to use the individual attribute values or values from the edge bundle table.

For the "with data" primitives that allow control over individual edges, the application controls edge visibility as follows:

- If the edge flag is off, edges are not displayed.
- If the edge flag is on, edge control is provided as follows:
  - If the ⟨*edge_flags*⟩ parameter for the "with data" primitive is set to NULL (no individual edge control data present), then all edges are displayed.

– If the ⟨*edge_flags*⟩ parameter for the "with data" primitive contains individual edge flags, then individual edges are displayed as specified.

SET EDGE FLAG creates a structure element that turns edge flags on and off for area–defining primitives. PHIGS uses this value when the *current edge flag ASF* entry in the traversal state list is set to individual.

SET EDGETYPE creates a structure element that specifies the edgetype. The list of edgetypes is identical to the list of linetypes.

SET EDGEWIDTH SCALE FACTOR creates a structure element that sets the scale factor used to calculate edgewidth. PHIGS uses this value when the *current edgewidth scale factor ASF* entry in the traversal state list is set to individual.

PHIGS multiplies the workstation–dependent nominal edgewidth by the edgewidth scale factor and then maps this value to the nearest available edgewidth. For example, when the edgewidth scale factor is less than or equal to 0.0, PHIGS uses the minimum edgewidth available on the workstation (that is, it displays the thinnest displayable line).

The following routines set the individual attribute for edge colour:

- SET EDGE COLOUR INDEX
- SET EDGE COLOUR

Both routines create structure elements. See Chapter 12 for a comparison of the two routines and for information on how PHIGS uses the corresponding ASF values.

Interior Shading Method

SET INTERIOR SHADING METHOD and SET BACK INTERIOR SHADING METHOD create structure elements that set the interior shading method for front– and back–facing polygons, respectively. PHIGS uses this value when the *current interior shading method ASF* entry or the *current back interior shading method ASF* entry in the traversal state list is set to individual.

The interior shading method has a visible effect on the following "with data" primitives:

- Fill area set with data; set of fill area sets with data
- Triangle strip with data; triangle set with data

- Quadrilateral mesh with data
- Non–uniform B–spline surface; non–uniform B–spline surface with data

The interior shading method controls whether PHIGS uses vertex normals for lighting calculations and vertex colours for interpolating colours across the primitive. Interior shading methods are described in Chapter 17.

Rendering Colour Model

SET RENDERING COLOUR MODEL creates a structure element that identifies the colour model in which colour interpolation is performed. The rendering colour model can be set only as an individual attribute. There is no corresponding bundle table entry. See Chapter 17 for more information on this routine. Note that this routine applies to polyline shading also.

Reflectance Model

When lighting is enabled, PHIGS applies a reflectance calculation to one or more points of an area–defining primitive to determine a colour at that point. The application can control the calculation method by specifying a **reflectance model** (also called a **lighting model**).

SET REFLECTANCE MODEL and SET BACK REFLECTANCE MODEL create structure elements that set the reflectance model for front– and back–facing facets, respectively. PHIGS uses these values when the value of the *current reflectance model ASF* or *current back reflectance model ASF* entry in the traversal state list is set to individual. See Chapter 17.

Reflectance Properties

The following attributes allow you to control the effects of reflectance on an area–defining primitive:

- The reflection type (default = simple (no shadows or mirror–like reflections))
- For simple reflectance property type:
  - Ambient reflection coefficient (default = 1.0)
  - Diffuse reflection coefficient (default = 1.0)

- Specular reflection coefficient (default = 1.0)
- Specular colour (default = white)
- Specular exponent (default = 0.0)

All reflectance property attributes are controlled as a group by a single aspect source flag, the *current reflectance properties ASF*. The setting of the *current reflectance properties ASF* entry in the traversal state list determines whether values are taken from the individual attribute setting or from the workstation reflectance bundle.

SET REFLECTANCE PROPERTIES and SET BACK REFLECTANCE PROPERTIES create structure elements that set the reflectance properties used for area–defining primitives. PHIGS uses this value when the *current reflectance properties ASF* entry or the *current back reflectance properties ASF* entry in the traversal state list is set to individual. See Chapter 17 for more information.

Surface Approximation Criteria

SET SURFACE APPROXIMATION CRITERIA creates a structure element that sets the surface approximation criteria type for the following primitives:

- Non–uniform B–spline surface; non–uniform B–spline surface with data
- Curved area–defining GDPs, such as circles and ellipses (implementation–dependent)

The surface approximation criteria type controls the smoothness of the curve (that is, how accurately the rendered surface matches the surface definition). Curves are usually rendered with lots of small straight lines, and the surface approximation criteria control the number and size of the lines. PHIGS uses this value when the *current surface approximation criteria ASF* entry in the traversal state list is set to individual. Refer to Chapter 20 for more information.

Parametric Surface Characteristics

SET PARAMETRIC SURFACE CHARACTERISTICS creates a structure element that sets the various parametric surface characteristics used to draw a non–uniform B–spline surface. PHIGS uses this value when the *current parametric surface characteristics ASF* entry in the traversal state list is set to individual. Refer to Chapter 20 for more information.

Back–facing Attributes

As noted, you can specify values for several different attributes of the back sides of area–defining primitives. These attributes are

- SET BACK INTERIOR INDEX
- SET BACK INTERIOR STYLE
- SET BACK INTERIOR STYLE INDEX
- SET BACK INTERIOR COLOUR
- SET BACK INTERIOR SHADING METHOD
- SET BACK REFLECTANCE MODEL
- SET BACK REFLECTANCE INDEX
- SET BACK REFLECTANCE PROPERTIES
- SET BACK DATA MAPPING METHOD

The routines for setting back–facing attributes are virtually identical to those for setting the front–facing attributes.

PHIGS determines the front and back faces of an area–defining primitive by examining the facet normal vector(s). The normal vector either is supplied by the application or is calculated by PHIGS based on the primitive's vertices. When rendering a filled area's front face, the front–face attributes are applied to fill it.

When rendering a fill area's back face, the situation is slightly more involved. Suppose, for example, that for some parts of your model, you want the front and back faces to be rendered with the same set of attributes, and for other parts of your model, with different sets of attributes. Of course, you could define and redefine the back–facing attributes multiple times, but there is a faster and more convenient way. The SET FACE DISTINGUISHING MODE routine allows you to turn the back–facing differentiation on and off at will: When it is on, back faces will be rendered with their own set of attributes; when it is off, they will be rendered as if they are front faces. See Chapter 15, *Front and Back Facet Processing*, for more information.

Don't confuse face culling with face distinguishing! Face culling is used to throw out faces based on their orientation. Face distinguishing is used to apply back–facing attributes to back–facing facets.

Bundled Attributes for Area–defining Primitives

The following attribute bundle tables apply to area–defining primitives:

- Data mapping bundle table
- Edge bundle table
- Interior bundle table
- Reflectance bundle table
- Parametric surface characteristics bundle table

This section describes the routines that set entries in those tables.

Use the SET INDIVIDUAL ASF routine to specify whether attributes should be taken from individual attribute values or from the currently selected entry of the appropriate bundle table.

Data Mapping Bundle Table

The SET DATA MAPPING REPRESENTATION routine sets the data mapping method values for a particular entry in the workstation data mapping bundle table. See Chapter 16.

Use SET DATA MAPPING INDEX and SET BACK DATA MAPPING INDEX to select a particular entry from the workstation data mapping bundle table.

Edge Bundle Table

There are two routines to set values in the workstation edge bundle table:

- SET EDGE REPRESENTATION defines an entry in the edge attribute bundle table. Each entry consists of the following:
  - An index value that identifies the entry in the bundle table
  - Edge flag
  - Edgetype

- Edgewidth scale factor
- Edge colour index

- SET EDGE REPRESENTATION PLUS also defines an entry in the edge attribute bundle table. This routine allows you to set additional values as defined for PHIGS PLUS. Each entry consists of the following:
  - An index value that identifies the entry in the bundle table
  - Edge flag
  - Edgetype
  - Edgewidth scale factor
  - Edge colour type (indexed or direct)
  - For indexed colour, an index into the workstation colour table
  - For direct colour, colour values from a specified colour model

SET EDGE INDEX creates a structure element that selects an entry from the edge bundle table.

Interior Bundle Table

There are two routines to set values in the workstation interior bundle table:

- SET INTERIOR REPRESENTATION defines an entry in the interior attribute bundle table. Each entry consists of the following:
  - An index value that identifies the entry in the bundle table
  - Interior style
  - Interior style index
  - Interior colour index

- SET INTERIOR REPRESENTATION PLUS also defines an entry in the interior attribute bundle table. This routine allows you to set additional values as defined for PHIGS PLUS. Each entry consists of the following:
  - An index value that identifies the entry in the bundle table
  - Interior style
  - Interior style index

- Interior colour type (indexed or direct)
- For indexed colour, an index into the workstation colour table
- For direct colour, colour values from a specified colour model
- Interior shading method

SET INTERIOR INDEX and SET BACK INTERIOR INDEX each create a structure element that selects an entry from the interior bundle table.

Reflectance Bundle Table

PHIGS PLUS maintains a reflectance bundle table for each open workstation. PHIGS PLUS uses values from the table when one of the following values in the traversal state list is set to bundled:

- *current reflectance model ASF* or *current back reflectance model ASF*
- *current reflectance properties ASF* or *current back reflectance properties ASF*

Use the SET REFLECTANCE REPRESENTATION routine to set the values for an entry in the workstation reflectance bundle table. See Chapter 17.

The SET REFLECTANCE INDEX and SET BACK REFLECTANCE INDEX routines select entries from the workstation reflectance table.

Parametric Surface Bundle Table

The SET PARAMETRIC SURFACE REPRESENTATION routine sets the parametric surface characteristic values for a particular entry in the workstation parametric surface characteristics bundle table. See Chapter 20 for a description of parametric surface characteristics.

Use the SET PARAMETRIC SURFACE INDEX routine to select a particular entry from the workstation parametric surface characteristics bundle table.

Chapter 11

Using Text

This chapter describes how to create text primitives and how to make use of the numerous text attributes.

Introduction

There are two basic kinds of text: **regular text** and **annotation text**.

Regular text is affected by all transformations: modelling, viewing, and workstation. Regular text is typically used for wording that is part of a defined scene (e.g., words on a billboard).

Annotation text always faces the viewer, regardless of the orientation of the image on the display. The *point* at which annotation text is rendered is affected by all transformations (like regular text), but the text itself, once positioned, is only affected by the workstation transformation. This means that the specified text is guaranteed to lie in the *xy*–plane of the display surface. Annotation text is typically used for labelling.

Annotation text also supports optional lead lines. A **lead line** ("lead" rhymes with "feed") is a line that extends from the text to some point associated with that text (that is, a pointer that "leads you" to the object). This is useful if there are many labels of annotation text; without lead lines, it would be difficult to tell which label went to which location or object on the image.

Other than these fundamental differences, regular text and annotation text have most other things in common. Therefore, in this chapter, statements will apply both to regular text and to annotation text unless otherwise noted.

Text is a planar primitive and is drawn in relation to a text plane. You can think of the text as enclosed in an imaginary parallelogram positioned on the text plane.

Each character is defined with respect to a box called a **character cell**. The character cell extends from left to right, bottom to top for every character. The reference lines (e.g., top, cap, left) are reference points for two attributes called *text alignment* and *text path*. The character usually resides in some subset of the character cell area. Most text is composed of individual character cells, arranged side by side, with no space between them.

There are three horizontal reference points to a character: left, center, and right. There are five vertical reference points to a character: bottom, base, half, cap, and top (see Figure 11–1).

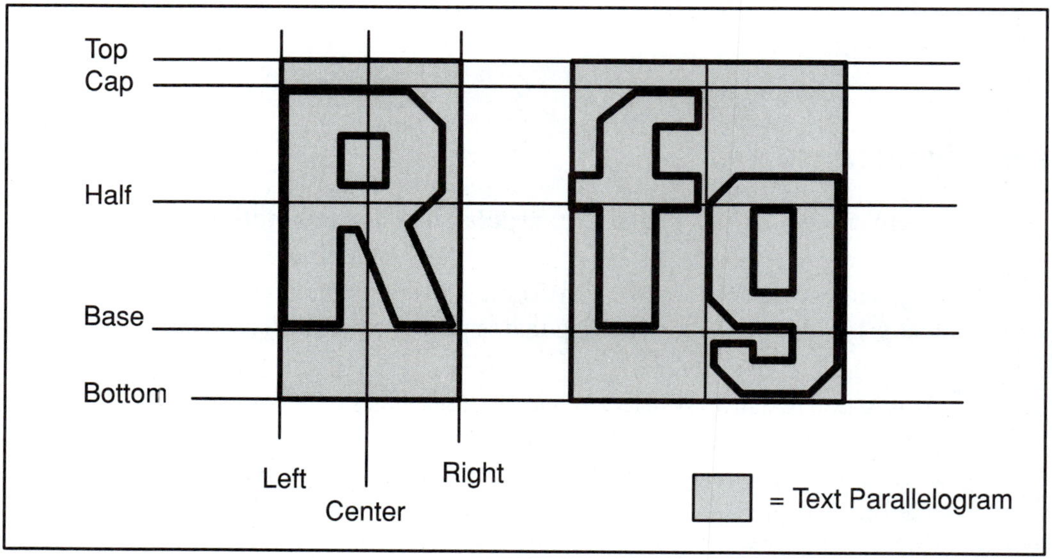

Figure 11–1. Text Reference Points

Regular 2D Text

As previously mentioned, we use the term "regular text" to distinguish between text and annotation text. Regular 2D text positions the text parallelogram on the *xy*–plane of the modelling coordinate system. You orient the text parallelogram on the plane by specifying the text position (in the definition of the primitive), text "up direction," text path, and text alignment (see Figure 11–2).

Use the character up vector attribute to rotate the parallelogram on the text plane. Use the text path attribute to specify the direction of the text (left to right, right to left, up, or down). Use the text alignment attribute to specify the alignment of the characters with respect to the text position.

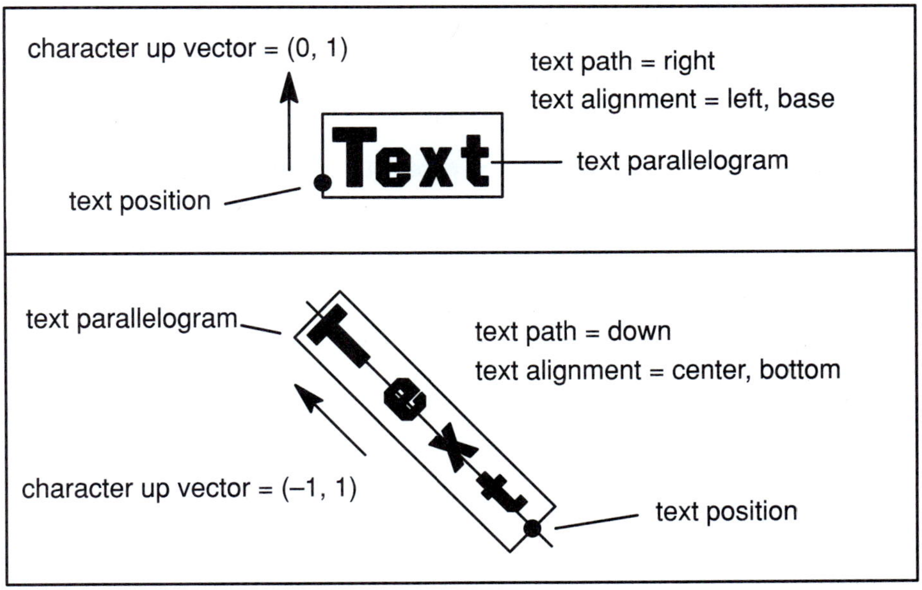

Figure 11–2. Regular 2D Text

The TEXT routine creates a structure element that, when traversed, renders the specified text at a given position on a plane defined in MCs. The calling signatures are as follows:

`call ptx(`*px*, *py*, *chars*`)` — Full FORTRAN 77 version

`call ptxs(`*px*, *py*, *string_length*, *chars*`)` — FORTRAN 77 subset version

C binding:

```
ptext(
   const PPoint      *text_pos,
   const char        *chars
);
```

where:

⟨*text_pos*⟩ is the text position in MCs for the C binding.

⟨*px*⟩ and ⟨*py*⟩ are the coordinates of the text position for the FORTRAN binding, in MCs.

⟨*string_length*⟩ is the length of the string (in characters) required for the FORTRAN 77 subset version of the routine.

⟨*chars*⟩ is the character string defined as follows:

- For the C binding, this parameter is defined as `char`.
- For the full FORTRAN 77 version, use `character*(*)`.
- For the FORTRAN 77 subset version, use `character*(80)`.

For example, the following C fragment creates a structure element that, when traversed, draws a text string at location (0.5, 1.0, 0.0):

```
Ppoint    Point;          /* one point */
...
Point.x = 0.5, Point.y = 1.0;
ptext(&Point, "Testing");
```

The following fragment creates a similar structure element for the full FORTRAN 77 version:

```
call ptx(0.5, 1.0, 'Testing')
```

Regular 3D Text

The TEXT 3 routine creates a structure element that allows you to position the text plane anywhere in the modelling coordinate system. The text plane is defined by a point (the text position) and two vectors, called the **first and second text direction vectors**. The text position and the two direction vectors define a text plane and a local coordinate system on that plane in which all geometric text attributes are measured; the coordinate system is known as the **text local coordinate** (**TLC**) system. The TLC system uses units of the same size as the current modelling coordinates.

The calling signatures for the TEXT 3 routine are as follows:

`call ptx3` (*px*, *py*, *pz*, *tdx*, *tdy*, *tdz*, *chars*)	Full FORTRAN 77 version
`call ptx3s` (*px*, *py*, *pz*, *tdx*, *tdy*, *tdz*, *lstr*, *chars*)	FORTRAN 77 subset version
`ptext3(`	C binding

```
ptext3(
   const PPoint3     *text_pos,
   const Pvec3       *text_dir[2],
   const char        *chars
);
```

where:

⟨*text_pos*⟩ is the text position in MCs for the C binding.

⟨*px*⟩, ⟨*py*⟩, and ⟨*pz*⟩ are the coordinates for the text position for the FORTRAN binding, expressed in MCs.

⟨*text_dir*⟩ contains the two text direction vectors in MCs for the C binding.

⟨*tdx*⟩, ⟨*tdy*⟩, and ⟨*tdz*⟩ contain *x*, *y*, and *z* values of the text direction vectors for the FORTRAN binding, expressed in MCs. Each parameter is a two–dimensional real array.

⟨*lstr*⟩ is the length of the string (in characters) required for the FORTRAN 77 subset version of the routine.

⟨*chars*⟩ is the character string. This parameter is the same as defined for the 2D text routine in the previous section.

The Text Local Coordinate System

The PHIGS standard defines the TLC as follows: "Let P be the text position and U and V be the first and second text direction vectors, respectively. The text plane is the plane that contains P and is perpendicular to $U \times V$. The origin of the text local coordinate system is at the point P. The positive *x*–axis of the text local coordinate system is parallel to U. Let T be a vector perpendicular to U and in the text plane. If $T \bullet V$ is positive, then the positive *y*–axis is parallel to T; otherwise, the positive *y*–axis is opposite T."

The easiest way to visualize the TLC is to place the text position at the modelling coordinate origin. In this case, the first text direction vector is the positive *x*–axis of the TLC and the second text direction vector is the positive *y*–axis. Once you have the text oriented in the proper direction, you can move the text position anywhere in modelling coordinates and the orientation will remain the same. That is how we positioned the text for the `spin_cube` program described earlier in this book. The following fragments are taken from that program.

This C fragment creates a 3D text string. Refer to the `spin_cube` program in Chapter 7 for the complete program and a picture.

```
static Ppoint3      RightTextPos = {1.0, -0.75, 0.75};
static Pvec3        RightTextOri[2] = {0, 0, -1, 0, 1, 0};
...
ptext3(&RightTextPos, RightTextOri, "Right");
```

The following fragment performs the same task for the FORTRAN binding:

```
real*4 px, py, pz                 { text position
real*4 tdx(2), tdy(2), tdz(2)     { text direction vectors
...
px=1.0            { text position
py=-0.75
pz=0.75
tdx(1)=0.0        { text direction vectors
tdy(1)=0.0
tdz(1)=-1.0
tdx(2)=0.0
tdy(2)=1.0
tdz(2)=0.0
call ptx3(px, py, pz, tdx, tdy, tdz, 'Right')  { 3D text
```

Annotation Text Primitives

Annotation text is a planar primitive and is always drawn in NPC space on a plane parallel to the display surface. You can think of annotation text as enclosed in an imaginary rectangle positioned on the annotation text plane.

The ANNOTATION TEXT RELATIVE and ANNOTATION TEXT RELATIVE 3 routines each creates a structure element that draws an annotation text string. The string is positioned on the *xy*–plane in NPC space that is specified by the *z* coordinate of the annotation point (which is zero for 2D annotation text).

In addition to an annotation text string, you specify the annotation text reference point as a location in modelling coordinate space. This is the point in the model to which the annotation text is referring (see Figure 11–3). You specify the annotation offset coordinates in NPC space. This offset, when added to the transformed reference point, yields the annotation point. This point forms the origin of the text local coordinate system (thereby determining the location of the annotation text).

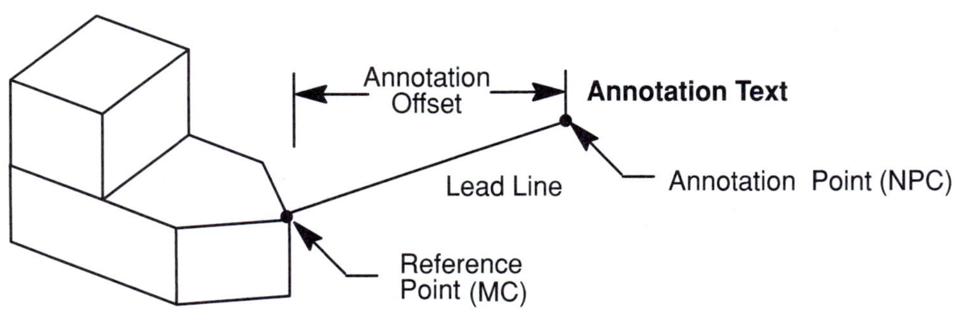

PHIGS uses the reference point and the annotation offset to calculate the annotation point.

Figure 11–3. Annotation Text

The calling signatures for the ANNOTATION TEXT RELATIVE routine are as follows (add *z* coordinates for the 3D routine):

`patr` (*refx*, *refy*, *offsetx*, *offsety*, *chars*) Full FORTRAN 77 binding

```
patrs (refx, refy, offsetx, offsety, lstr, chars)
```
FORTRAN 77 subset binding

```
panno_text_rel(
    const PPoint        *ref_point,
    const Pvec          *offset,
    const char          *chars
);
```
C binding

where:

⟨*ref_point*⟩ is the reference point in MCs for the C binding. This parameter is defined as `Ppoint` for 2D and `Ppoint3` for the 3D version.

⟨*offset*⟩ is the annotation text offset in NPCs for the C binding. This parameter is defined as `Pvec` for 2D and `Pvec3` for the 3D version.

⟨*refx*⟩, ⟨*refy*⟩, and ⟨*refz*⟩ for 3D are the coordinates for the text reference point for the FORTRAN binding, expressed in MCs.

⟨*offsetx*⟩, ⟨*offsety*⟩, and ⟨*offsetz*⟩ for 3D are the coordinates for the annotation text offset for the FORTRAN binding, expressed in NPCs.

⟨*lstr*⟩ is the length of the string (in characters) required for the FORTRAN 77 subset version of the routine.

⟨*chars*⟩ is the character string. This parameter is the same as defined for the 2D text routine earlier in this chapter.

The following fragment creates two 2D annotation text primitives with lead lines. The offset for each primitive is (0.15, 0.1) in NPC space.

```
      character*80 text1, text2

C Text structure
      call popst(Text)
      text1 = 'Polygon'
      text2 = 'Quad mesh'
      call psans(PLDLN)                  { use lead lines
      call psatch(0.02)                  { set annotation text height
      call patr ( 0.5, 0.8, 0.15, 0.1, text1)
      call patr ( 0.5, 0.5, 0.15, 0.1, text2)
      call pclst
```

See "Annotation Text Attributes," later in this chapter.

Inquiring the Text Capabilities of a Workstation

Use the following routines to determine the text capabilities of a given workstation type:

- INQUIRE ANNOTATION FACILITIES returns the following:
  - The number of available annotation text styles
  - The list of available annotation text styles
  - The number of available annotation text character heights
  - The minimum and maximum annotation text character heights
- INQUIRE TEXT FACILITIES returns the following:
  - The list of supported text fonts
  - The list of supported text precisions
  - the number of character heights supported
  - the minimum and maximum character heights
  - the number of character expansion factors supported
  - the minimum and maximum character expansion factors
  - the number of predefined entries in the workstation text bundle table

Inquiring the Text Extents

The INQUIRE TEXT EXTENTS routine helps answer the question, "Will this text string fit in the display area?" The routine expects the following input values:

- Workstation type
- Text font
- Character expansion factor
- Character spacing
- Character height

- Text path
- Horizontal and vertical text alignment values
- The text string

The INQUIRE TEXT EXTENTS routine returns the following:

- A text extent rectangle (two sets of *xy* values)
- A concatenation point offset (one *x* and one *y* value)

The **text extent rectangle** is the minimum area that completely encloses the text string (see Figure 11–2). These values are calculated in the text local coordinate system of the text primitive, assuming that the text position is at (0, 0) of the TLC. The values are independent of the character up vector and of all clipping and transformation values.

You can use the **concatenation point offset** to determine a position for a subsequent text string so that they both appear to be part of the same string. When concatenating text strings, use all of the same text attributes except for text alignment. Modify the text alignment according to the following rules:

- If the text path is right or left, use a value of "normal" for the horizontal component of the text alignment.
- If the text path is up or down, use a value of "normal" for the vertical component of the text alignment.

These rules also apply to annotation text alignment.

Text Attributes

The following lists the routines that set text and annotation text attributes. The rest of the chapter describes the routines.

- SET ANNOTATION STYLE specifies whether or not to draw a lead line from the object to the associated annotation text.
- SET CHARACTER EXPANSION FACTOR sets the character width by specifying a factor by which to multiply the default width. Applies both to text and annotation text.

- SET CHARACTER HEIGHT and SET ANNOTATION TEXT CHARACTER HEIGHT specify the height of subsequent character cells for text and annotation text, respectively.
- SET CHARACTER SPACING specifies the amount of space between adjacent characters. Applies both to text and annotation text.
- SET CHARACTER UP VECTOR and SET ANNOTATION TEXT CHARACTER UP VECTOR specify the angle of the normally vertical parts of characters for text and annotation text, respectively.
- SET TEXT ALIGNMENT and SET ANNOTATION TEXT ALIGNMENT specify the alignment of the text parallelogram (the minimally sized parallelogram that surrounds a block of text) for text and annotation text, respectively.
- SET TEXT COLOUR and SET TEXT COLOUR INDEX specify a colour for text. Both routines apply to text and annotation text.
- SET TEXT FONT specifies a font to be used for text. Applies both to text and annotation text.
- SET TEXT PATH and SET ANNOTATION TEXT PATH specify the direction taken in intercharacter spaces: right, left, down, or up.
- SET TEXT PRECISION sets the text precision to string, character, or stroke precision.
- SET TEXT REPRESENTATION and SET TEXT REPRESENTATION PLUS define entries in the text bundle table. Both routines apply to text and annotation text.
- SET TEXT INDEX selects an entry from the text bundle table. Applies both to text and annotation text.

Selecting Character Size and Shape

Shortly after text is rendered on an output device, it becomes obvious that some way of selecting the size and shape of the characters is needed. Text in certain parts of a plot is more "significant" and should be written in a larger size, while other parts should be smaller. If you need to squeeze a lot of text into a limited size, it would be handy to be able to make the characters narrower in order to fit them all in. PHIGS has routines for specifying these attributes.

Character Height

The calling signatures for SET CHARACTER HEIGHT are as follows:

```
call pschh(height)
```

```
pset_char_ht(
   Pfloat          height
);
```

where:

> ⟨*height*⟩ is the height of the character cell from bottom to top (not from base to cap), expressed in TLCs.

When SET CHARACTER HEIGHT is called, PHIGS also sets the character's width such that the character's shape remains the same, although the size has changed. That is, its aspect ratio–its width–to–height ratio specified by the font definition–remains constant. Therefore, when a character's height is doubled, for example, the character's width also doubles so as to keep the character's shape identical.

Use SET ANNOTATION TEXT CHARACTER HEIGHT to set the height for annotation text.

Character Width

The SET CHARACTER EXPANSION FACTOR routine allows alteration of the character width. It sets the width of subsequent characters not by specifying an absolute width, but by specifying a multiplier to be applied to the characters' default width as defined by the aspect ratio. In other words, every character has a default width based on that character's current height. If you want wider characters, you call SET CHARACTER EXPANSION FACTOR, passing to it a value greater than 1.0; if you want narrower characters, you pass a value less than 1.0. This value is multiplied by the default width to arrive at an absolute width for the characters, which is then used.

The calling signatures for SET CHARACTER EXPANSION FACTOR are as follows:

call pschxp (*factor*)

```
pset_char_expan(
   Pfloat              factor
);
```

where:

> ⟨*factor*⟩ is the multiplier applied to the default aspect ratio of the character cell.

The formula used by the SET CHARACTER EXPANSION FACTOR routine in calculating the character width is

$$\langle width \rangle = \langle expansion\_factor \rangle \times \langle font\_aspect\_ratio \rangle \times \langle char\_height \rangle$$

For example, passing a value of 1.5 will cause the characters to be 50% wider than the default width (for the current height) specified by the font definition.

The following program illustrates character height and expansion factor. In the first line, the program labels each character a little bigger than the previous one, and in the second line, each character is bit wider than the previous one.

```
#include <phigs.h>                    /* get PHIGS definitions for C */
#include <stdio.h>                    /* get standard I/O definitions */

main()                                       /* file "CharSize.c" */
{
Pint        WorkstnID = 1;              /* workstation identifier */
Pint        ConnID;                     /* connection identifier */
Pint        WorkstnType = POIDDX;       /* implementation-dependent */
Pint        TheStructure = 1;           /* structure ID */
char        *String, Str[2];            /* string holders */
float       Height = 0.0;               /* temporary variable: height */
float       Width = 0.05;               /* temporary variable: width */
float       X;                          /* x position holder */
```

```
Ppoint      Loc;                    /* location of text */
int         I;                      /* loop control variable */

popen_phigs(stderr, 0);             /* errors go to "stderr" */
pescape_u4("/dev/screen/phigs_window", &ConnID);
popen_ws(WcrkstnID, ConnID, WorkstnType);
popen_struct(TheStructure);
strcpy(Str, "?");                   /* put \0 into Str[1] */
/*--- show character height ---------------------------------------*/
String = "bigger and bigger";       /* initialize string */
Loc.x = 0.0, Loc.y = 0.7;           /* initial character location */
for (I = 0; I < 17; I++) {          /* loop for "bigger and bigger" */
    Height += 0.008;                /* increment height value */
    pset_char_ht(Height);
    Loc.x += Height * 0.7;          /* increment x position */
    Str[0] = String[I];            /* char -> null-terminated string */
    ptext(&Loc, Str);               /* define a character */
}
/*--- show character width ----------------------------------------*/
String = "wider and wider";         /* initialize string */
Loc.x = 0.0, Loc.y = 0.3;           /* initial character location */
for (I = 0; I < 15; I++) {          /* loop for "wider and wider" */
    Width += 0.06;                  /* increment width value */
    pset_char_expan(Width);         /* set character width */
    Loc.x += Width * 0.1;           /* increment x position */
    Str[0] = String[I];            /* char -> null-terminated string */
    ptext(&Loc, Str);               /* print a character */
}
pclose_struct();
ppost_struct(WorkstnID, TheStructure, 1.0);
pupd_ws(WorkstnID, PFLAG_PERFORM);  /* (regeneration flag) */
pclose_ws(WorkstnID);
pclose_phigs();
}
```

Figure 11–4 shows the output of the program.

Figure 11–4. Character Size and Width

The Up Vector

Every character has the attribute of **up vector**. The up vector is a vector that defines the direction of the "vertical" components of characters–those parts that usually aim straight up. The calling signatures for SET CHARACTER UP VECTOR are as follows:

```
call pschup(up_vector_x, up_vector_y)

pset_char_up_vec(
   const Pvec         *char_up_vector
);
```

where:

⟨*char_up_vector*⟩ is the up vector for text for the C binding.

⟨*up_vector_x*⟩ and ⟨*up_vector_y*⟩ are real numbers whose values, taken together, indicate a direction when interpreted within a Cartesian coordinate system.

The up vector is interpreted on the TLC plane; this is why only a 2D up vector is needed. Note that the magnitude of the numbers is irrelevant; the direction (1, 2) is identical to (2, 4).

The following example uses the character up vector to rotate text (the call to SET TEXT ALIGNMENT will be covered shortly):

```
#include <phigs.h>                     /* get PHIGS definitions for C */
#include <stdio.h>                     /* get standard I/O definitions */
#include <math.h>                        /* link with library "-lm" */
#define  deg             *M_PI/180.      /* convert degrees to radians */
main()                                     /* file "Rotate.c" */
{
Pint         WorkstnID = 1;            /* workstation-identifier */
Pint         ConnID;                   /* connection identifier */
Pint         WorkstnType = POIDDX;     /* implementation dependent */
Pint         TheStructure = 1;         /* structure ID  */
int          Angle;                    /* current rotation angle */
Pvec         UpVector;                 /* character up vector */
static Ptext_align  LeftHalf =        /* alignment for the left labels */
             {PHOR_LEFT, PVERT_HALF};
Ppoint       Loc;                      /* text location */
char         String[20];               /* string holder */

popen_phigs(stderr, 0);                /* errors go to "stderr" */
pescape_u4("/dev/screen/phigs_window", &ConnID);
popen_ws(WorkstnID, ConnID, WorkstnType);
popen_struct(TheStructure);
pset_char_ht(0.035);
pset_text_align(&LeftHalf);
Loc.x = Loc.y = 0.5;
for (Angle = 0; Angle <= 345; Angle += 15) {
    sprintf(String, "-----Angle=%d", Angle);
    UpVector.delta_x = cos(Angle deg);
    UpVector.delta_y = sin(Angle deg);
    pset_char_up_vec(&UpVector);
    ptext(&Loc, String);
}
pclose_struct();
ppost_struct(WorkstnID, TheStructure, 1.0);
pupd_ws(WorkstnID, PFLAG_PERFORM);  /* (regeneration flag) */
pclose_ws(WorkstnID);
pclose_phigs();
}
```

Figure 11–5 shows the output of the program.

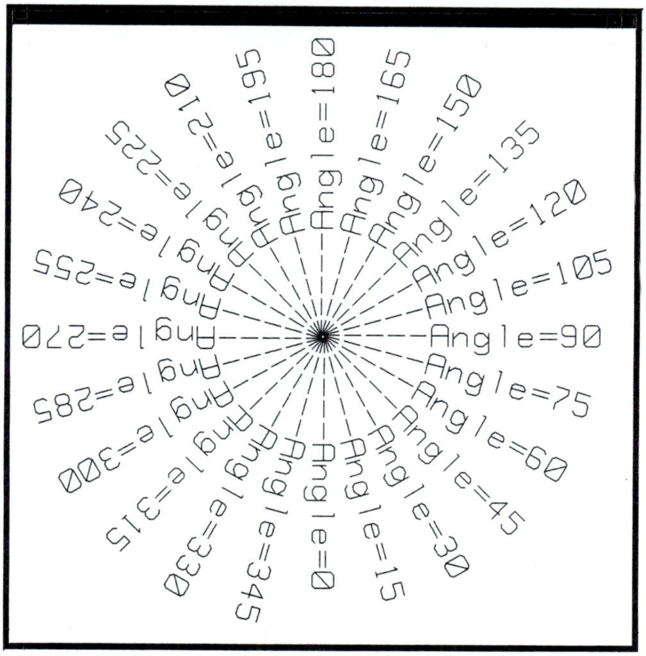

Figure 11–5. Text Rotation

It may be momentarily surprising to see that the text associated with 0° goes *down*, and not to the right, as 0° implies. This is because we were defining the *up* vector; i.e., the *vertical* parts of the characters go to the right.

For annotation text, use the SET ANNOTATION TEXT CHARACTER UP VECTOR routine.

Text Alignment

The need for control of text alignment is easily illustrated by the question, "If I move to (0, 0) and draw some text, which part of the text is at (0, 0)?" The need for controlling which part of text is at which point becomes painfully apparent if you remember ever using a graphics system that did not support text alignment. The simple matter of centering a title may have been either an annoying extra set of calculations based on the length of the label or a series of trial–and–error runs to get something that "looked good."

Based on the definition of a character cell, as described at the beginning of this chapter, those reference points on a character can be logically extended to relate to an entire text string.

Use SET TEXT ALIGNMENT to set the textual alignment. Its calling signatures are as follows:

```
call pstxal(h_alignment, v_alignment)
```

```
pset_text_align(
   const Ptext_align          *text_alignment
);
```

where:

⟨*text_alignment*⟩ is the text alignment for the C binding. This data type includes one horizontal alignment token and one vertical text alignment token (see list).

⟨*h_alignment*⟩ is the horizontal alignment value for the FORTRAN binding (see list).

⟨*v_alignment*⟩ is the vertical alignment value for the FORTRAN binding (see list).

Horizontal text alignment values are as follows:

- Normal (`PAHNOR, PHOR_NORM`)
- Left (`PALEFT, PHOR_LEFT`)
- Centered (`PACENT, PHOR_CTR`)
- Right (`PARITE, PHOR_RIGHT`)

Vertical text alignment values are as follows:

- Normal (PAVNOR, PVERT_NORM)
- Top (PATOP, PVERT_TOP)
- Cap (PACAP, PVERT_CAP)
- Half (PAHALF, PVERT_HALF)
- Base (PABASE, PVERT_BASE)
- Bottom (PABOTT, PVERT_BOTTOM)

Refer to the illustration in Figure 11–1. Also see the next section for information on "normal" alignment.

The following program demonstrates text alignment. It draws an "X" at the text location, and then labels the word "Test" with both the horizontal and vertical alignment set to specific values. That is, the "X" marks indicate the reference point of the respective labels. Figure 11–6 shows the output of this program.

Here is the program:

```
#include <phigs.h>                    /* get PHIGS definitions for C */
#include <stdio.h>                    /* get standard I/O definitions */

main()                                      /* file "Alignment.c" */
{
    Pint         WorkstnID = 1;             /* workstation identifier */
    Pint         ConnID;                    /* connection identifier */
    Pint         WorkstnType = POIDDX;      /* implementation-dependent */
    Pint         TheStructure = 1;          /* structure ID */
    static Ptext_align  CenterCap =         /* alignment for top labels */
                 {PHOR_CTR, PVERT_CAP};
    static Ptext_align  LeftHalf =         /* alignment for left labels */
                 {PHOR_LEFT, PVERT_HALF};
    Ptext_align Alignment;              /* alignment for middle labels */
    Ppoint       Loc;                       /* location of text strings */
    int          Halign, Valign;            /* loop control variables */
    float        H, V;                      /* temporary variables */
```

```
    popen_phigs(stderr, 0);              /* errors go to "stderr" */
    pescape_u4("/dev/screen/phigs_window", &ConnID);
    popen_ws(WorkstnID, ConnID, WorkstnType);
    popen_struct(TheStructure);
    /*--- do top labels -------------------------------------------*/
    pset_char_ht(0.015);
    pset_text_align(&CenterCap);
    Loc.y = 1.0;
    Loc.x = 0.1, ptext(&Loc, "TOP");     /* \                        */
    Loc.x = 0.3, ptext(&Loc, "CAP");     /*  \  Do the labels for    */
    Loc.x = 0.5, ptext(&Loc, "HALF");    /*   > vertical alignment   */
    Loc.x = 0.7, ptext(&Loc, "BASE");    /*  /  along top of plot.   */
    Loc.x = 0.9, ptext(&Loc, "BOTTOM"); /* /                        */
    /*--- do left labels ------------------------------------------*/
    pset_text_align(&LeftHalf);
    Loc.x = 0.0;
    Loc.y = 0.2, ptext(&Loc, "LEFT");    /* \  Labels for horizontal */
    Loc.y = 0.5, ptext(&Loc, "CTR");     /*  > alignment are along   */
    Loc.y = 0.8, ptext(&Loc, "RIGHT");   /* /  left edge of the plot.*/
    /*--- do letters in the middle -------------------------------*/
    pset_char_ht(0.03);
    pset_char_expan(0.8);
    for (Valign = PVERT_TOP; Valign <= PVERT_BOTTOM; Valign++) {
        for (Halign = PHOR_LEFT; Halign <= PHOR_RIGHT; Halign++) {
            V = Valign * 0.2 - 0.1;           /* calculate x value */
            H = Halign * 0.3 - 0.1;           /* calculate y value */
    DoLine(V + 0.01, H + 0.01, V - 0.01, H - 0.01);      /* NE to SW */
    DoLine(V + 0.01, H - 0.01, V - 0.01, H + 0.01);      /* SE to NW */
            Alignment.hor = Halign, Alignment.vert = Valign;
            pset_text_align(&Alignment);
            Loc.x = V, Loc.y = H;
            ptext(&Loc, "Test");
        }
    }
    pclose_struct();
    ppost_struct(WorkstnID, TheStructure, 1.0);
    pupd_ws(WorkstnID, PFLAG_PERFORM);  /* (regeneration flag) */
    pclose_ws(WorkstnID);
    pclose_phigs();
}
/*****************************************************************/
DoLine(X1, Y1, X2, Y2)
```

```
float   X1, Y1, X2, Y2;                    /* endpoints of line */
{
    Ppoint      LinePts[2];                /* xy values of polyline */
    Ppoint_list LineData;                  /* all data for polyline */

    LinePts[0].x = X1, LinePts[0].y = Y1;
    LinePts[1].x = X2, LinePts[1].y = Y2;
    LineData.num_points = 2, LineData.points = LinePts;
    ppolyline(&LineData);
}
```

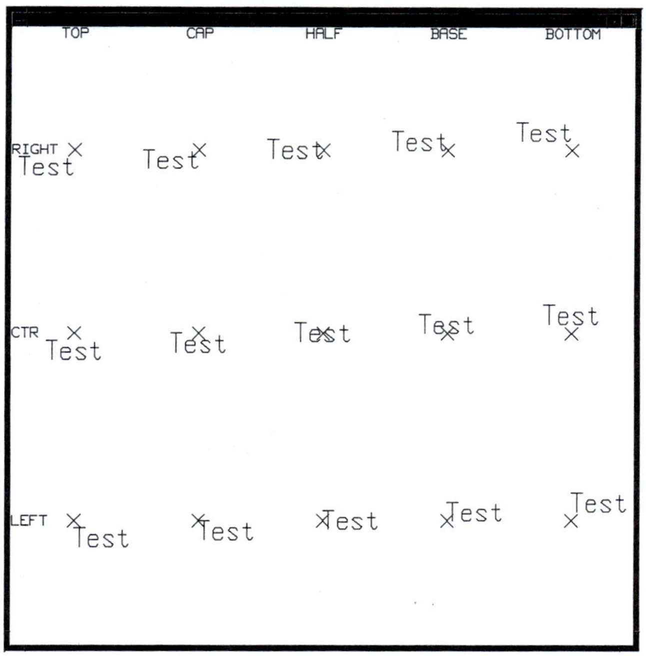

Figure 11–6. Text Alignment

Use SET ANNOTATION TEXT ALIGNMENT for annotation text.

Text Path

The **text path** is nothing more than where the next character is drawn relative to the previous character. In the usual case, after one character is drawn, the "pen" moves to the right in preparation for the next character. However, this default direction can be changed to left, down, or up if you so desire. The pertinent routine is SET TEXT PATH; its calling signatures are as follows:

```
call pstxp(path)
```

```
pset_text_path(
   Ptext_path          path
);
```

where:

⟨*path*⟩ is one of four possibilities:

- **Right** (`PRIGHT`, `PPATH_RIGHT`)
- **Left** (`PLEFT`, `PPATH_LEFT`)
- **Up** (`PUP`, `PPATH_UP`)
- **Down** (`PDOWN`, `PPATH_DOWN`)

Regardless of the text path, the first character in a string of text is drawn at the text position. The second and subsequent characters are drawn in positions that are dependent upon the text path, text alignment, character size and spacing, and so forth.

The following program uses the text path attribute:

```
#include <phigs.h>                         /* get PHIGS definitions for C */
#include <stdio.h>                         /* get standard I/O definitions */

main()                                         /* file "TextPath.c" */
{
Pint          WorkstnID = 1;               /* workstation identifier */
Pint          ConnID;                      /* connection identifier */
Pint          WorkstnType = POIDDX;        /* implementation-dependent */
Pint          TheStructure = 1;            /* structure ID  */
static Ppoint Loc = {                      /* text location */
```

```
            0.5, 0.7};

popen_phigs(stderr, 0);             /* errors go to "stderr" */
pescape_u4("/dev/screen/phigs_window", &ConnID);
popen_ws(WorkstnID, ConnID, WorkstnType);
popen_struct(TheStructure);
pset_char_ht(0.06);
pset_text_path(PPATH_RIGHT);
ptext(&Loc, " Right");
pset_text_path(PPATH_LEFT);
ptext(&Loc, " Left");
pset_text_path(PPATH_UP);
ptext(&Loc, " Up");
pset_text_path(PPATH_DOWN);
ptext(&Loc, " Down");
pclose_struct();
ppost_struct(WorkstnID, TheStructure, 1.0);
pupd_ws(WorkstnID, PFLAG_PERFORM);  /* (regeneration flag) */
pclose_ws(WorkstnID);
pclose_phigs();
}
```

Figure 11–7 shows the output of the program.

Figure 11–7. Text Path

For annotation text, use the SET ANNOTATION TEXT PATH routine.

Path–dependent Alignment

Another side of text alignment is that of "normal" alignment. Normal alignment is nothing more than a certain set of the alignment values, mentioned in the "Text Alignment" section, that are selected based on the current setting of the text path. Table 11–1 shows the alignment values used when normal alignment is selected.

Table 11–1. Text Path and Normal Alignment Values

Text Path	Normal, Horizontal, and Vertical Alignments
Right	(Left, Base)
Left	(Right, Base)
Up	(Center, Base)
Down	(Center, Top)

Text Density

This section discusses what we loosely describe as **text density**, which means, "With a given character size, how do you control how much text is in a specified area?"

Obviously, you can alter the amount of text that can fit in an area by changing the character height and width, for example, but with a fixed character size, the only other thing that will affect text density is the amount of space between characters.

Intracharacter Spacing

PHIGS allows you to specify the amount of space between characters (intracharacter spacing) by using the routine SET CHARACTER SPACING. The calling signatures are as follows:

```
call pschsp(spacing)
```

```
pset_char_space(
  Pfloat          spacing
);
```

where:

⟨*spacing*⟩ is a real number specifying the number of units of space between each pair of adjacent characters. The unit used is the current character height. Thus, a ⟨*spacing*⟩ of 0.4 causes a space that is four–tenths the current height of the character cell to be placed between every pair of adjacent characters.

An example of character spacing and how it affects textual output follows:

```
#include <phigs.h>                    /* get PHIGS definitions for C */
#include <stdio.h>                    /* get standard I/O definitions */

main()                                /* file "CharSpace.c" */
{
Pint      WorkstnID = 1;              /* workstation identifier */
Pint      ConnID;                     /* connection identifier */
Pint      WorkstnType = POIDDX;       /* implementation-dependent */
Pint      TheStructure = 1;           /* structure ID */
char      String[20];                 /* string holder */
```

```
Ppoint      Loc;                         /* location of text */
int         I;                           /* loop control variable */

popen_phigs(stderr, 0);                  /* errors go to "stderr" */
pescape_u4("/dev/screen/phigs_window", &ConnID);
popen_ws(WorkstnID, ConnID, WorkstnType);
popen_struct(TheStructure);
pset_char_ht(0.06);
pset_char_expan(0.45);
Loc.x = 0.0;
for (I = -1; I <= 4; I++) {
    pset_char_space(I * 0.25);
    sprintf(String, "Spacing: %4.2f", I * 0.25);
    Loc.y = (6 - I) * 0.1;
    ptext(&Loc, String);
}
pclose_struct();
ppost_struct(WorkstnID, TheStructure, 1.0);
pupd_ws(WorkstnID, PFLAG_PERFORM);  /* (regeneration flag) */
pclose_ws(WorkstnID);
pclose_phigs();
}
```

Figure 11–8 shows the output of the program.

Figure 11–8. Text Spacing

Text Fonts

Before we get started, some terminology is in order.

A **character set** is an ordered collection of graphical representations. It is typically used to describe an alphabet, a set of ideograms, or a set of symbols (glyphs). A character is any single member of a character set. The character is referenced by a unique bit combination, an ordered set of bits, within the character set. For example, the letter Z is referenced in the USASCII character set by the 8–bit character code 90 (`5A` hex). Examples of character sets include USASCII, Latin1, and a set of graphical symbols such as would be used by a CAD/CAM application. 7–bit and 16–bit character sets also exist. The PHIGS standard does not define routines to manipulate character sets. However, an implementation may provide escape routines to identify and switch between different character sets.

A **font** describes the stylistic appearance of the characters within the character set when they are rendered. Typically, the same font applied to different character sets describes the appearance of those characters in a similar way. Examples of fonts include **boldface** and *italic*. The PHIGS standard allows you to switch between different fonts.

Use the SET TEXT FONT routine to switch between different fonts. The calling signatures are

```
call pstxfn (font)
```

```
pset_text_font(
   Pint            font
);
```

where:

⟨*font*⟩ is an integer corresponding to the desired font. A value of 1 selects the default font.

The number of fonts supported by a workstation is implementation–dependent. The minimum number is 2. To find out how many fonts are available on your system, use INQUIRE TEXT FACILITIES. (This routine also returns the number of available character sets.)

Besides fonts such as boldface and italic, your implementation may also support proportional and nonproportional fonts. You may have noticed that computers are notorious for giving thin characters like "i," "l," and "." just as much space as wide characters, such as "W," "m," and "@." This is called *nonproportional text*. In a nonproportional font every letter gets the same amount of space, regardless of its size.

Most implementations also offer *proportional fonts*—where every letter takes only the amount of space it needs. The words in this paragraph are in a proportional font. In contrast, the sample programs are listed in a nonproportional font. Check your implementation documentation to see whether or proportional fonts are supported—they can greatly improve the readability of text.

Text Colour

The following routines set the individual text colour attribute:

- SET TEXT COLOUR INDEX
- SET TEXT COLOUR

Both of these routines create structure elements. Refer to Chapter 12 for a comparison of the two routines.

Text Precision

Text precision is used to select how close the text rendered on a workstation matches the text that is defined by the text attributes and the transformation and clipping that are in effect. PHIGS supports the following text precisions:

String

PHIGS generates the text character string using the requested font and aligns the text primitive at the requested text position. Character height, width, and expansion factor are evaluated as closely as possible, given the capabilities of the workstation. The implementation does not have to use the character up vector, base vector, text path, text alignment, and character–spacing values for this precision. It is up to the implementation to decide how to clip the text if part of the text string is out of the display area.

Character

PHIGS generates the text character string using the requested font and calculates the following values as closely as possible for each individual character:

- Character height
- Character width
- The up direction of the character up vector
- The baseline direction of the character base vector
- Character expansion factor

For character precision, PHIGS calculates the exact spacing used between character bodies, using the ideal character body. PHIGS calculates the character body from the text aspects and the font dimensions.

PHIGS determines the position of the resulting text extent parallelogram from the text alignment and the text position. Clipping is done on at least a character–by–character basis.

Stroke

PHIGS generates the text character string in the requested font and displays it at the text position by applying all of the text aspects. An implementation may choose to display the text by sending the output device a series of vectors to generate the desired characters. It may also choose to use another form, such as raster fonts. PHIGS clips the character string exactly at the clipping boundaries.

The routine for specifying the text precision is called SET TEXT PRECISION. The calling signatures are as follows:

```
call pstxpr(precision)
```

```
pset_text_prec(
   Ptext_prec          precision
);
```

where:

⟨*precision*⟩ is an integer specifying the desired text precision. Use one of the following values:

- **String** (`PSTRP, PPREC_STRING`)
- **Character** (`PCHARP, PPREC_CHAR`)
- **Stroke** (`PSTRKP, PPREC_STROKE`)

Text Bundles

If you require certain sets of text attributes repeatedly, you can define a **text bundle**. A text bundle is a large group of text attributes that can be invoked with a single selection. Thus, if you require two different strings of text to have different fonts, colours, expansion factors, spacing, and so forth, you can define bundle 1 to have the attributes for the first kind of text, and bundle 2 to have the attributes for the second kind of text. As many different bundles as required can be defined (the limit is implementation–dependent) and then selected by their integer indexes.

The text bundle table applies both to text and annotation text. There are two routines to set values in the workstation text bundle table:

- SET TEXT REPRESENTATION defines an entry in the text attribute bundle table. Each entry consists of the following:
  - An index value that identifies the entry in the bundle table
  - Text font
  - Text precision
  - Character expansion factor
  - Character spacing
  - Text colour index
- SET TEXT REPRESENTATION PLUS also defines an entry in the text attribute bundle table. This routine sets all of the values just listed. The only difference is that it allows you to specify the text colour as a general colour (either indexed or direct).

Recall that only nongeometric attributes can be included in an attribute bundle table. That is why there are no fields for character height, character up vector, text path, or text alignment.

SET TEXT INDEX creates a structure element that selects an entry from the text bundle table.

Use the SET INDIVIDUAL ASF routine to specify whether nongeometric text attributes should be taken from individual attribute values or from the currently selected entry of the text bundle table. The default (individual or bundled) is implementation–dependent.

Annotation Text Attributes

For annotation text, there are attributes that parallel those of regular text; the one–to–one correspondence is quite consistent.

The following routines are used in the same way as those described for regular text attributes:

- SET ANNOTATION TEXT CHARACTER UP VECTOR
- SET ANNOTATION TEXT PATH
- SET ANNOTATION TEXT ALIGNMENT

The following routines apply to both regular text and annotation text primitives:

- SET CHARACTER EXPANSION FACTOR
- SET CHARACTER SPACING
- SET TEXT COLOUR INDEX
- SET TEXT COLOUR
- SET TEXT FONT
- SET TEXT PRECISION

Annotation Text Style

The only exception – where annotation text offers a concept that regular text doesn't – is the area of lead lines. (Recall that a lead line extends from the annotation text to some point associated with that text; i.e., a pointer that "leads you" to the object.) This is useful if there are many labels of annotation text – without lead lines, it would be difficult to tell which label went to which location or object on the image. Figure 11–3 earlier in this chapter shows an example of a lead line.

Use the SET ANNOTATION STYLE routine to specufy whether or not to use lead lines. Its calling signatures are

```
call psans(annotation_style)
```

```
pset_anno_style(
  Pint            annotation_style
);
```

where:

⟨*annotation_style*⟩ can be one of the following values:

- Do not use lead lines (`PUNCON`, `PANNA_STYLE_UNCONNECTED`)
- Use lead lines (`PLDLN`, `PANNA_STYLE_LEAD_LINE`)

When lead lines are used, PHIGS connects the reference point and the annotation point with a line. The line uses the current polyline attributes.

INQUIRE ANNOTATION FACILITIES returns a list of available annotation styles.

Chapter 12

Using Colour

This chapter describes how to use PHIGS colour routines. Colour can be used for emphasis, for clarity, for realism, or just for presenting visually pleasing images. If you are careful in using colour, it will serve as a valuable tool for communication.

We have already dealt with the concept of "attribute" in Chapter 9, *Using Attributes*, and discovered, for example, that "text height" is an attribute of "text." Colour is another attribute that affects PHIGS primitives. PHIGS allows an application program to use colour in one of two ways:

- Define an entry in the workstation colour table and refer to the entry by an index value. This method is known as **indexed**, or **indirect colour specification**.
- Bypass the workstation colour table and specify colour values directly. Using this method, you specify the colour model to use, as well as the actual colour values. This method is known as **direct colour specification**.

You can use either method or a combination of the two methods, depending on the needs of your application program. For example, if you use certain colour values repeatedly, you could define them in the workstation colour table and then refer to them when needed by specifying an index into the table. If you dynamically change some colours in your application, you may find it more convenient to use direct specification for those colours.

Colour indices or direct colour values can be set as individual attributes or as part of an attribute bundle table. You tell PHIGS which to use by setting the appropriate attribute source flag.

A Little Historical Perspective

If you look through a list of PHIGS routines, you will see a large number that deal with colour. A short historical diversion will help to explain why there are so many colour routines.

"In the beginning," the PHIGS standard only had indexed colour specification. Direct colour specification was developed as part of PHIGS PLUS. PHIGS PLUS defines a colour selection mechanism known as **general colour**, in which the application can use either indirect or direct colour specification. Rather than replace the existing routines, PHIGS PLUS added new routines that could use general colour.

The easiest way to describe how to use PHIGS colour routines is to place them in two broad categories: before and after PHIGS PLUS. We take this approach in the following sections. Keep in mind that all of the routines are available to you and that you can use routines from either category, depending on the needs of your application.

Colour Specification before PHIGS PLUS

Before PHIGS PLUS there was only indexed colour specification (also known as indirect colour specification). With indexed colour specification, you define an entry in the workstation colour table and then reference the entry using an index into the table.

Defining an Entry in the Workstation Colour Table

Use SET COLOUR REPRESENTATION to associate a colour with an entry in the workstation colour table. Its calling signatures are as follows:

```
call pscr(workstation_id, colour_index, spec_size, colour_spec)
```

```
pset_colr_rep(
   Pint                workstation_id,
   Pint                colour_index,
   const Pcolr_rep     *colour_spec
);
```

where:

⟨*workstation_id*⟩ is the integer sent to the OPEN WORKSTATION routine.

⟨*colour_index*⟩ specifies the entry in the workstation colour table you want to define.

⟨*spec_size*⟩ is an integer specifying how many significant values are in the ⟨*colour_spec*⟩ array. This parameter is only used by the FORTRAN binding. For all colour models defined by the PHIGS standard, this value is 3.

⟨*colour_spec*⟩ specifies the colour components to put into the workstation colour table entry selected by ⟨*colour_index*⟩. For the C binding, this parameter is defined as `Pcolr_rep`. For the FORTRAN binding, this parameter is a real array with a sufficient number of elements to contain an entire colour specification (usually 3).

For example, to associate colour index 4 with red, you would define a real array, put the desired colour definition into it, and pass the array to the SET COLOUR REPRESENTATION routine. Assuming the current colour model is RGB (red, gree, blue), you might do it this way with the FORTRAN binding:

```
real  Red(3)
data Red /1., 0., 0./              ! red in RGB
...
call pscr(WkstnID, 4, 3, Red)      ! set colour representation
```

Here is similar code for the C binding:

```
static Prgb          Red = {1.0, 0.0, 0.0};
pset_colr_rep(WorkstnID, 4, &Red);
```

Or, if the current colour model is HSV (hue, saturation, value), you might say this for the FORTRAN binding:

```
real  Red(3)
data Red /0., 1., 1./              ! red in HSV
...
call pscr(WkstnID, 4, 3, Red)      ! set colour representation
```

Colour models are described later in this chapter.

Selecting an Entry from the Workstation Colour Table

This section describes how to use individual and bundled attribute specifications to select an entry from the workstation colour table.

Individual Attribute Specification

For individual attribute specification, the following SET ⟨*primitive type*⟩ COLOUR INDEX routines select entries from the workstation colour table:

- SET EDGE COLOUR INDEX
- SET INTERIOR COLOUR INDEX
- SET POLYLINE COLOUR INDEX
- SET POLYMARKER COLOUR INDEX
- SET TEXT COLOUR INDEX

PHIGS uses the entry in the workstation colour table specified by these routines when the associated attribute source flag is set to individual.

Bundled Attribute Specification

For bundled attributes, the following SET ⟨*primitive type*⟩ REPRESENTATION routines allow you to specify the colour index for an entry in the corresponding bundle table:

- SET POLYLINE REPRESENTATION
- SET POLYMARKER REPRESENTATION
- SET TEXT REPRESENTATION
- SET INTERIOR REPRESENTATION
- SET EDGE REPRESENTATION
- SET PATTERN REPRESENTATION

Aspect Source Flags

Table 9–4 lists the aspect source flag identifiers for "PHIGS before PHIGS PLUS." These values set the *current ⟨primitive type⟩ colour index ASF* entry in the traversal state list to either bundled or individual. For example, the following fragments set the *current polyline colour index ASF* entry in the traversal state list to bundled for the FORTRAN and C bindings:

```
call psiasf(PPLCI, PBUNDL)       { set individual ASF

pset_indiv_asf(PASPECT_LINE_COLR_IND, PASF_BUNDLED);
```

Besides setting the ASF value, you must also use a SET ⟨*primitive type*⟩ INDEX routine to select an entry from the corresponding bundle table.

Example

The following program adds a bundled attribute selection to the `hello_world` program presented in Chapter 2. We have numbered the following points of interest in the program:

1. We call the SET COLOUR REPRESENTATION routine twice to associate colour values with entries 2 and 3 in the workstation colour table.

2. We call SET POLYLINE REPRESENTATION to define entry 1 in the workstation polyline bundle table. We set the following values for entry 1 in the polyline bundle table:

   - linestyle = dashed
   - linewidth = 1.5
   - polyline colour index = 3

3. Before we create the first polyline element, we set the aspect source flag for linetype, linewidth, and polyline colour index to individual. Then we call SET POLYLINE COLOUR INDEX to select entry 2 in the workstation colour table:

```
call psiasf (PLN, PINDIV)     { set individual ASF (linestyle)
call psiasf (PLWSC, PINDIV)   { set individual ASF (scale factor)
call psiasf (PPLCI, PINDIV)   { set individual ASF (colour index)
call psplci(2)                { set line colour index
call ppl(5, Line1X, Line1Y)   { first polyline
```

4. Before we create the second polyline element, we change the aspect source flag for polyline colour index to bundled and select entry 1 from the polyline bundle table:

```
call psiasf (PPLCI, PBUNDL)      { set individual ASF
call pspli(1)                    { set polyline index
call ppl(5, Line2X, Line2Y)      { second polyline
```

Note that while PHIGS renders the second polyline with the colour index specified by entry 1 in the polyline bundle table, it *does not* use the linestyle or linewidth specified by entry 1 in the bundle table. This is because the attribute sources for linetype and linewidth are still set to individual.

```
program color    { program "color.ftn"
C This program draws a text string and two polylines
C and uses color values from the workstation colour table.
C It uses both bundled and individual sources for
C the polyline colour index.
C It waits for the user to press a key to exit.
%include '/sys/ins/phigs.ins.ftn'
      integer*4 WorkID     { workstation id
      integer*4 ConnectID  { connection id
      integer*4 StrucID     { structure ID
      real      Line1X(5), Line1Y(5) { points for line1
      real      Line2X(5), Line2Y(5) { points for line2
      integer*4 ChoiceStatus, ChoiceNum  { choice status and value
      integer*4 ColorIndex  { for workstation colour table
      integer*4 BundleIndex { for polyline bundle table
      real      Color(3)    { for defining a colour
      real      Lwidth      { line width
      parameter (StrucID=1)
      data Line1X /0.25, 0.75, 0.75, 0.25, 0.25/
      data Line1Y /0.25, 0.25, 0.75, 0.75, 0.25/
      data Line2X /0.2, 0.8, 0.8, 0.2, 0.2/
      data Line2Y /0.2, 0.2, 0.8, 0.8, 0.2/

      call popph(1, 0)                    { open PHIGS
      call popwk(WorkID, 1, POIDSX)       { open workstation
      ColorIndex= 2
      Color(1)=0.0
      Color(2)=1.0                        { RGB values for cyan
      Color(3)=1.0
1.    call pscr(WorkID, ColorIndex, 3, Color) { set color rep.
      ColorIndex= 3
```

```
      Color(1)=1.0
      Color(2)=1.0                     { RGB values for yellow
      Color(3)=0.0
      call pscr(WorkID, ColorIndex, 3, Color) { set color rep.
      Lwidth=1.5
      ColorIndex=3                  { set polyline representation
      BundleIndex=1                 { for polyline bundle table
2.    call psplr(WorkID, BundleIndex, PLDASH, Lwidth, ColorIndex)
C Build structure
      call popst(StrucID)              { open structure
                                       { set individual ASF values
3.     call psiasf (PPLCI, PINDIV)      {line colour index
      call psiasf (PLN, PINDIV)        { linetype
      call psiasf (PLWSC, PINDIV)      { scale factor
      call psiasf (PTXCI, PINDIV)      { text colour index
      call psplci(2)                   { set line colour index
      call ppl(5, Line1X, Line1Y)      { first polyline
4.    call psiasf (PPLCI, PBUNDL)      { set individual ASF
      call pspli(1)                    { set polyline index
      call ppl(5, Line2X, Line2Y)      { second polyline
      call pschh(0.04)                 { set character height
      call pstxci(3)                   { set text colour index
      call ptx(0.3, 0.5,'Hello World') { text
      call pclst                       { close the structure
C Display the structure
      call ppost(WorkID, StrucID, 1.0) { post structure
      call puwk(WorkID,PPERFO)         { update workstation
C Wait for user input
      call pschm(WorkID, 2, PREQU, PNECHO)           { set choice mode
      call prqch(WorkID, 2, ChoiceStatus, ChoiceNum) { request choice
C That's all, folks!
      call pclwk(WorkID)            { close the workstation
      call pclph                    { close PHIGS
      stop                          { stop processing
      end                           { end of main program
```

Colour Specification with PHIGS PLUS

PHIGS PLUS uses the concept of general colour to specify colour values. This allows an application either to specify an index into the workstation colour table or to use direct colour values from one of the supported colour models. The PHIGS PLUS C binding defines a structure named `Pgcolr` to specify a general colour:

```
Pgcolr
  typedef struct {
    Pint          colr_type;     /* colour type             */
    Pcolrv        colr_value;    /* colour value            */
} Pgcolr;
```

where:

⟨*colr_type*⟩ can take one of the following values:

- A value of indirect (`PCOLR_INDIRECT`)

  or

- A value that identifies a colour model:
  - `PCOLR_RGB` The RGB colour model
  - `PCOLR_CIELUV` The CIELUV (Commission Internationale de l'Eclairage) colour model
  - `PCOLR_HSV` The HSV colour model
  - `PCOLR_HLS` The HLS (hue, lightness, saturation) colour model
  - or an implementation–dependent value if the implementation supports other colour models.

If the colour type is indirect, then ⟨*colr_value*⟩ contains an index into the workstation colour table. If the colour type specifies a colour model, then ⟨*colr_value*⟩ contains the colour values of the colour (for example, red, green, and blue values for the RGB colour model).

The `Pcolrv` data type is defined as follows:

```
Pcolrv
  typedef union {
    Pint          colr_ind;      /* colour index            */
    Pcolr_rep     colr_rep;      /* colour representation   */
} Pcolrv;
```

See Appendix D for the definition of the `Pcolr_rep` data type.

Section 4.5.1 of the PHIGS PLUS standard has an illustration that shows how general colour specification works. We show a similar illustration in Figure 12–1.

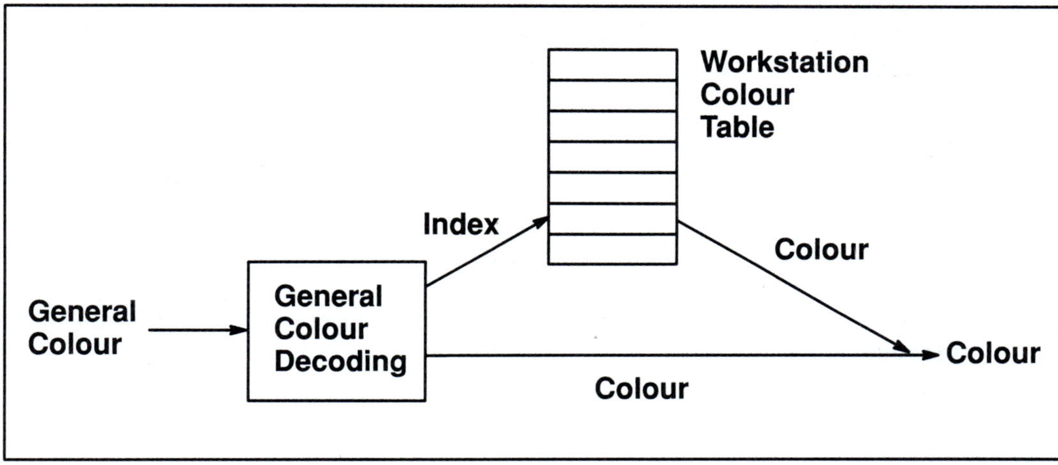

Figure 12–1. Resolving General Colour

All PHIGS PLUS routines that use colour allow general colour specification. PHIGS PLUS also enhances the functionality of a number of standard PHIGS routines by adding a new PHIGS PLUS version, explained next.

Individual Attribute Specification (General Colour)

For individual attribute specification, the SET ⟨*primitive type*⟩ COLOUR INDEX routines have a PHIGS PLUS counterpart: SET ⟨*primitive type*⟩ COLOUR. These routines allow general colour specification when the ASF for a ⟨*primitive type*⟩ colour is set to individual. The PHIGS PLUS routines are as follows:

- SET POLYLINE COLOUR
- SET POLYMARKER COLOUR

- SET TEXT COLOUR
- SET INTERIOR COLOUR
- SET BACK INTERIOR COLOUR
- SET EDGE COLOUR

The calling signatures of all these routines are identical. For example, the SET POLYLINE COLOUR routine is defined as follows for the C binding:

```
pset_line_colr (
   const Pgcolr   *colr   /* polyline colour */
);
```

Refer to the description of the `Pgcolr` data type earlier in this section.

The following fragment uses general colour to set the polyline colour attribute. PHIGS uses the values when the attribute source flag for polyline colour is set to individual. The example sets the polyline colour both by using a colour index and by specifying the colour with the RGB colour model.

```
Pgcolr   Colour;

popen_struct(Cube);                /* open structure               */
pset_indiv_asf(PASPECT_LINE_COLR_IND, PASF_INDIV);
/* use indirect colour specification */
Colour.colr_type = PCOLR_INDIRECT;
Colour.colr_value.colr_ind = 4;    /* entry 4 of wrkst. color table */
pset_line_colr(&Colour);           /* set polyline colour          */
.
. draw first polyline
.
/* use direct colour specification */
Colour.colr_type = PCOLR_RGB;
Colour.colr_value.colr_rep.rgb.red = 1.0;
Colour.colr_value.colr_rep.rgb.green = 0.0;
Colour.colr_value.colr_rep.rgb.blue = 0.0;
pset_line_colr(&Colour);           /* set polyline colour          */
.
. draw second polyline
.
pclose_struct();                   /* close structure              */
```

Bundled Attribute Specification (General Colour)

For bundled attribute specification, all of the SET ⟨*primitive type*⟩ REPRESENTATION routines have a PHIGS PLUS counterpart, SET ⟨*primitive type*⟩ REPRESENTATION PLUS, that uses general colour specification when the ASF for a ⟨*primitive type*⟩ colour is bundled during traversal. The PHIGS PLUS routines are as follows:

- SET POLYLINE REPRESENTATION PLUS
- SET POLYMARKER REPRESENTATION PLUS
- SET TEXT REPRESENTATION PLUS
- SET INTERIOR REPRESENTATION PLUS
- SET EDGE REPRESENTATION PLUS
- SET PATTERN REPRESENTATION PLUS

These routines set values in the same bundle tables as the corresponding SET ⟨*primitive type*⟩ REPRESENTATION routines. They just allow for additional fields as specified by PHIGS PLUS.

Attribute Source Flags

Table 9–5 lists the ASF identifiers for PHIGS PLUS. These values set the *current ⟨primitive type⟩ colour ASF* entry in the traversal state list to either bundled or individual. For example, the following fragments set the *current polyline colour ASF* entry in the traversal state list to bundled for the FORTRAN and C bindings:

```
call psiasf(PPLCOL, PBUNDL)      { set individual ASF
```

```
pset_indiv_asf(PASPECT_LINE_COLR, PASF_BUNDLED);
```

Besides setting the ASF value, you must also use a SET ⟨*primitive type*⟩ INDEX routine to select an entry from the corresponding bundle table.

The ASF identifier tells PHIGS to use the general colour specified by one of the following sources:

- If the ASF value is bundled, use the general colour specified by the currently selected entry from the appropriate bundle table.
- If the ASF value is individual, use the currently selected individual general colour value for the primitive type.

Recall that the general colour is either an index into the workstation colour table or a set of direct colour values from a specific colour model.

We recommend that if you are using bundled attributes, do not mix the new PHIGS PLUS routines with the older indexed–only routines, because it can get confusing as to which ASF value is in effect at a given time.

Colour Models

A **colour model** is a conceptual definition of a colour space in terms of explicit parameters. PHIGS supports the following colour models:

- **RGB** (red, green, blue)
- **CIELUV** (Commission Internationale de l'Eclairage)
- **HLS** (hue, lightness, saturation)
- **HSV** (hue, saturation, value)

Colour models are discussed in Appendix B. Refer to your implementation documentation to see which colour models are supported.

As with the individual colour attribute routines, PHIGS PLUS added new routines rather than modifying the existing colour model routines. The following paragraphs give a breakdown of the various colour model routines.

When you use *indirect* colour specification, use a SET COLOUR MODEL routine to specify the workstation colour model. Note that the colour model is needed only to define the colour model to be applied when setting or inquiring the workstation colour table. The following routines pertain to indirect colour specification:

- SET COLOUR MODEL sets the colour model for indirect colour specification. This routine sets the *current colour model* entry in the workstation state list.

- INQUIRE COLOUR MODEL returns the colour model in effect for indirect colour specification. The routine returns the value of the *current colour model* entry in the workstation state list.

- INQUIRE COLOUR MODEL FACILITIES returns the default colour model and the number of color models supported by the given workstation type.

Note that the SET COLOUR MODEL routine does not alter any colours already defined in the colour table, although it redefines the values as appropriate to match the new colour model. For example, if the current colour model is RGB and an entry of the colour representation table is (1, 0, 0), that entry defines red. If inquired, (1, 0, 0) will be returned. However, if the colour model is changed to HSV, the coordinate values for that entry will be returned as (0, 1, 1) – it still defines red, but the values will reflect the HSV representation of that colour.

When you use *direct* colour specification, you identify the colour model within the general colour parameter. Use the INQUIRE DIRECT COLOUR MODEL FACILITIES routine to determine how many colour models are available to you for direct colour specification.

When you use lighting and shading, you can specify the colour model to be used for colour interpolation (see Chapter 17 and Chapter 18). The following routines pertain to colour interpolation:

- SET RENDERING COLOUR MODEL sets the *current rendering colour model* entry in the traversal state list. This routine sets the colour model used for colour interpolation when using lighting and shading.

- INQUIRE RENDERING COLOUR MODEL FACILITIES returns the set of rendering colour models supported by a workstation.

Inquiring Colour Capabilities

The following routines allow an application to determine the capabilities of the device on which it is running:

- INQUIRE COLOUR FACILITIES returns the following information:
  - The number of available colour indices. This corresponds to the number of unique colours that a workstation supports (not necessarily simultaneously). A value of zero indicates a continuous range of colours (2^{24} colours).
  - Whether the workstation type supports colour or is monochromatic.
  - The number of indices corresponding to predefined colour table entries.
  - The primary colour chromaticity coefficients and luminance value for the primaries of the display device.
- INQUIRE WORKSTATION STATE TABLE LENGTHS returns the maximum number of entries that can be defined in each of the following PHIGS tables:
  - Polyline bundle table
  - Polymarker bundle table
  - Text bundle table
  - Interior bundle table
  - Edge bundle table
  - Pattern table
  - Colour table
  - View table

  You can use the value returned for the maximum number of entries in the colour table to ensure that you never use an invalid colour index.

  Note that the INQUIRE WORKSTATION STATE TABLE LENGTHS PLUS routine returns the maximum number of entries in the depth cue, light source, and colour mapping tables.

These routines require a workstation type as the first parameter. You should supply a specific workstation type, rather than a generic type to ensure that you get the correct values for the device. Refer to the example in Chapter 22, *Programming with PHIGS*.

Inquiring the Values of an Entry in the Workstation Colour Table

Colours in the colour representation table can be inquired via INQUIRE COLOUR REPRESENTATION. Its calling signatures are a little more complex than that of SET COLOUR REPRESENTATION:

```
 call pqcr(workstation_id, colour_index, spec_max, inquiry_type,
+ error, spec_size, colour_spec)
```

```
pinq_colr_rep(
   Pint                 workstation_id,
   Pint                 colour_index,
   Pinq_type            inquiry_type,
   Pint                 *error,
   Pcolr_rep            *colour_spec
);
```

where:

⟨*workstation_id*⟩ is the integer sent to the OPEN WORKSTATION routine.

⟨*colour_index*⟩ is an integer specifying which colour representation table entry you are interrogating.

⟨*spec_max*⟩ is an integer specifying how many elements have been allocated for the ⟨*colour_spec*⟩ array. This must be greater than or equal to 3 for the currently supported colour models. This parameter is required only for the FORTRAN binding.

⟨*inquiry_type*⟩ is an integer that returns the classification of colour returned. It will have one of two possible values:

- **Set** (`PSET, PINQ_SET`) indicates that the colour specification returned is exactly what the application originally set.
- **Realized** (`PREALI, PINQ_REALIZED`) indicates that the colour specification returned are those values used by the workstation. They may be slightly different than those values requested by the application.

⟨*error*⟩ is an integer that indicates any problems encountered in attempting to process the request. If no error occurred, ⟨*error*⟩ is 0.

⟨*spec_size*⟩ is an integer returning the number of components in ⟨*colour_spec*⟩. This will always be 3 for the colour models defined by the PHIGS standard, since they all have three values. This parameter is required only for the FORTRAN binding.

⟨*colour_spec*⟩ specifies the colour components of the workstation colour table entry selected by ⟨*colour_index*⟩ (assuming no error occurred). For the C binding, this parameter is defined as `Pcolr_rep` (see Appendix D). For the FORTRAN binding, this parameter is a real array with a sufficient number of elements to contain an entire colour specification (usually 3).

If the specified type of returned value is "Realized," and the entry has not been defined, PHIGS returns the colour associated with colour index 1. Note that PHIGS renders the colour defined by entry 1 if the referenced entry is undefined.

Background Colour

In the PHIGS standard, the background colour is the colour defined at entry 0 in the workstation colour table. If you wish to change the background colour to something other than the default black, just redefine entry 0 in the workstation colour table. Some implementations provide extensions that allow you to set the background colour for specific views.

Chapter 13

Name Sets and Filters

This chapter describes how to use name sets to make primitives eligible for name set highlighting, invisibility, and picking.

Highlighting allows you to emphasize an output primitive by changing its visual attributes. The way that primitives are highlighted is implementation-dependent. The most common way is to redraw the primitive in a different "highlight" colour. For example, the implementation may use workstation colour index 1 as the highlight colour for all primitives. As an extension to the PHIGS standard, some implementations support a workstation highlight table and a number of escape routines to define, select, and inquire entries in the table.

Invisibility has to do with selectively turning off the display of one or more primitives.

Picking allows the user to identify output primitives using a pick device such as a mouse button. See Chapter 14, *Graphical Input*, for an explanation of picking.

Name Sets

Name sets allow you to classify objects by name. While structure hierarchy is usually organized in terms of logical and/or spatial relationships, there are times when additional classification is necessary. For example, in a molecular modelling application, a chemist may want to view only the hydrogen atoms or only the oxygen atoms of a particular molecule. In an architectural package, an engineer may want to view only the electrical system on the third floor. Name sets give you this freedom without introducing additional complication to the structure hierarchy.

The following are some important points about using name sets. These topics are expanded upon later in the chapter.

- There are separate workstation filters for picking, invisibility, and highlighting.
- Each filter consists of an inclusion set (a list of names that are specifically enabled for an operation such as highlighting) and an exclusion set (a list of names that are specifically excluded from the operation).
- The current name set is defined in the CSS, through two structure elements:
  - An *add names to set* element adds names to the current name set.
  - A *subtract names from set* element subtracts names from the current name set.
- Name sets are identification attributes (see Chapter 9, *Using Attributes*). The current name set is an attribute applicable to all primitives.

Workstation Filters

At display time, the names in the current name set are compared to the workstation's invisibility, pick, and highlight filters (see Figure 13–1). Each filter consists of an inclusion set and an exclusion set of names that determine which primitives are eligible for the operation.

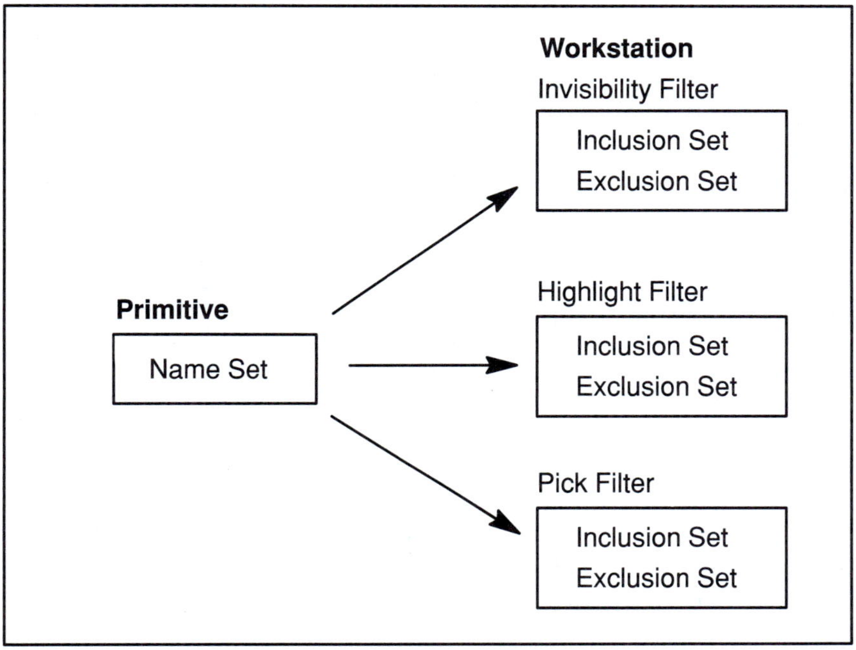

Figure 13–1. Name Sets and Workstation Filters

The workstation filters are part of the workstation state list. Therefore, you modify the filters outside of structure traversal. The following routines set the workstation filters:

- The SET INVISIBILITY FILTER routine defines the inclusion and exclusion filter name sets for invisibility.
- The SET HIGHLIGHTING FILTER routine defines the inclusion and exclusion filter name sets for highlighting.
- The SET PICK FILTER routine defines the inclusion and exclusion filter name sets for picking.

The following inquiry routines return the associated inclusion filter name set and the exclusion filter name set along with the number of elements in each:

- INQUIRE INVISIBILITY FILTER
- INQUIRE HIGHLIGHTING FILTER
- INQUIRE PICK DEVICE STATE
- INQUIRE PICK DEVICE STATE 3

Modifying the Current Name Set

The current name set is part of the traversal state list and is therefore only modifiable during structure traversal. The following CSS element-creating routines add and subtract names from the current name set:

- ADD NAMES TO SET
- REMOVE NAMES FROM SET

The value of the name set attribute associated with a given primitive is defined when a structure is traversed. When PHIGS encounters an *add names to set* structure element during traversal, it defines the name set for subsequent primitives as the union of the name set specified by the *add names to set* structure element and the current (inherited) name set. When a *remove names from set* structure element is encountered, all elements of the name set identified by the structure element are removed from the current name set.

When traversal begins, the current name set is empty. This means that the default for all primitives is that they are visible, not highlighted, and *not pickable*.

Use the INQUIRE PHIGS FACILITIES routine to inquire the number of available names for name sets. This value is defined in the PHIGS description table. The minimum range for a PHIGS implementation is from 0 to 63. Note that some implementations suggest that you keep the name set values as small as possible to improve performance.

Note that the SET * FILTER routines *replace* the old filters. However, the ADD/REMOVE routines *incrementally edit* the filters.

Defining the Workstation Filters

This section describes the relationship between the inclusion set, the exclusion set, and the current name set. In order for a primitive element to be eligible for a highlighting, invisibility, or picking operation, the name set associated with the primitive:

- Must have at least one member in the related inclusion filter
- Must not have any member in the related exclusion filter

If the inclusion and exclusion filters are empty, the primitive is not highlightable, cannot be made invisible (through name set functions), and cannot be picked. These relationships are expressed below. The symbol $\cap$ stands for intersection, and the symbol $\cup$ stands for union.

- For ADD NAMES TO SET:

  $C = C \cup N$ — The current set becomes the set union of the previous value of the current set and the specified name set.

- For REMOVE NAMES FROM SET:

  $C = C - N$ — The current set becomes the set difference of the previous value of the current set and the specified name set.

- Invisibility, highlighting, or pick filtering is performed if and only if:

  $(C \cap I \neq 0)$ AND $(C \cap E = 0)$

  There are names in the current set that are also in the include set, and there are no names in the current set that are also in the exclude set.

These relationships may seem confusing at first, but the actual use of name sets is quite straightforward. See the example at the end of the chapter.

PHIGS resets the related inclusion and exclusion filters each time you make a call to SET INVISIBILITY FILTER, SET PICK FILTER, or SET HIGHLIGHTING FILTER. To clear the filters and make all primitives ineligible for the operation, set both count values to 0. For example, the following examples use the FORTRAN binding:

`call pspkft(wkid, dev_no, 0, incl_set, 0, excl_set)`	clears the pick filter
`call pshlft(wkid, 0, incl_set, 0, excl_set)`	clears the highlighting filter
`call psivft(wkid, 0, incl_set, 0, excl_set)`	clears the invisibility filter

Name Set Example

This FORTRAN example demonstrates a simple use of name sets for highlighting and invisibility. The program uses text primitives to represent electrical and plumbing features on three floors of a building. The top half of Table 13–1 shows the output of the program.

Note that the text primitives "Electrical" and "Plumbing" are added to the CSS before any name sets are defined. Therefore, they do not have any name set attributes associated with them and are never eligible for highlighting or invisibility.

Table 13–1. Output from Name Set Example

First Frame	**Second Frame**	**Third Frame**

`Electrical Plumbing`
`Floor 1    Floor 1`
`Floor 2    Floor 2`
`Floor 3    Floor 3`
	`Electrical Plumbing`
	`Floor 1` `   Floor 1`
	`Floor 2    Floor 2`
	`Floor 3` `   Floor 3`
		`Electrical Plumbing`
		`Floor 1    Floor 1`

After first call to REDRAW ALL STRUCTURES Exclusion and inclusion sets are empty. Nothing is eligible for name set highlighting or invisi–bility.	After second call to REDRAW ALL STRUCTURES Highlighting inclusion set: [Electrical] Highlighting exclusion set: [Plumbing, Floor2]	After third call to REDRAW ALL STRUCTURES Invisibility inclusion set: [Electrical, Plumbing] Invisibility exclusion set: [Floor1]

The program works as follows:

- The program uses a keyboard choice device (choice device 2) to allow the program to pause until the operator presses a key. We use the REQUEST CHOICE routine to request the choice value. In the program, the REQUEST CHOICE routine follows each call to REDRAW ALL STRUCTURES.
- This example assumes that the implementation uses workstation colour table index 1 for the highlighting colour. That is why we set entry 1 in the workstation colour table to white. Check your implementation documentation for information on the default highlighting colour.
- There is one structure in the program, named `Root`.
- The program creates the text message "Press any key to continue" and the headings "Electrical" and "Plumbing" while the name set is empty. Since no name sets are associated with these elements, they cannot be eligible for highlighting or invisibility (they are always visible).
- The program adds and subtracts names from the current name set in order to associate a specific name set with each primitive.

The full program listing follows:

```
      program nameset    { nameset.ftn
C   DESCRIPTION: Demonstrates the use of name set attributes for
C                highlighting and invisibility.  Uses a keyboard choice
C                device to pause and let operator press key to continue.
%include '/sys/ins/phigs.ins.ftn'
       integer*4  BufferLength               { PHIGS buffer length
       integer*4  WorkID                     { workstation ID
       integer*4  ConnectID                { communication channel ID
       integer*4  Name(255)                  { name set
       integer*4  Root                       { structure ID
       parameter  (ConnectID=1)
       parameter  (BufferLength=0, WorkID=1)
       parameter  (Root=1)
       integer*4  IncludeSet(10), ExcludeSet(10) { name set variables
       integer*4  Floor1, Floor2, Floor3, Electrical, Plumbing
       parameter  (Floor1=1, Floor2=2, Floor3=3)
       parameter  (Electrical=4, Plumbing=5)
```

```
      integer*4  ChoiceStatus, ChoiceNum  { choice status and value
      character*80 message               { for displaying message
      real       White(3),Green(3),Yellow(3) { for defining colours
      data White  / 1.0, 1.0, 1.0 /
      data Green  / 0.0, 1.0, 0.0 /
      data Yellow / 1.0, 1.0, 0.0 /
      integer*4  ERRIND              { error indicator return value
C Open PHIGS and workstation
      call popph(1, BufferLength)
      call popwk(WorkID, ConnectID, POIDSX)
      call pscr(WorkID, 1, 3, White) { set colour representation
      call pscr(WorkID, 2, 3, Green)
      call pscr(WorkID, 3, 3, Yellow)
      call pschm(WorkID, 2, PREQU, PNECHO)   { set choice mode
C  Open the root structure
      call popst(Root)                     { open structure
C  Create message and category headings without name set attributes
      call pschh(0.03)                     { set text height
      call pstxci (2)                      { text colour index
      call ptx (0.02, 0.8, 'Press any key to continue')
      call pschh(0.05)                     { set text height
      call ptx (0.05, 0.6, 'ELECTRICAL')
      call ptx ( 0.6, 0.6, 'PLUMBING' )
      call pstxci (3)                      { text colour index
C Create name set attribute elements for each Electrical component
C   Current name set = empty
      Name(1) = Electrical
      Name(2) = Floor1
      call pads(2, Name)        { add Electrical, Floor1 to name set
C   Current name set = Electrical, Floor1
      call ptx (0.05, 0.5,'floor 1')
      Name(1) = Floor1
      call pres(1, Name)               { remove Floor1 from name set
      Name(1) = Floor2
      call pads(1, Name)                { add Floor2 to name set
C   Current name set = Electrical, Floor2
      call ptx (0.05, 0.4,'floor 2')
      call pres(1, Name)               { remove Floor2 from name set
      Name(1) = Floor3
      call pads(1, Name)                { add Floor3 to name set
C   Current name set = Electrical, Floor3
      call ptx (0.05, 0.3,'floor 3')
      Name(1) = Electrical
```

```
      call pres(1, Name)            { remove Electrical from name set
C   Current name set = Floor3
C   Create name set attribute elements for each Plumbing component
      Name(1) = Plumbing
      call pads(1, Name)                  { add Plumbing to name set
C   Current name set = Plumbing, Floor3
      call ptx (0.6, 0.3,'floor 3')
      Name(1) = Floor3
      call pres(1, Name)               { remove Floor3 from name set
      Name(1) = Floor2
      call pads(1, Name)                  { add Floor2 to name set
C   Current name set = Plumbing, Floor2
      call ptx (0.6, 0.4,'floor 2')
      call pres(1, Name)               { remove Floor2 from name set
      Name(1) = Floor1
      call pads(1, Name)                  { add Floor1 to name set
C   Current name set = Plumbing, Floor1
      call ptx (0.6, 0.5,'floor 1')
C Close the structure and post it to the workstation
      call pclst                          { close structure
      call ppost (WorkID, Root, 1.0)      { post structure
      call prst (WorkID, PALWAY)           { redraw all structures
      call prqch(WorkID, 2, ChoiceStatus, ChoiceNum) { request choice
C Highlight electrical on floors 1 and 3
      IncludeSet(1) = Electrical
      ExcludeSet(1) = Plumbing
      ExcludeSet(2) = Floor2
C Set highlighting filter
      call pshlft (WorkID, 1, IncludeSet, 2, ExcludeSet)
C Redraw all structures and request choice
      call prst (WorkID, PALWAY)           { redraw all structures
      call prqch(WorkID, 2, ChoiceStatus, ChoiceNum) { request choice
C Clear the highlighting filter
      call pshlft (WorkID, 0, IncludeSet, 0, ExcludeSet)
C Make electrical and plumbing on floors 2 and 3 invisible.
      IncludeSet(1) = Electrical
      IncludeSet(2) = Plumbing
      ExcludeSet(1) = Floor1
C Set invisibility filter
      call psivft (WorkID, 2, IncludeSet, 1, ExcludeSet)
C Redraw all structures and request choice
      call prst (WorkID, PALWAY)           { redraw all structures
      call prqch(WorkID, 2, ChoiceStatus, ChoiceNum) { request choice
```

```
call pupast(WorkID)                          { unpost all structures
call pclwk(WorkID)                           { close workstation
call pclph                                      { close PHIGS
stop
end
```

Chapter 14

Graphical Input

This chapter describes how to use PHIGS input routines to obtain graphical input from an end user (also called an operator). The PHIGS input model is based on the model established by the Graphics Kernel System (GKS). This is a flexible model that accepts input from many different kinds of physical or simulated devices and provides a smooth, natural flow of control between the operator and the application program.

The logical input devices described in this chapter are only supported on INPUT and OUTIN PHIGS workstation types (see Chapter 3, *Controlling PHIGS*). An INPUT workstation performs input only and does not perform graphical output (for example, a digitizing table). An OUTIN workstation accepts input from the operator and can perform graphical output. An example is a computer with a raster display device and some number of available input devices, including a keyboard, a pointer device (e.g., a mouse), and others such as a dial box or button box.

Selecting an Input Model for Your Application

Although the PHIGS standard has a flexible, easy-to-use input model, many applications decide to obtain input from the X Window system instead. This allows an application to customize its user interface using packages like Motif and X-widgets.

However, since PHIGS provides no tools for synchronizing X events with PHIGS events, we recommend that you use either all X input or all PHIGS input. If you plan to use all X input, do not use an OUTIN workstation type. Use an output-only workstation type instead. See "Picking with X Input" later in this chapter for more information on using PHIGS together with X.

Overview of PHIGS Input

An application program obtains graphical input from an operator by controlling the activity of one or more logical input devices. These devices deliver logical input values to the application program. The set of logical input values that apply to a particular device is called the **measure** of a device.

PHIGS identifies a logical input device by a workstation identifier, an input class, and a device number.

- The **workstation identifier** identifies an open workstation, of which the logical input device is a part.
- The **input class** determines the type of input value that the logical input device delivers. There are six input classes, as follows:
  - Locator
  - Stroke
  - Valuator
  - Choice
  - Pick
  - String
- The **device number** distinguishes different logical devices of the same input class on the same workstation. For example, there may be four locator devices, each with its own device number.

Implementation-dependent Features

The number of available logical input devices and the way in which they are supported are two of the most implementation-dependent aspects of PHIGS. Each implementation defines its own set of logical input devices within the framework of the PHIGS standard. For example, Table 14–1 lists an example set of logical input devices supported by one implementation. The first two columns in the table (the logical input class and the measure) are defined by the PHIGS standard. The second two columns show how one implementation chose to map the logical input classes to physical devices and software-simulated devices (the "popup" devices). See your implementation documentation for details about your system.

Table 14–1. Examples of Logical Input Classes and Physical/Simulated Devices

Defined by PHIGS		**Implementation-dependent Examples**	
Logical Input Class	**Logical Value (Measure) Returned**	**Logical Device Number**	**Physical or Simulated Device**
Locator	A position in world coordinates and a view index	1–3	Mouse buttons 1–3
Stroke	A sequence of positions in world coordinates and a view index	1–3	Mouse buttons 1–3
Valuator	A real number representing a dial's position	10–40	Dial box – Popup slider displays relative dial movement
Choice	A choice status and a nonnegative integer representing a selection from a number of choices	1 2 3 4 5–8 9–10	– Mouse-driven choice device – Keyboard-driven choice device – Function key choice device – Popup function box emulator – Popup choice menus – Physical function key box
Pick	A pick status, a pick path, and a pick path depth	1–3	Mouse buttons 1–3
String	An ASCII character string	1	Keyboard – Popup text string

Routine Names

The PHIGS FORTRAN binding includes a two–letter suffix in a routine name to indicate the particular input class. The abbreviations and examples of their use follow:

- Locator (`lc`)—for example, the name for GET LOCATOR is `pgtlc`.
- Stroke (`sk`)—for example, the name for GET STROKE is `pgtsk`.
- Valuator (`vl`)—for example, the name for GET VALUATOR is `pgtvl`.
- Choice (`ch`)—for example, the name for GET CHOICE is `pgtch`.

- Pick (`pk`)—for example, the name for GET PICK is `pgtpk`.
- String (`st`)—for example, the name for GET STRING is `pgtst`.

The PHIGS C binding also includes a syllable in routine names to indicate the particular input class. The abbreviations and examples of their use follow:

- Locator (`loc`)—for example, the name for GET LOCATOR is `pget_loc`.
- Stroke (`stroke`)—for example, the name for GET STROKE is `pget_stroke`.
- Valuator (`val`)—for example, the name for GET VALUATOR is `pget_val`.
- Choice (`choice`)—for example, the name for GET CHOICE is `pget_choice`.
- Pick (`pick`)—for example, the name for GET PICK is `pget_pick`.
- String (`string`)—for example, the name for GET STRING is `pget_string`.

Also, many of the PHIGS input routines have similar textual names that differ only with the type of input class. In this manual we often use the term ⟨*input_class*⟩ to indicate a group of routines. For example, the following routines can all be referred to as GET ⟨*input_class*⟩ routines:

- GET LOCATOR
- GET STROKE
- GET VALUATOR
- GET CHOICE
- GET PICK
- GET STRING

Summary of PHIGS Input Routines

Table 14–2 summarizes the different types of input routines.

Table 14–2. Input Routines

Routine	Description
INITIALIZE ⟨*input class*⟩	Defines the initial parameters for a logical input device.
SET ⟨*input class*⟩ MODE	Sets the operating mode and echo state for a particular device. There are three operating modes: Request, Sample, and Event. There are two echo modes: echo and no echo.
REQUEST ⟨*input class*⟩ (used for devices in Request mode)	Performs a request on a specified device. PHIGS prompts the operator for data and waits until the requested input has been entered or until a break action occurs.
SAMPLE ⟨*input class*⟩ (used for devices in Sample mode)	Immediately returns the current values associated with a specified device without waiting for user input.
AWAIT EVENT (used for devices in Event mode)	If input queue is empty, wait until an event occurs or until the time specified in a timeout parameter has elapsed. If there is at least one event report in the event queue, move the oldest event report in the queue to the PHIGS state list.
GET ⟨*input class*⟩ (used for devices in Event mode)	Used to examine an event report removed from the event queue by AWAIT EVENT.
FLUSH DEVICE EVENTS	Removes all entries in the event queue for a specified logical input device.
SET PICK IDENTIFIER	Creates a structure element that associates a pick identifier with subsequent primitives.
SET PICK FILTER	Sets the pick inclusion and exclusion filters.

The Logical Input Device Model

Each logical input device contains the following:

- Initial value
- Trigger and measure
- Prompt and echo type
- Echo area or echo volume
- Data record containing details about the prompt and echo type

The device's trigger and measure are defined by PHIGS. The application program can supply the initial value, echo area or volume, and data record. Depending on the implementation's definition of a device, the application can select from a list of predefined prompt and echo types.

Initial Values

Each logical input device has a set of initial values (for example, the initial locator position and view index for locator devices). When you open an OUTIN or INPUT workstation, PHIGS takes these initial values from the workstation description table. You can change the initial values by reinitializing the device. Refer to "Initializing Input Devices," later in this chapter.

Triggers and Measures

Each device that is in Request or Event mode (see "Operating Modes," later in this chapter) has an associated **trigger**, which the operator uses to indicate a value. An operator action (such as depressing a pointer device button) causes a trigger to "fire." A single trigger can be associated with more than one device. For example, a locator device and a pick device can both be triggered by the same mouse button.

Devices in Sample mode do not have a trigger. PHIGS automatically determines the current logical input values of the device each time the application calls the appropriate SAMPLE ⟨*input_class*⟩ routine.

As stated earlier in this chapter, the current logical input values associated with a given logical device are called the measure of the device. You can think of a measure as the state of an independent, active process (a measure process). The measure process is in existence whenever the device is taking part in an interaction; it does not exist otherwise. A measure process begins under the following circumstances:

- When a request is made of a device that is in Request mode (for example, when the application calls REQUEST LOCATOR)
- Whenever the application calls a SET ⟨*input_class*⟩ MODE routine to put the device in Sample or Event mode

The following summarizes the main points about a measure process:

- There can only be one measure process per logical input device.
- A measure process is active when you are in Sample or Event mode, or when you are making a "request" in Request mode.
- Each time you call SET ⟨*input_class*⟩ MODE with a mode parameter of Sample or Event, PHIGS stops any existing measure on that device and begins a new measure process.
- If you are in Request mode but are not making a request, there is no active measure process. The measure process begins when you call a REQUEST ⟨*input_class*⟩ routine and finishes after the operator satisfies the request or performs a break action.

Table 14–1, earlier in this chapter, lists the measure values returned by each logical input device.

Prompt and Echo Types—Displaying Logical Input Devices

Each logical input device has at least one "prompt and echo type, " or "PET." The following definitions explain the terms *prompt* and *echo*:

- A **prompt** is a cue to an operator, indicating that a particular logical input device is available.
- An **echo** is a cue that immediately notifies an operator of the measure of a logical input device.

- An **echo type** identifies the prompt and echo technique for a particular logical input device.

The prompt and echo types differ with each device. You select the prompt and echo type for a device in an INITIALIZE ⟨*input_class*⟩ routine. The following list shows some prompt and echo types that could be used to designate the current locator position for locator devices:

- Tracking cross
- Crosshair
- Rubber band line
- User-definable prompt made up of polyline or fill area primitives

See your implementation documentation for details on the prompt and echo types available on your system.

Echo Areas and Echo Volumes

Some logical input devices require an **echo area** (2D) or **echo volume** (3D) so PHIGS will know where to display the associated prompt or echo.

You specify the echo area or echo volume in an INITIALIZE ⟨*input_class*⟩ routine. PHIGS allows the application program to specify an echo area for 2D initialization routines and an echo volume for 3D initialization routines. The area is represented in device coordinates as x_{min}, x_{max}, y_{min}, and y_{max} (add z_{min} and z_{max} for echo volume). The type of measurement used for device coordinates is implementation-dependent. For example, one implementation may use approximate meters and another may use pixels. However, the value (0, 0, 0) is always at the bottom left-hand (rear) corner of the PHIGS display area.

If you need to specify an echo area or echo volume, first use INQUIRE DISPLAY SPACE SIZE or INQUIRE DISPLAY SPACE SIZE 3 to inquire the maximum area available for the echo area or echo volume, respectively, in device coordinates. See the picking example at the end of this chapter for sample code.

Note that some devices may ignore the echo area/volume parameter in an INITIALIZE ⟨*input_class*⟩ routine. In that case the input device (for example, a pick device) can display its prompt anywhere in the PHIGS display area. Check your implementation documentation for details on which logical input devices require echo area/volume information.

Coordinates Returned by Locator and Stroke Devices

Locator and stroke devices return world coordinate values. In order to do this, PHIGS automatically performs the reverse mapping from screen coordinates to world coordinates. This consists of using the inverse workstation transformation (DC to NPC) and the inverse viewing transformation (NPC to WC). Figure 14–1 illustrates the transformation.

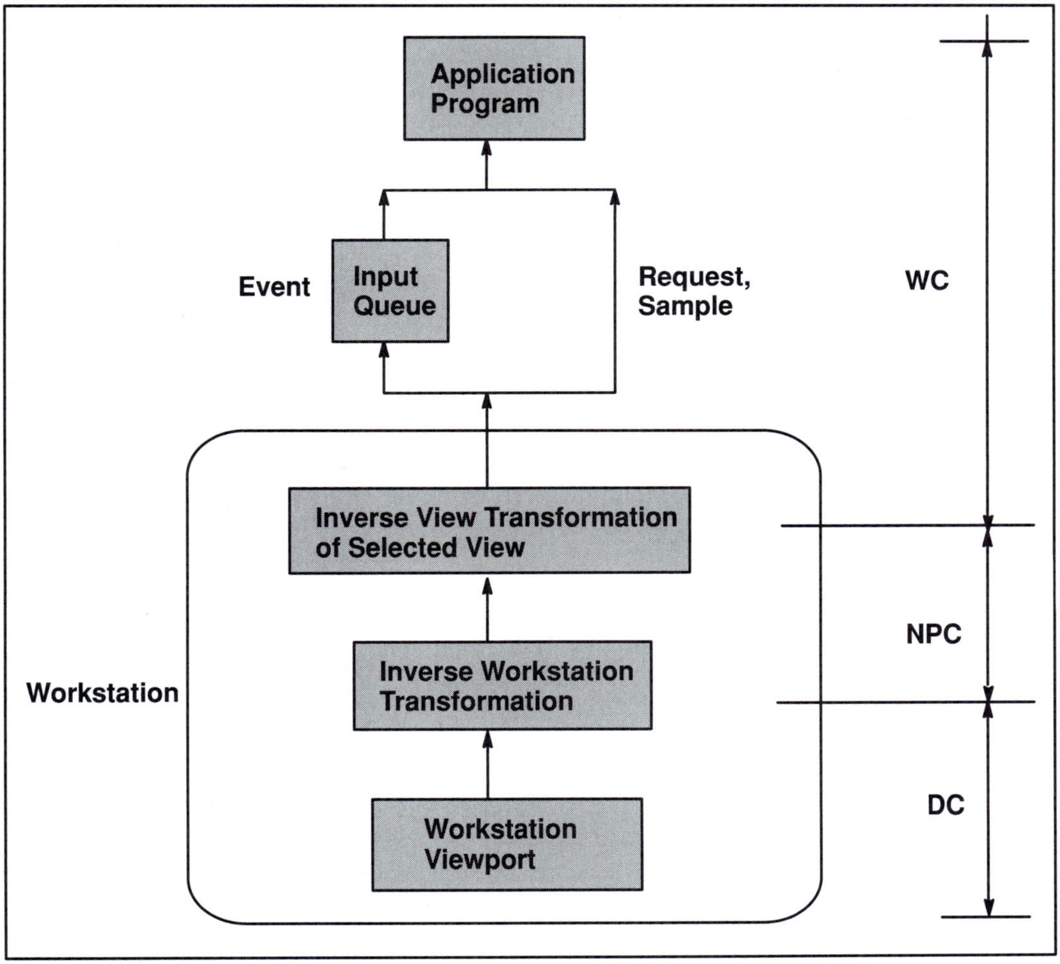

Figure 14–1. Transformation of Coordinate Input

Coordinate input can only be received from locations inside the portion of the workstation viewport into which the current workstation window is mapped.

PHIGS compares the coordinate input position in NPC coordinates to the current view clipping limits of the view transformations. It then finds the highest-priority view transformation whose current view clipping limits contain the coordinate position.

If you have overlapping views, PHIGS compares the corresponding *view transformation input priority* values in the workstation state list to determine which view has the highest priority. By default, views are prioritized according to their index number, with 0 being the highest priority, 1 being the second highest, and so forth. You can change this priority using the SET VIEW TRANSFORMATION INPUT PRIORITY routine. This routine takes the following input values:

- Workstation identifier
- Index of the view being adjusted
- Index of the reference view
- Flag indicating whether the view index should be higher (`PHIGHR, PRI_HIGHER`) or lower (`PLOWER, PRI_LOWER`) in relation to the reference view

Use the INQUIRE LIST OF VIEW INDICES routine to find out the current input priorities. View indices are returned in order of their input priorities. The first one has the highest priority.

Initializing Input Devices

When you open an OUTIN or INPUT workstation, PHIGS automatically initializes the available devices and puts them in Request mode. PHIGS gets the default values for the devices from the workstation description table.

Use an INITIALIZE ⟨*input_class*⟩ routine to reinitialize a device and change the initial values. The following routines initialize logical input devices:

- INITIALIZE LOCATOR
- INITIALIZE STROKE
- INITIALIZE VALUATOR
- INITIALIZE CHOICE
- INITIALIZE PICK
- INITIALIZE STRING

You can initialize a device only when it is in Request mode. PHIGS places all available devices in Request mode by default.

The PHIGS standard treats all logical input devices as 3D devices. However, the standard also provides 2D routines for each device. These 2D routines are a shorthand version of the 3D routines. The 2D initialize calls do not change the current *z* value of the echo value nor of the initial locator and stroke values.

See your implementation documentation for information on default initial values for logical input devices.

The number of available devices and the range of values those devices can accept are limited by the workstation type. The following routines are available to determine the available input device capabilities:

- INQUIRE NUMBER OF AVAILABLE LOGICAL INPUT DEVICES returns the number of supported devices of each logical input type for the specified workstation type.
- INQUIRE DEFAULT ⟨*input_class*⟩ DEVICE DATA returns information describing the default initial values for a particular logical device. There are 2D and 3D versions of this routine for each logical device type. The 2D versions discard the *z* data.

- INQUIRE ⟨*input_class*⟩ DEVICE STATE returns the current initial values and operating mode of a specific logical input device on a specified workstation. The 2D versions discard the *z* data.

Operating Modes

Each logical input device can be operated in three modes: Request, Sample, and Event. You obtain input from devices in different ways depending on the mode.

Use a SET ⟨*input_class*⟩ MODE routine to change the operating mode. A logical input device can only be in one operating mode at a time. The following routines set the operating mode for their corresponding device:

- SET LOCATOR MODE
- SET STROKE MODE
- SET VALUATOR MODE
- SET CHOICE MODE
- SET PICK MODE
- SET STRING MODE

The SET ⟨*input_class*⟩ MODE routines all take the same four input parameters. For example, the following calling signatures apply to the SET LOCATOR MODE routine:

```
call pslcm(wkstn_id, log_dev_no, mode, echo_switch)
```

```
pset_loc_mode(
    Pint            wkstn_id,
    Pint            log_dev_no,
    Pop_mode        mode,
    Pecho_switch    echo_switch
);
```

where:

⟨*wkstn_id*⟩ specifies the workstation identifier. The workstation must be open to use this routine.

⟨*log_dev_no*⟩ is the logical device number. This parameter identifies different devices of the same input class. For example, an implementation may support a different locator device for each button on a mouse.

⟨*mode*⟩ is the operating mode. Possible values are the following:

- **Request** (PREQU, POP_REQ)
- **Sample** (PSAMPL, POP_SAMPLE)
- **Event** (PEVENT, POP_EVENT)

⟨*echo_switch*⟩ is an echo switch that controls whether PHIGS displays the prompt and echo type associated with the device. Possible values are the following:

- **Echo mode off** (PNECHO, PSWITCH_NO_ECHO)
- **Echo mode on** (PECHO, PSWITCH_ECHO)

A prompt and echo type (set by an INITIALIZE ⟨*input_class*⟩ routine) determine how PHIGS displays the device.

Request Mode

Request mode is the default operating mode for each logical input device. In Request mode the application explicitly requests a value from an input device. There can be only one outstanding request at a time.

Each time you make a request of a device in Request mode, PHIGS begins a measure process and takes the initial measure from the initial values stored in the workstation state list for that device. Use an INITIALIZE ⟨*input_class*⟩ routine to change the initial measure.

Use a REQUEST ⟨*input_class*⟩ routine to request input from a device that is in Request mode. The REQUEST ⟨*input_class*⟩ routines are as follows:

- REQUEST LOCATOR
- REQUEST STROKE
- REQUEST VALUATOR
- REQUEST CHOICE

- REQUEST PICK
- REQUEST STRING

There are no 3D versions of the valuator, choice, pick, and string routines, because they do not return coordinate information. The 2D versions of the locator and stroke routines discard the *z* information.

The parameters for a REQUEST ⟨*input_class*⟩ routine differ depending on the type of information with which the device deals. For example, the following calling signatures apply to a REQUEST LOCATOR 3 routine:

```
call prqlc3(wkstn_id, log_dev_no, status, view_index, x, y, z)
```

```
preq_loc3(
    Pint            wkstn_id,
    Pint            log_dev_no,
    Pin_status      *status,
    Pint            *view_index,
    Ppoint3         *loc_position
);
```

where:

⟨*wkstn_id*⟩ and ⟨*log_dev_no*⟩ are input parameters that specify the workstation identifier and the locator device number.

⟨*status*⟩ is an output parameter that tells whether the request was successfully accomplished or whether a break action occurred. It can take one of these values:

- **None** (PNONE, PIN_STATUS_NONE). A break action occurred.
- **Success** (POK, PIN_STATUS_OK). The request was fulfilled.

⟨*view_index*⟩ is an output parameter that identifies the view in which the locator event occurred.

⟨*x*⟩, ⟨*y*⟩, and ⟨*z*⟩ are output parameters for the FORTRAN binding that identify the *x*, *y*, and *z* coordinates of the locator position, in world coordinates.

⟨*loc_position*⟩ is an output parameter for the C binding that identifies the *x*, *y*, and *z* coordinates of the locator position, in world coordinates.

When the application makes a request, PHIGS waits until the requested input has been entered or until a break action occurs. The break action is implementation-dependent. For example, the operator could initiate a break action by pressing a [Break] key. If a break occurs, the logical input value is not valid, and PHIGS returns a value of "none" in the ⟨*status*⟩ parameter.

Procedure for Using a Device in Request Mode

Use the following procedures to operate a device in Request mode.

- Use the INQUIRE ⟨*input_class*⟩ DEVICE STATE routine to obtain the current state of the logical input device. This routine returns the following:
  - Operating mode
  - Echo mode
  - Initial values
- If the device is not already in Request mode, use a SET ⟨*input_class*⟩ MODE routine to put the device in Request mode. If you want to display the associated prompt and echo type, set the echo mode to `PECHO`.
- If you want to change the initial values, use an INITIALIZE ⟨*input_class*⟩ routine to initialize the device. Note that you cannot initialize a device unless it is in Request mode.
- Use a REQUEST ⟨*input_class*⟩ routine to request the input value.
- When the REQUEST ⟨*input_class*⟩ routine returns, check the ⟨*status*⟩ parameter to determine if the operator aborted the request with a break action.

If a popup prompt is associated with a particular device, PHIGS automatically displays the popup while a request is pending.

Sample Mode

In Sample mode, PHIGS returns the measure of a device each time the application program asks for it, without waiting for or requiring operator action. PHIGS automatically maintains a measure for each device that is in Sample mode.

Each time you put a device in Sample mode, PHIGS initializes the measure from the initial values stored in the workstation state list for that device. Use an INITIALIZE ⟨*input_class*⟩ routine to change the initial measure.

Use a SAMPLE ⟨*input_class*⟩ routine to obtain the measure of a device that is in Sample mode. The SAMPLE ⟨*input_class*⟩ routines are as follows:

- SAMPLE LOCATOR
- SAMPLE STROKE
- SAMPLE VALUATOR
- SAMPLE CHOICE
- SAMPLE PICK
- SAMPLE STRING

There are no 3D versions of the valuator, choice, pick, and string routines, because they do not return coordinate information. The 2D versions of the locator and stroke routines discard the *z* information.

Devices in Sample mode do not have a trigger. PHIGS automatically reads the current logical input values of the device each time the application calls the appropriate SAMPLE ⟨*input_class*⟩ routine.

Procedure for Using a Device in Sample Mode

Use the following procedures to operate a device in Sample mode.

- Use the INQUIRE ⟨*input_class*⟩ DEVICE STATE routine to obtain the current state of the logical input device. This routine returns the following:
  - Operating mode
  - Echo mode
  - Initial values
- If you want to change the initial values, put the device in Request mode and then use an INITIALIZE ⟨*input_class*⟩ routine to initialize the device. Note that you cannot initialize a device unless it is in Request mode.
- Put the device in Sample mode. Use a SET ⟨*input_class*⟩ MODE routine. If you want to display the associated prompt and echo type, set the echo mode to `PECHO`.
- Repeatedly call a SAMPLE ⟨*input_class*⟩ routine to read the current measure of the device and take appropriate action.
- When you are through using the device (and no longer want the operator to see its echo), put the device in Request mode. Use a SET ⟨*input_class*⟩ MODE routine.

If a popup prompt is associated with a particular device, PHIGS automatically displays the popup the entire time that the device is in Sample mode.

Event Mode

The application program operates independently of any logical input devices that are in Event mode.

Each time you put a device in Event mode, PHIGS initializes the measure from the initial values stored in the workstation state list for that device. Use an INITIALIZE ⟨*input_class*⟩ routine to change the initial measure.

Each time the operator triggers a device that is in Event mode, PHIGS sends an event report to the **event queue**. PHIGS maintains one event queue for all devices that are in Event mode. Figure 14–2 illustrates how PHIGS uses the event queue.

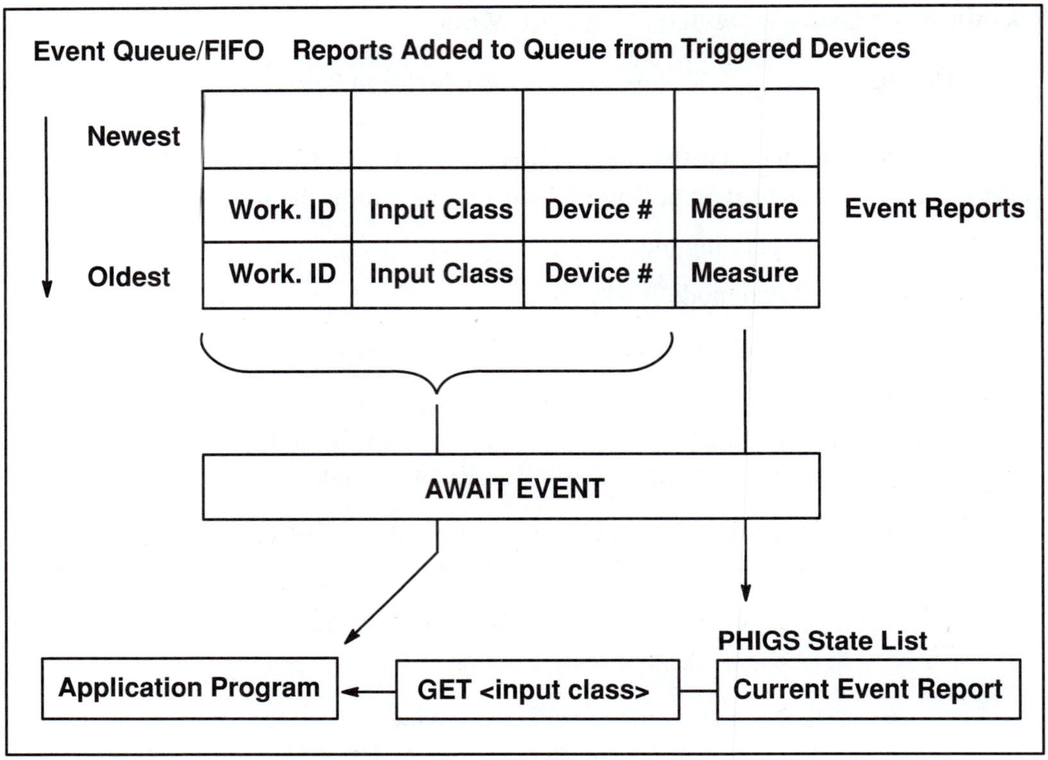

Figure 14–2. Event Queue

The Event Queue

The event queue is a FIFO (First In-First Out) queue that contains zero or more event reports. Each event report contains the workstation identifier, the input class and device number of the device that generated the event, and the corresponding measure. The number and type of values in the measure are dependent on the logical input device type.

Event reports are added to the queue when logical input devices in Event mode are triggered by the operator.

Removing Events from the Queue

The following routines remove event reports from the queue:

- AWAIT EVENT removes the oldest event report from the event queue and makes the information accessible to the application.

- FLUSH DEVICE EVENTS removes event reports from the queue that were generated by a specific device. The routine accepts a workstation identifier, an input class, and a device number. For example, you can delete all of the reports generated by locator device 2 on a specific workstation.
- CLOSE WORKSTATION removes all event reports in the queue generated by logical input devices on the workstation being closed.

The following section describes how to use the AWAIT EVENT routine to retrieve an event report.

Reading Event Reports

As previously mentioned, you can remove the oldest report from the event queue by calling the AWAIT EVENT routine. If the queue is empty, the AWAIT EVENT routine will wait for the next event or until an application-specified timeout period has elapsed.

The AWAIT EVENT routine returns the workstation identifier, input class, and device number. PHIGS stores the measure information (logical input values) in the current event report in the PHIGS state list. Use a GET ⟨*input_class*⟩ routine to examine the contents of this current event report.

The calling signatures for the AWAIT EVENT routine are as follows:

```
call pwait(timeout, wkstn_id, class, dev_no)
```

```
pawait_event(
   Pfloat          timeout,
   Pint            *wkstn_id,
   Pin_class       *class,
   Pint            *dev_no
);
```

where:

⟨*timeout*⟩ is the timeout period, in seconds. If a timeout occurs and there is still no entry in the event queue, PHIGS returns a value of None for the input class.

⟨*wkstn_id*⟩ is the workstation identifier.

⟨*class*⟩ indicates the class of input device that generated the event. Possible values are the following:

– None (`PNCLAS`, `PIN_NONE`). No input class has generated an event. (A timeout occurred.)

- Locator event (PLOCAT, PIN_LOC)
- Stroke event (PSTROK, PIN_STROKE)
- Valuator event (PVALUA, PIN_VAL)
- Choice event (PCHOIC, PIN_CHOICE)
- Pick event (PPICK, PIN_PICK)
- String event (PSTRIN, PIN_STRING)

⟨*dev_no*⟩ is the logical input device number of the device that generated the event.

As mentioned earlier, the AWAIT EVENT routine loads the oldest event report into the PHIGS state list. Use a GET ⟨*input_class*⟩ routine to examine the contents of the *current event report* in the PHIGS state list. Use the input class returned by the AWAIT EVENT routine to determine which GET ⟨*input_class*⟩ routine to use. Refer to the example later in this section.

The GET ⟨*input_class*⟩ routines are as follows:

- GET LOCATOR
- GET STROKE
- GET VALUATOR
- GET CHOICE
- GET PICK
- GET STRING

There are no 3D versions of the valuator, choice, pick, and string routines, because they do not return coordinate information. The 2D versions of the locator and stroke routines discard the z information.

Note that there is only one *current event report* in the PHIGS state list. So, if the application makes two calls to the AWAIT EVENT routine without calling a GET ⟨*input_class*⟩ routine in between, the first event will be lost.

Simultaneous Event Reports

When a trigger associated with more than one logical input device fires, all of the resulting event reports are entered into the queue and marked as a group of simultaneous event reports. The simultaneous reports must *all* fit in the queue, or none of them is added.

After the event report is removed (by calling AWAIT EVENT), if other reports in the same group of simultaneous events remain in the queue, PHIGS sets the *more simultaneous events* entry in the PHIGS state list to "more" (`PMORE`, `PSIMULT_MORE`). Use the INQUIRE MORE SIMULTANEOUS EVENTS routine to examine this value. If there are no more events, the routine returns a value of "no more" (`PNMORE`, `PSIMULT_NO_MORE`).

See the code fragment at the end of this section for an example of how to check for simultaneous event reports.

Input Queue Overflow

If the input queue becomes full, PHIGS does not queue up new events until the input queue is completely emptied (using AWAIT EVENT, FLUSH DEVICE EVENTS, or CLOSE WORKSTATION routines).

Procedure for Using a Device in Event Mode

Use the following procedures to operate a device in Event mode.

- Use the INQUIRE ⟨*input_class*⟩ DEVICE STATE routine to obtain the current state of the logical input device. This routine returns the following:
  - Operating mode
  - Echo mode
  - Initial values
- If you want to change the initial values, put the device in Request mode and then use an INITIALIZE ⟨*input_class*⟩ routine to initialize the device. Note that you cannot initialize a device unless it is in Request mode.
- Use a SET ⟨*input_class*⟩ MODE routine to put the device in Event mode. If you want to display the associated prompt and echo type, set the echo mode to `PECHO`.

- Use AWAIT EVENT to wait until an event is written into the input queue, or until a timeout occurs.
- Check the ⟨*class*⟩ output parameter of AWAIT EVENT to determine whether a timeout occurred (`PNCLAS`), or whether an event report was removed from the event queue.

  If an event report was removed from the event queue, test the ⟨*class*⟩ parameter to determine the class of the device generating the event and use the appropriate GET ⟨ *input class* ⟩ routine to return the logical input values (measure) in the current event report.
- Repeat the previous four steps as appropriate.
- When you are through using the device (and no longer want the operator to see its echo), use a SET ⟨*input_class*⟩ MODE routine to put the device in Request mode.

If a popup prompt is associated with a particular device, PHIGS automatically displays the popup the entire time that the device is in Event mode.

Event Mode Example

The following fragment shows how to use two locator devices in Event mode. We discuss the parameters later in the chapter. For now, just notice how the event loop operates. The program works as follows:

- If the operator triggers locator device 1, the program uses a GET LOCATOR 3 routine to retrieve the view identifier and the world coordinates of the locator position. Then the program prints out the information.
- If the operator triggers locator device 3, the program exits the event loop.
- If the operator waits for more than 60 seconds without triggering a locator device, the program exits the event loop. The floating-point value of 60.0 in the AWAIT EVENT routine signifies a timeout value of 60 seconds.

```
integer*4  WorkID, ReturnClass, ReturnDevice, view, ReturnID
real*4     TimeOut, x, y, z
parameter  (TimeOut=60.0)
   ...
C-- initialize locator devices 1 and 3 ------------------------------
pinlc3( WorkID, 1, 1, 0.0, 0.0, 0.0, 3, evol, 0, 0 )
pinlc3( WorkID, 3, 1, 0.0, 0.0, 0.0, 3, evol, 0, 0 )
C-- put locator devices 1 and 3 in event mode -----------------------
pslcm( WorkID, 1, PEVENT, PECHO )
pslcm( WorkID, 3, PEVENT, PECHO )
   ...
Done=.false.
do while (.not. Done)
 call pwait(TimeOut, ReturnID, ReturnClass, ReturnDevice)! await event
     if (ReturnClass .eq. PNCLAS) then  ! report timeout and quit
         print *, "One minute time out occured. Goodbye."
         Done=.true.
     endif
     if (( ReturnClass .eq. PLOCAT ) .and. (ReturnDevice .eq. 3)) then
         Done=.true.                    ! exit program
     endif
     if ((ReturnClass .eq. PLOCAT) .and. (ReturnDevice .eq. 1)) then
         call pgtlc3(view, x, y, z )    ! get locator
         print *, " view ID: ", view
         print *, "x = ", x
         print *, "y = ", y
         print *, "z = ", z
     endif
end do
```

Checking-for-Simultaneous-Events Example

This example shows how to deal with simultaneous events. For example, assume that pick device 1 and locator device 1 are both associated with the same mouse button. If both devices are placed in Event mode, two events can be generated at the same time when the operator presses mouse button 1.

The following fragment calls a function named `GetInfo` to act on the contents of the values of `ReturnClass` and `ReturnDevice`. The full `picking` program at the end of this chapter uses a similar technique.

This fragment calls the INQUIRE MORE SIMULTANEOUS EVENTS routine to determine whether or not there are any more events in the event queue. If there are, the fragment calls

AWAIT EVENT to remove the event from the queue. Then it sends the new values to the `GetInfo` function.

```
C
C Event Locp
C
      Done=.false.
      do while (.not. Done)
      call pwait(TimeOut,WorkIDOut,ReturnClass,ReturnDevice)

      if (ReturnClass .eq. PNCLAS) then { report timeout and quit}
        print *,"One minute time out occured. Goodbye."
        Done=.true.
      else
        print *," "
        call getinfo(ReturnClass,ReturnDevice, Done)
        call pqsim(ERRIND,MoreFlag)    { Check for more simul. events }
      do while (MoreFlag .eq. PMORE) { do while more events       }
        print *,"There was another simultaneous event:"
        call pwait(0,WorkIDOut,
     +   ReturnClass,ReturnDevice, Done)      { get next event       }
        call getinfo(ReturnClass,ReturnDevice)
        call pqsim(ERRIND,MoreFlag)     { check for more si-
mul. events}
           if (MoreFlag .eq. PNMORE) then
             print *,"end of simultaneous events"
           endif
      end do
      endif
      end do                 { end event loop            }
```

Picking

Picking is an important function for interactive graphics which allows an operator to select primitives displayed on the screen. Typically, a user wants to point at an object on the screen, click a button on a pointer device (e.g., a mouse) to make a selection, and then manipulate the selected object. The following are examples of the types of possible manipulations:

- Rotate, scale, or translate the object.
- Delete the object.
- Group the object with other objects in the scene.
- Separate the object from other objects in the scene.
- Change the colour of the object.
- Assign nonvisual values (such as weight, density, or other material properties) to the object.

Manipulation can take place only after an object has been identified. Picking is the functionality that makes that identification possible.

Picking with X Input

Several implementations support standard PHIGS picking in X Windows. However, it is difficult for an application to integrate PHIGS input for some operations with X input for other operations. Consequently, many applications may choose to use X events for all input when running in X Windows. Most PHIGS input devices can be supplanted by X input successfully, but picking, which involves a traversal of the CSS, cannot be emulated easily or with acceptable performance at the application level.

What is needed to support picking from X input is an entry point that performs only the pick traversal part of picking operations. This traversal is termed *direct pick* or *programmatic pick*. Several implementations support entry points for direct picking.

This chapter describes standard picking. Conceptually, direct picking is very similar to standard picking. See your implementation documentation to see if your system supports direct picking. Now, back to standard picking.

Pick Devices and Other Logical Input Devices

A pick device is similar to other logical input devices in several ways. The pick device can be placed in any of the three input operating modes: Request, Sample, or Event. Like other logical input devices, the pick device also has a trigger and a set of measure values.

The picking operation is also different from interactions with other logical input devices. Pick devices are the only logical input devices that interact with posted structure networks. The picking operation causes implicit traversal of the posted structures. This also means that the size of the structure network impacts picking performance.

Picking Terminology

The following terms describe the various aspects of picking:

Pick operation — The process of selecting primitive elements displayed on the screen. An operator uses a pick device (usually consisting of a cursor position and pointer device button) to identify a primitive. PHIGS returns a pick status, a pick path, and a pick path depth.

Pick status — A value that tells you whether a pick occurred.

Pick path — The traversal path to a picked primitive from its posted structure. The pick path contains the structure name, the pick identifier, and the element index of the structure element at each level in the hierarchy.

Pick path depth — The number of levels returned in the pick path.

Pick identifier — An integer name associated with one or more primitive elements. A pick identifier is an attribute set by a structure element. SET PICK IDENTIFIER creates the structure element.

Pick filter — A filter consisting of two name sets: a pick inclusion set and a pick exclusion set. PHIGS uses the pick filter to identify output primitives eligible for selection by a pick operation. This is based on the primitive's name set attribute. When traversal begins, no elements are eligible for picking. Traversal of structure elements that add and remove names from the name set can make elements eligible for picking.

Pick highlighting Emphasizing (for the purpose of picking) an output primitive by modifying its visual attributes. For example, redraw a line in a different colour.

Pick Path

In order to uniquely identify a picked primitive, PHIGS returns the entire traversal sequence from the posted structure to the picked primitive. Each successive level is invoked by an execute structure element. The picked primitive is the element at the lowest end of the pick path.

For each element in the pick path, PHIGS returns three values: a structure identifier, a pick ID, and an element index. The number of three-value entries in the pick path is called the pick path depth.

The REQUEST PICK, SAMPLE PICK, and GET PICK routines return a pick path.

For the C binding, define the pick path parameter as `Ppick_path` (see Appendix D).

For the FORTRAN binding, define the pick path parameter as a two-dimensional array of four-byte integers. For example, for a pick path depth of 1,024, declare the array as follows:

```
integer*4  ppath(3, 1024)
```

Note that a value much smaller than 1,024, such as 255 (or even 16), is often sufficient.

Figure 14–3 shows two simple structures and the pick path to one primitive. Assume that structure 1 is posted to the workstation. If an operator picks the third polyline in structure 2, the routines REQUEST PICK, SAMPLE PICK, and GET PICK return the pick path to that element. The third polyline is the fifth element in structure 2, so the element index for the bottom level is 5. Structure 2 is called by an execute structure element in structure 1 (element number 3 in structure 1).

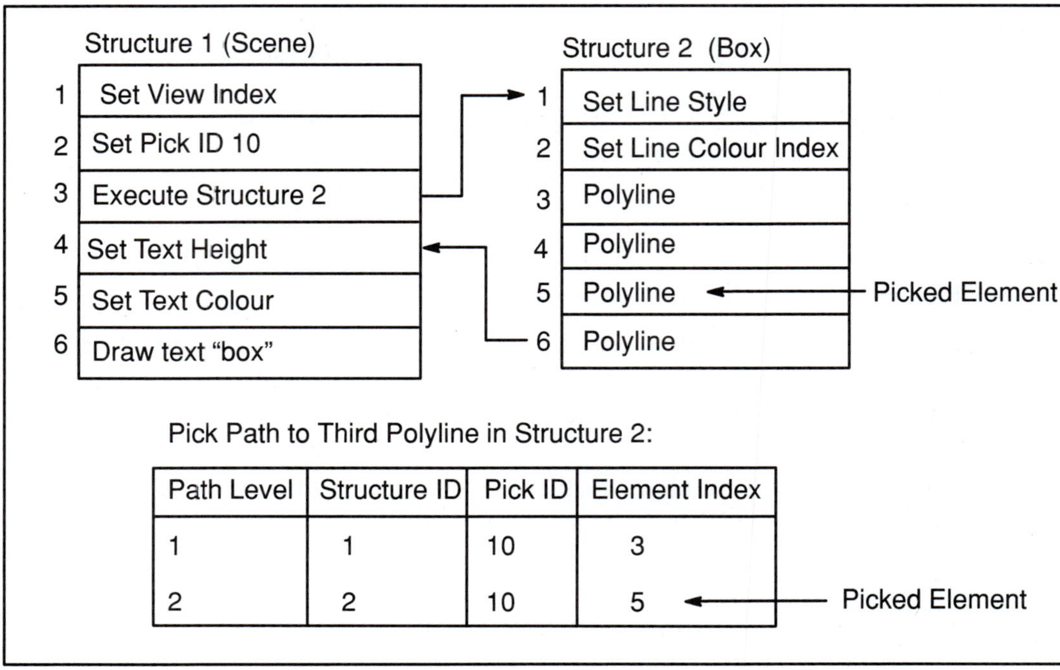

Figure 14–3. Pick Path Example

The example illustrated above uses the default pick path order of top-first (`PPOTOP`, `PORDER_TOP_FIRST`). You can reverse the order by changing the "pick path order" parameter in an INITIALIZE PICK routine. When you specify bottom-first (`PPOBOT`, `PORDER_BOTOM_FIRST`), the picked element is the first element returned in the pick path array.

Pick Identifiers

A pick identifier (pick ID) is an attribute that applies to all primitives. Pick IDs are set during structure traversal by a *set pick identifier* structure element. In essence, traversing a *set pick identifier* structure element associates an integer name with subsequently traversed primitives. PHIGS returns the pick identifier as part of the pick path.

Your application program can use pick IDs to keep track of primitive elements. Some implementations offer extension routines to allow you to set the element pointer to the next occurrence of a *set pick identifier* structure element during a structure editing session.

Use the SET PICK IDENTIFIER routine to set a pick identifier value. When PHIGS encounters a *set pick identifier* structure element during traversal, it sets the *current pick identifier* entry in the PHIGS traversal state list to the specified value. The current pick identifier is associated with subsequently traversed primitives until PHIGS encounters another *set pick identifier* element. The example at the end of this chapter uses pick IDs.

Pick Filters—Using Name Sets

The default state is that no primitives are eligible for picking! In order to make primitives eligible for picking, you must associate a name set with the primitive(s) and put the name set in the pick filter.

Use the ADD NAMES TO SET routine to create a structure element that adds a name to the current name set. Use REMOVE NAMES FROM SET to create a structure element that removes names from the current name set. See Chapter 13, *Name Sets and Filters*, for more information on name sets.

The SET PICK FILTER routine sets the inclusion and exclusion sets for subsequent pick measures. The routine associates the filter with a specified pick device. During a pick operation, PHIGS processes the pick filter against the current name set to determine whether primitives are pickable.

In order to be pickable, a primitive must be associated with a nonempty name set. At least one name in the associated name set must be in the filter's inclusion set, and none can be in the filter's exclusion set. A primitive is pickable only if *both* of the following statements are true:

- The inclusion set intersected with the current name set is nonempty.
- The exclusion set intersected with the current name set is empty.

You can use name sets selectively to make specific groups of primitives eligible for picking.

Making Primitives Eligible for Picking

One way to make all primitives pickable is to put an *add names to set* structure element in the top-level structure using the ADD NAMES TO SET routine. Then, before you perform the first pick operation, put the same name in the inclusion set of the pick filter using the SET PICK FILTER routine.

The following FORTRAN fragment makes everything in the structures named `Root` and `LineSquare` pickable.

```
integer*4  Incl(2), Excl(2)    ! include and exclude filters
integer*4  NameList(255)      ! namelist array for name sets
integer*4 Name1               ! name set element
parameter (Name1=1)
integer*4  WorkID             ! workstation ID
parameter (WorkID=1)
integer*4  PickDev            ! pick device number
parameter (PickDev=1)
integer*4  LineSquare, Root! structure names
parameter (LineSquare=1, Root=2)
!-- build root structure ---------------------------------------------
call popst(Root)              ! open structure
Namelist(1)=Name1             ! put Name1 in array
call pads(1, NameList)        ! add Name1 to current name set
call pexst(LineSquare)        ! execute LineSquare
call pclst                    ! close the structure
!-- put Name1 in pick filter ---------------------------------------
Incl(1)=Name1
call pspkft(WorkID, PickDev, 1, Incl, 0, Excl)
```

Using Pick Devices

When you open an OUTIN or INPUT workstation, PHIGS initializes the available pick devices (depending on the pointer device attached to the system) and puts them all in Request mode.

Prompt and Echo Type

The prompt for a pick device is implementation-dependent. For example, a prompt could be one of the available cursor patterns. Whatever prompt the implementation uses, as the operator moves the pointer device, PHIGS automatically updates its position on the screen.

The echo for a pick operation usually involves highlighting the primitive. Some implementations echo the primitives *before* they are picked to let you decide whether or not to pick the primitive. Others echo the primitives *after* they are picked.

The PHIGS standard defines three echo methods:

- Highlight the picked primitive.

- Highlight all primitives with the same pick identifier that are contained in the same structure as the picked primitive.
- Highlight the structure network containing the picked primitive.

Use INITIALIZE PICK to select a prompt and echo type.

Use the SET PICK MODE routine to turn the pick prompt and echo on or off. When the echo value is set to no echo, PHIGS does not highlight picked primitives and does not display the pick prompt.

Note that the highlighting feature used for pick echo is not related to the name set highlighting feature. See Chapter 13 for information on name set highlighting.

Pick Criteria

For a primitive to be eligible for a pick operation, it must have an associated name set, which must be in the pick inclusion set and not in the pick exclusion set (see "Pick Filters—Using Name Sets," earlier in this chapter). Also, a primitive must be in a posted structure network and be visible before it can be picked. Being visible means the following:

- The primitive must be within the workstation window.
- Depending on Hidden Line/Hidden Surface Removal, it must be visible on the screen.
- The primitive must fail the invisibility name set filter (See Chapter 13).

Modifying the Initial Values

The following initial values can be specified using the INITIALIZE PICK routine:

- Initial pick status
- Depth of the initial pick path
- Initial pick path
- Pick path order

- Prompt and echo type

The implementation may allow you to specify additional information such as a pick aperture or a pick highlight colour using the data record.

The implementation may or may not use the echo area/volume parameter in the INITIALIZE PICK routine. If it ignores this parameter, then pick devices can operate over the entire PHIGS graphics area.

Pick Aperture

A **pick aperture** is a region in NPC space used for testing candidate primitives during a pick operation. The aperture surrounds the cursor position. To be picked, at least some portion of the primitive must be within the pick aperture. A pick aperture is useful when you have a crowded scene and you want to ensure that the pick operation is restricted to an area immediately surrounding the cursor position.

The PHIGS standard leaves it up to the implementation to define the pick aperture. For example, the default pick aperture can be the size of the cursor. While every implementation has a default pick aperture, some allow the application to adjust the aperture programmatically. For example, the implementation can allow the specification of a pick aperture through the data record for the INITIALIZE PICK routine.

Controlling the Operating Mode

Use SET PICK MODE to change the operating mode for a pick device. The SET PICK MODE routine allows you to set the operating mode and the echo switch. The echo switch controls whether or not PHIGS highlights the picked primitive and displays the pick prompt. Recall that primitives are not eligible for picking until the name set pick filter criteria have been met.

Retrieving the Measure of a Pick Device

Use the following routines to retrieve the measure of a pick device (pick status, pick path, and pick path depth):

- In Request mode, use REQUEST PICK.
- In Sample mode, use SAMPLE PICK.
- In Event mode, use AWAIT EVENT and GET PICK. The AWAIT EVENT routine returns a value of `PPICK` or `PIN_PICK` when an event report belongs to the pick input class.

Picking and Event Mode Example

This example demonstrates the following:

- How to inquire the available PHIGS display area and use the information to define an echo volume for a logical input device
- How to use an event loop that allows an operator to interact with your application
- How to use picking, including how to examine the pick path returned by a pick operation
- How to use name sets to make certain primitives eligible for picking

Figure 14–4 shows the output of the program.

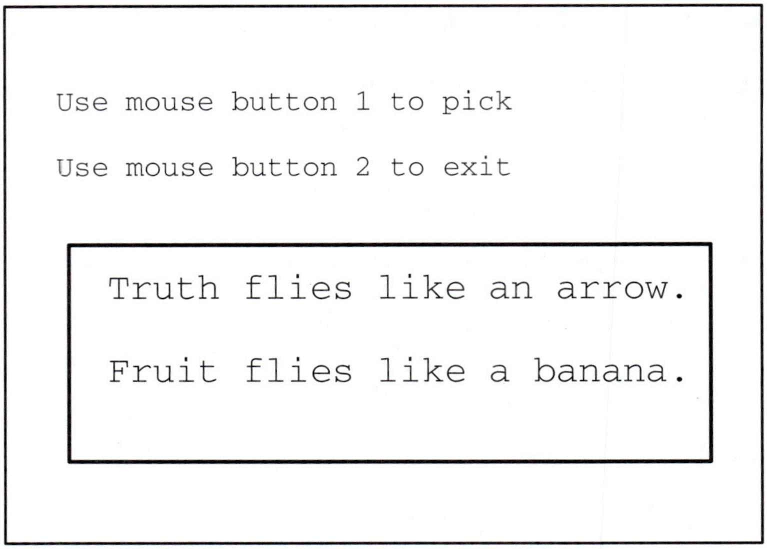

Figure 14–4. Output from picking Program

There are three structures in this program: `Scene`, `StrucA`, and `StrucB`. `StrucA` contains the fill area primitive (box around the quote text) and `StrucB` contains the quote from Groucho Marx. The following shows the contents of the three structures:

```
C Build Structure A
      call popst(StrucA)      { open structure
      call pspkid(20)         { set pick ID
      call psici(2)           { set interior colour index
      call pfa3(4,FAX,FAY,FAZ)  { fill area3 primitive
      call pclst              { close the structure
C Build Structure B
      text1 = 'Truth flies like an arrow.'
      text2 = 'Fruit flies like a banana.'
      call popst(StrucB)      { open structure
      call pspkid(30)         { set pick ID
      call pschh(0.03)        { set character height
      call pstxci(3)          { set text colour index
      call ptx(0.24, 0.5,text1) { text
      call ptx(0.24, 0.4,text2) { text
      call pclst              { close the structure
C Build Scene structure
```

```
      text3 = 'Use mouse button 1 to pick'
      text4 = 'Use mouse button 2 to exit'
      call popst(Scene)       { open structure
      call pschh(0.02)        { set character height
      call ptx(0.2, 0.8, text3)  { text
      call ptx(0.2, 0.75, text4) { text
      Namelist(1)=Name1       { put Name1 in array
C Nothing is pickable above this element since no name in name set
      call pads(1,NameList)  { add Name1 to current name set
      call pspkid(10)         { set pick ID
      call pexst(StrucA)      { execute structure
      call pexst(StrucB)      { execute structure
      call pclst              { close structure
```

Notice that the two text primitives in the `Scene` structure are placed before the *add names to set* structure element. Since these two text primitives do not have a name set attribute associated with them, they are not pickable.

The following fragment adds the name to the pick inclusion filter and therefore makes everything that follows the *add names to set* primitive pickable:

```
C Put Name1 in pick filter
      Incl(1)=Name1
      call pspkft(WorkID,Pointer,1,Incl,0,Excl)
```

Also notice that we have three pick IDs in the structure network. `Scene` has a pick ID of 10, `StrucA` has a pick ID of 20, and `StrucB` has a pick ID of 30. These values are returned as part of the pick path.

Defining the Echo Volume and Initializing Devices

This program defines an echo volume for the pick and locator device. It allows the two devices to display their prompts over the entire PHIGS display area. To do this we first call INQUIRE DISPLAY SPACE SIZE and then use the returned values to define the echo volume. Notice that we call INQUIRE WORKSTATION CONNECTION AND TYPE first to get the specific workstation type (see Chapter 3).

The INQUIRE DISPLAY SPACE SIZE routine returns values both in device coordinates and in raster units. It will depend on your implementation which values you use for the echo volume. This implementation (HP-PHIGS on Apollo Domain) requires that we use raster units. We subtract 1 from the maximum number of raster units to ensure that we are within the device limits. If you use device coordinates, you will probably not need to subtract anything, but if you do, it would be a much smaller amount.

The following fragment shows how we define the echo volume and initialize the devices:

```
C Inquire workstation connection and type
      call pqwkc(WorkID, ERRIND, ConnectID, SpecType)
C Inquire display space size 3
      call pqdsp3(SpecType,ERRIND,Unittype,
     + DX,DY,DZ,RX,RY,RZ)
C Specify echo size
      EchoVolume(1)=0.0
      EchoVolume(2)=RX-1.0
      EchoVolume(3)=0.0
      EchoVolume(4)=RY-1.0
      EchoVolume(5)=0.0
      EchoVolume(6)=RZ
C Initialize locator device
      LocDev=2
      call pinlc3( WorkID,     { workstation ID
     + LocDev,                 { device number
     + 0,                      { initial view index
     + 0.5, 0.5, 0.0,          { initial locator position (WC)
     + 3,                      { prompt echo type
     + EchoVolume,             { 3D volume for displaying prompt
     + Length,                 { length of data record
     + DATREC)                 { data record (not used)
C Initialize the pick device
      PickStatus=PNPICK
      Pointer=1
      PET=1
      call pinpk3(WorkID,      { workstation ID
     + Pointer,                { pick device number
     + PickStatus,             { initial pick status
     + PathDepth,              { initial pick path depth
     + PickPath,               { initial pick path
     + PET,                    { prompt echo type
     + EchoVolume,             { 3D volume for picking
     + Length,                 { length of data record
     + DATREC,                 { data record (not used)
     + PPOTOP)                 { return pick path top-first
```

The program uses locator device 2 and pick device 1. For this particular implementation, locator device 2 corresponds to mouse button 2, and pick device 1 corresponds to mouse button 1. The following is the printed output from the program after the four different mouse button clicks. Compare the returned pick paths to the contents of the structure network.

- Use mouse button 1 to pick the box (fill area primitive):

```
Pick Device:  1
 ReturnDepth:  2
  Structure No.:    1
  Pick ID:          10
  Element Offset:   6
  Structure No.:    2
  Pick ID:          20
  Element Offset:   3
```

- Use mouse button 1 to pick the text primitive with the text string, "Truth flies like an arrow":

```
Pick Device:  1
 ReturnDepth:  2
  Structure No.:    1
  Pick ID:          10
  Element Offset:   7
  Structure No.:    3
  Pick ID:          30
  Element Offset:   4
```

- Use mouse button 1 to attempt to pick the text primitive with this string, "Use mouse button 2 to exit":

```
Pick Device:  1
 No Pick. PickStatus:  2
```

  Recall that the two "informational" text strings are not pickable, because they have no associated name set attribute.

- Use mouse button 2 and click anywhere in the PHIGS display area. In this case the program prints the device number, view ID, world coordinates of the locator when the event occurred, and then exits the event loop and ends the program.

```
Locator Device: 2, view ID:  0
 coordinates =
```

```
         0.31
         0.67
         0.00
     Exiting program
    Fortran STOP
```

The complete listing of the program follows:

```
  program picking             { program "picking.ftn"
%include '/sys/ins/phigs.ins.ftn'
C This program demonstrates the use of picking in PHIGS.
C This is accomplished by the following steps:
C 1. Build a simple structure network consisting of
C    three structures: Scene, StrucA, and StrucB.
C 2. Initialize the mouse as picking device.
C 3. Initialize a locator device.
C 4. Use mouse button 1 to pick elements in the Scene.
C 5. Print the pick path and highlight the picked elements.
      integer*4 WorkID            { workstation ID
      integer*4 ConnectID         { connection ID
      integer*4 WorkType          { workstation type
      integer*4 SpecType          { specific workstation type
      integer*4 ERRIND            { error indicator
      integer*4 Unittype          { device unit type
      integer*4 RX,RY,RZ          { display space size in rasters
      integer*4 Pointer,LocDev    { input device numbers
      integer*4 Incl(2),Excl(2)   { include and exclude filters
      integer*4 NameList(255)     { namelist array for name sets
      integer*4 Scene, StrucA, StrucB { structure IDs
      parameter (Scene=1,StrucA=2, StrucB=3)
      integer*4 PET               { prompt echo type
      real      FAX(4), FAY(4), FAZ(4)    { points for fill area
      real      DX,DY,DZ          { display space size in DCs
      real      EchoVolume(6)     { echo volume limits
      integer*4 Length            { DATREC element return length
      parameter (Length=0)        { no data record elements
      character*80 DATREC(1)      { data record array
      character*80 text1, text2, text3, text4 { text strings
C Await event variables
      real      TimeOut           { timeout value for await event
      parameter (TimeOut=60)
      integer*4 WorkIDOut         { returned workstation ID
      integer*4 ReturnDevice      { returned device / await event
```

```
      integer*4 ReturnClass      { returned class / await event
      logical   Done             { loop control variable
      integer*4 Name1            { name for name set
      parameter (Name1=1)
      real Blue(3),White(3),Yellow(3),Red(3)
C Define basic data
      data FAX /0.2, 0.85, 0.85, 0.2/
      data FAY /0.25, 0.25, 0.6, 0.6/
      data FAZ /0.0,  0.0,  0.0,  0.0/
      data Blue   / 0.0, 0.0, 0.5 /
      data White  / 1.0, 1.0, 1.0 /
      data Yellow / 1.0, 1.0, 0.0 /
      data Red    / 1.0, 0.0, 0.0 /
      COMMON WorkID                      { workstation ID

      call popph(1, 0)                   { open PHIGS
      call popwk(WorkID, 1, POIBSX)  { open workstation
C Inquire workstation connection and type
      call pqwkc(WorkID, ERRIND, ConnectID, SpecType)
C Inquire display space size 3
      call pqdsp3(SpecType,ERRIND,Unittype,
     + DX,DY,DZ,RX,RY,RZ)
C Specify echo size
      EchoVolume(1)=0.0
      EchoVolume(2)=RX-1.0
      EchoVolume(3)=0.0
      EchoVolume(4)=RY-1.0
      EchoVolume(5)=0.0
      EchoVolume(6)=RZ
C Initialize locator device
      LocDev=2
      call pinlc3( WorkID,   { workstation ID
     + LocDev,               { device number
     + 0,                    { initial view index
     + 0.5, 0.5, 0.0,        { initial locator position (WC)
     + 3,                    { prompt echo type
     + EchoVolume,           { 3D volume for displaying prompt
     + Length,               { length of data record
     + DATREC)               { data record (not used)
C Initialize the pick device
      PickStatus=PNPICK
      Pointer=1
      PET=1
```

```
      call pinpk3(WorkID,    { workstation ID
     + Pointer,              { pick device number
     + PickStatus,           { initial pick status
     + PathDepth,            { initial pick path depth
     + PickPath,             { initial pick path
     + PET,                  { prompt echo type
     + EchoVolume,           { 3D volume for picking
     + Length,               { length of data record
     + DATREC,               { data record (not used)
     + PPOTOP)               { return pick path top-first
C Define the colours we'll be using
      call pscr(WorkID, 0, 3, Blue)    { background value
      call pscr(WorkID, 1, 3, White)   { highlight colour
      call pscr(WorkID, 2, 3, Yellow)  { for fill area colour
      call pscr(WorkID, 3, 3, Red)     { for text colour
C Build Structure A
      call popst(StrucA)      { open structure
      call pspkid(20)         { set pick ID
      call psici(2)           { set interior colour index
      call pfa3(4,FAX,FAY,FAZ)  { fill area3 primitive
      call pclst              { close the structure
C Build Structure B
      text1 = 'Truth flies like an arrow.'
      text2 = 'Fruit flies like a banana.'
      call popst(StrucB)      { open structure
      call pspkid(30)         { set pick ID
      call pschh(0.03)        { set character height
      call pstxci(3)          { set text colour index
      call ptx(0.24, 0.5,text1) { text
      call ptx(0.24, 0.4,text2) { text
      call pclst              { close the structure
C Build Scene structure
      text3 = 'Use mouse button 1 to pick'
      text4 = 'Use mouse button 2 to exit'
      call popst(Scene)       { open structure
      call pschh(0.02)        { set character height
      call ptx(0.2, 0.8, text3)  { text
      call ptx(0.2, 0.75, text4) { text
      Namelist(1)=Name1       { put Name1 in array
C Nothing is pickable above this element since no name in name set
      call pads(1,NameList)   { add Name1 to current name set
      call pspkid(10)         { set pick ID
      call pexst(StrucA)      { execute structure
```

```
      call pexst(StrucB)      { execute structure
      call pclst              { close structure
C Display the structure network
      call ppost(WorkID, Scene, 1.0)    { post structure
      call puwk(WorkID, PPERFO)         { update workstation
C Put Name1 in pick filter
      Incl(1)=Name1
      call pspkft(WorkID,Pointer,1,Incl,0,Excl)
      print *,"READY FOR PICK INPUT"
C Put devices in Event mode and enable echoing
      call pspkm(WorkID, Pointer, PEVENT, PECHO) { set pick mode
      call pslcm(WorkID, LocDev, PEVENT, PECHO)  { set locator mode
C Event loop
       Done=.false.
       do while (.not. Done)
        call pwait(TimeOut,WorkIDOut,ReturnClass,ReturnDevice)
        if (ReturnClass .eq. PNCLAS) then { report timeout and quit
         print *,"One minute timeout occured. Goodbye."
         Done=.true.
        else
         print *," "
         call GetInfo(ReturnClass,ReturnDevice, Done)
        endif
       end do
C Clean up and exit
      call pclwk(WorkID)     { close the workstation
      call pclph             { close PHIGS
      stop                   { stop processing
      end                    { end of main program
C*********************************************************************
C* GetInfo
C*********************************************************************
      subroutine GetInfo(ReturnClass,ReturnDevice, Done )
%include '/sys/ins/phigs.ins.ftn'
      integer*4 ReturnDevice { returned device / await event
      integer*4 ReturnClass  { returned class / await event
      logical   Done         { for exiting await event loop
      integer*4 Index        { looping variable
      integer*4 view         { returned view ID
      real      x, y, z      { returned view coordinates
      COMMON WorkID          { workstation ID
C Picking variables
      integer*4 PathDepth            { input pick path depth
```

```
      parameter(PathDepth=5)         { input pick path value
      integer*4 PickPath(3,PathDepth){ PickPath array
      integer*4 PickStatus           { return pick status
      integer*4 ReturnDepth          { return pick path depth

        if ((ReturnClass .eq. PLOCAT).and.(ReturnDevice .eq. 2))then
          call pgtlc3(view, x, y, z ) { get locator
          print *,"Locator Device: 2, view ID: ", view
          print *," coordinates = "
          write(6, '(6X, F4.2)') x, y, z
          Done=.true.
          print *,"Exiting program"
        endif
        if ( ReturnClass .eq. PPICK ) then
         print *,"Pick Device: ",ReturnDevice
C Call GET PICK
         call pgtpk(PathDepth, PickStatus, ReturnDepth, PickPath )
           if (PickStatus .eq. POK) then { print pick path }
               print *," ReturnDepth: ",ReturnDepth
             do 10 Index=1,ReturnDepth
               print *,"  Structure No.:  ",PickPath(1,Index)
               print *,"  Pick ID:        ",PickPath(2,Index)
               print *,"  Element Offset: ",PickPath(3,Index)
10           continue
           else
               print *," No Pick. PickStatus: ",PickStatus
           endif  { end 'if PickStatus .eq. POK'
        endif     { end 'if ReturnClass .eq. PPICK'
      return
      end
```

Chapter 15

Front and Back Facet Processing

This chapter describes the following:

- The PHIGS PLUS rendering pipeline
- Facet culling—excluding back-facing or front-facing portions of area-defining primitives from being displayed
- Facet distinguishing—specifying whether front or back attributes should be applied to the back-facing portions of area-defining primitives

Note that the PHIGS PLUS routines in Chapter 15–20 are only described for the C binding. See "Language Bindings, Fragments, and Pseudo-code" in the *Preface* for more information.

The PHIGS PLUS Rendering Pipeline

This chapter begins a discussion of the **rendering pipeline**. The discussion extends through the next several chapters. Each chapter describes different portions of the pipeline.

PHIGS PLUS introduced the concept of a rendering pipeline. As primitives travel through the pipeline, PHIGS performs a number of operations on the primitives (see Figure 15–1).

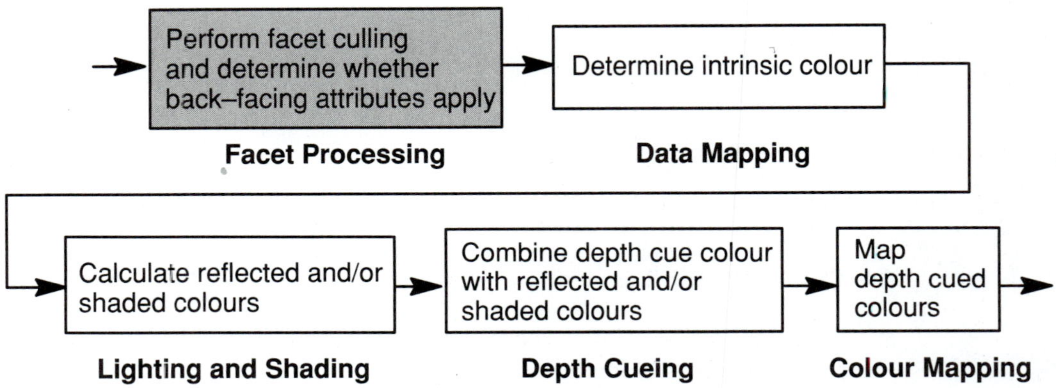

Figure 15–1. PHIGS PLUS Rendering Pipeline

The facet processing stage allows the application to specify whether the portions of area-defining primitives facing away from or facing toward the observer should be drawn or not. This is called **facet culling**. The facet processing stage also allows the application to specify whether the back-facing portions of area-defining primitives should have different attributes (different from the front-facing portions) applied to them.

The data mapping stage determines the source of intrinsic colour that will be associated with area-defining primitives. **Intrinsic colour** is the colour associated with a primitive before lighting calculations are applied. The source of intrinsic colour can be one of the following:

- Interior colour (attribute)
- Facet colour

- Application-supplied facet data
- Vertex colour
- Application-supplied vertex data

The facet and vertex data sources allow you to map application-specific information such as pressure or temperature to intrinsic colour. See Chapter 16, *INtrinsic Colour and Data Mapping*.

The lighting and shading stage is actually broken down into several separate stages, based on the interior shading method. The lighting stage uses a primitive's reflectance properties, orientation, and position in world coordinates to determine how a primitive's intrinsic colour is affected by lights, according to a reflectance model. The shading stage performs interpolation of colours (or other data) across the facets of area-defining primitives (and between the vertices of "polyline with colour" and "non-uniform B-spline curve with colour" primitives). See Chapter 17, *Lighting and Shading*.

The depth cueing stage modifies the colours of the shaded primitive by combining the primitive colour with a given depth cue colour based on the primitive's *z* components in NPC space. This allows an application to fade or intensify an image according to its depth. See Chapter 18, *Depth Cueing*.

The colour mapping stage allows an application either to display the colours calculated by the previous stages or to convert those colours into a set of application-defined colours. See Chapter 19, *Colour Mapping*.

Facet Culling for Area-Defining Primitives

Facet culling allows you to identify which facets of an area-defining primitive should not be seen and to instruct PHIGS to **cull**, or not draw them (the term *facet* is defined later in this section). Facet culling can improve rendering performance since it potentially cuts down on the number of primitive facets processed by the rendering pipeline.

PHIGS supports culling of front-facing or back-facing facets. Back-facing culling is the most common usage. This gives the effect of hidden surface removal for simple convex objects such as a sphere made up of fill area primitives.

Special effects can be achieved using front-facing culling. For example, an application can use front facet culling to expose the interior faces of a polygonal or polyhedral object. Culling is controlled by a structure element, so you can selectively insert elements to switch between front facet culling, back facet culling, and no culling.

Front facet culling is also useful if your application prefers to specify inward-pointing normals instead of outward facing (PHIGS's assumption). For example, Figure 15–2 shows two ways of defining a convex object. Each method uses eight primitives with facet normals. The left illustration uses outward-facing normals, and the right illustration uses inward-facing normals. Back facet culling is useful for the object on the left since it would mean that the portions facing away from the viewer would not be drawn. Front facet culling would be desirable on the right because the primitives with front-facing normals are at the back of the object.

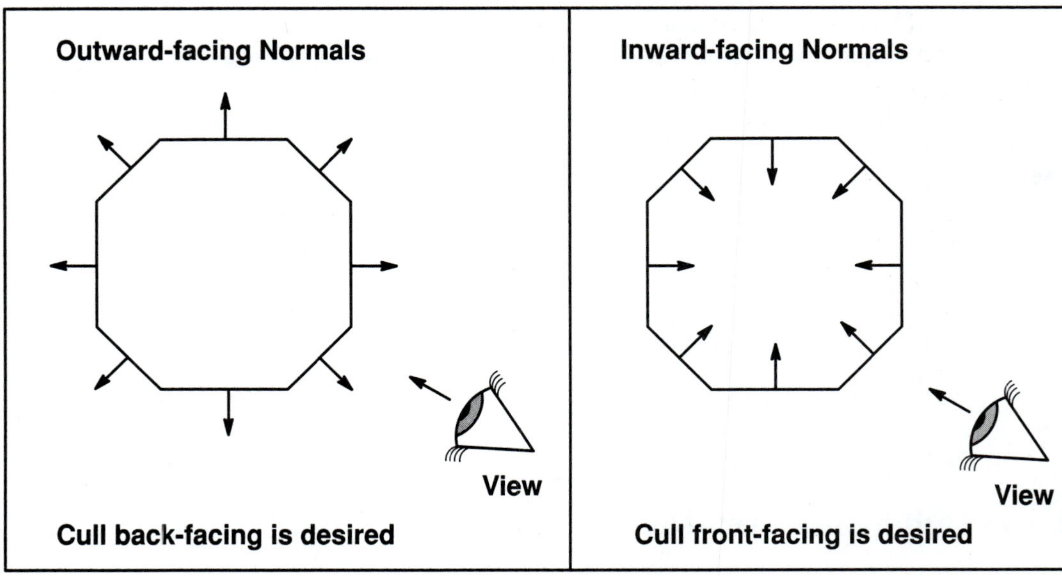

Figure 15–2. Eight Primitives with Facet Normals Forming a Convex Object

As mentioned, PHIGS supports facet culling for all area-defining primitives. The following lists the area-defining primitives:

- Fill area
- Fill area set

- Fill area set with data
- Set of fill area sets with data
- Cell array; cell array plus
- Triangle set with data
- Triangle strip with data
- Quadrilateral mesh with data
- Parametric surfaces (non-uniform B-spline surface and non-uniform B-spline surface with data)

Note that while parametric surfaces are not inherently faceted, PHIGS treats them as faceted surfaces in order to describe how they are displayed and how interior attributes are applied to them.

Setting the Facet Culling Mode

PHIGS supports facet culling through the use of a **facet culling mode**. The routine SET FACET CULLING MODE creates a structure element that selects the facet culling mode at traversal time. The C binding calling signature for the SET FACET CULLING MODE routine is

```
pset_facet_cull_mode(
  Pfacet_cull_mode    mode
);
```

where:

⟨*mode*⟩ specifies the facet culling mode. Use one of the following values:

- `PFACET_CULL_NONE`. No facet culling.
- `PFACET_CULL_BACKFACING`. Cull back-facing facets.
- `PFACET_CULL_FRONTFACING`. Cull front-facing facets.

For example, the following fragment causes back-facing facets to be discarded:

```
popen_struct(cube);                    /* open structure cube     */
pset_facet_cull_mode(PFACET_CULL_BACKFACING);
...
pclose_struct();                       /* close structure         */
```

Note that the facet culling mode cannot be controlled through bundled attributes.

Facets

PHIGS uses the concepts of facets and geometric normals to determine whether a portion of an area-defining primitive is front-facing or back-facing.

In PHIGS, area-defining primitives are conceptually subdivided into facets for the purposes of specifying data and applying attributes. The definition of each primitive's facets are as follows:

- The whole of a fill area or fill area set constitutes one facet.
- Each cell of a cell array or cell array plus constitutes one facet.
- Each fill area set in a "set of fill area sets" constitutes one facet.
- Each triangle in a triangle set or triangle strip constitutes one facet.
- Each quadrilateral in a quadrilateral mesh constitutes one facet.
- For parametric surfaces, it is up to the implementation to determine what the facets are. For example, each tesselated subprimitive of a parametric surface may constitute one facet. See your implementation documentation for details.

A facet is always considered a planar area. That is, a facet is assumed to lie in a plane. PHIGS applies a single test to that plane's normal to determine front versus back "facingness."

Figure 15–3 shows the facet information for a fill area set with data primitive.

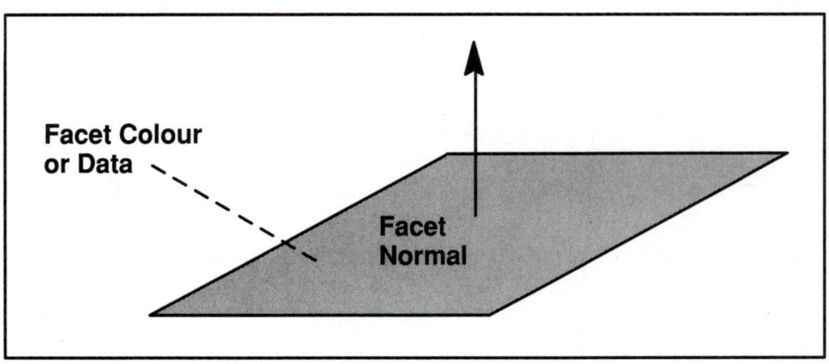

Figure 15–3. Fill Area Set with Data Facet and Vertex Information

Facet data in Figure 15–3 refers to application-specific information, such as temperature or pressure values, that you can include in the primitive definition. See Chapter 16.

Note that the vertices defining facets in a quadrilateral mesh, triangle strip, or a tesselated spline surface are usually not planar. For back facet and reflectance processing, PHIGS computes a normal vector for each facet if it is not supplied in the definition of the primitive.

Geometric Normals

PHIGS uses the **geometric normal** to determine if a facet is front-facing or back-facing. If a facet's geometric normal has a negative *z* component when transformed to NPC space, the facet is back-facing. Otherwise, the facet is front-facing.

The difference between a facet normal and a geometric normal is that a "facet normal" refers to a value supplied by the application. If the application supplies a facet normal value, PHIGS uses the value as the geometric normal. If the application does not supply a facet normal value, PHIGS calculates the geometric normal for each facet, using a method that depends on the primitive type.

The following primitives allow you to include facet normals in the primitive definition:

- Fill area set with data
- Set of fill area sets with data
- Triangle set with data
- Triangle strip with data
- Quadrilateral mesh with data

Note that vertex normals are not used for facet culling. They are used for lighting and shading (see Chapter 17).

How PHIGS Calculates the Geometric Normal

If the application does not supply facet normals (or if the primitive does not have facilities for specifying facet normals), then PHIGS calculates the geometric normal for each facet using one of several methods, depending on the primitive type. This section describes how PHIGS calculates the geometric normal for the following primitives:

- Fill area, fill area set, fill area set with data, set of fill area sets
- Triangle set (not triangle strip)
- Area-defining generalized drawing primitives (GDPs), such as circles and ellipses, if there are at least three points in the primitive definition

For information on how PHIGS calculates the geometric normal for other area-defining primitives, refer to Section 4.5.5 of the PHIGS PLUS standard.

For each of the area-defining primitives listed above, PHIGS computes a geometric normal for each facet by first determining three points (referred to as A, B, and C). Point A is the first point in the application-supplied list of vertices for each facet. Point B is the next point in the list that is not coincident with A. Point C is the next point in the list (after B) that is non-collinear with the line through A and B. For example, Figure 15–4 shows points A, B, and C for a fill area. (The primitive in Figure 15–4 is the front of the cube-with-the-corner-cut-off that we created in the "Single View Example" in Chapter 7, *Viewing and Workstation Transformations*.)

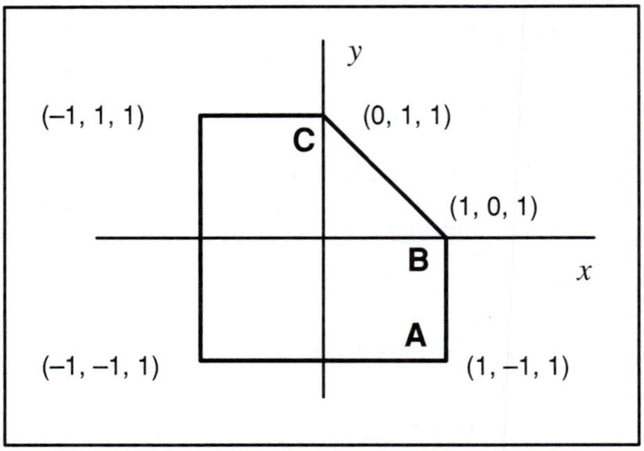

Figure 15–4. Points Used to Determine the Geometric Normal

The geometric normal is the normalized cross product of the following two vectors:

- The vector extending from A to B
- The vector extending from A to C

If PHIGS cannot find points A, B, and C in the vertex list, it determines that the primitive is degenerate. Whether or not a degenerate primitive is drawn is implementation dependent. In the case of a fill area set, PHIGS searches each of the lists of vertices until points A, B, and C are found.

Ordering the Points of an Area-defining Primitive

When PHIGS calculates the geometric normal, the normal's orientation (back-facing or front-facing) is determined by the order of points in the primitive definition. This is because PHIGS uses the points, in the order supplied, to calculate the various cross products. For the fill area, fill area set, triangle strip, and quadrilateral mesh, the order of the primitive's vertices determines the direction of the computed geometric normal. For the "set of fill area sets" and "triangle set" primitives, the order of indices determines the direction of the computed geometric normal. For the parametric surfaces, PHIGS determines the direction by the order of the surface's control points. This means that in the absence of a specified facet normal, an application indirectly controls the direction of the computed normal by the ordering of the data in the primitive.

A Word of Warning for the Reader

If you let PHIGS calculate the geometric normals, you need to be careful if you use modelling transformations to create reflections (where the determinant is less than 0). For example, assume that you construct a convex object with normals facing outward. Assume that the facets are defined as in Figure 15–4 using the same vertices. A, B, and C are as in Figure 15–4, and the computed normal is as follows:

$$\begin{aligned}(B - A) \times (C - A) &= (0, 1, 0) \times (-1, 2, 0) \\ &= (0, 0, 1)\end{aligned}$$

When you reflect (mirror) the object by the following matrix:

$$\begin{bmatrix} -1 & 0 & 0 \\ 0 & 1 & 0 \\ 0 & 0 & 1 \end{bmatrix}$$

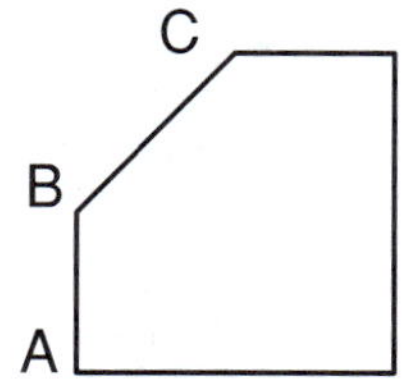

You get the following:

$$\begin{aligned}(B - A) \times (C - A) &= (0, 1, 0) \times (1, 2, 0) \\ &= (0, 0, -1)\end{aligned}$$

This is a now an inward-facing normal. Therefore, you need to use front-facet culling and reverse the use of front and back attributes!

Setting the Facet Distinguishing Mode

The following aspects have separate attributes for front and back facets:

- Data mapping method
- Interior colour
- Interior style
- Interior style index (selects an entry from workstation interior style table)
- Interior shading method
- Reflectance properties
- Reflectance model

Each of these aspects has a counterpart that is conditionally applied to back facets of area-defining primitives. The default is that PHIGS does not distinguish between front and back faces when applying attributes, treating all faces as "front." You can instruct PHIGS to distinguish between front and back faces by setting the *facet distinguishing mode* attribute.

The *facet distinguishing mode* attribute controls whether PHIGS distinguishes between front and back faces when applying attributes. The SET FACET DISTINGUISHING MODE routine creates a structure element that selects the facet distinguishing mode at traversal time. The C binding calling signature for the SET FACET DISTINGUISHING MODE routine is as follows:

```
pset_facet_disting_mode(
   Pfacet_disting_mode      mode
);
```

where:

⟨*mode*⟩ specifies the face distinguishing mode. Use one of the following values:

- `PFACET_DISTING_OFF`. Do not use back attributes. PHIGS uses the front facet attributes for both front and back facing facets of area-defining primitives. This is the default.

- `PFACET_DISTING_ON`. Use back attributes for the back facing facets of area-defining primitives.

For example, the following fragment turns on front and back facet distinguishing:

```
popen_struct(cube);                         /* open structure cube   */
pset_facet_disting_mode(PFACET_DISTING_ON);
.
.                              /* area-defining primitives go here   */
.
pclose_struct();                            /* close structure       */
```

Note that the *facet distinguishing mode* and *facet culling mode* attributes are independent of each other. PHIGS applies the facet culling mode regardless of the value of the facet distinguishing mode.

Back Facet Processing and the Workstation Bundle Tables

Both front- and back-facing facets of area-defining primitives obtain their attributes from the same bundle table. For example, the following routines apply to the interior bundle table:

- Use the following routines to define an entry in the interior bundle table:
  - SET INTERIOR REPRESENTATION
  - SET INTERIOR REPRESENTATION PLUS

  Both routines define entries in the same table. The PLUS routine defines additional fields defined by PHIGS PLUS.
- Use the following routines to select entries from the interior bundle table:
  - SET INTERIOR INDEX
  - SET BACK INTERIOR INDEX

The following describes how PHIGS uses front and back attributes in the interior bundle table. The same method applies to the other attribute tables that support front and back attributes.

- When you open an OUTPUT or OUTIN workstation, PHIGS uses values from the workstation description table to define the entries in the interior bundle table. The application program can use the SET INTERIOR REPRESENTATION or SET INTERI-

OR REPRESENTATION PLUS routine to redefine any of the values in the interior bundle table.

- During structure traversal, PHIGS uses the *current interior index* and the *current back interior index* (in the traversal state list) to select entries from the interior bundle table. Depending on the current facet distinguishing mode and the current facet culling mode, PHIGS uses the front and back interior index attributes when displaying respective portions of area-defining primitives. Each entry has a number of different aspects (for example, interior shading method, interior colour, and interior style). PHIGS decides which aspects from the table entry to use, based on the setting of the corresponding aspect source flags.

- If the application program specifies an entry that is not defined, then PHIGS uses entry 1 in the table.

By using this technique to select different entries in the tables for front- and back-facing portions of area-defining primitives, PHIGS avoids the problem of needing separate bundle tables for front and back attributes.

Table 15–1 lists the following:

- All of the front and back aspects
- The routines that set the individual attribute
- The routine that selects an entry from the associated bundle table
- The routines that define entries in the bundle table

Table 15–2 lists the C binding ASF identifiers for the aspects in Table 15–1. Use these values with a SET INDIVIDUAL ASF routine to select individual or bundled values for the aspect.

Table 15–1. Back and Front Aspect Routines

Name of Aspect	Individual Routine	Index Routine	Bundle Routine
Interior colour	pset_int_colr	pset_int_ind	pset_int_rep_plus
Interior style	pset_int_style	pset_int_ind	pset_int_rep_plus
Interior style index	pset_int_style_ind	pset_int_ind	pset_int_rep_plus
Int. shading method	pset_int_shad_method	pset_int_ind	pset_int_rep_plus
Back int. colour	pset_back_int_colr	pset_back_int_ind	pset_int_rep_plus
Back interior style	pset_back_int_style	pset_back_int_ind	pset_int_rep_plus
Back int. style index	pset_back_int_style_ind	pset_back_int_ind	pset_int_rep_plus
Back int. shad. method	pset_back_int_shad_method	pset_back_int_ind	pset_int_rep_plus
Reflectance model	pset_refl_model	pset_refl_ind	pset_refl_rep
Back reflec. model	pset_back_refl_model	pset_back_refl_ind	pset_refl_rep
Reflectance properties	pset_refl_props	pset_refl_ind	pset_refl_rep
Back reflec. properties	pset_back_refl_props	pset_back_refl_ind	pset_refl_rep
Data mapping method	pset_data_map_method	pset_dat_map_ind	pset_data_map_rep
Back data map. method	pset_back_data_map_method	pset_back_data_map_ind	pset_data_map_rep

Table 15–2. ASF Identifiers for Front and Back Aspects

Aspect	ASF Identifier
Interior colour	PASPECT_INT_COLR
Interior style	PASPECT_INT_STYLE
Interior stye index	PASPECT_INT_STYLE_IND
Interior shading method	PASPECT_INT_SHAD_METHOD
Back interior colour	PASPECT_BACK_INT_COLR
Back interior style	PASPECT_BACK_INT_STYLE
Back interior style index	PASPECT_BACK_INT_STYLE_IND
Back interior shading method	PASPECT_BACK_INT_SHAD_METHOD
Data mapping method	PASPECT_DATA_MAP_METHOD
Back data mapping method	PASPECT_BACK_DATA_MAP_METHOD
Reflectance properties	PASPECT_REFL_PROPS
Back reflectance properties	PASPECT_BACK_REFL_PROPS
Reflectance model	PASPECT_REFL_MODEL
Back reflectance model	PASPECT_BACK_REFL_MODEL

Chapter 16

Intrinsic Colour and Data Mapping

This chapter discusses the related concepts of intrinsic colour and data mapping. You only need to be concerned about intrinsic colours when you are performing lighting and shading. Data mapping is the process of selecting one or more intrinsic colours for a primitive.

Intrinsic Colour

The intrinsic colour is the colour associated with a primitive independent of lighting, depth cueing, and colour mapping.

The intrinsic colour can be derived from a number of different sources, depending on the primitive type. The following list shows the possible source(s) of intrinsic colour for each output primitive. Where there are multiple sources for the intrinsic colour, PHIGS uses the precedence shown in this list to select a source.

- Polymarker; text; annotation text
  - Polymarker, text, and annotation text colour aspect
- Polyline, non-uniform B-spline curve
  - Polyline colour aspect
- Polyline set with data
  - Vertex colours
  - Polyline colour aspect

- Non-uniform B-spline curve with colour
  - Colour spline
  - Polyline colour aspect
- Fill area; fill area set; non-uniform B-spline surface
  - Pattern representation (only if interior style is Pattern)
  - Interior colour aspect
- Fill area set with data; set of fill area set with data; triangle set with data; triangle strip with data; quadrilateral mesh with data; non-uniform B-spline surface with data
  - Pattern representation (only if interior style is Pattern)
  - Data mapping aspect can select interior colour, facet colour, facet data, vertex colour, or vertex data
  - Interior colour aspect
- Cell array; cell array plus
  - Cell colours
- Generalized drawing primitive (GDP)
  - Depends on the primitive

As you can see from this list, the "with data" area-defining primitives use the data mapping aspect as the source of the intrinsic colour if the interior style is not Pattern.

Data Mapping

Data mapping is used for determining the source of intrinsic colour for the "with data" area-defining primitives. Data mapping has the following components:

- It prioritizes the source of intrinsic colour (called a **source priority rule**). The available sources are as follows:
  - interior colour aspect
  - Facet colour
  - Application-supplied facet data
  - Vertex colour
  - Application-supplied vertex data
- It identifies the method used to convert application-supplied data, such as temperature or pressure, to colour.

Figure 16–1 shows the position of the data mapping stage in the rendering pipeline.

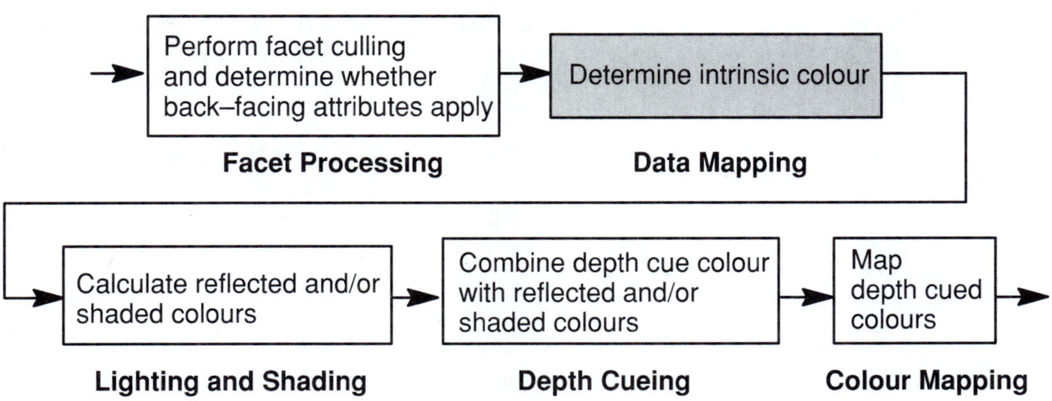

Figure 16–1. Data Mapping Stage of Rendering Pipeline

The application can specify facet colour, facet data, vertex colour, and vertex data as part of a "with data" area-defining primitive. Any of these optional values can be the source of intrinsic colour (in addition, of course, to the interior colour aspect). PHIGS determines the source on a primitive-by-primitive basis. Figure 16–2 shows how PHIGS selects the source of intrinsic colour. The application can have up to five elements in the source priority rule list. PHIGS checks each item in the list until it finds a match. If no match is found, interior colour aspect is used.

For example, an application could define a "fill area set with data" primitive with both facet colour and vertex colours. Then, at traversal time the application will specify whether to use facet colour, vertex colour, or interior colour aspect for the intrinsic colour by setting the data mapping attribute to Colour and setting the source priority rule list to contain a single element which is either Facet Colour, Vertex Colour, or Interior Colour Aspect. All three selectors could be listed; whichever one is first in the list will be used since the primitive has both facet and vertex colours.

Colour plate 2 (see colour insert) shows an application like we have been describing used with quadrilateral mesh and triangle strip primitives. In this example the primitives are defined once and then drawn in three different locations, each time using a different source of intrinsic colour.

As an another example, a finite element modeling application could associate values such as temperature or pressure with the facets or vertices of a primitive. Then, at traversal time the application could use the interior shading method and the data mapping method to instruct PHIGS to interpolate those values across the primitive and then map the results to a specific colour list. For example, the colour list could be a series of "colour ramps" going from blue to green, to yellow, to red, depicting increasing temperature values. Colour plate 1 shows two examples: One maps facet data to a colour list and the other maps vertex data to the same colour list.

In Figure 16–1 we listed data mapping as a separate stage in the rendering pipeline. However, in reality, interpolation can be applied to data values. Also, shading can spread vertex colours across a primitive, thereby determining the intrinsic colour. So, when interpolation occurs, the data mapping stage could be better represented as being part of the lighting and shading stage.

Note that data mapping is a relatively new feature in the PHIGS PLUS standard. If your implementation does not support data mapping, it may use another method for selecting the source of intrinsic colour for area-defining primitives. For example, it may depend on the shading method and on whether vertex colours or facet colours are specified in the primitive definition.

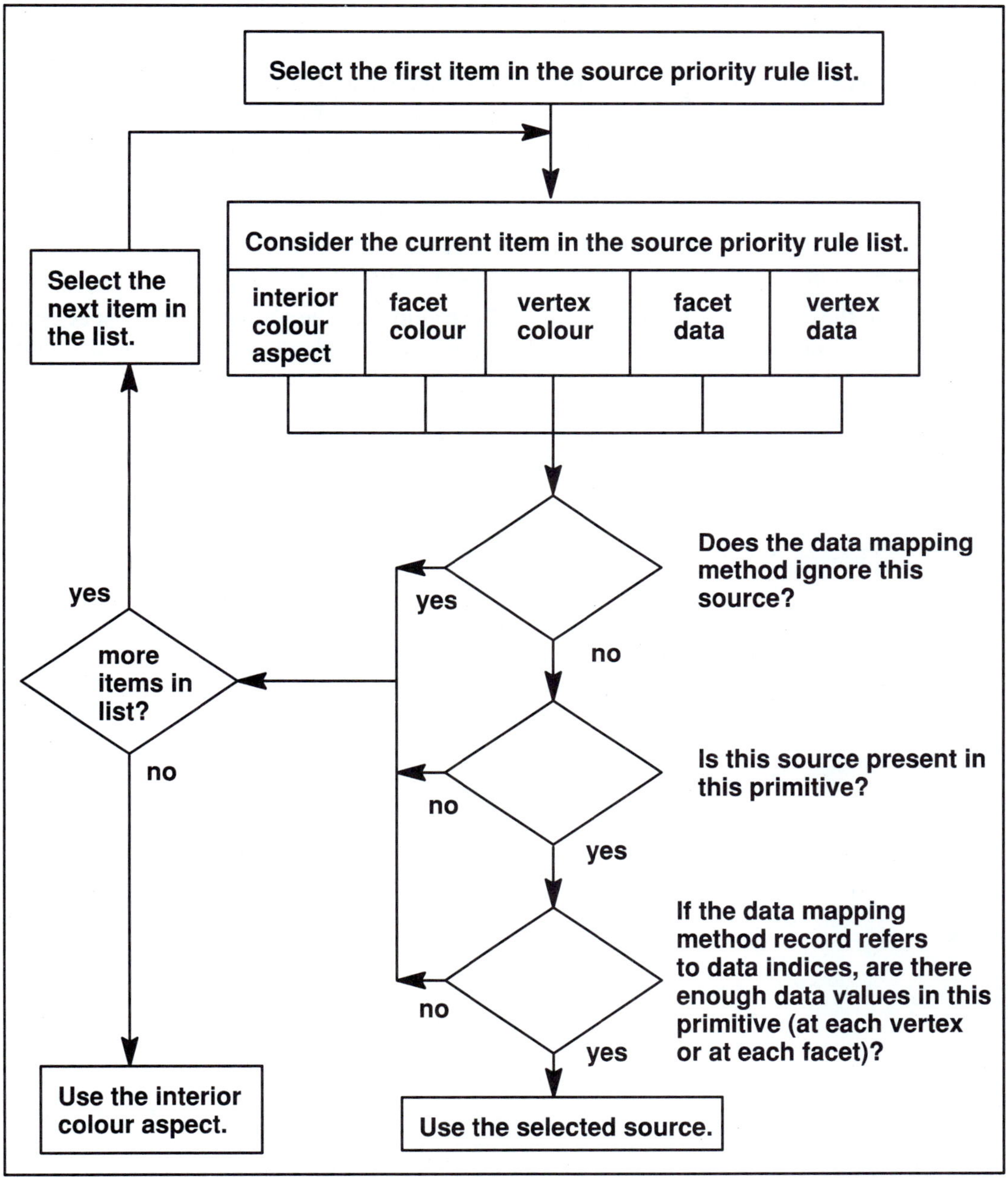

Figure 16–2. Determining the Source of Intrinsic Colour

Specifying a Data Mapping Method

You can set the data mapping method attribute via individual and bundled attributes. Also, if the face distinguishing mode is on, you can specify different attributes for the front and back of a facet. See the tables at the end of Chapter 15, *Front and Back Facet Processing*, for a list of routines.

Individual Attribute Specification (Data Mapping Method)

Use the SET DATA MAPPING METHOD routine for individual attribute specification. This routine creates a structure element that, when traversed, sets the *current data mapping method* entry in the traversal state list. PHIGS uses this value when the *current data mapping method ASF* entry in the traversal state list is set to individual.

The C binding calling signature for the SET DATA MAPPING METHOD routine is as follows:

```
pset_data_map_method(
   const Pdata_map_rep   *rep
);
```

where:

⟨*rep*⟩ is the data mapping method representation, in `Pdata_map_rep` format. The `Pdata_map_rep` data type is defined as follows:

```
Pdata_map_rep
 typedef struct {
   Pint              method;      /* data mapping method       */
   Psource_select_list  selectors; /* selector list            */
   union Pdata_map_rep_data {
    struct Pdata_map_rep_single_uniform {
      Pint         ind;         /* data value index          */
      Pfloat       lower_limit; /* lower range limit         */
      Pfloat       upper_limit; /* upper range limit         */
      Pint         colr_type;   /* colour type               */
      Pcolrv_list  colr_values; /* list of colour values     */
    } single_uniform;
    struct Pdata_map_rep_single_non_uniform {
      Pint         ind;         /* data value index          */
      Pfloat_list  range;       /* range boundaries          */
      Pint         colr_type;   /* colour type               */
      Pcolrv_list  colr_values; /* list of colour values     */
```

```
        } single_non_uniform;
        struct Pdata_map_rep_bi_uniform {
          Pint         inds[2];      /* data value indices      */
          Pfloat       lower_limit_a;/* lower limit of Ra range */
          Pfloat       upper_limit_a;/* upper limit of Ra range */
          Pfloat       lower_limit_b;/* lower limit of Rb range */
          Pfloat       upper_limit_b;/* upper limit of Rb range */
          Pint         colr_type;    /* colour type             */
          Pcolrv_set colr_values;/*list of color value lists    */
        } bi_uniform;
        struct Pdata_map_rep_bi_non_uniform {
          Pint         inds[2];     /* data value indices       */
          Pfloat_list  range_a;     /* Ra range boundaries      */
          Pfloat_set   range_b;     /* Rb range boundaries      */
          Pint         colr_type;   /* colour type              */
          Pcolrv_set   colr_values;/* array of colour values */
        } bi_non_uniform;
        ...                         /* implementation-defined   */
      } data;
    } Pdata_map_rep;
```

where:

`selectors` is a list of intrinsic colour source selectors. This is a list of flags that indicates the precedence that PHIGS should use when selecting a source of intrinsic colour. The values in the list are as follows:

- `PSOURCE_SELECT_COLR_ASPECT`. Use interior colour aspect as the source of intrinsic colour.
- `PSOURCE_SELECT_VERT_COLR`. Use vertex colour as the source of intrinsic colour.
- `PSOURCE_SELECT_VERT_DATA`. Use vertex data as the source of intrinsic colour.
- `PSOURCE_SELECT_FACET_COLR`. Use facet colour as the source of intrinsic colour.
- `PSOURCE_SELECT_FACET_DATA`. Use facet data as the source of intrinsic colour.

A given selector value is used only if the data-to-colour conversion rule is valid for the type of data. For example, `PSOURCE_SELECT_VERT_DATA` selects vertex data as the source of intrinsic colour only if the data-to-colour conversion rule is valid for the vertex data.

The order of values in the list indicates the precedence. The first value in the list has the highest precedence. During traversal, when PHIGS encounters a "with data" area-defining output primitive, it searches through the selector list until it finds a selector value that matches a source of intrinsic colour in the output primitive definition. Then it uses that value as the source of the intrinsic colour. Note that interior colour aspect always "matches." The application should end the list with `PSOURCE_SELECT_COLR_ASPECT`, since that value will always match.

The `method` field identifies the data-to-colour conversion rule used to convert application-specific data to colour. Each method expects specific values as defined in the `Pdata_map_rep` data type and by the current data-to-colour conversion rule. Fill in the appropriate fields, depending on the value of `method` (see "Using Data Mapping," later in this chapter). Note that the application-specific data we refer to here includes facet and vertex colour as well as facet and vertex data.

The related colour data types are as follows:

```
Pcolrv_list
 typedef struct {
   Pint           num_colrs;   /* number of colours          */
   Pcolrv_ptr     colrs;       /* list of colour values      */
} Pcolrv_list;

Pcolrv_ptr
 typedef union {
   Pint           *colr_inds;  /* pointer to colour indices */
   Pcolr_rep_ptr  colr_reps;   /* pointer to colour
                                  representations           */
} Pcolrv_ptr;

Pcolr_rep_ptr
 typedef union {
   Prgb           *rgb;
   Pcieluv        *cieluv;
   Phls           *hls;
   Phsv           *hsv;
   Pdata          *unsupp;
} Pcolr_rep_ptr;
```

```
Pcolrv_set
 typedef struct {
   Pint            num_lists;    /* # of colour value lists    */
   Pcolr_list      *colrs;       /* list of colour value
                                    lists                      */
} Pcolrv_set;
```

Use the SET BACK DATA MAPPING METHOD routine to set the data mapping method attribute for back-facing portions. The calling signature is similar to `pset_data_map_method`.

Bundled Attribute Specification (Data Mapping Method)

For bundled attribute specification, use the SET DATA MAPPING REPRESENTATION routine to set the data mapping method values for a particular entry in the workstation data mapping bundle table. A value is selected from this table, based on the current data mapping index, when the *current data mapping method ASF* is set to bundled. The C binding calling signature for the SET DATA MAPPING REPRESENTATION routine is as follows:

```
pset_data_map_rep(
Pint                     ws_id,
Pint                     index,
const Pdata_map_rep      *rep
);
```

where:

⟨*ws_id*⟩ identifies the workstation.

⟨*index*⟩ specifies an entry in the workstation data mapping table. This parameter identifies the workstation data mapping table entry to modify.

⟨*rep*⟩ is the data mapping method representation. See the definition of `Pdata_map_rep` earlier in this chapter.

Use the SET DATA MAPPING INDEX routine to control which entry from the data mapping bundle table is used for front-facing portions when the *current data mapping method ASF* is set to bundled.

Use the SET BACK DATA MAPPING INDEX routine to control which entry from the data mapping bundle table is used for back-facing portions when the *current back data mapping method ASF* is set to bundled.

Using Data Mapping

As mentioned earlier, the data mapping stage of the rendering pipeline has two components:

1. It prioritizes the source of intrinsic colour.

2 It identifies the method used to convert application-specific data, such as temperature or pressure, to colour.

There are five defined data mapping methods (numbered 1 through 5) that can be specified as the "rule" to convert application-specific data to colour. These are defined in the following subsections.

Method number 1 has a special purpose: It means "no conversion" and should be used when the application has no wish to use application-specific data as the colour source.

Data Mapping Method 1—Colour

Data mapping method 1 (`PDATA_MAP_METHOD_COLR`) is the traversal default and is the most commonly used method. It allows an application to specify whether to use interior colour, facet colour, or vertex colours as the source of intrinsic colour for "with data" area-defining primitives. With this data mapping method you specify a selector list and a data mapping method. Method 1 has no effect on application-specific data.

For example, assume that you define a quadrilateral mesh or triangle strip primitive with facet colours and vertex colours. At traversal time you can display the same primitive using interior colour, facet colour, or vertex colour just by setting the data mapping method and the appropriate interior shading method. By keeping the data-to-colour conversion rule to Colour and by changing the selector list, you can indicate which source you want to use at traversal time.

The following example draws a primitive three times using three different sources of intrinsic colour: interior colour, facet colour, and vertex colour.

The first two times the primitive is rendered, the interior shading method is set to None (no interpolation). This instructs PHIGS to render each facet with a single colour. The third time the interior shading method is set to Colour. This instructs PHIGS to interpolate vertex colour values across each facet.

```
Pdata_map_rep  rep;

rep.data.selectors.num = 1;
rep.data.seleectors.selectors[0] = PSOURCE_SELECT_COLR_ASPECT;
rep.method = PDATA_MAP_METHOD_COLR;

popen_struc(Scene);                 /* open structure              */
pset_view_ind(ViewIndex);           /* set view index              */
pset_int_style(PSTYLE_SOLID);       /* set interior style          */
pset_int_shad_method(PINT_SHAD_METHOD_NONE); /* int. shading method*/
pset_data_map_method(&rep);         /* set data mapping method     */
pexecute_struct(QuadMesh);          /* execute structure           */

rep.data.selectors[0] = PSOURCE_SELECT_FACET_COLOR; /* facet colour*/
pset_data_map_method(&rep);         /* set data mapping method     */
pexecute_struct(QuadMesh);          /* execute structure           */

rep.data.selectors[0] = PSOURCE_SELECT_VERT_COLR;
pset_data_map_method(&rep);            /* set data mapping method
*/
pset_int_shad_method(PINT_SHAD_METHOD_COLR);/* int. shading method */
pexecute_struct(QuadMesh);          /* execute structure           */
pclose_struc();                     /* close structure             */
```

Colour plate 2 (see colour insert) shows an example of this kind of data mapping using quadrilateral mesh and triangle strip primitives.

Note that in the above fragment the new primitive would be drawn over the old primitive each time since there is no change in the transformation to draw the primitive in a new location.

Data Mapping Methods 2 through 5—Using Application-Specific Data

Data mapping methods 2 through 5 support applications that need to convert application-specific data to colour values. For example, a finite element modeling application may have values for temperature or pressure associated with the facets or vertices of a primitive. Data mapping methods 2 through 5 allow the application to accomplish the following:

- Map facet or vertex data to an application-supplied colour list.
- Depending on the interior shading method, interpolate vertex data values across the primitive and then map the resulting values to an application-supplied colour list.

The application can have multiple data values associated with each facet or vertex. Figure 16–3 shows a triangle created by a "fill area set with data" primitive. Each vertex has a list of data values. The facet also has a list of data values denoted by $f_1 - f_j$. For example, the first value in each list could be a temperature value and the second could be a pressure value. You use an index value to tell PHIGS which value to use.

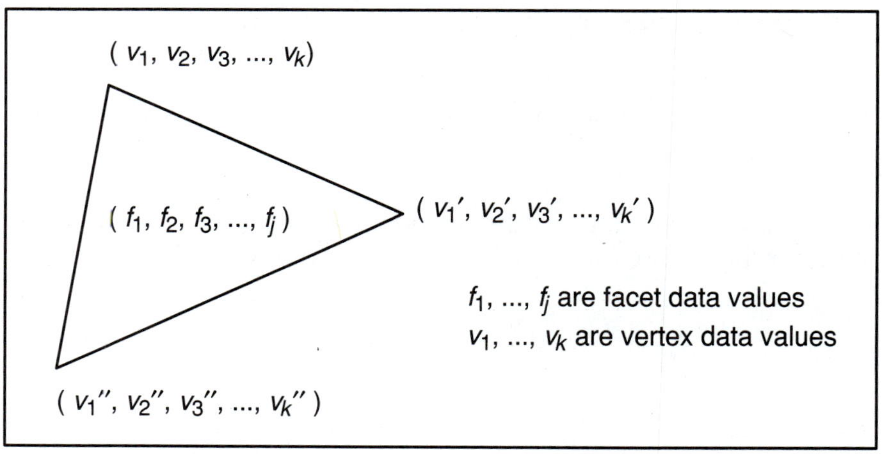

Figure 16–3. Application-Specific Data per Vertex

For data mapping methods 2 and 3, there is only one colour list. For those methods, you use one index value to specify which vertex data value or facet data value to use. Methods 4 and 5 support multiple colour lists. For those methods, you use a pair of indices to specify which two data values to use.

Methods 2 and 3 allow visualizing one data value at a time. For example, if you have pressure and temperature at each vertex, but the user wishes to concentrate on only a single value at a certain moment, use method 2 or 3.

Methods 4 and 5 are useful if you need to use more than one colour list. For example, if you had three types of materials that you wanted to display with temperature values, then you might want to use a different colour list for each material.

Methods 4 and 5 are also useful if you want to visualize two data values at the same time. For example, if the user wants to see both pressure and temperature distribution at the same time, you can use methods 4 and 5 and get effects that associate temperature with hue (red for hot, blue for cold) and associate pressure with saturation (desaturated for low pressure, saturated for high pressure).

The following sections describe data mapping methods 2 through 5.

Data Mapping Method 2—Single Value Uniform

This data mapping method (`PDATA_MAP_METHOD_SINGLE_UNIFORM`) allows you to specify a uniform range for mapping a given data value to a colour from a colour list. The application supplies the following information for this data mapping method:

- A selector list that prioritizes the sources of intrinsic colour. Source selector values other than `PSOURCE_SELECT_FACET_DATA` and `PSOURCE_SELECT_VERT_DATA` are ignored.
- A data mapping method value of 2 (single value uniform).
- An index that identifies the value to use from the facet list or vertex list (f_1–f_j or v_1–v_k in Figure 16–3). If this index is too big, the method is "not applicable" and the next colour source selector is examined.
- Two real values that indicate the portion of the application data values that will be divided into equal segments (for the purpose of mapping the data to colours). The first and last colours are targets for extreme data below or above the limits. For example, in Figure 16–4 we use values of 10.0 and 30.0 as limits, and we have four colours in the colour list. In this example, any value above 30 maps to red and any value below 10 maps to blue.
- A colour type that specifies which colour model to use for the colour list.
- A single colour list in `Pcolrv_list` format (defined earlier in this chapter). The length of the list implicitly specifies the number of gradations.

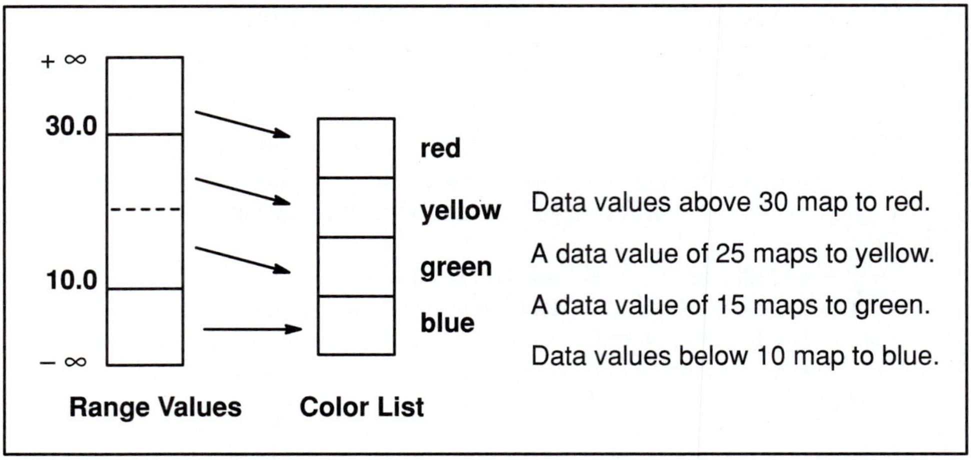

Figure 16–4. Examples of Range Values for Data Mapping Method 2

For example, let's assume that the first item in the colour selector list is PSOURCE_SELECT_VERT_DATA, the interior shading method is Data (interpolate application data values across the primitive), and that there are vertex data values in the primitive definition. In this case, PHIGS performs the following steps when it encounters the primitive structure element during traversal:

- Check the selector list to identify the first candidate for the source of intrinsic colour. It finds PSOURCE_SELECT_VERT_DATA.
- Reject the source of intrinsic colour if the data mapping method should ignore it.
- Check the index value to determine which vertex data values to use (v_1–v_k in Figure 16–3). Let's suppose the value is 2.
- Because the index value is 2, check that each vertex of the primitive has at least 2 pieces of application-specific data. If the primitive doesn't, the method is "not applicable" to the primitive and the next selector value would be examined. Let's suppose that each vertex does have 2 values.
- Since the shading method is Data in this example, interpolate the second vertex data values across the primitive (since the index is 2).
- Compare each of the resulting values with the range to select a value from the colour list.

- Use the values from the colour list as intrinsic colour values at the interpolated positions.
- Use the intrinsic colour values for any lighting calculations.

When using "non-uniform B-spline surface with data" primitives, the index value identifies a data spline from the list of data splines. PHIGS uses this data spline to determine the data values to map. This applies to data mapping methods 2–5.

Data Mapping Method 3—Single Value Non-uniform

This data mapping method (`PDATA_MAP_METHOD_SINGLE_NON_UNIFORM`) allows you to specify a series of non-uniform range limits that map data values to a colour list. The application supplies the following information for this data mapping method:

- A selector list that prioritizes the sources of intrinsic colour.
- A data mapping method value of 3 (single value non-uniform).
- An index value that identifies the value to use from the facet list or vertex list (f_1–f_j or v_1–v_k in Figure 16–3). If this index value is too big, the method is "not applicable" and the next selector is examined.
- A list of range boundaries. Each value within a given range will map to a single colour from the colour list. At least one value is required.
- A colour type that specifies which colour model to use for the colour list.
- A single colour list, in `Pcolrv_list` format (defined earlier in this chapter). At least two colour values are required.

A data value that falls within a specific range maps to a single colour from the colour list. Each range boundary identifies the lower limit of the range above it. The first range extends to negative infinity, and the last range extends to positive infinity. If there are n colours in the colour list, then the application supplies $n-1$ range limits.

For example, assume that you have data values from 0.0 to 40.0 and that you have four colours in the colour list. In this case, you can specify the ranges in either of the ways listed in Figure 16–5 (or in many other ways). For the right-hand example in Figure 16–5, we arbitrarily used range values of 5.0, 10.0, and 35.0. A data value of 15 in the right-hand example is in the third range and would map to the third colour in the colour list (yellow).

Note that the left-hand example in Figure 16–5 could also be performed by data mapping method 2.

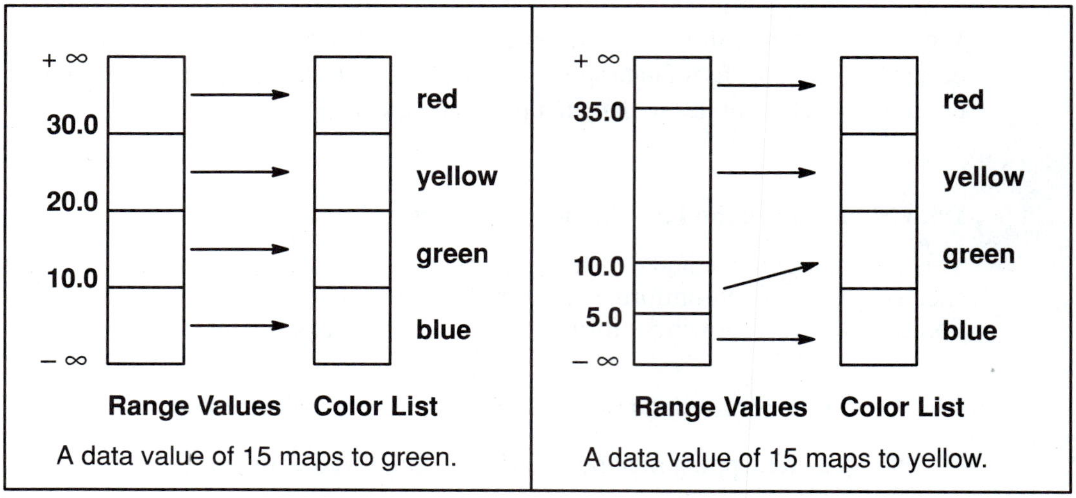

Figure 16–5. Examples of Range Values for Data Mapping Method 3

Data Mapping Method 4—Bivalue Uniform

This data mapping method (PDATA_MAP_METHOD_BI_UNIFORM) is similar to method 2 (single value uniform) except that it allows for multiple colour lists. Method 4 uses two of the data values from each facet list or vertex list (f_1–f_j or v_1–v_k in Figure 16–3). The first value, d_a, determines which colour list to use, and the second value, d_b, determines which colour to select from the list.

The application supplies the following information for this data mapping method:

- A selector list that prioritizes the sources of intrinsic colour.
- A data mapping method value of 4 (bivalue uniform).
- Two index values. The first index value selects the item from the list of data values (f_1–f_j or v_1–v_k in Figure 16–3) that will be used to determine the colour list C_i (see Figure 16–6). This item is called d_a.

The second index value selects the item from the list of data values that will be used to determine the colour to select from the colour list (this data value is called d_b). If either d_a or d_b is too large, the method is "not applicable" and the next colour source selector is examined.

- Two real values representing the lower and upper limits of the range R_a. R_a is the range for selecting the colour list.

- Two real values representing the lower and upper limits of the range R_b. These values indicate the portion of the application data that will be divided into equal segments (for the purpose of mapping the data to colours). For example, in Figure 16–6 we use values of 1.0 and 100.0 as limits. In this example, a data value of 50.0 would map halfway into the selected colour list.

- A colour type that specifies which colour model to use for the colour list.

- A set of colour lists in `Pcolrv_set` format (defined earlier in this chapter). Colour lists do not have to be of the same length.

Note that having lists of different lengths is useful for mapping out-of-bound values to a single colour (say, bright red can signify an out-of-range value). For example, assume that you need a 5×5 grid of colours. You can use seven colour lists to map the data as follows:

```
Colour list 1  (red)
Colour list 2  (red, C11, C12, C13, C14, C15, red)
Colour list 3  (red, C21, C22, C23, C24, C25, red)
Colour list 4  (red, C31, C32, C33, C34, C35, red)
Colour list 5  (red, C41, C42, C43, C44, C45, red)
Colour list 6  (red, C51, C52, C53, C54, C55, red)
Colour list 7  (red)
```

Example

As previously described, data mapping method 4 uses two ranges, R_a and R_b. R_a is used for selecting the colour list, and R_b is used to map data values to the selected colour list. Each range is used similarly to the single range in data mapping method 2.

In this example, let's assume that a primitive can be made up of three materials: water, plastic, and metal. In fact, let's assume that we have a large quadrilateral mesh primitive. Some facets represent water, some facets represent plastic, and some facets represent metal. We want to heat the primitive and display the temperature using colour values. Each material responds to heat differently, so we need a separate colour list for each material.

To accomplish this, each facet of the quadrilateral mesh can have two values. The first value indicates the type of material, and the second value indicates the temperature. By specifying the material type, we want to automatically select the colour list to use.

Figure 16–6 shows one facet of the quadrilateral mesh. The two data values associated with the facet are f_1 and f_2.

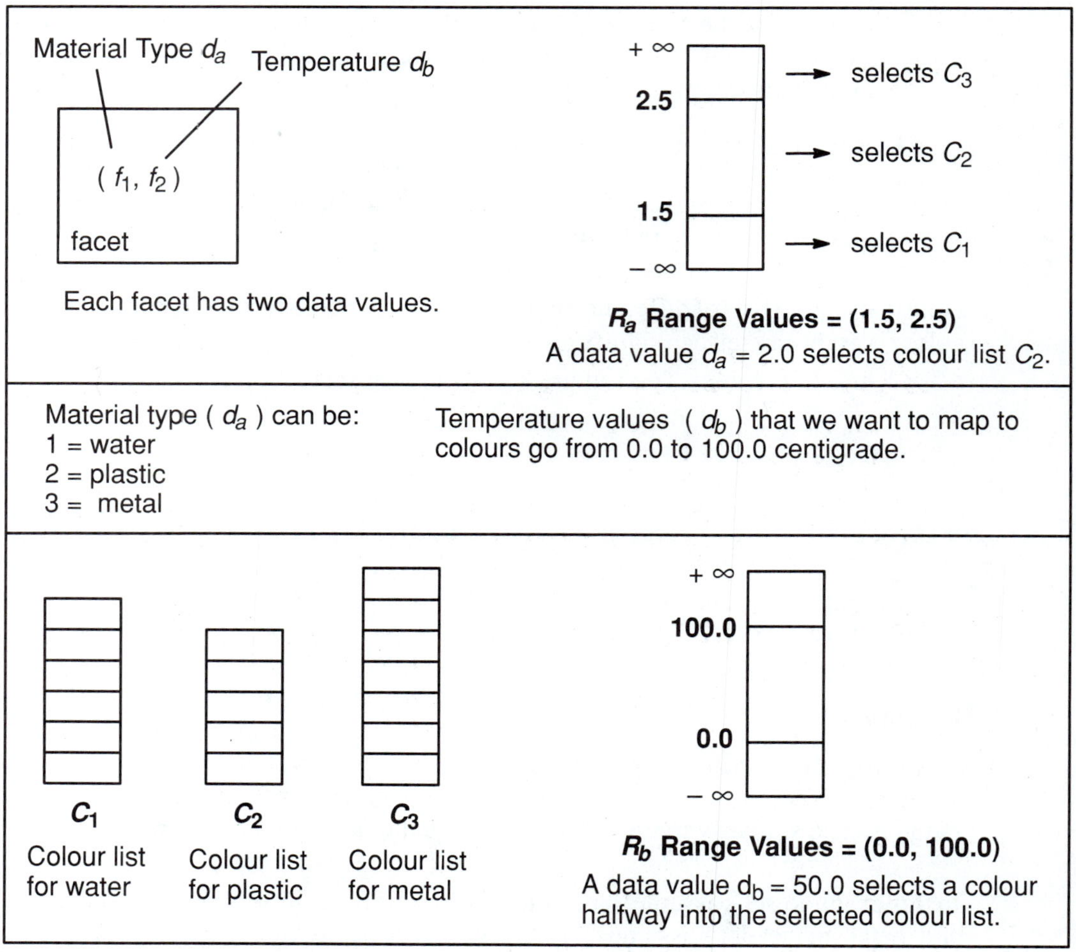

Figure 16–6. Example of Range Values for Data Mapping Method 4

For simplicity, let's assume that the values to identify the material can be 1 = water, 2 = plastic, and 3 = metal. Colour list C_1 is for water, C_2 is for plastic, and C_3 is for metal. Given this information, we can set up the range R_a using values of 1.5 and 2.5. Then values of $d_a = 1$ will map to C_1, values of $d_a = 2$ map to C_2 and values $d_a = 3$ map to C_3.

Let's assume that the temperature values we want to map to colours range from 0.0 to 100.0 degrees centigrade. Then we can specify range R_b as 0.0 and 100.0. For example, a value $d_b =$ 50.0 would map to a colour half way into the specified colour list.

Given the above information, here are the steps to access and utilize the values in Figure 16–6:

- Index 1 identifies d_a. This value identifies the material type. Depending on the material type PHIGS selects one of the colour lists from range R_a.
- Index 2 identifies d_b. This value specifies the temperature. PHIGS uses the range R_b to map the temperature into the colour list.
- Specify values 1.5 and 2.5 for range R_a.
- Specify values 0.0 and 100.0 for range R_b.

Data Mapping Method 5—Bivalue Non-uniform

This data mapping method (`PDATA_MAP_METHOD_BI_NON_UNIFORM`) is similar to method 3 (single value non-uniform) except that it allows for multiple colour lists. This data mapping method uses two of the data values from each facet list or vertex list (f_1–f_j or v_1–v_k in Figure 16–3). The first value, d_a, determines which colour list to use. The second value, d_b, determines which colour to select fromone of the colour lists.

There are two index values associated with data mapping method 5. The first and second index values select d_a and d_b from the data lists, respectively.

This method also uses the following:

- A list of range values referred to as R_a.
- A "list of lists" of range values named R_{b*}. The individual lists within R_{b*} are referred to as R_{b1}, R_{b2}, R_{b3}, etc.
- A "list of lists" of colour values, referred to as C_*. Individual colour lists are referred to as C_1, C_2, C_3, etc.

R_a is similar to the list of range boundaries used in data mapping method 3. PHIGS maps the first data value, d_a, into this list. Each range corresponds to a colour list and a range from R_{b*}. For example, if d_a falls below the first number in R_a, PHIGS uses the first colour list and R_{b1} (see Figure 16–7). If it falls between the first and second number, PHIGS uses the second colour list and R_{b2}. Each range boundary identifies the lower limit of the range above it. The first range extends to negative infinity and the last range extends to positive infinity. If there are n colour lists, then the application supplies $n-1$ range limits in R_a.

Each colour list is paired with a corresponding list of range values for d_b. So, when you specify a data value to select a colour list from R_a, you are also selecting the corresponding list of range values from the list of lists of range values R_{b*}. For example, in Figure 16–7, a data value, d_a, of 15 selects the second colour list, C_2, as well as the second list of range values, R_{b2}. Then a data value, d_b, of 25 selects the third colour in the C_2 colour list.

Likewise, a data value, d_a, of 5 selects the first colour list, C_1, as well as the first list of range values, R_{b1}. Then a data value, d_b, of 25 selects the second colour in colour list C_1.

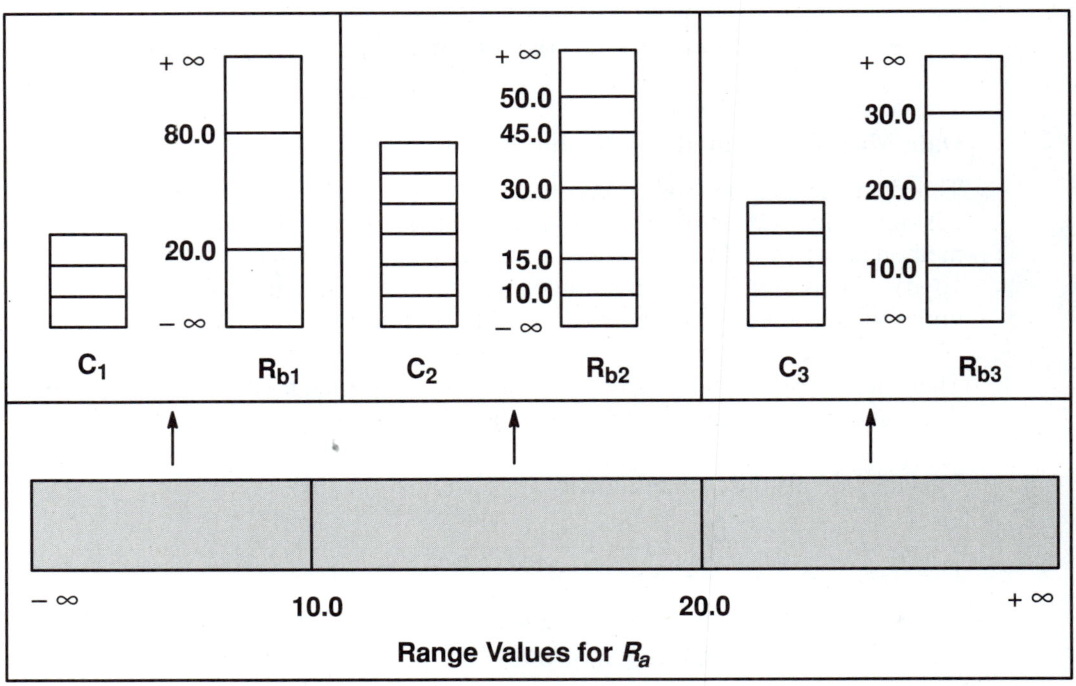

Figure 16–7. Specifying a Colour List and Range for Data Mapping Method 5

The application supplies the following information for this data mapping method:

- A selector list that prioritizes the sources of intrinsic colour. Source selector values other than PSOURCE_SELECT_FACET_DATA and PSOURCE_SELECT_VERT_DATA are ignored.
- A data mapping method value of 5 (bivalue non-uniform).
- Two index values. The first index value selects the item from the list of data values (f_1–f_j or v_1–v_k in Figure 16–3) that will be used to determine the colour list, C_i, and its associated range boundary list, R_{bi}. This data value is called d_a. The second index value selects the item from the list of data values that will be used to determine the colour to select from the colour list. This data value is called d_b.
- A list of range boundaries making up R_a. Values in each of the m ranges (defined by $m-1$ boundaries) will map to a single colour list from the set of available colour lists.
- A list of lists of range boundary values, R_{b*}. In each list of range boundaries, R_{bi}, range boundaries are specified in increasing order. Each list of range boundaries, R_{bi}, is associated with one of the colour lists. Each of the n ranges defined by the $n-1$ range boundaries in a list, R_{bi}, is associated with a single colour from the n colours in the corresponding list, C_i.
- A colour type that specifies which colour model to use for the colour list.
- An array of colour values in `Pcolrv_set` format (defined earlier in chapter) that contains all of the colour lists.

Chapter 17

Lighting and Shading

This chapter describes the lighting and shading portions of the PHIGS PLUS rendering pipeline. The input to this conceptual pipeline includes the primitives and the intrinsic colour values associated with the primitives. Figure 17–1 shows the rendering pipeline with a simplified version of the lighting and shading portion. In reality, the data mapping and lighting and shading stages may intermingle, depending on the interior shading method.

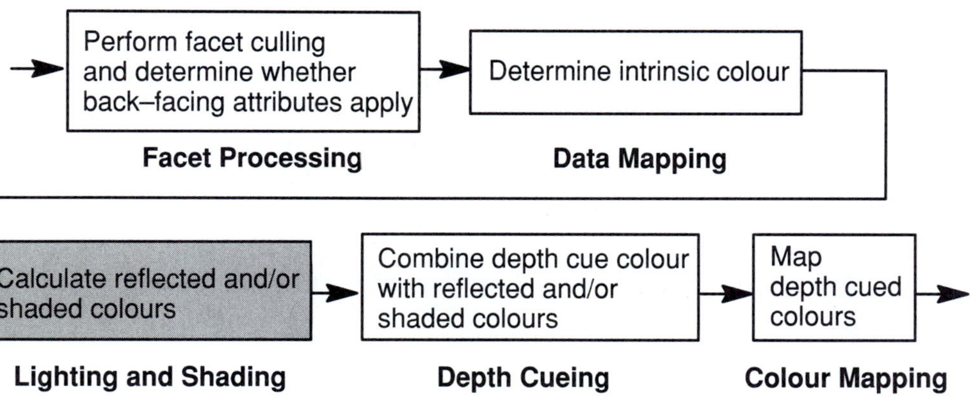

Figure 17–1. Rendering Pipeline

Lighting and shading can be applied to area-defining primitives. In addition, polyline set 3 with data primitives and non-uniform B-spline curve with colour primitives can utilize the shading stage of the rendering pipeline for interpolation of vertex colours. Cell array primitives are not shaded, but are affected by the lighting stage of the rendering pipeline.

Markers, text, annotation text, and the edges of area-defining primitives are not processed by the lighting and shading stages.

Lighting Overview

One of the most effective techniques for improving the realism of computer-generated images is the use of a **lighting model**, also called a **reflectance model**. Computer graphics systems use lighting models to imitate the ways in which light interacts with objects and how the human eye perceives this.

Modelling (visible) electromagnetic energy and the ways in which it interacts with matter and the human eye is a complex undertaking. The physics and physiology of visual perception have been studied by researchers for many years. Exact physical models are prohibitively complex and computationally expensive to implement in a computer graphics system. Thus, many of the lighting models used are simplified or empirically derived. For example, although true lights are almost always a *distributed source* of light (that is, light coming from an area of some nonzero size), in PHIGS they are modelled as *point sources* (that is, light coming from a point of zero size).

When light contacts an object, the light can be absorbed, transmitted, or reflected. Computer graphics systems are interested in the transmitted and reflected light, since those are what make an object visible. In this discussion, the primary interest is in reflected light. Note that PHIGS defines reflectance on a local basis. This means that interactions between objects, such as shadowing or mirror-like reflections, are not considered.

The intensity of light reflected and transmitted from an object is dependent upon the following:

- The wavelength of the light
- The angle at which the light strikes the object
- The angle between the surface of the object and a line to the eye
- The distance between the light and the object

If an object absorbs different wavelengths of light unequally, the light leaving the object will have a different colour than the incident light (the light hitting it). Further, depending on reflectance properties such as shininess, light is reflected in various ways. These dependencies are what give objects their colour.

PHIGS provides light sources of various kinds that you can turn on and off during traversal. These light sources fall into two main categories: **ambient** and **non-ambient**.

Ambient Light Sources

In the real world, ambient light is the light an object receives that is scattered from its surroundings. In a sense, the entire environment gives off light, and because of this, there is no static positional source for an ambient light.

In the PHIGS model, this concept corresponds to an ambient light source. When you turn an ambient light source on, it affects primitives in a scene independently of their position and orientation.

Only primitives traversed while a particular light source is turned on are affected by the light source. Therefore, if you want different types of ambient lights in a scene, you can turn one ambient light source off and turn another on. For example, objects you wish to appear to be in a darker corner of a room could have a darker ambient light associated with them.

Non-Ambient Light Sources

Non-ambient lights have a position in world coordinate space. If the position is very far away (conceptually at infinity), then we call it *parallel* (*directional*) *lighting*. Ignoring the real position of the light source makes the calculations easier.

Non-ambient light sources can have diffuse or specular effects on primitives. Diffuseness or specularity is a property of the object, as opposed to a property of the light. We talk about diffuse and specular reflections because they are reflections from an object. The ratio between the diffuse and specular reflections determines the shininess of an object. In PHIGS, we refer to the shininess or specularity as part of the reflectance properties of an object.

Ambient, Diffuse, and Specular Reflections

When performing lighting and shading, three types of light energy can contribute to the overall energy reflected from an object:

1. **Ambient reflection** is the light an object receives that is scattered from its surroundings. In a sense, the entire environment gives off light. If enabled, ambient light is constant across all surfaces, regardless of their position and orientation.

2. **Diffuse reflections** come from light emitted at non-ambient sources. Diffuse reflections from a surface scatter light equally in all directions, giving the surface a dull matte appearance from all viewing angles. Thus, the position of the observer is irrelevant as long as the object is visible. The direction and position of light sources relative to a surface determine how it is illuminated.

3. **Specular reflections** also come from light emitted at non-ambient sources. Specular reflections are the reflections that cause highlights on shiny objects. The intensity of specular reflections, unlike diffuse reflections, is highly dependent on the viewing angle of the observer. Since specular reflection scatters light in a directed way, the position of the light source and the position of the observer (eyepoint) are needed to determine the intensity of specular reflection seen by the observer.

PHIGS calculates the reflection components for contributions from each enabled light source and combines the components to determine the cumulative reflectance value at each point on a surface. Refer to "Light Source Calculations" later in this chapter for a discussion of the equations used.

Lighting and Shading Area-defining Primitives

This section describes the steps that are necessary to use lighting and shading for area-defining primitives, which are listed below.

- Fill area
- Fill area set
- Fill area set with data
- Set of fill area sets with data

- Cell array; cell array plus (lighting only)
- Triangle set with data
- Triangle strip with data
- Quadrilateral mesh with data
- Parametric surfaces (non-uniform B-spline surface and non-uniform B-spline surface with data)

Using Lighting and Shading

Use the following steps to control lighting and shading. Note that there are default values for each step.

- Set the *interior style* attribute to solid. For example:

  ```
  pset_int_style(PSTYLE_SOLID);
  ```

  The default interior style is implementation-dependent. See Chapter 10, *Output Primitives and Attributes*, for a description of the interior style attribute.

- Set the *rendering colour model* attribute. This identifies the model in which colour interpolation is performed (for example, RGB or HSV). The default value is 0, which specifies a workstation-dependent value.

- Set the facet culling mode and facet distinguishing mode. The facet culling mode allows you to specify whether or not to draw front- or back-facing facets of area-defining primitives. The facet distinguishing mode lets you assign different attributes to back- and front-facing facets of area-defining primitives. The default for facet culling is None, and the default for facet distinguishing is Off.

- Set the front and back *reflectance model* attributes. These define whether ambient, diffuse, and/or specular reflections are to be considered when PHIGS performs lighting calculations for the front and back facets of area-defining primitives. The default value is `PREFL_MODEL_NO_REFL`, which tells PHIGS, "Do not perform lighting calculations."

- Set the front and back *reflectance properties* attributes. These define the following values to be used in the lighting calculations:
  - Reflection type. The default is `PREFL_PROPS_SIMPLE_REFL` meaning no shadowing or mirror-like reflections. In this case PHIGS defines only the default value. Any other values are implementation-dependent.

- Ambient, diffuse, and specular reflection coefficients. Each default is 1.0.
- Specular colour, specified as a general colour. The default value for the index into the workstation colour table is 1. The default value for direct colour values is white.
- Specular exponent. The default value is 0.0.

- Define one or more light sources in the workstation light source table and turn on a set of light sources. The default is that no lights are defined and the light source state is Off.
- Set the front and back *interior shading method* attributes. The default value is `PINT_SHAD_METHOD_NONE` (shading method None), which produces a single reflected colour for each facet.

Note that the reflectance model and reflectance properties attributes can be set either individually or as part of an entry in the workstation reflectance bundle table. The interior shading method attribute can be set either individually or as part of an entry in the workstation interior bundle table.

The following sections describe these steps.

Specifying the Rendering Colour Model

The *rendering colour model* attribute identifies the model in which colour interpolation is performed. The calling signature for the SET RENDERING COLOUR MODEL routine is

```
pset_rend_colr_model(
  Pint                 model
);
```

where:

⟨*model*⟩ is the rendering colour model. Use one of the following values:

0 `PREND_COLR_MODEL_WS_DEP`. Workstation dependent colour model
1 `PREND_COLR_MODEL_RGB`. Red, green, blue
2 `PREND_COLR_MODEL_CIELUV`. *x* coefficient, *y* coefficient, *y* luminance
3 `PREND_COLR_MODEL_HSV`. Hue, saturation, value
4 `PREND_COLR_MODEL_HLS`. Hue, lightness, saturation

When a workstation does not support the requested colour model, PHIGS uses a value of 0 (which corresponds to the workstation-dependent colour model). The supported rendering colour models differ between implementations, although the RGB model is widely used. Use INQUIRE RENDERING COLOUR MODEL FACILITIES to determine the set of rendering colour models that a workstation supports.

The rendering colour model can be set only as an individual attribute. There is no corresponding bundle table entry. See Chapter 12, *Using Colour*, for more information on colour models. Note that interpolating the same colour using different colour models gets different results.

Specifying a Reflectance Model

When lighting is enabled, PHIGS applies a reflectance calculation to one or more points of a primitive to determine a colour at that point. The application can control the calculation method by specifying a reflectance model (also called a lighting model). The reflectance model attribute can specify one of the following conditions:

- Do not perform reflectance calculations.
- Use the ambient term of the reflectance calculations.
- Use the ambient and diffuse terms of the reflectance calculations.
- Use the ambient, diffuse, and specular terms of the reflectance calculations.

The more terms used in the reflectance equation, the more realistic the picture. However, there is a performance cost for the increased calculations at rendering time.

Refer to "Lighting Overview" earlier in this chapter for a description of ambient, diffuse, and specular reflections. Refer to "Light Source Calculations" later in this chapter for details on how PHIGS performs the lighting calculations.

If you do not make a call to set the reflectance model value, PHIGS uses "no reflectance calculation" as the default.

You can set the reflectance model attribute via individual and bundled attributes. Also, if the facet distinguishing mode is on, you can specify different attributes for the front and back of a facet. See Table 15–1 at the end of Chapter 15, *Front and Back Facet Processing*, for a list of routines.

Individual Attribute Specification (Reflectance Model)

Use the SET REFLECTANCE MODEL routine for individual attribute specification. This routine creates a structure element that, when traversed, sets the *current reflectance model* entry in the traversal state list. PHIGS uses this value when the *current reflectance model ASF* entry in the traversal state list is set to individual.

The calling signature for the SET REFLECTANCE MODEL routine is as follows:

```
pset_refl_model(
    Pint              refl_model
);
```

where:

⟨*refl_model*⟩ can be one of the following values:

- PREFL_MODEL_NO_REFL. No reflectance calculation.
- PREFL_MODEL_AMB_REFL. Use the ambient term.
- PREFL_MODEL_AMB_DIFF_REFL. Use the ambient and diffuse terms.
- PREFL_MODEL_AMB_DIFF_SPEC_REFL. Use ambient, diffuse, and specular terms of the reflectance calculations.

For example, the following fragment sets the reflectance model value to use the ambient and diffuse terms of the reflectance calculation:

```
popen_struct(cube);          /* open structure cube      */
pset_refl_model(PREFL_MODEL_AMB_DIFF_REFL);
...
pclose_struct();             /* close structure          */
```

Use the SET BACK REFLECTANCE MODEL routine to set the reflectance model attribute for back-facing portions.

Bundled Attribute Specification (Reflectance Model)

For bundled attribute specification, use the `refl_model` field in the SET REFLECTANCE REPRESENTATION routine to specify the reflectance model. PHIGS uses this value when the *current reflectance model ASF* is set to bundled. The SET REFLECTANCE INDEX routine selects the entry from the reflectance bundle table. Refer to the description of the workstation reflectance table in the following section, "Setting the Reflectance Properties."

Use the SET BACK REFLECTANCE INDEX routine to select an entry to be used for back-facing portions when the *current back reflectance model ASF* is set to bundled.

Setting the Reflectance Properties

The following reflectance properties attributes allow you to control the effects of reflectance on an area-defining primitive:

- The reflection type (default = simple (no shadowing or mirror-like reflections))
- Ambient reflection coefficient (default = 1.0)
- Diffuse reflection coefficient (default = 1.0)
- Specular reflection coefficient (default = 1.0)
- Specular colour (default = white)
- Specular exponent (default = 0.0)

All six reflectance properties attributes are controlled as a group by a single aspect source flag, the *current reflectance properties ASF*. The setting of the *current reflectance properties ASF* in the traversal state list determines whether values are taken from the individual attribute setting or from the workstation reflectance bundle. See Table 15–1 at the end of Chapter 15 for a list of routines.

Individual Attribute Specification (Reflectance Properties)

For individual attribute specification, use the SET REFLECTANCE PROPERTIES routine to set the reflectance properties attribute for front-facing portions of area-defining primitives. The calling signature for the SET REFLECTANCE PROPERTIES routine is as follows:

```
pset_refl_props(
    const Prefl_prop          *refl_prop
);
```

where:

⟨*refl_prop*⟩ specifies the reflectance properties data. The `Prefl_prop` data type is defined as follows:

```
Prefl_prop
 typedef struct {
   Pint            type;         /* reflectance property type */
   union Prefl_prop_data {
    struct Prefl_prop_simple_refl {
      Pfloat       amb_coeff;    /* ambient reflection coeff. */
      Pfloat       diff_coeff;   /* diffuse refl. coeff.      */
      Pfloat       spec_coeff;   /* specular refl. coeff.     */
      Pgcolr       spec_colr;    /* specular colour           */
      Pfloat       spec_exp;     /* specular exponent         */
    } simple_refl;
    ...                          /* implementation-defined    */
   } data;
} Prefl_prop;
```

where:

`type` specifies either the default simple reflection, `PREFL_PROPS_SIMPLE_REFL`, or an implementation-dependent type. PHIGS only defines the default type (simple reflection with no shadowing or mirror-like reflections).

`amb_coeff` is the ambient reflection coefficient. This parameter specifies the percentage of ambient light reflected by an area. It must be in the range [0, 1], inclusive, where 0 represents no reflection and 1 represents 100% reflection.

`diff_coeff` is the diffuse reflection coefficient. This parameter specifies the percentage of light from non-ambient sources diffusely reflected by an area. It must be in the range [0, 1], inclusive, where 0 represents no reflection and 1 represents 100% reflection.

`spec_coeff` is the ambient reflection coefficient. This parameter specifies the percentage of light from non-ambient sources specularly reflected by an area. It must be in the range [0, 1], inclusive, where 0 represents no reflection and 1 represents 100% reflection.

`spec_colr` is the specular colour, in `Pgcolr` format (see Chapter 16, *Intrinsic Colour and Data Mapping*). The specular colour is specified as a general colour, meaning that it is either represented as an index into the workstation colour table or as a set of colour components from a particular colour model (for example, RGB triplets).

`spec_exp` is the specular exponent. This parameter specifies how "shiny" the surface is. The specular exponent can have values greater than or equal to 0, where larger values specify a shinier surface. Refer to "Manipulating the Specular Exponent" later in this section for more information.

The fragment listed below sets the following reflectance properties:

- Use ambient, diffuse, and specular reflection coefficients of 1.0.
- Set the specular colour to gray (using (0.4, 0.4, 0.4) in the RGB colour model).
- Set the specular exponent to 20.0.
- Set the reflectance model to 4, so all three of the reflectance terms will be used in the lighting calculations.

```
Prefl_prop   rep;
...
rep.type = PREFL_PROPS_SIMPLE_REFL;
rep.data.simple_refl.amb_coeff = 1.0;
rep.data.simple_refl.diff_coeff = 1.0;
rep.data.simple_refl.spec_coeff = 1.0;
/* use direct RGB colour */
rep.data.simple_refl.spec_colr.colr_type = PCOLR_RGB;
rep.data.simple_refl.spec_colr.colr_value.colr_rep.rgb.red = 0.4;
rep.data.simple_refl.spec_colr.colr_value.colr_rep.rgb.green = 0.4;
rep.data.simple_refl.spec_colr.colr_value.colr_rep.rgb.blue = 0.4;
rep.data.simple_refl.spec_exp = 20.0;

popen_struct(scene);                /* open structure              */
/* set reflectance model*/
pset_refl_model(PREFL_MODEL_AMB_DIFF_SPEC_REFL);
pset_refl_props(&rep);              /* set reflectance properties  */
...
pclose_struct();                    /* close structure             */
```

Use the SET BACK REFLECTANCE PROPERTIES routine to set the reflectance properties attributes for back-facing portions.

Implementation-defined Reflectance Types

PHIGS only defines reflectance type `PREFL_PROPS_SIMPLE_REFL`. An implementation can define different reflection types as values less than 0. Possible implementation-defined reflection types might include the following:

- Different reflectance equations (for example, the equations suggested by PHIGS do not include a square term)

- Coefficients per colour band
- Allowances for transparency

Refer to your implementation documentation to see if your system supports any additional reflection types.

Manipulating the Specular Exponent

The specular exponent is a nonnegative number that indicates an area's shininess: the higher the specular exponent, the shinier the area. This means that the higher the specular exponent, the closer the surface is to a perfect reflector in its reflective properties. For a high specular exponent, highlights are less diffuse, more well-defined, and actually end up being smaller than those on a less specular (lower exponent) surface. So an area with a specular exponent of 1.0 should appear brighter (if it's got a high-intensity specular colour like white) but less shiny or mirror-like than an area with an exponent of 255. You may find that specular highlights look more natural or intuitively correct with spot light sources that have a reasonable spread angle, rather than positional light sources. Light sources are described later in this chapter.

Bundled Attribute Specification (Reflectance Properties)

PHIGS maintains a reflectance bundle table for each open workstation. This reflectance table is used for both the reflectance model and the reflectance properties. PHIGS uses values from the table when the *current reflectance properties ASF* is set to bundled.

Use the SET REFLECTANCE REPRESENTATION routine to set the values for an entry in the workstation reflectance bundle table. The SET REFLECTANCE INDEX routine selects the entry from the workstation reflectance table.

Use the SET BACK REFLECTANCE INDEX routine to select an entry to be used for back-facing portions when the *current back reflectance index ASF* is set to bundled.

Defining an Entry in the Workstation Reflectance Table

The calling signature for the SET REFLECTANCE REPRESENTATION routine is as follows:

```
pset_refl_rep(
   Pint              ws_id,
   Pint              index,
   const Prefl_rep   *rep
);
```

where:

⟨*ws_id*⟩ identifies the workstation.

⟨*index*⟩ specifies the entry in the table that will be modified.

⟨*rep*⟩ is the reflectance representation for this entry. The `Prefl_rep` data type is defined as follows:

```
Prefl_rep
 typedef struct {
   Pint              refl_model;      /* reflectance model       */
   Prefl_prop        refl_prop;   /* reflectance property data */
 } Prefl_rep;
```

Refer to the description of SET REFLECTANCE PROPERTIES earlier in this chapter for a description of `Prefl_prop`.

When you open an OUTPUT or OUTIN workstation, PHIGS uses values from the workstation description table to define the entries in the reflectance bundle table. The application program can use the SET REFLECTANCE REPRESENTATION routine to redefine any of the values in the reflectance bundle table.

During structure traversal, PHIGS uses the *current reflectance index* and the *current back reflectance index* (in the traversal state list) to select entries from the reflectance bundle table. Depending on the current facet distinguishing and facet culling modes, PHIGS uses the front- and back-reflectance index attributes when displaying respective portions of area-defining primitives. Each entry has a number of different aspects (for example, specular colour and specular exponent). PHIGS decides which aspects from the table entry to use based on the setting of the corresponding aspect source flags.

If the application program specifies an entry that is not defined, PHIGS uses entry 1 in the table.

Setting the Interior Shading Method

You control the shading method for area-defining primitives by setting the *interior shading method* attribute. This attribute can take one of five values.

The main difference between the five shading methods has to do with what information (if any) is interpolated across the facet. The name of each shading method indicates the information that is interpolated. Table 17–1, at the end of the section, compares the amount of calculation performed at each vertex and at each interpolated point across the facet.

For methods 2 through 5 to perform interpolation, the application must supply at least one of the following: vertex normals, vertex colour, or vertex data.

If the application supplies vertex normals, PHIGS uses those values as reflectance normals. If not specified, the normal at each vertex is the geometric normal of the facet with which that vertex is associated when the facet is being rendered. Refer to "Facet Culling for Area-defining Primitives" in Chapter 15 for a discussion of geometric normals.

This section describes how the five interior shading methods are used for interior style SOLID. HOLLOW primitives are treated as solid except that only the interior edges are drawn. EMPTY primitives are not lit or shaded. Check your implementation documentation for the way your implementation deals with interior styles HATCH and PATTERN.

Shading Method 1: None (No Interpolation)

This shading method (`PINT_SHAD_METHOD_NONE`) is sometimes called *constant*, or *flat shading* because it produces a single reflected colour for each facet of an area-defining primitive. When reflectance calculations are enabled, PHIGS uses the following procedure to render each facet:

1. Determine the intrinsic colour for the facet.
2. Calculate the reflected colour for the facet using the geometric normal, the intrinsic colour, and the active light sources.
3. Duplicate the single colour over the entire facet.

This method usually uses either facet colour or interior colour as the source of the intrinsic colour. If vertex colour or vertex data is used, then PHIGS chooses a point on the facet, interpolates the data values to that point, and then determines the intrinsic colour.

Shading Method 2: Colour

The constant value for this method is (`PINT_SHAD_METHOD_COLR`). When PHIGS renders a facet using this method, it interpolates the realized vertex colours across each facet. This method is commonly referred to as *smooth shading*, or *Gouraud shading* (see Gouraud, H., (1971). *Computer Display of Curved Surfaces*, Ph.D. Thesis, University of Utah).

When reflectance calculations are enabled, PHIGS uses the following procedure to render each facet:

1. Determine the intrinsic colour at each vertex.
2. Calculate the reflected colour at each vertex using the intrinsic colour at the vertex, the reflectance normal, and the active light sources.
3. Interpolate the reflected vertex colours across the facet.

You can get very realistic results with shading method Colour as long as the facets are fairly small (in DC space). With large facets, shading methods 3 through 5 will give more realistic results, but at increasingly high computational costs.

Shading Method 3: Data

The constant value for this method is (`PINT_SHAD_METHOD_DATA`). This shading method allows the application to interpolate data mapping information at a lower computational cost than methods 4 or 5 (see Chapter 16). When reflectance calculations are enabled, PHIGS uses the following procedure to render each facet:

1. Calculate any reflectance terms that are independent of intrinsic colour for each vertex (using the reflectance normals). For example, if specular reflections are enabled, PHIGS can calculate the specular reflectance contribution from the light sources at each vertex since the specular contribution does not use the intrinsic colour (it uses the specular colour).

2. Interpolate the reflectance terms across the entire facet.

3. Determine an intrinsic colour at each interpolated position. If vertex colours or vertex data are the source of the intrinsic colour, PHIGS interpolates those values across the primitive so that a value is derived for each interpolated position. PHIGS then maps each value to a colour according to the method indicated by the data mapping method.

4. Calculate a reflected colour at each interpolated position using the interpolated reflectance terms, the corresponding intrinsic colour, and the light source information.

Shading Method 4: Data and Dot

The constant value for this method is (`PINT_SHAD_METHOD_DATA_DOT`). When reflectance calculations are enabled, PHIGS uses the following procedure to render each facet:

1. Use the reflectance normal to calculate the following dot products for each vertex:
   - One for each positional or spot light, if lighting is enabled
   - One toward the eye
2. Interpolate the dot products across the facet.
3. Determine an intrinsic colour at each interpolated position. If vertex colours or vertex data are the source of the intrinsic colour, PHIGS interpolates those values as described for shading method 3.
4. Calculate a reflected colour at each interpolated position using the interpolated dot products, the corresponding intrinsic colour, and the active light sources.

Shading Method 5: Data and Normal

The constant value for this method is (PINT_SHAD_METHOD_DATA_NORM). This is the most time-expensive method, but it can give the best quality image, particularly if the direction of the vertex normals for a single facet varies a great deal. When reflectance calculations are enabled, PHIGS uses the following procedure to render each facet:

1. Interpolate the reflectance normals across the primitive.
2. Determine an intrinsic colour at each interpolated position. If vertex colours or vertex data are the source of the intrinsic colour, PHIGS interpolates those values as described for shading method 3.
3. Calculate a reflected colour at each interpolated point using the interpolated reflectance normal, the corresponding intrinsic colour, and the active light sources.

The following example describes a case where the Data and Normal shading method would be more useful than the other methods. In this example the ideal surface being approximated by a facet bows outward, with the center being exactly perpendicular to the light source and the sides equally bent away from the light source. All of the other methods only recognize the angles of the sides, which are equal, and interpolate an even colour across the face. Only the Data and Normal method recognizes that the angles are the same but in opposite directions, and shows a bright spot when interpolating from one side to the other. (Note that this problem can be overcome for the other shading methods if small facets are used.)

Table 17–1 compares the calculations performed for shading methods Colour through Data and Normal.

Table 17–1. Comparison of Calculations Performed by Shading Methods

Shading Method	Perform Calculations per Vertex	Perform Calculations at Interpolated Points
Colour	reflectance calculation resulting in colour	Perform colour interpolation per point
Data	reflectance calculation terms independent of intrinsic colour	Determine intrinsic colour and complete reflectance calculation
Data and Dot	dot products calculation	Interpolate dot products and data or colours across facets, determine intrinsic colour, and complete reflectance calculation
Data and Normal	none	Interpolate normals and data or colours across facets, determine intrinsic colour, and calculate reflected colour

Setting the Interior Shading Method Attribute

You can set the interior shading method attribute via individual and bundled attributes. Also, if the facet distinguishing mode is on, you can specify different attributes for the front and back of a facet. See Table 15–1 in Chapter 15 for a list of routines.

Individual Attribute Specification (Interior Shading Method)

For individual attribute specification, use the SET INTERIOR SHADING METHOD routine to select the interior shading method used for area-defining primitives. This routine creates a structure element that, when traversed, sets the *current interior shading method* entry in the traversal state list. PHIGS uses this value when the *current interior shading method ASF* is set to individual.

The calling signature for the SET INTERIOR SHADING METHOD routine is as follows:

```
pset_int_shad_method(
  Pint                  method
);
```

where:

⟨*method*⟩ can be one of the following values:

1 PINT_SHAD_METHOD_NONE
2 PINT_SHAD_METHOD_COLR
3 PINT_SHAD_METHOD_DATA
4 PINT_SHAD_METHOD_DATA_DOT
5 PINT_SHAD_METHOD_DATA_NORM

These values are described earlier in this section. Check your implementation documentation to see how many shading methods are supported, and check for specific details on using each method.

The following fragment sets the interior shading method to Colour:

```
popen_struct(cube);          /* open structure cube              */
pset_int_shad_method(PINT_SHAD_METHOD_COLR);
...
pclose_struct();             /* close structure                  */
```

Use the SET BACK INTERIOR SHADING METHOD routine to set the interior shading method attribute for back-facing portions.

Bundled Attribute Specification (Interior Shading Method)

For bundled attribute specification, use the `shad_method` field in the SET INTERIOR REPRESENTATION PLUS routine to specify the interior shading method. PHIGS uses this value when the *current interior shading method ASF* is set to bundled. The SET INTERIOR INDEX routine selects the entry from the interior bundle table.

Use the SET BACK INTERIOR INDEX routine to select an entry to be used for back-facing portions when the *current back interior shading method ASF* is set to bundled. The calling signature is similar to that for SET INTERIOR INDEX.

Refer to Chapter 10 for a description of SET INTERIOR REPRESENTATION PLUS.

Defining and Selecting Light Sources

PHIGS supports multiple light sources through the use of a workstation light source table. Use SET LIGHT SOURCE REPRESENTATION to define or modify an entry in the table. Use SET LIGHT SOURCE STATE to select entries from the table. The SET LIGHT SOURCE STATE routine creates a structure element that activates and deactivates multiple entries in the table at traversal time.

PHIGS specifies that the minimum number of entries available in the light source table is 5. The actual number varies with each implementation.

An implementation can select the equations that it uses to calculate the effect of light sources on an object. However, PHIGS recommends a set of equations to use. These are presented later in this chapter in the section entitled "Light Source Calculations."

Defining an Entry in the Workstation Light Source Table

The calling signature for the SET LIGHT SOURCE REPRESENTATION routine is as follows:

```
pset_light_source_rep(
   Pint                     ws_id,
   Pint                     index,
   const Plight_source_rep  *rep
);
```

where:

⟨*ws_id*⟩ identifies the workstation.

⟨*index*⟩ specifies an entry in the light source table. This parameter identifies the workstation light source table entry to be modified.

⟨*rep*⟩ is the light source representation for this entry. The `Plight_source_rep` data type is defined as follows:

```
Plight_source_rep
  typedef struct {
   Pint          type;            /* light source type       */
   union Plight_source_rep_data {
    struct Plight_source_rep_amb {
      Pgcolr    colr;             /* light source colour     */
    } amb;
    struct Plight_source_rep_dir {
      Pgcolr    colr;             /* light source colour     */
      Pvec3     dir;              /* light source direction  */
    } dir;
    struct Plight_source_rep_pos {
      Pgcolr    colr;        /* light source colour           */
      Ppoint3   pos;         /* light source position         */
      Pfloat    c1;          /* light source atten. coeff.    */
      Pfloat    c2;          /* light source atten. coeff.    */
    } pos;
    struct Plight_source_rep_spot {
      Pgcolr    colr;        /* light source colour           */
      Ppoint3   pos;         /* light source position         */
      Pvec3     dir;         /* light source direction        */
      Pfloat    concent_exp; /* concentration exponent        */
      Pfloat    c1;          /* light source atten. coeff.    */
      Pfloat    c2;          /* light source atten. coeff.    */
      Pfloat spread_angle    /* light source spread angle     */
    } spot;
    ...                      /* implementation-defined        */
   } data;
} Plight_source_rep;
```

where:

`type` identifies the light source type. This field takes one of the following values:

1 `PLIGHT_SOURCE_AMB` **Ambient**. An ambient light source has a light source colour and affects primitives independently of their orientation and position.

2 `PLIGHT_SOURCE_DIR` **Directional**. A directional light source has a light source colour and a light source direction. The light source direction is the direction of the light from the light source.

3 `PLIGHT_SOURCE_POS` **Positional**. A positional light source has a light source colour, a light source position, and two attenuation coefficients.

4 PLIGHT_SOURCE_SPOT **Spot**. A spot light source has a light source colour, a light source position, a light source direction, two attenuation coefficients, a concentration exponent, and a spread angle.

The remainder of the Plight_source_rep structure defines each light source type. Fill in the appropriate fields depending on the value of type. The following subsections describe the different light source types and show how to fill in the various fields.

You specify light source colour as a general colour. See Chapter 16 for a description of the Pgcolr data type.

Ambient Light Source

Conceptually, ambient lighting is the light an object receives that is scattered back from its surroundings. In reality, this is a distributed light source, and an exact model would be both extremely complex and computationally expensive. Therefore, PHIGS models ambient lighting as a constant, diffuse reflection from all sides of the object, regardless of the position or orientation of the object or other light sources.

Ambient light sources have a light source colour and affect area-defining primitives independently of their orientation and position. The light source colour is the only information needed when an ambient light source is defined. This value is specified as a general colour.

For example, the following fragment shows how to define a dim gray ambient light source. You should experiment with the intensity of an ambient light. If you make it too bright, it will overpower the other lights in the scene and make the image appear too light.

```
Pint                WorkID = 1, index = 1;
Plight_source_rep   rep;

rep.type = PLIGHT_SOURCE_AMB; /* ambient light source type */
rep.data.amb.colr.colr_type = PCOLR_RGB;    /* use direct RGB
                                                colour values */
rep.data.amb.colr.colr_value.colr_rep.rgb.red = 0.1;
rep.data.amb.colr.colr_value.colr_rep.rgb.green = 0.1;
rep.data.amb.colr.colr_value.colr_rep.rgb.blue = 0.1;
pset_light_source_rep(WorkID, index, &rep);
```

Directional Light Source

Directional light sources have a light source colour and a light source direction. Since the light source is conceptually at infinity, the light travels as parallel rays. Thus, the direction of the light is the same for all objects, regardless of their position. The light direction is indicated by a unit vector pointing in the direction the light travels. The light source direction is specified as a 3D vector in world coordinates.

For example, the following fragment defines a directional light source with a blue colour and a direction vector of (0.0, 0.0, –1.5):

```
Pint               WorkID = 1, index = 2;
Plight_source_rep  rep;

rep.type = PLIGHT_SOURCE_DIR; /* directional light source type     */
rep.data.dir.colr.colr_type = PCOLR_RGB;   /* use direct RGB
                                              colour values */
rep.data.dir.colr.colr_value.colr_rep.rgb.red = 0.0;
rep.data.dir.colr.colr_value.colr_rep.rgb.green = 0.0;
rep.data.dir.colr.colr_value.colr_rep.rgb.blue = 1.0;
rep.data.dir.dir.delta_x = 0.0;          /* light source direction  */
rep.data.dir.dir.delta_y = 0.0;
rep.data.dir.dir.delta_z = -1.5;
pset_light_source_rep(WorkID, index, &rep);
```

Positional Light Source

You can think of a positional light source as a light bulb of zero size at a given position in world coordinates. Light emanates in all directions from a positional light source, so objects all around the light source are illuminated.

The rays from a positional light source are not parallel, and the position of an object with respect to the light source affects the angle at which light strikes the object's surface. A positional light source is typically located relatively close to the viewing area because it would otherwise have an effect very much like the computationally simpler directional light source.

Positional light sources have a light source colour, light source position, and two attenuation coefficients. The **attenuation coefficients** determine how the light's brightness falls off from the light source to the point on the object being lit. Attenuation coefficients are often used to model how the intensity of light falls off as the light travels through different media, such as fog, water, or air. Typical values might be as follows:

- Coefficient 1 = 1.0 and coefficient 2 = 0.0 to effect no attenuation.
- Coefficient 1 = 1.0 and coefficient 2 = 1/*d* where *d* is the distance at which you expect the light to be half of its original intensity.

Refer to "Lighting Calculations," later in this chapter, for a description of how attenuation coefficients are used in the lighting calculations.

For example, the following fragment defines a positional light source with a red colour, attenuation coefficients 1.0 and 0.0, and a position of (0.0, 1.5, 0.0):

```
Pint                 WorkID = 1, index = 3;
Plight_source_rep    rep;

rep.type = PLIGHT_SOURCE_POS;    /* positional light source type */
rep.data.pos.colr.colr_type = PCOLR_RGB;/* use direct RGB
                                          colour values.data*/
rep.data.pos.colr.colr_value.colr_rep.rgb.red = 1.0;
rep.data.pos.colr.colr_value.colr_rep.rgb.green = 0.0;
rep.data.pos.colr.colr_value.colr_rep.rgb.blue = 0.0;
rep.data.pos.c1 = 1.0;     /* attenuation coefficients   */
rep.data.pos.c2 = 0.0;
rep.data.pos.pos.x = 0.0;     /* light source position*/
rep.data.pos.pos.y = 1.5;
rep.data.pos.pos.z = 0.0;

pset_light_source_rep(WorkID, index, &rep);
```

Spot Light Source

A spot light source is conceptually a point light source with a cone of influence (see Figure 17–2). This cone of influence is determined by the light source direction and a spread angle. If a point lies outside the cone of influence, its colour is not affected by that light source.

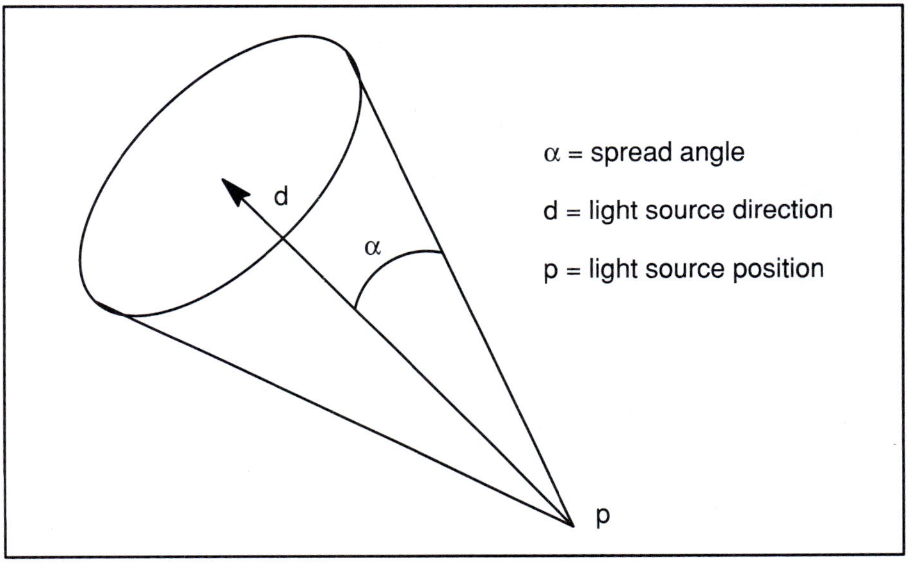

Figure 17–2. Spot Light Cone of Influence

Spot light sources have a light source colour, light source position, light source direction, attenuation coefficients, concentration exponent, and spread angle.

The spread angle defines the width of the cone of influence. It is measured in radians from the light source directional vector. The concentration exponent describes how the spot light brightness falls off from the center of the beam to the side.

The attenuation coefficients determine how the light's brightness falls off from the light source to the point on the object being lit. Refer to the description of attenuation coefficients under "Positional Light Sources," earlier in this section.

If you want a spot light to have a natural "falling off" effect across an object, make sure that the object being lit contains multiple facets. This is important because, depending on the spread angle and the concentration exponent, the amount of light falling on one particular portion of an object can be vastly different from the amount falling on a different portion. For shading methods 1 and 2, light source equations are applied, at most, at every vertex of an object, so a single fill area representing an object being lit by a spot light is insufficient. For shading methods 3, 4, and 5, lighting calculations are performed at every interpolated point across the facet, so it is not as important that an object contain multiple facets. For most implementations, it is more expensive in terms of performance to use shading methods 3 through 5 than it is to define more, smaller facets and use shading method 2 to get the same amount of realism in the rendering.

Turning Light Sources On and Off

Use SET LIGHT SOURCE STATE to select entries from the workstation light source table. This routine creates a structure element that activates and deactivates multiple entries in the table at traversal time. The calling signature for the SET LIGHT SOURCE STATE routine is as follows:

```
pset_light_source_st(
   const Pint_list        *act_list,
   const Pint_list        *deact_list
);
```

where:

⟨*act_list*⟩ is an array that identifies the entries in the workstation light source table that should be turned on.

⟨*deact_list*⟩ is an array that identifies the entries in the workstation light source table that should be turned off.

When traversal begins, all lights are turned off by default. The SET LIGHT SOURCE STATE routine adds or subtracts light sources from the existing set of light sources that are on in the workstation state list.

Example

The fragment listed in this example performs the following operations:

- Turns on light sources 1, 2, 3, and 4 and renders Area Primitive A.

- Turns off light sources 2 and 4 and turns on light sources 13 and 16. Then renders Area Primitive B.

```
Pint        Scene;
Pint_list   LightsOnA, LightsOnB, LightsOffB, EmptyList;
Pint        MyArray1[10], MyArray2[10], MyArray3[10];

LightsOnA.ints = MyArray1;              /* set up pointer  */
LightsOnA.num_ints = 4;
LightsOnA.ints[0] = 1;  LightsOnA.ints[1]=2;  LightsOnA.ints[2]=3;
LightsOnA.ints[3] = 4;

LightsOnB.ints = MyArray2;              /* set up pointer  */
LightsOnB.num_ints = 2;
LightsOnB.ints[0] = 13;  LightsOnB.ints[1]=16;

LightsOffB.ints = MyArray3;             /* set up pointer  */
LightsOffB.num_ints=2;
LightsOffB.ints[0] = 2;  LightsOffB.ints[1] = 4;

EmptyList.ints = MyArray1;
EmptyList.num_ints = 0;

popen_struct(Scene);                    /* open structure Scene */
pset_light_source_st(&LightsOnA,&EmptyList);
/* draw Area Primitive A */
pset_light_source_st(&LightsOnB, &LightsOffB);
/* draw Area Primitive B */
pclose_struct();/* close structure */
```

Assuming that no other light sources are already turned on, Area Primitive A is rendered using lights 1, 2, 3, and 4. Area Primitive B is rendered using lights 1, 3, 13, and 16. This assumes that these lights have been defined as described earlier in this chapter.

If you try to turn on a light that has not been defined, PHIGS ignores the request for that particular light source.

Lighting Example 1—Constant Shading

This example uses lighting and the default shading method None to display the cube-with-the-corner-cut-off that we have presented before. The example defines four light sources: a gray ambient light, a red directional light, and two positional lights defined as blue and green. Colour plate 3 (see colour insert) shows the final output of the program.

This section describes how the program works.

First we create the object and set the facet culling, interior colour, and edge attributes:

- Our object must be represented as area-defining primitives. In this case we use fill area set primitives because we want to display edges.
- Avoid drawing the primitives that face away from you. Use the SET FACET CULLING MODE routine to enable back-facet culling.
- In this example we use a white object in order to show the effects of coloured lights. We use the SET INTERIOR COLOUR INDEX routine to set the fill area sets primitives' intrinsic colour (the colour before lighting effects are taken into account). The following fragment sets entry 4 in the workstation colour table to white. Then it opens the `Scene` structure, turns on back-facet culling, sets the interior style to solid, and sets the interior colour index to 4:

```
Pint          Scene = 2;      /* structure identifier          */
Pint          ViewIndex = 1;  /* view index                    */
Pint          WorkID = 1;     /* workstation ID                */
Pcolr_rep     Color;
...
Color.rgb.red = 1.0;  Color.rgb.green = 1.0; /* white */
Color.rgb.blue = 1.0;
pset_colr_rep(WorkID, 4, &Color);
...
popen_struct(Scene);                /* open structure            */
pset_view_ind(ViewIndex);           /* set view index            */
pset_facet_cull_mode(PFACET_CULL_BACKFACING); /* set facet
                                       cull mode                 */
pset_int_style(PSTYLE_SOLID);       /* set interior style        */
pset_int_colr_ind(4);               /* set interior color index  */
...
pclose_struct();                    /* close structure           */
```

- We use the default shading method None for this example (each fill area set primitive gets a single colour), so there is no need to call the SET INTERIOR SHADING METHOD routine.

- Since we are using the interior colour as the source of intrinsic colour, there is no need to call SET DATA MAPPING METHOD. Interior colour is the default source of intrinsic colour for area-defining primitives.

Next we specify the terms that PHIGS should use in the reflectance calculations and define and turn on the appropriate light sources:

- Use the value `PREFL_MODEL_AMB_DIFF_REFL` in the SET REFLECTANCE MODEL routine to instruct PHIGS to use ambient and diffuse reflections in the reflectance equation:

  ```
  pset_refl_model(PREFL_MODEL_AMB_DIFF_REFL);
  ```

- We use the default ambient and diffuse reflection coefficients in the reflectance equation, so there is no need to call the SET REFLECTANCE PROPERTIES routine (the default values are both 1.0).

- This particular object is centered around (0.0, 0.0, 0.0) in world coordinates. We define the following light sources to shine on the object:

  - A gray ambient light source.
  - A red positional light source shining down on the object from (0.0, 1.5, 0.0).
  - A blue directional light source shining directly at the front of the object. The vector representing the direction is (0.0, 0.0, –1.5).
  - A green-coloured positional light source shining toward the left side of the object. The light source position is (–1.5, 0.0, 0.0).

  We use SET LIGHT SOURCE REPRESENTATION to define the different light sources. The fragments for defining the first three light sources are listed under the descriptions of the individual light source types earlier in this section and are not repeated here. The following fragment defines light source number 4 as a green, positional light source:

```
Pint        WorkID = 1, index = 4;
Plight_source_rep  rep;

rep.type = PLIGHT_SOURCE_POS;    /* positional light source type */
rep.data.pos.colr.colr_type = PCOLR_RGB;/* use direct RGB
                                         colour values          */
rep.data.pos.colr.colr_value.colr_rep.rgb.red = 0.0;
rep.data.pos.colr.colr_value.colr_rep.rgb.green = 1.0;
rep.data.pos.colr.colr_value.colr_rep.rgb.blue = 0.0;
rep.data.pos.c1 = 1.0;           /* attenuation coefficients  */
rep.data.pos.c2 = 0.0;
rep.data.pos.pos.x = -1.5;       /* light source position     */
rep.data.pos.pos.y = 0.0;
rep.data.pos.pos.z = 0.0;
pset_light_source_rep(WorkID, index, &rep);
```

After defining the locations, colours, and intensities of the lights, you must specify which ones to use at the moment. After all, the fact that a light is in the room doesn't mean that the light is on. You have to flip the light switch. The following fragment shows the entire `Scene` structure, including the SET LIGHT SOURCE STATE routine that turns on light sources 1 through 4:

```
Pint_list     LightsOn, LightsOff;
Pint        MyArray[10];
...
LightsOn.ints = MyArray;/* set up pointer  */
LightsOn.num_ints = 4;
LightsOn.ints[0] = 1;  LightsOn.ints[1] = 2;  LightsOn.ints[2] = 3;
LightsOn.ints[3] = 4;

LightsOff.ints = MyArray;
LightsOff.num_ints = 0;


popen_struct(Scene);                        /* open structure        */
pset_view_ind(ViewIndex);                   /* set view index        */
pfacet_cull_mode(PFACET_CULL_BACKFACING);   /* set facet cull mode   */
pset_int_style(PSTYLE_SOLID);               /* set interior style    */
pset_int_colr_ind(4);                  /* set interior color index   */
pset_refl_model(PREFL_MODEL_AMB_DIFF_REFL);    /* set reflect. model*/
/* set light source state */
pset_light_source_st(&LightsOn, &LightsOff);
pexecute_struct(Cube);                      /* execute structure     */
pclose_struct();                            /* close structure       */
```

Lighting Example 2—Smooth Shading with Vertex Normals

This example uses ambient, diffuse, and specular reflections, as well as user-supplied vertex normals for smooth shading. Colour plate 4 (see colour insert) shows the output of the program.

In this example, we model a sphere. A sphere of radius 1.0 is a convenient object to model in an example where the user supplies vertex normals, because (if the sphere is defined around (0, 0, 0) in modelling coordinates) the *x*, *y*, and *z* values of locations on the surface are the same as the *x*, *y*, and *z* values of the normal to the surface at that point.

The program works as follows:

- We have a `Scene` structure that executes a `Sphere` structure twice. The `Sphere` structure builds the object using fill area set 3 with data primitives, centered around the modelling coordinate origin.
- The first time we execute the `Sphere` structure, the interior shading method is None (constant shading).
- Then we change the interior shading method to Colour (smooth shading) and execute the `Sphere` structure again in a different location. In order to draw the object in a new position, we use the BUILD TRANSFORMATION MATRIX 3 routine to build a transformation matrix, supplying it scaling, rotation, and translation information. Then we replace the local transformation using the SET LOCAL TRANSFORMATION 3 routine.
- Since we are using the interior colour as the source of intrinsic colour, there is no need to call SET DATA MAPPING METHOD. Interior colour is the default source of intrinsic colour for area-defining primitives.

Make the following calls to enable specular reflections:

- Supply a value of `PREFL_MODEL_AMB_DIFF_SPEC_REFL` to the SET REFLECTANCE MODEL routine to create a structure element that instructs PHIGS to use ambient, diffuse, and specular reflections in the lighting equation as shown:

  ```
  pset_refl_model(PREFL_MODEL_AMB_DIFF_SPEC_REFL);
  ```

- Use SET REFLECTANCE PROPERTIES to modify values used in the interior reflectance equation. In the following fragment we call SET REFLECTANCE PROPERTIES in order to set the specular highlight colour to a light gray and set the specular exponent to 20.0.

```
Prefl_prop      refl_prop;
...
refl_prop.type = PREFL_PROPS_SIMPLE_REFL;
refl_prop.data.simple_refl.amb_coeff = 1.0;
refl_prop.data.simple_refl.diff_coeff = 1.0;
refl_prop.data.simple_refl.spec_coeff = 1.0;
/* use direct RGB colour */
refl_prop.data.simple_refl.spec_colr.colr_type = PCOLR_RGB;
refl_prop.data.simple_refl.
     spec_colr.colr_value.colr_rep.rgb.red = 0.4;
refl_prop.data.simple_refl.
     spec_colr.colr_value.colr_rep.rgb.green= 0.4;
refl_prop.data.simple_refl.
     spec_colr.colr_value.colr_rep.rgb.blue = 0.4;
refl_prop.data.simple_refl.spec_exp = 20.0;
...
pset_refl_props(&refl_prop); /* set reflectance properties   */
```

- Instruct PHIGS to use vertex normals by specifying interior shading method Colour:

```
pset_int_shad_method(PINT_SHAD_METHOD_COLR);
```

- Define and turn on the light sources. Use SET LIGHT SOURCE REPRESENTATION to define entries in the light source table. Use SET LIGHT SOURCE STATE to turn on the lights. The following fragment defines light source table entry 2 and turns on light source entries 1 through 3. The definitions for entries 1 and 2 are not shown. Entry 1 is an ambient light with values (0.65, 0.65, 0.65). Entry 2 is a directional light with direction (–10.0, –10.0, 0.0) and colour (0.9, 0.9, 0.9).

```
Pint                WorkID = 1, index = 2;
Pint_list           LightsOn,LightsOff;
Plight_source_rep   light_src_rep;
Pint                MyArray[10];
...
LightsOn.ints=MyArray;              /* set up pointer  */
LightsOn.num_ints=3;
LightsOn.ints[0] = 1;  LightsOn.ints[1] = 2;  LightsOn.ints[2] = 3;
LightsOff.ints = MyArray;
LightsOff.num_ints = 0;

light_src_rep.type = PLIGHT_SOURCE_DIR; /* directional light */
light_src_rep.data.dir.colr.colr_type = PCOLR_RGB;
```

```
light_src_rep.data.dir.colr.colr_value.colr_rep.rgb.red = 0.9;
light_src_rep.data.dir.colr.colr_value.colr_rep.rgb.green = 0.9;
light_src_rep.data.dir.colr.colr_value.colr_rep.rgb.blue = 0.9;
light_src_rep.data.dir.dir.delta_x = 10.0; /* light source direc.*/
light_src_rep.data.dir.dir.delta_y = 10.0;
light_src_rep.data.dir.dir.delta_z = -10.0;
...
pset_light_source_rep(WorkID, index, &light_src_rep);

popen_struct(Scene); /* open structure  */
pset_light_source_st(&LightsOn, &LightsOff);
...
pclose_struct();/* close structure */
```

The following fragment shows the entire `Scene` structure. We change the local transformation matrix each time we execute the `Sphere` structure. This is done to rotate the sphere and to place it in a new position.

```
Ppoint3    point = {0.0, 0.0, 0.0};
Pvec3      trans1 = {-0.4, 0.4, 0.4};
Pvec3      trans2 = { 0.4, -0.4, 0.4};
Pfloat     x_angle = -60.0, y_angle = 30.0; z_angle = -5.0;
Pvec3      scale = {0.5, 0.5, 0.5};
Pint       errind;
Pmatrix3   matrix1, matrix2;
/* for changing degrees to radians */
float      DegreesToRadians = 3.14159265/180.0;

popen_struct(Scene);               /* open structure     */
pset_view_ind(ViewIndex);          /* set view index     */
pfacet_cull_mode(PFACET_CULL_BACKFACING);
pset_int_style(PSTYLE_SOLID);      /* set interior style */
pset_refl_model(PREFL_MODEL_AMB_DIFF_SPEC_REFL);
pset_refl_props(&refl_prop);
/* set light source state */
pset_light_source_st(&LightsOn, &LightsOff);
pbuild_tran_matrix3(&point; &trans1,
                x_angle*DegreesToRadians,
                y_angle*DegreesToRadians,
                z_angle*DegreesToRadians,
                &scale, &errind, matrix1);
if(errind != 0){printf("error in pbuild_tran_matrix %d\n", errind);}
pset_local_tran3(matrix1, PTYPE_REPLACE);
pset_int_shad_method(PINT_SHAD_METHOD_NONE);
pexecute_struct(Sphere);           /* execute structure */
```

```
pbuild_tran_matrix3(&point; &trans2,
                    x_angle*DegreesToRadians,
                    y_angle*DegreesToRadians,
                    z_angle*DegreesToRadians,
                    &scale, &errind, matrix2);
if(errind != 0){printf("error in pbuild_tran_matrix %d\n", errind);}
pset_local_tran3(matrix2,PTYPE_REPLACE);
pset_int_shad_method(PINT_SHAD_METHOD_COLR);
pexecute_struct(Sphere);             /* execute structure */
pclose_struct();                     /* close structure   */
```

Colour plate 4 (see colour insert) shows the output of the program. The image on the left shows shading method None (constant shading). The sphere has specular reflections, but shading method None ignores vertex normals. Specular highlighting is enabled, but each facet receives only one colour. The image on the right uses shading method Colour, which takes the vertex normals into account. In this case colours are interpolated across each facet, and the specular highlights are more realistic.

Notice that although the front of the sphere on the right is smoothed, the silhouette has flat spots. Smoothing the silhouette requires a more exact approximation of the object (that is, use more area-defining primitives of smaller size or use a non-uniform B-spline primitive).

Eyepoint Calculations for Specular Highlighting

When using specular reflection with smooth shading, PHIGS needs to determine the position of the viewer, or the eyepoint. Since specular reflections are highly dependent on the angles between the light source, the surface normal, and the eye position, the eye position must be part of the reflection calculation.

The PHIGS PLUS standard does not specify a way to let the application specify an eyepoint. However, some implementations allow eyepoint specification as an extension to the standard. This can improve performance, as described in the next paragraph.

If the application program does not provide a way for an application to specify an eyepoint explicitly, PHIGS calculates the eyepoint by performing a reverse mapping through the current viewing transformation. This is a time-expensive operation. Some implementations allow the application to supply the eyepoint explicitly. In this way the application program calculates the eyepoint once and stores the results for repeated use. Refer to your user documentation to determine whether your implementation allows you to set the eyepoint.

Typically, you should make the eyepoint value equal to the center of perspective projection (if you are using perspective) for the view. Also, since each view has its own eyepoint, make sure that you calculate an eyepoint for each view.

Light Source Calculations

This section is not needed in order to use lighting and shading, but it gives a detailed explanation of the light source calculations recommended by PHIGS PLUS (see Annex C of the PHIGS PLUS standard).

Table 17–2 shows the mathematical symbols, descriptions, data types, and source for each value. Figure 17–3 shows a graphical representation of some of the relevant symbols. After the table, the formulae are presented with relevant comments.

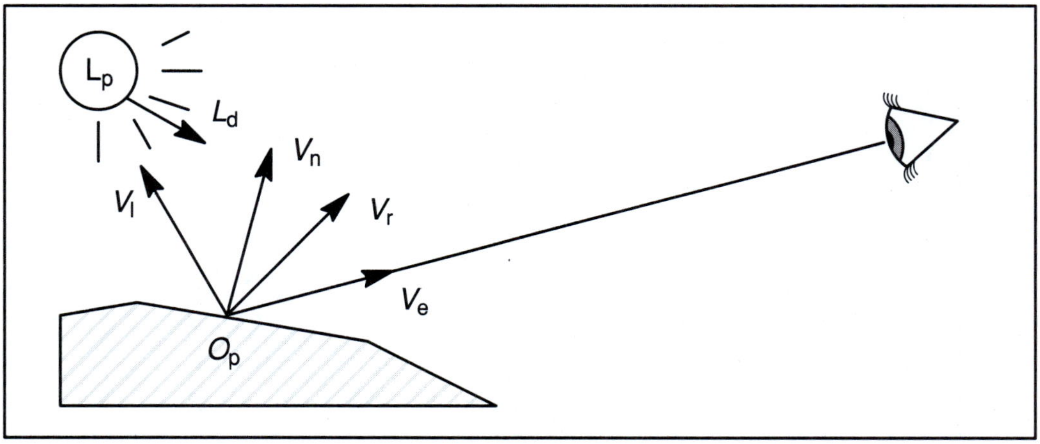

Figure 17–3. Graphical Representation of the Mathematical Symbols in Table 17–1

Note that PHIGS PLUS recommends that the implementation perform lighting calculations in world coordinate space. This section assumes that world coordinate space is used.

Table 17–2. Variable Definitions for Reflectance Equation

Symbol	Description	Data Type	Source
L_d	Light source direction	3xR	1
L_c	Light source colour	COLRV	1
L_p	Light source position	3xR	1
L_e	Light source concentration exponent	R	1
$C1$, $C2$	Attenuation coefficients	R	1
A_s	Spread angle	R	1
L_a	Light attenuation	R	2
O_p	Object position	3xR	3
O_c	Object intrinsic colour	COLRV	4
O_s	Object specular colour	COLRV	5
O_e	Object specular exponent	R	5
K_a	Ambient reflection coefficient	R	5
K_d	Diffuse reflection coefficient	R	5
K_s	Specular reflection coefficient	R	5
V_e	Unit vector from object to eyepoint	3xR	2
V_r	Unit reflection vector from object	3xR	2
V_l	Unit vector from object to light source	3xR	2
V_n	Unit normal vector of object	NORM	3
C_a	Ambient contribution from light source	COLRV	2
C_d	Diffuse contribution from light source	COLRV	2
C_s	Specular contribution from light source	COLRV	2

1 = light source representation (SET LIGHT SOURCE REPRESENTATION)
2 = calculated by PHIGS
3 = explicit or derived from object geometry by PHIGS
4 = intrinsic colour (see Chapter 16)
5 = surface or back reflectance properties (SET REFLECTANCE PROPERTIES or bundled)

R = 4-byte real

COLRV = colour value, in `Pgcolr` format—depending on the colour type, either an integer index or a set of real values corresponding to a specific colour model

NORM = three real values specifying the coordinates of a unit normal vector

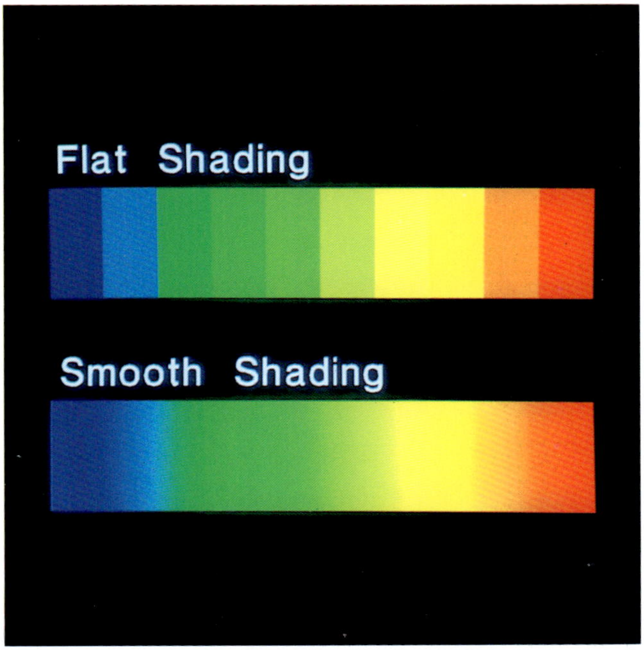

Colour Plate 1. Using Facet and Vertex Colour Intensities to Access the Colour List

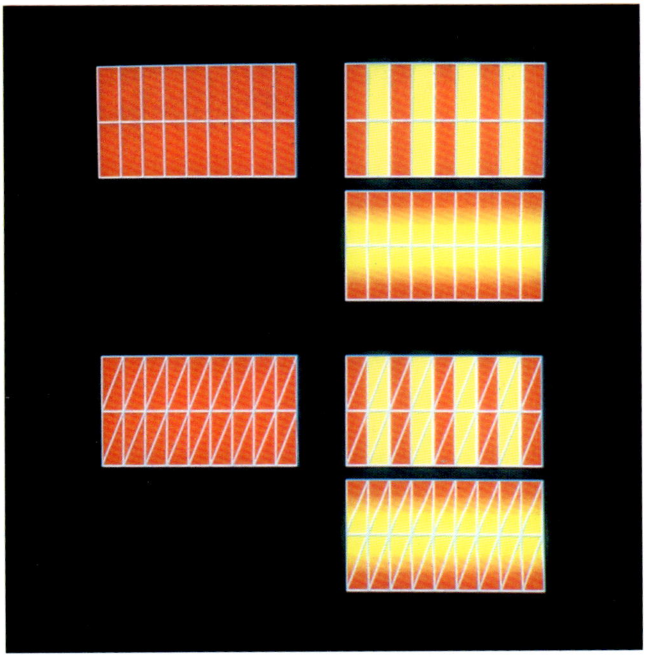

Colour Plate 2. Quadrilateral Mesh and Triangle Strip Primitives with Intrinsic Colour

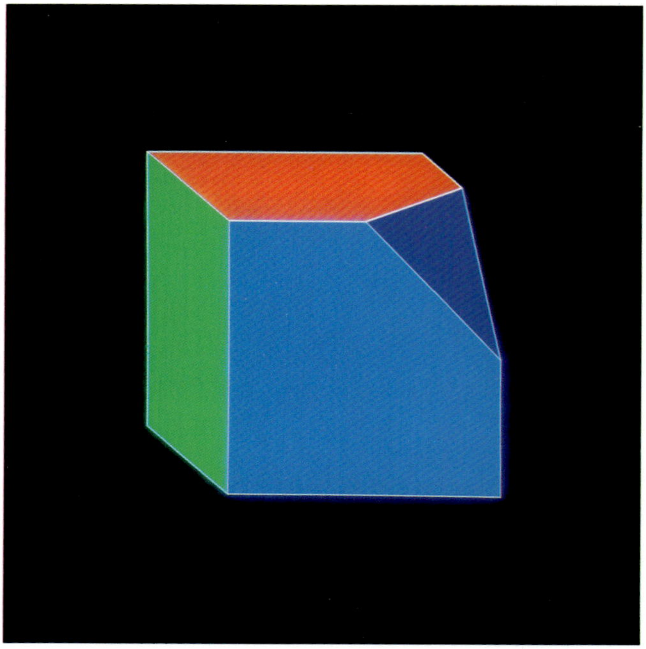

Colour Plate 3. Lighting Applied to Fill-area Set Primitives

Colour Plate 4. Constant-shading and Smooth-shading a Sphere

Colour Plate 5. Vertex Colour Interpolation

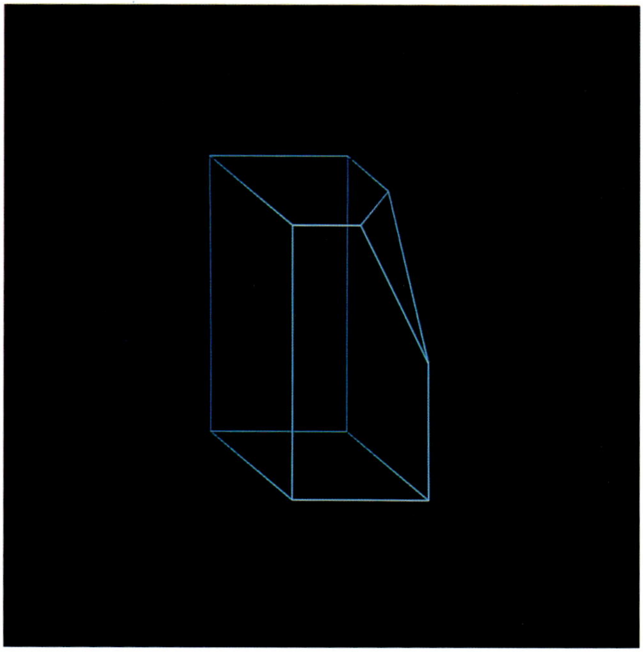

Colour Plate 6. Depth-cued Wireframe Image

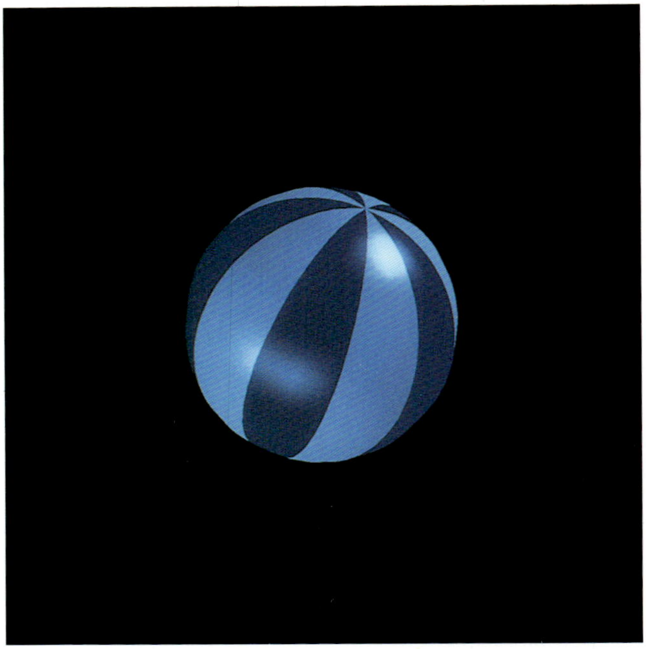

Colour Plate 7. Using Colour Mapping for Gray-scale Shading

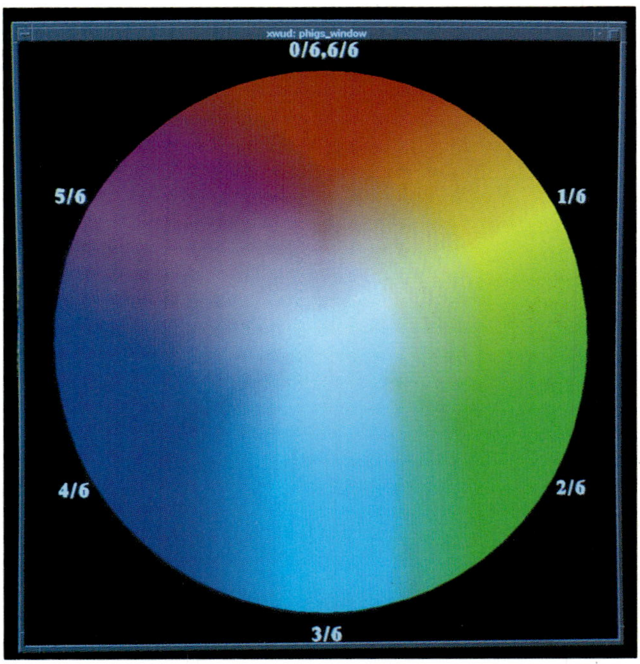

Colour Plate 8. HSV Colour Wheel

The result of the reflectance calculation evaluated at a point on a primitive is a single colour. The colour is the sum of the individual components, $C_a + C_d + C_s$, of all the currently active light sources as shown below:

$$\sum_{i=1}^{i=n} (C_{a,i} + C_{d,i} + C_{s,i}),\ n = \text{total number of active light sources}$$

where C_a is the ambient contribution from a light source, C_d is the diffuse contribution, and C_s is the specular contribution.

The application specifies one of the following calculation methods:

1. No reflectance calculation. In this method, colour is not affected by the lighting portion of the rendering pipeline.
2. Use the ambient term of the reflectance calculation.
3. Use the ambient and diffuse terms of the reflectance calculation.
4. Use the ambient, diffuse, and specular terms of the reflectance calculation.

Refer to "Controlling the Reflectance Calculations," earlier in this chapter, for more information.

Ambient Light Sources

PHIGS models ambient lighting as a constant, diffuse reflection from all sides of the object, regardless of the position or orientation of the object or light sources.

The equations used to calculate ambient light reflection are as follows:

$$C_a = K_a L_c O_c$$

$$C_d = 0$$

$$C_s = 0$$

Directional Light Sources

Directional light sources have a light source colour and a light source direction. Since the light source is conceptually at infinity, the light travels as parallel rays. Thus, the direction of the light is the same for all objects, regardless of their position. The light direction is indicated by a unit vector pointing in the direction the light travels. The light source direction is specified as a 3D vector in world coordinates.

The equations used to calculate the directional light reflection are as follows:

$$C_a = 0$$

$$C_d = K_d L_c O_c \vec{V_n} \bullet \vec{V_l}$$

$$C_s = K_s O_s L_c (\vec{V_e} \bullet \vec{V_r})^{O_e}$$

Positional Light Sources

You can think of a positional light source as a light bulb of zero size at a given position in world coordinates. Light emanates in all directions from a positional light source, so objects all around the light source are illuminated as long as they are visible.

The rays from a positional light source are not parallel, and the position of an object with respect to the light source affects the angle at which light strikes the object's surface. A positional light source is typically located relatively close to the viewing area.

Positional light sources have a light source colour, a light source position, and two attenuation coefficients. The equations used to calculate the positional light reflection are as follows:

$$C_a = 0$$

$$C_d = K_d O_c L_c \vec{V_n} \bullet \vec{V_l} \; L_a$$

$$C_s = K_s O_s L_c (\vec{V_e} \bullet \vec{V_r})^{O_e} \; L_a$$

Spot Light Sources

A spot light source is conceptually a point light source with a cone of influence (see Figure 17–2, earlier in this chapter). This cone of influence is determined by the light source direction and a spread angle. If a point lies outside the cone of influence, its colour is not affected by that light source.

Spot light sources have a light source colour, light source position, light source direction, attenuation coefficients, concentration exponent, and spread angle. The equations used to calculate the spot light reflection are as follows:

$$C_a = 0$$

$$C_d = K_d\, O_c\, L_c\, \vec{V_n} \bullet \vec{V_l}\, (\vec{L_d} \bullet -\vec{V_l})^{L_e}\, L_a$$

$$C_s = K_s\, O_s\, L_c\, (\vec{V_e} \bullet \vec{V_r})^{O_e}\, (\vec{L_d} \bullet -\vec{V_l})^{L_e}\, L_a$$

Light Attenuation

The light attenuation factor (L_a) is used in several of these light source equations. The light attenuation factor models the physical world by decreasing the contribution of light intensity as the distance between the light source and the object increases. Although light intensity in the real world falls off with the square of the distance, inverse square attenuations have been found to give poor results in computed images. Therefore, the following formula is used:

$$L_a = 1 / (C1 + C2\, |\vec{O_p} - \vec{L_p}|)$$

where:

L_a is the attenuation factor of the light.

$C1$ and $C2$ are the attenuation coefficients.

O_p is the position of the object being lit.

L_p is the position of the light source.

$|\vec{O_p} - \vec{L_p}|$ is the distance between the object and the light source.

The value of L_a is truncated to 1.0, if necessary, to prevent it from increasing the total intensity of the image.

Use the SET LIGHT SOURCE REPRESENTATION routine to define the light attenuation coefficients and the light source position.

Reflection Vector

PHIGS uses a reflection vector (V_r) for specular colour calculations. The following formula is used to calculate the reflection vector:

$$V_r = 2 (\vec{V_n} \bullet \vec{V_l}) \vec{V_n} - \vec{V_l}$$

The reflection normal (V_n) defines the orientation of a primitive at a certain point for the purposes of evaluating a reflectance vector at that point. If vertex normals are supplied with the primitive data, they are used as reflectance normals. Otherwise, PHIGS uses the geometric normal.

Handling Light Overflow

When you start shining multiple light sources onto surfaces that have specular reflections enabled, it is easy to have the reflectance calculations produce a value (for example, in RGB) that is greater than 1.0. This is called a **light overflow**. For example, with ambient and several light sources on an object, it is possible to have the total amount of reflected light much greater than 1.0, despite the fact that 1.0 is the largest value that has meaning in the RGB colour system. This presents a problem, because if the resultant value is greater than 1.0, it is not really "light."

Check your user documentation to see how the implementation reacts when a light overflow occurs. For example, if an RGB colour value exceeds 1.0, the implementation may truncate the value to 1.0. When this happens, a colour that is predominantly one hue will tend to become white (desaturate).

You can use the reflection coefficients to control intensity overflows. Reflection coefficients can be set by the following routines:

- For individual attribute specification, use SET REFLECTANCE PROPERTIES.

- For bundled attribute specification, use SET REFLECTANCE REPRESENTATION.

Refer to "Setting the Reflectance Properties," earlier in this chapter, for information on how to use these routines.

Alternatively, you can diminish the intensity of the lights (this may be the easiest thing to do).

Using Vertex Colours

This section describes how to use vertex colour for "with data" primitives that allow vertex colour information in the primitive definition. Vertex colour can be included in the primitive definition for the following primitives:

- Polyline set with data
- Fill area set with data
- Set of fill area sets with data
- Triangle set with data
- Triangle strip with data
- Quadrilateral mesh with data
- Non-uniform B-spline curve with colour
- Non-uniform B-spline surface with data

PHIGS defines colour interpolation as the linear interpolation of colour coordinates across line segments or polygons. In this section we are concerned with interpolation of vertex colours.

PHIGS interpolates vertex colour values across a primitive when the following conditions are met:

- The data mapping method specifies that vertex colour should be used as the source of intrinsic colour.
- Vertex colour and/or vertex normals are supplied in the primitive definition.

- The vertex data flag in the primitive definition tells PHIGS that vertex colour exists.
- For area-defining primitives, use interior shading methods 2 through 5.
- For polyline set 3 with colour and non-uniform B-spline curve with colour primitives, use polyline shading method 2 (Colour).

Note that interpolation of colours across a primitive is also evident under the following circomstances:

- When non-ambient light sources are active and only vertex normals are supplied
- When application-supplied vertex data is present and the data mapping method and shading methods are set correctly (see Chapter 16).

Lighting and Vertex Colour Interpolation

You can use vertex colour interpolation without enabling any light sources. In fact, vertex colour interpolation is often used without light sources in order to display accurate colour values without the added effects of lighting. Refer to "Setting the Interior Shading Method," earlier in this chapter, for more information.

Using Vertex Colour with Line Primitives

Polyline set 3 with data and non-uniform B-spline curve with colour primitives can utilize the shading method portion of the rendering pipeline for interpolation of vertex colours.

You can control whether PHIGS draws these primitives with or without vertex colour interpolation by setting the *polyline shading method*. The polyline shading method is an attribute that can take one of the values described below:

- `PLINE_SHAD_METHOD_NONE`—**None**. Do not interpolate colours across line segments. If vertex colours are given for the polyline, the *i*th vertex colour determines the colour of the *i*th polyline segment. If you don't specify vertex colours, PHIGS uses the current polyline colour aspect (see "Attributes and Aspects" in Chapter 9, *Using Attributes*).
- `PLINE_SHAD_METHOD_COLR`—**Colour**. If vertex colours are available, PHIGS uses the current rendering colour model and interpolates the colours along the line

segments. If vertex colours are not present, PHIGS colours the entire polyline in a single colour determined by the current polyline colour aspect.

Note that PHIGS applies the linetype attribute after shading. The linetype attribute acts like a masking operation, making it possible to produce nonsolid, shaded lines.

You can set the polyline shading method attribute via individual and bundled attributes. Depending on the value of the *current polyline shading method ASF* entry in the traversal state list, PHIGS uses either the individual attribute value (called the *current polyline shading method)* or a value from the workstation polyline bundle table. Use the following routines to set and select the attribute value:

- For individual attribute specification, use the SET POLYLINE SHADING METHOD routine. This routine places a *set polyline shading method* structure element in the CSS.
- For bundled attribute specification, use the `shad_method` field in the SET POLYLINE REPRESENTATION PLUS routine to set the polyline shading method for a particular entry in the workstation polyline bundle table.
- Use the SET POLYLINE INDEX routine to select a particular entry from the workstation polyline bundle table. This routine places a *set polyline index* structure element in the CSS.
- Use the SET INDIVIDUAL ASF routine to set the *current polyline shading method ASF* entry in the traversal state list to either individual or bundled. This routine places a *set individual ASF* structure element in the CSS. The ASF identifier value is `PASPECT_LINE_COLR`.

Individual Attribute Specification (Polyline Colour Interpolation)

For individual attribute specification, use the SET POLYLINE SHADING METHOD routine. This routine creates a structure element that, when traversed, sets the *current polyline shading method* entry in the traversal state list. PHIGS uses this value when the *current polyline shading method ASF* entry in the traversal state list is set to individual.

The calling signature for the SET POLYLINE SHADING METHOD routine is as follows:

```
pset_line_shad_method(
   Pint                    method
);
```

where:

⟨*method*⟩ can take one of the following values:

- PLINE_SHAD_METHOD_NONE. **None**
- PLINE_SHAD_METHOD_COLR. **Colour**

The values are described earlier in this section. For example, the following fragment sets the interior shading method to Colour:

```
popen_struct(cube);            /* open structure cube          */
pset_line_shad_method(PLINE_SHAD_METHOD_COLR);
...
pclose_struct();               /* close structure              */
```

Bundled Attribute Specification (Polyline Colour Interpolation)

For bundled attribute specification, use the shad_meth field in the SET POLYLINE REPRESENTATION PLUS routine. The shad_meth field sets the polyline shading method for a given entry in the workstation polyline bundle table. PHIGS uses this value when the *current polyline shading method ASF* is set to bundled. The SET POLYLINE INDEX routine selects the entry from the bundle table.

Refer to Chapter 10, *Output Primitives and Attributes*, for a description of the SET POLYLINE REPRESENTATION PLUS routine.

Using Vertex Colour Interpolation with Area-defining Primitives

The example in this section applies vertex colours to the front of the cube-with-the-corner-cut-off. In this case we use fill area set 3 with data primitives in order to define the primitive with vertex colour values. Colour plate 5 (see colour insert) shows the output of the complete program.

This program does not use any lighting routines. Lighting is not necessary for vertex colour interpolation. The necessary components are vertex colours, interior style solid, and an appropriate shading method. In this case we use shading method 2 (Colour).

The program works as follows:

- We use two structures: `Scene` and `Cube`. The `Cube` structure creates the geometry and the primitives have associated vertex colours. The following fragment shows how the program defines the front face of the object:

```
Pint          colr_type = PCOLR_RGB;      /* RGB colour model   */
Pfacet        facet_data = {0, NULL, NULL, NULL};
Pedge_flag_set  edge_data;
static Ppoint3  VertexPoints[5] = {
                1.0, -1.0, 1.0,
                1.0, 0.0, 1.0,
                0.0, 1.0, 1.0,
                -1.0, 1.0, 1.0,
                -1.0, -1.0, 1.0 };
static Pcolrv_ptr  VertexColours[5] = {
                1.0, 0.0, 1.0,            /* magenta           */
                1.0, 0.5, 1.0,            /* light magenta     */
                1.0, 1.0, 0.5             /* light yellow      */
                1.0, 1.0, 0.0,            /* yellow            */
                1.0, 0.0, 0.0 };          /* red               */
static  Pvertex3_list VertexList = {
        5, 0, /* # data */                /* number of vertices   */
        VertexPoints, VertexColours, NULL, NULL};
static  Pvertex3_set  VertexSet = { 1, &VertexList};
...
pfill_area_set3_data(colr_type, &facet_data, &edge_data,
                        &VertexSet);
```

Figure 17–4 shows the geometry created by the above fragment. This is the same geometry we used in Chapter 15 to show how PHIGS calculates a geometric normal.

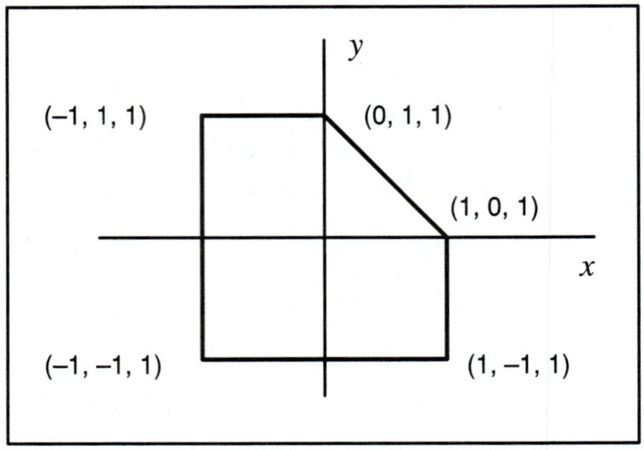

Figure 17–4. Front Face of the Cube-with-the-corner-cut-off

- We set the interior style and interior shading method within the `Scene` structure. We also use the `Scene` structure to set the data mapping method. We use a data mapping method of Colour and specify that vertex colour is the source of intrinsic colour. The following fragment shows the contents of the `Scene` structure:

```
Pdata_map_rep rep;            /* for data mapping method       */
...

rep.selectors.num = 1;
/* use interior colour        */
rep.selectors.selectors[0] = PSOURCE_SELECT_VERT_COLR;
/* use data mapping method Colour  */
rep.method = PDATA_MAP_METHOD_COLR;

popen_struct(Scene);          /* open structure cube           */
pset_view_ind(1);             /* set view index                */
pset_data_map_method(&rep);   /* set data mapping method       */
pset_int_style(PSTYLE_SOLID); /* set interior style            */
/* set interior shading method  */
pset_int_shad_method(PINT_SHAD_METHOD_COLR);
pset_edge_flag(PEDGE_ON);     /* set edge flag                 */
pset_edge_colr_ind(1);        /* set edge colour index         */
pexecute_struct(Cube);        /* execute structure             */
pclose_struct();              /* close structure               */
```

In this example we do not use individual edge flags per vertex. However, we turn on the edge flag so that all edges are displayed. Then we select an appropriate edge colour—in this case we use index 2 in the workstation colour table, which we have previously set to black.

Tips for Using Lighting and Shading

In order to create high-quality images, the application program needs to make the following choices:

- Select the most appropriate primitives and attributes.
- Decide upon the amount of computational cost for rendering that your application can sustain.

The following sections describe some specific areas to which an application program should pay careful attention.

Use Planar Geometry and Data

While a number of PHIGS primitives allow you to create multi-faceted primitives, you should make sure that individual facets are planar. PHIGS does not define the effects produced by nonplanar geometry or nonplanar intrinsic colour data. Implementations make allowances for non-planar data and geometry, but in general, applying lighting calculations to nonplanar data and geometry can lead to unexpected results.

Shading Methods and Primitive Size

As an application programmer, you need to make decisions about how much time your application can take to produce a high-quality image. The more computationally expensive the shading method, the longer it takes to produce the final image. You may be able to use a less time-expensive shading method if you use more, smaller primitives to define the model. For example, when using fill area set with data primitives to define a sphere, the more primitives you use to define the sphere, the smoother the resulting image.

In general, when using vertex data, using more, smaller primitives results in a smoother, more accurate image. It may be a good idea to give the user control of both the size of the primitives and the shading methods.

Rigid versus Non-rigid Transformations

Transformations that affect the appearance of an image can be grouped into two main areas:

- **Rigid transformations** change the relative positions of the objects and the observer. An example of a rigid transformation is a transformation matrix that moves or rotates an object or scales the object using equal amounts in x, y, and z. Such a transformation does not alter the surface normals of the object.
- **Non-rigid transformations** change the overall shape of an object and can therefore change or distort the surface normals of the object. An example of a non-rigid transformation is a scaling matrix in which the scale factors for x, y, and z are not equal (called *anisotropic scaling*). For example, you can use an anisotropic scaling matrix to distort a sphere into an egg-shaped object.

The problem with non-rigid transformations is that they distort the meaningfulness of the vertex normals. When using lighting and shading, you should avoid using non-rigid transformations in the modelling matrix. (The modelling matrix is the point at which you define the geometry and position it in world coordinates.) This is because when PHIGS performs shading calculations, the values are dependent on the way the area-defining primitive is facing (that is, the normal to the surface). PHIGS also uses the normal when determining whether or not a primitive is back-facing or front-facing (for culling purposes).

If you want to use non-rigid transformations, try using them in the viewing transformation (the transformation from world coordinates to normalized projection coordinates). If you use non-rigid transformations in the modelling matrix when performing lighting and shading, it may produce unexpected results. Some implementations make allowances for non-rigid transformations, and others do not.

While we're on the subject of rigid and non-rigid transformations, we should mention that mirroring is a rigid transformation with which you have to be careful. See the discussion of mirroring transformations in the section entitled "Geometric Normals" in Chapter 15.

Chapter 18

Depth Cueing

This chapter describes the depth cueing stage of the PHIGS PLUS rendering pipeline (see Figure 18–1).

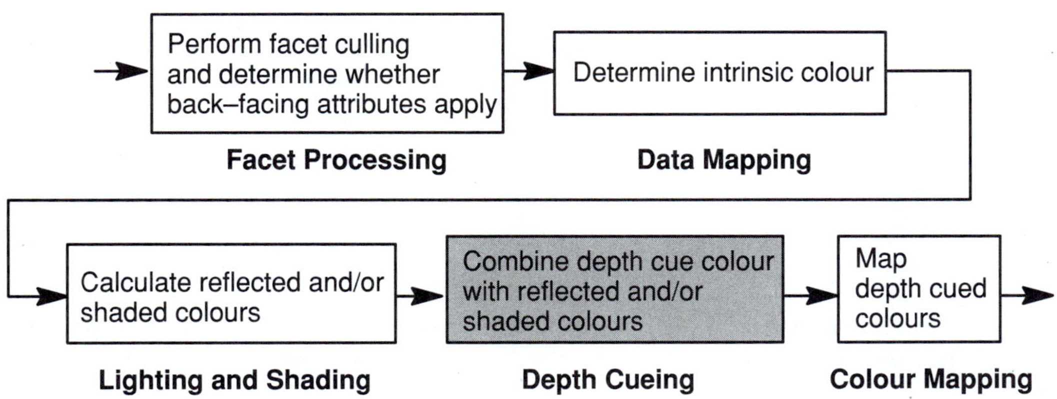

Figure 18–1. Rendering Pipeline

Depth cueing allows you to add perceptual depth information to an image. When depth cueing is enabled, the intensity, or brightness, of an image can vary with the NPC space *z* component of the primitives in the image. This allows an application program to either fade or intensify the image with depth.

By fading or intensifying the image with depth, you can differentiate the depth of an image relative to the observer. A common use is to apply depth cueing to an image so that the parts closer to the observer are brighter than the parts farther away.

Figure 18–2 shows a 3D object drawn in wireframe style without depth cueing. As you can see, the main drawback to a wireframe image is that you can often see the far side of the object as easily as the near side. This makes it hard to tell which side is closer to you (in fact, with a little mental effort, you may be able to "turn the object inside out" reversing back and front). Most real objects are not transparent, and even when partially transparent, they often contain visual clues as to which portions are closest to the observer.

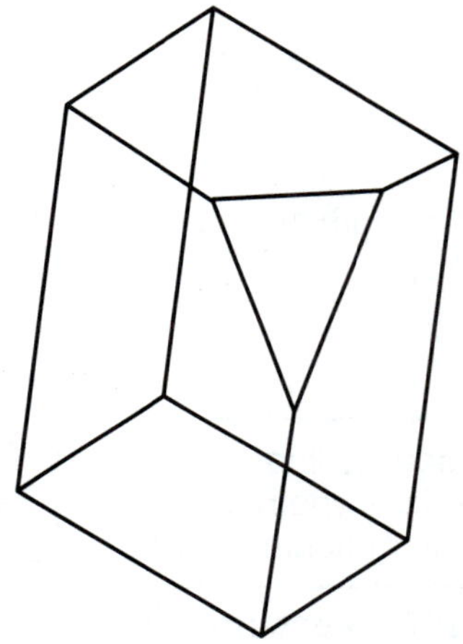

Figure 18–2. Wireframe Image with No Depth Cueing

Colour plate 6 (see colour insert) shows a wireframe image displayed with depth cueing. Notice how much easier it is to tell which portions of the image are closer.

Depth cueing is commonly used with wireframe images. However, because of its position in the rendering pipeline, depth cueing also can be used in a scene after lighting and shading have been applied.

Using Depth Cueing

An application controls depth cueing through the workstation depth cue table. The SET DEPTH CUE REPRESENTATION routine defines or changes an entry in the table. The calling signature for the SET DEPTH CUE REPRESENTATION routine is as follows:

```
pset_depth_cue_rep(
    Pint                    wk_id,
    Pint                    index,
    const Pdepth_cue_rep    *rep
);
```

where:

⟨*wk_id*⟩ identifies the workstation.

⟨*index*⟩ identifies the entry being modified in the depth cue table. The number of entries in the table is implementation-dependent. The minimum number of entries is 1.

⟨*rep*⟩ is the information being stored for this table entry, in `Pdepth_cue_rep` format. The data type `Pdepth_cue_rep` is defined as follows:

```
Pdepth_cue_rep
 typedef struct {
   Pdepth_cue_mode         mode;
   Pfloat                  ref_planes[2];
   Pfloat                  scale[2];
   Pgcolr                  gcolr;
 } Pdepth_cue_rep;
```

where:

`mode` can be one of the following values:

- `PDEPTH_CUE_SUPPR`. Do not use depth cueing.
- `PDEPTH_CUE_ALLOWED`. Use depth cueing.

`ref_planes` is an array of two real values that identify the position of the depth cue reference planes. Both values represent z values in NPC space.

`scale` is an array of two real values (in the range [0.0, 1.0], inclusive) that specifies the extent of the colour change. The two scale factors specify the mixing ratio of the primitive colour and the depth cue colour.

`gcolr` is the colour into which the objects gradually fade or intensify, in `Pgcolr` format. The depth cue colour is specified as a general colour, meaning that it is represented either as an index into the workstation colour table or as a set of colour values from a particular colour model (for example, RGB triplets). See Chapter 12, *Using Colour*, for a description of `Pgcolr`.

The SET DEPTH CUE INDEX routine creates a structure element that selects an entry from the workstation depth cue table. The C binding calling signature for the SET DEPTH CUE INDEX routine is as follows:

```
pset_depth_cue_ind(
   Pint                 index
);
```

where:

⟨*index*⟩ specifies an entry in the depth cue table.

When traversal begins, PHIGS sets the default depth cue index to 1. Depth cue entry 1 contains predefined values and specifies that depth cueing is disabled. Other entries in the workstation depth cue table may also contain predefined entries, depending on the implementation.

Depth cueing applies to all output primitives. Since depth cueing is controlled by a structure element, it is possible to have several different depth cueing colours, reference planes, and scaling factors in a scene at the same time. However, keep in mind that if primitives with different depth cueing effects are in the same picture, the effect may be confusing.

Depth Cue Scaling

In the following discussion, the term "primitive colour" is the colour of the primitive as it enters the depth cue stage of the rendering pipeline. This is the intrinsic colour of the primitive with any appropriate lighting and shading applied. The "depth cue colour" is the colour specified by the currently selected entry of the workstation depth cue table.

The two depth cue scale factors are values in the range [0.0, 1.0], inclusive. These scale factors are applied to the two depth cue reference planes and define the mixture of primitive and depth cue colours at their respective planes. The reference planes are the front and back relative to NPC *z* space.

The actual method used for depth cueing is left up to the implementation. However, PHIGS PLUS suggests a practical method. The following discussions of depth cue scaling and depth cue equations describe this method.

The two depth cue reference planes together with the depth cue scale factors define a piecewise linear mapping that determines how the depth cue colour is mixed with the primitive colour at any given point on the NPC *z* plane. Points lying between the reference planes have their colour blended with the depth cue colour based on their position relative to the reference planes. Points lying outside the reference planes have their colour blended as though they were lying on the reference plane (see Figure 18–3).

For example, if the front scale factor is *x,* the colour at the front plane is (100 * x)% primitive colour and (100 * (1 – x))% depth cue colour. The back scale factor works similarly with the back plane. The depth cue scale factor used at a specific *z* value in between the front and back depth cue planes is determined from a linear interpolation of the front and back scale factors.

Figure 18–3 shows an example of the interpolation of colour values for a front scale factor of 0.9 and a back scale value of 0.2. You can see from this example that when a primitive lies outside the depth cue mapping range, its intensity scale value becomes a constant.

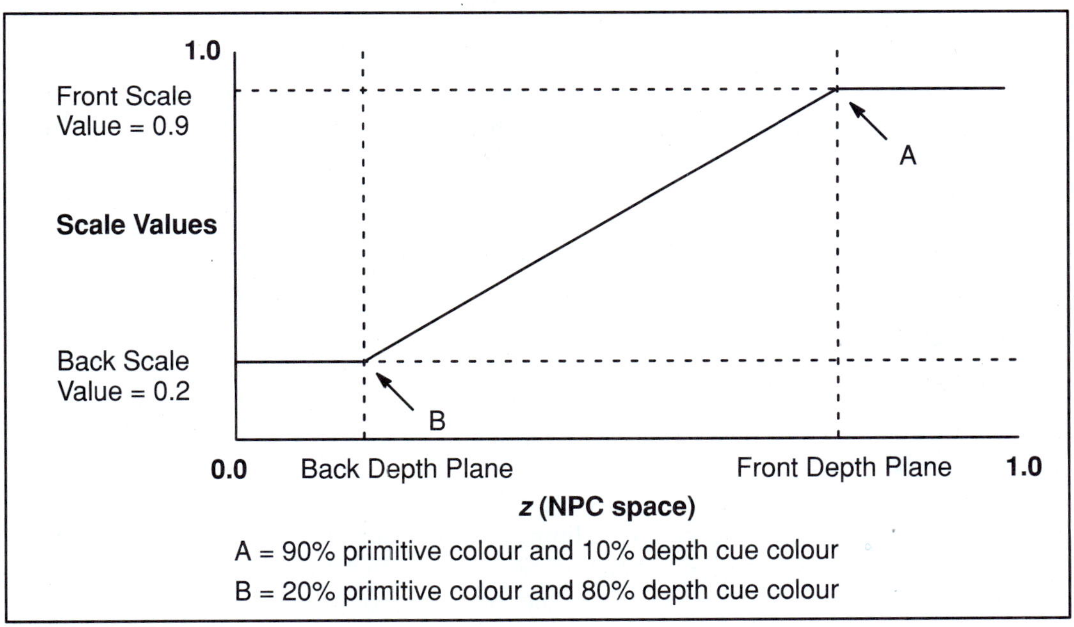

Figure 18–3. Depth Cue Scaling Example

Intensity Values beyond the Depth Cue Reference Planes

PHIGS PLUS suggests that the amount of depth cueing for primitives that lie in front of the front plane be the same as that directly at the front plane. Likewise, the amount of depth cueing for primitives that lie beyond the back plane is the same as that directly at the back plane.

When an object crosses one of the reference planes, the depth cueing of the vertices that lie beyond the reference plane are determined by the depth cue scale factor at the reference plane. PHIGS implementations have two choices in this case:

- Create extra vertices at the plane intersections. This has the effect of clamping the depth cue scaling at the plane intersections. This is the most accurate implementation of the suggested form of depth cueing. However, it may affect performance since the implementation must create extra vertices.
- Do not create extra vertices. In this case, when a primitive crosses the depth cue planes, the transition does not occur at the defined depth cue planes. Instead, the transition is a function of the intensity derivative and the distance of the given vertex from the depth cue planes.

  In this case, if the primitives cross one of the depth cue reference planes, then the resulting image may have distorted depth cueing. This distortion is usually only detectable when two large adjacent primitives have a large difference in *z* values that extend beyond the reference planes. If this presents a problem for your application, you can either make the depth cue reference planes equal to the front and back view-clipping planes or ensure that the depth cue planes are beyond the NPC *z* extents of the primitives.

Check your implementatioin documentation to determine which case applies to you.

Recommendations

Use the following guidelines until you determine values that more closely match the needs of your application:

- The easiest way to select values for the depth cue reference planes is to use the *z* values of the view clipping limits. These values are set by the SET VIEW REPRESENTATION 3 routine and can be retrieved by INQUIRE VIEW REPRESENTATION 3. The default values are 1.0 for the front and 0.0 for the back.
- For the best results you should use values that are close to the NPC *z* extents of the object being displayed. This is because if you have a small object in the middle of a large depth cue range, the depth cueing may not be very noticeable.

- For symmetrical objects (for example, spheres, cones, and cylinders), better depth cueing effects may be obtained by placing the back reference plane at the center axis of the object. For example, the following illustration shows a scene where the back reference is moved to the center of the object.

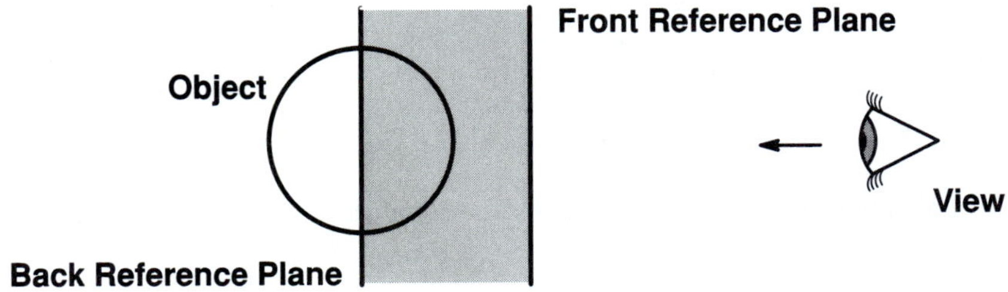

  In the above illustration, the shaded area shows the portion of the model affected by depth cueing. The brightest effect will be at the front of the object (if the front scaling value is higher than the back scaling value).

- Base your depth cue colour on the colour of the primitive and on the background colour. Many applications fade the object into the background colour or into a colour such as gray, or black, or a foggy colour, such as a foggy brown.

Depth Cueing Equations

The depth cueing equations are presented here for readers who are interested in the equations that PHIGS PLUS recommends (see Annex E of PHIGS PLUS standard).

The scaling of a point between the front and back depth cue reference planes is determined by a linear interpolation of the depth cue scale factors between the reference planes. Any points in front of the front depth cue reference plane or behind the back depth cue reference plane are rendered using a constant depth cue scale factor as indicated by the following equations.

Definitions

C = component of input colour
C_d = component of depth cue colour
C' = component of resultant colour
Z = depth cue of point (in NPC)
P_f = z coordinate of front reference plane (in NPC)
P_b = z coordinate of back reference plane (in NPC)

S_f = front scale factor
S_b = back scale factor
r = the blending factor that defines how much of each colour will be blended together

Equations

If Z is in front of P_f, then the following equation defines C':

$$C' = S_f\,C_i + (1 - S_f)C_d$$

If Z is behind P_b, then the following equation defines C':

$$C' = S_b\,C_i + (1 - S_b)C_d$$

If Z is between P_f and P_b, then the following equation defines C':

$$C' = r\,C_i + (1 - r)C_d$$

where:

$$r = S_b + (Z - P_b)\frac{S_f - S_b}{P_f - P_b}$$

Depth Cueing Example

The following example shows how to set an entry in the workstation depth cue table. The output from the complete program is shown in colour plate 6 (see colour insert).

In this example, after the viewing and workstation transformations are applied, the geometry lies between 0.25 and 0.75 in NPC space. So, if we set the back depth cue reference plane to 0.25 and the front depth cue reference plane to 0.75, we achieve the maximum depth cueing effect. Alternatively, we could set the front and back reference planes to the *z* values of the view-clipping limits. This would guarantee that the object would be depth cued, but the effect would not be as dramatic.

This example defines entry number 2 in the workstation depth cue table because it may be helpful for the application to keep entry 1 for disabling depth cueing. The fragment sets the following values for entry 2:

- Depth cue reference planes of 0.25 (back) and 0.75 (front).
- Front depth cue scale factor = 1.0. The front reference plane will use 0% of the depth cue colour and 100% of the primitive colour.

- Back depth cue scale factor = 0.0. The back reference plane will use 100% of the depth cue colour and 0% of the primitive colour.

- A depth cue colour of gray (RGB colour model value (0.4, 0.4, 0.4)). The primitive colour is white, so the objects fades from white to gray.

The following fragment defines entry 2 in the workstation depth cue table. Then it uses the SET DEPTH CUE INDEX routine to create a structure element that selects the entry:

```
int      WorkID = 1;      /* workstation ID                          */
int      index = 2;       /* index into workstation depth cue table  */
int      ViewID = 1;      /* index into workstation view table       */
int      Shape = 1;       /* structure identifier                    */
int      Scene = 2;       /* structure identifier                    */
Pdepth_cue_rep  rep;      /* the depth cue representation            */

/* *** define workstation depth cue table entry "1" ************     */
rep.mode = PDEPTH_CUE_ALLOWED;  /* enable depth cueing               */
rep.ref_planes[0] = 0.25;  /* Use z values close to object for       */
rep.ref_planes[1] = 0.75;  /* depth cue reference planes.            */
rep.scale[0] = 0.0;    /* Back scale factor uses 0% primitive
                          color and therefore, 100% depth cue color. */
rep.scale[1] = 1.0; /* front scale factor uses 100% primitive color*/

rep.gcolor.colr_type = PCOLR_RGB;  /* use direct RGB colour values */
rep.gcolor.colr_value.colr_rep.rgb.red = 0.4;
rep.gcolor.colr_value.colr_rep.rgb.green = 0.4;
rep.gcolor.colr_value.colr_rep.rgb.blue = 0.4;

/* set depth cue representation for entry 2 */
pset_depth_cue_rep(WorkID, index, &rep);

popen_struct(Scene);             /* open structure                  */
pset_view_ind(ViewID);           /* set view index                  */
pset_depth_cue_ind(index);       /* set depth cue index             */
pexecute_struct(Shape);          /* execute structure               */
pclose_struct();                 /* close structure                 */
```

Chapter 19

Colour Mapping

This chapter describes how to use the colour mapping stage of the rendering pipeline (see Figure 19–1). Colour mapping is provided to allow a final mapping of primitive colours to workstation-specific colours. The default is a one-to-one mapping that does not require any specific action on the application's part.

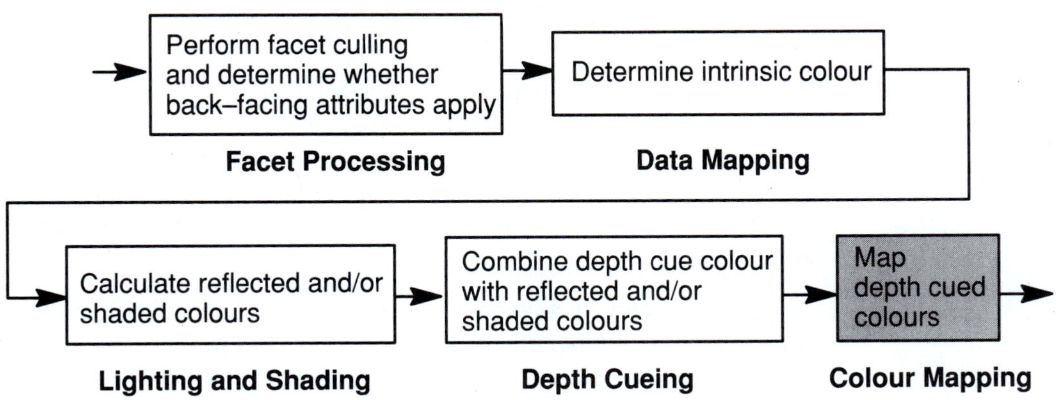

Figure 19–1. The Rendering Pipeline

Colour Mapping Methods

The colour mapping stage uses one of three colour mapping methods—true colour, pseudo colour, or pseudo-n—to determine the final output colours of a primitive.

- When the **true colour** method is in effect, PHIGS attempts to render the colours of a primitive exactly as they were processed by the previous stages of the rendering pipeline.
- When the **pseudo colour** method is in effect, PHIGS converts each output colour (from the previous stage of the rendering pipeline) to a single integer index. PHIGS uses the index to select a colour from an application-specified list of pseudo colours.
- When the **pseudo-n** method is in effect, PHIGS converts each output colour (from the previous stage of the rendering pipeline) to a set of indices. PHIGS uses these indices to select individual colour coordinates from several application-specified lists. For example, there are three lists for the RGB colour model: one for red, one for green, and one for blue values.

In all three cases, the resulting colours are workstation-dependent.

As mentioned earlier, the true colour method is the default method. The following are some common uses for the pseudo colour and pseudo-n methods:

- When shading with a small number of colours, you can use one of the pseudo colour methods to increase the number of shades used (on a system with a limited amount of available colours). For example, an application shading with one colour could use the pseudo colour method to set up a colour ramp with as many shades of that colour as it needs. In this chapter, we show how to perform gray scale shading using this method.
- An application can take advantage of the pseudo colour mapping methods when it needs to display a number of exact shades of a colour. For example, a finite element modelling application may need to display a number of exact shades of several colours to create a stress diagram. The application could store several colour ramps in a colour list and then have PHIGS convert the colours resulting from the lighting and shading and/or depth cueing stages to those exact shades.

  Note that another way to accomplish this effect would be to use vertex or facet data in the data mapping stage of the rendering pipeline (see Chapter 16, *Intrinsic Colour and Data Mapping*).

The Workstation Colour Mapping Table

The colour mapping stage uses the workstation colour mapping table (different from the workstation colour table).

The SET COLOUR MAPPING INDEX routine creates a structure element that selects an entry from the table at traversal time. The SET COLOUR MAPPING REPRESENTATION routine defines or changes an entry in the table. The C binding calling signature for the SET COLOUR MAPPING REPRESENTATION routine is as follows:

```
pset_colr_map_rep(
    Pint                    wkid,
    Pint                    index,
    const Pcolr_map_rep     *rep
);
```

where:

⟨*wkid*⟩ is the workstation identifier.

⟨*index*⟩ is an index into the workstation colour mapping table. This parameter identifies the colour mapping table entry to be modified.

⟨*rep*⟩ is the colour mapping representation for this entry. The `Pcolr_map_rep` data type is defined as follows:

```
Pcolr_map_rep
 typedef struct {
  Pint            method;       /* colour mapping method      */
  union Pcolr_map_rep_data {
   struct Pcolr_map_rep_pseudo {
     Pint         model;        /* colour model               */
     Pfloat_list  weight_vector;/* weight vector values       */
     Pcolrv_list  colrs;        /* list of colour values      */
   } pseudo;
   struct Pcolr_map_rep_pseudo_N {
     Pint         model;        /* colour model               */
     Pfloat_set   colrs;        /* list of lists of colour
                                   coordinates                */
   } pseudo_N;
```

```
        ...
        } data;         /* implementation-defined               */
    } Pcolr_map_rep;
```

where:

`method` identifies the colour mapping method. This field takes one of the following values:

1 `PCOLR_MAP_METHOD_TRUE` **True colour** outputs colours identical to those input from the previous stage of the rendering pipeline.

2 `PCOLR_MAP_METHOD_PSEUDO` **Pseudo colour** converts each colour from the previous stage of the rendering pipeline to a single integer index. PHIGS uses the index to select a colour from the list of colours specified in the `pseudo` portion of `Pcolr_map_rep`.

3 `PCOLR_MAP_METHOD_PSEUDO_N` **Pseudo colour n** converts each colour from the previous stage of the rendering pipeline to a set of indices. PHIGS uses these indices to select individual colour coordinates from the lists of coordinates specified in the `pseudo_N` portion of `Pcolr_map_rep`.

`model` identifies the colour model to use as the colour mapping colour model. This field takes one of the following values:

```
1 PMODEL_RGB
2 PMODEL_CIELUV
3 PMODEL_HSV
4 PMODEL_HLS
```

See Chapter 12, *Using Colour*, for more information on colour models.

The number of dimensions in the colour model determines how many weight vector values there are and how many coordinates there are for each colour in the colour list. For example, if the colour model is RGB, then there will be three weight vector values and three colour coordinates for each colour. In fact, all of the colour models listed for the `model` field contain three colour coordinates. The only time you will need a different number is if the implementation defines its own colour model.

`weight_vector` identifies the weight vector used for the pseudo colour method. These values are used for weighted averaging. PHIGS applies the weight vector to the colour resulting from the previous stage of the rendering pipeline in order to determine an index into the pseudo colour list.

`colrs` is defined differently for pseudo colour and pseudo-n colour mapping methods (see next section).

Using the "colrs" Field

For the **pseudo colour** method, `colrs` is a single list of colour coordinates, in `Pcolrv_list` format. Each entry in the list is specified by a number of real values. All of the colour models listed in `model` require three coordinates. For example, if the colour model is RGB, then each entry in the list has three values, representing red, green, and blue colour coordinates.

So, for the **pseudo colour** method, ⟨*rep*⟩ contains the colour model, the number of colours in the list, and a list of the colours.

For the **pseudo-n** method, there is a separate list for each dimension of the colour model. PHIGS determines a given colour by selecting one entry from each list. For example, if the colour model is RGB, there will be three lists. In this case PHIGS uses a value from the first list as the red component, a value from the second list as the blue component, and a value from the third list as the green component.

The `Pfloat_set` data type and its related data type `Pfloat_list` are defined as:

```
Pfloat_list
 typedef struct {
   Pint         num_floats;      /* number of Pfloats in list */
   Pfloat       *floats;         /* list of floats            */
} Pfloat_list;

Pfloat_set
 typedef struct {
   Pint         num_lists;       /* number of float lists     */
   Pfloat_list *floats;          /* list of float lists       */
} Pfloat_set;
```

The lists are stored consecutively in the `floats` field. Recall that PHIGS retrieves a different colour coordinate from each list. So, for the RGB colour model you would store the values as follows for a list with 10 colours: red1, red2, ..., red10, green1, green2, ..., green10, blue1, blue2, ..., blue10.

The Weight Vector

This section describes how PHIGS uses the weight vector to select an entry from the application's pseudo colour list. For simplicity, let's assume the colour model is RGB. This means that each colour value has three colour coordinates and that there are three values for the weight vector.

During traversal, when pseudo colour mapping is in effect, PHIGS uses the following procedure to achieve the mapping from an RGB colour output by the previous stage of the rendering pipeline to an entry in the list of pseudo colours. The values *R*, *G*, and *B* represent the coordinates of the colour output from the previous stage of the rendering pipeline.

1. If the rendering colour model is different from the colour mapping colour model, convert the colour to the colour mapping colour model.

2. If necessary, normalize the colour components so that each is in the range [0, 1], inclusive.

3. Normalize the weight vector, W, by dividing it by the sum of its components, (W1 + W2 + W3). This ensures that the sum of the weight vector components will not exceed 1.0.

4. Calculate the following, rounded to the nearest integer:

   $$J = (L - 1)(\mathrm{W1} * R + \mathrm{W2} * G + \mathrm{W3} * B) + 1$$

   where *L* is the number of colours in the pseudo colour list; W1, W2, and W3 are the components of the weight vector; and *R*, *G*, and *B* are the output RGB colour values at any given point on the primitive.

5. Use *J* as an index to select one of the entries in the list of pseudo colours.

6. Output the selected colour.

PHIGS uses the absolute values of the weight vector components. If the application supplies the weight vector (0.0, 0.0, 0.0), all colours will resolve to the first colour in the pseudo colour range supplied in the data record.

Example—Gray-Scale Shading

The example described in this section uses the RGB colour model and converts RGB colour values from the lighting and shading stage of the rendering pipeline to varying shades of gray (from dark gray to white). The intensity of the gray at any point on the primitive depends on the colour of the primitive after it has passed through the lighting and shading and depth cue stages.

You can experiment with gray-scale shading as an alternative to the true colour mapping method. Colour gradations caused by lighting and shading can be very smooth, depending on the size of your pseudo colour list (a colour list with 100 colours gives good results).

This example uses the same sphere discussed in Chapter 17, *Lighting and Shading* in the section entitled "Lighting Example 2—Smooth Shading with Vertex Normals," to demonstrate specular highlighting. We use more fill area primitives (50 around the axis as opposed to 20 in the sphere in Chapter 17) in order to achieve a smoother image. Colour plate 7 (see colour insert) shows the image created from this example.

The following subsections describe how the program works.

Defining an Entry in the Colour Mapping Table

This example redefines entry 1 in the workstation colour mapping table as follows:

- Colour mapping method = pseudo colour
- Weight vector = (0.3, 0.59, 0.11) (more about this later)
- Pseudo colour list = a list of 100 colours consisting of a "ramp" from black to white

The program uses a subroutine named `ColourMap1` for defining the entries in the colour mapping table. The following fragment shows how `ColourMap1` builds the colour list and defines workstation colour mapping table entry 1:

```
Pint          WorkID, CMapEntry = 1, i, j = 0;
Pcolr_map_rep rep;
Pfloat        red, green, blue;
Pfloat        weight_vector[3];

/* **** set colour mapping representation 1 ************ */

ColourMap1() /* create a gray-scale ramp */
{
   rep.method = PCOLR_MAP_METHOD_PSEUDO;
   rep.pseudo.model = PMODEL_RGB;           /* RGB colour model */
   rep.pseudo.weight_vector.num_floats = 3;
   weight_vector[0] = 0.3;                  /* red value    */
   weight_vector[1] = 0.59;                 /* green value  */
   weight_vector[2] = 0.11;                 /* blue value   */
   rep.pseudo.weight_vector.floats = weight_vector;
   rep.pseudo.colrs.num_colrs = 100;

   red = 0.0; green = 0.0; blue = 0.0;

   for (i = 0; i < 100; i++) {
      red = red+0.01;           /* increase red from 0.0 to 1.0    */
      green = green+0.01;       /* increase green from 0.0 to 1.0  */
      blue = blue+0.01;         /* increase blue from 0.0 to 1.0   */
      if (red > 1.0) red = 1.0;
      if (green > 1.0) green = 1.0;
      if (blue > 1.0) blue = 1.0;
      rep.pseudo.colrs.colrs.colr_reps.rgb[j].red = red;
      rep.pseudo.colrs.colrs.colr_reps.rgb[j].green = green;
      rep.pseudo.colrs.colrs.colr_reps.rgb[j].blue = blue;
      j=j+1
   }

rep.pseudo.colrs.num_colrs = 1;          /* one colour list         */
pset_colr_map_rep(WorkID, index, &rep); /* set colour mapping rep. */

} /* end ColourMap1 */
```

Selecting an Entry from the Colour Mapping Table

In order to use an entry in the colour mapping table, you must insert a *set colour mapping index* structure element into the appropriate structure:

```
Pint Scene, CMapEntry = 1;

popen_struct(Scene);                /* open structure                 */
pset_colr_map_ind(CMapEntry);       /* set colour mapping index       */
...
pclose_struct();                    /* close structure                */
```

Using the Weight Factor

As we mentioned earlier, this example uses a weight factor of (0.3, 0.59, 0.11). Now let's see how this weight factor affects a particular RGB colour value that has just come from the lighting and shading and depth cueing stages. We will arbitrarily choose a light blue colour (0.4, 0.4, 0.8).

As described in "The Weight Vector" section earlier in this chapter, PHIGS uses the following formula to calculate the index (J) into the colour list:

$$J = (L - 1) (\mathrm{W1} * R + \mathrm{W2} * G + \mathrm{W3} * B) + 1$$

With a 100-element pseudo colour list, a weight vector of (0.3, 0.59, 0.11), and RGB colour values of (0.4, 0.4, 0.8), we get the following solution to the equation:

$$J = (100 - 1) (0.3*0.4 + 0.59*0.4 + 0.11*0.8) + 1$$

$$J = 99 * (0.12 + 0.236 + 0.088) + 1$$

$$J = 99 * 0.444 + 1$$

$$J = 44.956$$

PHIGS rounds the value to the nearest integer and uses that number as the index into the colour list. In this case the entry is 45, which translates to (0.44, 0.44, 0.44) in our pseudo colour list.

Since the weight vector components in this example add up to 1.0, we don't have to consider the fact that PHIGS normalizes the weight vector before beginning the calculations.

You can see that as you give different values to the weight vector, it will change the resulting index value (*J*). In this case we use a weight vector of (0.3, 0.59, 0.11) because it closely imitates how our eyes react to red, green, and blue light, respectively. We see green light the best, and blue registers the least amount. The vector (0.3, 0.59, 0.11) is actually the weight vector used to create the luminance vector in the NTSC broadcast standard (used in television broadcasting).

Differences between Implementations

PHIGS expects an implementation to support the *true colour* colour mapping method. The other two methods are optional. Check your implementation documentation to see which methods are supported, and check for any special details about how the implementation performs colour mapping. The following are some areas to check:

- How many colour mapping methods are supported? Use INQUIRE COLOUR MAPPING FACILITIES to find out.
- How many entries are in the colour mapping table? Use INQUIRE LIST OF COLOUR MAPPING INDICES or INQUIRE WORKSTATION STATE TABLE LENGTHS PLUS to find out.
- What is the total number of colours available to the implementation? This will depend on the number of colours that the device can display simultaneously. For example, on some implementations the total number of pseudo colours defined across all entries of the workstation colour mapping table cannot exceed the number of colours defined in the workstation colour table. Use INQUIRE COLOUR FACILITIES.
- Can the first entry be modified by the application? PHIGS suggests that the first entry should not be modifiable.
- What is the default colour mapping method that the implementation puts into effect when the application opens a workstation that supports colour mapping? Use INQUIRE PREDEFINED COLOUR MAPPING REPRESENTATION.
- Can you use more than one colour mapping method per traversal? Since colour mapping may change the entries in the device's colour map(s), changing the colour mapping method during traversal could affect colours rendered before the change. In other words, it might have the effect of changing the colours of primitives already displayed on the screen.

  Some implementations support multiple colour mapping methods per traversal. This allows an application to render a scene with different colour mapping representations. For example, you could render most of a scene with the *true colour* colour mapping method and then render one particular object using the *pseudo colour* mapping method.

- Does the implementation process the view background colour through the colour mapping stage? Some implementations process the view background colour the same as primitive colours. This means that the background colour will get modified when it passes through the colour mapping stage for the pseudo colour methods. If this is true, then you can make allowances by setting the first entry in the pseudo colour list to the desired background colour. Then make sure that the background colour always uses the first entry in the list. The next section describes this in more detail.

The Background Colour

If your implementation processes the background colour through the colour mapping stage, then you can use the technique described here to ensure getting the right background colour every time.

- First, make sure that the application program uses a black view background colour. This is the default on many systems.
- Then, set the first entry in the pseudo colour list to the colour you want to use for the background colour.

When PHIGS processes the colour black (0.0, 0.0, 0.0) through the colour mapping stage, we get entry 1 in the pseudo colour list. For example, assuming we have a pseudo colour list of 152, PHIGS processes a colour of black as follows:

$$J = (152 - 1) (1.0*(0.0) + 0.0*0.0 + 0.0*0.0) + 1$$

$$J = 1.0$$

So, whatever colour you used for the first entry in the pseudo colour list will be the entry used for the background colour.

Chapter 20

B–Splines

Introduction

In many solid modelling software packages, complex objects are made by combining simpler objects such as cubes, spheres, cones, cylinders, and so forth. In addition, many solid modellers allow the user to specify free-form surfaces. If the system uses a different primitive for each of these shapes, a large amount of code is needed to handle combining these primitives into the final object. **B-splines** provide a solution to this problem. With B-splines, it is possible to represent both the simple geometric shapes and the free-form surfaces. Thus, the solid modeller needs to handle only one primitive for all objects.

This chapter discusses PHIGS' implementation of B-splines, and does not address much theory. If you desire more information, these introductory texts are recommended:

- Foley, J. D., and Van Dam, A. (1990). *Computer Graphics: Principles and Practices*, 2nd ed., Reading, MA: Addison-Wesley.
- Newman W.F., and Sproull, R.F. (1979). *Principles of Interactive Computer Graphics*, Ch.21, New York, NY: McGraw-Hill.
- Rogers, D. F., and Alan, J. A. (1976). *Mathematical Elements for Computer Graphics*, Chs, 4–6, New York, NY: McGraw-Hill.

More detailed information can be found in Volume 17 of the 1985 SIGGRAPH course notes.

B-splines have many useful mathematical properties that can be exploited in graphics applications:

- A non-rational B-spline curve or surface can be rotated, translated, and scaled in XY or XYZ space by applying the transformation matrix only to the control points.
- B-spline surfaces are often rendered using facets. It is possible to compute a true surface normal at each vertex of each facet.
- Each segment of a curve or each patch of a surface lies within the convex hull of the control points affecting that segment or patch.
- It is possible to add control points to a B-spline curve or surface without changing the order of the B-spline.
- Moving a control point affects the curve or surface only in the vicinity of the control point.
- B-splines can represent any piecewise polynomial that satisfies the continuity constraints at the boundaries between segments/patches. In particular, **Bezier patches** are a special case of a B-spline with the number of knots at the start and end of the parameter range equal to the order and no other knots.
- There are several ways to compute points along a B-spline without actually evaluating the polynomial functions repeatedly. These ways include *forward differencing* and *recursive subdivision*.

Because the spline representation is so much more compact than a filled-area representation, there are other advantages as well. For example:

- Much more of a complex object or precomputed animated sequence will fit in main memory at one time. This results in increased speed because less use is made of the virtual memory system of the host.
- If spline calculations are done in a graphics accelerator, there is less data to send from the host to the accelerator.

A graphics accelerator may perform the job of generating the filled-area mesh needed to display the surface, thus saving the host from having to do this job and probably doing the job faster than the host could do it. Also, since the graphics accelerator does the mesh computation, the resolution at display time is not fixed in the database.

The exception to this is when Bezier patches are combined: The result is still a Bezier curve or surface, but there are now interior knots of multiplicity *order* −1.

Yet another advantage to the spline representation is the ability to use trimming curves. These are curves that allow you to "trim off" portions of a spline surface.

In the remainder of this chapter, please bear with us as we introduce a lot of jargon; discussions about splines seem to have their own unique vocabulary.

What's a B-Spline Look Like, Anyway?

The mathematical concept of the spline comes from its physical counterpart: the draftsman's spline. This is a long, narrow strip of wood, plastic, or other flexible material that is used like a user-modifiable French curve. The spline is held in place by lead weights, called *ducks*. When the number and location of the ducks are varied, the spline can be made to pass through the desired data points. Thus, the spline describes smooth curves between the anchored points.

There are many forms of splines: B-splines, Bezier splines, interpolating splines, Hermite splines, etc. PHIGS supports (non-uniform, non-rational, and rational) B-splines and all subsets of B-splines, e.g., Bezier splines. The "B" in the name "B-spline" stands for "basis," because B-splines form a basis of the spline vector space.

As mentioned, B-splines can be used to create free-form curves and surfaces. The mathematically defined curve or surface is defined and/or influenced by a set of points called control points (analogous to the ducks in the physical system), so named because the points control the shape of the curve or surface.

Splines are polynomial curves placed end to end: They are piecewise polynomials. The curves themselves can have varying degrees; that is, the highest exponent in the polynomial equation can be

- 1, in which case the curve is **linear**
- 2, in which case the curve is **quadratic**
- 3, in which case the curve is **cubic**
- 4, in which case the curve is **quartic**
- 5, in which case the curve is **quintic**

The order of a spline curve is 1 greater than the degree of polynomial required to build it (see Table 20–1).

Table 20–1. Spline Orders

Spline Order Name	Degree	Order
Linear	1	2
Quadratic	2	3
Cubic	3	4
Quartic	4	5
Quintic	5	6

Thus, a quintic spline is a sixth-order curve.

Use INQUIRE B-SPLINE SURFACE FACILITIES and INQUIRE CURVE FACILITIES to determine the maximum order supported by the implementation.

The PHIGS routine to draw a spline curve is NON-UNIFORM B-SPLINE CURVE 3:

```
pnon_uniform_b_spline_curve3(
    const Pcurve_geom_spline    *curve_spline
);
```

where:

⟨*curve_spline*⟩ is a pointer to a structure of type `Pcurve_geom_spline`:

```
typedef struct {
    Pint                    order;
    Pfloat_list             knots;
    Pfloat                  low_limit;
    Pfloat                  high_limit;
    Prationality            rationality;
    Pctrl_point3_list       ctrl_points;
} Pcurve_geom_spline
```

where:

`order` is an integer that specifies the spline order, as described above.

`knots` specifies the knot vector. Knots will be covered later in the chapter. The `Pfloat_list` type is

```
typedef struct {
    Pint        num_floats;
    Pfloat      *floats;
} Pfloat_list;
```

`low_limit` and `high_limit` specify the beginning and ending points for the independent variable *t* in the parametric equations used to calculate the spline curve.

`rationality` specifies whether the spline curve is to be rational or non-rational. Rationality is also covered later in the chapter. The `Prationality` type is

```
typedef enum {
    PB_SPLINE_NON_RATIONAL;
    PB_SPLINE_RATIONAL;
} Prationality;
```

`ctrl_points` specifies the size of the control point array, and the array's values themselves. The `Pctrl_point3_list` type is

```
typedef struct {
    Pint            num_points;
    Ppoint3_ptr     points;
} Pctrl_point3_list;
```

The `Ppoint3_ptr` type is

```
typedef union {
  Ppoint3       *point3;      /* standard 3D point: XYZ */
  Phomo_point4  *homo_point4;  /* 3D homogeneous point: XYZW */
} Ppoint3_ptr;
```

The `Phomo_point4` type is

```
typedef struct {
    Pfloat      wx;   /* wx coordinate           */
    Pfloat      wy;   /* wy coordinate           */
    Pfloat      wz;   /* wz coordinate           */
    Pfloat      w;    /* homogenous coordinate   */
} Phomo_point4;
```

Order, Please?

The following code fragment shows the orders of splines that PHIGS supports: linear, quadratic, cubic, quartic, and quintic—orders 2, 3, 4, 5, and 6, respectively. There are seven control points.

```
...
Pcurve_geom_spline  MyCurve;
Pfloat              KnotVectorData[13];
static Ppoint3      ControlPointData[7] = {
                    {0.1, 0.3, 0.0},
                    {0.3, 0.7, 0.0},
                    {0.4, 0.4, 0.0},
                    {0.5, 0.6, 0.0},
                    {0.6, 0.3, 0.0},
                    {0.8, 0.4, 0.0},
                    {0.9, 0.6, 0.0}};
...
MyCurve.order = 6;                          /* quintic */
MakeKnotVector(KnotVectorData);             /* user routine does knots */
MyCurve.knots.num_floats = 13;
MyCurve.knots.floats = KnotVectorData;
MyCurve.low_limit = 0.0;
MyCurve.high_limit = 8.0;
MyCurve.rationality = PB_SPLINE_NON_RATIONAL;
MyCurve.ctrl_points.num_points = 7;
MyCurve.ctrl_points.points.point = ControlPointData;
pnon_uniform_b_spline_curve3(&MyCurve);
...
```

Figure 20–1 shows what the output of such a program could look like.

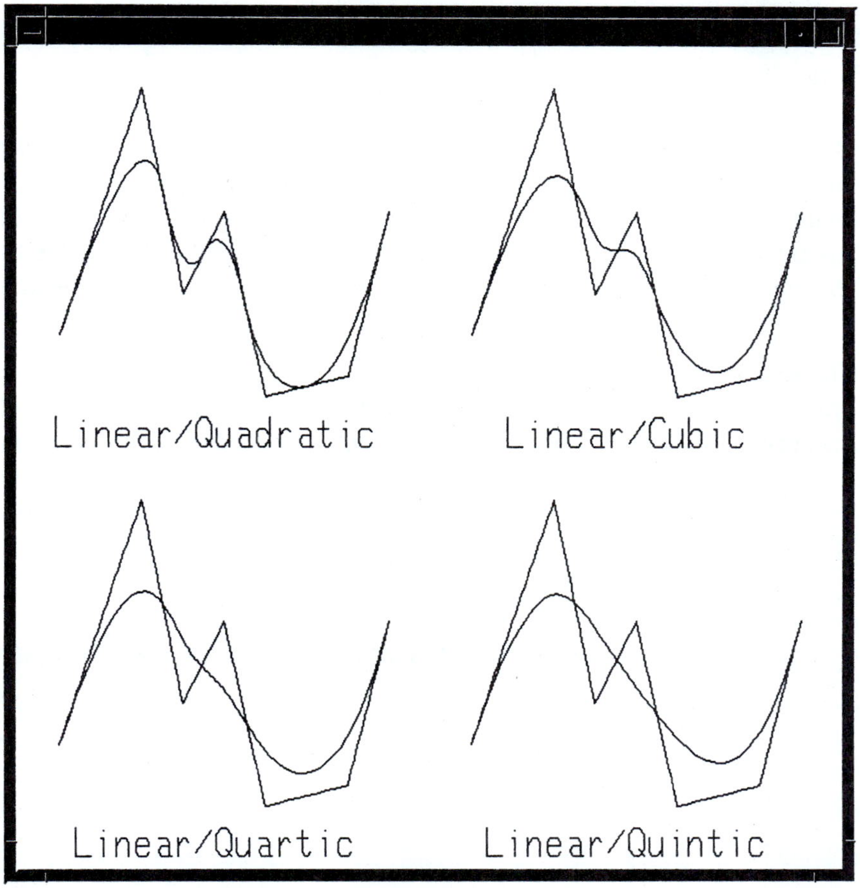

Figure 20–1. Linear, Quadratic, Cubic, Quartic, and Quintic B-Splines

As you can see, the higher the order of the curve, the "tighter" it is; in other words, the curve gets farther from the control points. By the way, the control points' locations are shown by the endpoints of the segments in the linear spline.

Notice how the linear spline is nothing more than a connect-the-dots exercise. You could get the same effect with a polyline. However, there are some significant advantages to straight lines having a spline representation. One such advantage is that you don't have to include a check for a special case: "If linear, then polyline, else spline"; a spline will work regardless.

Local Controllability

One nice feature of B-splines is that they allow local control. That is, when one part of the curve is changed, the others remain unchanged. In a real-world situation of designing a mechanical part, it would indeed be frustrating to have the shape *almost* right—where only one small area needs its shape updated but when you update that small area, the rest of the object changes shape. B-splines provide the ability to limit changes to a relatively small region.

The screen image in Figure 20–2 illustrates this local controllability. Five third-order (quadratic) spline curves were drawn, each with ten control points. The sets of control points for the curves are identical for each curve except for the *y* value of the seventh point, which goes from 0.1 through 0.5. You'll notice that the only part of the curve that is different from rendition to rendition is the part immediately surrounding the relocated control point.

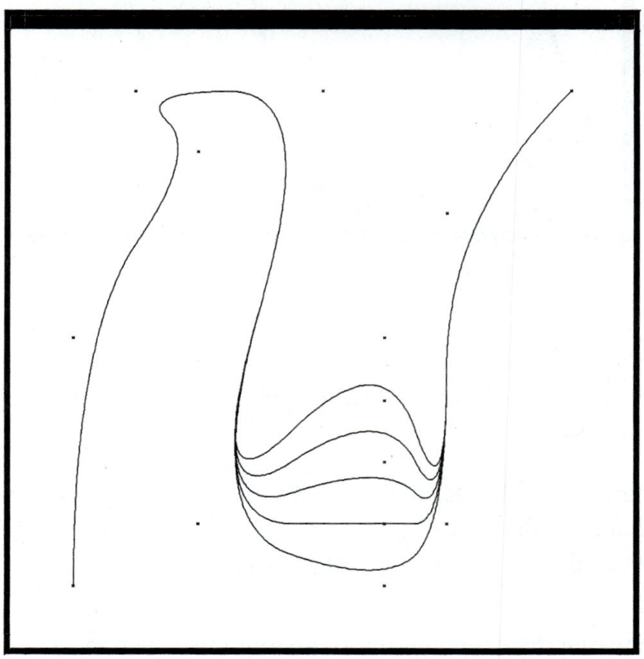

Figure 20–2. Local Control in B-Spline Curves

Multiplicity of Control Points

Judging from the previous two examples, you might get the impression that control points can be just about anywhere. That is true: They can even be *on top of one another*.

If you have a spline curve controlled by a certain set of control points, each point controls the curve a certain amount. You can increase the amount of influence at a specific location or in a certain direction by having control points close together. The ultimate in togetherness is having two or more points at exactly the same location; something slightly unusual happens in such a case.

If you experiment with the previous examples, you may notice that a curve gets "sharper"—its radius of curvature decreases—where multiple control points are close together. In the extreme case, where multiple control points are coincident, the radius of curvature of the curve can go to zero. This results in a **cusp**, or slope discontinuity, in the curve. At this sharp point the slope of the curve is undefined.

The number of control points that must be coincident in order to cause a discontinuity varies with the order of the curve: It is one less than the order of the curve (or, equal to the degree of the curve). Thus, a linear curve, whose order is 2, need only have one coincident point at each point in order to generate a discontinuity. In other words, *every* point makes a discontinuity. A quadratic curve, whose order is 3, needs two coincident points; a cubic curve, whose order is 4, needs three; a quartic curve whose order is 5, needs four; and a quintic curve, whose order is 6, needs five.

A Mathematical Digression

In this section, we go deeper into the mathematical foundation of B-spline curves. Understanding this section is not necessary in order to use B-splines, but the math is presented in case you want to see some of the derivations of the spline concepts.

It was stated previously that B-splines can be used to represent both curves and surfaces. To continue in the same vein as the rest of the chapter, the simpler concepts—spline curves—are dealt with first. Spline surfaces (simply, two-dimensional extensions of spline curves) are covered later. Note that in this context, a spline curve is considered one-dimensional because it is a line, even though the line can be curved and may extend into two or three dimensions. In the same way, a spline *surface* is considered two-dimensional because it is a plane, even though it may extend into three dimensions and may be curved in space.

Parametric Curves

Curves drawn by graphics applications are frequently drawn parametrically. With this scheme, the points along a curve in the xy plane are described by two functions, say $x(t)$ and $y(t)$, where t is the parameter that is allowed to vary over some range, often from 0 to 1. For each value of t, it is possible to compute a value for x and a value for y. A curve in three-dimensional space is described by three functions, $x(t)$, $y(t)$, and $z(t)$. The use of parametric curves permits curves that are multivalued, and it avoids problems with portions of curves having infinite slope.

Polynomials are frequently used to define parametric curves. In this case, the functions $x(t)$, $y(t)$, and $z(t)$ are polynomials in t. The largest exponent in the polynomial determines the degree of the polynomial. If the largest exponent is 5, the polynomial is quintic. Quintic polynomials are sufficient for most graphics applications. They are a good compromise when such factors as computational stability, computational speed, memory requirements, and the ability to represent arbitrary curves are considered.

In applications where complex or free-form curves and surfaces are required, it is not possible for one parametric curve to represent adequately the desired curve. In these cases, the desired curve is represented by several parametric curves joined together. For example, the first section of the curve may be represented by one set of polynomials, say $x_1(t)$, $y_1(t)$, $z_1(t)$, with t varying from 0 to 1, and the last section of the curve may be represented by a second set of polynomials, say $x_2(t)$, $y_2(t)$, $z_2(t)$, with t varying from 1 to 2. This is called a **piecewise polynomial curve**, and the individual parametric curves are referred to as **segments**.

Continuity

Another important consideration in curve definition includes the order (or degree) of continuity at the points where curve segments meet:

- Zero-order (or "positional") continuity means that the two curves involved merely touch, or have the same value at the transition point. Zero-order continuity is used to define sharp edges.
- First-order continuity means that the first derivatives (with respect to the parameter) of the meeting curves are equal at the transition point. Geometrically, this can usually be seen as equal slopes in the curves where they meet. However, in some unusual cases (like the cusp example), there can be apparent discontinuities in XYZ space even though the derivatives with respect to the parameter are continuous (and equal to 0).

- Higher-order continuity is achieved when higher-order derivatives (with respect to the parameter) are constant across the meeting point; in general, a transition is said to have *n*th-order continuity if all derivatives up to the *n*th derivatives are equal for both curve segments at the point where they meet.

In other words:

- If both segments give the same values for x, y, and z at the joint, the curve has **positional continuity** across the joint.
- If, in addition, the *slope* of both segments is the same at the joint, the curve has **first-derivative continuity** at the joint.
- If, in addition, the *rate of change of the slope* of the two segments is the same at the joint, the curve has **second -derivative continuity** at the joint. With quintic polynomials, it is possible to get fourth-derivative continuity at the joints. This is adequate for many graphics applications and is therefore the highest-degree curve supported by PHIGS.

The higher the degree of the polynomials used in the segments, the higher the degree of continuity attainable at the joints. The higher the order of continuity at such joints, the smoother the transition will appear. The order of continuity possible at joints for general curves is proportional to the order of the polynomials used to represent the curve segments. Therefore, higher-order polynomials are desirable to produce smooth joints (although smooth joints can be produced with lower-order polynomials also, with proper control point location).

However, higher-order polynomials do have drawbacks. One major disadvantage is that they tend to vary more severely and may amplify minor variations in control point location, or even oscillate between joints. In most cases, it is desirable for splines to have a "variation-diminishing" effect, i.e., the curve should smooth small variations in the location of the control points. Quintic polynomials offer a good compromise of smoothness, versatility, and joint continuity, and are most often used for splines.

Polynomials and B-Splines

So what do polynomial curves have to do with B-splines? B-splines are simply piecewise polynomial functions that can be specified to have the desired continuity at the joints between segments. B-splines can be specified in terms of three parameters:

- The **order**, which is simply one plus the degree of the desired polynomial. For example, the order of a quintic polynomial is six.

- A knot vector, which is the set of values of the parameter t at which joints occur (B-splines are parametric curves; the parameter is t). If a value occurs only once in a knot vector, it is referred to as a **single knot**. If the value occurs n times, the knot is said to have a multiplicity of n. For example, the knot vector [0, 0, 0, 1, 2, 3, 4, 4, 4] specifies several things:
  - That the ends of the curve are at $t = 0$ and $t = 4$
  - There are **segments** between 0 and 1, 1 and 2, 2 and 3, and 3 and 4
  - There are **joints** between segments at $t = 1$, $t = 2$, and $t = 3$
  - The **multiplicities** of the endpoints (0 and 4) are 3; there are three 0s and three 4s. The multiplicities of the points at the segment joints are all 1.
- A set of control points, which, as we've seen, affects the shape of the resultant curve.

Why would anyone want more than one knot at a joint? This is the way that continuity is controlled at the joint (or the end). The number of knots at a point must be less than or equal to the order of the curve. If a single knot occurs at a point, the curve has continuity through the (⟨*order*⟩ – 2)th-derivative at that point. For each additional knot at the joint, the continuity is reduced by one derivative. For example, if the order is 4, the curve has second-derivative continuity at single knots, first-derivative continuity at double knots, positional continuity at triple knots, and no continuity at knots of multiplicity four. *No* continuity? In this case, the position of the curve can be specified without regard to the adjoining segment.

One other aspect of knot vectors needs to be explained. Knots are either uniform or nonuniform. Uniform knots occur when all the differences between any two adjacent pairs of values (which are not endpoints) in the knot vector are the same. The first and last values in the knot vector are allowed to occur more than once. For example, the knot vector [0, 0, 0, 1, 2, 3, 4, 4, 4] specifies uniform knots. The knot vectors [0, 0, 0, 1, 1, 2, 2, 3, 3, 4, 4, 4] and [0, 0, 0, 1, 3, 4, 4, 4] specify nonuniform knots.

There are many reasons for wanting the ability to specify nonuniform knots. Among these are the ability to control the continuity at each joint, the ability to control how much the parameter changes across each segment, and the ability to split segments into smaller pieces.

Specification of the order and knot vector for a B-spline curve defines a set of blending functions used to form the final curve. The number of blending functions for each segment is always equal to the order of the B-spline. Furthermore, each blending function is nonzero only over a very limited range. A blending function that starts on knot value i ends on knot value i +

⟨*order*⟩. For example, if ⟨*order*⟩ = 4 and the knot vector is [0, 0, 0, 0, 1, 2, 3, 4, 4, 4, 4], the first blending function starts at 0 and ends at 1, the second blending function starts a 0 and ends at 2, the third blending function starts at 0 and ends at 3, the fourth starts at 0 and ends at 4, the fifth starts at 1 and ends at 4, and so on. Figure 20–3 illustrates this.

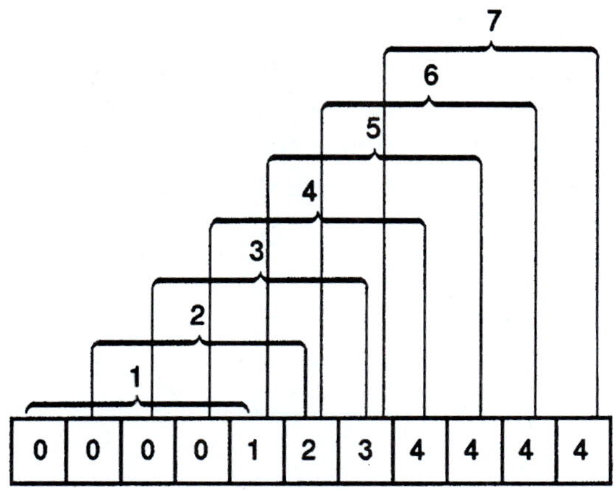

Figure 20–3. Blending Functions

It is also worth noting that the blending functions sum to unity over the entire parameter range. For example, the point at the end of a curve is 100% controlled by the first knot; the point at the first joint is 75% controlled by knot 1 and 25% by knot 2; the point at the second joint, 50% by knot 1, 25% each by knots 2 and 3; the point, the point and the third joint, 25% by each of the first 4 knots; and so forth.

So how is the final curve specified? A weight is assigned to each blending function. The final curve is the weighted sum of the blending functions. For each function $x(t)$, $y(t)$, and $z(t)$, the weights are the x, y, and z coordinates of the control points. The control points are points in XYZ space that the B-spline curve should be close to. Just *how* close depends on the multiplicity of the knots at each joint. If knots of multiplicity equal to the order are specified at the start and end of the B-spline, the curve will go through the first and last control points. The shape of the B-spline curve can be manipulated by moving the control points around. And here is an important point: *The number of control points for a B-spline curve is equal to the number of knots minus the order.*

Knot Vectors

A knot vector is a series of values that control how the blending functions are applied to the control points. In all cases of knot vector values x_i, the relationship $x_i \leq x_{i+1}$ holds for all x_i. Thus, for example, [0, 1, 2, 3, 4] or [0, 0, 0, 1, 2, 3, 3, 3] are valid knot vectors, but [0, 1, 2, 3, 2, 3, 4] is not.

How do you figure out what the values in the knot vector should be? Say, for example, that you want to design the shape of a mechanical part: one jaw of a standard staple remover. You have a rough idea of its shape, in an angular sort of way, and what you want is a spline to smooth out these rough edges. You make a simple sketch of your idea, which looks like this:

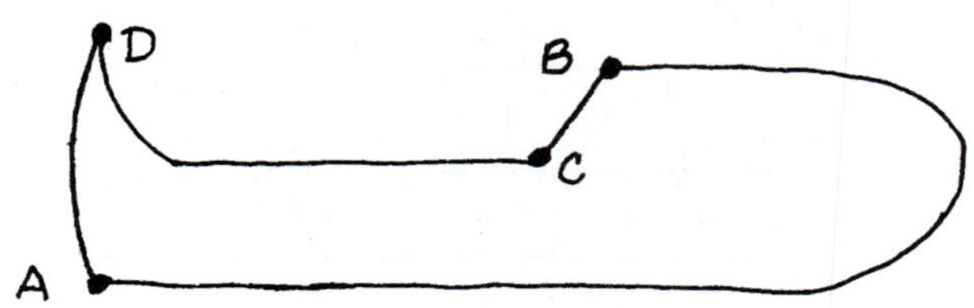

Figure 20–4. Hand-drawn Sketch of Staple-Remover's Jaw

From the previous example program, is it obvious that a linear spline is not going to be enough; it makes no curves at all. We must use at least a quadratic spline in order to get the curves: Let's say quadratic is sufficient. But there *are* some straight areas on the pattern. How can you get one curve to be partly quadratic and partly linear? This is where knot vectors come in.

In our example of a staple-remover jaw, it might be easier to do the various sections of the shape one at a time and then connect them together. Let's start at the lower left-hand corner. There are four sections needed (there could be more or less, but let's go with four):

- The section from A to B. This contains a straight section, a curve, and another straight section.
- The section from B to C. This is a simple straight section.

- The section from C to D. This has a straight part followed by a curve.
- The section from D back to A. This is one curve.

From A to B

As mentioned, the section from A to B is a curve between two straight segments. We need to figure out how many knots we need in the knot vector for this section.

A quadratic spline (unless altered by an appropriate knot vector) has osculation points at the midpoints of the lines connecting the control points. That is, the midpoint of each line composing the polygon of control points is tangent to the quadratic curve (this is illustrated earlier in the chapter in Figure 20–2). This has two implications in our application:

- There must be a control point at each end of each straight section. Since there are two straight sections (see Figure 20–4), there must be four control points for the straight parts.
- There must be *two* control points that cause the curved part. One is insufficient because the quadratic curve, attempting to be tangent to every line of the enclosing control point polygon, would cause curves in the parts we want to be straight.

The result of the above is that there must be six control points—three on the bottom, three on the top, thus (we are using only *x* and *y* data; *z* isn't needed, because it's a 2D curve, and *w* isn't needed, because it's a non-rational spline):

```
static Ppoint3      ControlPointData1[6] = {
                    {0.1, 0.1, 0.0},
                    {0.7, 0.1, 0.0},
                    {0.9, 0.1, 0.0},
                    {0.9, 0.3, 0.0},
                    {0.7, 0.3, 0.0},
                    {0.6, 0.3, 0.0}};
```

Note that the first three points are collinear, as are the last three.

A Rule

When working with splines, one rule must always be followed. This rule was stated earlier in this chapter in the section titled "A Mathematical Digression." However, since that section was optional reading, the rule is restated here:

$$\langle knots \rangle = \langle control\_points \rangle + \langle order \rangle$$

In this part of the example:

- We have six control points: $\langle control\_points \rangle = 6$.
- We want a quadratic curve: $\langle order \rangle = 3$.
- The required number of knots: $\langle knots \rangle = 6 + 3 = 9$.

Our example requires four segments for this portion of the staple-remover jaw:

- The first straight part
- The first half of the curved part (up to the point where the curve is tangent to the vertical line connecting the third and fourth control points)
- The second half of the curved part (from the point where the curve is tangent to the vertical line to the second straight part)
- The second straight part

Knot vectors typically go from 0 through the number of segments in the curve. Since we have four segments in this part of the curve, the values should go from 0 to 4. But we already saw that 9 knots are required; 0 through 4 only gives us 5. Where do the others come from?

Unless they use an appropriate knot vector, non-linear spline curves do not touch the endpoints of the frame of control points. This touching of the ends can be ensured by duplicating the first and last knots to a multiplicity equal to the order of the curve. Since our curve is of order three, the first and last knots should exist in triplicate.

Finally, then, the knot vector for the first section of the outline of the staple-remover jaw looks like this: [0, 0, 0, 1, 2, 3, 4, 4, 4]. The curve itself, based on the above control points and knot vector, looks like the image in Figure 20–5.

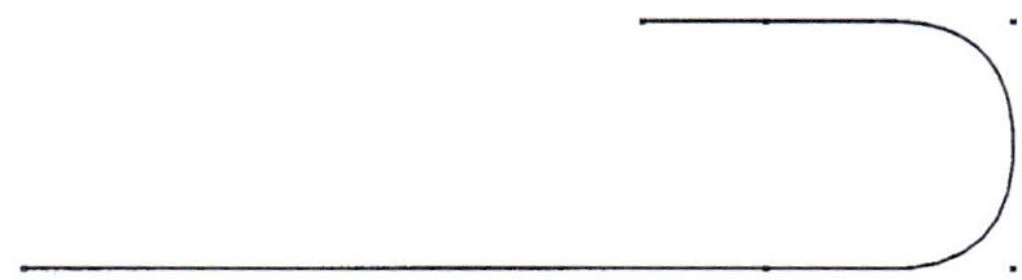

Figure 20–5. Staple-Remover Jaw: Part I

From B to C

The second section of the outline of the staple-remover jaw is simpler than the first. It consists of one straight line. However, two control points are not sufficient. Since this is a quadratic curve, there need to be two sections comprising the defining polygon of control points, so the two endpoints of the curve can be tangent to the two segments.

In this case, just put an extra control point somewhere between the two ends; just where doesn't matter, as long as they are collinear. They must be collinear to ensure a straight line.

The control points should be

```
static Ppoint3       ControlPointData2[3] = {
                     {0.6,  0.3,  0.0},
                     {0.55, 0.25, 0.0},
                     {0.5,  0.2,  0.0}};
```

Again, the precise placement of the middle control point is not cast in concrete; it can be anywhere between the other two, as long as they are collinear.

And because ⟨*knots*⟩ = ⟨*control_points*⟩ + ⟨*order*⟩, we need six knots. There is only one span between the endpoints; thus, the knot vector's values go from 0 to 1. The endpoints must be in triplicate to ensure the curve reaching them. The resultant knot vector is [0, 0, 0, 1, 1, 1]. Figure 20–6 shows the second portion of the curve.

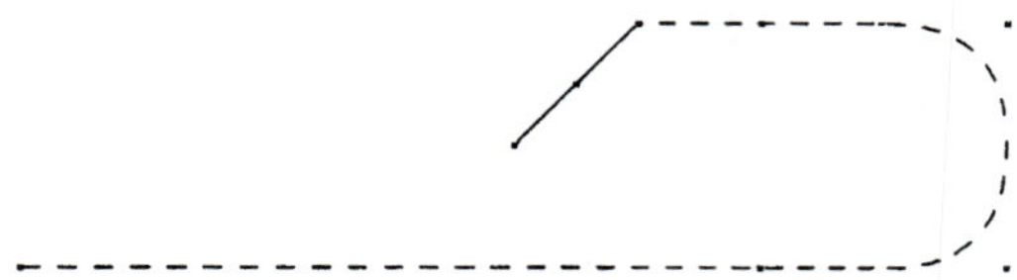

Figure 20–6. Staple-Remover Jaw: Part II

From C to D

The third section of the outline of the staple-remover jaw consists of a straight portion followed by one curve. Similar to the first section (from A to B), a straight line smoothly connected to a curve requires three collinear points for the straight part, and then the point(s) for the curved part.

The control points should be

```
static Ppoint3        ControlPointData3[4] = {
                      {0.5,  0.2, 0.0},
                      {0.2,  0.2, 0.0},
                      {0.12, 0.2, 0.0},
                      {0.1,  0.3, 0.0}};
```

Because ⟨*knots*⟩ = ⟨*control_points*⟩ + ⟨*order*⟩, we need seven knots. There are two spans between the endpoints; thus, the knot vector's values go from 0 to 2. As usual with a quadratic curve, the endpoints must be in triplicate to ensure the curve reaching them. The resultant knot vector is [0, 0, 0, 1, 2, 2, 2]. Figure 20–7 shows the third portion of the curve.

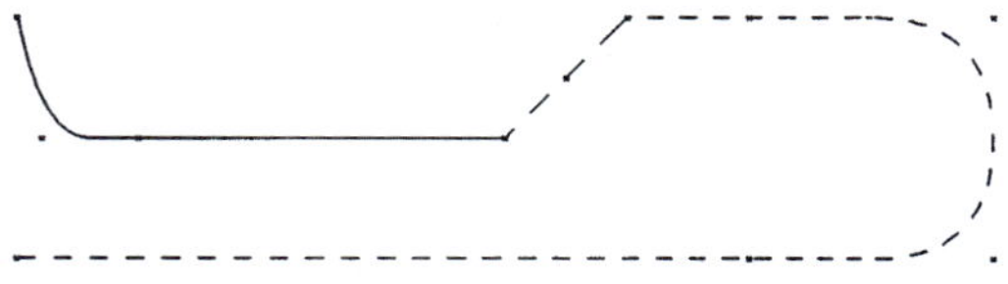

Figure 20–7. Staple-Remover Jaw: Part III

From D Back to A

The fourth section of the outline of the staple-remover jaw consists of one curve. This section of the jaw's outline has no straight sections; thus, there is no need for collinear points. The control points should be

```
static Ppoint3       ControlPointData4[3] = {
                     {0.1,   0.3,  0.0},
                     {0.07,  0.2,  0.0},
                     {0.1,   0.1,  0.0}};
```

There is only one segment, even though it is curved; thus, the knot vector's values go from 0 to 1. The resultant knot vector is [0, 0, 0, 1, 1, 1]. Figure 20–8 shows the fourth portion of the curve.

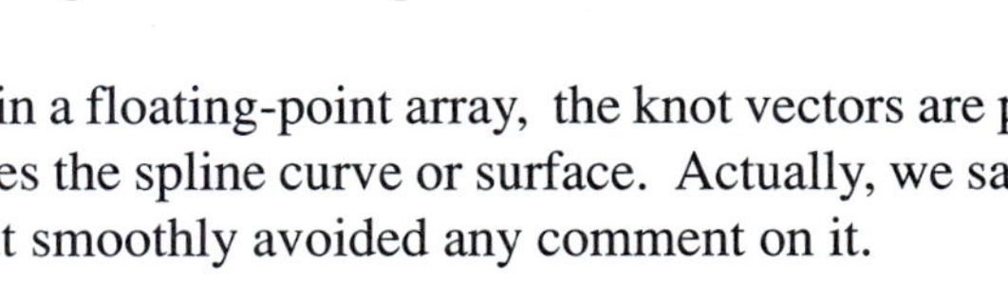

Figure 20–8. Staple-Remover Jaw: Part IV

After you define them in a floating-point array, the knot vectors are passed to PHIGS via the same routine that creates the spline curve or surface. Actually, we saw this in the code fragment shown earlier, but smoothly avoided any comment on it.

The Entire Shape

Let's put these sets of control points and knot vectors into a coded form that could actually draw the shape. Here is the code fragment:

```
...
static Ppoint3       ControlPointData1[6] = {
                     {0.1, 0.1, 0.0},
                     {0.7, 0.1, 0.0},
                     {0.9, 0.1, 0.0},
                     {0.9, 0.3, 0.0},
                     {0.7, 0.3, 0.0},
                     {0.6, 0.3, 0.0}};
static Ppoint3       ControlPointData2[3] = {
                     {0.6,  0.3,  0.0},
                     {0.55, 0.25, 0.0},
                     {0.5,  0.2,  0.0}};
static Ppoint3       ControlPointData3[4] = {
                     {0.5,  0.2, 0.0},
                     {0.2,  0.2, 0.0},
                     {0.12, 0.2, 0.0},
                     {0.1,  0.3, 0.0}};
static Ppoint3       ControlPointData4[3] = {
                     {0.1,  0.3, 0.0},
                     {0.07, 0.2, 0.0},
                     {0.1,  0.1, 0.0}};
static Pfloat KnotVector1data[9] =
                       {0.0, 0.0, 0.0, 1.0, 2.0, 3.0, 4.0, 4.0, 4.0};
static Pfloat KnotVector2data[6] = {0.0, 0.0, 0.0, 1.0, 1.0, 1.0};
static Pfloat KnotVector3data[7] = {0.0, 0.0, 0.0, 1.0,
                                    2.0, 2.0, 2.0};
static Pfloat KnotVector4data[6] = {0.0, 0.0, 0.0, 1.0, 1.0, 1.0};
...
MyCurve1.knots.num_floats = 9;
MyCurve1.knots.floats = KnotVector1data;
MyCurve2.knots.num_floats = 6;
MyCurve2.knots.floats = KnotVector2data;
MyCurve3.knots.num_floats = 7;
MyCurve3.knots.floats = KnotVector3data;
MyCurve4.knots.num_floats = 6;
MyCurve4.knots.floats = KnotVector4data;
...
```

Combining Curves into One

The previous implementation of the staple-remover jaw works, but it is somewhat clumsy. It would be better to connect all the small pieces of the curve into one larger one. To combine multiple small curves into a larger one that draws the same shape, you need to address two areas:

- Concatenating the respective sets of control points
- Concatenating the respective knot vectors

Concatenating Control Points

Concatenating control points is basically trivial: Just concatenate, and remove redundancies thereby introduced. To illustrate, take the first two of the sets of control points in our code fragment:

```
static Ppoint3      ControlPointData1[6] = {
                    {0.1, 0.1, 0.0},
                    {0.7, 0.1, 0.0},
                    {0.9, 0.1, 0.0},
                    {0.9, 0.3, 0.0},
                    {0.7, 0.3, 0.0},
                    {0.6, 0.3, 0.0}};
```

and

```
static Ppoint3      ControlPointData2[3] = {
                    {0.6,  0.3,  0.0},
                    {0.55, 0.25, 0.0},
                    {0.5,  0.2,  0.0}};
```

Since the first series of control points ends at (0.6, 0.3, 0.0), and the second series starts at the same point, remove one of those points, and consider the numbers a single new set of control points:

```
static Ppoint3      ControlPointData1[8] = {
                    {0.1,  0.1,  0.0},
                    {0.7,  0.1,  0.0},
                    {0.9,  0.1,  0.0},
```

```
{0.9,  0.3,  0.0},
{0.7,  0.3,  0.0},
{0.6,  0.3,  0.0},
{0.55, 0.25, 0.0},
{0.5,  0.2,  0.0}};
```

Similar operations would be carried out to concatenate the other sets of control points.

Concatenating Knot Vectors

Concatenating knot vectors is a bit trickier than concatenating the control points. It can be done if two constraints are met:

- The knots at the endpoints have multiplicity equal to the order of the curve.
- All individual curves have the same order. That is, for example, you cannot combine the knot vectors of a quadratic curve and a cubic curve (at least, with this simple algorithm).

Assuming these two conditions are satisfied, there are four steps required to combine two knot vectors into one:

1. Remove the entire last group of equal values from the first knot vector.
2. Remove the first *element* from the first group of equal values in the second knot vector.
3. Add n to each element in the second knot vector, where n is the value of the elements removed in Step 1.
4. Consider the knot vectors one.

Let's carry out this process for our example.

- Concatenate knot vectors [0, 0, 0, 1, 2, 3, 4, 4, 4] and [0, 0, 0, 1, 1, 1].
  - Step 1: Knot vector #1 becomes [0, 0, 0, 1, 2, 3].
  - Step 2: Knot vector #2 becomes [0, 0, 1, 1, 1].
  - Step 3: Knot vector #2 becomes [4, 4, 5, 5, 5].

- Step 4: The new knot vector is [0, 0, 0, 1, 2, 3, 4, 4, 5, 5, 5].

- Concatenate the knot vector [0, 0, 0, 1, 2, 3, 4, 4, 5, 5, 5] (obtained by concatenating the first two knot vectors) and the knot vector [0, 0, 0, 1, 2, 2, 2].
  - Step 1: Knot vector #1 becomes [0, 0, 0, 1, 2, 3, 4, 4].
  - Step 2: Knot vector #2 becomes [0, 0, 1, 2, 2, 2].
  - Step 3: Knot vector #2 becomes [5, 5, 6, 7, 7, 7].
  - Step 4: The new knot vector is [0, 0, 0, 1, 2, 3, 4, 4, 5, 5, 6, 7, 7, 7].

- Concatenate the knot vector [0, 0, 0, 1, 2, 3, 4, 4, 5, 5, 6, 7, 7, 7] (obtained by concatenating the first three knot vectors) and the knot vector [0, 0, 0, 1, 1, 1].
  - Step 1: Knot vector #1 becomes [0, 0, 0, 1, 2, 3, 4, 4, 5, 5, 6].
  - Step 2: Knot vector #2 becomes [0, 0, 1, 1, 1].
  - Step 3: Knot vector #2 becomes [7, 7, 8, 8, 8].
  - Step 4: The new knot vector is [0, 0, 0, 1, 2, 3, 4, 4, 5, 5, 6, 7, 7, 8, 8, 8].

Now, putting these concatenated sets of control points and concatenated knot vectors into our pseudo-code, we have:

```
static Ppoint3      ControlPointData[13] = {
                    {0.1,  0.1,  0.0},
                    {0.7,  0.1,  0.0},
                    {0.9,  0.1,  0.0},
                    {0.9,  0.3,  0.0},
                    {0.7,  0.3,  0.0},
                    {0.6,  0.3,  0.0},
                    {0.55, 0.25, 0.0},
                    {0.5,  0.2,  0.0},
                    {0.2,  0.2,  0.0},
                    {0.12, 0.2,  0.0},
                    {0.1,  0.3,  0.0},
                    {0.07, 0.2,  0.0},
                    {0.1,  0.1,  0.0}};
static KnotVectorData[16] = {0.0, 0.0, 0.0, 1.0, 2.0, 3.0, 4.0, 4.0,
                    5.0, 5.0, 6.0, 7.0, 7.0, 8.0, 8.0, 8.0};
    ...
MyCurve.knots.num_floats = 16;
MyCurve.knots.floats = KnotVectorData;
```

And the output would be something like the illustration in Figure 20–9 (the control point locations are marked with a polymarker primitive).

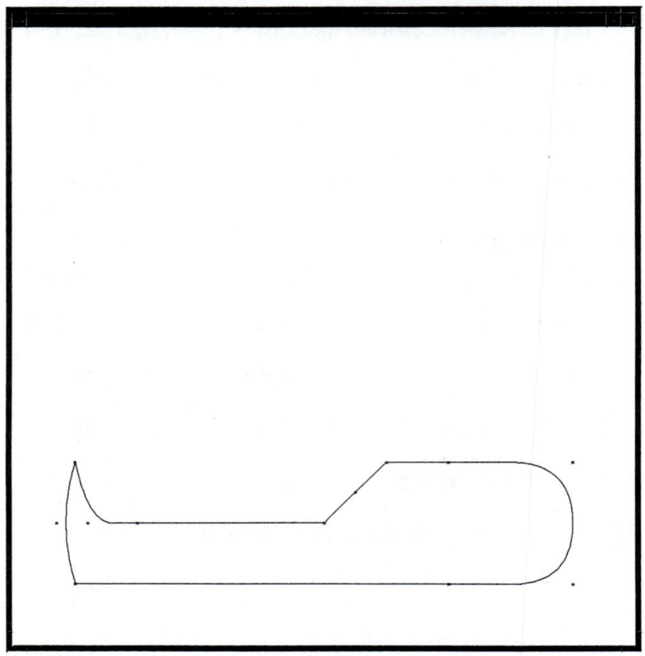

Figure 20–9. The Staple Remover Jaw

Multiplicity of Knots

The concept of multiplicity of control points is similar to the concept of multiplicity of knots within a knot vector. We saw in the example of the staple-remover jaw that it was permissible to have knots of multiplicity greater than 1 in the interior of a knot vector, but not much was said about what was accomplished by doing it.

The concept of multiple knots is intimately associated with the degree of continuity between adjacent parts of a spline curve. To recap the discussion of continuity at joints (in "A Mathematical Digression," earlier in this chapter), let's look again at the three kinds of continuity available with PHIGS' B-splines:

- If both segments give the same values for x, y, and z at the joint, the curve has positional continuity ("zeroeth-derivative") across the joint.
- If, in addition, the slope of both segments is the same at the joint, the curve has first-derivative continuity at the joint.
- If, in addition, the rate of change of the slope of the two segments is the same at the joint, the curve has second-derivative continuity at the joint.
- And so forth, up to fourth-derivative continuity.

This is how the multiplicity of knots is connected with continuity: For every duplication of a knot value, the continuity at that joint is lessened by one. Again, this continuity is with respect to the parameter space (u or v), and *not* necessarily real space (x, y, and z). For example, in a cubic curve:

- Interior knots with a multiplicity of 1 cause second-derivative continuity across the joint. That is, the rates of change of slope of the two curves are the same at the joint.
- Interior knots with a multiplicity of 2 cause first-derivative continuity across the joint. That is, the slopes of the two curves are the same at the joint.
- Interior knots with a multiplicity of 3 cause zeroeth-derivative (positional) continuity across the joint. That is, the locations of the two curves are the same at the joint.
- Interior knots with a multiplicity of 4 cause no continuity across the joint. That is, there are two disjoint curves with no apparent relationship.

Similar things happen for quadratic curves: Singular knots cause first-derivative continuity, duplicate knots cause positional continuity, and triplicate knots cause no continuity. Also similar are the linear curves: Singular knots cause positional continuity, and duplicate knots cause no continuity. In this way, you can cause sharp corners (also known as cusps or "knuckles") in a spline curve regardless of the order of the spline.

Three-dimensional Spline Curves

So far, we've been discussing only two-dimensional spline curves. At first, one might think that if you get into three dimensions, you must start talking about surfaces, but this is not the case. A curve, being merely a line, need not be restricted to a plane. The only difference between drawing a 2D and a 3D spline curve is the *z* data that you pass to the spline routines. So far, we have been setting all the *z* values to a single value (zero); this results in a 2D spline curve, confined to a plane.

To generate a spline curve that extends into three dimensions, merely give different values to the *z* array.

Bezier Knots

There is a subset of B-splines that is known as Bezier splines. For this special set of B-splines, the knots at the beginning and end of the knot sequence have a multiplicity equal to the order of the curve (this ensures that the curve will pass through the beginning and ending control points), and all interior knots have multiplicity of ⟨*order*⟩ – 1.

In addition to these requirements, the ⟨*knots*⟩ = ⟨*control_points*⟩ + ⟨*order*⟩ rule still holds. Thus, you do not have *complete* freedom to add and/or delete control points and/or knots. For example, suppose you have a three-span quadratic Bezier curve with seven control points: Its knot vector would be [0, 0, 0, 1, 1, 2, 2, 3, 3, 3]. The rule is satisfied. At this point, you *cannot* add a single control point and still have a Bezier curve; either the rule would be violated, or the number of control points or knots would be wrong. However, you can add *two* control points (and the associated two knots) and still have a Bezier curve.

Thus, to generate curves and surfaces with the Bezier form, merely create control point arrays and knot vectors that satisfy the above conditions.

Specifying a Spline's Smoothness

It was mentioned earlier in the chapter that there is no memory-consumption penalty for rendering a spline curve with high resolution as opposed to low resolution—the same control points are used for all resolutions. There is a calculation-time penalty for greater resolution, however. Regardless of resolution, memory is constant for a given spline curve. The tradeoff occurs between image accuracy and calculation time. The choice you make depends on your application.

The resolution of spline curves and surfaces is controlled by the routines SET CURVE APPROXIMATION CRITERIA and SET SURFACE APPROXIMATION CRITERIA, respectively:

```
pset_curve_approx_crit(
   const Pcurve_approx_crit   *data
);

pset_surf_approx_crit(
   const Psurf_approx_crit    *data
);
```

Parametric Surface Characteristics

As mentioned earlier, B-spline surfaces are created parametrically and, thus, when PHIGS renders such a surface, parametric surface attributes are applied.

The SET PARAMETRIC SURFACE CHARACTERISTICS routine sets the various attributes defined for B-spline surfaces:

```
pset_param_surf_chars(
   const Pparam_surf_chars    *data
);
```

where:

⟨*data*⟩ is a pointer to a data record of type `Pparam_surf_chars`:

```
typedef struct {
  Pint                      type;
  union Pparam_surf_chars_data {
```

```
        struct Pparam_surf_iosparam {
          Pplacement placement;  /*curve placement:
                                     uniform or non-uniform */
          Pint        num_u_curves; /* curve count in u direction */
          Pint        num_v_curves;/* curve count in v direction */
        } isoparam;
        struct Pparam_surf_level_mc {
          Ppoint3     origin;   /* origin point */
          Pvec3          dir;      /* direction vector */
          Pfloat_list    params;   /* parameter list */
        } level_mc;
        struct Pparam_surf_level_wc {
          Ppoint3        origin;   /* origin point */
          Pvec3          dir;      /* direction vector */
          Pfloat_list    params;   /* parameter list */
        } level_wc;
         ...                       /* implementation-defined */
      } data;
    } Pparam_surf_chars;
```

Spline Surfaces

The logical extension of a spline curve is a **spline surface**. A spline surface is only marginally more difficult to understand than a spline curve; you just define two families of spline curves: one for each direction on the surface.

If you'll remember the discussions on spline curves, there were *x*, *y*, and *z* values in the arrays of control points, and there was an associated knot vector. In defining a spline surface, there will be a rectangular *grid* represented in the *x*, *y*, and *z* values' arrays of control points, and *two* knot vectors. The two knot vectors are for travelling along the two dimensions of the rectangular representation of control points. That is, one knot vector is used to define one family of curves, and the other is used to define the other, "perpendicular" family of curves.

Spline surfaces can be thought of—conceptually, not mathematically—merely as a large number of spline curves very close together. The curve, using the *u* knot vector, moves in a direction perpendicular to its length and describes a series of "parallel" curves. Then, using the *v* knot vector, another series of "parallel" curves is generated "perpendicular" to the first set of curves. When viewed together, these two sets of curves look like a piece of window screen with various bumps and dents along its surface.

The PHIGS routine for drawing spline surfaces is similar to those of drawing spline curves; there is merely another direction to include in the statement. The calling signature of the NON-UNIFORM B-SPLINE SURFACE 3 routine is

```
pnon_uniform_b_spline_surf3(
   const Psurf_geom_spline       *spline_data,
   const Ptrim_curve_loop_list   *trim_curves
);
```

where:

⟨*spline_data*⟩ is a pointer to a data record of type `Psurf_geom_spline`:

```
typedef struct {
  Pint                  u_order;
  Pint                  v_order;
  Pfloat_list           u_knots;
  Pfloat_list           v_knots;
  Prationality          rationality;
  Pctrl_point3_array    ctrl_points;
} Psurf_geom_spline;
```

where:

`Pctrl_point3_array` is a data record of the following type:

```
typedef struct {
  Pint_size    dims;
  Ppoint3_ptr  points;
} Pctrl_point3_array;

typedef struct {
    Pint       size_x;
    Pint       size_y;
} Pint_size;
```

⟨*trim_curves*⟩ is a pointer to a data record of type `Ptrim_curve_loop_list`:

```
typedef struct {
  Pint              num_trim_loops;
```

```
  Ptrim_curve_loop *trim_loops;
} Ptrim_curve_loop_list;

typedef struct {
  Pint           num_trim_curves;
  Ptrim_curve    *trim_curves;
} Ptrim_curve_loop;

typedef struct {
  Pcurve_approx_crit              approx_crit;
  Pvis_flag                       visibility_flag;
  Pint                            order;
  Pfloat_list                     knots;
  Pfloat                          low_limit;
  Pfloat                          high_limit;
  Prationality                    rationality;
  Pctrl_point_list                ctrl_points;
} Ptrim_curve
```

Trimming curves are covered in the next section.

Note that, unlike `u_order` and `v_order`, there is no `u_rationality` and `v_rationality`; that is, you cannot specify a spline surface that is rational in one direction and nonrational in the other. The surface is either rational in both directions or nonrational in both directions.

Figure 20–10 shows what a spline surface looks like. The solid line mesh shows the edges of the polygons making up the surface, and the dotted line mesh shows the control point locations.

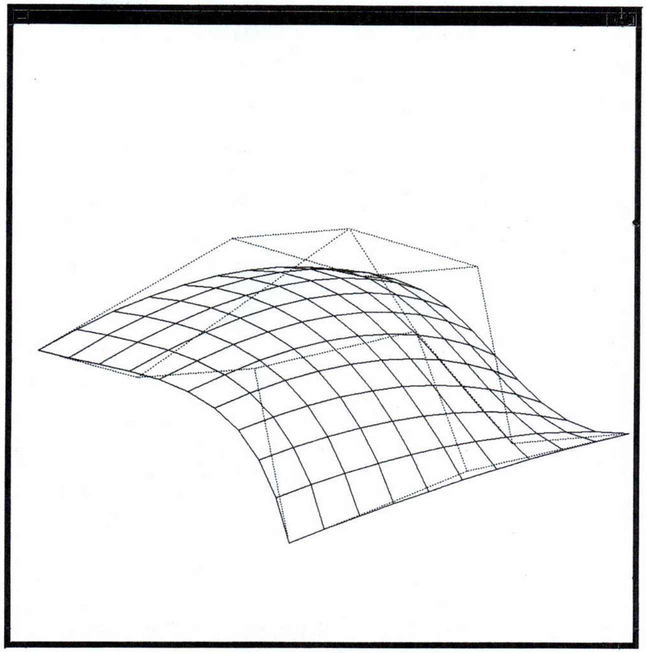

Figure 20–10. Wire-mesh Representation of a B-Spline Surface

Trimming Curves

If an application uses B-splines to represent the surfaces of solid objects, one other operation is essential. The need for this arises from such simple operations as drilling a hole in an object. A way is needed to tell the computer not to display the piece of the surface inside the drill hole.

In the general case, this is done by sending the graphics processor a description of the surface and of all the pieces that should be cut off of the surface. These descriptions are called **trimming curves**, and they are also represented as B-splines. Using B-splines to represent trimming curves allows both simple geometric shapes and more complex shapes resulting from the intersection of two objects to be represented with one primitive. In addition, the representation is compact, and one description is sufficient no matter what the size of the object on the screen.

This is a powerful feature of PHIGS' B-spline functionality. As stated, a trimming curve is just a spline curve, which we've discussed throughout this chapter. It is defined identically to any other spline curve, with the following exception: The control points are defined in *uv* space (more about this later).

In order for a "hole" to be defined in a B-spline surface, the trimming curve(s) must form a closed loop. This is similar to defining a polygon, as opposed to a polyline: The polygon must form a closed loop, so that it has an interior and an exterior. With trimming curves, a closed loop can be defined by one or more separate trimming curves, defined tail-to-head, as long as the trimming curves together form a closed loop.

Rules for Trimming Curves

Several rules must be followed when defining trimming curves. Note that some of the rules assume that the computer uses a graphics accelerator to perform some of the calculations.

Control Points

Trimming curves must be defined in the parameter space (*not* the XYZ space) of the surface being trimmed. That is, the control points of a trimming curve must have values in the range of the *u* and *v* knot vectors for the surface.

For example, if the *u* and *v* knot vectors are [0, 0, 0, 1, 2, 3, 3, 3] and [0, 0, 1, 2, 2, 3, 4, 4], respectively, the control points for any trimming curves for this surface should define curves that do not extend outside of the 0–3 and 0–4 range, respectively.

Closed Loops

All trimming curves must form closed loops. A loop can be a single trimming curve whose ends are touching, or it can be made up of multiple open trimming curves connected in a head-to-tail fashion.

No Overlapping Trimming Curves

Trimming curves cannot intersect or overlap each other in the *uv* parameter space. Intersecting trimming curves must be combined by the user into a single closed loop that represents the net effect of the individual intersecting curves.

Trimming curves may intersect each other in the XYZ space, for example, in a case like a sphere where a line in *uv* space maps into a point in XYZ space.

Which Part Is Retained?

If the parameter space for a surface is right-handed (i.e., if the cross product of *u* and *v* points toward you), everything on and to the left of a trimming curve is kept and everything to the right of the trimming curve is trimmed off. "Left" and "right" are determined by traversing the trimming curve from the minimum to the maximum value of the parameter. If the parameter space for a surface is left-handed, everything on and to the right of the trimming curve is kept. The first trimming curve defined for a surface must always be counterclockwise.

The Edges of a Surface

If the edges of a trimmed surface are visible, a trimming curve must be put around the surface on the edge of the surface. An untrimmed surface is assumed to be entirely visible.

Small Trimming Curves

B-spline surface patches are rendered as many individual polygons. If a trimming curve represents a loop that is so small it fits entirely into a single polygon, the trimming curve has no effect.

Curve Capacity

The graphics accelerator can handle only a limited number of trimming curve segments for each patch. If a patch contains too many trimming curve segments, the patch is subdivided by the PHIGS software until each subpatch contains few enough segments to be displayed. Thus, from the user's point of view, there is no limit to the number of trimming curves per patch.

Rendering Capabilities

When a B-spline surface is rendered, it is first tessellated into a fill area set. The filled areas generated by the graphics accelerator for B-spline surfaces are handled in much the same way as user-defined filled areas. They can be smooth-shaded using all of the light source features; they can be filled and edged; they are subject to the user-defined clip limits and hidden-surface removal. Perspective projections, depth cueing, and back-facet culling can also be used with B-spline surfaces. See "Parametric Surface Characteristics," earlier in this chapter, for more information.

Use INQUIRE TRIMMING CURVE FACILITIES to determine the maximum trimming curve order supported by the implementation.

Trimming Curve Examples

The following code fragments show how trimming curves work. Starting with the "wire-mesh" example from earlier in the chapter, we'll trim it in two ways:

- Cut a teardrop-shaped hole in it.
- Cut off everything *except* the teardrop-shaped piece.

Making a Teardrop-shaped Hole

The following things must be done to make the teardrop-shaped hole:

Define the Trimming Curves

Two trimming curves are needed. One is for the hole (where the surface stops), and one is for the perimeter of the surface itself. This second curve is necessary because PHIGS needs to know where the surface *starts* so it doesn't get confused when the inner trimming curve says where it stops.

Since the part of the surface to the right of the curve is trimmed off, and that to the left is retained, the teardrop hole should be defined in a clockwise manner, while the curve that defines the perimeter of the surface should be defined in a counterclockwise manner. Thus, the "ring" of the surface is consistently labelled as something to keep.

```
static Ppoint               EdgeControlPointData[5] = {
                            {0.0, 0.0},
                            {1.0, 0.0},
                            {1.0, 1.0},
                            {0.0, 1.0},
                            {0.0, 0.0}};
static Pctrl_point_list   EdgeControlPoints={5, EdgeControlPointData};
static Ppoint               InnerControlPointData[4] = {
                            {0.35, 0.05},
                            {0.25, 0.95},
                            {0.95, 0.95},
                            {0.35, 0.05}};
static Pctrl_point_list     InnerControlPoints={4,
                            InnerControlPointData};
```

Note that all of these values are defined with respect to the parameter space. That is, since both knot vectors for the surface go from 0.0 to 1.0, all trimming curves for this surface must also lie on this surface.

Sending the Trimming Curves to PHIGS

After the trimming curves are defined, they must be sent to PHIGS. As mentioned, there are two trimming curves in our program. They are installed along with the spline curve data:

```
...
Ptrim_curve_loop_list        TrimCurveLoopList;
Ptrim_curve_loop             TrimCurveLoops[2];
Ptrim_curve                  EdgeCurve, InnerCurve;
static Pfloat                EdgeKnots[7] = {
                             0.0, 0.0, 1.0, 2.0, 3.0, 4.0, 4.0};
static Pfloat                InnerKnots[8] = {
                             0.0, 0.0, 0.0, 0.0, 1.0, 1.0, 1.0, 1.0};
static Ppoint                EdgeControlPointData[5] = {
                             {0.0, 0.0},
                             {1.0, 0.0},
                             {1.0, 1.0},
                             {0.0, 1.0},
                             {0.0, 0.0}};
static Ppoint                InnerControlPointData[4] = {
                             {0.35, 0.05},
                             {0.25, 0.95},
                             {0.95, 0.95},
                             {0.35, 0.05}};

...
EdgeCurve.approx_data.type = PCURVE_APPROX_CHORDAL_SIZE_DC;
EdgeCurve.approx_data.chordal_size_dc.approx = 0.01;
EdgeCurve.visibility_flag = PVIS_ON;
EdgeCurve.order = 2;                /* linear */
EdgeCurve.knots.num_floats = 7;
EdgeCurve.knots.floats = EdgeKnots;
EdgeCurve.low_limit = 0.0;
EdgeCurve.high_limit = 4.0;
EdgeCurve.rationality = PB_SPLINE_NON_RATIONAL;
EdgeCurve.ctrl_points.num_points = 5;
EdgeCurve.ctrl_points.points.point = EdgeControlPointData;
```

```
InnerCurve.approx_data.type = PCURVE_APPROX_CHORDAL_SIZE_DC;
InnerCurve.approx_data.chordal_size_dc.approx = 0.01;
InnerCurve.vis_flag = PVIS_ON;
InnerCurve.order = 3;                /* cubic */
InnerCurve.knots.num_floats = 8;
InnerCurve.knots.floats = InnerKnots;
InnerCurve.low_limit = 0.0;
InnerCurve.high_limit = 1.0;
InnerCurve.rationality = PB_SPLINE_NON_RATIONAL;
InnerCurve.ctrl_points.num_points = 4;
InnerCurve.ctrl_points.points.point = InnerControlPointData;


TrimCurveLoops[0].num_trim_curves = 1;
TrimCurveLoops[0].trim_curves = &EdgeCurve;
TrimCurveLoops[1].num_trim_curves = 1;
TrimCurveLoops[1].trim_curves = &InnerCurve;
TrimCurveLoopList.num_trim_loops = 2;
TrimCurveLoopList.trim_loops = TrimCurveLoops;
```

Figure 20–11 shows a B-spline surface with a hole trimmed out:

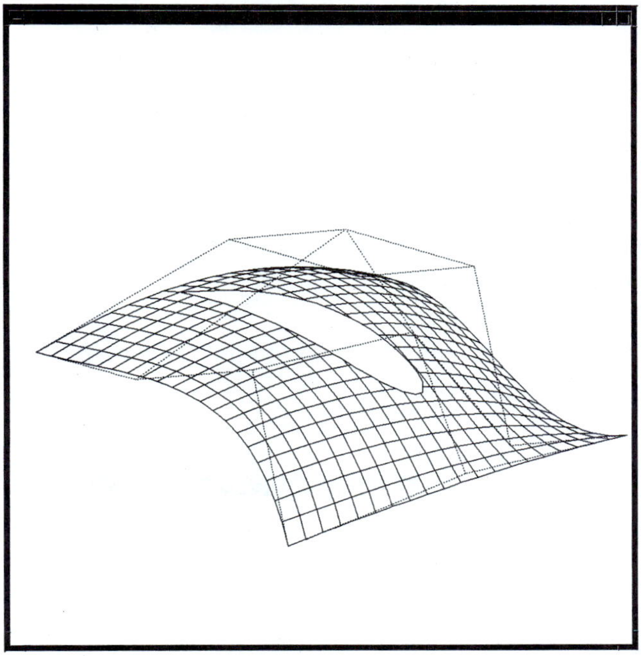

Figure 20–11. B-Spline Surface with Hole Trimmed Out

Keeping the Teardrop; Tossing the Rest

To trim the *outside* of the surface off, keeping only the teardrop, is slightly simpler than making the hole. The reason is that one fewer trimming curve must be defined: the outside edge.

The trimming curve that makes the teardrop itself must be changed, however. Now that we're *keeping* the teardrop, rather than throwing it away, we must define the trimming curve's control points in reverse order. The reason for this is that the surface to the *left* of the curve is kept, and we want to keep the surface on the other side this time. Thus, the curve becomes

```
static Ppoint               EdgeControlPointData[5] = {
                            {0.0, 0.0},
                            {1.0, 0.0},
                            {1.0, 1.0},
                            {0.0, 1.0},
                            {0.0, 0.0}};
static Ppoint               InnerControlPointData[4] = {
```

```
{0.35, 0.05},
{0.95, 0.95},
{0.25, 0.95},
{0.35, 0.05}};
```

Other than this change, and removing the requirements of the `Edge` trimming curve, the program would be unchanged.

Figure 20–12 shows an example of the output of such a program: The teardrop shape is kept, and the rest is trimmed off.

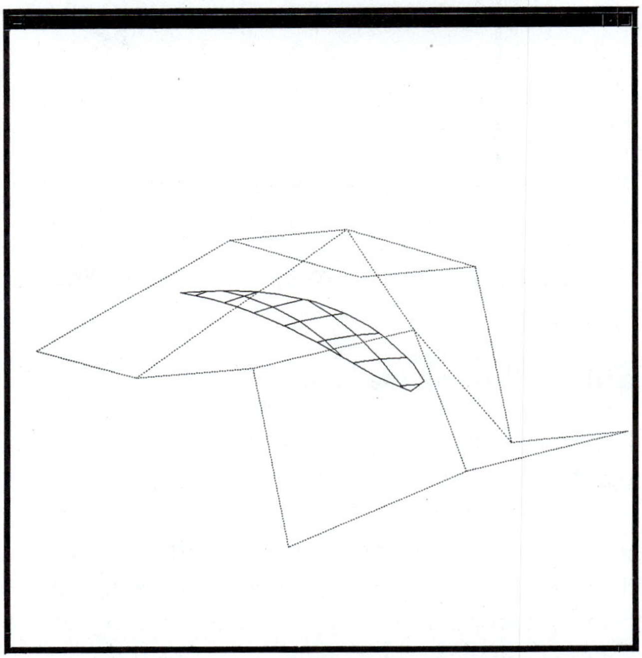

Figure 20–12. B-Spline Surface with Outer Parts Trimmed

Rational Splines

One of the developments in the use of splines in computer graphics has been the introduction of **rational splines.** Rational splines differ from non-rational splines in that they have weights associated with each control point. These individual weights affect the magnitude of the influence that each control point exerts on the curve. (For more detailed information concerning rational splines, see Tiller, W. (1983). "Rational B-Splines for Curve and Surface Representation," *IEEE Computer Graphics and Applications*, September, pp. 61–69.)

The form of the coordinates of a rational spline looks similar to the data points discussed in Chapter 6, *Modelling Transformations*. If you'll remember, an extra coordinate, called the **homogeneous coordinate**, was added to the right end of a data point representation. Usually, the value of the homogeneous coordinate was 1.0.

In the same way, B-splines can have homogeneous coordinates or not have them. If homogeneous coordinates are not present (a non-rational spline), the results are the same as having a rational spline with all the homogeneous coordinates equal to 1.0.

In non-rational splines (the kind discussed already), each control point has the same "pull"; that is, no one control point could affect the curve any more than any other control point. With rational splines, however, the homogeneous coordinate specifies a "weight" (like a kind of "antigravity"), and the greater the value of the homogeneous coordinate, the less the pull of the associated control point. That is, the greater the weight, the closer the function is to zero: $x_t = X_t / H_t$; thus, $x(t)$ goes to 0 as $H(t)$ goes to infinity; assuming $X(t)$ is fixed. This added control allows a greater range of curves to be represented. For example, rational splines can represent all conic sections exactly, while parabolas are the only conic sections accurately representable with non-rational splines.

When the control points are defined for rational splines, an additional value is included with the normal Cartesian coordinates, namely a weight, represented by w. This concept is similar to the use of homogeneous coordinates for points in other data structures used in other computer graphics.

Rational B-splines cannot be rotated, scaled, or translated merely by applying the transformations to the control points. Matrix transformations must be applied to each point on the curve or to each vertex of the polygons making up the curve or surface. This is taken care of automatically by PHIGS. However, if the control points are transformed before being sent to the pipeline, there will be unpredictable results.

The Math

A rational B-spline is the ratio of two polynomials. A rational B-spline curve is specified as four B-spline curves: $X(t)$, $Y(t)$, $Z(t)$, and $W(t)$. The points traced out in XYZ space are given by:

$$x_i = X_i / W_i$$

$$y_i = Y_i / W_i$$

$$z_i = Z_i / W_i$$

The function $W(t)$ is constrained to be greater than zero over the range of t for which it is defined. Nonrational B-splines are clearly a subset of rational B-splines for which $W(t) = 1.0$.

Conic Sections

One useful application of rational B-splines is that of drawing conic sections; specifically, circles and ellipses. It is impossible to represent a circle exactly with non-rational splines, although you can approximate it by having your control points in the shape of a many-sided regular polygon.

For example, to make a perfect circle of unit radius centered on the origin (see Figure 20–13) the control points and knot vector must be set up as follows:

- There are nine control points, arranged one at the edge of each octant, with the first and last coincident. (The octants are 45-degree-wide sections that converge at the origin.)
- The control points on the axes have the normal xy values, and a homogeneous coordinate of 1. The control points in the middle of the quadrants have x and y magnitudes of $\sqrt{2}/2$, also known as sin(45°) or cos(45°), with signs appropriate for the quadrant. The homogeneous coordinates are $\sqrt{2}/2$.

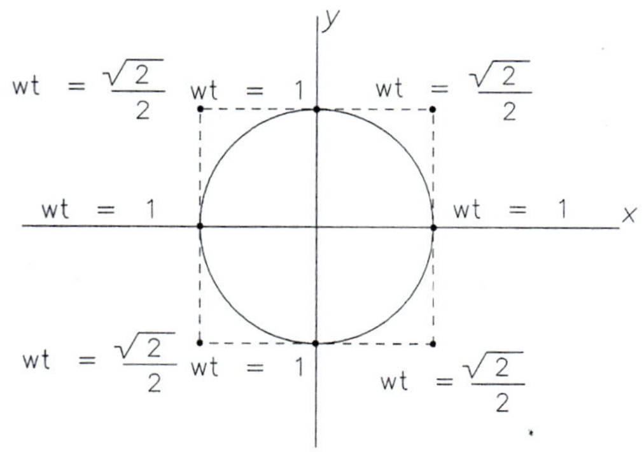

Figure 20–13. Conic Section Control Points

- The knot vector is set up to interpolate the control points that are on the *x* and *y* axes: [0, 0, 0, 1, 1, 2, 2, 3, 3, 4, 4, 4].

Defining a rational B-spline as such results in a perfect circle.

Chapter 21

Metafiles

PHIGS supports two models for storing graphical data:

- Archive files store structure networks for later reuse by a PHIGS application
- **Metafiles** are used to store and exchange the pictures created by the traversal of structures in the CSS

While the contents of an archive file can only be used by PHIGS, the contents of a metafile can be used by other applications. For example, a typical use of a metafile in PHIGS is to create a file that can be spooled to a printer. Another use is to exchange data between a PHIGS system and a non-PHIGS graphics system.

PHIGS defines a format for archive files but does not define a format for metafiles. However, it recommends a standard format called **computer graphics metafile** (**CGM**). CGM is widely used in the computer industry for exchanging graphics data between different computer vendors' equipment. The CGM specification is a graphics standard for storing the description of graphics images in a file. A CGM file does not contain pixel information; instead, it contains graphics primitives that reconstruct the picture. A CGM interpreter is often used to transfer or print these images to hardcopy.

One problem with using CGM is that it does not support 3D primitives. Implementations usually resolve this difference by projecting the 3D data to 2D before storing it in the CGM file. This can be done by applying all PHIGS modelling and viewing transformations, including perspective, to the primitives as they are rendered to a metafile output workstation.

The usage of metafiles is very implementation-dependent. This chapter gives a brief overview of the main topics. See your implementation documentation for details.

Using Metafile Workstations

The PHIGS standard supports the general notion of metafiles though metafile output (MO) and metafile input (MI) workstations. An MO workstation captures static picture definitions to a metafile. An MI workstations allows the reading and interpretation of a metafile.

To open an MO or MI workstation you typically specify the following information via the OPEN WORKSTATION routine:

- Identify the metafile in the connection ID parameter
- Identify either MO or MI workstation in the workstation type parameter

The mapping between a filename that represents a metafile and a numeric connection ID is one of the things that the PHIGS standard leaves up to the implementation. Implementations often define an escape routine to provide this mapping. For example, HP-PHIGS provides an extension routine named CREATE CONNECTION IDENTIFIER FOR FILENAME, named `pescape_u4`, that allows the application to create a connection identifier for a file that can be used with OPEN WORKSTATION. It also defines an MO workstation type as `PWMO`. The following fragment opens an MO workstation:

```
Pint        WorkstnID = 1;          /* workstation identifier      */
Pint        ConnID;                 /* connection identifier       */
Pint        WorkstnType = PWMO;     /* metafile output workstation */
popen_phigs(stderr, 0);             /* open PHIGS                  */
                                    /* errors go to "stderr"       */
pescape_u4("/dev/screen/phigs_window", &ConnID);
popen_ws(WorkstnID, ConnID, WorkstnType); /* open workstation      */
...
```

Writing Information to a Metafile

As mentioned, an MO workstation captures static picture definitions to a metafile. In the model of picture generation that many PHIGS implementations use, whenever a PHIGS routine that causes a regeneration is invoked, a picture is output to the metafile. That picture is generated from the structure networks posted to the MO workstation. The metafile picture reflects the content of those structures together with various workstation states that have been set for the MO workstation. The metafile can contain multiple pictures, each generated by a separate PHIGS regeneration.

The default value of the display update state on an MO workstation is usually WAIT/NIVE (see Chapter 4, *Posting Structures and Controlling Picture Changes*). Under this state, the metafile picture is generated only when you make an explicit request through a routine such as UPDATE WORKSTATION or REDRAW ALL STRUCTURES. If you change the display update state the metafile picture might be generated more frequently because of implicit regenerations. Since metafile picture generation can consume a large amount of file storage, you should exercise caution when changing the display update states from the default.

The application can also store its own data in a metafile using the WRITE ITEM TO METAFILE routine. This routine accepts a workstation identifier, a metafile item type, and a data record.

Reading Information from a Metafile

When you open an MI workstation, the first item in the metafile becomes the **current item**. Use the following routines to obtain information from a metafile:

- GET ITEM FROM METAFILE returns the item type and the size of the current item.
- READ ITEM FROM METAFILE returns the data record associated with an item. You supply the size returned by GET ITEM FROM METAFILE. This routine also increments the current item value.
- INTERPRET ITEM decodes the information in the data record.

The following are examples of metafile elements that can become the current item:

- Primitives
- Primitive attribute values

- Application data
- Pattern table or colour table modifications

Since the CSS is the only portion of PHIGS capable of accepting picture information, your application must open an appropriate structure when interpreting a metafile primitive, primitive attribute value, or application data. Depending on the edit mode, PHIGS will insert one or more structure elements in the open structure when it executes an INTERPRET ITEM routine.

Chapter 22

Programming with PHIGS

This chapter covers the following aspects of writing application programs with PHIGS:

- Device-independent programming
- Improving performance
- Using the FORTRAN binding

Device-independent Programming

This section describes the following:

- How to use the PHIGS description table when porting from one PHIGS implementation to another
- How to use the workstation description table to write application programs that take advantage of different capabilities on different machines

Inquiring the PHIGS Description Table

When porting from one PHIGS implementation to another, you can determine a number of implementation-specific parameters and limits by inquiring values from the PHIGS description table. This section describes the routines that inquire values from the PHIGS description table.

The INQUIRE LIST OF AVAILABLE WORKSTATION TYPES routine returns the list of available workstation types.

The INQUIRE PHIGS FACILITIES routine returns the following information:

- The maximum number of simultaneously open workstations
- The maximum number of simultaneously open archive files
- The maximum number of available names for name sets
- The number of available character sets
- The list of available character sets
- The maximum lengths of the normal and inverted filter lists used for incremental spatial search (see Chapter 5, *Using Structures*)

The INQUIRE MODELLING CLIPPING FACILITIES routine returns the following information:

- The number of distinct planes in the modelling clipping volume
- The number of modelling clipping operators
- The available modelling clipping operators

Refer to the end of Chapter 5 for information on modelling clipping.

The INQUIRE GENERALIZED STRUCTURE ELEMENT FACILITIES routine returns the following information:

- The number of available generalized structure elements (GSEs)
- The list of GSE identifiers

- The workstation-dependency indicators for the list of available GSEs. This parameter specifies whether or not support for the generalized structure element is workstation-dependent.

Inquiring the Workstation Description Table

You can determine the capabilities of PHIGS on a particular workstation by inquiring values from the workstation description table. Some of the important points are summarized as follows:

- Each generic workstation type has its own descriptive table of values, called a workstation description table (WDT) (see Chapter 3, *Controlling PHIGS*).
- In addition, when you open a workstation on a particular device, PHIGS determines a number of additional values that are particular to the device. A specific WDT exists to describe further each open workstation.

The PHIGS standard provides a full set of values in the WDT so that the application can almost always inquire whether a device supports a particular operation before it calls the PHIGS routine to perform the operation.

Workstation description table values typically do not change over the lifetime of a workstation. The following routines return values from the workstation description table:

- INQUIRE PREDEFINED ⟨*attribute*⟩ REPRESENTATION routines return the predefined values associated with a particular entry in an attribute table. Note that these values are equivalent to the values in the workstation state list until the application explicitly sets the attribute table's values differently.
- INQUIRE ⟨*attribute*⟩ FACILITIES routines return information on the availability and capabilities of certain attributes on a particular workstation type. For example, INQUIRE POLYLINE FACILITIES returns the available linetypes, linewidths, and the number of predefined entries in the polyline bundle table for a given workstation type.

There are also a number of other routines that return values from the WDT (see Appendix A).

Use the following procedure to inquire values from a specific workstation description table:

1. Open a workstation using one of the predefined generic types. For example:

```
 integer*4 WorkID, errind, ConnectID
...
 call popwk(WorkID, ConnectID, POIDDX)
```

   The above fragment uses an implementation-specific value (`POIDDX`) to open the workstation.

2. Call the INQUIRE WORKSTATION CONNECTION AND TYPE routine to get the specific workstation type. For example:

```
 integer*4 SpecificType
...
 call pqwkc(WorkID, errind, ConnectID, SpecificType)
 if (errind .ne. 0) print *,"error in pqwkc: ",errind
```

3. Pass the specific type value to any of the workstation description table inquiry routines (see the following example).

Example

On a given PHIGS implementation, different output devices are usually identified as different workstation types (see Chapter 3). If you plan to run your application on a number of different workstation types, it is useful to determine the size of the workstation attribute tables before you define values for the tables. This example shows you how to do that. First, let's look at the routines that return the sizes of the workstation attribute tables:

- INQUIRE WORKSTATION STATE TABLE LENGTHS returns the size of the standard PHIGS workstation attribute tables:
  - Polyline bundle table
  - Marker bundle table
  - Text bundle table
  - Interior bundle table
  - Edge bundle table

- Pattern table
- Colour table
- View table

- INQUIRE WORKSTATION STATE TABLE LENGTHS PLUS returns the size of the additional tables defined by PHIGS PLUS:
  - Data mapping table
  - Reflectance table
  - Parametric surface table
  - Light source table
  - Depth cue table
  - Colour mapping table

The following fragment determines the size of the standard workstation attribute tables for a specific workstation type. Then it prints out the size of the corresponding workstation colour table.

```
 integer*4  WorkID, errind, ConnectID, SpecificType
 integer*4  PolyBundl,MarkerBundl, TextBundl
 integer*4  InterBundl, EdgeBundl, PatternTbl
 integer*4  ColourTbl, ViewTbl
 ...
 call popwk(WorkID, ConnectID, POIDDX)
 call pqwkc(WorkID, errind, ConnectID,   ! inq. wkstn. conn. type
+  SpecificType)
 if (errind .ne. 0) print *,"error indicator #: ",errind
 call pqwksl(SpecificType, errind, ! inq wkstn state tbl lengths
+  PolyBundl, MarkerBundl, TextBundl, InterBundl, EdgeBundl,
+  PatternTbl, ColourTbl, ViewTbl)
 print *, "number of colour table entries: ", ColourTbl
```

In the above fragment, the `ColourTbl` parameter returns the number of workstation colour table indices available to the application program on an opened workstation. The application program can use this value to ensure that it never uses an invalid colour index.

The following is the entire program using the C binding:

```
#include <phigs.h>                  /* get PHIGS definitions for C   */
#include <stdio.h>                  /* get standard I/O definitions  */

main()                                    /* file "InqTables.c"      */
{
    Pint        WorkstnID = 1;            /* workstation identifier  */
    Pint        ConnID, *ConnPtr;         /* connection identifier   */
    Pint        WorkstnType = POIDDX;     /* implementation-dependent*/
    Pint        TheStructure = 1;         /* structure ID            */
    Pstore      *Store;                   /* storage area            */
    Pint        Error;                    /* error-return variable   */
    Pint        SpecificType;           /* specific workstation type */
    Pws_st_tables Tables;        /* workstation state table lengths*/

    popen_phigs(stderr, 0);               /* errors go to "stderr"   */
    pescape_u4("/dev/screen/phigs_window", &ConnID);
    popen_ws(WorkstnID, ConnID, WorkstnType);
    pcreate_store(&Error, &Store);        /* allocate storage memory */
    if (Error) {
        printf("Error %d in pcreate_store; terminating.\n", Error);
        exit(1);
    }
    pinq_ws_conn_type(WorkstnID, Store, &Error, &ConnPtr,
                      &SpecificType);
    pinq_ws_st_table(SpecificType, &Error, &Tables);
    if (Error) {
        printf("Error %d in pinq_ws_st_table; terminating.\n", Error);
        exit(1);
    }
    printf("Number of colour table entries: %d\n", Tables.colr_reps);
    pclose_ws(WorkstnID);
    pclose_phigs();
}
```

Tips for Device-independent Programming

To write a program that adapts to the various PHIGS and workstation differences that can exist, you may have to structure your application program to include different algorithms for the various differences that can exist. For example, if the number of available colours on different devices varies greatly, you may want to incorporate the ability to differentiate primitives with aspects other than colour (for example, when less colours are available, differentiate line primitives with colour *and* linetype).

Given the large number of differences that can exist among workstations, it is not practical to handle all the contingencies that the WDT can indicate. Instead, you must carefully make decisions of which potential device differences you are willing to handle and which differences you are willing to assume won't arise or which your program will decline to handle (for example, by early termination). For these latter differences, you can document that your application requires certain workstation characteristics.

In making such decisions, base your strategy on the set of devices and workstation types on which you are planning to support your application. For example, if you never plan to run your application on more than one workstation type, you can program the application assuming that certain WDT values will be constant. On the other hand, if your application is to run on all workstation types on all graphics devices supported by your PHIGS implementation, you will need to write code to query at least the WDT values that can differ across these workstations and to supply algorithms that can handle these differences. Continuing the example, if your application is to run on more than one PHIGS implementation, you will need to inquire even more WDT values and some PHIGS description table values, and provide additional logic to handle the differences.

The PHIGS standard gives wide latitude on what a workstation has to support. There is a minimum set of functionality, but an implementation can differ widely from the full set. PHIGS PLUS adds even more functionality for which workstation support can vary. Device-independent programming not only will aid you in handling device differences among workstations on a given PHIGS implementation, but will also greatly reduce efforts in porting to other vendors PHIGS implementations (or to new workstations introduced by your implementation).

Improving Performance

This section describes several general areas where program speed may be increased. Some involve disabling capabilities you don't need at the moment, and others involve selecting the most efficient way to perform a given task.

Because of the differences between PHIGS implementations, some of these tips may yield large performance improvements, while some may yield little or no improvement. Experiment to see which benefit your application.

Structure Editing

Grouping edits to a structure (that is, performing a long sequence of edits to structure A, then a long sequence to structure B) is often faster than switching between structures multiple times.

Structure Networks

The following tips apply to the efficient use of structure networks:

- PHIGS requires a potentially large amount of traversal state information to be saved when a structure is instanced (executed) during traversal. This has to do mainly with saving and restoring attribute information. For this reason, make sure that there are enough drawing primitives in each structure to make traversal of the structure worthwhile.
- Don't set attributes needlessly. For example, don't insert a *set line colour* structure element before every polyline if the line colour is not changing.

Use the structure hierarchy in a natural manner; let a single structure map to a single graphical entity that can be manipulated as a unit. While this may not improve performance, it often makes programs easier to design and maintain. There are two broad styles: breaking the structure network at articulation points (transformation matrices), and breaking the network at attribute points (places where it is natural to specify attributes on a per-instance basis).

Lighting Performance

The following may affect lighting performance:

- The more light sources that are active, the slower the rendering speed.
- Increasing the number of reflectance calculations may decrease rendering performance. For example, using just ambient lighting is probably faster than using ambient

and diffuse. Using ambient, diffuse, and specular is probably slower than using just ambient and diffuse.

- Using a more computationally expensive shading method may decrease rendering performance. See Table 17–1 at the end of "Setting the Interior Shading Method" in Chapter 17 for a comparison of the calculations for each shading method. Also see "Tips for Lighting and Shading" in Chapter 17.

Name Sets

Enable name set highlighting only when you are using it. This means that the highlighting name set inclusion filter should be empty unless you are actually using highlighting techniques. If the inclusion filter is empty (default), the system does not have to check name set elements as they are encountered.

The same logic applies to the name set invisibility and picking filters. If all inclusion and exclusion filters are empty (this is the default), you will probably get your best performance. See Chapter 13, *Name Sets and Filters*.

Keep the names in the name set compact and numerically small. For example, use names {1, 2, 5, 8, 9} rather than {1, 20, 500, 8000, 90000} or {10001, 10002, 10005, 10008, 10009}.

Viewing

The following tips apply to viewing. See Chapter 7, *Viewing and Workstation Transformations*.

- Perspective projection may be slower than parallel projection.
- If your implementation supports the "posting to views" extensions to the PHIGS standard, and if that model is appropriate for your application, use the extensions instead of posting structures to the workstation. In the posting to views model, you do not use structure elements to change the current viewing parameters, but rather the viewing parameters are associated with individual viewports.

Primitives

In general, try to define geometry using the smallest number of primitives possible. For example, one fill area set can define a number of (coplanar) polygonal areas. Also, one polyline with many segments may provide better performance than many polylines with one segment.

Quadrilateral Mesh and Triangle Strip Primitives

When representing a curved surface, one quadrilateral mesh or triangle strip primitive usually gives better performance than representing the same area using many fill area primitives. See Chapter 10, *Output Primitives and Attributes*.

Text

Fonts made up of polylines may provide better performance than fonts made up of fill areas (called bitmap fonts). See your implementation documentation for a description of supported fonts.

Changing the text font as little as possible may improve performance. For example, group all of your text using a particular font together, preceded by a single call to SET TEXT FONT.

Face Culling and Hidden Surface Removal

Culling back-facing area-defining primitives may increase rendering performance. On the other hand, using hidden surface removal (HLHSR) may decrease rendering performance. See Chapter 15, *Front and Back Facet Processing* and Chapter 8, *Hidden Line/Hidden Surface Removal*.

Application-level Clipping

If you can determine, at the application level, that an object is entirely outside the clipping limits, you can increase rendering performance by not posting the associated structures.

For example, suppose you have a section of code that draws 10,000 polylines. If there is a way to determine that all these lines are outside the clip limits, you will save time otherwise spent clipping the 10,000 lines. Of course, if the application-level checking takes more time than the clipping, there is no performance gain. Note that proper use of structure hierarchy can often help in this area. See Chapter 5.

Regeneration

Use UPDATE WORKSTATION rather than REDRAW ALL STRUCTURES.

For high frame-rate applications, a smaller workstation viewport will decrease the amount of time spent clearing the display surface.

Colour Mapping

Colour mapping methods "pseudo colour" and "pseudo colour n" may be slower than colour mapping method "true colour". See Chapter 19, *Colour Mapping*.

X Windows

On workstations that display in X windows, keep the X window used for rendering the PHIGS display in front of other windows. Avoid nonrectangular window shapes whenever possible.

Using FORTRAN

This section covers the following topics:

- FORTRAN binding names
- Data records
- The FORTRAN 77 subset binding

FORTRAN Binding Names

The PHIGS FORTRAN binding restricts names to six characters which makes for some pretty unusual-looking names. Each routine name begins with `p` for PHIGS, and the remaining letters are abbreviations for the main function of the routine. For example, OPEN becomes `op`, UPDATE becomes `u`, and WORKSTATION becomes `wk`. Thus, open workstation becomes `popwk` and update workstation becomes `puwk`. Clause 4 of the PHIGS FORTRAN binding lists the abbreviations.

The FORTRAN 77 Subset Binding

PHIGS defines two bindings for FORTRAN, one for full FORTRAN 77 and another for the FORTRAN 77 subset. The binding for the FORTRAN 77 subset takes into account the following restrictions imposed by the subset:

- Routines in the full FORTRAN 77 binding can have arguments of type `CHARACTER*(*)`. In the subset version, these routines must have arguments of type `CHARACTER*80`.

- A number of routines that use character strings need an additional parameter in the subset version that specifies the number of characters in the string. When this happens, there is a specific version of the routine that is distinguished by the addition of a final "`s`" on the name.

PACK DATA RECORD and UNPACK DATA RECORD are examples of the first case. There is only one PACK DATA RECORD routine, but character string entries are defined differently depending on whether or not you are using the subset.

The TEXT 3 routine is an example of the second case. There are two distinct routines: `ptx3` and `ptx3s`. See Chapter 11, *Using Text*.

Using Data Records with the FORTRAN Binding

A number of PHIGS routines have a **data record** parameter. Data records serve two purposes in PHIGS:

- They allow additional implementation-dependent data, which is not defined in the standard parameter list, to be passed to PHIGS routines. For example, the generalized drawing primitive (GDP) routine has a data record parameter, and the implementation can define the contents of the data record for each primitive.
- For the FORTRAN language, they provide a method to pack unsimilar data types into the same data element, very much like C structures or unions.

For the FORTRAN binding, use the PACK DATA RECORD routine to load information into a data record. Data records can consist of integers, reals, and character strings.

The calling signature for PACK DATA RECORD is as follows:

`call pprec` (*num_ints*, *IntArray*, *num_reals*, *RealArray*, *num_strings*, *StrLengths*,
\+ *StringArray*, *MaxLenDatrec*, *Error*, *ldr*, *data_record*)

where:

⟨*num_ints*⟩ is the number of entries in the integer array. This parameter is an integer.

⟨*IntArray*⟩ is the integer array. For the FORTRAN 77 subset version, this must be the size specified in ⟨*num_ints*⟩. For the full FORTRAN version, it can be any size.

⟨*num_reals*⟩ is the number of entries in the real array. This parameter is an integer.

⟨*RealArray*⟩ is the real array. For the FORTRAN 77 subset version, this must be the size specified in ⟨*num_reals*⟩. For the full FORTRAN version, it can be any size.

⟨*num_strings*⟩ is the number of character string entries. This parameter is an integer.

⟨*StrLengths*⟩ is an integer array. Each entry specifies the length of the corresponding string in the string array. For the FORTRAN 77 subset version, the size of the array must be ⟨*num_strings*⟩. For the full FORTRAN version, it can be any size.

⟨*StringArray*⟩ is the character string array. For the FORTRAN 77 subset version, this must be declared as `CHARACTER*80`. For the full FORTRAN version, it can be any size.

⟨*MaxLenDatrec*⟩ is the number of 80-byte blocks the application allocates for the data record.

The following are output parameters:

⟨*Error*⟩ is an error indicator.

⟨*ldr*⟩ is the actual length of the data record. This is the number of 80-byte array elements used in the data record.

⟨*data_record*⟩ is the returned data record.

You pass the data record and its actual length to the appropriate PHIGS routine. Use UNPACK DATA RECORD to unpack a data record created by `pprec`.

Example

The PACK DATA RECORD routine makes data records easy to use. Your main concerns as an application programmer are to supply the correct number of integer, real, and string values and to make sure that the values are in the correct order.

This example is taken from the program that creates a circle GDP in Chapter 23. It supplies the following information to the circle data record:

- The data record requires one integer value and one real value. There are no string values, so we specify that the number of strings is 0.
- The single integer value identifies the number of points needed to define the circle (for this particular GDP, only one point is needed).

- The real value specifies the radius of the circle.

The above information is specific to HP-PHIGS. Other implementations may use different data record values to define a similar circle.

The following fragment opens the structure, packs the data record, and passes the data record to the GDP routine:

```
integer*4 TheStructure              ! display list structure root
parameter (TheStructure=1)          ! value chosen by the user
real CenterX(1), CenterY(1)         ! for center point
data CenterX /.5/, CenterY /.5/ ! define location of center
character*80 DataRec(2)             ! data record array
integer*4 DataRecSize               ! returned size of data record
integer*4 IntArray(10)              ! integer array
real RealArray(10)                  ! real array
character*80 StrArray(10)           ! dummy string array
integer*4 Error                     ! error-return variable
...
call popst(TheStructure)            ! open display list structure
IntArray(1)=1                       ! # of pts. to specify circle
RealArray(1)=.4                     ! radius of circle
call pprec (1, IntArray, 1, RealArray, ! pack data record
+  0, 80, StrArray, 2, Error, DataRecSize, DataRec)
if (Error .ne. 0) then
print *,"Error", Error, "in pprec."
stop
endif
call pgdp (1, CenterX, CenterY, -10, DataRecSize,
+          DataRec)                 ! create GDP
call pclst                          ! close display list structure
```

In the above fragment the –10 value identifies a circle GDP for HP-PHIGS. Note that PACK DATA RECORD does not create a structure element, so the `pprec` routine could have been placed before the OPEN STRUCTURE routine with the same effect.

There is another pack data record example in Chapter 23, in the section entitled “Using ESCAPE.”

PHIGS PLUS Pack and Unpack Routines

PHIGS PLUS defines the following additional routines for packing and unpacking data:

- PACK COLOUR SPLINE CURVE
- UNPACK COLOUR SPLINE CURVE
- PACK COLOUR SPLINE SURFACE
- UNPACK COLOUR SPLINE SURFACE
- PACK DATA SPLINE SURFACE
- UNPACK DATA SPLINE SURFACE
- PACK TRIMMING CURVE
- UNPACK TRIMMING CURVE

See your implementation documentation for information on using these routines.

Using "INQUIRE LIST OF ..." Routines

There are a number of routines that start with "INQUIRE LIST OF ...." For the FORTRAN binding, these routines return the number of items in the list and one item from the list. To get the entire list, you call the routine multiple times. For example, the FORTRAN binding calling signature for the INQUIRE LIST OF AVAILABLE WORKSTATION TYPES routine is as follows:

`call pqewk` (*n*, *error*, *number*, *type*)

where:

⟨*n*⟩ is the requested element in the list.

The following parameters are output parameters:

⟨*error*⟩ is an error indicator.

⟨*number*⟩ is the number of entries in the list of available workstation types.

⟨*type*⟩ is the ⟨*n*⟩th element in the list of available workstation types.

Use the following procedure to determine all of the available elements in the list:

1. Call the routine a first time with ⟨*n*⟩ equal to 0 to find out how many items are in the list of available workstation types.
2. Call the routine ⟨*number*⟩ times, passing it values from 1 to ⟨*number*⟩, to determine all of the supported values.

Chapter 23

Extensions

Introduction

In many cases, developers of an implementation of an ISO or ANSI standard encounter a dilemma where there are two mutually exclusive requirements they must simultaneously meet: They want to develop standardized software because of its inherent portability, but state-of-the-art software and hardware support very useful capabilities and performance-improvement features that are not yet standard. Two responses to this dilemma are to

- Develop standard software that is very portable, but supports none of the advanced, nonstandard features.
- Develop software that implements the advanced features but is inherently nonstandard.

As you can imagine, both of these options are unacceptable to most software developers. If they choose the first option, they sacrifice the flashy images, high performance, or ease of use only possible with state-of-the-art techniques—those techniques that make people want to buy their product. On the other hand, if they choose the second option, they sacrifice the compatibility and portability, only possible with standard software, which make people want to buy their product. But in this case, the product is considered proprietary, and therefore probably won't work well with other software and hardware.

The resolution of these problems is for the providers of the implementation to write software in which the state-of-the-art functionality and performance are "half-supported." That is, routines will be made available for the application programmer to use, but they will be accessed through an obviously "back-door" method—a method that, while it certainly works, does not introduce routine names that are likely to interfere with the standard as it develops in the future. In other words, you can temporarily *escape* from the boundaries imposed by the standard. Then, as the standard is developed over time, a particular functionality may, if appropriate, become "officially" supported, and have an "official" routine name instead of the temporary one assigned to "escape" the previous support limitations. PHIGS supports this approach with the following:

- The ESCAPE routine
- Generalized drawing primitives (GDPs and GDP3s)
- Generalized structure elements (GSEs)

Note that these features are part of the PHIGS standard itself. That is, within the definition of the PHIGS standard, ESCAPE, GDP, and GSE are officially supported mechanisms to allow implementations to add value to the standard by supporting useful, but as yet nonstandard, functionality.

Using ESCAPE

The rationale for the ESCAPE function is explained in the previous section. The calling signature of ESCAPE for the C binding is

```
pescape(
    Pint                      func_id,
    const Pescape_in_data     *in_data,
    Pstore                    *store,
    Pescape_out_data          **out_data
);
```

where:

⟨*func_id*⟩ is an integer that specifies the requested functionality, out of the many available. This value is a negative number if it is an implementation-defined feature.

⟨*in_data*⟩ is a pointer to a structure containing the data necessary for accomplishing the requested task. The contents differ, depending on ⟨*func_id*⟩. The actual definition of this structure type is implementation-dependent.

⟨*store*⟩ is a "handle" to a block of dynamically allocated memory, whose purpose is to contain the output data. The amount of data space needed is unknown prior to the call; hence, the dynamic allocation. ⟨*store*⟩ is pointed to by ⟨*out_data*⟩.

⟨*out_data*⟩ is a pointer that points to the dynamically allocated memory referenced by ⟨*store*⟩. The contents of this memory, defined by ESCAPE, depend on the value of ⟨*func_id*⟩ and the current state of the PHIGS system. Like ⟨*in_data*⟩, the actual definition of the ⟨*out_data*⟩ type is implementation-dependent.

The calling signature of ESCAPE for the FORTRAN binding is

```
 call pesc(func_id, in_data_rec_len, in_data_rec, out_data_rec_max_len,
+ out_data_rec_len, out_data_rec)
```

where:

⟨*func_id*⟩ is an integer that specifies the requested functionality, out of the many available. This value is a negative number if it is an implementation-defined feature.

⟨*in_data_rec_len*⟩ is an integer specifying the size of ⟨*in_data_rec*⟩, expressed in 80-byte blocks (e.g., FORTRAN's `character*80`). The size of the data record is returned by PACK DATA RECORD. You can set ⟨*in_data_rec_len*⟩ to 0 if no input data record is defined.

⟨*in_data_rec*⟩ is an array of bytes whose effective length is 80 × ⟨*in_data_rec_len*⟩. The contents differ, depending on ⟨*func_id*⟩. Use PACK DATA RECORD to define this array.

⟨*out_data_rec_max_len*⟩ is the size of the ⟨*out_data_rec*⟩ array the application allocates, expressed in 80-byte blocks.

⟨*out_data_rec_len*⟩ is the actual number of 80-byte blocks needed to store the information to be returned in ⟨*out_data_rec*⟩. This value is computed by ESCAPE. If ESCAPE determines this to be greater than ⟨*out_data_rec_ max_len*⟩, an error is generated, and ⟨*out_data_rec*⟩ is not changed.

⟨*out_data_rec*⟩ is an array of 80-byte blocks of data whose contents, defined by ESCAPE, depend on the value of ⟨*func_id*⟩. The data in ⟨*out_data_rec*⟩ should be interpreted using UNPACK DATA RECORD. See Chapter 22, *Programming with PHIGS*, for information on data records.

For example, HP-PHIGS has an escape that allows you to set the dithering value for a particular workstation (the value determines how many shades are used for dithering). Suppose you wanted to set the dithering value of a particular workstation to 8. This functionality does not have a standard routine defined for it, but it can be accessed via ESCAPE. The HP-PHIGS reference page for ESCAPE says that this functionality is associated with a ⟨*func_id*⟩ value of –240. The reference page has this to say about ⟨*func_id*⟩ –240:

```
-240: SET DITHERING VALUE
  Pertinent PACK DATA RECORD (PPREC) arguments:
  INTEGER IL = 2            Number of integer values
  INTEGER IA(2)             1. Workstation identifier
                            2. Dithering value
```

This tells us that in order to use the SET DITHERING VALUE functionality, we must define an integer array at least two elements long, and define the first element to be the workstation identifier, and the second element to be the desired dithering value. Also, by virtue of their absence, we can deduce that no real arrays or string arrays are used at all. After PACK DATA RECORD converts the arrays into the data record, we pass it to ESCAPE.

The following code fragment illustrates how to put this knowledge to use:

```
 integer*4              IntArray(2), Dummy
 integer*4              ErrorReturn, DataRecLen
 character*80           DataRec(10)
   ...
 IntArray(1)=WkstnID    ! workstation ID
 IntArray(2)=8          ! desired dither value
 call pprec(2, IntArray,! integer array
+  0, Dummy,            ! real array unused
+  0, 0, Dummy,         ! string array unused
+  10,                  ! data record max. length
+  ErrorReturn,         ! error-return variable
+  DataRecLen,          ! actual space used
+  DataRec)               ! data record itself
 if (ErrorReturn .ne. 0) then ! if error occurred...
   (deal with error condition)
 else
   call pesc(-240,      ! -240 -> set dither value
+    DataRecLen, DataRec,  ! pass encoded data
+    0, 0, Dummy)       ! output data record unused
 end if
```

Individual Entry Points

The ESCAPE routine is PHIGS' generic entry point for accessing nonstandard functionality. However, many PHIGS implementations also offer a second, preferred way of accessing these nonstandard functionalities: the convenient *optional* entry points defined by the PHIGS standard. This approach involves calling a dedicated, single-purpose routine.

These single-purpose routines correlate to the various values of ⟨*func_id*⟩ that can be sent to ESCAPE. For example, the standard naming convention for the FORTRAN binding is to use the characters "`pue`" and append a three-digit number equal to the absolute value of the ⟨*func_id*⟩ that would be passed to ESCAPE to accomplish the same function. The standard naming convention for the C binding is to do the same thing using with the characters "`pescape_u`". The exact routine names are not really important, as long as there is an unambiguous, one-to-one mapping between the ⟨*func_id*⟩ passed to ESCAPE and the special-purpose routine, and the names do not conflict with the rules put forth in the standard.

Using the special-purpose routines is "preferred" because the ESCAPE routine, not knowing which ⟨*func_id*⟩ will ultimately be passed to it, must contain the code to accomplish *every possible task* that could be requested. Since it is extremely unlikely that *every* possible task will be called for, this generality results in greater memory usage and decreased performance, both of which are avoided if the special-purpose routines are used.

Generalized Drawing Primitives

The PHIGS standard allows an implementation to define additional output primitives. PHIGS provides a mechanism called generalized drawing primitives (GDPs) to allow the implementation to present the new primitives in a standard format. The following are examples of GDPs:

- Circle
- Circular arc
- Ellipse
- Elliptical arc
- 2D polyline set

The way that you specify a GDP is implementation dependent. For example, a circle could be defined in a number of different ways, including a center point and a radius, a center point and a peripheral point, or three peripheral points.

The implementation selects the set of attributes that are most applicable to the GDP. It can specify that zero or more sets of polyline, polymarker, text, annotation text, and interior or edge attributes apply to a given GDP. For example, a circle can be treated as an area-defining primitive, and a circular arc can be treated as a line primitive. Whether or not individual or bundled attributes apply to the primitive depends on the appropriate attribute source flags. View index, HLHSR identifier, pick identifier, and name set attributes always apply to GDPs.

Implementations may allow the application to specify the GDP through the GENERALIZED DRAWING PRIMITIVE or GENERALIZED DRAWING PRIMITIVE 3 routine. The implementation may also supply alternative individual entry GDP point routines (see "Using Escapes" earlier in this chapter). If individual entry points are provided, they may be preferable with regard to execution time, structure element creation time, and code space requirements.

The calling signature for GENERALIZED DRAWING PRIMITIVE is as follows (add *z* values for the 3D routine):

```
call pgdp(num_pts, x_values, y_values, identifier, ldr, data_record)
```

```
pgdp(
    const Ppoint_list   *point_list,
    Pint                identifier,
    const Pgdp_data     *gdp_data
);
```

where:

⟨*point_list*⟩ is the point list for the C binding.

⟨*identifier*⟩ is the GDP identifier. This value is implementation-dependent.

⟨*gdp_data*⟩ is the GDP data record for the C binding.

The following parameters are for the FORTRAN binding:

⟨*num_pts*⟩ is the number of points in the GDP.

⟨*x_values*⟩ and ⟨*y_values*⟩ are the *x* and *y* coordinates required by the GDP, expressed in modelling coordinates.

⟨*ldr*⟩ is the dimension of the data record array. This is the number of 80-byte elements forming the data record. The size of the data record is dependent on the particular GDP.

The PACK DATA RECORD routine returns this value when you use that routine to build the data record. If the GDP has no data record values, set ⟨*ldr*⟩ to 0, and PHIGS will ignore the record.

⟨*data_record*⟩ is the data record. This parameter contains different information based on which GDP you select. Use the PACK DATA RECORD routine to form this data record. See Chapter 22 for information on data records.

GDPs do not generate errors during traversal. If the implementation does not recognize the GDP type, it ignores the structure element.

Using the GENERALIZED DRAWING PRIMITIVE Routine

This example shows how to use the GENERALIZED DRAWING PRIMITIVE routine with the FORTRAN binding. It shows how HP-PHIGS creates a 2D circle GDP. The example uses the following implementation-dependent information:

- For HP-PHIGS, the circle identifier is –10.
- For HP-PHIGS, the following information is required by the circle data record:
  - number of integers = 1 (the number of points needed to define the circle)
  - number of reals = 1 (the radius value)
  - number of strings = 0

The program draws a large, unfilled circle in the middle of the window (see Figure 23–1). The full listing follows:

```
include 'phigs.f1.h'            ! get the PHIGS aliases
program CircleGDP               ! program "CircleGDP.f"
include 'phigs.f2.h'            ! get the PHIGS constants

integer*4 WorkstnID             ! workstation identifier
parameter (WorkstnID=1)         ! value chosen by the user
integer*4 ConnID                ! connection identifier
integer*4 WorkstnType           ! workstation type
parameter (WorkstnType=POIDDX)  ! implementation-dependent
integer*4 TheStructure          ! display list structure root
parameter (TheStructure=1)      ! value chosen by the user
```

```
real CenterX(1), CenterY(1)      ! for center point
data CenterX /.5/, CenterY /.5/ ! define location of center
character*80 DataRec(2)          ! data record array
integer*4 DataRecSize            ! returned size of data record
integer*4 IntArray(10)           ! integer array
real RealArray(10)               ! real array
character*80 StrArray(10)        ! dummy string array
integer*4 Error                  ! error-return variable
integer*4 fdopen                 ! to get file descriptor

call popph(fdopen(fnum(7), 'w'//char(0)), 0)    ! open PHIGS
call pue004('/dev/screen/phigs_window', ConnID)! get connection ID
call popwk(WorkstnID, ConnID, WorkstnType)      ! open workstation
call popst(TheStructure)                ! open display list structure
IntArray(1)=1                           ! # of pts. to specify circle
RealArray(1)=.4                         ! radius of circle

call pprec (1, IntArray, 1, RealArray, ! pack data record
+  0, 0, StrArray, 2, Error, DataRecSize, DataRec)
if (Error .ne. 0) then
print *,"Error", Error, "in pprec."
stop
endif
call pgdp (1, CenterX, CenterY, -10, DataRecSize,
+           DataRec)                    ! create GDP
call pclst          ! close display list structure
call ppost(WorkstnID, TheStructure, 1.)! mark structure for display
call puwk(WorkstnID, PPERFO)            ! update the workstation
call pclwk(WorkstnID)                   ! close workstation
call pclph                              ! close PHIGS
stop                                    ! stop processing
end                                     ! end of program
```

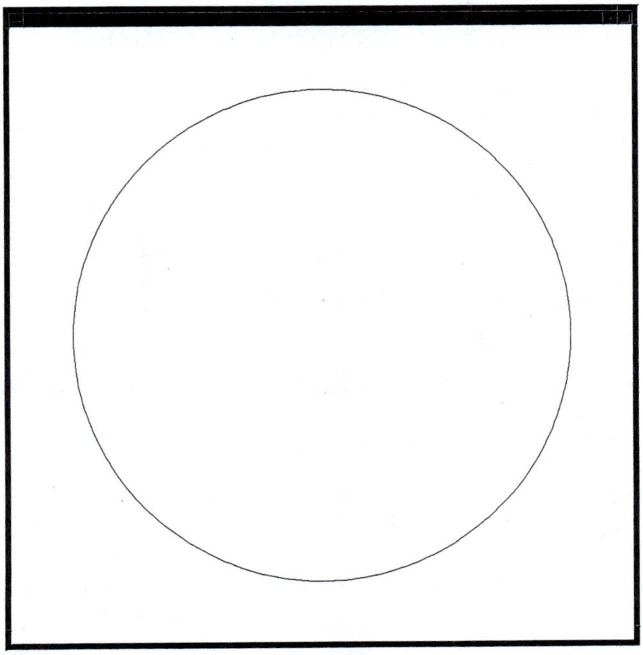

Figure 23–1. Circle Drawn by the GDP

Generalized Structure Element (GSE)

PHIGS provides a standard mechanism that allows implementations to add their own specialized structure elements (other than GDPs). The mechanism is called a generalized structure element (GSE). This allows an implementation to add special control and attribute-related structure elements that are not defined by the PHIGS standard.

For example, the PHIGS standard defines a highlighting feature that can be turned on and off using name sets. However, it does not define a method for selecting different highlight options such as using different colours for different primitives. An implementation could define a highlight table and then add an escape routine for modifying entries in the table. Then it could provide a GSE for selecting an entry from the table at traversal time.

GSEs do not create output primitives. PHIGS provides the generalized drawing primitive (GDP) for that purpose.

The calling signatures for the GENERALIZED STRUCTURE ELEMENT routine are as follows:

```
call pgse(gse_id, ldr, gse_datrec)
```

```
pgse(
    Pint                    gse_id,
    const Pgse_data         *gse_data
);
```

where:

⟨*gse_id*⟩ is an integer that identifies the specific type of generalized structure element.

⟨*gse_data*⟩ is the generalized structure element data for the C binding.

⟨*ldr*⟩ is the dimension of the data record for the FORTRAN binding. This parameter specifies the number of 80-byte blocks required to store the GSE's data.

⟨*gse_datrec*⟩ is the generalized structure element data record for the FORTRAN binding. Use PACK DATA RECORD to pack a variety of integers, floating-point numbers, and strings into the data record before sending it to the GSE routine.

The data will contain whatever information is necessary for the definition of the generalized structure element. For example, if the element selects an entry from an implementation-defined workstation highlight table, the only necessary information would be a single integer value, the index.

GSEs do not generate errors during traversal. If the implementation does not recognize the GSE type, it ignores the structure element.

Note that two different implementations might use the same GSE (or GDP) ID for entirely different elements. Likewise, two different implementations might use different GSE or GDP IDs for the same element. If you are concerned about making your application portable between different PHIGS implementations, you should limit your use of GSEs and GDPs.

Chapter 24

Using PHIGS with X Windows

Introduction

A computer's working capacity can be divided between several processes, each of which has its own dedicated area—its own **window**—of the display for input and/or output. This is perhaps the major benefit of a windowing system. The user can address each window at will and cause programmatic input and/or output to be associated with a particular window. The X11 Window System ("X Window System" is a trademark of the Massachusetts Institute of Technology) is a powerful window system. Many PHIGS implementations run on X11.

This chapter suggests some methods for running PHIGS programs with the X Window System. It is assumed at this point that you have a working knowledge of PHIGS and a working knowledge of X11 used individually; this chapter deals with using them together. Specifically, this chapter:

- Explains how to deal with X events, such as "expose" and "resize" events.
- Describes how to take a PHIGS program and run it in a previously existing window. Because such a program does not call Xlib procedures, it is called *window-dumb*. This is in contrast to *window-smart* programs.
- Provides development details for creating window-smart PHIGS programs, which make Xlib window calls. Window-smart programs create and manipulate their own windows; these windows last only for the duration of the program.

X Documentation

This chapter covers only the simpler aspects of running PHIGS in an X11 environment; there are many topics that, because of their level of complexity, are outside the scope of this manual. For much more detailed information on using X11, see the following documents:

- Jones, O. *Introduction to the X Window System*, Englewood Cliffs, NJ: Prentice Hall.
- Asente, P. J., and Swick, R.R. *The X Window System Toolkit*, Bedford, MA: Digital Press.
- *The Definitive Guides to the X Window System,* Volumes 0 – 5, Sebastopol, CA: O'Reilly and Associates.
- Gaskins, T. (1992). *PHIGS Programming Manual*, Sebastopol, CA: O'Reilly and Associates.
- Kosko, L. (1992). *PHIGS Reference Manual*, Sebastopol, CA: O'Reilly and Associates.

Refer to your own PHIGS implementation documentation for device-specific information relating to PHIGS and X.

Notation Conventions

As in the rest of this book, PHIGS routine names are written in small caps (for example, OPEN PHIGS). X Window System routines are written using both upper and lower case (for example, XGetVisualInfo). Values returned by and supplied to X routines are written in computer font (for example, `PseudoColor` visual).

PHIGS Operation in the X Window Environment

Depending on your PHIGS implementation, you may be able to run a PHIGS program on one machine and send its output through the network to another machine's X server.

When PHIGS is running within an X window environment, there are no restrictions on which other applications may be running simultaneously in other X windows; there are no direct interactions between PHIGS and other applications running under X. However, there are *indirect* interactions such as competition for limited X resources (such as input and colour maps) and system resources.

Several statements should be made pertaining to interactions between PHIGS and X Windows:

- On a single computer, multiple processes can be running PHIGS applications simultaneously. They do not interfere with each other, as there is no interaction (other than through archiving or metafiles) between the PHIGS functions of each process.
- Several windows of an X display can have a PHIGS workstation opened to it. These workstations can be opened by a single PHIGS process or by multiple PHIGS processes; either way will work.
- There is no restriction placed on the relationship of PHIGS windows to other windows: PHIGS windows may have any window as parent and may have arbitrary windows as children. PHIGS windows will behave properly when partially or fully obscured by other windows (although performance may be affected in a partially obscured window).
- The number of visuals supported by PHIGS is implementation-dependent.
- The number of PHIGS workstations that can be opened from a single PHIGS process is implementation-dependent.
- If multiple PHIGS workstations are opened simultaneously to a single window, the results are undefined.
- When a PHIGS workstation is rendering, all other PHIGS workstations and processes may be blocked. For example, if one PHIGS process initiates a complex set of primitives that requires five seconds to render, and another PHIGS process tries to display a popup menu, the second process may have to wait until the entire five-second period has elapsed.

Creating Windows

When you create windows for your PHIGS application or X programming, both the visual class and the depth of the window must be taken into consideration. You need to select a visual/depth pair based on the PHIGS capabilities you need in conjunction with implementation-dependent constraints on the workstation type.

The Visual Class

The X11 Window System developed by MIT supports six visual classes; they determine how colour is used in X11 windows. The following lists the six visual classes:

- `PseudoColor`
- `DirectColor`
- `StaticGray`
- `GrayScale`
- `StaticColor`
- `TrueColor`

The visual class of a window is established at window creation time and is not changeable thereafter. The visual class ultimately assigned to the window may not be the one you requested; it depends on the requested window depth and the current server mode. If you plan to run your program on a variety of devices, you may have to structure your application program to include different algorithms for the various differences in visual classes that can exist.

When creating a window of a particular configuration, you must specify the correct depth, in addition to specifying a valid visual. Thus, to get a 24-bit window, the depth must be 24 and the visual must be the visual returned from XGetVisualInfo corresponding to the 24-bit, `DirectColor` visual. You can also use XMatchVisualInfo to list the available visuals.

Your implementation documentation should list the different characteristics of the PHIGS workstations when opened to a window of a particular depth and visual class. With this information, you can intelligently choose an X server configuration and the depth and visual class of a window in which to open a PHIGS workstation. An application that needs to be portable should try to implement "rules" to match available visuals to its needs. It may also have to try several workstations if the implementation limitations are not hardcoded or configurable.

Handling X Events

PHIGS applications running in X windows should, at a minimum, consider handling X exposure (`Expose`) and resize (`ConfigureNotify`) events. This section covers the basics of handling these events, including some alternatives for handling resize events.

NOTE: Some implementations handle expose and resize automatically.

To capture these events, your application will need first to tell the X server that it wishes to receive them. This can be done by setting the `event_mask` member of the `XSetWindowAttributes` structure which is passed in when XCreateWindow or XChangeWindowAttributes is invoked, or the `event_mask` can be passed in when XSelectInput is invoked. The `event_mask` needs to include the `ExposureMask` to capture exposure events and the `StructureNotifyMask` to capture changes in the window structure, which includes resize events.

The simplest way to receive events is to loop on XNextEvent, which returns an event as soon as one is received. However, this is most appropriate for an application that is driven by an input event loop. Refer to your X documentation for further information on sophisticated event-queue handling.

Capturing X Events and PHIGS Input

If your application both uses PHIGS event-mode input and is running in an X window, you will need to watch both the PHIGS event queue and the X event queue. However, this is not recommended because it is not possible to handle both X and PHIGS input events asynchronously. The main problem is that time-ordering is not guaranteed. Some implementations have a two-process model, and others have mergeable event queues. This is one of the reasons we recommend you use X rather than PHIGS for your input.

If you do choose to capture both PHIGS input and X input, the following code fragment shows how your application might do this. In this example, the application is processing both PHIGS pick events and X exposure and resize events. The program loops on the pick events, processing all X events during each loop. Although it is not shown, the application must also have some way of allowing the user to break out of the loop.

```
void Loop(wkid, pick_device, display, window)
int  wkid;                              /* workstation ID */
int  pick_device;                       /* pick device no. */
```

```
Display *display;                       /* server display ID */
Window  window;                         /* X window ID */
{
    static int  event_class = PNCLAS; /* PHIGS event class */
    int    event_wkid;                  /* PHIGS event workstation */
    int    event_device;                /* PHIGS event device */
    static int  status = CONTINUE;      /* loop status */
    XSelectInput(display, window,       /* receive these X events */
      ExposureMask | StructureNotifyMask);     :
    pset_pick_mode(wkid, pick_device,
                POP_EVENT, PSWITCH_ECHO); /* set pick mode */
    do {          /* loop */
        while (event_class == PNCLAS) {    /* wait for a pick event */
            ProcessXEvents(wkid, display); /* process X events */
            pawait_event(0.0, &event_wkid, /* look for pick events */
              &event_class, &event_device);
        }
        ProcessPickEvent();         /* process the pick event */
        event_class = PNCLAS;       /* reset the pick-occurred flag */
    } while (status == CONTINUE)    /* loop */
}
void ProcessXEvents(wkid, display)
int  wkid;                          /* workstation ID */
Display *display;                   /* server display ID */
{
    XEvent event;                   /* X event */
    while (XEventsQueued(display, QueuedAfterReading))  /* get all
    {                                                    X events */
        XNextEvent(display, &event); /* fetch the next X event */
        switch (event.type) {       /* select on event type */
            case MapNotify:         /* window mapped */
            case Expose:            /* window exposed */
                ProcessExposure(); /* process now visible window */
                break;
            case ConfigureNotify:  /* window resized */
                ProcessResize();   /* process resized window */
                break;
            default:
                break;
        }
    }
}
```

Exposure Events

When you receive an exposure event for your window receiving PHIGS output, the contents of the window may be undefined unless the window has backing-store capabilities and PHIGS can draw into the backing store. If your implementation does not support backing store, regenerate the PHIGS image by invoking REDRAW ALL STRUCTURES.

Resize Events

Each implementation has its own default behavior when the user shrinks the size of the window. For example, by default HP-PHIGS maps the upper left-hand corner of the display space to the window. HP-PHIGS does not automatically adjust the viewport to account for the new window size. If the display surface is smaller than the window, the viewport will cover only a portion of the window now, whereas if the display surface were larger, a portion of the viewport would fill the window, but the display surface would be clipped by the window. Other implementations automatically resize the viewport when the user resizes the window. See your implementation documentation for details.

An Implementation-dependent Example

Although this example is specific to HP-PHIGS, it gives you an idea of the issues involved when resizing windows.

On HP-PHIGS, an X11 window of any size up to 32,767 × 32,767 pixels can be created. When PHIGS opens a workstation in this window, PHIGS automatically learns the window size. Invoke INQUIRE DISPLAY SPACE SIZE or INQUIRE DISPLAY SPACE SIZE 3 to determine the size, in device coordinates and pixels, of the window at the time PHIGS was opened to it. The window size at OPEN WORKSTATION is referred to as the **display space size** of the workstation. This value doesn't change for the lifetime of the workstation.

When a window is resized after the PHIGS workstation is opened to it, there is no way for PHIGS to realize the window has changed size. Inquiries of the display space size will return the size of the window at the time PHIGS was opened to it, rather than the current size of the window.

Rendering will continue to the resized window, with the display space anchored to the upper left-hand corner of the window. Because PHIGS is unaware of the resize, no scaling will be done to the graphics. However, the graphics will be clipped to the window boundaries. In other words, when a workstation is first opened, the X window exactly "covers" the display space. If the window is resized smaller, it only covers the upper left corner of the display space. If the window is sized larger, it covers more than the display space.

Although PHIGS is not aware of the resize event, your application can capture the event and take action to fit the graphics better into the new window size. Several options for this are described ahead. Note that on HP-PHIGS it is never possible to enlarge the display space beyond its size at the time the workstation was opened. For this reason, we recommend your application create and open a PHIGS workstation in the largest window that could be usable during the lifetime of the workstation. If you wish to display a smaller window initially, create the window, open the PHIGS workstation to it, decrease the size of the window, and then map the window, making it visible for the first time.

Capturing Resize Events

The application captures resize events through XNextEvent, which returns the `ConfigureNotify` X11 event. Window size information in pixels is provided with the event. Conversions between pixels and device coordinates (DCs), which are usually approximate meters, can be made easily since the display space inquiries return the display space size in both units.

Another point to notice is that the workstation transformation is isotropic. This means if the workstation window aspect ratio (height/width) and workstation viewport aspect ratio differ, the workstation window cannot entirely fill the viewport. Instead, the larger of the height or width will be fully fit to the viewport, and the smaller will be proportionately fit to the viewport, with the excess area being rendered in black. It is a good idea to start with your workstation window and workstation viewport using the same aspect ratio so there is no portion of the viewport which cannot be rendered to. Note also that if the workstation window does not fill the viewport, it is anchored at the lower left of the display surface (as specified in PHIGS). It is important to note that PHIGS computes the "placement" of the workstation window to viewport mapping whenever either is changed.

Note also there is no need to consider the z coordinate when making resize calculations. The window can only be resized in x and y, not in z.

Each implementation has its own default behavior when the user shrinks the size of the X window. Some implementations automatically adjust the viewport to account for the new window size, and others do not.

One possibility for handling the resize event is to refit the views within the adjusted viewport to take best advantage of the X window's dimensions. This is analogous to refitting subwindows to a window, as is discussed in X documentation. However, this may disturb the layout of the display. Disturbance of the user interface and other visibility factors must be considered.

Uniform Scaling

Uniform scaling is a commonly used method for handling resize events. This method scales the graphics to best fit the adjusted viewport without sacrificing the original aspect ratio of the graphics. This results in the full image being visible but uniformly scaled down to fit as well as possible in the newly sized window. If the workstation window and X window don't have the same aspect ratio, some of the X window will not be used.

Uniform scaling is accomplished by simply adjusting the viewport to cover the newly sized window. The workstation window is unchanged, so PHIGS performs its normal maximizing of the workstation window in the viewport. Thus, you continue to view the entire image. The graphics are not "stretched" (non-uniformly scaled) since the workstation transformation is isotropic; changing the workstation viewport only cannot result in non-uniform scaling.

See the "Window-Smarter" example later in this chapter.

The "Focus Window" and What It Means

In an X Window environment, there is a concept called **focus**. A window that is focused has a resource—such as the keyboard or the device colour map—associated with it. These two resources can obtain the focus independently, or together, according to your configuration. The term "focus" is used because the window in question is often the focus of interaction or of the user's attention.

The focus policies of the keyboard and the colour map are governed by the window manager and can be either of these two options:

- XNextEvent, which returns `explicit`, meaning that a specific request must be made for focus to be granted; for example, when the mouse button is clicked while the pointer is in a window
- `pointer`, meaning that focus is granted when the mouse pointer enters a window; no click is necessary

In addition, the colour map focus policy can be set to `keyboard`, which means "grant colour map focus to whichever window currently has keyboard focus." See your window manager's documentation for more details.

The remainder of this chapter assumes that the window manager's focus policies are both set to `pointer`.

The focus window also comes into play in the context of PHIGS. On some devices, the image in a nonfocused window may appear to be rendered with erroneous colours. This occurs when multiple processes requiring different X colour maps are sharing the same hardware colour map; the currently focused process determines the contents of the shared hardware colour map. To correct the colours in any particular window, simply focus that window.

Application developers are encouraged to design colour-map cooperation into their application programs. Suggestions for implementing colour map cooperation are

- Use the X11 colour maps and colour map calls whenever possible. See *The Definitive Guides to the X Window System* for some excellent advice on cell allocation; for example, cells may be acquired by RGB.
- Initialize a few identical entries in all colour maps and use these colours for borders, foreground/background, text, and any other commonly displayed information.
- Minimize the number of different X colour maps used. This will minimize the competition for limited hardware resources. Also, look at standard colour map properties; they facilitate sharing.

A major problem for PHIGS PLUS in X is that the most natural colour mapping method is true colour mapping. This requires a "ramp" of colour values in the colour map, such as those described by standard colour maps.

Window Managers and Pointer Buttons

One problem you may encounter when running PHIGS programs that receive input from the X11 pointer device is that the window manager being run may actually prevent PHIGS from seeing the clicks of the mouse button. For example, some systems implement their explicit-focus policy by grabbing all button presses that occur while the X cursor is over a window. Therefore, if a user moves the pointer over a PHIGS window and presses a mouse button, the PHIGS program will not see the button press, because X has "grabbed" it. However, most window managers allow users to reconfigure the window manager's button bindings in order to allow programs to receive input from the X11 pointer device.

Input devices work similarly to output devices, in the context of the focus window: Only the program running in the focused window is logically connected to the input devices. The "keyboard focus policy" is logically extrapolated into the "input focus policy." Suppose, for example, you have two PHIGS programs running simultaneously in two different windows, and they both use a graphical input device. To which program is the input device connected? Again, it is connected to the current input focus window.

Running A Window-Dumb PHIGS Program with X11

A **window-dumb program** is defined as one that does not make Xlib calls. The X11 window to which the program sends its output must be created before the program runs. We mention this topic mainly because many of the sample programs in this book use this technique. It allows us to keep the length of the program as short as possible.

The way that you create an X window is implementation-dependent. Keep in mind that when you create a window, X restricts you to certain combinations of depths and visual classes according to the device and X server configuration you are using. Not all of these windows that can be created are supported by PHIGS workstations.

Once the destination window has been created, an association between the PHIGS program and the window must be made. To allow the window-dumb program to access the X11 window, you have to tell PHIGS the name of the window to which output should go. This process is implementation-dependent. For example, HP-PHIGS supports an extension routine, named CREATE CONNECTION IDENTIFIER FOR FILENAME, that does the job:

```
call pue004('/dev/screen/phigs_window', ConnID)  ! FORTRAN binding

pescape_u4("/dev/screen/phigs_window", &ConnID);     /* C binding */
```

This routine returns the integer connection identifier (`ConnID`), which is subsequently passed to OPEN WORKSTATION.

We use this technique frequently in the programs shown in this book. Many of them use the following code, which uses the concepts just described:

```
call pue004('/dev/screen/phigs_window', ConnID)  ! get connection ID
call popwk(WorkstnID, ConnID, WorkstnType)       ! open workstation

pescape_u4("/dev/screen/phigs_window", &ConnID);/* C binding */
popen_ws(WorkstnID, ConnID, WorkstnType);
```

The first line assigns the previously created window `phigs_window` a connection identifier, and the second line associates that connection identifier with a workstation of the type specified by `WorkstnType`. Workstation types are implementation-dependent. In this book we often use the HP-PHIGS token `POIDSX`, which stands for "**P**HIGS **O**UT**I**N **D**irect Mode **S**ingle-buffered **X** Window".

Window-Smart Examples

Window-smart programs create and manipulate their own windows; these windows last only for the duration of the program. This section presents two window-smart examples. One is a very simple example and the other handles exposure and resize events.

A Simple Window-Smart Example

This simple example creates an X window and uses an implementation-dependent escape routine, CREATE CONNECTION IDENTIFIER FOR X11 WINDOW (`pue005, pescape_u5`) to create a connection between PHIGS and the X window. Then it opens a PHIGS workstation in the window and displays some simple graphics (a single line). The program uses the PHIGS input routine REQUEST CHOICE to decide when to exit the program.

```
#include <phigs.h>           /* get PHIGS definitions for C       */
#include <X11R4/X11/X.h>     /* get common X window definitions   */
#include <X11/Xlib.h>        /* get C routine definitions for X   */
#include <X11/Xutil.h>       /* get X utilities                   */
#include <stdio.h>           /* get standard I/O definitions      */

Display        *display;          /* X display identifier         */
Window         WindowID;          /* X window identifier          */

main()                            /* file "WindowSmart.c"         */
{
    Pint       WorkstnID = 1;     /* workstation identifier       */
    Pint       ConnID;            /* connection identifier        */
    Pint       WorkstnType = POIDDX;  /* implementation-dependent */
    Pint       TheStructure = 1;  /* structure ID                 */
    int        TheLine = 1;       /* structure root               */
    static Ppoint LinePoints[2] = {   /* line from SW to NE       */
               {0.0, 0.0}, {1.0, 1.0}};
    static Ppoint_list LineData = {
               2, LinePoints};
    int        ChoiceStatus, ChoiceNum;/* choice status and value */

    popen_phigs(stderr, 0);              /* errors go to "stderr"   */
    MakeXWindow();/*(&display, &WindowID);    /* make X window      */
    pue005(display, WindowID, &ConnID); /* get connection ID        */
    popen_ws(WorkstnID, ConnID, WorkstnType);  /* open workstation */
```

```
    popen_struct(TheLine);          /* open display list structure  */
    ppolyline(&LineData);           /* polyline with 2 points       */
    pclose_struct();                /* close display list structure */
    ppost_struct(WorkstnID, TheLine, 1.0);      /* post structure   */
    pupd_ws(WorkstnID, PFLAG_PERFORM);  /* update workstation       */
/*--- make keyboard a choice device so "Press [Return]..." works --*/
    pset_choice_mode(WorkstnID, 2, POP_REQ, PSWITCH_NO_ECHO);
/* request choice */
    preq_choice(WorkstnID, 2, &ChoiceStatus, &ChoiceNum);
    pclose_ws(WorkstnID);           /* close workstation            */
    pclose_phigs();                 /* close PHIGS                  */
}
/*****************************************************************/
MakeXWindow()
{
    int         screen, Border, Background;  /* X sundries         */

    if ((display = XOpenDisplay(NULL)) == NULL) {   /* use $DISPLAY*/
 fprintf(stderr, "XOpenDisplay: can't open %s\n", XDisplayName(NULL));
        exit(1);
    }
    screen = DefaultScreen(display);        /* get default screen   */
    Border = BlackPixel(display, screen);  /* define foreground     */
    Background = WhitePixel(display, screen);  /* define background*/
    WindowID = XCreateSimpleWindow(display,    /* make the window  */
      RootWindow(display, screen),          /*   parent window      */
50, 50, 300, 300, 3, Border, Background); /* location, size, colors*/
    XMapWindow(display, WindowID);          /* realize window       */
    XFlush(display);
}
```

A Window-Smarter Example

The example in this section illustrates the basic steps that might be taken in a window-smart application. Here is a detailed list of the steps you might take in your window-smart application:

1. Invoke XOpenDisplay. This establishes the client/server connection and supplies the display identifier.

2. Fetch the identifier for the default screen that will be used by the `DefaultScreen` macro.

3. Fetch a visual. In the example given, a match for an eight-plane `PseudoColor` visual is found by invoking XMatchVisualInfo. There is a visual with these characteristics supported on most PHIGS devices; however, there are some exceptions. For example, if you are using a gray-scale device, you need to look for a visual with a `GrayScale` rather than `PseudoColor` visual class. If you are using a device with 24 planes, you should look for a 24-plane `DirectColor` visual.

4. Create a colour map. Some implementations automatically allocate and initialize entries in the colour map. See your implementation documentation for details. Do not create a colour map when using a `TrueColor` or `StaticColor` visual.

5. Create a window. Note that you can prepare for any window resizing the user might do by creating the window to fill the screen. The width and height for such a window can be determined easily by using the `XDisplayWidth` and `XDisplayHeight` macros. Also, notice you can specify a minimal border (width of zero and in the background colour) since the window manager will most likely provide the borders. If you are going to size the window down, do it after opening the workstation.

6. Register with the X server which X events you will be processing by invoking XSelectInput. In the example we look for exposure, resize, and button-press events.

7. Open a PHIGS workstation to the window. Most implementations require that you create a connection ID between the X window and the PHIGS workstation.

8. Map the window. Now that the window is located and sized where you want it, map the window to make it visible.

9. Define a loop to process X events. This particular example handles exposure and resize events. Notice the mapping of the window will generate the exposure event

that will render the image for the first time. Button-press events are also received, providing a way in this example for an X event to be received that indicates the user has finished using the program.

This example illustrates the uniform scaling strategy for handling resize events (see "Resize Events," earlier in this chapter). The following steps were taken to implement the uniform scaling strategy:

1. The pixel-to-DC conversion factor was calculated once, as soon as the workstation was opened, by invoking INQUIRE DISPLAY SPACE SIZE. This routine returns the display surface size in both pixels and DCs, making it easy to calculate the conversion factor.

2. When a resize event is received, the window's new width and height are converted from pixels to DCs. The viewport is then reset to continue mapping to the upper left-hand corner of the display surface and to have exactly the same width and height as the X window.

The example renders a model that is just a red fill area. The model is defined to fill completely the *xy* plane of both the view and the workstation window. You can resize, iconify, obscure, and expose the window to see the effects on the model. To exit the program, depress a pointer button within the window when the window is focused.

Note that the example assumes that the implementation automatically defines entry 2 in the workstation colour table as red. Your implementation may not automatically allocate entries in the workstation colour table, or it may allocate different colours.

As you will see when executing the program, the red box, which is defined to illustrate the workstation window, will always be fully visible. Since the viewport is anchored to the bottom left-hand corner of the window, the box will appear in the lower left of the window, as opposed to the entire window, whenever the workstation window and workstation viewports don't match.

Before executing the program, you may have to define the environment variable `DISPLAY` to identify the X server used for display. See your implementation documentation for details.

Here is the source code for the program:

```
#include <phigs.h>          /* get PHIGS definitions */
#include <X11R4/X11/X.h>    /* get common X window definitions */
#include <X11/Xlib.h>       /* get C routine definitions for X */
#include <X11/Xutil.h>      /* get X window utilities */
#include <X11/XHPlib.h>     /* get HP-specific X definitions */
#include <stdio.h>          /* get standard I/O definitions */

main()                                     /* file "WindowSmarter.c" */
{
    /*--- X-windows-related variables ---------------------------------------*/
    Display              *display;         /* X display identifier */
    Window               parent;           /* window ID of parent window */
    Window               window;           /* window ID of window of interest */
    int                  screen;           /* id of X display screen */
    int                  LocX, LocY;       /* location of UL corner of window */
    int                  Width, Height;    /* width and height of window */
    int                  BorderWidth;      /* window of border */
    int                  depth;            /* depth of window */
    int                  Class;            /* class of window (Input? Output?) */
    long                 ValueMask;        /* for red values for window */
    XSetWindowAttributes attributes;       /* other window creation attributes */
    int                  VisualClass;      /* requested visual class of window */
    Visual               *visual;          /* actual visual class of window */
    XVisualInfo          VisualInfo;       /* contains assorted visual info */
    Colormap             ColorMap;         /* colour map ID for window */
    XEvent               event;            /* X event type */
    /*--- PHIGS-related variables -------------------------------------------*/
    Pint                 WorkstnID = 1;    /* workstation ID */
    static Pint          GenWkstnType = POIDSX;  /* generic workstation type */
    Pint                 ConnID;           /* connection ID */
    Pint                 *ConnIDptr;       /* ditto, but for pinq_ws_conn_type */
    Pint                 SpecWkstnType;    /* specific workstation type */
    Pint                 BoxStructure=1;   /* structure ID for object drawn */
    Pdisp_space_size     DispSize;         /* size of display in various units */
    Plimit               Viewport;         /* structure for viewport data */
    Pstore               *Store;           /* storage area */
    int                  ErrInd;           /* error-return indicator */
    /*--- process-related variables -----------------------------------------*/
    float                PixelToDC;        /* conversion factor: pixels to DCs */
    float                DCwidth;          /* window width, PHIGS DCs (meters) */
    float                DCheight;        /* window height, PHIGS DCs (meters) */
```

```
static Ppoint       ShapeData[4] =  {0.0,0.0, 0.0,1.9, 1.9,1.9, 1.9,0.0};
static Ppoint_list  Shape =         {4, ShapeData};
static Prgb         Red =           {1.0, 0.0, 0.0};  /* RGB for red */

/*=== set up the X display ========================================*/
display = XOpenDisplay(NULL);
if (!display) {
    printf("ERROR:  Failed to open default display\n");
    exit(1);
}
screen = DefaultScreen(display);
/*--- create 8-plane PseudoColor window, child of root ----------------*/
parent = RootWindow(display, screen);      /* works on most configs. */
LocX = 0;  LocY = 0;
Width = XDisplayWidth(display, screen);
Height = XDisplayHeight(display, Height);
BorderWidth = 0;
depth = 8;
Class = InputOutput;
VisualClass = PseudoColor;
if (!XMatchVisualInfo(display, screen, depth, VisualClass, &VisualInfo))
    printf("ERROR:  Couldn't find a matching visual\n");
visual = VisualInfo.visual;
ValueMask = CWBorderPixel | CWColormap | CWBackPixel;
ColorMap = XCreateColormap(display, parent, visual, AllocNone);
attributes.colormap = ColorMap;
attributes.border_pixel = 0;
attributes.background_pixel = 0;
window = XCreateWindow(display, parent, LocX, LocY, Width, Height,
  BorderWidth, depth, Class, visual, ValueMask, &attributes);
/*--- capture exposure and resize events ------------------------------*/
XSelectInput(display, window,
  ExposureMask | StructureNotifyMask | ButtonPressMask);
XSync(display, False);
/*=== set up PHIGS ================================================*/
popen_phigs(stderr, 0);
pescape_u5(display, window, &ConnID);      /* get conn. ID for window */
/*--- open the workstation ----------------------------------------*/
popen_ws(WorkstnID, ConnID, GenWkstnType);
pset_colr_rep(WorkstnID, 2, &Red);
/*--- determine pixel-to-DC conversion factor for resize algorithm -----*/
pcreate_store(&ErrInd, &Store);
if (ErrInd)
```

```
    printf("Error %d in pcreate_store\n", ErrInd), exit(1);
pinq_ws_conn_type(WorkstnID, Store, &ErrInd, &ConnIDptr, &SpecWkstnType);
if (ErrInd)
    printf("Error %d in pinq_ws_conn_type\n", ErrInd), exit(1);
pinq_disp_space_size(SpecWkstnType, &ErrInd, &DispSize);
if (ErrInd)
    printf("Error %d in pinq_disp_space_size\n", ErrInd), exit(1);
PixelToDC = (float)DispSize.size_dc.size_x / DispSize.size_raster.size_x;
/*--- resize the window down to application size -----------------------*/
Width = 600;  Height = 400;
XResizeWindow(display, window, Width, Height);
/*--- map the window, making it visible for the first time -------------*/
XMapWindow(display, window);
XSync(display, False);
/*--- create a structure with a large red box --------------------------*/
popen_struct(BoxStructure);
pset_int_colr_ind(2);
pset_int_style(PSTYLE_SOLID);
pfill_area(&Shape);
pclose_struct();
/*--- post the model to the workstation --------------------------------*/
ppost_struct(WorkstnID, BoxStructure, 1.0);
/*--- loop on X events for the rest of the program ---------------------*/
while (True) {
    XNextEvent(display, &event);
    switch (event.type) {
        /*--- regenerate when an exposure event is captured ------------*/
        case Expose:
            predraw_all_structs(WorkstnID, PFLAG_ALWAYS);
            break;
        /*--- adjust viewport when a resize event is captured ----------*/
        case ConfigureNotify:
            DCwidth = (float) event.xconfigure.width * PixelToDC;
            DCheight = (float) event.xconfigure.height * PixelToDC;
            Viewport.x_min = 0.0;
            Viewport.y_min = DispSize.size_dc.size_y - DCheight;
            Viewport.x_max = DCwidth;
            Viewport.y_max = DispSize.size_dc.size_y;
            pset_ws_vp(WorkstnID, &Viewport);
            break;
        /*--- close up shop when the window is clicked/closed ----------*/
        case ButtonPress:
            pclose_ws(WorkstnID);           /* close workstation */
```

```
                pclose_phigs();                         /* close PHIGS */
                exit(0);
                break;
            /*--- ignore all other events ----------------------------------*/
            default:
                break;
        }
    }
}
```

Intermixing PHIGS and X11 I/O

Mixing PHIGS and X11 Output

It is possible to mix PHIGS and X11 output in the same window; however, there are certain rules to abide by when writing such applications. While these rules may not be universal for all implementations, they are good general rules for mixing PHIGS and X.

Both PHIGS and X11 have buffered output. The use of Xlib operations in a PHIGS window is only defined within certain constraints:

- Following each sequence of X11 operations and before any PHIGS operation that could cause a picture change (i.e., a change in the CSS or the workstation state), XSync must be called. The update and deferral modes can be used to control regenerations in response to changes, but X must be synced before explicit regeneration.
- Following each sequence of PHIGS operations that may cause a picture change and before any X11 operation, REDRAW ALL STRUCTURES must be called; UPDATE WORKSTATION is not adequate when mixing output.

It can be assumed X rendering will be directed to at least the visible buffer; that is, X rendering will be immediately visible over the currently displayed PHIGS image.

Mixing PHIGS and X rendering is not a fully supported behavior. Although we believe you should see the previously predicted behavior when you follow the guidelines, we do not guarantee it. It would be a good idea to test thoroughly your application's usage of PHIGS and X output mixing on each X server, window, and PHIGS workstation configuration that you support. You may consider providing a mechanism for the user to indicate that the PHIGS image should be regenerated if his or her window has been corrupted.

Mixing PHIGS and X11 Input

There may be problems mixing PHIGS and X input because it is not possible to handle both X and PHIGS input events asynchronously. The earlier scheme shown for mixing X event-handling and PHIGS input can be extended to cover some cases of mixed input.

PEX

When the designers of the X window system were doing their development work at MIT, they concentrated their effort on the lower-level aspects of a window system: networked window management, input, and simple 2D output. This was a large enough task in itself. They made a deliberate decision to postpone the more complicated aspects of a full-featured windowing system until "later." Now, some years later, X is very successful and has become a de facto standard windowing product in the worldwide workstation market. "Later" has arrived.

With the 2D version of X windows firmly entrenched, the designers are concentrating their efforts on those more difficult aspects of windowing previously postponed: 3D graphics and image processing. Simultaneously, PHIGS is starting to gain widespread acceptance as a standard, portable graphics system; hence, the 3D enhancements to the current X Windows System were temporarily associated with the 3D portion of PHIGS. From this association came the name **PEX**, which meant "**P**HIGS **E**xtensions to **X**." Since that time, the enhancements to the X Window System have been more generally applicable than just to PHIGS, so the original meaning of PEX has been dropped, although the name "PEX" has stuck nonetheless. However, the PEX extension retains many of the capabilities and features of PHIGS and PHIGS PLUS.

PEX Processing

In an X Windows environment, an X server runs continuously. The server is the program that is responsible for receiving and acting upon requests from application processes, or X clients. These clients can connect to and send requests to any device on the network that is also running an X server process. The form of the information passed between X servers and X clients is precisely defined by the X protocol specification, and if the information conforms to that specification, network transparency will result. That is, it is indiscernible by the user whether or not the X client is executing on the local machine, or on another machine connected via the network. This makes truly portable code possible: As long as the applications conform to the X protocol, they can communicate effectively with machines from other vendors without being rewritten, recompiled, or even relinked. Similarly, PEX is in fact a set of additional protocol requests that perform PHIGS-like 3D graphics operations.

The PEX Pipeline

The transformation pipeline for PEX is similar to that of PHIGS, but understandably, there is some added functionality required in order to deal with the network transparency and window environment. Figure 24–1 shows the PEX transformation pipeline.

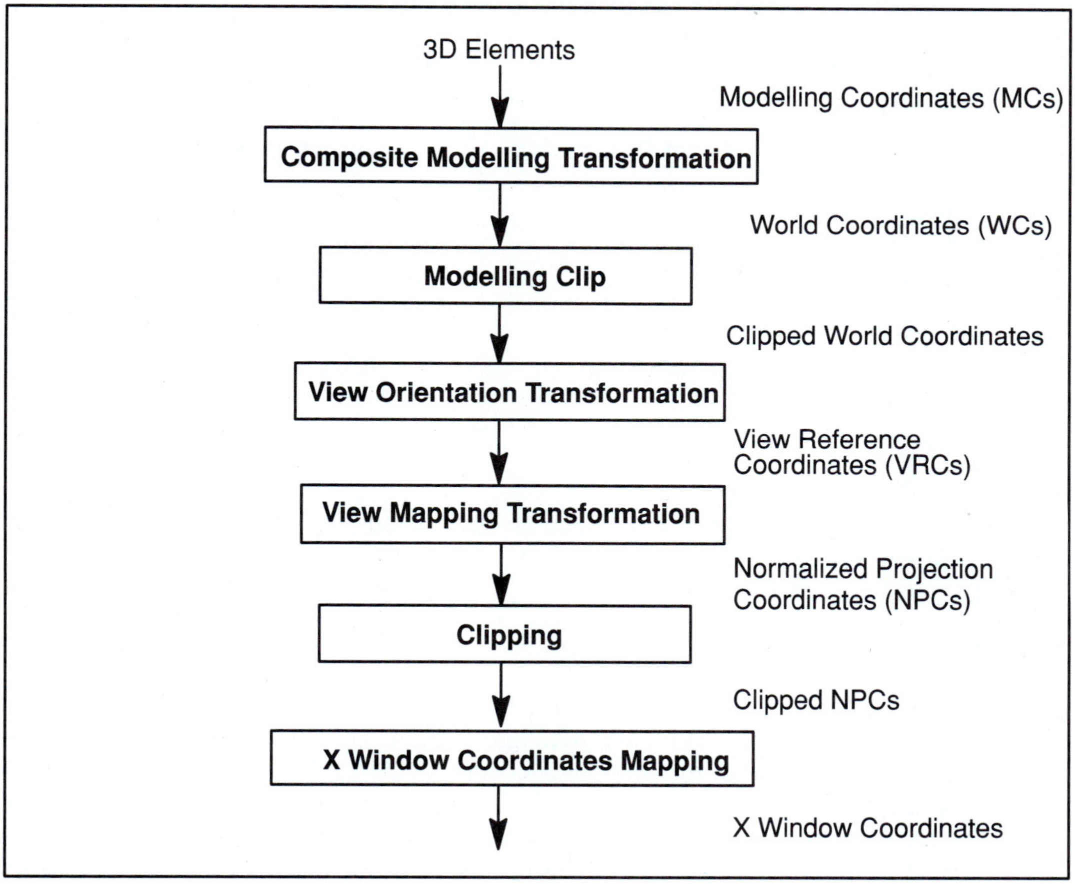

Figure 24–1. The PEX Transformation Pipeline

PEX uses the rendering pipeline defined by PHIGS PLUS. A powerful feature of the rendering pipeline is its ability to perform colour transformations, in addition to geometric transformations. Just as geometric information is transformed to pixel locations, colours are also transformed into pixel colours. And, like geometric information after having been passed through the pipeline, colours passing through the pipeline often come out of the pipeline quite different than they went in—colours can be modified from light-source position and colour, object orientation, depth cueing, and so forth. Figure 24–2 shows the PHIGS PLUS rendering pipeline.

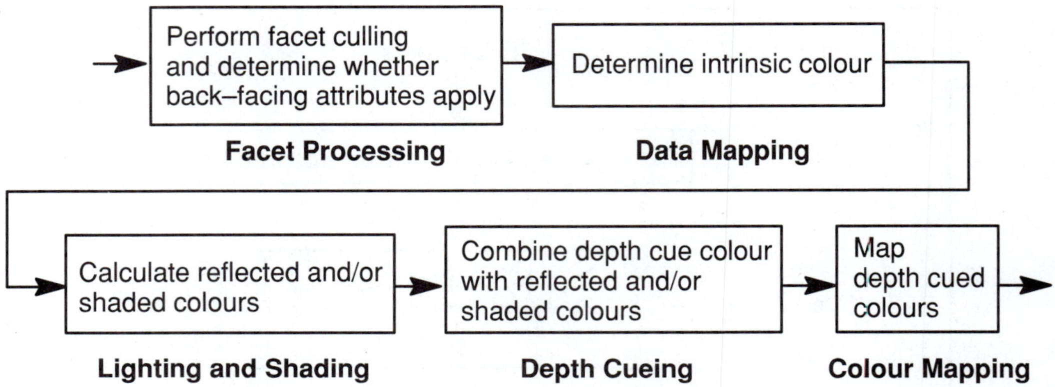

Figure 24–2. PHIGS PLUS Rendering Pipeline

Note that at this writing, no version of PEX includes a data mapping stage. However, data mapping is proposed as part of PEX Version 6.0.

Structures

Like PHIGS, PEX supports a structure-traversal mode of operation during its rendering: The hierarchical database is transformed into a single, one-dimensional stream of output primitives. One advantage to a structure network, or display list, is that the hierarchical structure makes organization and manipulation easier. However, one disadvantage to the hierarchical structure network is that it can consume enormous amounts of memory; not all devices can spare such copious amounts of memory. Also, some implementations do not require structure editing operations to perform modelling or attribute changes. For these implementations, the overhead of maintaining a structure network may be unnecessary.

To address this problem, PEX was designed to support an "immediate mode"; that is, as soon as primitives are encountered, they are rendered. This is different from the structure-network mode, in which the primitives are stored for later rendering. Note that an immediate mode is also being proposed as part of the PHIGS standard.

Where Do We Go from Here?

PEX was designed to provide the capabilities of PHIGS and other 3D graphics standards in the network-transparent, device-independent X environment. As more and more organizations are creating implementations of it on their respective types of hardware, we should be seeing its functionality more commonly used all the time. Judging from its acceptance so far, it shouldn't be long.

There is a sample implementation of PEX called PEX SI available from MIT. Several vendors already have products that use PHIGS in PEX, and others are developing products that will use it. PEXlib is another programming interface that bears the same relationship to PEX protocol as Xlib does to X protocol.

PEX 5.0 is the version currently available in PEX SI and in vendor's products. At this writing, PEX 5.1 is in public review and PEX Version 6.0 is just getting started.

Refer to the *Bibliography* for a list of PEX documentation.

Appendix A

PHIGS Lists

This appendix contains the following lists:

- A list of PHIGS element types
- A list of PHIGS routines sorted by function
- A list of PHIGS routines sorted in alphabetical order

Element Types

The following list contains all the element types as returned from INQUIRE CURRENT ELEMENT TYPE AND SIZE and INQUIRE ELEMENT TYPE AND SIZE.

FTN	C Binding Name	Value/Description
PENIL	PELEM_NIL	1 element pointer is pointing to element 0
PEPL3	PELEM_POLYLINE3	2 polyline 3
PEPL	PELEM_POLYLINE	3 polyline
PEPM3	PELEM_POLYMARKER3	4 polymarker 3
PEPM	PELEM_POLYMARKER	5 polymarker
PETX3	PELEM_TEXT3	6 text 3
PETX	PELEM_TEXT	7 text
PEATR3	PELEM_ANNO_TEXT_REL3	8 annotation text relative 3

FTN	C Binding Name	Value/Description
PEATR	PELEM_ANNO_TEXT_REL	9 annotation text relative
PEFA3	PELEM_FILL_AREA3	10 fill area 3
PEFA	PELEM_FILL_AREA	11 fill area
PEFAS3	PELEM_FILL_AREA_SET3	12 fill area set 3
PEFAS	PELEM_FILL_AREA_SET	13 fill area set
PECA3	PELEM_CELL_ARRAY3	14 cell array 3
PECA	PELEM_CELL_ARRAY	15 cell array
PEGDP3	PELEM_GDP3	16 generalized drawing primitive 3
PEGDP	PELEM_GDP	17 generalized drawing primitive
PEPLI	PELEM_LINE_IND	18 set polyline index
PEPMI	PELEM_MARKER_IND	19 set polymarker index
PETXI	PELEM_TEXT_IND	20 set text index
PEII	PELEM_INT_IND	21 set interior index
PEEDI	PELEM_EDGE_IND	22 set edge index
PELN	PELEM_LINETYPE	23 set linetype
PELWSC	PELEM_LINEWIDTH	24 set linewidth scale factor
PEPLCI	PELEM_LINE_COLR_IND	25 set polyline colour index
PEMK	PELEM_MARKER_TYPE	26 set marker type
PEMKSC	PELEM_MARKER_SIZE	27 set marker size scale factor
PEPMCI	PELEM_MARKER_COLR_IND	28 set polymarker colour index
PETXFN	PELEM_TEXT_FONT	29 set text font
PETXPR	PELEM_TEXT_PREC	30 set text precision
PECHXP	PELEM_CHAR_EXPAN	31 set character expansion factor
PECHSP	PELEM_CHAR_SPACE	32 set character spacing
PETXCI	PELEM_TEXT_COLR_IND	33 set text colour index
PECHH	PELEM_CHAR_HT	34 set character height
PECHUP	PELEM_CHAR_UP_VEC	35 set character up vector
PETXP	PELEM_TEXT_PATH	36 set text path
PETXAL	PELEM_TEXT_ALIGN	37 set text alignment
PEATCH	PELEM_ANNO_CHAR_HT	38 set annotation text character height
PEATCU	PELEM_ANNO_CHAR_UP_VEC	39 set annotation text character up vector
PEATP	PELEM_ANNO_PATH	40 set annotation text path
PEATAL	PELEM_ANNO_ALIGN	41 set annotation text alignment
PEANST	PELEM_ANNO_STYLE	42 set annotation style
PEIS	PELEM_INT_STYLE	43 set interior style
PEISI	PELEM_INT_STYLE_IND	44 set interior style index

FTN	C Binding Name	Value/Description
PEICI	PELEM_INT_COLR_IND	45 set interior colour index
PEEDFG	PELEM_EDGE_FLAG	46 set edge flag
PEEDT	PELEM_EDGETYPE	47 set edgetype
PEEWSC	PELEM_EDGEWIDTH	48 set edgewidth scale factor
PEEDCI	PELEM_EDGE_COLR_IND	49 set edge colour index
PEPA	PELEM_PAT_SIZE	50 pattern size
PEPRPV	PELEM_PAT_REF_POINT_VECS	51 pattern reference point and vectors
PEPARF	PELEM_PAT_REF_POINT	52 pattern reference point
PEADS	PELEM_ADD_NAMES_SET	53 add names to set
PERES	PELEM_REMOVE_NAMES_SET	54 remove names from set
PEIASF	PELEM_INDIV_ASF	55 set individual ASF
PEHRID	PELEM_HLHSR_ID	56 set hlhsr identifier
PELMT3	PELEM_LOCAL_MODEL_TRAN3	57 set local transformation 3
PELMT	PELEM_LOCAL_MODEL_TRAN	58 set local transformation
PEGMT3	PELEM_GLOBAL_MODEL_TRAN3	59 set global transformation 3
PEGMT	PELEM_GLOBAL_MODEL_TRAN	60 set global transformation
PEMCV3	PELEM_MODEL_CLIP_VOL3	61 set modelling clipping volume 3
PEMCV	PELEM_MODEL_CLIP_VOL	62 set modelling clipping volume
PEMCLI	PELEM_MODEL_CLIP_IND	63 set modelling clipping indicator
PERMCV	PELEM_RESTORE_MODEL_CLIP_VOL	64 restore modelling clipping volume
PEVWI	PELEM_VIEW_IND	65 set view index
PEEXST	PELEM_EXEC_STRUCT	66 execute structure
PELB	PELEM_LABEL	67 label
PEAP	PELEM_APPL_DATA	68 application data
PEGSE	PELEM_GSE	69 generalized structure element
PEPKID	PELEM_PICK_ID	70 set pick identifier
/* end of PHIGS enumerations */		
/* start of PHIGS PLUS enumerations */		
PEPLS3	PELEM_POLYLINE_SET3_COLR	71 polyline set 3 with colour
PEFSD3	PELEM_FILL_AREA_SET3_DATA	72 fill area set 3 with data
PEFSD	PELEM_FILL_AREA_SET_DATA	73 fill area set with data
PECA3P	PELEM_CELL_ARRAY3_PLUS	74 cell array 3 plus
PESFS3	PELEM_SET_OF_FILL_AREA_SETS3_DATA	75 set of fill area sets 3 with data

FTN	C Binding Name	Value/Description
PESFSD	PELEM_SET_OF_FILL_AREA_SETS_DATA	
		76 set of fill area sets with data
PETS3D	PELEM_TRI_SET3_DATA	77 triangle set 3 with data
PETSD	PELEM_TRI_SET_DATA	78 triangle set with data
PEST3D	PELEM_TRI_STRIP3_DATA	79 triangle strip 3 with data
PETSTD	PELEM_TRI_STRIP_DATA	80 triangle strip with data
PEQM3D	PELEM_QUAD_MESH3_DATA	81 quadrilateral mesh 3 with data
PEQMD	PELEM_QUAD_MESH_DATA	82 quadrilateral mesh with data
PEBC3	PELEM_NON_UNIFORM_B_SPLINE_CURVE3	
		83 non-uniform B-spline curve
PEBC3C	PELEM_NON_UNIFORM_B_SPLINE_CURVE3_COLR	
		84 non-uniform B-spline curve w/colour
PEBS3	PELEM_NON_UNIFORM_B_SPLINE_SURF3	
		85 non-uniform B-spline surface
PEBS3D	PELEM_NON_UNIFORM_B_SPLINE_SURF3_DATA	
		86 non-uniform B-spline surface w/data
PEDMI	PELEM_DATA_MAP_IND	87 set data mapping index
PERFI	PELEM_REFL_IND	88 set reflectance index
PEBII	PELEM_BACK_INT_IND	89 set back interior index
PEBSDMI	PELEM_BACK_DATA_MAP_IND	90 set back data mapping index
PEBRFI	PELEM_BACK_REFL_IND	91 set back reflectance index
PEPRSI	PELEM_PARAM_SURF_IND	92 set parametric surface index
PEPLC	PELEM_LINE_COLR	93 set polyline colour
PEPLSM	PELEM_LINE_SHAD_METHOD	94 set polyline shading method
PEPMC	PELEM_MARKER_COLR	95 set polymarker colour
PETXC	PELEM_TEXT_COLR	96 set text colour
PEFDM	PELEM_FACET_DISTING_MODE	97 set facet distinguishing mode
PEFCM	PELEM_FACET_CULL_MODE	98 set facet culling mode
PEIC	PELEM_INT_COLR	99 set interior colour
PEISM	PELEM_INT_SHAD_METHOD	100 set interior shading method
PEDMM	PELEM_DATA_MAP_METHOD	101 set data mapping method
PERFP	PELEM_REFL_PROPS	102 set reflectance properties
PERFM	PELEM_REFL_MODEL	103 set reflectance model
PEBIS	PELEM_BACK_INT_STYLE	104 set back interior style
PEBISI	PELEM_BACK_INT_STYLE_IND	105 set back interior style index
PEBIC	PELEM_BACK_INT_COLR	106 set back interior colour

FTN	C Binding Name	Value/Description
PEBISM	PELEM_BACK_INT_SHAD_METHOD	107 set back interior shading method
PEBDMM	PELEM_BACK_DATA_MAP_METHOD	108 set back data mapping method
PEBRFP	PELEM_BACK_REFL_PROPS	109 set back reflectance properties
PEBRFM	PELEM_BACK_REFL_MODEL	110 set back reflectance model
PELSS	PELEM_LIGHT_SOURCE_STATE	111 set light source state
PEEDC	PELEM_EDGE_COLR	112 set edge colour
PECAC	PELEM_CURVE_APPROX_CRIT	113 set curve approximation criteria
PESAC	PELEM_SURF_APPROX_CRIT	114 set surface approximation criteria
PEPSC	PELEM_PARAM_SURF_CHARS	115 set parametric surface characteristics
PERCM	PELEM_REND_COLR_MODEL	116 set rendering colour model
PEDCI	PELEM_DEPTH_CUE_IND	117 set depth cue index
PECMI	PELEM_COLR_MAP_IND	118 set colour mapping index

PHIGS Routines Listed by Function

The following list shows the PHIGS routine name followed by the FORTRAN and the C binding names.

Control Routines

	FTN	C Binding
CLOSE PHIGS	pclph	pclose_phigs
CLOSE WORKSTATION	pclwk	pclose_ws
MESSAGE	pmsg, pmsgs	pmessage
OPEN PHIGS	popph	popen_phigs
OPEN WORKSTATION	popwk	popen_ws
REDRAW ALL STRUCTURES	prst	predraw_all_structs
SET DISPLAY UPDATE STATE	psdus	pset_disp_upd_st
UPDATE WORKSTATION	puwk	pupd_ws

Primitive Routines

	FTN	C Binding
ANNOTATION TEXT RELATIVE	patr, patrs	panno_text_rel
ANNOTATION TEXT RELATIVE 3	patr3, patr3s	panno_text_rel3
CELL ARRAY	pca	pcell_array
CELL ARRAY 3 PLUS	pca3p	pcell_array3_plus
CELL ARRAY 3	pca3	pcell_array3
FILL AREA	pfa	pfill_area
FILL AREA 3	pfa3	pfill_area3

FILL AREA SET	pfas	pfill_area_set
FILL AREA SET 3	pfas3	pfill_area_set3
FILL AREA SET WITH DATA	pfasd	pfill_area_set_data
FILL AREA SET 3 WITH DATA	pfas3d	pfill_area_set3_data
GENERALIZED DRAWING PRIMITIVE	pgdp	pgdp
GENERALIZED DRAWING PRIMITIVE 3	pgdp3	pgdp3
NON-UNIFORM B-SPLINE CURVE 3	pbsc	pnon_uniform_b_spline_curve3
NON-UNIFORM B-SPLINE CURVE 3 WITH COLOUR	pbscc	pnon_uniform_b_spline_curve3_colr
NON-UNIFORM B-SPLINE SURFACE 3	pbss	pnon_uniform_b_spline_surf3
NON-UNIFORM B-SPLINE SURFACE 3 WITH DATA	pbssd	pnon_uniform_b_spline_surf3_data
POLYLINE	ppl	ppolyline
POLYLINE 3	ppl3	ppolyline3
POLYLINE SET 3 WITH COLOUR	ppls3c	ppolyline_set3_colr
POLYMARKER	ppm	ppolymarker
POLYMARKER 3	ppm3	ppolymarker3
QUADRILATERAL MESH WITH DATA	pqmd	pquad_mesh_data
QUADRILATERAL MESH 3 WITH DATA	pqm3d	pquad_mesh3_data
SET OF FILL AREA SETS WITH DATA	psfasd	pset_of_fill_area_sets_data
SET OF FILL AREA SETS 3 WITH DATA	psfas3	pset_of_fill_area_sets3_data
TEXT	ptx, ptxs	ptext
TEXT 3	ptx3, ptx3s	ptext3

TRIANGLE SET WITH DATA	ptsd	ptri_set_data
TRIANGLE SET 3 WITH DATA	pts3d	ptri_set3_data
TRIANGLE STRIP WITH DATA	ptstd	ptri_strip_data
TRIANGLE STRIP 3 WITH DATA	ptst3d	ptri_strip3_data

Attribute Specification Routines

Select Entries from Workstation Bundle Tables

SET BACK DATA MAPPING INDEX	psbdmi	pset_back_data_map_ind
SET BACK INTERIOR INDEX	psbii	pset_back_int_ind
SET BACK REFLECTANCE INDEX	psbrfi	pset_back_refl_ind
SET EDGE INDEX	psedi	pset_edge_ind
SET DATA MAPPING INDEX	psdmi	pset_data_map_ind
SET INTERIOR INDEX	psii	pset_int_ind
SET PARAMETRIC SURFACE INDEX	pspsi	pset_param_surf_ind
SET POLYLINE INDEX	pspli	pset_line_ind
SET POLYMARKER INDEX	pspmi	pset_marker_ind
SET TEXT INDEX	pstxi	pset_text_ind
SET REFLECTANCE INDEX	psrfi	pset_refl_ind

Select Entries from Workstation Attribute Tables That Are Not Bundle Tables

SET BACK INTERIOR STYLE INDEX	psbisi	pset_back_int_style_ind
SET COLOUR MAPPING INDEX	pscmi	pset_colr_map_ind
SET DEPTH CUE INDEX	psdci	pset_depth_cue_ind

SET LIGHT SOURCE STATE	pslss	pset_light_source_st
SET INTERIOR STYLE INDEX	psisi	pset_int_style_ind
SET VIEW INDEX	psvwi	pset_view_ind

Individual Attribute Selection

Individual Attributes: Namesets

ADD NAMES TO SET	pads	padd_names_set
REMOVE NAMES FROM SET	pres	premove_names_set

Individual Attributes: Lines

SET LINETYPE	psln	pset_linetype
SET LINEWIDTH SCALE FACTOR	pslwsc	pset_linewidth
SET POLYLINE COLOUR	psplc	pset_line_colr
SET POLYLINE COLOUR INDEX	psplci	pset_line_colr_ind
SET POLYLINE SHADING METHOD	psplsm	pset_line_shad_method

Individual Attributes: Markers

SET MARKER SIZE SCALE FACTOR	psmksc	pset_marker_size
SET MARKER TYPE	psmk	pset_marker_type
SET POLYMARKER COLOUR	pspmc	pset_marker_colr
SET POLYMARKER COLOUR INDEX	pspmci	pset_marker_colr_ind

Individual Attributes: Text

SET ANNOTATION STYLE	psans	pset_anno_style
SET ANNOTATION TEXT ALIGNMENT	psatal	pset_anno_align

SET ANNOTATION TEXT CHARACTER HEIGHT	psatch	pset_anno_char_ht
SET ANNOTATION TEXT CHARACTER UP VECTOR	psatcu	pset_anno_char_up_vec
SET ANNOTATION TEXT PATH	psatp	pset_anno_path
SET CHARACTER EXPANSION FACTOR	pschxp	pset_char_expan
SET CHARACTER HEIGHT	pschh	pset_char_ht
SET CHARACTER SPACING	pschsp	pset_char_space
SET CHARACTER UP VECTOR	pschup	pset_char_up_vec
SET TEXT ALIGNMENT	pstxal	pset_text_align
SET TEXT COLOUR	pstxc	pset_text_colr
SET TEXT COLOUR INDEX	pstxci	pset_text_colr_ind
SET TEXT FONT	pstxfn	pset_text_font
SET TEXT PATH	pstxp	pset_text_path
SET TEXT PRECISION	pstxpr	pset_text_prec

Individual Attributes: Area-defining Primitives

SET BACK DATA MAPPING METHOD	psbdmm	pset_back_data_map_method
SET BACK INTERIOR COLOUR	psbic	pset_back_int_colr
SET BACK INTERIOR SHADING METHOD	psbism	pset_back_int_shad_method
SET BACK INTERIOR STYLE	psbis	pset_back_int_style
SET BACK INTERIOR STYLE INDEX	psbisi	pset_back_int_style_ind
SET BACK REFLECTANCE PROPERTIES	psbrfp	pset_back_refl_props
SET BACK REFLECTANCE MODEL	psbrfm	pset_back_refl_model
SET DATA MAPPING METHOD	psdmm	pset_data_map_method
SET EDGE COLOUR	psedc	pset_edge_colr
SET EDGE COLOUR INDEX	psedci	pset_edge_colr_ind

SET EDGE FLAG .... psedfg pset_edge_flag
SET EDGETYPE .... psedt pset_edgetype
SET EDGEWIDTH SCALE FACTOR .... psewsc pset_edgewidth
SET FACET CULLING MODE .... psfcm pset_facet_cull_mode
SET FACET DISTINGUISHING MODE .... psfdm pset_facet_disting_mode
SET INTERIOR COLOUR .... psic pset_int_colr
SET INTERIOR COLOUR INDEX .... psici pset_int_colr_ind
SET REFLECTANCE MODEL .... psrfm pset_refl_model
SET INTERIOR SHADING METHOD .... psism pset_int_shad_method
SET INTERIOR STYLE .... psis pset_int_style
SET INTERIOR STYLE INDEX .... psisi pset_int_style_ind
SET PATTERN REFERENCE POINT AND VECTORS .... psprpv pset_pat_ref_point_vecs
SET PATTERN REFERENCE POINT .... psparf pset_pat_ref_point
SET PATTERN SIZE .... pspa pset_pat_size
SET REFLECTANCE PROPERTIES .... psrfp pset_refl_props

Individual Attributes: B-Splines

SET CURVE APPROXIMATION CRITERIA .... pscac pset_curve_approx_criteria
SET PARAMETRIC SURFACE CHARACTERISTICS .... pspsc pset_param_surf_chars
SET SURFACE APPROXIMATION CRITERIA .... pssac pset_surf_approx_crit

Aspect Source Flag Setting

SET INDIVIDUAL ASF .... psiasf pset_indiv_asf

Workstation Attribute Table Definition

Workstation Bundle Table Definition

SET DATA MAPPING REPRESENTATION	psdmr	pset_data_map_rep
SET DEPTH CUE REPRESENTATION	psdcr	pset_depth_cue_rep
SET EDGE REPRESENTATION	psedr	pset_edge_rep
SET EDGE REPRESENTATION PLUS	psedp	pset_edge_rep_plus
SET INTERIOR REPRESENTATION	psir	pset_int_rep
SET INTERIOR REPRESENTATION PLUS	psip	pset_int_rep_plus
SET PARAMETRIC SURFACE REPRESENTATION	pspsr	pset_param_surf_rep
SET POLYLINE REPRESENTATION	psplr	pset_line_rep
SET POLYLINE REPRESENTATION PLUS	psplp	pset_line_rep_plus
SET POLYMARKER REPRESENTATION	pspmr	pset_marker_rep
SET POLYMARKER REPRESENTATION PLUS	pspmp	pset_marker_rep_plus
SET REFLECTANCE REPRESENTATION	psrfr	pset_refl_rep
SET TEXT REPRESENTATION	pstxr	pset_text_rep
SET TEXT REPRESENTATION PLUS	pstxrp	pset_text_rep_plus

Workstation Attribute Tables Definition (for Tables That Are Not Bundle Tables)

SET COLOUR MAPPING REPRESENTATION	pscmr	pset_colr_map_rep
SET COLOUR REPRESENTATION	pscr	pset_colr_rep
SET DEPTH CUE REPRESENTATION	psdcr	pset_depth_cue_rep
SET LIGHT SOURCE REPRESENTATION	pslsr	pset_light_source_rep
SET PATTERN REPRESENTATION PLUS	pspap	pset_pat_rep_plus
SET PATTERN REPRESENTATION	pspar	pset_pat_rep
SET VIEW REPRESENTATION	psvwr	pset_view_rep
SET VIEW REPRESENTATION 3	psvwr3	pset_view_rep3

Workstation Filter Definition

SET HIGHLIGHTING FILTER	pshlft	pset_highl_filter
SET INVISIBILITY FILTER	psivft	pset_invis_filter
SET PICK FILTER	pspkft	pset_pick_filter

Colour Model Control

SET COLOUR MODEL	pscmd	pset_colr_model
SET RENDERING COLOUR MODEL	psrcm	pset_rend_colr_model

HLHSR Attributes

SET HLHSR IDENTIFIER	pshrid	pset_hlhsr_id
SET HLHSR MODE	pshrm	pset_hlhsr_mode

Modelling Transformations

SET GLOBAL TRANSFORMATION	psgmt	pset_global_tran
SET GLOBAL TRANSFORMATION 3	psgmt3	pset_global_tran3
SET LOCAL TRANSFORMATION	pslmt	pset_local_tran
SET LOCAL TRANSFORMATION 3	pslmt3	pset_local_tran3

Modelling Clipping

RESTORE MODELLING CLIPPING VOLUME	prmcv	prestore_model_clip_vol
SET MODELLING CLIPPING INDICATOR	psmcli	pset_model_clip_ind
SET MODELLING CLIPPING VOLUME	psmcv	pset_model_clip_vol
SET MODELLING CLIPPING VOLUME 3	psmcv3	pset_model_clip_vol3

View Operations

SET VIEW INDEX	psvwi	pset_view_ind
SET VIEW REPRESENTATION	psvwr	pset_view_rep
SET VIEW REPRESENTATION 3	psvwr3	pset_view_rep3
SET VIEW TRANSFORMATION INPUT PRIORITY	psvtip	pset_view_tran_in_pri

Workstation Transformation

SET WORKSTATION VIEWPORT	pswkv	pset_ws_vp
SET WORKSTATION VIEWPORT 3	pswkv3	pset_ws_vp3
SET WORKSTATION WINDOW	pswkw	pset_ws_win
SET WORKSTATION WINDOW 3	pswkw3	pset_ws_win3

Utility Routines to Support Modelling

BUILD TRANSFORMATION MATRIX	pbltm	pbuild_tran_matrix
BUILD TRANSFORMATION MATRIX 3	pbltm3	pbuild_tran_matrix3
COMPOSE MATRIX	pcom	pcompose_matrix
COMPOSE MATRIX 3	pcom3	pcompose_matrix3
COMPOSE TRANSFORMATION MATRIX	pcotm	pcompose_tran_matrix
COMPOSE TRANSFORMATION MATRIX 3	pcotm3	pcompose_tran_matrix3
ROTATE	pro	protate
ROTATE X	prox	protate_x
ROTATE Y	proy	protate_y
ROTATE Z	proz	protate_z
SCALE	psc	pscale
SCALE 3	psc3	pscale3

TRANSFORM POINT	ptp	ptran_point
TRANSFORM POINT 3	ptp3	ptran_point3
TRANSLATE	ptr	ptranslate
TRANSLATE 3	ptr3	ptranslate3

Utility Routines to Support Viewing

EVALUATE VIEW MAPPING MATRIX	pevmm	peval_view_map_matrix
EVALUATE VIEW MAPPING MATRIX 3	pevmm3	peval_view_map_matrix3
EVALUATE VIEW ORIENTATION MATRIX	pevom	peval_view_ori_matrix
EVALUATE VIEW ORIENTATION MATRIX 3	pevom3	peval_view_ori_matrix3

Structure Routines

Structure Content Routines

APPLICATION DATA	pap	pappl_data
CLOSE STRUCTURE	pclst	pclose_struct
COPY ALL ELEMENTS FROM STRUCTURE	pcelst	pcopy_all_elems_struct
DELETE ELEMENT	pdel	pdel_elem
DELETE ELEMENT RANGE	pdelra	pdel_elem_range
DELETE ELEMENTS BETWEEN LABELS	pdellb	pdel_elems_labels
EMPTY STRUCTURE	pemst	pempty_struct
EXECUTE STRUCTURE	pexst	pexec_struct
GENERALIZED STRUCTURE ELEMENT	pgse	pgse
LABEL	plb	plabel
OFFSET ELEMENT POINTER	posep	poffset_elem_ptr
OPEN STRUCTURE	popst	popen_struct

SET EDIT MODE	psedm	pset_edit_mode
SET ELEMENT POINTER	psep	pset_elem_ptr
SET ELEMENT POINTER AT LABEL	pseplb	pset_elem_ptr_label

Structure Manipulation Routines

CHANGE STRUCTURE IDENTIFIER	pcstid	pchange_struct_id
CHANGE STRUCTURE IDENTIFIER AND REFERENCES	pcstir	pchange_struct_id_refs
CHANGE STRUCTURE REFERENCES	pcstrf	pchange_struct_refs
DELETE ALL STRUCTURES	pdas	pdel_all_structs
DELETE STRUCTURE	pdst	pdel_struct
DELETE STRUCTURE NETWORK	pdsn	pdel_struct_net

Structure Display Routines

POST STRUCTURE	ppost	ppost_struct
UNPOST ALL STRUCTURES	pupast	punpost_all_structs
UNPOST STRUCTURE	pupost	punpost_struct

Structure Archiving Routines

ARCHIVE ALL STRUCTURES	parast	par_all_structs
ARCHIVE STRUCTURES	parst	par_structs
ARCHIVE STRUCTURE NETWORKS	parsn	par_struct_nets
CLOSE ARCHIVE FILE	pclarf	pclose_ar_file
DELETE ALL STRUCTURES FROM ARCHIVE	pdasar	pdel_all_structs_ar
DELETE STRUCTURES FROM ARCHIVE	pdstar	pdel_structs_ar
DELETE STRUCTURES NETWORKS FROM ARCHIVE	pdsnar	pdel_struct_nets_ar
OPEN ARCHIVE FILE	poparf	popen_ar_file
RETRIEVE ALL STRUCTURES	prast	pret_all_structs

RETRIEVE STRUCTURE IDENTIFIERS	prsid	pret_struct_ids
SET CONFLICT RESOLUTION	pscnrs	pset_conf_res
RETRIEVE ALL STRUCTURES	prast	pret_all_structs
RETRIEVE PATHS TO ANCESTORS	prepan	pret_paths_ances
RETRIEVE PATHS TO DESCENDANTS	prepde	pret_paths_descs
RETRIEVE STRUCTURE IDENTIFIERS	prsid	pret_struct_ids
RETRIEVE STRUCTURE NETWORKS	presn	pret_struct_nets
RETRIEVE STRUCTURES	prest	pret_structs

Input Routines

Pick Identifier And Filter

SET PICK FILTER	pspkft	pset_pick_filter
SET PICK IDENTIFIER	pspkid	pset_pick_id

Initialization

INITIALIZE CHOICE	pinch	pinit_choice
INITIALIZE CHOICE 3	pinch3	pinit_choice3
INITIALIZE LOCATOR	pinlc	pinit_loc
INITIALIZE LOCATOR 3	pinlc3	pinit_loc3
INITIALIZE PICK	pinpk	pinit_pick
INITIALIZE PICK 3	pinpk3	pinit_pick3
INITIALIZE STRING	pinst	pinit_string
INITIALIZE STRING 3	pinst3	pinit_string3
INITIALIZE STROKE	pinsk	pinit_stroke
INITIALIZE STROKE 3	pinsk3	pinit_stroke3

INITIALIZE VALUATOR	pinvl	pinit_val
INITIALIZE VALUATOR 3	pinvl3	pinit_val3

Setting Mode

SET CHOICE MODE	pschm	pset_choice_mode
SET LOCATOR MODE	pslcm	pset_loc_mode
SET PICK MODE	pspkm	pset_pick_mode
SET STRING MODE	psstm	pset_string_mode
SET STROKE MODE	psskm	pset_stroke_mode
SET VALUATOR MODE	psvlm	pset_val_mode

Request Routines

REQUEST CHOICE	prqch	preq_choice
REQUEST LOCATOR	prqlc	preq_loc
REQUEST LOCATOR 3	prqlc3	preq_loc3
REQUEST PICK	prqpk	preq_pick
REQUEST STRING	prqst	preq_string
REQUEST STROKE	prqsk	preq_stroke
REQUEST STROKE 3	prqsk3	preq_stroke3
REQUEST VALUATOR	prqvl	preq_val

Sample Routines

SAMPLE CHOICE	psmch	psample_choice
SAMPLE LOCATOR	psmlc	psample_loc
SAMPLE LOCATOR 3	psmlc3	psample_loc3
SAMPLE PICK	psmpk	psample_pick
SAMPLE STRING	psmst	psample_string

SAMPLE STROKE	psmsk	psample_stroke
SAMPLE STROKE 3	psmsk3	psample_stroke3
SAMPLE VALUATOR	psmvl	psample_val

Event Routines

AWAIT EVENT	pwait	pawait_event
FLUSH DEVICE EVENTS	pflush	pflush_events
GET CHOICE	pgtch	pget_choice
GET LOCATOR	pgtlc	pget_loc
GET LOCATOR 3	pgtlc3	pget_loc3
GET PICK	pgtpk	pget_pick
GET STRING	pgtst	pget_string
GET STROKE	pgtsk	pget_stroke
GET STROKE 3	pgtsk3	pget_stroke3
GET VALUATOR	pgtvl	pget_val

Metafile Routines

WRITE ITEM TO METAFILE	pwitm	pwrite_item
GET ITEM TYPE FROM METAFILE	pqtitm	pget_item_type
READ ITEM FROM METAFILE	prditm	pread_item
INTERPRET ITEM	piitm	pinterpret_item

Inquiry Routines

Inquiry Routines for Operating State Values

INQUIRE ARCHIVE STATE VALUE	pqars	pinq_ar_st
INQUIRE STRUCTURE STATE VALUE	pqstrs	pinq_struct_st
INQUIRE SYSTEM STATE VALUE	pqsys	pinq_sys_st
INQUIRE WORKSTATION STATE VALUE	pqwkst	pinq_ws_st

Inquiry Routines for PHIGS Description Table

INQUIRE GENERALIZED STRUCTURE ELEMENT FACILITIES	pqgsef	pinq_gse_facs
INQUIRE LIST OF AVAILABLE WORKSTATION TYPES	pqewk	pinq_list_avail_ws_types
INQUIRE MODELLING CLIPPING FACILITIES	pqmclf	pinq_model_clip_facs
INQUIRE PHIGS FACILITIES	pqphf	pinq_phigs_facs

Inquiry Routines for PHIGS State List

INQUIRE ALL CONFLICTING STRUCTURES	pqcst	pinq_all_conf_structs
INQUIRE ARCHIVE FILES	pqarf	pinq_ar_files
INQUIRE CONFLICTING STRUCTURES IN NETWORK	pqcstn	pinq_conf_structs_net
INQUIRE CONFLICT RESOLUTION	pqcnrs	pinq_conf_res
INQUIRE EDIT MODE	pqedm	pinq_edit_mode
INQUIRE MORE SIMULTANEOUS EVENTS	pqsim	pinq_more_simult_events
INQUIRE SET OF OPEN WORKSTATIONS	pqopwk	pinq_open_wss
INQUIRE STRUCTURE IDENTIFIERS	pqsid	pinq_struct_ids

Inquiry Routines for Workstation Description Table

INQUIRE ANNOTATION FACILITIES	pqanf	pinq_anno_facs
INQUIRE B-SPLINE SURFACE FACILITIES	pqcbssf	pinq_b_spline_surf_facs

INQUIRE COLOUR FACILITIES	pqcf	pinq_colr_facs
INQUIRE COLOUR MAPPING FACILITIES	pqcmf	pinq_colr_map_facs
INQUIRE COLOUR MAPPING METHOD FACILITIES	pqcmmf	pinq_colr_map_method_facs
INQUIRE COLOUR MODEL FACILITIES	pqcmdf	pinq_colr_model_facs
INQUIRE CURVE FACILITIES	pqcvf	pinq_curve_facs
INQUIRE DATA MAPPING FACILITIES	pqdmf	pinq_data_map_facs
INQUIRE DEFAULT DISPLAY UPDATE STATE	pqddus	pinq_def_disp_upd_st
INQUIRE DEFAULT LOCATOR DEVICE DATA 3	pqdlc3	pinq_def_loc_data3
INQUIRE DEFAULT LOCATOR DEVICE DATA	pqdlc	pinq_def_loc_data
INQUIRE DEFAULT PICK DEVICE DATA 3	pqdpk3	pinq_def_pick_data3
INQUIRE DEFAULT PICK DEVICE DATA	pqdpk	pinq_def_pick_data
INQUIRE DEFAULT STRING DEVICE DATA 3	pqdst3	pinq_def_string_data3
INQUIRE DEFAULT STRING DEVICE DATA	pqdst	pinq_def_string_data
INQUIRE DEFAULT STROKE DEVICE DATA 3	pqdsk3	pinq_def_stroke_data3
INQUIRE DEFAULT STROKE DEVICE DATA	pqdsk	pinq_def_stroke_data
INQUIRE DEFAULT VALUATOR DEVICE DATA 3	pqdvl3	pinq_def_val_data3
INQUIRE DEFAULT VALUATOR DEVICE DATA	pqdvl	pinq_def_val_data
INQUIRE DEPTH CUE FACILITIES	pqdcf	pinq_depth_cue_facs
INQUIRE DIRECT COLOUR MODEL FACILITIES	pqdcmf	pinq_direct_colr_model_facs
INQUIRE DISPLAY SPACE SIZE 3	pqdsp3	pinq_disp_space_size3
INQUIRE DISPLAY SPACE SIZE	pqdsp	pinq_disp_space_size
INQUIRE DYNAMICS OF STRUCTURES	pqdstr	pinq_dyns_structs
INQUIRE DYNAMICS OF WORKSTATION ATTRIBUTES	pqdswa	pinq_dyns_ws_attrs
INQUIRE DYNAMICS OF WORKSTATION PLUS	pqdcwp	pinq_dyns_ws_plus
INQUIRE EDGE FACILITIES	pqedf	pinq_edge_facs
INQUIRE GENERALIZED DRAWING PRIMITIVE 3	pqgdp3	pinq_gdp3

INQUIRE GENERALIZED DRAWING PRIMITIVE	pqgdp	pinq_gdp
INQUIRE HLHSR IDENTIFIER FACILITIES	pqhrif	pinq_hlhsr_id_facs
INQUIRE HLHSR MODE FACILITIES	pqhrmf	pinq_hlhsr_mode_facs
INQUIRE INTERIOR FACILITIES PLUS	pqifp	pinq_int_facs_plus
INQUIRE INTERIOR FACILITIES	pqif	pinq_int_facs
INQUIRE LIGHT SOURCE FACILITIES	pqlsf	pinq_light_source_facs
INQUIRE LIST OF AVAILABLE GENERALIZED DRAWING PRIMITIVES 3	pqegd3	pinq_list_avail_gdp3
INQUIRE LIST OF AVAILABLE GENERALIZED DRAWING PRIMITIVES	pqegdp	pinq_list_avail_gdp
INQUIRE LIST OF AVAILABLE GENERALIZED STRUCTURE ELEMENTS	pqegse	pinq_list_avail_gse
INQUIRE MODELLING CLIPPING FACILITIES	pqmclf	pinq_model_clip_facs
INQUIRE NUMBER OF AVAILABLE LOGICAL INPUT DEVICES	pqli	pinq_num_avail_in
INQUIRE NUMBER OF DISPLAY PRIORITIES SUPPORTED	pqdp	pinq_num_disp_pris
INQUIRE PARAMETRIC SURFACE FACILITIES	pqpsf	pinq_param_surf_facs
INQUIRE PARAMETRIC SURFACE REPRESENTATION	pqpsr	pinq_param_surf_rep
INQUIRE PATTERN FACILITIES	pqpaf	pinq_pat_facs
INQUIRE PATTERN REPRESENTATION PLUS	pqparp	pinq_pat_rep_plus
INQUIRE POLYLINE FACILITIES PLUS	pqplfp	pinq_line_facs_plus
INQUIRE POLYLINE FACILITIES	pqplf	pinq_line_facs
INQUIRE POLYMARKER FACILITIES	pqpmf	pinq_marker_facs
INQUIRE PREDEFINED COLOUR MAPPING REPRESENTATION	pqpcmr	pinq_pred_colr_map_rep
INQUIRE PREDEFINED COLOUR REPRESENTATION	pqpcr	pinq_pred_colr_rep
INQUIRE PREDEFINED DATA MAPPING REPRESENTATION	pqpdmr	pinq_pred_data_map_rep
INQUIRE PREDEFINED DEPTH CUE REPRESENTATION	pqpdcr	pinq_pred_depth_cue_rep
INQUIRE PREDEFINED EDGE REPRESENTATION PLUS	pqpedp	pinq_pred_edge_rep_plus
INQUIRE PREDEFINED EDGE REPRESENTATION	pqpedr	pinq_pred_edge_rep
INQUIRE PREDEFINED INTERIOR REPRESENTATION PLUS	pqpip	pinq_pred_int_rep_plus
INQUIRE PREDEFINED INTERIOR REPRESENTATION	pqpir	pinq_pred_int_rep

INQUIRE PREDEFINED LIGHT SOURCE REPRESENTATION	pqplsr	pinq_pred_light_source_rep
INQUIRE PREDEFINED PARAMETRIC SURFACE REPRESENTATION	pqppsr	pinq_pred_param_surf_rep
INQUIRE PREDEFINED PATTERN REPRESENTATION PLUS	pqppap	pinq_pred_pat_rep_plus
INQUIRE PREDEFINED PATTERN REPRESENTATION	pqppar	pinq_pred_pat_rep
INQUIRE PREDEFINED POLYLINE REPRESENTATION PLUS	pqpplp	pinq_pred_line_rep_plus
INQUIRE PREDEFINED POLYLINE REPRESENTATION	pqpplr	pinq_pred_line_rep
INQUIRE PREDEFINED POLYMARKER REPRESENTATION PLUS	pqppmp	pinq_pred_marker_rep_plus
INQUIRE PREDEFINED POLYMARKER REPRESENTATION	pqppmr	pinq_pred_marker_rep
INQUIRE PREDEFINED REFLECTION REPRESENTATION	pqprfr	pinq_pred_refl_rep
INQUIRE PREDEFINED TEXT REPRESENTATION PLUS	pqptxp	pinq_pred_text_rep_plus
INQUIRE PREDEFINED TEXT REPRESENTATION	pqptxr	pinq_pred_text_rep
INQUIRE PREDEFINED VIEW REPRESENTATION	pqpvwr	pinq_pred_view_rep
INQUIRE RENDERING COLOUR MODEL FACILITIES	pqrcmf	pinq_rend_colr_model_facs
INQUIRE REFLECTION FACILITIES	pqrff	pinq_refl_facs
INQUIRE REFLECTION REPRESENTATION	pqrfr	pinq_refl_rep
INQUIRE RENDERING COLOUR MODEL FACILITIES	pqrcmf	pinq_rend_colr_model_facs
INQUIRE TEXT EXTENT	pqtxx, pqtxxs	pinq_text_extent
INQUIRE TEXT FACILITIES	pqtxf	pinq_text_facs
INQUIRE TRIMMING CURVE FACILITIES	pqtcf	pinq_trim_curve_facs
INQUIRE VIEW FACILITIES	pqvwf	pinq_view_facs
INQUIRE WORKSTATION CATEGORY	pqwkca	pinq_ws_cat
INQUIRE WORKSTATION CLASSIFICATION	pqwkcl	pinq_ws_class

INQUIRE WORKSTATION STATE TABLE LENGTHS PLUS	pqwslp	pinq_ws_st_table_length_plus
INQUIRE WORKSTATION STATE TABLE LENGTHS	pqwksl	pinq_ws_st_table

Inquiry Routines for Workstation State List

INQUIRE CHOICE DEVICE STATE 3	pqchs3	pinq_choice_st3
INQUIRE CHOICE DEVICE STATE	pqchs	pinq_choice_st
INQUIRE COLOUR MAPPING REPRESENTATION	pqcmr	pinq_colr_map_rep
INQUIRE COLOUR MAPPING STATE	pqcms	pinq_colr_map_st
INQUIRE COLOUR MODEL	pqcmd	pinq_colr_model
INQUIRE COLOUR REPRESENTATION	pqcr	pinq_colr_rep
INQUIRE DATA MAPPING REPRESENTATION	pqdmr	pinq_data_map_rep
INQUIRE DEPTH CUE REPRESENTATION	pqdcr	pinq_depth_cue_rep
INQUIRE DISPLAY UPDATE STATE	pqdus	pinq_disp_upd_st
INQUIRE EDGE REPRESENTATION PLUS	pqedp	pinq_edge_rep_plus
INQUIRE EDGE REPRESENTATION	pqedr	pinq_edge_rep
INQUIRE HIGHLIGHTING FILTER	pqhlft	pinq_highl_filter
INQUIRE HLHSR MODE	pqhrm	pinq_hlhsr_mode
INQUIRE INTERIOR REPRESENTATION PLUS	pqip	pinq_int_rep_plus
INQUIRE INTERIOR REPRESENTATION	pqir	pinq_int_rep
INQUIRE INVISIBILITY FILTER	pqivft	pinq_invis_filter
INQUIRE LIGHT SOURCE REPRESENTATION	pqlsr	pinq_light_source_rep
INQUIRE LIST OF COLOUR INDICES	pqeci	pinq_list_colr_inds
INQUIRE LIST OF COLOUR MAPPING INDICES	pqecmi	pinq_list_colr_map_inds
INQUIRE LIST OF DATA MAPPING INDICES	pqedmi	pinq_list_data_map_inds
INQUIRE LIST OF DEPTH CUE INDICES	pqedci	pinq_list_depth_cue_inds
INQUIRE LIST OF EDGE INDICES	pqeedi	pinq_list_edge_inds
INQUIRE LIST OF INTERIOR INDICES	pqeii	pinq_list_int_inds

INQUIRE LIST OF LIGHT SOURCE INDICES	pqelsi	pinq_list_light_source_inds
INQUIRE LIST OF PARAMETRIC SURFACE INDICES	pqepsi	pinq_list_param_surf_inds
INQUIRE LIST OF PATTERN INDICES	pqepai	pinq_list_pat_inds
INQUIRE LIST OF POLYLINE INDICES	pqepli	pinq_list_line_inds
INQUIRE LIST OF POLYMARKER INDICES	pqepmi	pinq_list_marker_inds
INQUIRE LIST OF REFLECTANCE INDICES	pqerf	pinq_list_refl_inds
INQUIRE LIST OF TEXT INDICES	pqetxi	pinq_list_text_inds
INQUIRE LIST OF VIEW INDICES	pqevwi	pinq_list_view_inds
INQUIRE LOCATOR DEVICE STATE 3	pqlcs3	pinq_loc_st3
INQUIRE LOCATOR DEVICE STATE	pqlcs	pinq_loc_st
INQUIRE PATTERN REPRESENTATION	pqpar	pinq_pat_rep
INQUIRE PICK DEVICE STATE 3	pqpks3	pinq_pick_st3
INQUIRE PICK DEVICE STATE	pqpks	pinq_pick_st
INQUIRE POLYLINE REPRESENTATION PLUS	pqplp	pinq_line_rep_plus
INQUIRE POLYLINE REPRESENTATION	pqplr	pinq_line_rep
INQUIRE POLYMARKER REPRESENTATION PLUS	pqpmp	pinq_marker_rep_plus
INQUIRE POLYMARKER REPRESENTATION	pqpmr	pinq_marker_rep
INQUIRE POSTED STRUCTURES	pqpost	pinq_posted_structs
INQUIRE STRING DEVICE STATE 3	pqsts3	pinq_string_st3
INQUIRE STRING DEVICE STATE	pqsts	pinq_string_st
INQUIRE STROKE DEVICE STATE 3	pqsks3	pinq_stroke_st3
INQUIRE STROKE DEVICE STATE	pqsks	pinq_stroke_st
INQUIRE TEXT REPRESENTATION PLUS	pqtxp	pinq_text_rep_plus
INQUIRE TEXT REPRESENTATION	pqtxr	pinq_text_rep
INQUIRE TRIMMING CURVE FACILITIES	pqtcf	pinq_trim_curve_facs
INQUIRE VALUATOR DEVICE STATE 3	pqvls3	pinq_val_st3

INQUIRE VALUATOR DEVICE STATE	pqvls	pinq_val_st
INQUIRE VIEW REPRESENTATION	pqvwr	pinq_view_rep
INQUIRE WORKSTATION CONNECTION AND TYPE	pqwkc	pinq_ws_conn_type
INQUIRE WORKSTATION TRANSFORMATION 3	pqwkt3	pinq_ws_tran3
INQUIRE WORKSTATION TRANSFORMATION	pqwkt	pinq_ws_tran

Inquiry Routines for Structure State List

INQUIRE SET OF WORKSTATIONS TO WHICH POSTED	pqwkpo	pinq_wss_posted

Inquiry Routines for Structure Content

ELEMENT SEARCH	pels	pelem_search
INCREMENTAL SPATIAL SEARCH 3	piss3	pincr_spa_search3
INCREMENTAL SPATIAL SEARCH	piss	pincr_spa_search
INQUIRE CURRENT ELEMENT CONTENT	pqceco	pinq_cur_elem_content
INQUIRE CURRENT ELEMENT TYPE AND SIZE	pqcets	pinq_cur_elem_type_size
INQUIRE ELEMENT CONTENT	pqeco	pinq_elem_content
INQUIRE ELEMENT POINTER	pqep	pinq_elem_ptr
INQUIRE ELEMENT TYPE AND SIZE	pqets	pinq_elem_type_size
INQUIRE OPEN STRUCTURE	pqopst	pinq_open_struct
INQUIRE PATHS TO ANCESTORS	pqpan	pinq_paths_ances
INQUIRE PATHS TO DESCENDANTS	pqpde	pinq_paths_descs
INQUIRE STRUCTURE STATUS	pqstst	pinq_struct_status

Inquiry Routines for PHIGS Error State List

INQUIRE ERROR HANDLING MODE	pqerhm	pinq_err_hand_mode
INQUIRE INPUT QUEUE OVERFLOW	pqiqov	pinq_in_overf

Error Routines

EMERGENCY CLOSE PHIGS	peclph	pemergency_close_phigs
ERROR HANDLING	perhnd	perr_hand
ERROR LOGGING	perlog	perr_log
SET ERROR HANDLING MODE	pserhm	pset_err_hand_mode

Special Interface

ESCAPE	pesc	pescape

FORTRAN Binding Utility Routines

PACK COLOUR SPLINE CURVE	ppcsc	N/A
UNPACK COLOUR SPLINE CURVE	pucsc	N/A
PACK COLOUR SPLINE SURFACE	ppcss	N/A
UNPACK COLOUR SPLINE SURFACE	pucss	N/A
PACK DATA RECORD	pprec	N/A
UNPACK DATA RECORD	purec	N/A
PACK DATA SPLINE SURFACE	ppdss	N/A
UNPACK DATA SPLINE SURFACE	pudss	N/A
PACK TRIMMING CURVE	pptc	N/A
UNPACK TRIMMING CURVE	putc	N/A

C Binding Utility Routines

CREATE STORE	N/A	pcreate_store
DELETE STORE	N/A	pdel_store
SET ERROR HANDLING	N/A	pset_err_hand

Routines Listed in Alphabetical Order

Routine Name	FTN	C Binding
ADD NAMES TO SET	pads	padd_names_set
ANNOTATION TEXT RELATIVE 3	patr3, patr3s	panno_text_rel3
ANNOTATION TEXT RELATIVE	patr, patrs	panno_text_rel
APPLICATION DATA	pap	pappl_data
ARCHIVE ALL STRUCTURES	parast	par_all_structs
ARCHIVE STRUCTURE NETWORKS	parsn	par_struct_nets
ARCHIVE STRUCTURES	parst	par_structs
AWAIT EVENT	pwait	pawait_event
BUILD TRANSFORMATION MATRIX 3	pbltm3	pbuild_tran_matrix3
BUILD TRANSFORMATION MATRIX	pbltm	pbuild_tran_matrix
CELL ARRAY 3 PLUS	pca3p	pcell_array3_plus
CELL ARRAY 3	pca3	pcell_array3
CELL ARRAY	pca	pcell_array
CHANGE STRUCTURE IDENTIFIER AND REFERENCES	pcstir	pchange_struct_id_refs
CHANGE STRUCTURE IDENTIFIER	pcstid	pchange_struct_id
CHANGE STRUCTURE REFERENCES	pcstrf	pchange_struct_refs
CLOSE ARCHIVE FILE	pclarf	pclose_ar_file
CLOSE PHIGS	pclph	pclose_phigs
CLOSE STRUCTURE	pclst	pclose_struct
CLOSE WORKSTATION	pclwk	pclose_ws
COMPOSE MATRIX 3	pcom3	pcompose_matrix3

COMPOSE MATRIX	pcom	pcompose_matrix
COMPOSE TRANSFORMATION MATRIX 3	pcotm3	pcompose_tran_matrix3
COMPOSE TRANSFORMATION MATRIX	pcotm	pcompose_tran_matrix
COPY ALL ELEMENTS FROM STRUCTURE	pcelst	pcopy_all_elems_struct
CREATE STORE	N/A	pcreate_store
DELETE ALL STRUCTURES FROM ARCHIVE	pdasar	pdel_all_structs_ar
DELETE ALL STRUCTURES	pdas	pdel_all_structs
DELETE ELEMENT RANGE	pdelra	pdel_elem_range
DELETE ELEMENT	pdel	pdel_elem
DELETE ELEMENTS BETWEEN LABELS	pdellb	pdel_elems_labels
DELETE STORE	N/A	pdel_store
DELETE STRUCTURE NETWORK	pdsn	pdel_struct_net
DELETE STRUCTURE	pdst	pdel_struct
DELETE STRUCTURES FROM ARCHIVE	pdstar	pdel_structs_ar
DELETE STRUCTURES NETWORKS FROM ARCHIVE	pdsnar	pdel_struct_nets_ar
ELEMENT SEARCH	pels	pelem_search
EMERGENCY CLOSE PHIGS	peclph	pemergency_close_phigs
EMPTY STRUCTURE	pemst	pempty_struct
ERROR HANDLING	perhnd	perr_hand
ERROR LOGGING	perlog	perr_log
ESCAPE	pesc	pescape
EVALUATE VIEW MAPPING MATRIX 3	pevmm3	peval_view_map_matrix3
EVALUATE VIEW MAPPING MATRIX	pevmm	peval_view_map_matrix
EVALUATE VIEW ORIENTATION MATRIX 3	pevom3	peval_view_ori_matrix3
EVALUATE VIEW ORIENTATION MATRIX	pevom	peval_view_ori_matrix
EXECUTE STRUCTURE	pexst	pexec_struct
FILL AREA 3	pfa3	pfill_area3
FILL AREA SET 3 WITH DATA	pfas3d	pfill_area_set3_data

FILL AREA SET 3	pfas3	pfill_area_set3
FILL AREA SET WITH DATA	pfasd	pfill_area_set_data
FILL AREA SET	pfas	pfill_area_set
FILL AREA	pfa	pfill_area
FLUSH DEVICE EVENTS	pflush	pflush_events
GENERALIZED DRAWING PRIMITIVE 3	pgdp3	pgdp3
GENERALIZED DRAWING PRIMITIVE	pgdp	pgdp
GENERALIZED STRUCTURE ELEMENT	pgse	pgse
GET CHOICE	pgtch	pget_choice
GET ITEM TYPE FROM METAFILE	pqtitm	pget_item_type
GET LOCATOR 3	pgtlc3	pget_loc3
GET LOCATOR	pgtlc	pget_loc
GET PICK	pgtpk	pget_pick
GET STRING	pgtst	pget_string
GET STROKE 3	pgtsk3	pget_stroke3
GET STROKE	pgtsk	pget_stroke
GET VALUATOR	pgtvl	pget_val
INCREMENTAL SPATIAL SEARCH 3	piss3	pincr_spa_search3
INCREMENTAL SPATIAL SEARCH	piss	pincr_spa_search
INITIALIZE CHOICE 3	pinch3	pinit_choice3
INITIALIZE CHOICE	pinch	pinit_choice
INITIALIZE LOCATOR 3	pinlc3	pinit_loc3
INITIALIZE LOCATOR	pinlc	pinit_loc
INITIALIZE PICK 3	pinpk3	pinit_pick3
INITIALIZE PICK	pinpk	pinit_pick
INITIALIZE STRING 3	pinst3	pinit_string3
INITIALIZE STRING	pinst	pinit_string
INITIALIZE STROKE 3	pinsk3	pinit_stroke3

INITIALIZE STROKE	pinsk	pinit_stroke
INITIALIZE VALUATOR 3	pinvl3	pinit_val3
INITIALIZE VALUATOR	pinvl	pinit_val
INQUIRE ALL CONFLICTING STRUCTURES	pqcst	pinq_all_conf_structs
INQUIRE ANNOTATION FACILITIES	pqanf	pinq_anno_facs
INQUIRE ARCHIVE FILES	pqarf	pinq_ar_files
INQUIRE ARCHIVE STATE VALUE	pqars	pinq_ar_st
INQUIRE B-SPLINE SURFACE FACILITIES	pqbssf	pinq_b_spline_surf_facs
INQUIRE CHOICE DEVICE STATE 3	pqchs3	pinq_choice_st3
INQUIRE CHOICE DEVICE STATE	pqchs	pinq_choice_st
INQUIRE COLOUR FACILITIES	pqcf	pinq_colr_facs
INQUIRE COLOUR MAPPING FACILITIES	pqcmf	pinq_colr_map_facs
INQUIRE COLOUR MAPPING METHOD FACILITIES	pqcmmf	pinq_colr_map_method_facs
INQUIRE COLOUR MAPPING REPRESENTATION	pqcmr	pinq_colr_map_rep
INQUIRE COLOUR MAPPING STATE	pqcms	pinq_colr_map_st
INQUIRE COLOUR MODEL FACILITIES	pqcmdf	pinq_colr_model_facs
INQUIRE COLOUR MODEL	pqcmd	pinq_colr_model
INQUIRE COLOUR REPRESENTATION	pqcr	pinq_colr_rep
INQUIRE CONFLICT RESOLUTION	pqcnrs	pinq_conf_res
INQUIRE CONFLICTING STRUCTURES IN NETWORK	pqcstn	pinq_conf_structs_net
INQUIRE CURRENT ELEMENT CONTENT	pqceco	pinq_cur_elem_content
INQUIRE CURRENT ELEMENT TYPE AND SIZE	pqcets	pinq_cur_elem_type_size
INQUIRE CURVE FACILITIES	pqcvf	pinq_curve_facs
INQUIRE DATA MAPPING FACILITIES	pqdmf	pinq_data_map_facs
INQUIRE DATA MAPPING REPRESENTATION	pqdmr	pinq_data_map_rep
INQUIRE DEFAULT CHOICE DEVICE DATA 3	pqdch3	pinq_def_choice_data3
INQUIRE DEFAULT CHOICE DEVICE DATA	pqdch	pinq_def_choice_data

INQUIRE DEFAULT DISPLAY UPDATE STATE	pqddus	pinq_def_disp_upd_st
INQUIRE DEFAULT LOCATOR DEVICE DATA 3	pqdlc3	pinq_def_loc_data3
INQUIRE DEFAULT LOCATOR DEVICE DATA	pqdlc	pinq_def_loc_data
INQUIRE DEFAULT PICK DEVICE DATA 3	pqdpk3	pinq_def_pick_data3
INQUIRE DEFAULT PICK DEVICE DATA	pqdpk	pinq_def_pick_data
INQUIRE DEFAULT STRING DEVICE DATA 3	pqdst3	pinq_def_string_data3
INQUIRE DEFAULT STRING DEVICE DATA	pqdst	pinq_def_string_data
INQUIRE DEFAULT STROKE DEVICE DATA 3	pqdsk3	pinq_def_stroke_data3
INQUIRE DEFAULT STROKE DEVICE DATA	pqdsk	pinq_def_stroke_data
INQUIRE DEFAULT VALUATOR DEVICE DATA 3	pqdvl3	pinq_def_val_data3
INQUIRE DEFAULT VALUATOR DEVICE DATA	pqdvl	pinq_def_val_data
INQUIRE DEPTH CUE FACILITIES	pqdcf	pinq_depth_cue_facs
INQUIRE DEPTH CUE REPRESENTATION	pqdcr	pinq_depth_cue_rep
INQUIRE DIRECT COLOUR MODEL FACILITIES	pqdcmf	pinq_direct_colr_model_facs
INQUIRE DISPLAY SPACE SIZE 3	pqdsp3	pinq_disp_space_size3
INQUIRE DISPLAY SPACE SIZE	pqdsp	pinq_disp_space_size
INQUIRE DISPLAY UPDATE STATE	pqdus	pinq_disp_upd_st
INQUIRE DYNAMICS OF STRUCTURES	pqdstr	pinq_dyns_structs
INQUIRE DYNAMICS OF WORKSTATION ATTRIBUTES	pqdswa	pinq_dyns_ws_attrs
INQUIRE DYNAMICS OF WORKSTATION PLUS	pqdcwp	pinq_dyns_ws_plus
INQUIRE EDGE FACILITIES	pqedf	pinq_edge_facs
INQUIRE EDGE REPRESENTATION PLUS	pqedp	pinq_edge_rep_plus
INQUIRE EDGE REPRESENTATION	pqedr	pinq_edge_rep
INQUIRE EDIT MODE	pqedm	pinq_edit_mode
INQUIRE ELEMENT CONTENT	pqeco	pinq_elem_content
INQUIRE ELEMENT POINTER	pqep	pinq_elem_ptr
INQUIRE ELEMENT TYPE AND SIZE	pqets	pinq_elem_type_size

INQUIRE ERROR HANDLING MODE	pqerhm	pinq_err_hand_mode
INQUIRE GENERALIZED DRAWING PRIMITIVE 3	pqgdp3	pinq_gdp3
INQUIRE GENERALIZED DRAWING PRIMITIVE	pqgdp	pinq_gdp
INQUIRE GENERALIZED STRUCTURE ELEMENT FACILITIES	pqgsef	pinq_gse_facs
INQUIRE HIGHLIGHTING FILTER	pqhlft	pinq_highl_filter
INQUIRE HLHSR IDENTIFIER FACILITIES	pqhrif	pinq_hlhsr_id_facs
INQUIRE HLHSR MODE FACILITIES	pqhrmf	pinq_hlhsr_mode_facs
INQUIRE HLHSR MODE	pqhrm	pinq_hlhsr_mode
INQUIRE INPUT QUEUE OVERFLOW	pqiqov	pinq_in_overf
INQUIRE INTERIOR FACILITIES PLUS	pqifp	pinq_int_facs_plus
INQUIRE INTERIOR FACILITIES	pqif	pinq_int_facs
INQUIRE INTERIOR REPRESENTATION PLUS	pqip	pinq_int_rep_plus
INQUIRE INTERIOR REPRESENTATION	pqir	pinq_int_rep
INQUIRE INVISIBILITY FILTER	pqivft	pinq_invis_filter
INQUIRE LIGHT SOURCE FACILITIES	pqlsf	pinq_light_source_facs
INQUIRE LIGHT SOURCE REPRESENTATION	pqlsr	pinq_light_source_rep
INQUIRE LIST OF AVAILABLE GENERALIZED DRAWING PRIMITIVES 3	pqegd3	pinq_list_avail_gdp3
INQUIRE LIST OF AVAILABLE GENERALIZED DRAWING PRIMITIVES	pqegdp	pinq_list_avail_gdp
INQUIRE LIST OF AVAILABLE GENERALIZED STRUCTURE ELEMENTS	pqegse	pinq_list_avail_gse
INQUIRE LIST OF AVAILABLE WORKSTATION TYPES	pqewk	pinq_list_avail_ws_types
INQUIRE LIST OF COLOUR INDICES	pqeci	pinq_list_colr_inds
INQUIRE LIST OF COLOUR MAPPING INDICES	pqecmi	pinq_list_colr_map_inds
INQUIRE LIST OF DATA MAPPING INDICES	pqedmi	pinq_list_data_map_inds
INQUIRE LIST OF DEPTH CUE INDICES	pqedci	pinq_list_depth_cue_inds
INQUIRE LIST OF EDGE INDICES	pqeedi	pinq_list_edge_inds
INQUIRE LIST OF INTERIOR INDICES	pqeii	pinq_list_int_inds
INQUIRE LIST OF LIGHT SOURCE INDICES	pqelsi	pinq_list_light_source_inds

INQUIRE LIST OF PARAMETRIC SURFACE INDICES	pqepsi	pinq_list_param_surf_inds
INQUIRE LIST OF PATTERN INDICES	pqepai	pinq_list_pat_inds
INQUIRE LIST OF POLYLINE INDICES	pqepli	pinq_list_line_inds
INQUIRE LIST OF POLYMARKER INDICES	pqepmi	pinq_list_marker_inds
INQUIRE LIST OF REFLECTANCE INDICES	pqerf	pinq_list_refl_inds
INQUIRE LIST OF TEXT INDICES	pqetxi	pinq_list_text_inds
INQUIRE LIST OF VIEW INDICES	pqevwi	pinq_list_view_inds
INQUIRE LOCATOR DEVICE STATE 3	pqlcs3	pinq_loc_st3
INQUIRE LOCATOR DEVICE STATE	pqlcs	pinq_loc_st
INQUIRE MODELLING CLIPPING FACILITIES	pqmclf	pinq_model_clip_facs
INQUIRE MORE SIMULTANEOUS EVENTS	pqsim	pinq_more_simult_events
INQUIRE NUMBER OF AVAILABLE LOGICAL INPUT DEVICES	pqli	pinq_num_avail_in
INQUIRE NUMBER OF DISPLAY PRIORITIES SUPPORTED	pqdp	pinq_num_disp_pris
INQUIRE OPEN STRUCTURE	pqopst	pinq_open_struct
INQUIRE PARAMETRIC SURFACE FACILITIES	pqpsf	pinq_param_surf_facs
INQUIRE PARAMETRIC SURFACE REPRESENTATION	pqpsr	pinq_param_surf_rep
INQUIRE PATHS TO ANCESTORS	pqpan	pinq_paths_ances
INQUIRE PATHS TO DESCENDANTS	pqpde	pinq_paths_descs
INQUIRE PATTERN FACILITIES	pqpaf	pinq_pat_facs
INQUIRE PATTERN REPRESENTATION PLUS	pqparp	pinq_pat_rep_plus
INQUIRE PATTERN REPRESENTATION	pqpar	pinq_pat_rep
INQUIRE PHIGS FACILITIES	pqphf	pinq_phigs_facs
INQUIRE PICK DEVICE STATE 3	pqpks3	pinq_pick_st3
INQUIRE PICK DEVICE STATE	pqpks	pinq_pick_st
INQUIRE POLYLINE FACILITIES PLUS	pqplfp	pinq_line_facs_plus
INQUIRE POLYLINE FACILITIES	pqplf	pinq_line_facs
INQUIRE POLYLINE REPRESENTATION PLUS	pqplp	pinq_line_rep_plus

INQUIRE POLYLINE REPRESENTATION	pqplr	pinq_line_rep
INQUIRE POLYMARKER FACILITIES	pqpmf	pinq_marker_facs
INQUIRE POLYMARKER REPRESENTATION PLUS	pqpmp	pinq_marker_rep_plus
INQUIRE POLYMARKER REPRESENTATION	pqpmr	pinq_marker_rep
INQUIRE POSTED STRUCTURES	pqpost	pinq_posted_structs
INQUIRE PREDEFINED COLOUR MAPPING REPRESENTATION	pqpcmr	pinq_pred_colr_map_rep
INQUIRE PREDEFINED COLOUR REPRESENTATION	pqpcr	pinq_pred_colr_rep
INQUIRE PREDEFINED DATA MAPPING REPRESENTATION	pqpdmr	pinq_pred_data_map_rep
INQUIRE PREDEFINED DEPTH CUE REPRESENTATION	pqpdcr	pinq_pred_depth_cue_rep
INQUIRE PREDEFINED EDGE REPRESENTATION PLUS	pqpedp	pinq_pred_edge_rep_plus
INQUIRE PREDEFINED EDGE REPRESENTATION	pqpedr	pinq_pred_edge_rep
INQUIRE PREDEFINED INTERIOR REPRESENTATION PLUS	pqpip	pinq_pred_int_rep_plus
INQUIRE PREDEFINED INTERIOR REPRESENTATION	pqpir	pinq_pred_int_rep
INQUIRE PREDEFINED LIGHT SOURCE REPRESENTATION	pqplsr	pinq_pred_light_source_rep
INQUIRE PREDEFINED PARAMETRIC SURFACE REPRESENTATION	pqppsr	pinq_pred_param_surf_rep
INQUIRE PREDEFINED PATTERN REPRESENTATION PLUS	pqppap	pinq_pred_pat_rep_plus
INQUIRE PREDEFINED PATTERN REPRESENTATION	pqppar	pinq_pred_pat_rep
INQUIRE PREDEFINED POLYLINE REPRESENTATION PLUS	pqpplp	pinq_pred_line_rep_plus
INQUIRE PREDEFINED POLYLINE REPRESENTATION	pqpplr	pinq_pred_line_rep
INQUIRE PREDEFINED POLYMARKER REPRESENTATION PLUS	pqppmp	pinq_pred_marker_rep_plus
INQUIRE PREDEFINED POLYMARKER REPRESENTATION	pqppmr	pinq_pred_marker_rep
INQUIRE PREDEFINED REFLECTION REPRESENTATION	pqprfr	pinq_pred_refl_rep
INQUIRE PREDEFINED TEXT REPRESENTATION PLUS	pqptxp	pinq_pred_text_rep_plus
INQUIRE PREDEFINED TEXT REPRESENTATION	pqptxr	pinq_pred_text_rep
INQUIRE PREDEFINED VIEW REPRESENTATION	pqpvwr	pinq_pred_view_rep
INQUIRE REFLECTION FACILITIES	pqrff	pinq_refl_facs

INQUIRE REFLECTION REPRESENTATION	pqrfr	pinq_refl_rep
INQUIRE RENDERING COLOUR MODEL FACILITIES	pqrcmf	pinq_rend_colr_model_facs
INQUIRE SET OF OPEN WORKSTATIONS	pqopwk	pinq_open_wss
INQUIRE SET OF WORKSTATIONS TO WHICH POSTED	pqwkpo	pinq_wss_posted
INQUIRE STRING DEVICE STATE 3	pqsts3	pinq_string_st3
INQUIRE STRING DEVICE STATE	pqsts	pinq_string_st
INQUIRE STROKE DEVICE STATE 3	pqsks3	pinq_stroke_st3
INQUIRE STROKE DEVICE STATE	pqsks	pinq_stroke_st
INQUIRE STRUCTURE IDENTIFIERS	pqsid	pinq_struct_ids
INQUIRE STRUCTURE STATE VALUE	pqstrs	pinq_struct_st
INQUIRE STRUCTURE STATUS	pqstst	pinq_struct_status
INQUIRE SYSTEM STATE VALUE	pqsys	pinq_sys_st
INQUIRE TEXT EXTENT	pqtxx, pqtxxs	pinq_text_extent
INQUIRE TEXT FACILITIES	pqtxf	pinq_text_facs
INQUIRE TEXT REPRESENTATION PLUS	pqtxp	pinq_text_rep_plus
INQUIRE TEXT REPRESENTATION	pqtxr	pinq_text_rep
INQUIRE TRIMMING CURVE FACILITIES	pqtcf	pinq_trim_curve_facs
INQUIRE VALUATOR DEVICE STATE 3	pqvls3	pinq_val_st3
INQUIRE VALUATOR DEVICE STATE	pqvls	pinq_val_st
INQUIRE VIEW FACILITIES	pqvwf	pinq_view_facs
INQUIRE VIEW REPRESENTATION	pqvwr	pinq_view_rep
INQUIRE WORKSTATION CATEGORY	pqwkca	pinq_ws_cat
INQUIRE WORKSTATION CLASSIFICATION	pqwkcl	pinq_ws_class
INQUIRE WORKSTATION CONNECTION AND TYPE	pqwkc	pinq_ws_conn_type
INQUIRE WORKSTATION STATE TABLE LENGTHS PLUS	pqwslp	pinq_ws_st_table_length_plus

INQUIRE WORKSTATION STATE TABLE LENGTHS	pqwksl	pinq_ws_st_table
INQUIRE WORKSTATION STATE VALUE	pqwkst	pinq_ws_st
INQUIRE WORKSTATION TRANSFORMATION 3	pqwkt3	pinq_ws_tran3
INQUIRE WORKSTATION TRANSFORMATION	pqwkt	pinq_ws_tran
INTERPRET ITEM	piitm	pinterpret_item
LABEL	plb	plabel
MESSAGE	pmsg, pmsgs	pmessage
NON-UNIFORM B-SPLINE CURVE 3 WITH COLOUR	pbscc	pnon_uniform_b_spline_curve3_colr
NON-UNIFORM B–SPLINE CURVE 3	pbsc	pnon_uniform_b_spline_curve3
NON–UNIFORM B-SPLINE SURFACE 3 WITH DATA	pbssd	pnon_uniform_b_spline_surf3_data
NON-UNIFORM B-SPLINE SURFACE 3	pbss	pnon_uniform_b_spline_surf3
OFFSET ELEMENT POINTER	posep	poffset_elem_ptr
OPEN ARCHIVE FILE	poparf	popen_ar_file
OPEN PHIGS	popph	popen_phigs
OPEN STRUCTURE	popst	popen_struct
OPEN WORKSTATION	popwk	popen_ws
PACK COLOUR SPLINE CURVE	ppcsc	N/A
PACK COLOUR SPLINE SURFACE	ppcss	N/A
PACK DATA RECORD	pprec	N/A
PACK DATA SPLINE SURFACE	ppdss	N/A
PACK TRIMMING CURVE	pptc	N/A
POLYLINE 3	ppl3	ppolyline3
POLYLINE SET 3 WITH COLOUR	ppls3c	ppolyline_set3_colr

POLYLINE	ppl	ppolyline
POLYMARKER 3	ppm3	ppolymarker3
POLYMARKER	ppm	ppolymarker
POST STRUCTURE	ppost	ppost_struct
QUADRILATERAL MESH 3 WITH DATA	pqm3d	pquad_mesh3_data
QUADRILATERAL MESH WITH DATA	pqmd	pquad_mesh_data
READ ITEM FROM METAFILE	prditm	pread_item
REDRAW ALL STRUCTURES	prst	predraw_all_structs
REMOVE NAMES FROM SET	pres	premove_names_set
REQUEST CHOICE	prqch	preq_choice
REQUEST LOCATOR 3	prqlc3	preq_loc3
REQUEST LOCATOR	prqlc	preq_loc
REQUEST PICK	prqpk	preq_pick
REQUEST STRING	prqst	preq_string
REQUEST STROKE 3	prqsk3	preq_stroke3
REQUEST STROKE	prqsk	preq_stroke
REQUEST VALUATOR	prqvl	preq_val
RESTORE MODELLING CLIPPING VOLUME	prmcv	prestore_model_clip_vol
RETRIEVE ALL STRUCTURES	prast	pret_all_structs
RETRIEVE PATHS TO ANCESTORS	prepan	pret_paths_ances
RETRIEVE PATHS TO DESCENDANTS	prepde	pret_paths_descs
RETRIEVE STRUCTURE IDENTIFIERS	prsid	pret_struct_ids
RETRIEVE STRUCTURE NETWORKS	presn	pret_struct_nets
RETRIEVE STRUCTURES	prest	pret_structs
ROTATE X	prox	protate_x
ROTATE Y	proy	protate_y
ROTATE Z	proz	protate_z
ROTATE	pro	protate

SAMPLE CHOICE	psmch	psample_choice
SAMPLE LOCATOR 3	psmlc3	psample_loc3
SAMPLE LOCATOR	psmlc	psample_loc
SAMPLE PICK	psmpk	psample_pick
SAMPLE STRING	psmst	psample_string
SAMPLE STROKE 3	psmsk3	psample_stroke3
SAMPLE STROKE	psmsk	psample_stroke
SAMPLE VALUATOR	psmvl	psample_val
SCALE 3	psc3	pscale3
SCALE	psc	pscale
SET ANNOTATION STYLE	psans	pset_anno_style
SET ANNOTATION TEXT ALIGNMENT	psatal	pset_anno_align
SET ANNOTATION TEXT CHARACTER HEIGHT	psatch	pset_anno_char_ht
SET ANNOTATION TEXT CHARACTER UP VECTOR	psatcu	pset_anno_char_up_vec
SET ANNOTATION TEXT PATH	psatp	pset_anno_path
SET BACK DATA MAPPING INDEX	psbdmi	pset_back_data_map_ind
SET BACK DATA MAPPING METHOD	psbdmm	pset_back_data_map_method
SET BACK INTERIOR COLOUR	psbic	pset_back_int_colr
SET BACK INTERIOR INDEX	psbii	pset_back_int_ind
SET BACK INTERIOR SHADING METHOD	psbism	pset_back_int_shad_method
SET BACK INTERIOR STYLE INDEX	psbisi	pset_back_int_style_ind
SET BACK INTERIOR STYLE	psbis	pset_back_int_style
SET BACK REFLECTANCE INDEX	psbrfi	pset_back_refl_ind
SET BACK REFLECTANCE MODEL	psbrfm	pset_back_refl_model
SET BACK REFLECTANCE PROPERTIES	psbrfp	pset_back_refl_props
SET CHARACTER EXPANSION FACTOR	pschxp	pset_char_expan

SET CHARACTER HEIGHT	pschh	pset_char_ht
SET CHARACTER SPACING	pschsp	pset_char_space
SET CHARACTER UP VECTOR	pschup	pset_char_up_vec
SET CHOICE MODE	pschm	pset_choice_mode
SET COLOUR MAPPING INDEX	pscmi	pset_colr_map_ind
SET COLOUR MAPPING REPRESENTATION	pscmr	pset_colr_map_rep
SET COLOUR MODEL	pscmd	pset_colr_model
SET COLOUR REPRESENTATION	pscr	pset_colr_rep
SET CONFLICT RESOLUTION	pscnrs	pset_conf_res
SET CURVE APPROXIMATION CRITERIA	pscac	pset_curve_approx_criteria
SET DATA MAPPING INDEX	psdmi	pset_data_map_ind
SET DATA MAPPING METHOD	psdmm	pset_data_map_method
SET DATA MAPPING REPRESENTATION	psdmr	pset_data_map_rep
SET DEPTH CUE INDEX	psdci	pset_depth_cue_ind
SET DEPTH CUE REPRESENTATION	psdcr	pset_depth_cue_rep
SET DISPLAY UPDATE STATE	psdus	pset_disp_upd_st
SET EDGE COLOUR INDEX	psedci	pset_edge_colr_ind
SET EDGE COLOUR	psedc	pset_edge_colr
SET EDGE FLAG	psedfg	pset_edge_flag
SET EDGE INDEX	psedi	pset_edge_ind
SET EDGE REPRESENTATION PLUS	psedp	pset_edge_rep_plus
SET EDGE REPRESENTATION	psedr	pset_edge_rep
SET EDGETYPE	psedt	pset_edgetype
SET EDGEWIDTH SCALE FACTOR	psewsc	pset_edgewidth
SET EDIT MODE	psedm	pset_edit_mode
SET ELEMENT POINTER AT LABEL	pseplb	pset_elem_ptr_label
SET ELEMENT POINTER	psep	pset_elem_ptr

SET ERROR HANDLING MODE	pserhm	pset_err_hand_mode
SET ERROR HANDLING	N/A	pset_err_hand
SET FACET CULLING MODE	psfcm	pset_facet_cull_mode
SET FACET DISTINGUISHING MODE	psfdm	pset_facet_disting_mode
SET GLOBAL TRANSFORMATION 3	psgmt3	pset_global_tran3
SET GLOBAL TRANSFORMATION	psgmt	pset_global_tran
SET HIGHLIGHTING FILTER	pshlft	pset_highl_filter
SET HLHSR IDENTIFIER	pshrid	pset_hlhsr_id
SET HLHSR MODE	pshrm	pset_hlhsr_mode
SET INDIVIDUAL ASF	psiasf	pset_indiv_asf
SET INTERIOR COLOUR INDEX	psici	pset_int_colr_ind
SET INTERIOR COLOUR	psic	pset_int_colr
SET INTERIOR INDEX	psii	pset_int_ind
SET INTERIOR REPRESENTATION PLUS	psip	pset_int_rep_plus
SET INTERIOR REPRESENTATION	psir	pset_int_rep
SET INTERIOR SHADING METHOD	psism	pset_int_shad_method
SET INTERIOR STYLE INDEX	psisi	pset_int_style_ind
SET INTERIOR STYLE	psis	pset_int_style
SET INVISIBILITY FILTER	psivft	pset_invis_filter
SET LIGHT SOURCE REPRESENTATION	pslsr	pset_light_source_rep
SET LIGHT SOURCE STATE	pslss	pset_light_source_st
SET LINETYPE	psln	pset_linetype
SET LINEWIDTH SCALE FACTOR	pslwsc	pset_linewidth
SET LOCAL TRANSFORMATION 3	pslmt3	pset_local_tran3
SET LOCAL TRANSFORMATION	pslmt	pset_local_tran
SET LOCATOR MODE	pslcm	pset_loc_mode
SET MARKER SIZE SCALE FACTOR	psmksc	pset_marker_size
SET MARKER TYPE	psmk	pset_marker_type

SET MODELLING CLIPPING INDICATOR	psmcli	pset_model_clip_ind
SET MODELLING CLIPPING VOLUME 3	psmcv3	pset_model_clip_vol3
SET MODELLING CLIPPING VOLUME	psmcv	pset_model_clip_vol
SET OF FILL AREA SET 3 WITH DATA	psfas3	pset_of_fill_area_sets3_data
SET OF FILL AREA SET WITH DATA	psfasd	pset_of_fill_area_sets_data
SET PARAMETRIC SURFACE CHARACTERISTICS	pspsc	pset_param_surf_chars
SET PARAMETRIC SURFACE INDEX	pspsi	pset_param_surf_ind
SET PARAMETRIC SURFACE REPRESENTATION	pspsr	pset_param_surf_rep
SET PATTERN REFERENCE POINT AND VECTORS	psprpv	pset_pat_ref_point_vecs
SET PATTERN REFERENCE POINT ...	psparf	pset_pat_ref_point
SET PATTERN REPRESENTATION PLUS	pspap	pset_pat_rep_plus
SET PATTERN REPRESENTATION	pspar	pset_pat_rep
SET PATTERN SIZE	pspa	pset_pat_size
SET PICK FILTER	pspkft	pset_pick_filter
SET PICK IDENTIFIER	pspkid	pset_pick_id
SET PICK MODE	pspkm	pset_pick_mode
SET POLYLINE COLOUR INDEX	psplci	pset_line_colr_ind
SET POLYLINE COLOUR	psplc	pset_line_colr
SET POLYLINE INDEX	pspli	pset_line_ind
SET POLYLINE REPRESENTATION PLUS	psplp	pset_line_rep_plus
SET POLYLINE REPRESENTATION	psplr	pset_line_rep
SET POLYLINE SHADING METHOD	psplsm	pset_line_shad_method
SET POLYMARKER COLOUR INDEX	pspmci	pset_marker_colr_ind
SET POLYMARKER COLOUR	pspmc	pset_marker_colr
SET POLYMARKER INDEX	pspmi	pset_marker_ind
SET POLYMARKER REPRESENTATION PLUS	pspmp	pset_marker_rep_plus

SET POLYMARKER REPRESENTATION	pspmr	pset_marker_rep
SET REFLECTANCE INDEX	psrfi	pset_refl_ind
SET REFLECTANCE MODEL	psrfm	pset_refl_model
SET REFLECTANCE PROPERTIES	psrfp	pset_refl_props
SET REFLECTANCE REPRESENTATION	psrfr	pset_refl_rep
SET RENDERING COLOUR MODEL	psrcm	pset_rend_colr_model
SET STRING MODE	psstm	pset_string_mode
SET STROKE MODE	psskm	pset_stroke_mode
SET SURFACE APPROXIMATION CRITERIA	pssac	pset_surf_approx_crit
SET TEXT ALIGNMENT	pstxal	pset_text_align
SET TEXT COLOUR INDEX	pstxci	pset_text_colr_ind
SET TEXT COLOUR	pstxc	pset_text_colr
SET TEXT FONT	pstxfn	pset_text_font
SET TEXT INDEX	pstxi	pset_text_ind
SET TEXT PATH	pstxp	pset_text_path
SET TEXT PRECISION	pstxpr	pset_text_prec
SET TEXT REPRESENTATION PLUS	pstxp	pset_text_rep_plus
SET TEXT REPRESENTATION	pstxr	pset_text_rep
SET VALUATOR MODE	psvlm	pset_val_mode
SET VIEW INDEX	psvwi	pset_view_ind
SET VIEW REPRESENTATION 3	psvwr3	pset_view_rep3
SET VIEW REPRESENTATION	psvwr	pset_view_rep
SET VIEW TRANSFORMATION INPUT PRIORITY	psvtip	pset_view_tran_in_pri
SET WORKSTATION VIEWPORT 3	pswkv3	pset_ws_vp3
SET WORKSTATION VIEWPORT	pswkv	pset_ws_vp
SET WORKSTATION WINDOW 3	pswkw3	pset_ws_win3
SET WORKSTATION WINDOW	pswkw	pset_ws_win
TEXT 3	ptx3, ptx3s	ptext3

TEXT	ptx, ptxs	ptext
TRANSFORM POINT 3	ptp3	ptran_point3
TRANSFORM POINT	ptp	ptran_point
TRANSLATE 3	ptr3	ptranslate3
TRANSLATE	ptr	ptranslate
TRIANGLE SET 3 WITH DATA	pts3d	ptri_set3_data
TRIANGLE SET WITH DATA	ptsd	ptri_set_data
TRIANGLE STRIP 3 WITH DATA	ptst3d	ptri_strip3_data
TRIANGLE STRIP WITH DATA	ptstd	ptri_strip_data
UNPACK DATA RECORD	purec	N/A
UNPACK COLOUR SPLINE CURVE	pucsc	N/A
UNPACK COLOUR SPLINE SURFACE	pucss	N/A
UNPACK DATA SPLINE SURFACE	pudss	N/A
UNPACK TRIMMING CURVE	putc	N/A
UNPOST ALL STRUCTURES	pupast	punpost_all_structs
UNPOST STRUCTURE	pupost	punpost_struct
UPDATE WORKSTATION	puwk	pupd_ws
WRITE ITEM TO METAFILE	pwitm	pwrite_item

Appendix B

PHIGS Colour Models

Introduction

In order for a computer to deal with any particular concept, that concept must be defined in quantifiable terms. Representing colour is no exception: All the aspects of colour that are required to be dealt with accurately on a programmatic basis must be defined in some rational, self-consistent manner. This has been done for computers several times and, not surprisingly, there are several different approaches to manipulating and representing colours on a machine that cannot really perceive or understand what colour is.

The first step in defining a colour model for a computer is to define a **colour space**. A colour space is a geometric representation of colours, finite in extent, and usually defined in three dimensions. Once this colour space is defined, actual values are applied at various points in that space. The locations of these values, and the axes along which they are placed, are selected in such a way as to allow unambiguous colour selection for any valid combination of selector values. A colour space, combined with a defined colour-selection mechanism, is called a **colour model**. In other words, colour models define a colour-coordinate system and a finite volume of space within which each describable colour is represented by a point.

PHIGS Colour Handling

In PHIGS, colours are specified by selecting a colour model and then specifying the colour-selecting coordinates in the colour space of that model. Every open workstation has an associated colour model in effect, which is specified by the *current colour model* entry in the workstation state list.

The PHIGS standard refers to several different colour models. Some of them are required for a standard-conformant PHIGS implementation; others are optional. These models are described in subsequent sections.

According to the PHIGS standard, colour models are associated with numbers as follows:

- Colour models less than 1 are implementation-dependent.
- Colour models 1 through 4 are predefined as RGB, CIELUV, HSV, and HLS, respectively (these descriptions follow). RGB and CIELUV are required to be available for a PHIGS implementation to be standard-conformant; HSV and HLS, on the other hand, can be omitted from an implementation without sacrificing standards conformance.

The colour models available on any particular workstation can be inquired by the routine INQUIRE COLOUR MODEL FACILITIES.

PHIGS Colour Models

This section describes the four colour models used by the PHIGS standard.

RGB Colour Model

In working with colour, most computer displays have three electron guns. These guns shoot electrons at a substance called a phosphor, which glows when electrons hit it. There is one phosphor for each electron gun: red, green, and blue. All visible colours can be generated through various combinations of these three colours. Thus, red, green, and blue are called the *additive primary colours*. The RGB colour model is the easiest model for an implementation to support since it so closely matches the hardware.

As you might expect, "RGB" stands for red/green/blue. Since there are three components, they can be conceptualized as the three perpendicular axes necessary to represent points in three-dimensional space. Thus, there are a red axis, a green axis, and a blue axis, and every possible colour can be represented by just three values: one for each of the red, green, and blue components. Figure B–1 illustrates the RGB colour cube.

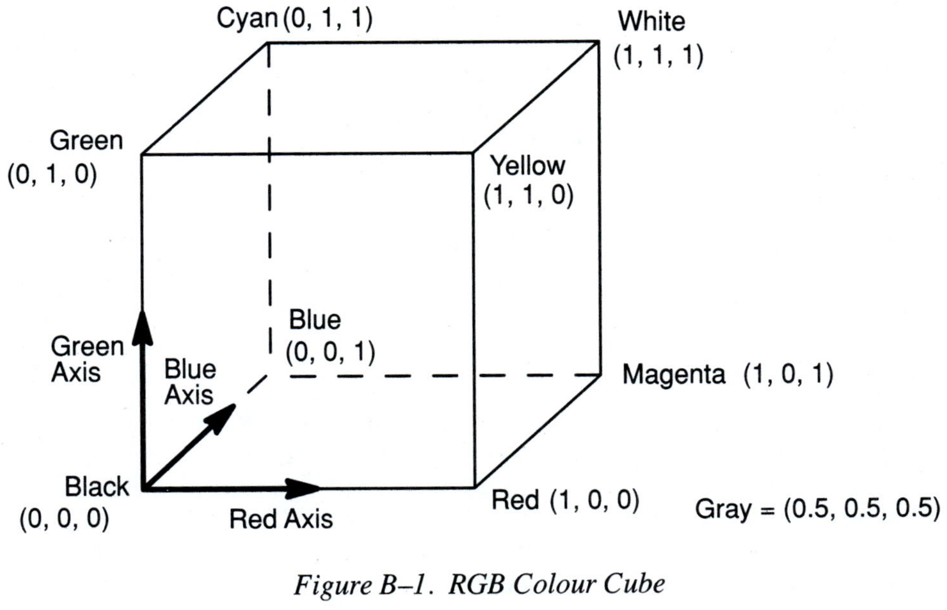

Figure B–1. RGB Colour Cube

The RGB colour cube describes an additive colour system. In an additive colour system, colour is generated by mixing varying amounts of the primary colours (more on this later).

Since we need a computer model of the colour model, we need to represent the model in some mathematical form. If there is an absence of a particular colour, let us denote this by saying that colour has a brightness (or intensity) of 0.0. And, for the sake of convenience, let us consider the greatest possible brightness to be 1.0. At this point, our colour model can be represented by the unit cube shown above, in which each dimension designates the value of one of the colours red, green, or blue.

The corner of the cube at which the colour axes start, reasonably enough, is called (0, 0, 0). This is called the origin, and the eye would perceive this as black. The opposite corner, one unit away along each axis, represents the colour in which red, green, and blue are at their brightest. This point is called (1, 1, 1), and the eye perceives this as white. Indeed, if the red, green, and blue components of a colour are all equal (between 0 and 1), the resultant colour is a shade of gray, somewhere along the continuum between black and white.

This RGB colour model is convenient, and it bears a strong resemblance to the hardware with which it is used. Every piece of display hardware can represent at least a subset of this colour model. Again, every possible colour can be represented by a trio of coordinates: one for each of the red, green, and blue components.

By referring to the colour cube in Figure B–1, you can see that you change from red to yellow by adding increasing amounts of green. Orange is midway between yellow and red, or roughly (1.0, 0.5, 0.0). You can experiment by adding different amounts of green until you find a suitable orange colour. Table B–1 lists the RGB values for a number of frequently used colours.

Experiment with different values to get the shade you want. For example, green can range from a vivid green colour (0.1, 1.0, 0.1) to a faint light green (0.9, 1.0, 0.9).

Using the RGB Colour Model

An important point to remember when dealing with the RGB colour model is that you are not mixing paint, but rather you are mixing colours in the visible light spectrum. The lighter you want a colour to be, the closer the red, green, and blue values should be to 1.0. For example, pure blue is (0.0, 0.0, 1.0), and a light blue is (0.75, 0.75, 1.0). This is like taking a colour close to white (0.75, 0.75, 0.75) and adding a small amount of blue to get (0.75, 0.75, 1.0). To get a darker blue, put the red and green values closer to 0, for example, (0.2, 0.2, 1.0).

In general, to get a darker colour, put the values closer to 0. For example, going from (0.0, 0.0, 1.0) to (0.0, 0.0, 0.4) changes from pure bright blue to pure dark blue. Also, going from (1.0, 0.0, 1.0) to (0.6, 0.0, 0.6) changes from magenta to a darker purple (see Table B–1).

Table B–1. Sample RGB Colour Values

Colour Value			Visible Colour
R	**G**	**B**	
0.0	0.0	0.0	Black
1.0	1.0	1.0	White
1.0	0.0	0.0	Red
0.0	1.0	0.0	Pure green
0.75	1.0	0.75	Light green
0.0	0.4	0.0	Dark green
0.0	0.0	1.0	Pure blue
0.75	0.75	1.0	Light blue
0.0	0.0	0.4	Dark pure blue
0.0	1.0	1.0	Cyan
1.0	1.0	0.0	Yellow
1.0	0.0	1.0	Magenta
1.0	0.75	1.0	Light purple
0.6	0.0	0.6	Dark purple

The following example creates a grid of 11 × 11 fill area primitives to illustrate one side of the RGB colour cube. You can get a finer gradation of colour using more (and smaller) primitives and smaller colour increments.

```
      program rgb_side
C   DESCRIPTION:
C     This program draws an 11 x 11 grid of fill area primitives
C     and assigns colours to match one side of the
C     RGB colour cube: Red   = 1.0
C                      Green = 0.0 to 1.0
C                      Blue  = 0.0 to 1.0
```

```
%include '/sys/ins/phigs.ins.ftn'
      integer*4 Scene, WorkID, i, j, n
      parameter (Scene=1, WorkID=2)
      real      BoxX(4),BoxY(4), red, green, blue
      real      Color(3)
      data boxx /0.05, 0.05, 0.1, 0.1/
      data boxy /0.0, 0.05, 0.05, 0.0/

      call popph (1, 0)                {open PHIGS
      call popwk (WorkID, 1, DPWODS)   { open workstation
      call pscmd (WorkID,PRGB)         { set colour model to RGB
C *****************************************************************
C Load the colour map
      red = 1.0
      green = -0.1            {so first time through value is 0
      n = 1      {start at colour index 1}
      DO i=1,11
        green = green + 0.1
        blue = -0.1      {so first time through value will be 0
        DO j = 1,11
          blue = blue + 0.1
          if (green .GT. 1.0) green = 1.0
          if (blue .GT. 1.0) blue = 1.0
           Color(1)=red
           Color(2)=green
           Color(3)=blue
           call pscr(WorkID, n, 3, Color)  {set colour rep.
          n = n+1
        enddo
      enddo
C *************************************************************
      call popst(Scene)              {open structure
      call psis(PSOLID)              {set interior style
      n =1
      do i = 1,11
        BoxY(1) = BoxY(1) + 0.05     {increment y values each time
        BoxY(2) = BoxY(2) + 0.05     {through the loop
        BoxY(3) = BoxY(3) + 0.05
        BoxY(4) = BoxY(4) + 0.05
        BoxX(1) = 0.05          {reset x values before inner loop
        BoxX(2) = 0.05
        BoxX(3) = 0.1
        BoxX(4) = 0.1
```

```
          do j = 1,11
            BoxX(1) = BoxX(1) + 0.05
            BoxX(2) = BoxX(2) + 0.05
            BoxX(3) = BoxX(3) + 0.05
            BoxX(4) = BoxX(4) + 0.05
            call psici(n)              {set interior colour index
            call pfa(4,BoxX,BoxY)      {fill area primitive
            n = n +1
          enddo
        enddo
        call pclst                     {close structure
C *************************************************************
        call ppost (WorkID, Scene, 1.0)       {post structure}
        call puwk(WorkID,PPERFO)              {update workstation
C Wait here until carriage return to exit.
        READ *
        call pupost (WorkID, Scene)           {close and exit
        call pclwk (WorkID)
        call pclph
        stop
        end
```

CIELUV Colour Model

"CIE" is an abbreviation for the Commission Internationale de l'Eclairage. It is used to refer to the CIE universal colour definition system used as a colour model. The current version of the CIE colour model is the product of several revisions over the last six decades.

The CIELUV model provides a device-independent method for specifying colours. It is based on the properties of the "average" human visual system, as opposed to those of any particular output device.

CIELUV colours are specified by the luminance value, y, and the u', v' chromaticity coordinates. These parameters can take values from 0.0 to 1.0, although only a subset of describable colours is physically realizable by any actual output device. Black is represented by a luminance value of zero.

The u', v' chromaticity diagram is shown in Figure B–2. For more information on this colour model, refer to Appendix I of the PHIGS standard.

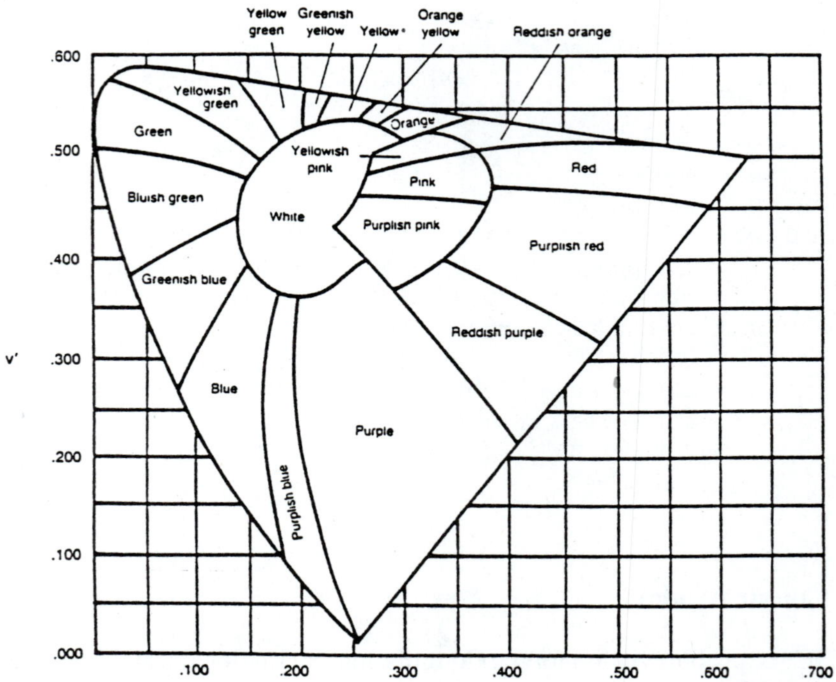

Figure B–2. CIE LUV Colour Model

HSV Colour Model

The colour cube is very useful for working with physical systems based on colour primaries. They are not always intuitive, though. The HSV (hue, saturation, and value) model is closer to the intuitive model of colour used by artists and is very effective for interactive colour selection. It is similar in concept to the methods used by artists for mixing paints, where pure hues are selected, and then white and black are mixed to dilute the colour and/or darken it.

The three parameters used in the HSV colour model represent hue (the pure colour to be worked with), saturation (the ratio of the pure colour mixed with white), and luminosity value (the brightness per unit area).

The HSV colour space, unlike the RGB colour *cube*, is a colour *cone*. It resides in a cylindrical coordinate system; i.e., a coordinate system in which a polar coordinate system represents the xy plane, and it is combined with the z-axis from a rectangular coordinate system.

Figure B–3 illustrates the HSV colour cone. Colour plate 8 (see colour insert) shows a top view of the cone.

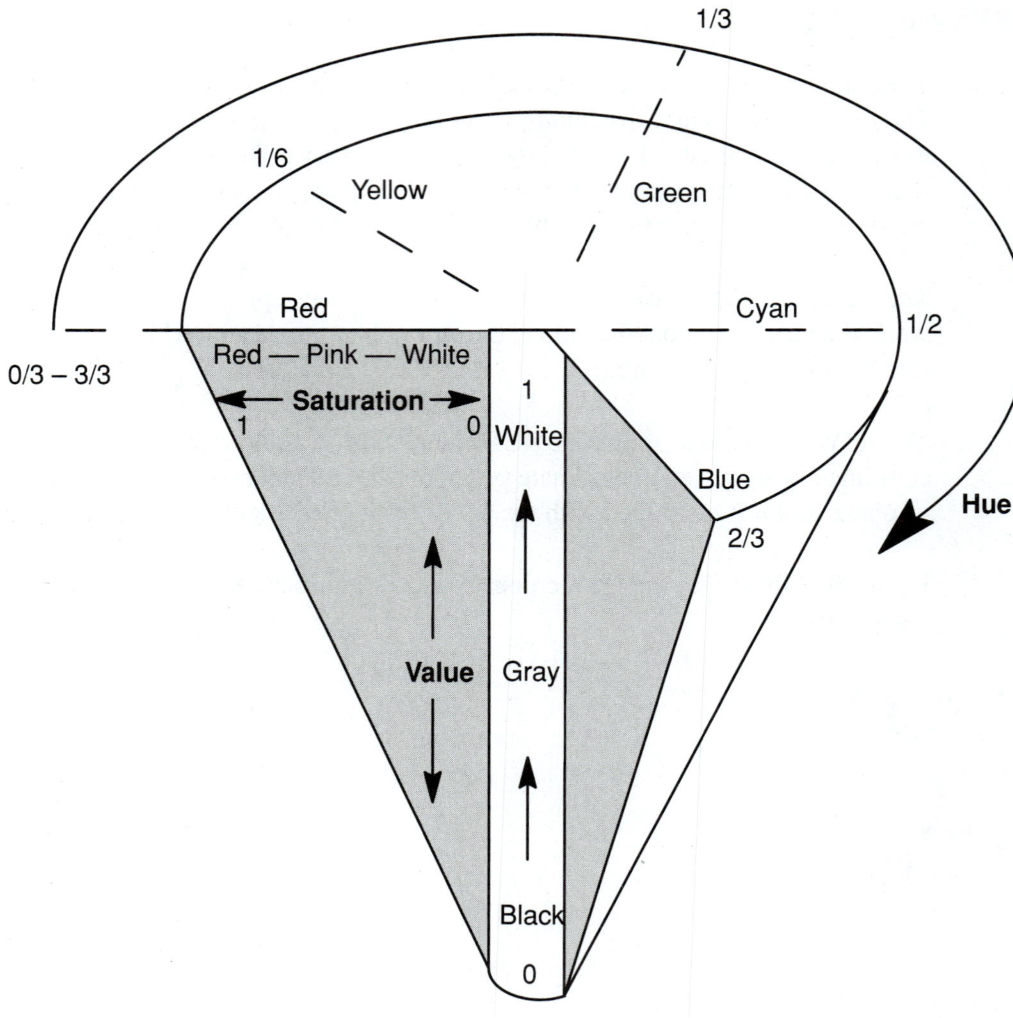

Figure B–3. The HSV Colour Cone

There are four characteristics of the HSV cylindrical colour space that need to be understood:

- The coordinates are normalized; that is, they range from a minimum value of 0.0 through a maximum value of 1.0. Any combination of the three values is legal, as long as they are all in the 0–1 range.

- **Hue** is the angular coordinate; i.e., how far around the circle are we? The common colours red, yellow, green, cyan, blue, and magenta are located at integer multiples of 1/6 around the circle.

- **Saturation** is the radial coordinate; i.e., how far from the axis of the cone are we? Note that the range of legal saturation values does not change depending on the value of luminosity, as the cone shape implies. A saturation value of 1.0 when the luminosity value is 0.0 is just as legal as a saturation of 1.0 when the luminosity is 1.0. Thus, a cylindrical shape would perhaps be a clearer model (this is discussed later). The cone shape illustrates that as the luminosity decreases, the *visible change* caused by the hue and saturation also decreases.

- The **luminosity** value is the altitude above the polar coordinate plane; i.e., how far above the "floor" of the coordinate system (the point of the cone) are we? The "luminosity value" is abbreviated "value" in the name HSV; however, "value" doesn't indicate what *kind* of entity it is quantifying ("Give me the value." "The value of what?"). Thus, we will use the term "luminosity" in order to distinguish this value from other values.

The HSV cone rests point-down on a black point (luminosity value = 0) and extends upward, with increasing altitude representing increasing luminosity (brightness). Whenever the luminosity value is at 0, saturation and hue do not matter (although any normalized values are still legal); all resultant colours are black. White is at the center of the top of the cone (luminosity value = 1, saturation = 0). Whenever saturation is 0, the value of hue does not matter; all resultant colours are some shade of gray. The center line of the cylinder (saturation = 0) connects the black point of the cone (luminosity value=0, saturation=0) with white (luminosity value = 1, saturation = 0) through a series of gray steps (luminosity value = 0–1, saturation = 0). The outer surface of the cone (saturation = 1) represents fully saturated colour.

Be aware that this conical conceptual model can be misleading. From looking at the model, its radius at the top implies (correctly) that when the luminosity value is 1, the saturation (represented by radius) can take on any value between 0 and 1, inclusive. However, from looking at the same model, its radius at the bottom implies (incorrectly) that when the luminosity value is 0, the saturation (represented by radius) must also be 0 and, in general, that the saturation value cannot exceed the luminosity value. This is *not* the case. Moreover, the conical shape implies that at a luminosity value of 0.5, a saturation of 0.5 represents fully saturated colour. This is also not the case. In spite of the misleading conical shape, the HSV model uses true cylindrical coordinates, and you can specify saturation values anywhere in the 0–1 range regardless of the luminosity value.

The conical shape of the HSV colour model can serve to remind you of this general guideline: The smaller the luminosity value, the less *noticeable* any change in hue or saturation will be in the resultant image.

Table B–2 lists several sample HSV values. In the table, most of the saturation and value components remain constant. To create lighter colours, decrease the saturation component. To create darker (less bright) colours, decrease the value component. Notice that red can be represented by a hue of 0.0 or a hue of 1.0, since red is the start and end of the colour wheel (going around the top of the colour cone in Figure B–3).

Table B–2. Sample HSV Colour Values

Colour Value			**Visible Colour**
H	**S**	**V**	
1.00	1.0	0.0	Black
0.00	0.0	1.0	White
0.00	1.0	1.0	Red
1.00	1.0	1.0	Red
0.16	1.0	1.0	Yellow
0.33	1.0	1.0	Green
0.50	1.0	1.0	Cyan
0.66	1.0	1.0	Blue
0.83	1.0	1.0	Magenta

The following example shows what happens when you keep saturation and luminosity value constant at 1.0, and change the hue from 0 to 1 in 0.025 increments. The program creates a row of 40 fill area primitives and assigns a different HSV colour to each primitive.

```
         program HSV
C DESCRIPTION:
C  This program draws a row of 40 polygons and assigns
C  a different HSV colour to each polygon.  The program
C  demonstrates what happens when you keep saturation
C  at 1, value at 1, and increase hue from 0.0 to 1.0
C  (in 0.025 increments). Colours change in increments
C  as follows: cyan-->blue-->magenta-->red.
%include '/sys/ins/phigs.ins.ftn'
      integer*4 Scene, WorkID, i
      parameter (Scene=1, WorkID=2)
      real BoxX(4), BoxY(4), Hue, Saturation, Value
      real Color(3)
      data BoxX /-1.0, -1.0, -0.95, -0.95/
      data BoxY /-0.4, 0.4, 0.4, -0.4/

      call popph (1, 0)                {open PHIGS
      call popwk (WorkID, 1, DPWODS) { open workstation
      call pscmd (WorkID,PHSV)         { set colour model to HSV
C ***********************************************************
C Load the colour map
      Saturation = 1.0
      Value = 1.0
      Hue   = 0.0
      do i=1,40
        Color(1)=Hue
        Color(2)=Saturation
        Color(3)=Value
        call pscr(WorkID, i, 3, Color) {set colour rep.
        Hue = Hue + 0.025
        if (Hue .GT. 1.0) Hue = 1.0  {to protect against
                                       { values like 1.000000001
      enddo
C ************************************************************
      call popst(Scene)                {open structure
      call psis(PSOLID)                {set interior style
        do i = 1,40
          call psici (i)               {set interior colour
          call pfa(4,BoxX,BoxY)        {fill area primitive
          BoxX(1) = BoxX(1) + 0.05
          BoxX(2) = BoxX(2) + 0.05
          BoxX(3) = BoxX(3) + 0.05
          BoxX(4) = BoxX(4) + 0.05
```

```
           enddo
          call pclst                      {close structure
C **************************************************************
         call ppost (WorkID, Scene, 1.0)      {post structure
         call puwk(WorkID,PPERFO)             {update workstation
C Wait here til carriage return to exit.
         READ *
         call pupost (WorkID, Scene)          {close and exit
         call pclwk (WorkID)
         call pclph
         stop
         end
```

HLS Colour Model

The HLS (hue/lightness/saturation) model is a double-ended colour cone.

- The hue is the angle about the axis of the cone, in fractions of a circle.
- The saturation is the radius of the cone.
- The lightness (intensity or brightness) is the height of the cone.

The angle, radius, and height range from 0.0 to 1.0. Each point within the cone defines a unique colour with a hue value (angle), a saturation value (radius), and a lightness value (height). Figure B–4 illustrates the HLS colour cone.

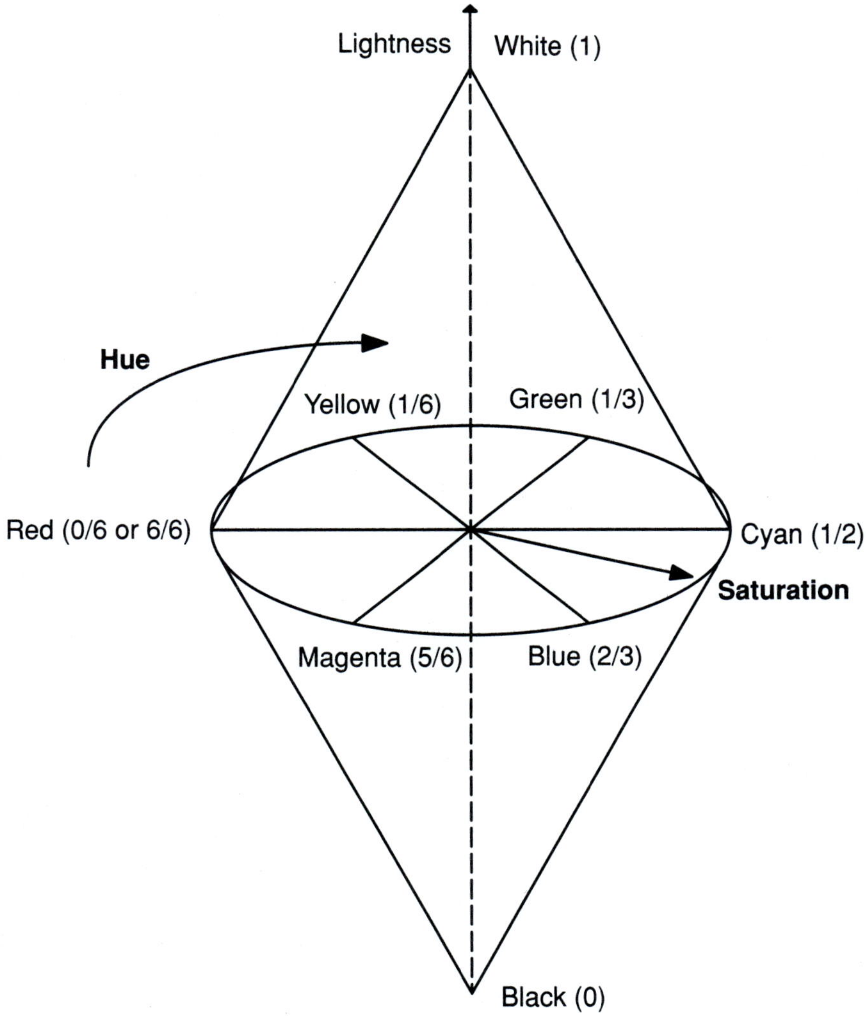

Figure B–4. The HLS Colour Cone

Appendix C

Sample Programs

This appendix contains listings of programs that either were too long for the main text or are C or FORTRAN binding versions of programs in the text. These programs are available online, as described at the beginning of Chapter 2, *An Introduction to PHIGS*.

Also refer to "Some comments about FORTRAN Comments" in the *Preface* and "Some Implementation-dependent Aspects" of the Programs in Chapter 2.

Progressive Example Program

This section lists the FORTRAN version of the progressive example described in Chapter 2, *An Introduction to PHIGS*. The C binding version is listed at the end of Chapter 2.

```
include 'phigs.f1.h'                   ! get the PHIGS aliases
program TicLabels                      ! program "TicLabels.f"
include 'phigs.f2.h'                   ! get the PHIGS constants

integer*4 WorkstnID                    ! workstation identifier
parameter (WorkstnID=1)                ! value chosen by the user
integer*4 ConnID                       ! connection identifier
integer*4 WorkstnType                  ! workstation type
parameter (WorkstnType=POIDDX)         ! out/in, direct, dbl bfr, X
integer*4 TheCurve                     ! display list structure root
parameter (TheCurve=1)                 ! value chosen by the user
```

```
      real       X(100), Y(100)                   ! points for polyline
      integer*4 SimplexSansSerif                  ! sent to "pstxfn"
      parameter (SimplexSansSerif=-2)
      integer*4 BoldSansSerif                     ! sent to "pstxfn"
      parameter (BoldSansSerif=-4)
      integer*4 I                                 ! loop control variable
      character*5 Strng                           ! the text to be labelled
      integer*4 fdopen                            ! to get file descriptor

      call popph(fdopen(fnum(7), 'w'//char(0)), 0)       ! open PHIGS
      call pue004('/dev/screen/phigs_window', ConnID)    ! get connection ID
      call popwk(WorkstnID, ConnID, WorkstnType)! open workstation
      call DefineView(WorkstnID, 1,               ! mapping for view index 1:
     + 0., 1., 0., 1.,                            !   window: 0-1, 0-1
     + .12, .98, .1, .88,                         !   viewport: in a subset
     + .false.)                                   !   don't clip at view window
      call DefineView(WorkstnID, 2,               ! mapping for view index 2:
     + 0., 1., 0., 1., 0., 1., 0., 1.,            !   window & viewpt: 0-1, 0-1
     + .true.)                                    !   clip at view window
      call DefineView(WorkstnID, 3,               ! mapping for view index 3:
     + 0., 1., 0., 1.,                            !   window: 0-1, 0-1
     + .12, .98, .1, .88,                         !   viewport: in a subset
     + .true.)                                    !   clip at view window
      call popst(TheCurve)                        ! open display list structure
      !=== create the labels ==========================================+======
      call psvwi(2)                               ! set view index to 2
      !--- do the main title ------------------------------------------+------
      call pstxfn(BoldSansSerif)                  ! set text font
      call pstxal(PACENT, PATOP)                  ! text alignment: center, top
      call pschh(.05)                             ! set character height in TLCs
      call pschsp(0.)                             ! set character spacing
      call ptx(.5, 1., 'VOLTAGE VARIANCE')        ! define the text
      !--- do the x-axis title ----------------------------------------+------
      call pstxfn(SimplexSansSerif)               ! set text font
      call pstxal(PACENT, PABOTT)                 ! text alignment: center,bottom
      call pschh(.03)                             ! set character height in TLCs
      call ptx(.5, 0., 'Time (seconds)')          ! define the text
      !--- do the y-axis title ----------------------------------------+------
      call pschup(-1., 0.)                        ! up vector straight left
      call pstxal(PACENT, PATOP)                  ! text alignment: center, top
      call ptx(0., .5, 'Voltage')                 ! define the text
      !=== graph the data =============================================+======
      call psvwi(1)                               ! set view index to 1
```

```
      call DefineRectangle(0., 1., 0., 1.)       ! frame the viewport
      open(unit=9, file='data')                  ! open the data file
      do I=1, 100                                ! for each point...
         read(9, *, end=20) X(I), Y(I)           ! read the x, y values
      end do
   20 close(9)                                   ! close the data file
      call ppl(100, X, Y)                        ! polyline with 100 points
      !--- define the tic marks -----------------------------------------+------
      call psvwi(3)                              ! set view index to 3
      call DefineTics('X', 0., 0., 1., .01, .01, 5)
      call DefineTics('X', 1., 0., 1., .01, .01, 5)
      call DefineTics('Y', 0., 0., 1., .01, .01, 5)
      call DefineTics('Y', 1., 0., 1., .01, .01, 5)
      !--- label the X tic marks ----------------------------------------+-------
      call psvwi(1)                              ! set view index to 1
      call pschup(0., 1.)                        ! up vector straight up
      call pschh(0.02)                           ! in a y range of 0-1
      call pschxp(1.)                            ! set char. expansion factor
      call pstxal(PACENT, PATOP)                 ! text alignment: center, top
      do I=0,100,10                              ! for each major tick along x
         write(unit=Strng, fmt='(f4.2)') I*.01 ! create the string to label
         call ptx(I*.01, 0., Strng)              ! define an x tic label
      end do
      !--- label the Y tic marks ----------------------------------------+-------
      call pstxal(PARITE, PAHALF)                ! text alignment: right, half
      do I=0,100,10                              ! for each major tick along y
         write(unit=Strng, fmt='(f4.2)') I*.01 ! create the string to label
         call ptx(0., I*.01, Strng)              ! define a y tic label
      end do
      call pclst                                 ! close display list structure
      !--- post the image and close up shop ------------------------------------
      call ppost(WorkstnID, TheCurve, 1.0)       ! mark structure for display
      call puwk(WorkstnID, PPERFO)               ! update the workstation
      call pclwk(WorkstnID)                      ! close workstation
      call pclph                                 ! close PHIGS
      stop                                       ! stop processing
      end                                        ! end of program
!********************************************************************************
      subroutine DefineView(WorkstnID, ViewIndex,
     +  Wxmin, Wxmax, Wymin, Wymax, Vxmin, Vxmax, Vymin, Vymax,
     +  ClipAtWindow)
      include 'phigs.f2.h'                       ! get the PHIGS constants
      integer*4 WorkstnID                        ! workstation identifier
```

```
      integer*4 ViewIndex                     ! the view being defined
      real      Wxmin, Wxmax, Wymin, Wymax    ! view window limits
      real      Vxmin, Vxmax, Vymin, Vymax    ! projection viewport limits
      logical   ClipAtWindow                  ! window (or display surface?)

      integer*4 ErrorReturn                   ! error return variable
      real      WindowLimits(4)               ! window limits as passed in
      real      ViewportLimits(4)             ! viewport limits as passed in
      real      ClipLimits(4)                 ! clip limits (set to viewport)
      real      ViewMappingMatrix(3,3)        ! view mapping matrix
      real      Identity(3,3)                 ! default view orient. matrix
      data      Identity /1., 0., 0.,
     +                    0., 1., 0.,
     +                    0., 0., 1./

      WindowLimits(1)=Wxmin                   ! \
      WindowLimits(2)=Wxmax                   !  \  put individual values
      WindowLimits(3)=Wymin                   !  /  into a "limits" array
      WindowLimits(4)=Wymax                   ! /
      ViewportLimits(1)=Vxmin                 ! \
      ViewportLimits(2)=Vxmax                 !  \  put individual values
      ViewportLimits(3)=Vymin                 !  /  into a "limits" array
      ViewportLimits(4)=Vymax                 ! /
      if (ClipAtWindow) then
          ClipLimits(1)=ViewportLimits(1)     ! \
          ClipLimits(2)=ViewportLimits(2)     !  \  make the clip limits
          ClipLimits(3)=ViewportLimits(3)     !  /  equal to viewport
          ClipLimits(4)=ViewportLimits(4)     ! /
      else
          ClipLimits(1)=0.                    ! \
          ClipLimits(2)=1.                    !  \  make the clip limits
          ClipLimits(3)=0.                    !  /  equal to display surface
          ClipLimits(4)=1.                    ! /
      end if
      call pevmm(WindowLimits, ViewportLimits, ! evaluate view mapping matrix
     + ErrorReturn, ViewMappingMatrix)
      if (ErrorReturn .ne. 0) then            ! did we get an error?
          print *,"Error", ErrorReturn, "occurred during ",
     +      "call to Evaluate View Mapping Matrix (pevmm)."
          stop
      end if
      call psvwr(WorkstnID, ViewIndex,        ! set view representation
     + Identity, ViewMappingMatrix,           ! view orient., view mapping
```

```
     + ClipLimits, PCLIP)                           ! "PCLIP" = "turn clipping on"
      return                                        ! return to calling context
      end                                           ! end of subroutine
!*****************************************************************************
      subroutine DefineRectangle(Xmin, Xmax, Ymin, Ymax)
      real      Xmin, Xmax, Ymin, Ymax              ! rectangle's limits
      include 'phigs.f2.h'                          ! get the PHIGS constants

      real      X(5), Y(5)                          ! outline of rectangle

      X(1)=Xmin                                     ! lower left corner's x value
      Y(1)=Ymin                                     ! lower left corner's y value
      X(2)=Xmax                                     ! lower right corner's x value
      Y(2)=Ymin                                     ! lower right corner's y value
      X(3)=Xmax                                     ! upper right corner's x value
      Y(3)=Ymax                                     ! upper right corner's y value
      X(4)=Xmin                                     ! upper left corner's x value
      Y(4)=Ymax                                     ! upper left corner's y value
      X(5)=Xmin                                     ! lower left corner's x value
      Y(5)=Ymin                                     ! lower left corner's y value
      call ppl(5, X, Y)                             ! polyline
      return                                        ! return to calling context
      end                                           ! end of subroutine
!*****************************************************************************
      subroutine DefineTics(Axis, Location, Start, End, Delta, Size,
     + Major)
      character Axis                        ! which axis are the tics for?
      real      Location                    ! where is this line of tics located?
      real      Start                       ! where do the tics start?
      real      End                         ! where do they end?
      real      Delta                       ! draw a tic every how often?
      real      Size                        ! how big should the tics be?
      integer*4 Major                       ! how often does a major tic occur?
      integer*4 Tic                         ! which tic are we on?
      real      X(2), Y(2)                  ! both ends of a tic mark
      real      CurrentX, CurrentY          ! loop control variables
      real      Length                      ! length of current tic mark

      if ((Axis .eq. 'x') .or. (Axis .eq. 'X')) then
          CurrentX=Start                    ! initialize x position
          Tic=0                             ! which tic are we on?
          do while (CurrentX .le. End)
              if (mod(Tic, Major) .ne. 0) then
```

```
            Length=Size           ! short tic...
        else
            Length=Size*2.        ! ...or long one?
        endif
        X(1)=CurrentX             ! x location: bottom of tic mark
        Y(1)=Location-Length      ! y location: bottom of tic mark
        X(2)=CurrentX             ! x location: top of tic mark
        Y(2)=Location+Length      ! y location: top of tic mark
        call ppl(2, X, Y)         ! define the tic
        Tic=Tic+1                 ! increment the tic counter
        CurrentX=CurrentX+Delta
    end do
else
    if ((Axis .eq. 'y') .or. (Axis .eq. 'Y')) then
        CurrentY=Start            ! initialize y position
        Tic=0                     ! which tic are we on?
        do while (CurrentY .le. End)
            if (mod(Tic, Major) .ne. 0) then
                Length=Size       ! short tic...
            else
                Length=Size*2.    ! ...or long one?
            endif
            X(1)=Location-Length  ! x location: left end of tic
            Y(1)=CurrentY         ! y location: left end of tic
            X(2)=Location+Length  ! x location: right end of tic
            Y(2)=CurrentY         ! y location: right end of tic
            call ppl(2, X, Y)     ! define the tic
            Tic=Tic+1             ! increment the tic counter
            CurrentY=CurrentY+Delta
        end do
    endif
endif
return
end
```

Inquire Structure Contents Program

This section lists the C and FORTRAN binding versions of the inquire structure contents program described in Chapter 5, *Using Structures.*

C Binding Version of Inquuire Structure Program

```
#include <phigs.h>                         /* get HP-PHIGS definitions for C */
#include <stdio.h>                         /* get standard I/O definitions */

main()                                     /* file "InqStructs.c" */
{
    Pint        WorkstnID = 1;             /* workstation identifier */
    Pint        ConnID;                    /* connection identifier */
    Pint        WorkstnType = POIDDX;      /* out/in, direct, dbl. bufr., Xwindow */
    Pint        StructureID = 1;           /* structure ID (chosen by user) */
    static Ppoint3 SquarePts[4] = {
        0.25, 0.25, 0.0,
        0.75, 0.25, 0.0,
        0.75, 0.75, 0.0,
        0.25, 0.75, 0.0};
    static Ppoint_list3 Square = {
        4, SquarePts};
    static Ppoint TextLocation = {0.3, 0.5};
    Pelem_type  ElementType;
    Pint        Error;                     /* error-return variable */
    Pin_status  ChoiceStatus;              /* returned from "preq_choice" */
    Pint        ChoiceNum;                 /* choice value */
    Pint        ElementPos, NumElements, CurrentElement, ElementSize;
    static char ElementNames[][28] = {
        "PELEM_ALL",                       "PELEM_NIL",
        "PELEM_POLYLINE3",                 "PELEM_POLYLINE",
        "PELEM_POLYMARKER3",               "PELEM_POLYMARKER",
        "PELEM_TEXT3",                     "PELEM_TEXT",
        "PELEM_ANNO_TEXT_REL3",            "PELEM_ANNO_TEXT_REL",
        "PELEM_FILL_AREA3",                "PELEM_FILL_AREA",
        "PELEM_FILL_AREA_SET3",            "PELEM_FILL_AREA_SET",
        "PELEM_CELL_ARRAY3",               "PELEM_CELL_ARRAY",
        "PELEM_GDP3",                      "PELEM_GDP",
        "PELEM_LINE_IND",                  "PELEM_MARKER_IND",
        "PELEM_TEXT_IND",                  "PELEM_INT_IND",
```

```
    "PELEM_EDGE_IND",                  "PELEM_LINETYPE",
    "PELEM_LINEWIDTH",                 "PELEM_LINE_COLR_IND",
    "PELEM_MARKER_TYPE",               "PELEM_MARKER_SIZE",
    "PELEM_MARKER_COLR_IND",           "PELEM_TEXT_FONT",
    "PELEM_TEXT_PREC",                 "PELEM_CHAR_EXPAN",
    "PELEM_CHAR_SPACE",                "PELEM_TEXT_COLR_IND",
    "PELEM_CHAR_HT",                   "PELEM_CHAR_UP_VEC",
    "PELEM_TEXT_PATH",                 "PELEM_TEXT_ALIGN",
    "PELEM_ANNO_CHAR_HT",              "PELEM_ANNO_CHAR_UP_VEC",
    "PELEM_ANNO_PATH",                 "PELEM_ANNO_ALIGN",
    "PELEM_ANNO_STYLE",                "PELEM_INT_STYLE",
    "PELEM_INT_STYLE_IND",             "PELEM_INT_COLR_IND",
    "PELEM_EDGE_FLAG",                 "PELEM_EDGETYPE",
    "PELEM_EDGEWIDTH",                 "PELEM_EDGE_COLR_IND",
    "PELEM_PAT_SIZE",                  "PELEM_PAT_REF_POINT_VECS",
    "PELEM_PAT_REF_POINT",             "PELEM_ADD_NAMES_SET",
    "PELEM_REMOVE_NAMES_SET",          "PELEM_INDIV_ASF",
    "PELEM_HLHSR_ID",                  "PELEM_LOCAL_MODEL_TRAN3",
    "PELEM_LOCAL_MODEL_TRAN",          "PELEM_GLOBAL_MODEL_TRAN3",
    "PELEM_GLOBAL_MODEL_TRAN",         "PELEM_MODEL_CLIP_VOL3",
    "PELEM_MODEL_CLIP_VOL",            "PELEM_MODEL_CLIP_IND",
    "PELEM_RESTORE_MODEL_CLIP_VOL",    "PELEM_VIEW_IND",
    "PELEM_EXEC_STRUCT",               "PELEM_LABEL",
    "PELEM_APPL_DATA",                 "PELEM_GSE",
    "PELEM_PICK_ID"};

popen_phigs(stderr, 0);              /* errors go to "stderr" */
pescape_u4("/dev/screen/phigs_window", &ConnID);
popen_ws(WorkstnID, ConnID, WorkstnType);
ppost_struct(WorkstnID, StructureID, 1.0);
/*---- define the structure -------------------------------------------*/
popen_struct(StructureID);
pset_int_style(PSTYLE_HOLLOW);
pfill_area3(&Square);
pset_char_ht(0.04);
ptext(&TextLocation, "Hello World");
pclose_struct();
/*---- display the structure ------------------------------------------*/
ppost_struct(WorkstnID, StructureID, 1.0);
pupd_ws(WorkstnID, PFLAG_PERFORM);
/*---- make keyboard a choice device so "[Return] to go on." works ------*/
printf("Press [Return] to continue.\n");
pset_choice_mode(WorkstnID, 2, POP_REQ, PSWITCH_NO_ECHO);
```

```
    preq_choice(WorkstnID, 2, &ChoiceStatus, &ChoiceNum);
    /*---- edit the structure -------------------------------------------*/
    pset_edit_mode(PEDIT_REPLACE);
    popen_struct(StructureID);
    pinq_elem_ptr(&Error, &ElementPos);
    if (Error) {
        printf("Error %d in pinq_elem_ptr; terminating.", Error);
        exit(1);
    }
    printf("Number of elements in structure: %d\n", ElementPos);
    NumElements = ElementPos;
    for (CurrentElement = 1; CurrentElement <= NumElements; CurrentElement++){
        pset_elem_ptr(CurrentElement);
        pinq_cur_elem_type_size(&Error, &ElementType, &ElementSize);
        if (Error) {
            printf("Error %d in pinq_cur_elem_type_size; terminating.",Error);
            exit(1);
        }
        printf("---------------------------------------------------------\n");
        printf("Element type: %d (%s)\n", ElementType,
          ElementNames[ElementType]);
        if (ElementType == PELEM_INT_STYLE)     /* if int. style, replace */
            pset_int_style(PSTYLE_SOLID);
        GetInfo(ElementType);
    }
    pclose_struct();
    pupd_ws(WorkstnID, PFLAG_PERFORM);
    pclose_ws(WorkstnID);
    pclose_phigs();
}
/*************************************************************************/
/*  Note that the routine below deals only with element types uses in this  */
/*  program: integers, floats, text, and a 3D point list.  These examples   */
/*  are sufficient to communicate the technique.  Other types may added by  */
/*  the user as necessary.                                                   */
/*************************************************************************/
GetInfo(ElementType)
Pelem_type      ElementType;
{
    Pstore      *Store;                 /* storage area */
    Pint        Error;                  /* error-return variable */
    Pelem_data  *ElementData;           /* the data */
```

```
pcreate_store(&Error, &Store);        /* allocate storage memory */
if (Error) {
    printf("Error %d in pcreate_store; terminating.\n", Error);
    exit(1);
}
pinq_cur_elem_content(Store, &Error, &ElementData);
if (Error) {
    printf("Error %d in pinq_cur_elem_content; terminating.\n", Error);
    exit(1);
}
switch (ElementType) {
    case PELEM_ALL:                                /* 0 */            break;
    case PELEM_NIL:                                /* 1 */            break;
    case PELEM_POLYLINE3:                          /* 2 */            break;
    case PELEM_POLYLINE:                           /* 3 */            break;
    case PELEM_POLYMARKER3:                        /* 4 */            break;
    case PELEM_POLYMARKER:                         /* 5 */            break;
    case PELEM_TEXT3:                              /* 6 */            break;
    case PELEM_TEXT:                               /* 7 */
        ElemText("Text", ElementData->text.pos,
          ElementData->text.char_string);                             break;
    case PELEM_ANNO_TEXT_REL3:                     /* 8 */            break;
    case PELEM_ANNO_TEXT_REL:                      /* 9 */            break;
    case PELEM_FILL_AREA3:                         /* 10 */
        ElemPtLst3("Fill Area 3", &(ElementData->point_list3));       break;
    case PELEM_FILL_AREA:                          /* 11 */           break;
    case PELEM_FILL_AREA_SET3:                     /* 12 */           break;
    case PELEM_FILL_AREA_SET:                      /* 13 */           break;
    case PELEM_CELL_ARRAY3:                        /* 14 */           break;
    case PELEM_CELL_ARRAY:                         /* 15 */           break;
    case PELEM_GDP3:                               /* 16 */           break;
    case PELEM_GDP:                                /* 17 */           break;
    case PELEM_LINE_IND:                           /* 18 */           break;
    case PELEM_MARKER_IND:                         /* 19 */           break;
    case PELEM_TEXT_IND:                           /* 20 */           break;
    case PELEM_INT_IND:                            /* 21 */           break;
    case PELEM_EDGE_IND:                           /* 22 */           break;
    case PELEM_LINETYPE:                           /* 23 */           break;
    case PELEM_LINEWIDTH:                          /* 24 */           break;
    case PELEM_LINE_COLR_IND:                      /* 25 */           break;
    case PELEM_MARKER_TYPE:                        /* 26 */           break;
    case PELEM_MARKER_SIZE:                        /* 27 */           break;
    case PELEM_MARKER_COLR_IND:                    /* 28 */           break;
```

```
case PELEM_TEXT_FONT:                  /* 29 */          break;
case PELEM_TEXT_PREC:                  /* 30 */          break;
case PELEM_CHAR_EXPAN:                 /* 31 */          break;
case PELEM_CHAR_SPACE:                 /* 32 */          break;
case PELEM_TEXT_COLR_IND:              /* 33 */          break;
case PELEM_CHAR_HT:                    /* 34 */
    ElemFloat("Character height", ElementData->float_data);   break;
case PELEM_CHAR_UP_VEC:                /* 35 */          break;
case PELEM_TEXT_PATH:                  /* 36 */          break;
case PELEM_TEXT_ALIGN:                 /* 37 */          break;
case PELEM_ANNO_CHAR_HT:               /* 38 */          break;
case PELEM_ANNO_CHAR_UP_VEC:           /* 39 */          break;
case PELEM_ANNO_PATH:                  /* 40 */          break;
case PELEM_ANNO_ALIGN:                 /* 41 */          break;
case PELEM_ANNO_STYLE:                 /* 42 */          break;
case PELEM_INT_STYLE:                  /* 43 */
    ElemInt("Interior style", ElementData->int_style);       break;
case PELEM_INT_STYLE_IND:              /* 44 */          break;
case PELEM_INT_COLR_IND:               /* 45 */          break;
case PELEM_EDGE_FLAG:                  /* 46 */          break;
case PELEM_EDGETYPE:                   /* 47 */          break;
case PELEM_EDGEWIDTH:                  /* 48 */          break;
case PELEM_EDGE_COLR_IND:              /* 49 */          break;
case PELEM_PAT_SIZE:                   /* 50 */          break;
case PELEM_PAT_REF_POINT_VECS:         /* 51 */          break;
case PELEM_PAT_REF_POINT:              /* 52 */          break;
case PELEM_ADD_NAMES_SET:              /* 53 */          break;
case PELEM_REMOVE_NAMES_SET:           /* 54 */          break;
case PELEM_INDIV_ASF:                  /* 55 */          break;
case PELEM_HLHSR_ID:                   /* 56 */          break;
case PELEM_LOCAL_MODEL_TRAN3:          /* 57 */          break;
case PELEM_LOCAL_MODEL_TRAN:           /* 58 */          break;
case PELEM_GLOBAL_MODEL_TRAN3:         /* 59 */          break;
case PELEM_GLOBAL_MODEL_TRAN:          /* 60 */          break;
case PELEM_MODEL_CLIP_VOL3:            /* 61 */          break;
case PELEM_MODEL_CLIP_VOL:             /* 62 */          break;
case PELEM_MODEL_CLIP_IND:             /* 63 */          break;
case PELEM_RESTORE_MODEL_CLIP_VOL:     /* 64 */          break;
case PELEM_VIEW_IND:                   /* 65 */          break;
case PELEM_EXEC_STRUCT:                /* 66 */          break;
case PELEM_LABEL:                      /* 67 */          break;
case PELEM_APPL_DATA:                  /* 68 */          break;
case PELEM_GSE:                        /* 69 */          break;
```

```
        case PELEM_PICK_ID:                     /* 70 */                break;
    }
}
/****************************************************************************/
ElemInt(Name, Value)
char    *Name;
Pint    Value;
{
    printf("%s: %d\n", Name, Value);
}
/****************************************************************************/
ElemFloat(Name, Value)
char    *Name;
Pfloat  Value;
{
    printf("%s: %5.2f\n", Name, Value);
}
/****************************************************************************/
ElemText(Name, Pos, Value)
char            *Name;
Ppoint          Pos;
char            *Value;
{
    printf("%s: \"%s\" at (%5.3f, %5.3f)\n", Name, Value, Pos.x, Pos.y);
}
/****************************************************************************/
ElemPtLst3(Name, Value)
char            *Name;
Ppoint_list3    *Value;
{
    int         I;                      /* loop control variable */

    printf("%s (%d points):\n", Name, Value->num_points);
    for (I = 0; I < Value->num_points; I++)
        printf("  (%5.3f, %5.3f, %5.3f)\n", Value->points[I].x,
          Value->points[I].y, Value->points[I].z);
}
```

FORTRAN Binding Version of Inquire Structure Program

```
      include 'phigs.f1.h'                      ! get the HP-PHIGS aliases
      program InqStructs                        ! program "InqStructs.f"
      include 'phigs.f2.h'                      ! get the HP-PHIGS constants

      integer*4 WorkstnID                       ! workstation identifier
      parameter (WorkstnID=1)                   ! value chosen by the user
      integer*4 ConnID                          ! connection identifier
      integer*4 WorkstnType                     ! workstation type
      parameter (WorkstnType=POIDDX)            ! out/in, direct, dbl. bfr., X
      integer*4 StructureID                     ! structure identifier
      parameter (StructureID=1)                 ! value chosen by the user
      integer*4 Error                           ! error-return variable
      integer*4 ChoiceStatus, ChoiceNum         ! choice status and value
      real      AreaX(4), AreaY(4), AreaZ(4)    ! points for fill area
      data      AreaX /0.25, 0.75, 0.75, 0.25/  ! points for fill area
      data      AreaY /0.25, 0.25, 0.75, 0.75/
      data      AreaZ /0.0,  0.0,  0.0,  0.0/
      integer*4 ElementType, IntSize, RealSize, StringSize
      integer*4 ElementPos, NumElements, CurrentElement
      character*6 ElementNames(105)
      data      ElementNames /'PENIL','PEPL3',  'PEPL',   'PEPM3',
     +  'PEPM',   'PETX3',  'PETX',   'PEATR3', 'PEATR',  'PEFA3',
     +  'PEFA',   'PEFAS3', 'PEFAS',  'PECA3',  'PECA',   'PEGDP3',
     +  'PEGDP',  'PEPLI',  'PEPMI',  'PETXI',  'PEII',   'PEEDI',
     +  'PELN',   'PELWSC', 'PEPLCI', 'PEMK',   'PEMKSC', 'PEPMCI',
     +  'PETXFN', 'PETXPR', 'PECHXP', 'PECHSP', 'PETXCI', 'PECHH',
     +  'PECHUP', 'PETXP',  'PETXAL', 'PEATCH', 'PEATCU', 'PEATP',
     +  'PEATAL', 'PEANST', 'PEIS',   'PEISI',  'PEICI',  'PEEDFG',
     +  'PEEDT',  'PEEWSC', 'PEEDCI', 'PEPA',   'PEPRPV', 'PEPARF',
     +  'PEADS',  'PERES',  'PEIASF', 'PEHRID', 'PELMT3', 'PELMT',
     +  'PEGMT3', 'PEGMT',  'PEMCV3', 'PEMCV',  'PEMCLI', 'PERMCV',
     +  'PEVWI',  'PEEXST', 'PELB',   'PEAP',   'PEGSE',  'PEPKID',
     +  'PEPSD3', 'PEFAD3', 'PEFSD3', 'PECAP3', 'PETSD3', 'PEQMD3',
     +  'PESFSD', 'PENBSC', 'PENBSS', 'PEDPCI', 'PECMI',  'PERCM',
     +  'PEAPR',  'PEBAPR', 'PEPLSM', 'PEBIS',  'PEBISI', 'PEISM',
     +  'PEBISM', 'PEIRE',  'PEBIRE', 'PELSS',  'PEFDM',  'PEFCM',
     +  'PEPLC',  'PEPMC',  'PETC',   'PEIC',   'PEBIC',  'PEEC',
     +  'PECAC',  'PETCAC', 'PESAC',  'PEPSC',  'PEBPSC'/
      integer*4 fdopen                          ! to get file descriptor

      call popph(fdopen(fnum(7), 'w'//char(0)), 0)      ! open PHIGS
```

```
call pue004('/dev/screen/phigs_window', ConnID)   ! get connection ID
call popwk(WorkstnID, ConnID, WorkstnType)! open workstation
call ppost(WorkstnID, StructureID, 1.)    ! mark structure for display
!--- define the structure ------------------------------------------------
call popst(StructureID)                   ! open structure
call psis(PHOLLO)                         ! set interior colour index
call pfa3(4, AreaX, AreaY, AreaZ)         ! fill area 3 primitive
call pschh(0.04)                          ! set character height
call ptx(0.3, 0.5, 'Hello World')         ! text
call pclst                                ! close the structure
!--- display the structure -----------------------------------------------
call ppost(WorkstnID, StructureID, 1.0)   ! post structure
call puwk(WorkstnID, PPERFO)              ! update workstation
!--- make keyboard a choice device so "[Return] to go on." works -------
print *, "Press [Return] to continue."
call pschm(WorkstnID, 2, PREQU, PNECHO)   ! set choice mode on keyboard
call prqch(WorkstnID, 2, ChoiceStatus, ChoiceNum) ! request choice
!--- edit the structure --------------------------------------------------
call psedm(PREPLC)                        ! set edit mode: replace
call popst(StructureID)                   ! open structure
call pqep(Error, ElementPos)              ! inquire element pointer
if (Error .ne. 0) then
    print *, "Error", Error, " in pqcets; terminating."
    stop
endif
print *, "Number of elements in structure: ", ElementPos
NumElements=ElementPos
do CurrentElement=1, NumElements
    call psep(CurrentElement)             ! set element pointer
    call pqcets(Error, ElementType,       ! inquire element type, size
+     IntSize, RealSize, StringSize)
    if (Error .ne. 0) then
        print *, "Error", Error, " in pqcets; terminating."
        stop
    endif
    print *, "-----------------------------------------------------"
    print *, "Element type: ", ElementType,
+     " (", ElementNames(ElementType), ")"
    if (ElementType .eq. PEIS) then       ! if int. style, replace it
        call psis(PSOLID)                 ! set interior style
    endif
    call GetInfo
end do
```

```
      call pclst                                  ! close the structure
      call puwk(WorkstnID, PPERFO)                ! update the workstation
      call pclwk(WorkstnID)                       ! close workstation
      call pclph                                  ! close PHIGS
      stop                                        ! stop processing
      end                                         ! end of program
!******************************************************************************
      subroutine GetInfo
      include 'phigs.f2.h'                        ! get the PHIGS constants

      integer*4         Error, I
      integer*4         IntSize, RealSize, StrSize
      integer*4         Ints(100)
      real              Reals(100)
      integer*4         StrLen(100), Length
      character*80      String, Strings(100)

      call pqceco(100, 100, 100,                  ! inq. current element content
     +  Error, IntSize, Ints, RealSize, Reals, StrSize, StrLen, Strings)
      if (Error .ne. 0) then
          print *, "Error", Error, " in pqceco, terminating."
          stop
      endif
      !--- print the integers ---------------------------------------------
      print *, "  Number of integers: ", IntSize
      if (IntSize .gt. 0) then
          print *, "    Integers:"
          do I=1, IntSize
              write(6, '(6X, I2)') Ints(I)
          end do
      end if
      !--- print the reals ------------------------------------------------
      print *, "  Number of reals: ", RealSize
      if (RealSize .gt. 0) then
          print *, "    Reals:"
          do i=1, RealSize
              write(6, '(6X, F4.2)') Reals(I)
          end do
      endif
      !--- print the strings ----------------------------------------------
      print *, "  Number of strings: ", StrSize
      if (StrSize .gt. 0) then
          print *, "    Strings:"
```

```
    do I=1, StrSize
        Length=StrLen(I)
        String=Strings(I)
        print *, '       "', String(1:Length), '"'
    end do
end if
return
end
```

Bicycle Animation Program

This section lists the C binding and FORTRAN binding versions of the bicycle animation program described in Chapter 6, *Modelling Transformations.*

C Binding Version of Bicycle Animation Program

```
#include <phigs.h>                         /* get PHIGS definitions for C */
#include <stdio.h>                         /* get standard I/O definitions */
#include <math.h>                          /* link with library "-lm" */

#define  Spokes        30                 /* number of spokes, sides on rim */
#define  dTheta        (2*M_PI/Spokes)    /* angle between spokes */
#define  dX            -0.003             /* speed of moving bike */
#define  deg           *M_PI/180.         /* convert degrees to radians */

main()                                     /* file "Bicycle.c" */
{
    Pint        WorkstnID = 1;            /* workstation identifier */
    Pint        ConnID;                    /* connection identifier */
    Pint        WorkstnType = POIDDX;      /* implementation-dependent */

    Pint        Bike = 1, Wheel = 2, Frame = 3; /* structure IDs */
    float       WheelAngle;                /* current rotation of wheels */
    float       Xpos;                      /* current position of bike */
    static Ppoint FramePoints[] = {
                -0.95,-1.03, -0.87,-1.05, -0.60,-0.33,  /* fork */
                -0.05,-1.05,  1.00,-1.05,  0.55, 0.00,  /* rear triangle */
                 0.50,-0.10,  0.85,-0.95,  0.08,-0.95, 0.60, 0.10,
                 0.70, 0.10,  0.73, 0.15,  0.70, 0.20,  /* seat */
                 0.37, 0.20,  0.34, 0.15,  0.51, 0.13,
                -0.01,-0.92, -0.56,-0.20, -0.52,-0.10,  /* front triangle */
                 0.40,-0.10,  0.44, 0.00, -0.51, 0.00,
                -0.45, 0.15, -0.10, 0.15, -0.10, 0.20,  /* handlebars */
                -0.50, 0.20};
    static Ppoint_list FrameData = {26, FramePoints};
    Ppoint      SpokeData[2], RimData[Spokes + 1];
    Ppoint_list Spoke, Rim;
    static Ppoint LocalOrigin = {0.0, 0.0};     /* for rotation/scaling */
    static Pvec TransF = {-0.9, -1.0};          /* front wheel translation */
    static Pvec TransR = { 0.9, -1.0};          /* rear wheel translation */
```

```
static Pvec Scale = {0.5, 0.5};                   /* reduce to half size */
Ppoint        TempLoc;                            /* for text only */
Pvec          TempScale;                          /* for text only */
Pvec          TempTrans;                          /* for text only */
/*--- transformation matrix variables ----------------------------------*/
Pmatrix       Translation[3][3],Scaling[3][3];/* transformation matrices */
Pmatrix       Matrix[3][3];                       /* temporary matrix */
Pint          Error;                              /* error-return variable */
int           I;                                  /* loop control variable */
float         Theta;                              /* temporary variable */

popen_phigs(stderr, 0);                           /* errors go to "stderr" */
pescape_u4("/dev/screen/phigs_window", &ConnID);
popen_ws(WorkstnID, ConnID, WorkstnType);
pset_disp_upd_st(WorkID, PDEFER_WAIT, PMODE_NIVE);
ppost_struct(WorkstnID, Bike, 1.0);              /* mark struct. for display */
/*=== define all CSS structures ========================================*/
/*--- define the "Frame" structure -------------------------------------*/
popen_struct(Frame);
pfill_area(&FrameData);
pbuild_tran_matrix(&LocalOrigin, &TransF, 0.0, &Scale, &Error, Matrix);
pset_local_tran(Matrix, PTYPE_REPLACE);
pexec_struct(Wheel);
pbuild_tran_matrix(&LocalOrigin, &TransR, 0.0, &Scale, &Error, Matrix);
pset_local_tran(Matrix, PTYPE_REPLACE);
pexec_struct(Wheel);
pclose_struct();
/*--- define the "Wheel" structure -------------------------------------*/
popen_struct(Wheel);
Rim.points = RimData;
for (I = 0; I <= Spokes; I++) {
    Theta = I * dTheta;                           /* calculate required angle */
    Rim.points[I].x = cos(Theta);                 /* x=r*cos(Theta) where r=1 */
    Rim.points[I].y = sin(Theta);                 /* y=r*sin(Theta) where r=1 */
}
Rim.num_points = Spokes + 1;
ppolyline(&Rim);
Spoke.num_points = 2;
Spoke.points = SpokeData;
for (I = 0; I < Spokes; I++) {
    Theta = I * dTheta;                           /* calculate required angle */
    Spoke.points[0].x = 0.0;                      /* \  Start defining each */
    Spoke.points[0].y = 0.0;                      /*  \ spoke from the center */
```

```
    Spoke.points[1].x = cos(Theta);          /*  / and proceed */
    Spoke.points[1].y = sin(Theta);          /* /  rimward. */
    ppolyline(&Spoke);
}
pclose_struct();
/*--- define the "Bike" structure -------------------------------------*/
popen_struct(Bike);
pset_char_ht(0.04);
TempLoc.x = 0.1, TempLoc.y = 0.8;
ptext(&TempLoc, "Joe's Bike Shop");
TempScale.delta_x = TempScale.delta_y = 0.25;
pscale(&TempScale, &Error, Scaling);
TempTrans.delta_x = TempTrans.delta_y = 0.6;
ptranslate(&TempTrans, &Error, Translation);
pcompose_matrix(Translation, Scaling, &Error, Matrix);
pset_local_tran(Matrix, PTYPE_REPLACE);
pexec_struct(Frame);
pclose_struct();
/*=== display the stucture ============================================*/
ppost_struct(WorkstnID, Bike, 1.0);
pset_edit_mode(PEDIT_REPLACE);
Xpos = 1.4;                                  /* first location for bike */
WheelAngle = 0.0;                            /* first angle for wheels */
for (Xpos = 1.4; Xpos > -0.36; Xpos += dX) {
    /*--- first, open "Bike" structure and move the frame --------------*/
    popen_struct(Bike);
    pset_elem_ptr(3);                        /* bike xform is element #3 */
    TempTrans.delta_x = Xpos, TempTrans.delta_y = 0.6;
    ptranslate(&TempTrans, &Error, Translation);
    pcompose_matrix(Translation, Scaling, &Error, Matrix);
    pset_local_tran(Matrix, PTYPE_REPLACE);
    pclose_struct();
    /*--- next, open the "Frame" structure and rotate the wheels -------*/
    popen_struct(Frame);
    pbuild_tran_matrix(&LocalOrigin, &TransR, WheelAngle deg, &Scale,
      &Error, Matrix);
    pset_elem_ptr(2);                        /* fr. wheel xform is ele. 2 */
    pset_local_tran(Matrix, PTYPE_REPLACE);
    pbuild_tran_matrix(&LocalOrigin, &TransF, WheelAngle deg, &Scale,
      &Error, Matrix);
    pset_elem_ptr(4);                        /* bk. wheel xform is ele. 4 */
    pset_local_tran(Matrix, PTYPE_REPLACE);
    WheelAngle -= dX * 3000/(2 * M_PI);      /* increment wheel angle */
```

```
        pclose_struct();
        pupd_ws(WorkstnID, PFLAG_PERFORM);
    }
    pclose_ws(WorkstnID);
    pclose_phigs();
}
```

FORTRAN Binding Version of Bicycle Animation Program

```
      include 'phigs.f1.h'                        ! get the PHIGS aliases
      program Bicycle                             ! program "Bicycle.f"
      include 'phigs.f2.h'                        ! get the PHIGS constants

      integer*4 WorkstnID                         ! workstation identifier
      parameter (WorkstnID=1)                     ! value chosen by the user
      integer*4 ConnID                            ! connection identifier
      integer*4 WorkstnType                       ! workstation type
      parameter (WorkstnType=POIDDX)              ! out/in, direct, dbl bfr, X
      integer*4 Bike, Wheel, Frame                ! \ structure IDs
      parameter (Bike=1, Wheel=2, Frame=3)        ! / (defined by user)
      real      WheelAngle                        ! current rotation of wheels
      real      Xpos                              ! current position of bike
      real      pi, dTheta, dX                    ! required constants
      integer*4 Spokes                            ! \ specifies number of spokes
      parameter (Spokes=20)                       ! / and number of sides on rim
      parameter (pi=3.14159265358979323846)       ! circumference/diameter
      parameter (dTheta=2*pi/Spokes)              ! angle between spokes
      parameter (dX=-.003)                        ! speed of moving bike
      real      FAreaX(26), FAreaY(26)            ! points for fill area (frame)
      real      PolylineX(100), PolylineY(100)    ! points for circles (wheels)
      real      SpokeX(2), SpokeY(2)              ! points for spokes
      data      FAreaX /-0.95, -0.87, -0.60,                    ! fork
     +            -0.05, 1.00, 0.55, 0.50, 0.85, 0.08, 0.60,    ! r. triangle
     +            0.70, 0.73, 0.70, 0.37, 0.34, 0.51,           ! seat
     +            -0.01, -0.56, -0.52, 0.40, 0.44, -0.51,       ! fr. triangle
     +            -0.45, -0.10, -0.10, -0.50/                   ! handlebars
      data      FAreaY /-1.03, -1.05, -0.33,                    ! fork
     +            -1.05, -1.05, 0.00, -0.10, -0.95, -0.95, 0.10,! r. triangle
     +            0.10, 0.15, 0.20, 0.20, 0.15, 0.13,           ! seat
     +            -0.92, -0.20, -0.10, -0.10, 0.00, 0.00,       ! fr. triangle
     +            0.15, 0.15, 0.20, 0.20/                       ! handlebars
      !--- transformation matrix variables ------------------------------++++++
      real      Translation(3,3), Scaling(3,3)  ! transformation matrices
```

```
real      Matrix(3,3)                    ! temporary matrix
real      TransXf, TransXr, TransY, Scale ! front/rear transl., scaling
parameter (TransXf=-0.9, TransXr=0.9, TransY=-1.0, Scale=0.5)
integer*4 Error                          ! error-return variable
integer*4 I                              ! loop control variable
real      Theta                          ! temporary variable
integer*4 fdopen                         ! to get file descriptor
real      rad, d                         ! \ for converting degrees
rad(d)=   (d*pi/180.0)                   ! / to radians

call popph(fdopen(fnum(7), 'w'//char(0)), 0)      ! open PHIGS
call pue004('/dev/screen/phigs_window', ConnID)   ! get connection ID
call popwk(WorkstnID, ConnID, WorkstnType)        ! open workstation
call psdus(WorkstnID, PWAITD, PNIVE)     ! set display update state
call ppost(WorkstnID, Bike, 1.)          ! mark structure for display
!=== define all CSS structures ====================================++++++
!--- define the "Frame" structure ----------------------------------++++++
call popst(Frame)                        ! open structure
call pfa(26, FAreaX, FAreaY)             ! fill area primitive
call pbltm(0.0, 0.0, 0.0, 0.0, 0.0, 0.0, 0.0, Error, Matrix)
call pslmt(Matrix, PCREPL)               ! set local transformation
call pexst(Wheel)                        ! execute structure
call pslmt(Matrix, PCREPL)               ! set local transformation
call pexst(Wheel)                        ! execute structure
call pclst                               ! close structure
!--- define the "Wheel" structure ----------------------------------++++++
call popst(Wheel)                        ! open structure
do I=1, Spokes+1                         ! define the wheel rim
    Theta=(I-1)*dTheta                   ! calculate required angle
    PolylineX(I)=cos(Theta)              ! x=r*cos(Theta) where r=1
    PolylineY(I)=sin(Theta)              ! y=r*sin(Theta) where r=1
end do
call ppl(Spokes+1, PolylineX, PolylineY) ! 2D polyline
do I=0, Spokes                           ! define the spokes
    Theta=(I-1)*dTheta                   ! calculate required angle
    SpokeX(1)=0.0                        ! \  start defining each
    SpokeY(1)=0.0                        !  \ spoke from the center,
    SpokeX(2)=cos(Theta)                 !  / and then proceed
    SpokeY(2)=sin(Theta)                 ! /  rimward.
    call ppl(2, SpokeX, SpokeY)          ! 2D polyline
end do
call pclst                               ! close structure
!--- define the "Bike" structure -----------------------------------++++++
```

```
call popst(Bike)                              ! open structure
call pschh(0.04)                              ! set character height
call ptx(0.1, 0.8, 'Joe''s Olde Bike Shoppe')     ! 2D text
call psc(0.25, 0.25, Error, Scaling)              ! scale
call ptr(0.6, 0.6, Error, Translation)            ! translate
call pcom(Translation, Scaling, Error, Matrix)    ! concatenate matrices
call pslmt(Matrix, PCREPL)                    ! set local transform
call pexst(Frame)                             ! execute structure
call pclst                                    ! close the structure
!=== display the stucture ========================================++++++
call ppost(WorkstnID, Bike, 1.0)              ! post structure
call psedm(PREPLC)                            ! set edit mode to replace
Xpos=1.4                                      ! starting location for bike
WheelAngle=0.0                                ! starting rotation for wheels
do while (Xpos .gt. -.36)                     ! loop for structure editing
    !--- first, open "Bike" structure and move the frame ---------++++++
    call popst(Bike)                          ! open structure
    call psep(3)                              ! bike xform is element #3
    call ptr(Xpos, 0.6, Error, Translation)! build translation matrix
    call pcom(Translation, Scaling, Error, Matrix)! concatenate matrices
    call pslmt(Matrix, PCREPL)                ! set local transform
    call pclst()                              ! close structure
    Xpos=Xpos+dX                              ! increment X value
    !--- next, open the "Frame" structure and rotate the wheels --++++++
    call popst(Frame)                         ! open structure
    call pbltm(0.0, 0.0, TransXr,             ! build matrix
+     TransY, rad(WheelAngle), Scale, Scale, Error, Matrix)
    call psep(2)                              ! front wheel xform is ele. #2
    call pslmt(Matrix, PCREPL)                ! set local transform
    call psep(4)                              ! back wheel xform is ele. #4
    call pbltm(0.0, 0.0, TransXf,             ! build matrix
+     TransY, rad(WheelAngle+5.), Scale, Scale, Error, Matrix)
    call pslmt(Matrix, PCREPL)                ! set local transform
    WheelAngle=WheelAngle-dX*3000/(2*pi)      ! increment wheel angle
    call pclst()                              ! close structure
    call puwk(WorkstnID, PPERFO)              ! update workstation
end do                                        ! end of movement loop
call pclwk(WorkstnID)                         ! close workstation
call pclph                                    ! close PHIGS
stop                                          ! stop processing
end                                           ! end of program
```

SingleView Program

This section lists the FORTRAN version of the `SingleView` program described in Chapter 7, *Viewing and Workstation Transformations*. The C version is in Chapter 7.

```
      include 'phigs.f1.h'              ! get the PHIGS aliases
      program SingleView                ! file "SingleView.f"
      include 'phigs.f2.h'              ! get the PHIGS constants

      integer*4 WorkstnID               ! workstation ID
      parameter (WorkstnID=1)
      integer*4 ConnID                  ! communication channel ID
      integer*4 Error                   ! error indicator
      integer*4 Scene, Cube             ! structure IDs
      parameter (Scene=1, Cube=2)
!---- viewing variables -----------------------------------------------
      real      WindowLimits(4)          !  window limits
      real      ViewportLimits(6)        !  viewport limits
      real      ClipLimits(6)            !  clipping limits
      data      WindowLimits    /-1.75, 1.75, -1.75, 1.75/
      data      ViewportLimits  /0., 1., 0., 1., 0., 1./
      data      ClipLimits      /0., 1., 0., 1., 0., 1./
      real      PRPx, PRPy, PRPz         !  projection reference point
      parameter (PRPx=0., PRPy=0., PRPz=1.)
      real      ViewPlnDist              !  view plane distance
      real      BackPlnDist              !  back plane distance
      real      FrontPlnDist             !  front plane distance
      parameter (ViewPlnDist=0., BackPlnDist=-5., FrontPlnDist=5.)
      real      Orientation(4,4), Mapping(4,4)
!---- working variables -----------------------------------------------
      real      Angle                   ! rotation angle for editing structure
      real      Replacement(4,4), Ymat(4,4), Xmat(4,4)
      integer*4 I                       ! loop control variable
      integer*4 fdopen                  ! to get file descriptor

      call popph(fdopen(fnum(7), 'w'//char(0)), 0)       ! open PHIGS
      call pue004('/dev/screen/phigs_window', ConnID)    ! get connection ID
      call popwk(WorkstnID, ConnID, POIDDX)              ! open workstation
!---- define view 1 ---------------------------------------------------
      call pevom3(                      ! evaluate view orientation matrix
     +  0.0, 0.0, 0.0,                  ! view reference point
     +  0.4, 0.3, 1.0,                  ! view plane normal
```

```
  +  0.0, 1.0, 0.0,                     ! view up vector
  +  Error, Orientation)                ! returned items
   if (Error .ne. 0) then
       print *,"Error",Error,"in pevom3; terminating."
       stop
   endif
   call pevmm3(                         ! evaluate view mapping matrix
  +  WindowLimits, ViewportLimits, PPARL, PRPx, PRPy, PRPz,
  +  ViewPlnDist, BackPlnDist, FrontPlnDist, Error, Mapping)
   if (Error .ne. 0) then
       print *,"Error",Error,"in pevmm3; terminating."
       stop
   endif
   call psvwr3(                         ! set view representation
  +  WorkstnID, 1, Orientation, Mapping, ClipLimits,
  +  PCLIP, PCLIP, PCLIP)
   !--- create the structure ------------------------------------------------
   call BuildCube(Cube)
   call prox(0.0, Error, Replacement)! rotate in x (make identity matrix)
   call popst(Scene)                    ! open structure
   call psvwi(1)                        ! set view index
   call pslmt3(Replacement, PCREPL)     ! set local transformation matrix
   call pexst(Cube)                     ! execute structure
   call pclst                           ! close structure
   call ppost(WorkstnID, Scene, 1.0)    ! post structure Scene
   call puwk(WorkstnID, PPERFO)         ! update workstation
   call prox(0.0, Error, Xmat)          ! rotate in x (make identity matrix)
   call prox(0.0, Error, Ymat)          ! rotate in x (make identity matrix)
   call prox(0.0, Error, Replacement)! rotate in x (make identity matrix)
   call psedm(PREPLC)                   ! set edit mode (to "replace")
   call popst(Scene)                    ! open structure
   do 10 i=0,360
       Angle = I * 0.017453292          ! convert degrees to radians
       !--- create matrices for rotation in x and y ----------------------
       call proy(Angle, Error, Ymat) ! rotate in x
       call prox(Angle, Error, Xmat) ! rotate in y
       call pcom3(Xmat, Ymat, Error, Replacement)     ! concatenate matrices
       call psep(2)                     ! set element pointer to 2
       call pslmt3(Replacement, PCREPL)! set local transformation matrix
       call prst(WorkstnID, PALWAY)     ! redraw all structures
10 continue                             ! end of "do" loop
   call pclst()                         ! close structure
   call pclwk(WorkstnID)                ! close workstation
```

```
      call pclph                          ! close PHIGS
      end
!*******************************************************************************
      subroutine BuildCube(Cube)
      include 'phigs.f2.h'                ! get the PHIGS constants
      integer*4 Cube

      integer*4 NumPoints(1)              ! index array
      !--- Truncated cube data.  Points are defined in anti-clockwise order --
      !--- so that front faces point out from origin.  -----------------------
      real      TopX(5), TopY(5), TopZ(5)
      data      TopX /-1., -1.,  0.,  1.,  1./
      data      TopY / 1.,  1.,  1.,  1.,  1./
      data      TopZ /-1.,  1.,  1.,  0., -1./
      real      TopDirX(2), TopDirY(2), TopDirZ(2)
      data      TopDirX /1.,0./, TopDirY /0.,0./, TopDirZ /0.,-1./
      real      BottomX(4), BottomY(4), BottomZ(4)
      data      BottomX /-1., -1.,  1.,  1./
      data      BottomY /-1., -1., -1., -1./
      data      BottomZ / 1., -1., -1.,  1./
      real      RightX(5), RightY(5), RightZ(5)
      data      RightX / 1.,  1.,  1.,  1.,  1./
      data      RightY /-1.,  1.,  1.,  0., -1./
      data      RightZ /-1., -1.,  0.,  1.,  1./
      real      RightDirX(2), RightDirY(2), RightDirZ(2)
      data      RightDirX /0.,0./, RightDirY /0.,1./, RightDirZ /-1.,0./
      real      LeftX(4), LeftY(4), LeftZ(4)
      data      LeftX /-1., -1., -1., -1./
      data      LeftY /-1.,  1.,  1., -1./
      data      LeftZ / 1.,  1., -1., -1./
      real      FrontX(5), FrontY(5), FrontZ(5)
      data      FrontX / 1.,  1.,  0., -1., -1./
      data      FrontY /-1.,  0.,  1.,  1., -1./
      data      FrontZ / 1.,  1.,  1.,  1.,  1./
      real      FrontDirX(2), FrontDirY(2), FrontDirZ(2)
      data      FrontDirX /1.,0./, FrontDirY /0.,1./, FrontDirZ /0.,0./
      real      BackX(4), BackY(4), BackZ(4)
      data      BackX /-1., -1.,  1.,  1./
      data      BackY /-1.,  1.,  1., -1./
      data      BackZ /-1., -1., -1., -1./
      real      CornerX(3), CornerY(3), CornerZ(3)
      data      CornerX /1.,  1.,  0./
      data      CornerY /0.,  1.,  1./
```

```
data      CornerZ /1.,  0.,  1./

call popst(Cube)                    ! open structure
call psfcm(PBKFC)                   ! set face-cull mode: back-facing
call pschh(.4)                      ! set character height
call pschxp(.8)                     ! set character expansion factor
!--- do top of cube -------------------------------------------------------
NumPoints(1)=5
call pfas3(1, NumPoints, TopX, TopY, TopZ)           ! fill area set 3
call ptx3(-.75, 1., 0., TopDirX, TopDirY, TopDirZ, 'Top')
!--- do bottom of cube ----------------------------------------------------
NumPoints(1)=4
call pfas3(1, NumPoints, BottomX, BottomY, BottomZ)  ! fill area set 3
!--- do right side of cube ------------------------------------------------
NumPoints(1)=5
call pfas3(1, NumPoints, RightX, RightY, RightZ)     ! fill area set 3
call ptx3(1., -.75, .75, RightDirX, RightDirY, RightDirZ, 'Right')
!--- do left side of cube -------------------------------------------------
NumPoints(1)=4
call pfas3(1, NumPoints, LeftX, LeftY, LeftZ)        ! fill area set 3
!--- do front of cube -----------------------------------------------------
NumPoints(1)=5
call pfas3(1, NumPoints, FrontX, FrontY, FrontZ)     ! fill area set 3
call ptx3(-.75, -.75, 1., FrontDirX, FrontDirY, FrontDirZ,'Front')
!--- do back of cube ------------------------------------------------------
NumPoints(1)=4
call pfas3(1, NumPoints, BackX, BackY, BackZ)        ! fill area set 3
!--- do truncated corner of cube ------------------------------------------
NumPoints(1)=3
call pfas3(1, NumPoints, CornerX, CornerY, CornerZ)  ! fill area set 3
call pclst                                   ! close structure
return
end
```

Pilot's-Eye View Program

This section lists the C and FORTRAN versions of the pilot's-eye view program described in Chapter 7, *Viewing and Workstation Transformations.*

C Binding Version of Pilot's-Eye View Program

```
#include <phigs.h>                      /* get PHIGS definitions for C */
#include <stdio.h>                      /* get standard I/O definitions */
#include <math.h>                       /* link with library "-lm" */

#define  deg    *M_PI/180               /* convert degrees to radians */

Pint    SceneID = 1, PlaneID = 2, CircleID = 3, CylinderID = 4,
        ConeID = 5, SphereID = 6, SquareID = 7, CubeID = 8;
main()                                  /* file "ZoomView.c" */
{
    Pint         WorkstnID = 1;         /* workstation identifier */
    Pint         ConnID;                /* connection identifier */
    Pint         WorkstnType = POIDDX;  /* out/in, direct, dbl. bfr., Xwindow */
    Pint         Error;                 /* error indicator */
    float        CenterX = 5.0, CenterY = 5.0;   /* center-of-image rotation */
    Pmatrix3     M1, M2, M3, M4, M;     /* transformation matrices */
    Pvec3        XformVec1, XformVec2;  /* for scalings and translations */
    static Pvec3 ZeroVec = {0.0, 0.0, 0.0};      /* all-zeroes vector */
    static Pvec3 OneVec =  {1.0, 1.0, 1.0};      /* all-ones vector */
    float        X, Y, Z;               /* temporary position variables */
    float        X1, Y1, Z1, X2, Y2, Z2; /* position last time/this time */
    float        VelX1, VelY1, VelZ1;   /* velocity last time */
    float        VelX2, VelY2, VelZ2;   /* velocity this time */
    float        AccelX1, AccelY1, AccelZ1;      /* acceleration last time */
    float        AccelX2, AccelY2, AccelZ2;      /* acceleration this time */
    int          I;                     /* loop control variable */

    /*=== open PHIGS and workstation ======================================= */
    popen_phigs(stderr, 0);                      /* errors go to "stderr" */
    pescape_u4("/dev/screen/phigs_window", &ConnID);
    popen_ws(WorkstnID, ConnID, WorkstnType);
    /*=== define all needed structures ===================================== */
    /*---- define the "floor" plane ------------------------------------------*/
    popen_struct(PlaneID);                       /* open structure  */
```

```
Plane(0.0, 10.0, 1.0, 0.0, 10.0, 2.0);        /* define plane */
pclose_struct();                                /* close structure */
/*---- define the 2D shapes with supporting roles ---------------------*/
popen_struct(CircleID);                         /* open structure */
SupinePolygon(24);                              /* define a "circle" */
pclose_struct();                                /* close structure */
popen_struct(SquareID);                         /* open structure */
SupinePolygon(4);                               /* define a square */
pclose_struct();                                /* close structure */
/*---- define the cylinder --------------------------------------------*/
popen_struct(CylinderID);                       /* open structure  */
Cylinder(1.0, 0.2, 1.0, 0.1);                   /* define cylinder */
pclose_struct();                                /* close structure */
/*---- define the cone ------------------------------------------------*/
popen_struct(ConeID);                           /* open structure */
Cone(1.0, 2.0, 0.05);                           /* define cone */
pclose_struct();                                /* close structure */
/*---- define the sphere ----------------------------------------------*/
popen_struct(SphereID);                         /* open structure  */
Sphere(1.0, 5.0);                               /* define sphere */
pclose_struct();                                /* close structure */
/*---- define the cube ------------------------------------------------*/
popen_struct(CubeID);                           /* open structure */
Cube(sqrt(2.0)/2, 0.1, 1.0, 0.1);               /* define cube */
pclose_struct();                                /* close structure */
/*=== define the scene ============================================== */
popen_struct(SceneID);
pset_view_ind(1);
pexec_struct(PlaneID);
/*---- cone -----------------------------------------------------------*/
XformVec1.delta_x = 5.0, XformVec1.delta_y = 1.0, XformVec1.delta_z = 0.0;
ptranslate3(&XformVec1, &Error, M);
pset_local_tran3(M, PTYPE_REPLACE);
pexec_struct(ConeID);
/*---- cylinders ------------------------------------------------------*/
XformVec1.delta_x = 2.0, XformVec1.delta_y = 8.0, XformVec1.delta_z = 0.0;
ptranslate3(&XformVec1, &Error, M);
pset_local_tran3(M, PTYPE_REPLACE);
pexec_struct(CylinderID);               /* short, fat cylinder */
XformVec1.delta_x = 0.0, XformVec1.delta_y = 0.0, XformVec1.delta_z =-0.5;
ptranslate3(&XformVec1, &Error, M);
XformVec1.delta_x = 0.4, XformVec1.delta_y = 0.4, XformVec1.delta_z = 2.0;
pscale3(&XformVec1, &Error, M1);
```

```
AppendTransformation(M, M1);
protate_x(90 deg, &Error, M1);
AppendTransformation(M, M1);
protate_z(30 deg, &Error, M1);
AppendTransformation(M, M1);
XformVec1.delta_x = 2.3, XformVec1.delta_y = 8.3, XformVec1.delta_z = 1.4;
ptranslate3(&XformVec1, &Error, M1);
AppendTransformation(M, M1);
pset_local_tran3(M, PTYPE_REPLACE);
pexec_struct(CylinderID);           /* tall, thin cylinder */
/*---- spheroids ------------------------------------------------------*/
pbuild_tran_matrix3(&ZeroVec, &OneVec, 45 deg, 0.0, 0.0, &OneVec,
  &Error, M);
pset_local_tran3(M, PTYPE_REPLACE);
pexec_struct(SphereID);             /* sphere */
XformVec1.delta_x = 8.0, XformVec1.delta_y = 6.0, XformVec1.delta_z = 2.0;
XformVec2.delta_x = 0.5, XformVec2.delta_y = 0.5, XformVec2.delta_z = 2.0;
pbuild_tran_matrix3(&ZeroVec, &XformVec1, 0.0, 0.0, 0.0, &XformVec2,
  &Error, M);
pset_local_tran3(M, PTYPE_REPLACE);
pexec_struct(SphereID);             /* prolate spheroid */
XformVec1.delta_x = 5.0, XformVec1.delta_y = 1.0, XformVec1.delta_z = 2.5;
XformVec2.delta_x = 1.0, XformVec2.delta_y = 1.0, XformVec2.delta_z = 0.5;
pbuild_tran_matrix3(&ZeroVec, &XformVec1, 0.0, 0.0, 0.0, &XformVec2,
  &Error, M);
pset_local_tran3(M, PTYPE_REPLACE);
pexec_struct(SphereID);             /* oblate spheroid */
/*---- cubes ----------------------------------------------------------*/
protate_z(45 deg, &Error, M);
XformVec1.delta_x = 2.0, XformVec1.delta_y = 1.0, XformVec1.delta_z = 1.0;
pscale3(&XformVec1, &Error, M1);
AppendTransformation(M, M1);
protate_x(90 deg, &Error, M1);
AppendTransformation(M, M1);
protate_z(30 deg, &Error, M1);
AppendTransformation(M, M1);
XformVec1.delta_x = 8.0, XformVec1.delta_y = 3.0, XformVec1.delta_z = 0.5;
ptranslate3(&XformVec1, &Error, M1);
AppendTransformation(M, M1);
pset_local_tran3(M, PTYPE_REPLACE);
pexec_struct(CubeID);               /* bottom block */
protate_z(45 deg, &Error, M1);
protate_y(90 deg, &Error, M2);
```

```
pcompose_matrix3(M2, M1, &Error, M3);
protate_z(50 deg, &Error, M4);
pcompose_matrix3(M4, M3, &Error, M1);
XformVec1.delta_x = 7.8, XformVec1.delta_y = 2.5, XformVec1.delta_z = 1.5;
ptranslate3(&XformVec1, &Error, M2);
pcompose_matrix3(M2, M1, &Error, M);
pset_local_tran3(M, PTYPE_REPLACE);
pexec_struct(CubeID);                 /* top cube */
pclose_struct();                      /* close structure */
/*=== move around/in the scene ======================================= */
ppost_struct(WorkstnID, SceneID, 1.0);      /* post structure */
/*---- go around the scene once ----------------------------------------*/
for (I = 0; I <= 360; I += 2) {
    PolarToRectangular(25.0, (I-90) deg, 80 deg, &X, &Y, &Z);
    DefineCameraView(WorkstnID, 1,   /* workstation ID, view number */
      X + CenterX, Y + CenterY, Z,   /* PRP (point looked from) */
      5.0, 5.0, 0.0,                 /* VRP (point looked at) */
      30.0, PTYPE_PERSPECT,          /* field of view, proj. type */
      0.0, 0.0, 1.0);                /* up vector */
    pupd_ws(1, PFLAG_PERFORM);       /* update workstation */
}
/*---- look down on the scene from above -------------------------------*/
pset_disp_upd_st(WorkstnID, PDEFER_ASAP, PMODE_NIVE);
for (I = 80; I >= 4; I--) {
    PolarToRectangular(25.0, -90 deg, I deg, &X, &Y, &Z);
    DefineCameraView(WorkstnID, 1,   /* workstation ID, view number */
      X + CenterX, Y + CenterY, Z,   /* PRP (point looked from) */
      5.0, 5.0, 0.0,                 /* VRP (point looked at) */
      30.0, PTYPE_PERSPECT,          /* field of view, proj. type */
      0.0, 0.0, 1.0);                /* up vector */
}
for (I = 4; I <= 90; I += 2) {
    PolarToRectangular(25.0, -90 deg, I deg, &X, &Y, &Z);
    DefineCameraView(WorkstnID, 1,   /* workstation ID, view number */
      X + CenterX, Y + CenterY, Z,   /* PRP (point looked from) */
      5.0, 5.0, 0.0,                 /* VRP (point looked at) */
      30.0, PTYPE_PERSPECT,          /* field of view, proj. type */
      0.0, 0.0, 1.0);                /* up vector */
}
/*---- move into the scene ---------------------------------------------*/
X1 = X + CenterX; Y1 = Y + CenterY; Z1 = Z; /* starting point of move */
X2 = 7.0; Y2 = 10.0; Z2 = 1.0;             /* ending point of move */
for (I = 0; I <= 100; I++) {
```

```
    X = (100-I)*X1*0.01 + I*X2*0.01;          /* \  Move linearly from  */
    Y = (100-I)*Y1*0.01 + I*Y2*0.01;          /*  > point 1 to point 2, */
    Z = (100-I)*Z1*0.01 + I*Z2*0.01;          /* /  in 101 easy steps.  */
    DefineCameraView(WorkstnID, 1,  /* workstation ID, view number */
      X, Y, Z,                      /* PRP (point looked from) */
      5.0, 5.0, 0.0,                /* VRP (point looked at) */
      30.0, PTYPE_PERSPECT,         /* field of view, proj. type */
      0.0, 0.0, 1.0);               /* up vector */
}
/*---- look up at the the cone/spheroid juncture ----------------------*/
X1 = 5.0; Y1 = 5.0; Z1 = 0.0;       /* starting point of pan/tilt */
X2 = 5.0; Y2 = 1.0; Z2 = 2.0;       /* ending point of pan/tilt */
for (I = 0; I <= 50; I++) {
    X = (50-I)*X1*0.02 + I*X2*0.02; /* \  Move linearly from point */
    Y = (50-I)*Y1*0.02 + I*Y2*0.02; /*  > 1 to point 2, in 51 */
    Z = (50-I)*Z1*0.02 + I*Z2*0.02; /* /  easy steps. */
    DefineCameraView(WorkstnID, 1,  /* workstation id, view number */
      7.0, 10.0, 1.0,               /* PRP (point looked from) */
      X, Y, Z,                      /* VRP (point looked at) */
      30.0, PTYPE_PERSPECT,         /* field of view, proj. type */
      0.0, 0.0, 1.0);               /* up vector */
}
/*---- zoom in on the cone/spheroid juncture -------------------------*/
for (I = 60; I >= 4; I--) {
    DefineCameraView(WorkstnID, 1,  /* workstation ID, view number */
      7.0, 10.0, 1.0,               /* PRP (point looked from) */
      X2, Y2, Z2,                   /* VRP (point looked at) */
      I * 0.5, PTYPE_PERSPECT,      /* field of view, proj. type */
      0.0, 0.0, 1.0);               /* up vector */
}
for (I = 4; I <= 270; I += 2) {
    DefineCameraView(WorkstnID, 1,  /* workstation ID, view number */
      7.0, 10.0, 1.0,               /* PRP (point looked from) */
      X2, Y2, Z2,                   /* VRP (point looked at) */
      I * 0.5, PTYPE_PERSPECT,      /* field of view, proj. type */
      0.0, 0.0, 1.0);               /* up vector */
}
for (I = 270; I >= 120; I--) {
    DefineCameraView(WorkstnID, 1,  /* workstation ID, view number */
      7.0, 10.0, 1.0,               /* PRP (point looked from) */
      X2, Y2, Z2,                   /* VRP (point looked at) */
      I * 0.5, PTYPE_PERSPECT,      /* field of view, proj. type */
      0.0, 0.0, 1.0);               /* up vector */
```

```
    }
    /*---- fly away as in an airplane ------------------------------------*/
    AccelX1 = 0.0; AccelY1 = 0.0; AccelZ1 = 1.0;
    for (I = 0; I <= 1082; I++) {
        /*---- devise a complex, but smooth, steadily rising flight path ---*/
        X2 = 5 - 1.5*sin((I*1.7) deg) - 0.9*cos((I*0.34) deg);
        Y2 = 4 + (I*0.004 + 1)*cos((I*1.3 + 15) deg) + 0.5*sin((I*1.6) deg);
        Z2 = I * 0.003;
        VelX2 = X2-X1, VelY2 = Y2-Y1, VelZ2 = Z2-Z1;
        AccelX2 = VelX2-VelX1, AccelY2 = VelY2-VelY1, AccelZ2 = VelZ2-VelZ1;
        if (I > 3) {            /* ignore anomalous values */
            DefineCameraView(WorkstnID,1,/* workstation ID, view number */
              X1, Y1, Z1,               /* PRP (point looked from) */
              X2, Y2, Z2,               /* VRP (point looked at) */
              90.0, PTYPE_PERSPECT,     /* field of view, proj. type */
              AccelX1, AccelY1, 0.003); /* up vector */
        }
        X1 = X2, Y1 = Y2, Z1 = Z2;
        VelX1 = VelX2, VelY1 = VelY2, VelZ1 = VelZ2;
        AccelX1 = AccelX2, AccelY1 = AccelY2, AccelZ1 = AccelZ2;
    }
    pupd_ws(WorkstnID, PFLAG_PERFORM);  /* (regeneration flag) */
    pclose_ws(WorkstnID);
    pclose_phigs();
}
/*************************************************************************/
Plane(Xmin, Xmax, dX, Ymin, Ymax, dY)
float   Xmin, Xmax, Ymin, Ymax;         /* defines size of floor */
float   dX, dY;                         /* size of tiles in floor */
{
    float       X, Y;                   /* loop control variables */

    X = Xmin;
    while (X <= Xmax + 0.00001) {
        OneLine(X, Ymin, 0.0, X, Ymax, 0.0);
        X = X + dX;
    }
    Y = Ymin;
    while (Y <= Ymax + 0.00001) {
        OneLine(Xmin, Y, 0.0, Xmax, Y, 0.0);
        Y = Y + dY;
    }
}
```

```
/*************************************************************************/
OneLine(X1, Y1, Z1, X2, Y2, Z2)
float   X1, Y1, Z1, X2, Y2, Z2;          /* point 1, point 2 */
{
    Ppoint_list3        PointList;       /* entirety of data for POLYLINE 3 */
    Ppoint3             Points[2];       /* xyz data for POLYLINE 3 */

    Points[0].x = X1, Points[0].y = Y1, Points[0].z = Z1;
    Points[1].x = X2, Points[1].y = Y2, Points[1].z = Z2;
    PointList.num_points = 2;
    PointList.points = Points;
    ppolyline3(&PointList);
}
/*************************************************************************/
SupinePolygon(Sides)
int             Sides;                   /* number of sides of polygon */
{
    Ppoint_list3        PointList;       /* entirety of data for POLYLINE 3 */
    Ppoint3             Points[360];     /* xyz data for POLYLINE 3 */
    int                dTheta, I, Index;/* loop control variables */
    float               Theta;           /* temporary variable */

    dTheta = 360/Sides;                  /* degrees per side */
    Index = 0;                           /* for array subscripts */
    for (I = 0; I <= 360; I += dTheta) {
        Theta = I deg;                   /* convert degrees to radians */
        Points[Index].x = cos(Theta);    /* \                      */
        Points[Index].y = sin(Theta);    /*  > calculate xyz data */
        Points[Index].z = 0.0;           /* /                      */
        Index++;                         /* increment array subscript */
    }
    PointList.num_points = Sides + 1;
    PointList.points = Points;
    ppolyline3(&PointList);
}
/*************************************************************************/
Cylinder(Radius, dRadius, Height, dHeight)
float   Radius;                          /* radius of cylinder */
float   dRadius;                         /* dist. between circles in top/btm. */
float   Height;                          /* total height of cylinder */
float   dHeight;                         /* dist. between layers in cylinder */
{
    Pmatrix3    M1, M2, M;               /* transformation matrices */
```

```
    Pvec3         XformVec;                   /* for C binding */
    int           Error;                      /* error-return variable */
    float         R, Z;                       /* loop control variables */

    R = dRadius;                              /* initial radius */
    while (R <= Radius) {
        /*--- do bottom first ----------------------------------------------*/
        XformVec.delta_x = XformVec.delta_y = R;
        XformVec.delta_z = 1.0;
        pscale3(&XformVec, &Error, M1);
        pset_local_tran3(M1, PTYPE_REPLACE);
        pexec_struct(CircleID);
        /*--- do top --------------------------------------------------------*/
        XformVec.delta_x = XformVec.delta_y = 0.0;
        XformVec.delta_z = Height;
        ptranslate3(&XformVec, &Error, M2);
        pcompose_matrix3(M1, M2, &Error, M);
        pset_local_tran3(M, PTYPE_REPLACE);
        pexec_struct(CircleID);
        R += dRadius;                         /* increment the radius */
    }
    Z = 0.0;
    XformVec.delta_x = XformVec.delta_y = Radius;
    XformVec.delta_z = 1.0;
    pscale3(&XformVec, &Error, M1);
    while (Z <= Height) {
        XformVec.delta_x = XformVec.delta_y = 0.0;
        XformVec.delta_z = Z;
        ptranslate3(&XformVec, &Error, M2);
        pcompose_matrix3(M1, M2, &Error, M);
        pset_local_tran3(M, PTYPE_REPLACE);
        pexec_struct(CircleID);
        Z += dHeight;                         /* increment the height */
    }
}
/***************************************************************************/
Cone(Radius, Height, dHeight)
float           Radius;                       /* radius of sphere */
float           Height;                       /* height of whole cone */
float           dHeight;                      /* distance between rings */
{
    Pmatrix3      M1, M2, M;                  /* transformation matrices */
    Pvec3         XformVec;                   /* for C binding */
```

```
    int         Error;                    /* error-return variable */
    float       Z, R;                     /* loop control variable */

    Z = dHeight;                          /* initial height */
    while (Z <= Height) {
        R = Radius * ((Height - Z)/Height);
        XformVec.delta_x = XformVec.delta_y = R;
        XformVec.delta_z = 1.0;
        pscale3(&XformVec, &Error, M1);
        XformVec.delta_x = XformVec.delta_y = 0;
        XformVec.delta_z = Z;
        ptranslate3(&XformVec, &Error, M2);
        pcompose_matrix3(M1, M2, &Error, M);
        pset_local_tran3(M, PTYPE_REPLACE);
        pexec_struct(CircleID);
        Z += dHeight;                     /* increment the height */
    }
}
/***********************************************************************/
Sphere(Radius, dPhi)
float           Radius;                   /* radius of sphere */
float           dPhi;                     /* angular dist. between latitudes */
{
    Pmatrix3    M1, M2, M;                /* transformation matrices */
    Pvec3       XformVec;                 /* for C binding */
    int         Error;                    /* error-return variable */
    float       Phi, R, Z;                /* loop control variables */

    Phi = dPhi;                           /* initial radius */
    while (Phi < 180.0) {
        R = Radius * sin(Phi deg);
        Z = Radius * cos(Phi deg);
        XformVec.delta_x = XformVec.delta_y = R;
        XformVec.delta_z = 1.0;
        pscale3(&XformVec, &Error, M1);
        XformVec.delta_x = XformVec.delta_y = 0.0;
        XformVec.delta_z = Z;
        ptranslate3(&XformVec, &Error, M2);
        pcompose_matrix3(M1, M2, &Error, M);
        pset_local_tran3(M, PTYPE_REPLACE);
        pexec_struct(CircleID);
        Phi += dPhi;                      /* increment Phi */
    }
```

```
}
/*************************************************************************/
Cube(Distance, dDistance, Height, dHeight)
float           Distance;               /* center-to-corner distance */
float           dDistance;              /* dist. between vert. in top/btm. */
float           Height;                 /* total height of cube */
float           dHeight;                /* distance between layers in cube */
{
    Pmatrix3    M1, M2, M;              /* transformation matrices */
    Pvec3       XformVec;               /* for C binding */
    int         Error;                  /* error-return variable */
    float       Dist, Z;                /* loop control variables */

    Dist = dDistance;                   /* initial radius */
    while (Dist <= Distance) {
        /*--- do bottom first ------------------------------------------*/
        XformVec.delta_x = XformVec.delta_y = Dist;
        XformVec.delta_z = 1.0;
        pscale3(&XformVec, &Error, M1);
        pset_local_tran3(M1, PTYPE_REPLACE);
        pexec_struct(SquareID);
        /*--- do top ---------------------------------------------------*/
        XformVec.delta_x = XformVec.delta_y = 0.0;
        XformVec.delta_z = Height;
        ptranslate3(&XformVec, &Error, M2);
        pcompose_matrix3(M1, M2, &Error, M);
        pset_local_tran3(M, PTYPE_REPLACE);
        pexec_struct(SquareID);
        Dist += dDistance;              /* increment the radius */
    }
    Z = 0.0;
    XformVec.delta_x = XformVec.delta_y = Distance;
    XformVec.delta_z = 1.0;
    pscale3(&XformVec, &Error, M1);
    while (Z <= Height) {
        XformVec.delta_x = XformVec.delta_y = 0.0;
        XformVec.delta_z = Z;
        ptranslate3(&XformVec, &Error, M2);
        pcompose_matrix3(M1, M2, &Error, M);
        pset_local_tran3(M, PTYPE_REPLACE);
        pexec_struct(SquareID);
        Z += dHeight;                   /* increment the height */
    }
```

```
}
/***************************************************************************/
DefineCameraView(WorkstnID, ViewNo, PRPx, PRPy, PRPz, VRPx, VRPy, VRPz,
  FieldOfView, ProjType, VUPx, VUPy, VUPz)
int             WorkstnID, ViewNo;      /* workstn id, view to be defined */
float           PRPx, PRPy, PRPz;       /* proj. ref. pt. (point looked from) */
float           VRPx, VRPy, VRPz;       /* view ref. pt. (point looked at) */
float           FieldOfView;            /* "zoomness" in degrees */
Pproj_type      ProjType;               /* parallel or perspective? */
float           VUPx, VUPy, VUPz;       /* view up vector */
{
    Pview_map3  MapStruct;              /* structure for view mapping info */
    Ppoint3     ViewRefPt;              /* view reference point */
    Pvec3       ViewNrmVc, ViewUpVec;   /* view normal/up vectors */
    Pmatrix3    Mapping;                /* view mapping matrix */
    Pmatrix3    Orientation;            /* view orientation matrix */
    float       Distance;               /* distance from PRP to VRP */
    float       Wndw;                   /* window limits */
    Pview_rep3  ViewRep;                /* view representation */
    int         Error;                  /* error-return variable */
    int         I, J;                   /* loop control variables */

    ViewRefPt.x = VRPx, ViewRefPt.y = VRPy, ViewRefPt.z = VRPz;
    ViewNrmVc.delta_x = PRPx - VRPx;    /* \  view plane normal determined  */
    ViewNrmVc.delta_y = PRPy - VRPy;    /*  > by projection reference point */
    ViewNrmVc.delta_z = PRPz - VRPz;    /* /  and view reference point.     */
    ViewUpVec.delta_x = VUPx, ViewUpVec.delta_y = VUPy,
      ViewUpVec.delta_z = VUPz;
    peval_view_ori_matrix3(&ViewRefPt, &ViewNrmVc, &ViewUpVec, &Error,
      Orientation);
    if (Error != 0){
        printf("Error %d in peval_view_ori_matrix3; terminating.\n", Error);
        exit(1);
    }
    Distance = sqrt((PRPx-VRPx)*(PRPx-VRPx) + (PRPy-VRPy)*(PRPy-VRPy) +
      (PRPz-VRPz)*(PRPz-VRPz));
    Wndw = Distance * tan(FieldOfView deg/2);   /* FOV controls window size */
    MapStruct.win.x_min =               /* \                              */
      MapStruct.win.y_min = -Wndw;      /*  \ This assumes a square window */
    MapStruct.win.x_max =               /*  / (aspect ratio = 1.00).      */
      MapStruct.win.y_max = Wndw;       /* /                              */
    MapStruct.proj_vp.x_min = MapStruct.proj_vp.y_min =
      MapStruct.proj_vp.z_min = 0.0;
```

```
    MapStruct.proj_vp.x_max = MapStruct.proj_vp.y_max =
      MapStruct.proj_vp.z_max = 1.0;
    MapStruct.proj_type = ProjType;
    MapStruct.proj_ref_point.x = 0.0, MapStruct.proj_ref_point.y = 0.0,
      MapStruct.proj_ref_point.z = Distance;
    MapStruct.view_plane = 0.0;
    MapStruct.back_plane = -1E3 * Distance;      /* virtually infinite */
    MapStruct.front_plane = Distance - 0.01;     /* right in front of eye pt. */
    peval_view_map_matrix3(&MapStruct, &Error, Mapping);
    if (Error != 0){
        printf("Error %d in peval_view_map_matrix3; terminating.\n", Error);
        exit(1);
    }
    for (I = 0; I < 4; I++)
        for (J = 0; J < 4; J++) {
            ViewRep.ori_matrix[I][J] = Orientation[I][J];
            ViewRep.map_matrix[I][J] = Mapping[I][J];
        }
    ViewRep.clip_limit.x_min = 0.0;
    ViewRep.clip_limit.x_max = 1.0;
    ViewRep.clip_limit.y_min = 0.0;
    ViewRep.clip_limit.y_max = 1.0;
    ViewRep.clip_limit.z_min = 0.0;
    ViewRep.clip_limit.z_max = 1.0;
    ViewRep.xy_clip = ViewRep.back_clip = ViewRep.front_clip = PIND_CLIP;
    pset_view_rep3(WorkstnID, ViewNo, &ViewRep);
}
/**************************************************************************/
PolarToRectangular(R, Theta, Phi, X, Y, Z)
float   R, Theta, Phi;          /* input: 3D polar (spherical) coords. */
float   *X, *Y, *Z;             /* output: 3D rect. (Cartesian) coords. */
{
    *X = R * sin(Phi) * cos(Theta);
    *Y = R * sin(Phi) * sin(Theta);
    *Z = R * cos(Phi);
}
/**************************************************************************/
AppendTransformation(MainTransform, Appendix)
Pmatrix3        MainTransform;  /* the transformation to be appended to */
Pmatrix3        Appendix;       /* the transformation to be appended */
{
    Pmatrix3    Temp;           /* temporary matrix holder */
    int         Error;          /* error indicator */
```

```
    int         I, J;           /* loop control variables */

    pcompose_matrix3(Appendix, MainTransform, &Error, Temp);
    for (I = 0; I < 4; I++)                         /* \  Copy result matrix  */
        for (J = 0; J < 4; J++)                     /*  > back into the first */
            MainTransform[I][J] = Temp[I][J];       /* /  argument matrix.    */
}
```

FORTRAN Binding Version of Pilot's-Eye View Program

```
      include 'phigs.f1.h'               ! get the PHIGS aliases
      program ZoomView                   ! file "ZoomView.f"
      include 'phigs.f2.h'               ! get the PHIGS constants

      integer   WorkstnID                ! workstation ID
      parameter (WorkstnID=1)            ! user-selectable value
      integer   ConnID                   ! communication channel ID
      integer   Error                    ! error indicator
      !--- define structure IDs -----------------------------------------
      integer   SceneID, PlaneID, CircleID, CylinderID, ConeID
      integer   SphereID, SquareID, CubeID
      common    /StructureIDs/ SceneID, PlaneID, CircleID, CylinderID
      common    /StructureIDs/ ConeID, SphereID, SquareID, CubeID
      data      SceneID, PlaneID, CircleID, CylinderID /1, 2, 3, 4/
      data      ConeID, SphereID, SquareID, CubeID /5, 6, 7, 8/

      real      CenterX, CenterY         ! center-of-image rotation
      data      CenterX /5./, CenterY /5./
      real      M1(4,4), M2(4,4), M3(4,4), M4(4,4), M(4,4)      ! matrices
      real      X, Y, Z                          ! temporary position variables
      real      X1, Y1, Z1, X2, Y2, Z2           ! position last time/this time
      real      VelX1, VelY1, VelZ1              ! velocity last time
      real      VelX2, VelY2, VelZ2              ! velocity this time
      real      AccelX1, AccelY1, AccelZ1        ! acceleration last time
      real      AccelX2, AccelY2, AccelZ2        ! acceleration this time
      integer   I                        ! loop control variable
      integer   fdopen                   ! to get file descriptor

      real      rad, deg                         ! type the statement function
      rad(deg)= ((deg)*3.14159265358979/180.)    ! convert degrees to radians

      !=== open PHIGS and workstation ====================================
      call popph(fdopen(fnum(7), 'w'//char(0)), 0)      ! open PHIGS
```

```
call pue004('/dev/screen/phigs_window', ConnID)   ! get connection ID
call popwk(WorkstnID, ConnID, POIDDX)     ! open workstation
!=== define all needed structures =========================================
!--- define the "floor" plane ---------------------------------------------
call popst(PlaneID)                       ! open structure
call Plane(0., 10., 1., 0., 10., 2.)      ! define plane
call pclst                                ! close structure
!--- define the 2D shapes with supporting roles ----------------------------
call popst(CircleID)              ! open structure
call SupinePolygon(24)            ! define a "circle"
call pclst                        ! close structure
call popst(SquareID)              ! open structure
call SupinePolygon(4)             ! define a square
call pclst                        ! close structure
!--- define the cylinder --------------------------------------------------
call popst(CylinderID)            ! open structure
call Cylinder(1., .2, 1., .1)     ! define cylinder
call pclst                        ! close structure
!--- define the cone ------------------------------------------------------
call popst(ConeID)                ! open structure
call Cone(1., 2., .05)            ! define cone
call pclst                        ! close structure
!--- define the sphere ----------------------------------------------------
call popst(SphereID)              ! open structure
call Sphere(1., 5.)               ! define sphere
call pclst                        ! close structure
!--- define the cube ------------------------------------------------------
call popst(CubeID)                ! open structure
call Cube(sqrt(2.)/2, .1, 1., .1) ! define cube
call pclst                        ! close structure
!=== define the scene =====================================================
call popst(SceneID)
call psvwi(1)
call pexst(PlaneID)
!--- cone -----------------------------------------------------------------
call ptr3(5., 1., 0., Error, M)
call pslmt3(M, PCREPL)
call pexst(ConeID)
!--- cylinders ------------------------------------------------------------
call ptr3(2., 8., 0., Error, M)
call pslmt3(M, PCREPL)
call pexst(CylinderID)            ! short, fat cylinder
call ptr3(0., 0., -.5, Error, M)
```

```
call psc3(.4, .4, 2., Error, M1)
call AppendTransformation(M, M1)
call prox(rad(90), Error, M1)
call AppendTransformation(M, M1)
call proz(rad(30), Error, M1)
call AppendTransformation(M, M1)
call ptr3(2.3, 8.3, 1.4, Error, M1)
call AppendTransformation(M, M1)
call pslmt3(M, PCREPL)
call pexst(CylinderID)           ! tall, thin cylinder
!--- spheroids ----------------------------------------------------
call pbltm3(0.,0.,.0, 1.,1.,1., rad(45),0.,0., 1.,1.,1., Error, M)
call pslmt3(M, PCREPL)
call pexst(SphereID)             ! sphere
call pbltm3(0.,0.,.0, 8.,6.,2., 0.,0.,0., .5,.5,2., Error, M)
call pslmt3(M, PCREPL)
call pexst(SphereID)             ! prolate spheroid
call pbltm3(0.,0.,.0, 5.,1.,2.5, 0.,0.,0., 1.,1.,.5,
+  Error, M)
call pslmt3(M, PCREPL)
call pexst(SphereID)             ! oblate spheroid
!--- cubes ---!----------------------------------------------------
call proz(rad(45), Error, M)
call psc3(2., 1., 1., Error, M1)
call AppendTransformation(M, M1)
call prox(rad(90), Error, M1)
call AppendTransformation(M, M1)
call proz(rad(30), Error, M1)
call AppendTransformation(M, M1)
call ptr3(8., 3., .5, Error, M1)
call AppendTransformation(M, M1)
call pslmt3(M, PCREPL)
call pexst(CubeID)               ! bottom block
call proz(rad(45), Error, M1)
call proy(rad(90), Error, M2)
call pcom3(M2, M1, Error, M3)
call proz(rad(50), Error, M4)
call pcom3(M4, M3, Error, M1)
call ptr3(7.8, 2.5, 1.5, Error, M2)
call pcom3(M2, M1, Error, M)
call pslmt3(M, PCREPL)
call pexst(CubeID)               ! top cube
call pclst                       ! close structure
```

```
!=== move around/in the scene ==========================================
call ppost(WorkstnID, SceneID, 1.0)       ! post structure
!--- go around the scene once ------------------------------------------
do I=0,360,2
    call PolarToRectangular(25., rad(I-90), rad(80), X, Y, Z)
    call DefineCameraView(WorkstnID, 1,   ! workstation ID, view number
+     X+CenterX, Y+CenterY, Z,            ! PRP (point looked from)
+     5., 5., 0.,                         ! VRP (point looked at)
+     30., PPERS,                         ! field of view, proj. type
+     0., 0., 1.)                         ! up vector
    call puwk(1, PPERFO)                  ! update workstation
end do
!--- look down on the scene from above --------------------------------
call psdus(WorkstnID, PASAP, PNIVE)       ! Set the display update state
do I=80,4,-2
    call PolarToRectangular(25., rad(-90), rad(I), X, Y, Z)
    call DefineCameraView(WorkstnID, 1,   ! workstation ID, view number
+     X+CenterX, Y+CenterY, Z,            ! PRP (point looked from)
+     5., 5., 0.,                         ! VRP (point looked at)
+     30., PPERS,                         ! field of view, proj. type
+     0., 0., 1.)                         ! up vector
end do
do I=4,90,2
    call PolarToRectangular(25., rad(-90), rad(I), X, Y, Z)
    call DefineCameraView(WorkstnID, 1,   ! workstation ID, view number
+     X+CenterX, Y+CenterY, Z,            ! PRP (point looked from)
+     5., 5., 0.,                         ! VRP (point looked at)
+     30., PPERS,                         ! field of view, proj. type
+     0., 0., 1.)                         ! up vector
end do
!--- move into the scene -----------------------------------------------
X1=X+CenterX                              ! \  The point looked from at
Y1=Y+CenterY                              !  > the beginning of the
Z1=Z                                      ! /  camera movement.
X2=7.                                     ! \  The point looked from at
Y2=10.                                    !  > the end of the camera
Z2=1.                                     ! /  movement.
do I=0,100
    X=(100-I)*X1*.01+I*X2*.01             ! \  Move linearly from point
    Y=(100-I)*Y1*.01+I*Y2*.01             !  > 1 to point 2, in 101
    Z=(100-I)*Z1*.01+I*Z2*.01             ! /  easy steps.
    call DefineCameraView(WorkstnID, 1,   ! workstation ID, view number
+     X, Y, Z,                            ! PRP (point looked from)
```

```
+      5., 5., 0.,                          ! VRP (point looked at)
+      30., PPERS,                          ! field of view, proj. type
+      0., 0., 1.)                          ! up vector
 end do
 !--- look up at the the cone/spheroid juncture -------------------------
 X1=5.                                      ! \  The point looked at at
 Y1=5.                                      !  > the beginning of the
 Z1=0.                                      ! /  camera pan/tilt.
 X2=5.                                      ! \  The point looked at at
 Y2=1.                                      !  > the end of the camera
 Z2=2.                                      ! /  pan/tilt.
 do I=0,50
     X=(50-I)*X1*.02+I*X2*.02               ! \  Move linearly from point
     Y=(50-I)*Y1*.02+I*Y2*.02               !  > 1 to point 2, in 51
     Z=(50-I)*Z1*.02+I*Z2*.02               ! /  easy steps.
     call DefineCameraView(WorkstnID, 1,    ! workstation ID, view number
+      7., 10., 1.,                         ! PRP (point looked from)
+      X, Y, Z,                             ! VRP (point looked at)
+      30., PPERS,                          ! field of view, proj. type
+      0., 0., 1.)                          ! up vector
 end do
 !--- zoom in on the cone/spheroid juncture ----------------------------
 do I=60,4,-1
     call DefineCameraView(WorkstnID, 1,    ! workstation ID, view number
+      7., 10., 1.,                         ! PRP (point looked from)
+      X2, Y2, Z2,                          ! VRP (point looked at)
+      I*.5, PPERS,                         ! field of view, proj. type
+      0., 0., 1.)                          ! up vector
 end do
 do I=4,270,2
     call DefineCameraView(WorkstnID, 1,    ! workstation ID, view number
+      7., 10., 1.,                         ! PRP (point looked from)
+      X2, Y2, Z2,                          ! VRP (point looked at)
+      I*.5, PPERS,                         ! field of view, proj. type
+      0., 0., 1.)                          ! up vector
 end do
 do I=270,120,-1
     call DefineCameraView(WorkstnID, 1,    ! workstation ID, view number
+      7., 10., 1.,                         ! PRP (point looked from)
+      X2, Y2, Z2,                          ! VRP (point looked at)
+      I*.5, PPERS,                         ! field of view, proj. type
+      0., 0., 1.)                          ! up vector
 end do
```

```
      !--- fly away as in an airplane ---------------------------------------
      AccelX1=0.
      AccelY1=0.
      AccelZ1=1.
      do I=0,1082
          !--- devise a complex, but smooth, steadily rising flight path ---
          X2=5-1.5*sin(rad(I*1.7))-.9*cos(rad(I*.34))
          Y2=4+(I*.004+1)*cos(rad(I*1.3+15))+.5*sin(rad(I*1.6))
          Z2=I*.003
          VelX2=X2-X1
          VelY2=Y2-Y1
          VelZ2=Z2-Z1
          AccelX2=VelX2-VelX1
          AccelY2=VelY2-VelY1
          AccelZ2=VelZ2-VelZ1
          if (I .gt. 3) then                   ! ignore anomalous values
              call DefineCameraView(WorkstnID,1,! workstation ID, view number
     +          X1, Y1, Z1,                     ! PRP (point looked from)
     +          X2, Y2, Z2,                     ! VRP (point looked at)
     +          90., PPERS,                     ! field of view, proj. type
     +          AccelX1, AccelY1, .003)         ! up vector
          end if
          X1=X2
          Y1=Y2
          Z1=Z2
          VelX1=VelX2
          VelY1=VelY2
          VelZ1=VelZ2
          AccelX1=AccelX2
          AccelY1=AccelY2
          AccelZ1=AccelZ2
      end do
      call pclwk(WorkstnID)             ! close workstation
      call pclph                        ! close PHIGS
      stop
      end
!*****************************************************************************
      subroutine Plane(Xmin, Xmax, dX, Ymin, Ymax, dY)
      real      Xmin, Xmax, Ymin, Ymax  ! defines size of floor
      real      dX, dY                  ! size of tiles in floor
      include 'phigs.f2.h'              ! get the PHIGS constants

      real      X, Y                    ! loop control variables
```

```
      X=Xmin
      do while (X .le. Xmax+.00001)
          call OneLine(X, Ymin, 0., X, Ymax, 0.)
          X=X+dX
      end do
      Y=Ymin
      do while (Y .le. Ymax+.00001)
          call OneLine(Xmin, Y, 0., Xmax, Y, 0.)
          Y=Y+dY
      end do
      return
      end
!*****************************************************************************
      subroutine OneLine(X1, Y1, Z1, X2, Y2, Z2)
      real      X1, Y1, Z1, X2, Y2, Z2

      real      X(2), Y(2), Z(2)

      X(1)=X1
      Y(1)=Y1
      Z(1)=Z1
      X(2)=X2
      Y(2)=Y2
      Z(2)=Z2
      call ppl3(2, X, Y, Z)
      return
      end
!*****************************************************************************
      subroutine SupinePolygon(Sides)
      integer   Sides                    ! number of sides of polygon

      real      X(360), Y(360), Z(360)   ! xyz data for POLYLINE 3
      integer   dTheta, I, Index         ! locp control variables
      real      Theta                    ! temporary variable

      real      rad, deg                         ! type the statement function
      rad(deg)= ((deg)*3.14159265358979/180.)    ! convert degrees to radians

      dTheta=360/Sides                   ! degrees per side
      Index=1                            ! for array subscripts
      do I=0, 360, dTheta                ! for each side...
          Theta=rad(I)                   !   convert degrees to radians
```

```
        X(Index)=cos(Theta)          !   \
        Y(Index)=sin(Theta)          !    > calculate xyz data
        Z(Index)=0.                  !   /
        Index=Index+1                !   increment array subscript
      end do
      call ppl3(Sides+1, X, Y, Z)    ! polyline 3
      return
      end
!***************************************************************************
      subroutine Cylinder(Radius, dRadius, Height, dHeight)
      real      Radius               ! radius of cylinder
      real      dRadius              ! distance between circles in top/btm
      real      Height               ! total height of cylinder
      real      dHeight              ! distance between layers in cylinder
      include 'phigs.f2.h'           ! get the PHIGS constants

      integer   SceneID, PlaneID, CircleID, CylinderID, ConeID
      integer   SphereID, SquareID, CubeID
      common    /StructureIDs/ SceneID, PlaneID, CircleID, CylinderID
      common    /StructureIDs/ ConeID, SphereID, SquareID, CubeID

      real      M1(4,4), M2(4,4), M(4,4)! transformation matrices
      integer   Error                ! error-return variable
      real      R, Z                 ! loop control variables

      R=dRadius                      ! initial radius
      do while (R .le. Radius)
        !--- do bottom first ------------------------------------------
        call psc3(R, R, 1., Error, M1)! scale 3
        call pslmt3(M1, PCREPL)      ! set local transformation 3
        call pexst(CircleID)         ! execute structure
        !--- then do top ----------------------------------------------
        call ptr3(0., 0., Height, Error, M2)        ! translate 3
        call pcom3(M1, M2, Error, M) ! compose matrix 3
        call pslmt3(M, PCREPL)       ! set local transformation 3
        call pexst(CircleID)         ! execute structure
        R=R+dRadius                  ! increment the radius
      end do
      Z=0.
      call psc3(Radius, Radius, 1., Error, M1)  ! scale 3
      do while (Z .le. Height)
        call ptr3(0., 0., Z, Error, M2)             ! translate 3
        call pcom3(M1, M2, Error, M) ! compose matrix 3
```

```
        call pslmt3(M, PCREPL)          ! set local transformation 3
        call pexst(CircleID)            ! execute structure
        Z=Z+dHeight                     ! increment the height
    end do
    return
    end
!***********************************************************************
    subroutine Cone(Radius, Height, dHeight)
    real      Radius                    ! radius of sphere
    real      Height                    ! height of whole cone
    real      dHeight                   ! distance between rings
    include 'phigs.f2.h'                ! get the PHIGS constants

    integer   SceneID, PlaneID, CircleID, CylinderID, ConeID
    integer   SphereID, SquareID, CubeID
    common    /StructureIDs/ SceneID, PlaneID, CircleID, CylinderID
    common    /StructureIDs/ ConeID, SphereID, SquareID, CubeID

    real      M1(4,4), M2(4,4), M(4,4)! transformation matrices
    integer   Error                     ! error-return variable
    real      Z, R                      ! loop control variable

    Z=dHeight                           ! initial height
    do while (Z .le. Height)
        R=Radius*((Height-Z)/Height)
        call psc3(R, R, 1., Error, M1)! scale 3
        call ptr3(0., 0., Z, Error, M2)       ! translate 3
        call pcom3(M1, M2, Error, M)    ! compose matrix 3
        call pslmt3(M, PCREPL)          ! set local transformation 3
        call pexst(CircleID)            ! execute structure
        Z=Z+dHeight                     ! increment the height
    end do
    return
    end
!***********************************************************************
    subroutine Sphere(Radius, dPhi)
    real      Radius                    ! radius of sphere
    real      dPhi                      ! angular distance between latitudes
    include 'phigs.f2.h'                ! get the PHIGS constants

    integer   SceneID, PlaneID, CircleID, CylinderID, ConeID
    integer   SphereID, SquareID, CubeID
    common    /StructureIDs/ SceneID, PlaneID, CircleID, CylinderID
```

```
      common    /StructureIDs/ ConeID, SphereID, SquareID, CubeID

      real      M1(4,4), M2(4,4), M(4,4)! transformation matrices
      integer   Error                   ! error-return variable
      real      Phi, R, Z               ! loop control variables

      real      rad, deg                        ! type the statement function
      rad(deg)= ((deg)*3.14159265358979/180.)   ! convert degrees to radians

      Phi=dPhi                          ! initial radius
      do while (Phi .lt. 180.)
          R=Radius*sin(rad(Phi))
          call psc3(R, R, 1., Error, M1)! scale 3
          Z=Radius*cos(rad(Phi))
          call ptr3(0., 0., Z, Error, M2)       ! translate 3
          call pcom3(M1, M2, Error, M)  ! compose matrix 3
          call pslmt3(M, PCREPL)        ! set local transformation 3
          call pexst(CircleID)          ! execute structure
          Phi=Phi+dPhi                  ! increment Phi
      end do
      return
      end
!*****************************************************************************
      subroutine Cube(Distance, dDistance, Height, dHeight)
      real      Distance                ! center-to-corner distance
      real      dDistance               ! distance between vertices in top/btm
      real      Height                  ! total height of cube
      real      dHeight                 ! distance between layers in cube
      include 'phigs.f2.h'              ! get the PHIGS constants

      integer   SceneID, PlaneID, CircleID, CylinderID, ConeID
      integer   SphereID, SquareID, CubeID
      common    /StructureIDs/ SceneID, PlaneID, CircleID, CylinderID
      common    /StructureIDs/ ConeID, SphereID, SquareID, CubeID

      real      M1(4,4), M2(4,4), M(4,4)! transformation matrices
      integer   Error                   ! error-return variable
      real      Dist, Z                 ! loop control variables

      Dist=dDistance                            ! initial radius
      do while (Dist .le. Distance)
          !--- do bottom first -------------------------------------------
          call psc3(Dist, Dist, 1., Error, M1)! scale 3
```

```
        call pslmt3(M1, PCREPL)        ! set local transformation 3
        call pexst(SquareID)           ! execute structure
        !--- then do top -----------------------------------------------------
        call ptr3(0., 0., Height, Error, M2)          ! translate 3
        call pcom3(M1, M2, Error, M)   ! compose matrix 3
        call pslmt3(M, PCREPL)         ! set local transformation 3
        call pexst(SquareID)           ! execute structure
        Dist=Dist+dDistance            ! increment the "radius"
    end do
    Z=0.
    call psc3(Distance, Distance, 1., Error, M1)      ! scale 3
    do while (Z .le. Height)
        call ptr3(0., 0., Z, Error, M2)               ! translate 3
        call pcom3(M1, M2, Error, M)   ! compose matrix 3
        call pslmt3(M, PCREPL)         ! set local transformation 3
        call pexst(SquareID)           ! execute structure
        Z=Z+dHeight                    ! increment the height
    end do
    return
    end
!*************************************************************************
    subroutine DefineCameraView(WorkstnID, ViewNo, PRPx, PRPy, PRPz,
   +  VRPx, VRPy, VRPz, FieldOfView, ProjType, VUPx, VUPy, VUPz)
    integer   WorkstnID, ViewNo        ! workstation ID, view to be defined
    real      PRPx, PRPy, PRPz         ! proj. ref. point (point looked from)
    real      VRPx, VRPy, VRPz         ! View ref. point (point looked at)
    real      FieldOfView              ! "zoomness" in degrees
    integer   ProjType                 ! parallel or perspective?
    real      VUPx, VUPy, VUPz         ! view up vector
    include 'phigs.f2.h'               ! get the PHIGS constants

    real      VPNx, VPNy, VPNz         ! view plane normal
    real      FPD, BPD                 ! front/back place distance
    real      Mapping(4,4)             ! view mapping matrix
    real      Orientation(4,4)         ! view orientation matrix
    real      Distance                 ! distance from PRP to VRP
    real      Wndw, Window(4)          ! window limits
    real      Viewport(6)              ! viewport limits
    real      ClipLimits(6)            ! clip limits
    data      Viewport   /0.0, 1.0, 0.0, 1.0, 0.0, 1.0/
    data      ClipLimits /0.0, 1.0, 0.0, 1.0, 0.0, 1.0/
    integer   Error                    ! error-return variable
```

```
      real      rad, deg                           ! type the statement function
      rad(deg)= ((deg)*3.14159265358979/180.)      ! convert degrees to radians

      VPNx=PRPx-VRPx                         ! \  View plane normal determined by
      VPNy=PRPy-VRPy                         !  > projection reference point and
      VPNz=PRPz-VRPz                         ! /  view reference point.
      call pevom3(VRPx, VRPy, VRPz, VPNx, VPNy, VPNz, VUPx, VUPy, VUPz,
     +  Error, Orientation)
      if (Error .ne. 0) then
          print *, "Error", Error, " in pevom3; terminating."
          stop
      end if
      Distance=sqrt((PRPx-VRPx)**2+(PRPy-VRPy)**2+(PRPz-VRPz)**2)
      Wndw=Distance*tan(rad(FieldOfView)/2)     ! FOV determines window size
      Window(1)=-Wndw                        ! \
      Window(2)=Wndw                         !  \ This assumes a square window
      Window(3)=-Wndw                        !  / (aspect ratio = 1.00).
      Window(4)=Wndw                         ! /
      FPD=Distance-0.001                     ! right in front of eyepoint
      BPD=-1E3*Distance                      ! virtually infinite
      call pevmm3(Window, Viewport, ProjType, 0., 0., Distance,
     +  0., BPD, FPD, Error, Mapping)
      if (Error .ne. 0) then
          print *, "Error", Error, " in pevmm3; terminating."
          stop
      end if
      call psvwr3(WorkstnID, ViewNo, Orientation, Mapping, ClipLimits,
     +  PCLIP, PCLIP, PCLIP)
      return
      end
!*****************************************************************************
      subroutine PolarToRectangular(R, Theta, Phi, X, Y, Z)
      real      R, Theta, Phi                ! input: 3D polar (spherical) coords.
      real      X, Y, Z                      ! output: 3D rect. (Cartesian) coords.

      X=R*sin(Phi)*cos(Theta)
      Y=R*sin(Phi)*sin(Theta)
      Z=R*cos(Phi)
      return
      end
!*****************************************************************************
      subroutine AppendTransformation(MainTransform, Appendix)
      real      MainTransform(4,4)          ! the transformation to be appended to
```

```
real      Appendix(4,4)            ! the transformation to be appended

real      Temp(4,4)                ! temporary matrix holder
integer   Error                    ! error indicator
integer   I, J                     ! loop control variables

call pcom3(Appendix, MainTransform, Error, Temp)
do I=1,4                                     ! \
    do J=1,4                                 !  \  Copy the result matrix
        MainTransform(I,J)=Temp(I,J)         !   > back into the first
    end do                                   !  /  argument matrix.
end do                                       ! /
return
end
```

Four Views Program

This section lists the C and FORTRAN binding versions of the four–views program described in Chapter 7, *Viewing and Workstation Transformations*.

C Binding Version of Four-Views Program

```
#include <phigs.h>                        /* get PHIGS definitions for C */
#include <stdio.h>                        /* get standard I/O definitions */

#define CopyMatrix(src,dest)     {int    I, J;                              \
                                  for (I = 0; I < 4; I++)                   \
                                      for (J = 0; J < 4; J++)               \
                                          dest[I][J] = src[I][J];           \
                                 }
#define CheckError(err, rtn)     if (err) {                                 \
                                     fprintf(stderr, "Error %d in %s; %s",  \
                                     err, rtn, "terminating.\n");           \
                                     exit(1);                               \
                                 }

main()                                    /* file "FourViews.c" */
{
    Pint        WorkstnID = 1;            /* workstation identifier */
    Pint        ConnID;                   /* connection identifier */
    Pint        WorkstnType = POIDDX;     /* out/in, direct, dbl. bfr., Xwindow */
```

```
Pint        Scene = 1, Cube = 2;     /* structure IDs */
Pint        Error;                   /* error indicator */
Pmatrix3    ViewMapMatrix;           /* from "peval_view_map_matrix3" */
Pmatrix3    ViewOriMatrix;           /* from "peval_view_ori_matrix3" */
/*--- viewing parameters for View 1 -------------------------------------*/
static Pview_map3   ViewMapping1 = {/* sent to "peval_view_map_matrix3" */
  {-1.75, 1.75, -1.75, 1.75},        /* window limits */
  {0.5, 1.0, 0.5, 1.0, 0.0, 1.0},    /* projection viewport limits */
  PTYPE_PERSPECT,                    /* perspective projection */
  {0.0, 0.0, 10.0},                  /* projection reference point */
  0.0, -2.5, 2.5};                   /* view/back/front plane distances */
static Ppoint3      ViewRefPt1 = {0.0, 0.0, 0.0};
static Pvec3        ViewNormVec1 = {0.4, 0.3, 1.0};
static Pvec3        ViewUpVec1 = {0.0, 1.0, 0.0};
static Plimit3      ClipLimits1 = {0.5, 1.0, 0.5, 1.0, 0.0, 1.0};
Pview_rep3          ViewRep1;
/*--- viewing parameters for View 2 -------------------------------------*/
static Pview_map3   ViewMapping2 = {/* sent to "peval_view_map_matrix3" */
  {-1.25, 1.25, -1.25, 1.25},        /* window limits */
  {0.0, 0.5, 0.5, 1.0, 0.0, 1.0},    /* projection viewport limits */
  PTYPE_PARAL,                       /* parallel projection */
  {0.0, 0.0, 10.0},                  /* projection reference point */
  0.0, -2.5, 2.5};                   /* view/back/front plane distances */
static Ppoint3      ViewRefPt2 = {0.0, 0.0, 0.0};
static Pvec3        ViewNormVec2 = {0.0, 0.5, 0.0};
static Pvec3        ViewUpVec2 = {0.0, 0.0, -1.0};
static Plimit3      ClipLimits2 = {0.0, 0.5, 0.5, 1.0, 0.0, 1.0};
Pview_rep3          ViewRep2;
/*--- viewing parameters for View 3 -------------------------------------*/
static Pview_map3   ViewMapping3 = {/* sent to "peval_view_map_matrix3" */
  {-1.25, 1.25, -1.25, 1.25},        /* window limits */
  {0.0, 0.5, 0.0, 0.5, 0.0, 1.0},    /* projection viewport limits */
  PTYPE_PARAL,                       /* parallel projection */
  {0.0, 0.0, 10.0},                  /* projection reference point */
  0.0, -2.5, 2.5};                   /* view/back/front plane distances */
static Ppoint3      ViewRefPt3 = {0.0, 0.0, 0.0};
static Pvec3        ViewNormVec3 = {0.0, 0.0, 0.5};
static Pvec3        ViewUpVec3 = {0.0, 1.0, 0.0};
static Plimit3      ClipLimits3 = {0.0, 0.5, 0.0, 0.5, 0.0, 1.0};
Pview_rep3          ViewRep3;
/*--- viewing parameters for View 4 -------------------------------------*/
static Pview_map3   ViewMapping4 = {/* sent to "peval_view_map_matrix3" */
  {-1.25, 1.25, -1.25, 1.25},        /* window limits */
```

```
  {0.5, 1.0, 0.0, 0.5, 0.0, 1.0},    /* projection viewport limits */
  PTYPE_PARAL,                       /* parallel projection */
  {0.0, 0.0, 10.0},                  /* projection reference point */
  0.0, -2.5, 2.5};                   /* view/back/front plane distances */
static Ppoint3      ViewRefPt4 = {0.0, 0.0, 0.0};
static Pvec3        ViewNormVec4 = {0.8, 0.0, 0.0};
static Pvec3        ViewUpVec4 = {0.0, 1.0, 0.0};
static Plimit3      ClipLimits4 = {0.5, 1.0, 0.0, 0.5, 0.0, 1.0};
Pview_rep3          ViewRep4;

popen_phigs(stderr, 0);              /* errors go to "stderr" */
pescape_u4("/dev/screen/phigs_window", &ConnID);
popen_ws(WorkstnID, ConnID, WorkstnType);
/*--- set up View 1 (upper right) ---------------------------------------*/
peval_view_map_matrix3(&ViewMapping1, &Error, ViewMapMatrix);
CheckError(Error, "peval_view_map_matrix3");
peval_view_ori_matrix3(&ViewRefPt1, &ViewNormVec1, &ViewUpVec1, &Error,
  ViewOriMatrix);                                      /*  +---+---+  */
CheckError(Error, "peval_view_ori_matrix3");           /*  |   | X |  */
CopyMatrix(ViewOriMatrix, ViewRep1.ori_matrix);        /*  +---+---+  */
CopyMatrix(ViewMapMatrix, ViewRep1.map_matrix);        /*  |   |   |  */
ViewRep1.clip_limit = ClipLimits1;                     /*  +---+---+  */
ViewRep1.xy_clip = ViewRep1.back_clip = ViewRep1.front_clip = PIND_CLIP;
pset_view_rep3(WorkstnID, 1, &ViewRep1);
/*--- set up View 2 (upper left) ----------------------------------------*/
peval_view_map_matrix3(&ViewMapping2, &Error, ViewMapMatrix);
CheckError(Error, "peval_view_map_matrix3");
peval_view_ori_matrix3(&ViewRefPt2, &ViewNormVec2, &ViewUpVec2, &Error,
  ViewOriMatrix);                                      /*  +---+---+  */
CheckError(Error, "peval_view_ori_matrix3");           /*  | X |   |  */
CopyMatrix(ViewOriMatrix, ViewRep2.ori_matrix);        /*  +---+---+  */
CopyMatrix(ViewMapMatrix, ViewRep2.map_matrix);        /*  |   |   |  */
ViewRep2.clip_limit = ClipLimits2;                     /*  +---+---+  */
ViewRep2.xy_clip = ViewRep2.back_clip = ViewRep2.front_clip = PIND_CLIP;
pset_view_rep3(WorkstnID, 2, &ViewRep2);
/*--- set up View 3 (lower left) ----------------------------------------*/
peval_view_map_matrix3(&ViewMapping3, &Error, ViewMapMatrix);
CheckError(Error, "peval_view_map_matrix3");
peval_view_ori_matrix3(&ViewRefPt3, &ViewNormVec3, &ViewUpVec3, &Error,
  ViewOriMatrix);                                      /*  +---+---+  */
CheckError(Error, "peval_view_ori_matrix3");           /*  |   |   |  */
CopyMatrix(ViewOriMatrix, ViewRep3.ori_matrix);        /*  +---+---+  */
CopyMatrix(ViewMapMatrix, ViewRep3.map_matrix);        /*  | X |   |  */
```

```
    ViewRep3.clip_limit = ClipLimits3;                      /*  +---+---+  */
    ViewRep3.xy_clip = ViewRep3.back_clip = ViewRep3.front_clip = PIND_CLIP;
    pset_view_rep3(WorkstnID, 3, &ViewRep3);
    /*--- set up View 4 (lower right) ---------------------------------------*/
    peval_view_map_matrix3(&ViewMapping4, &Error, ViewMapMatrix);
    CheckError(Error, "peval_view_map_matrix3");
    peval_view_ori_matrix3(&ViewRefPt4, &ViewNormVec4, &ViewUpVec4, &Error,
      ViewOriMatrix);                                       /*  +---+---+  */
    CheckError(Error, "peval_view_ori_matrix3");            /*  |   |   |  */
    CopyMatrix(ViewOriMatrix, ViewRep4.ori_matrix);         /*  +---+---+  */
    CopyMatrix(ViewMapMatrix, ViewRep4.map_matrix);         /*  |   | X |  */
    ViewRep4.clip_limit = ClipLimits4;                      /*  +---+---+  */
    ViewRep4.xy_clip = ViewRep4.back_clip = ViewRep4.front_clip = PIND_CLIP;
    pset_view_rep3(WorkstnID, 4, &ViewRep4);
    /*--- draw all four views -----------------------------------------------*/
    BuildCube(Cube);
    popen_struct(Scene);
    pset_view_ind(1);   pexec_struct(Cube);
    pset_view_ind(2);   pexec_struct(Cube);
    pset_view_ind(3);   pexec_struct(Cube);
    pset_view_ind(4);   pexec_struct(Cube);
    pclose_struct();
    ppost_struct(WorkstnID, Scene, 1.0);
    pupd_ws(WorkstnID, PFLAG_PERFORM);
    pclose_ws(WorkstnID);
    pclose_phigs();
}
/***************************************************************************/
BuildCube(StructID)
int      StructID;                       /* structure ID for cube structure */
{
    static Ppoint3 TopPoints[5]     = {-1,1,-1, -1,1,1, 0,1,1, 1,1,0, 1,1,-1};
    static Ppoint_list3 Top         = {5, TopPoints};
    static Ppoint3 BottomPoints[4]  = {-1,-1,1, -1,-1,-1, 1,-1,-1, 1,-1,1};
    static Ppoint_list3 Bottom      = {4, BottomPoints};
    static Ppoint3 RightPoints[5]   = {1,-1,-1, 1,1,-1, 1,1,0, 1,0,1, 1,-1,1};
    static Ppoint_list3 Right       = {5, RightPoints};
    static Ppoint3 LeftPoints[4]    = {-1,-1,1, -1,1,1, -1,1,-1, -1,-1,-1};
    static Ppoint_list3 Left        = {4, LeftPoints};
    static Ppoint3 FrontPoints[5]   = {1,-1,1, 1,0,1, 0,1,1, -1,1,1, -1,-1,1};
    static Ppoint_list3 Front       = {5, FrontPoints};
    static Ppoint3 BackPoints[4]    = {-1,-1,-1, -1,1,-1, 1,1,-1, 1,-1,-1};
    static Ppoint_list3 Back        = {4, BackPoints};
```

```
    static Ppoint3 CornerPoints[3] = {1,0,1, 1,1,0, 0,1,1};
    static Ppoint_list3 Corner     = {3, CornerPoints};
    static Ppoint_list3 CubePoints[7];
    Ppoint_list_list3   Cube;
    /*--- text locations and orientations ----------------------------------*/
    static Ppoint3      TopTextPos = {-0.75, 1.0, 0.0};
    static Pvec3        TopTextOri[2] = {1,0,0,  0,0,-1};
    static Ppoint3      RightTextPos = {1.0, -0.75, 0.75};
    static Pvec3        RightTextOri[2] = {0,0,-1,  0,1,0};
    static Ppoint3      FrontTextPos = {-0.75, -0.75, 1.0};
    static Pvec3        FrontTextOri[2] = {1,0,0,  0,1,0};
    int                 I;              /* loop control variable */

    CubePoints[0] = Top;        CubePoints[1] = Bottom;
    CubePoints[2] = Right;      CubePoints[3] = Left;
    CubePoints[4] = Front;      CubePoints[5] = Back;
    CubePoints[6] = Corner;
    popen_struct(StructID);
    psfcm(1);                           /* set face-culling: back-facing */
    Cube.num_point_lists = 1;
    for (I = 0; I < 7; I++) {
        Cube.point_lists = &(CubePoints[I]);
        pfill_area_set3(&Cube);
    }
    pset_char_ht(0.4);
    pset_char_expan(0.7);
    ptext3(&TopTextPos, TopTextOri, "Top");
    ptext3(&RightTextPos, RightTextOri, "Right");
    ptext3(&FrontTextPos, FrontTextOri, "Front");
    pclose_struct();
}
```

FORTRAN Binding Version of Four-Views Program

```
      program four_views
C     description: This program draws an object with pfas3 primitives
C                  and displays the object in four views.
%include '/sys/ins/phigs.ins.ftn'

C Variables
      integer*4   BufferLength               { currently unused
      integer*4   WorkID                     { workstation ID
      integer*4   ConnectID                  { communication channel ID
      integer*4   ERRIND                     { error indicator
      integer*4   status
      real*4      Color(3)                   { for color table values
      parameter(BufferLength=0, WorkID=1)
      integer*4   Scene, Cube                { structure IDs
      parameter(Scene=1, Cube=2)
C Viewing variables
      real        vwrx, vwry, vwrz
      real        vpnx, vpny, vpnz
      real        vupx, vupy, vupz
      real        wdw_lim(4)
      real        vp_lim(6)
      real        clip_lim(6)
      real        pjrx, pjry, pjrz  { projection reference point
      real        vpld              { view plane distance
      real        bpld              { back plane distance
      real        fpld              { front plane distance
C View orientation and view mapping matrices
      real*4 Orientation(4,4), Mapping(4,4)
      real*4 LineX(5), LineY(5), LineZ(5)
C Input variables
      integer*4 ChoiceStatus, ChoiceNum { choice status and value

C Open PHIGS and workstation
      call popph(1, BufferLength)              { open PHIGS
      ConnectID=1
      call popwk(WorkID, ConnectID, POIDSX)     { open workstation
      call psdus(WorkID,PWAITD,PNIVE)          { set display update state
C Define views
      pjrx  = 0.0          { projection reference point
      pjry  = 0.0          { in viewing reference coordinates
      pjrz  = 10.0
```

```
      vpld  =  0.0            { view plane distance
      bpld  = -2.5            { back plane distance
      fpld  =  2.5            { front plane distance

C *** Define Workstation View Table Entry '1' ***

      vwrx = 0.0             { view reference point
      vwry = 0.0
      vwrz = 0.0
      vpnx = 0.4             { view plane normal
      vpny = 0.3
      vpnz = 1.0
      vupx = 0.0             { view up vector
      vupy = 1.0
      vupz = 0.0
      wdw_lim(1)  = -1.75    { window limits
      wdw_lim(2)  =  1.75
      wdw_lim(3)  = -1.75
      wdw_lim(4)  =  1.75
                              { relative position of view 1
      vp_lim(1)   =  0.5     {     ______________
      vp_lim(2)   =  1.0     {    |       |      |
      vp_lim(3)   =  0.5     {    |       |  X   |
      vp_lim(4)   =  1.0     {    |       |      |
      vp_lim(5)   =  0.0     {    |--------------|
      vp_lim(6)   =  1.0     {    |       |      |
C                             {    |       |      |
      clip_lim(1) =  0.5     {    |_______|______|
      clip_lim(2) =  1.0
      clip_lim(3) =  0.5
      clip_lim(4) =  1.0
      clip_lim(5) =  0.0
      clip_lim(6) =  1.0
      call pevom3(vwrx, vwry, vwrz, vpnx, vpny, vpnz,
     +            vupx, vupy, vupz, ERRIND, Orientation)
      call pevmm3(wdw_lim, vp_lim, PPARL, pjrx, pjry, pjrz,
     +            vpld, bpld, fpld, ERRIND, Mapping)
      call psvwr3(WorkID, 1, Orientation, Mapping, clip_lim,
     +            PCLIP, PCLIP, PCLIP)

C *** Define Workstation View Table Entry '2' ***

      vwrx = 0.0             { view reference point
```

```
      vwry = 0.0
      vwrz = 0.0
      vpnx = 0.0               { view plane normal
      vpny = 0.5
      vpnz = 0.0
      vupx = 0.0               { view up vector
      vupy = 0.0
      vupz = -1.0
      wdw_lim(1)  = -1.5    { window limits
      wdw_lim(2)  =  1.5
      wdw_lim(3)  = -1.5
      wdw_lim(4)  =  1.5
                             { relative position of view 2
      vp_lim(1)   =  0.0     {      ______________
      vp_lim(2)   =  0.5     {     |      |       |
      vp_lim(3)   =  0.5     {     |  X   |       |
      vp_lim(4)   =  1.0     {     |      |       |
      vp_lim(5)   =  0.0     {     |--------------|
      vp_lim(6)   =  1.0     {     |      |       |
C                            {     |      |       |
      clip_lim(1) =  0.0     {     |______|_______|
      clip_lim(2) =  0.5
      clip_lim(3) =  0.5
      clip_lim(4) =  1.0
      clip_lim(5) =  0.0
      clip_lim(6) =  1.0
      call pevom3(vwrx, vwry, vwrz, vpnx, vpny, vpnz,
     +            vupx, vupy, vupz, ERRIND, Orientation)
      call pevmm3(wdw_lim, vp_lim, PPARL, pjrx, pjry, pjrz,
     +            vpld, bpld, fpld, ERRIND, Mapping)
      call psvwr3(WorkID, 2, Orientation, Mapping, clip_lim,
     +            PCLIP, PCLIP, PCLIP)

C *** Define Workstation View Table Entry '3' ***

      vwrx = 0.0               { view reference point
      vwry = 0.0
      vwrz = 0.0
      vpnx = 0.0               { view plane normal
      vpny = 0.0
      vpnz = 0.5
      vupx = 0.0               { view up vector
      vupy = 1.0
```

```
      vupz = 0.0
      wdw_lim(1)   = -1.5    { window limits
      wdw_lim(2)   =  1.5
      wdw_lim(3)   = -1.5
      wdw_lim(4)   =  1.5
                              { relative position of view 3
      vp_lim(1)    =  0.0     {      _______________
      vp_lim(2)    =  0.5     {     |       |       |
      vp_lim(3)    =  0.0     {     |       |       |
      vp_lim(4)    =  0.5     {     |       |       |
      vp_lim(5)    =  0.0     {     |---------------|
      vp_lim(6)    =  1.0     {     |       |       |
C                             {     |   X   |       |
      clip_lim(1) =  0.0      {     |_______|_______|
      clip_lim(2) =  0.5
      clip_lim(3) =  0.0
      clip_lim(4) =  0.5
      clip_lim(5) =  0.0
      clip_lim(6) =  1.0
      call pevom3(vwrx, vwry, vwrz, vpnx, vpny, vpnz,
     +            vupx, vupy, vupz, ERRIND, Orientation)
      call pevmm3(wdw_lim, vp_lim, PPARL, pjrx, pjry, pjrz,
     +            vpld, bpld, fpld, ERRIND, Mapping)
      call psvwr3(WorkID, 3, Orientation, Mapping, clip_lim,
     +            PCLIP, PCLIP, PCLIP)


C *** Define Workstation View Table Entry '4' ***

      vwrx = 0.0              { view reference point
      vwry = 0.0
      vwrz = 0.0
      vpnx = 0.8              { view plane normal
      vpny = 0.0
      vpnz = 0.0
      vupx = 0.0              { view up vector
      vupy = 1.0
      vupz = 0.0
      wdw_lim(1)   = -1.5    { window limits
      wdw_lim(2)   =  1.5
      wdw_lim(3)   = -1.5
      wdw_lim(4)   =  1.5
                              { relative position of view 4
```

```
      vp_lim(1)    =  0.5      {       ______________
      vp_lim(2)    =  1.0      {     |       |       |
      vp_lim(3)    =  0.0      {     |       |       |
      vp_lim(4)    =  0.5      {     |       |       |
      vp_lim(5)    =  0.0      {     |---------------|
      vp_lim(6)    =  1.0      {     |       |       |
C                              {     |       |   X   |
      clip_lim(1) =  0.5       {     |_______|_______|
      clip_lim(2) =  1.0
      clip_lim(3) =  0.0
      clip_lim(4) =  0.5
      clip_lim(5) =  0.0
      clip_lim(6) =  1.0
      call pevom3(vwrx, vwry, vwrz, vpnx, vpny, vpnz,
     +            vupx, vupy, vupz, ERRIND, Orientation)
      call pevmm3(wdw_lim, vp_lim, PPARL, pjrx, pjry, pjrz,
     +            vpld, bpld, fpld, ERRIND, Mapping)
      call psvwr3(WorkID, 4, Orientation, Mapping, clip_lim,
     +            PCLIP, PCLIP, PCLIP)

C ***************************************************************
      call BuildCube(Cube)

      call popst(Scene)        { open structure
      LineX(1)=0.0             { Since PHIGS does not have facilities
      LineY(1)=1.0             { for defining view borders,
      LineX(2)=0.0             { this code draws 2D lines in
      LineY(2)=0.0             { view 0 to simulate view borders.
      LineX(3)=1.0             { These lines work for this example
      LineY(3)=0.0             { because we have split up the available
      LineX(4)=1.0             { NPC area into four equal viewports.
      LineY(4)=1.0
      LineX(5)=0.0
      LineY(5)=1.0
      call ppl(5, LineX, LineY)
      LineX(1)=0.0
      LineY(1)=0.5
      LineX(2)=1.0
      LineY(2)=0.5
      call ppl(2, LineX, LineY)
      LineX(1)=0.5
      LineY(1)=1.0
      LineX(2)=0.5
```

```
      LineY(2)=0.0
      call ppl(2, LineX, LineY)
      call psvwi(1)                     { set view index
      call pexst(Cube)                  { execute structure
      call psvwi(2)                     { set view index
      call pexst(Cube)                  { execute structure
      call psvwi(3)                     { set view index
      call pexst(Cube)                  { execute structure
      call psvwi(4)                     { set view index
      call pexst(Cube)                  { execute structure
      call pclst                        { close structure

      call ppost(WorkID, Scene, 1.0)    { post structure Scene
      call puwk(WorkID, PPERFO)         { update workstation
C Wait for user
      call pschm(WorkID, 2, PREQU, PNECHO)          { set choice mode
      call prqch(WorkID, 2, ChoiceStatus, ChoiceNum) { request choice
C     call phg_$print_workstation(WorkID, 'print.ps', 8,0,
C    +     8.5, 11.0,errind, status)
      call pupast(WorkID)               { unpost all structures
      call pclwk(WorkID)                { close workstation
      call pclph                        { close PHIGS
      end

C***************************************************
      subroutine BuildCube(Cube)
      integer*4 Cube
%include '/sys/ins/phigs.ins.ftn'
      integer*4 npl      { number of fill areas in a fill area set
      integer*4 ixa(2)   { index array
                         { For example, if there are two fill areas
                         { in the fill area set, each with 4 points,
                         { then ixa(1)=4 and ixa(2)=8.
                         { In this example, there is only one fill area in each
                         { fill area set, so we only use ixa(1).
      real*4 px, py, pz                 { text position
      real*4 tdx(2), tdy(2), tdz(2)     { text direction vectors
C x, y, and z components of point lists for object.
C Points are in a counterclockwise order so that front
C faces are pointing out from origin.
      real Topx(5)
      data Topx /-1.0, -1.0, 0.0, 1.0, 1.0/
      real Topy(5)
```

```
data Topy /1.0, 1.0, 1.0, 1.0, 1.0/
real Topz(5)
data Topz /-1.0, 1.0, 1.0, 0.0, -1.0/

real Bottomx(4)
data Bottomx /-1.0, -1.0, 1.0, 1.0/
real Bottomy(4)
data Bottomy /-1.0, -1.0, -1.0, -1.0/
real Bottomz(4)
data Bottomz /1.0, -1.0, -1.0, 1.0/

real Rightx(5)
data Rightx /1.0, 1.0, 1.0, 1.0, 1.0/
real Righty(5)
data Righty /-1.0, 1.0, 1.0, 0.0, -1.0/
real Rightz(5)
data Rightz /-1.0, -1.0, 0.0, 1.0, 1.0/

real Leftx(4)
data Leftx /-1.0, -1.0, -1.0, -1.0/
real Lefty(4)
data Lefty /-1.0, 1.0, 1.0, -1.0/
real Leftz(4)
data Leftz /1.0, 1.0, -1.0, -1.0/

real Frontx(5)
data Frontx /1.0, 1.0, 0.0, -1.0, -1.0/
real Fronty(5)
data Fronty /-1.0, 0.0, 1.0, 1.0, -1.0/
real Frontz(5)
data Frontz /1.0, 1.0, 1.0, 1.0, 1.0/

real Backx(4)
data Backx /-1.0, -1.0, 1.0, 1.0/
real Backy(4)
data Backy /-1.0, 1.0, 1.0, -1.0/
real Backz(4)
data Backz /-1.0, -1.0, -1.0, -1.0/

real Cornerx(3)
data Cornerx /1.0, 1.0, 0.0/
real Cornery(3)
data Cornery /0.0, 1.0, 1.0/
```

```
real Cornerz(3)
data Cornerz /1.0, 0.0, 1.0/

call popst(Cube)                  { open structure
call psfcm(PBKFC)                 { cull back-facing polygons
call pschh(0.4)                   { set character height
npl=1                             { one fill area in each fill area set
ixa(1)=5                          { 5 points in the fill area
call pfas3(npl, ixa, Topx, Topy, Topz)  { fill area set 3
px=-0.75            { text position
py=1.0              { origin of local text coordinate system
pz=0.0
tdx(1)=1.0          { text direction vectors
tdy(1)=0.0
tdz(1)=0.0
tdx(2)=0.0
tdy(2)=0.0
tdz(2)=-1.0
call ptx3(px, py, pz, tdx, tdy, tdz, 'Top')     { 3D text

ixa(1)=4            { 4 points in the fill area
call pfas3(npl, ixa, Bottomx, Bottomy, Bottomz) { fill area set 3

ixa(1)=5
call pfas3(npl, ixa, Rightx, Righty, Rightz)
px=1.0              { text position
py=-0.75
pz=0.75
tdx(1)=0.0          { text direction vectors
tdy(1)=0.0
tdz(1)=-1.0
tdx(2)=0.0
tdy(2)=1.0
tdz(2)=0.0
call ptx3(px, py, pz, tdx, tdy, tdz, 'Right')  { 3D text

ixa(1)=4
call pfas3(npl, ixa, Leftx, Lefty, Leftz)

ixa(1)=5            { 5 points in the fill area
call pfas3(npl, ixa, Frontx, Fronty, Frontz)   { fill area set 3
px=-0.75            { text position
py=-0.75
```

```
      pz=1.0
      tdx(1)=1.0          { text direction vectors
      tdy(1)=0.0
      tdz(1)=0.0
      tdx(2)=0.0
      tdy(2)=1.0
      tdz(2)=0.0
      call ptx3(px, py, pz, tdx, tdy, tdz, 'Front')  { 3D text

      ixa(1)=4            { 4 points in the fill area
      call pfas3(npl, ixa, Backx, Backy, Backz)      { fill area set 3

      ixa(1)=3            { 3 points in the fill area
      call pfas3(npl, ixa, Cornerx, Cornery, Cornerz) { fill area set 3
      call pclst          { close structure
      return
      end
C end BuildCube
```

Text Programs

This section lists the FORTRAN versions of the text programs in Chapter 11, *Using Text*.

Character Size

```
      include 'phigs.f1.h'               ! get the PHIGS aliases
      program CharSize                   ! file "CharSize.f"
      include 'phigs.f2.h'               ! get the PHIGS constants

      integer*4  WorkstnID               ! workstation identifier
      parameter (WorkstnID=1)            ! value chosen by the user
      integer*4  ConnID                  ! connection identifier
      integer*4  WorkstnType             ! workstation type
      parameter (WorkstnType=POIDDX)     ! implementation-dependent
      real  Height, Width                ! height/width holders
      real  X                            ! x position holder
      character*20 String                ! string holder
      integer*4  I                       ! loop control variable
      integer*4 fdopen                   ! to get file descriptor

      call popph(fdopen(fnum(7), 'w'//char(0)), 0)     ! open PHIGS
```

```
call pue004('/dev/screen/phigs_window', ConnID) ! get connection ID
call popwk(WorkstnID, ConnID, WorkstnType)      ! open workstation
call popst(1)                        ! open display list structure
! - - show character height  - - - - - - - - - - - - - -+- - -
Height=0.                            ! initial character height
String='bigger and bigger'    ! initialize string
X=0.                          ! X-position holder
do I=1, 17                    ! loop for "bigger and bigger"
    Height=Height+.008        ! increment height value
    call pschh(Height)        ! set character height
    X=X+Height*0.7            ! increment x position
    call ptx(X, .7, String(I:I))! define a character
end do                        ! end of loop
! - - show character width  - - - - - - - - - - - - - -+- - -
Width=.05                     ! initial character height
String='wider and wider'      ! initialize string
X=0.                          ! X-position holder
do I=1, 15                    ! loop for "wider and wider"
    Width=Width+.06           ! increment width value
    call pschxp(Width)        ! set character width
    X=X+Width*.1              ! increment X position
    call ptx(X, .3, String(I:I))   ! print a character
end do                        ! end of loop
call pclst                    ! close display list structure
call ppost(WorkstnID, 1, 1.)  ! send picture to display
call puwk(WorkstnID, PPERFO)  ! update the workstation
call pclwk(WorkstnID)         ! close workstation
call pclph                    ! close PHIGS
stop                          ! stop processing
end                           ! end of program
```

Rotate

```
include 'phigs.f1.h'             ! get the PHIGS aliases
program Rotate                   ! file "Rotate.f"
include 'phigs.f2.h'             ! get the PHIGS constants

integer*4  WorkstnID             ! workstation identifier
parameter (WorkstnID=1)          ! value chosen by the user
integer*4  ConnID                ! connection identifier
integer*4  WorkstnType           ! workstation type
parameter (WorkstnType=POIDDX)   ! implementation-dependent
integer*4  Angle                 ! current rotation angle
```

```
character*20 String             ! string holder
integer*4 fdopen                ! to get file descriptor
real rad, deg                   ! type the statement function
rad(deg)=  ((deg)*3.14159265358979/180.) ! convert degrees to radians

call popph(fdopen(fnum(7), 'w'//char(0)), 0)  ! open PHIGS
call pue004('/dev/screen/phigs_window', ConnID)  ! get connection ID
call popwk(WorkstnID, ConnID, WorkstnType)! open workstation
call popst(1)                   ! open display list structure
call pschh(0.035)               ! set character size
call pstxal(PALEFT, PAHALF)     ! set text alignment
do Angle=0,345,15               ! every 15 degrees
   write(unit=String, fmt='("---Angle=",i3)') Angle
   call pschup(cos(rad(real(angle))),sin(rad(real(Angle))))
   call ptx(.5, .5, String)
end do
call pclst                      ! close display list structure
call ppost(WorkstnID, 1, 1.)    ! send picture to display
call puwk(WorkstnID, PPERFO)    ! update the workstation
call pclwk(WorkstnID)           ! close workstation
call pclph                      ! close PHIGS
stop                            ! stop processing
end                             ! end of program
```

Alignment

```
include 'phigs.f1.h'          ! get the PHIGS aliases
program Alignment             ! file "Alignment.f"
include 'phigs.f2.h'          ! get the PHIGS constants

integer*4  WorkstnID          ! workstation identifier
parameter (WorkstnID=1)       ! value chosen by the user
integer*4  ConnID             ! connection identifier
integer*4  WorkstnType        ! workstation type
parameter (WorkstnType=POIDDX)  ! implementation-dependent
real H, V                     ! temporary time savers
integer*4  Halign, Valign     ! loop control variables
integer*4 fdopen              ! to get file descriptor

call popph(fdopen(fnum(7), 'w'//char(0)), 0)      ! open PHIGS
call pue004('/dev/screen/phigs_window', ConnID)  ! get connection ID
call popwk(WorkstnID, ConnID, WorkstnType)        ! open workstation
```

```
call popst(1)                   ! open display list structure
!-- do top labels -----------------------+---
call pschh(0.015)               ! set character height
call pstxal(PACENT, PACAP)      ! set text alignment
call ptx(.1, 1., "PATOP")       ! \
call ptx(.3, 1., "PACAP")       !  \  Do labels for vertical
call ptx(.5, 1., "PAHALF")      !   L alignment along the top
call ptx(.7, 1., "PABASE")      !  /  of the plot (more room).
call ptx(.9, 1., "PABOTT")      ! /
!-- do left labels ----------------------+---
call pstxal(PALEFT, PAHALF)     ! set text alignment
call ptx(0., .25, "PALEFT")     ! \  Do labels for horizontal
call ptx(0., .55, "PACENT")     !  L alignment along the left
call ptx(0., .85, "PARITE")     ! /  edge of the plot.
!-- do letters in the middle -----------------+---
call pschh(.03)                 ! set character height
call pschxp(.8)                 ! set char. expansion factor
do Valign=PATOP,PABOTT          ! for each vert. alignment...
Halign=PALEFT, PARITE           ! for each horiz. alignment...
 V=Valign*.2-.1                 ! calculate x value
 H=Halign*.3-.1                 ! calculate y value
 call DoLine(V+.01, H+.01, V-.01, H-.01)! line from NE to SW
 call DoLine(V+.01, H-.01, V-.01, H+.01)! line from SE to NW
        call pstxal(Halign, Valign)     ! set text alignment
        call ptx(V, H, "Test")          ! plot the text
    end do
end do
call pclst                      ! close display list structure
call ppost(WorkstnID, 1, 1.)    ! send picture to display
call puwk(WorkstnID, PPERFO)    ! update the workstation
call pclwk(WorkstnID)           ! close workstation
call pclph                      ! close PHIGS
stop                            ! stop processing
end                             ! end of program
!***********************************************************+*****
subroutine DoLine(X1, Y1, X2, Y2)
real X1, Y1, X2, Y2             ! endpoints of line
real X(2), Y(2)                 ! arrays for polyline

X(1)=X1                         ! \
Y(1)=Y1                         !  \  Put simple values
X(2)=X2                         !  /  into arrays.
Y(2)=Y2                         ! /
```

```
call ppl(2, X, Y)              ! polyline
return                         ! Return to calling context
end                            ! of subroutine.
```

Text Path

```
include 'phigs.f1.h'           ! get the PHIGS aliases
program TextPath               ! file "TextPath.f"
include 'phigs.f2.h'           ! get the PHIGS constants

integer*4  WorkstnID           ! workstation identifier
parameter (WorkstnID=1)        ! value chosen by the user
integer*4  ConnID              ! connection identifier
integer*4  WorkstnType         ! workstation type
parameter (WorkstnType=POIDDX)   ! implementation-dependent
integer*4 fdopen               ! to get file descriptor

call popph(fdopen(fnum(7), 'w'//char(0)), 0)     ! open PHIGS
call pue004('/dev/screen/phigs_window', ConnID) ! get connection ID
call popwk(WorkstnID, ConnID, WorkstnType)      ! open workstation
call popst(1)                  ! open display list structure
call pschh(.06)                ! set character height
call pstxp(PRIGHT)             ! set text path
call ptx(.5, .7, " Right")     ! write text with current path
call pstxp(PLEFT)              ! set text path
call ptx(.5, .7, " Left")      ! write text with current path
call pstxp(PUP)                ! set text path
call ptx(.5, .7, " Up")        ! write text with current path
call pstxp(PDOWN)              ! set text path
call ptx(.5, .7, " Down")      ! write text with current path
call pclst                     ! close display list structure
call ppost(WorkstnID, 1, 1.)   ! send picture to display
call puwk(WorkstnID, PPERFO)   ! update the workstation
call pclwk(WorkstnID)          ! close workstation
call pclph                     ! close PHIGS
stop                           ! stop processing
end                            ! end of program
```

Character Spacing

```
include 'phigs.f1.h'           ! get the PHIGS aliases
program CharSpace              ! file "CharSpace.f"
include 'phigs.f2.h'           ! get the PHIGS constants
```

```
integer*4  WorkstnID            ! workstation identifier
parameter (WorkstnID=1)         ! value chosen by the user
integer*4  ConnID               ! connection identifier
integer*4  WorkstnType          ! workstation type
parameter (WorkstnType=POIDDX)    ! implementation-dependent
character*20 String             ! string holder
integer*4  I                    ! loop control variable
integer*4 fdopen                ! to get file descriptor

call popph(fdopen(fnum(7), 'w'//char(0)), 0)     ! open PHIGS
call pue004('/dev/screen/phigs_window', ConnID) ! get connection ID
call popwk(WorkstnID, ConnID, WorkstnType)      ! open workstation
call popst(1)                   ! open display list structure
call pschh(.06)                 ! set character height
call pschxp(.45)                ! set char. expansion factor
do I=-1,4
    call pschsp(I*.25)          ! set character spacing
    write(unit=String, fmt='("Spacing: ",f4.2)') I*.25
    call ptx(0., (6-I)*.1, String) ! label the text
end do
call pclst                      ! close display list structure
call ppost(WorkstnID, 1, 1.)    ! send picture to display
call puwk(WorkstnID, PPERFO)    ! update the workstation
call pclwk(WorkstnID)           ! close workstation
call pclph                      ! close PHIGS
stop                            ! stop processing
end                             ! end of program
```

Appendix D
C Binding Data Types

This appendix lists in alphabetical order the data types for the basic PHIGS C binding. PHIGS PLUS data types are not included since the PHIGS PLUS C binding is not finalized as of this writing. See the section entitled "Language Bindings, Fragments, and Pseudo-code" in the *Preface*.

A

Par_file

```
typedef struct {
  Pint                 id;
  char              *name;
} Par_file;
```

Par_file_list

```
typedef struct {
  Pint        num_ar_files;
  Par_file       *ar_files;
} Par_file_list;
```

Par_st

```
typedef enum {
  PST_ARCL,
  PST_AROP
} Par_st;
```

Pasf

```
typedef enum {
  PASF_BUNDLED,
  PASF_INDIV
} Pasf;
```

Pattrs

```
typedef enum {
  PATTR_LINE,
  PATTR_MARKER,
  PATTR_TEXT,
  PATTR_INT,
  PATTR_EDGE
} Pattrs;
```

C

Pchoice_data

```
typedef struct {
  union Pchoice_pets {
    struct Pchoice_pet_r1 {
      Pint              dummy;
    } pet_r1;
    struct Pchoice_pet_r2 {
      Pint            num_prompts;
      Ppr_switch       *prompts;
    } pet_r2;
    struct Pchoice_pet_r3 {
      Pint            num_strings;
      char              **strings;
    } pet_r3;
    struct Pchoice_pet_r4 {
```

```
      Pint             num_strings;
      char               **strings;
    } pet_r4;
    struct Pchoice_pet_r5 {
      Pint               struct_id;
      Pint            num_pick_ids;
      Pint               *pick_ids;
    } pet_r5;
  } pets;
} Pchoice_data;
```

Pchoice_data3

```
typedef struct {
  union Pchoice3_pets {
    struct Pchoice3_pet_r1 {
      Pint               dummy;
    } pet_r1;
    struct Pchoice3_pet_r2 {
      Pint             num_prompts;
      Ppr_switch          *prompts;
    } pet_r2;
    struct Pchoice3_pet_r3 {
      Pint             num_strings;
      char               **strings;
    } pet_r3;
    struct Pchoice3_pet_r4 {
      Pint             num_strings;
      char               **strings;
    } pet_r4;
    struct Pchoice3_pet_r5 {
      Pint               struct_id;
      Pint            num_pick_ids;
      Pint               *pick_ids;
    } pet_r5;
  } pets;
} Pchoice_data3;
```

Pcieluv

```
typedef struct {
  Pfloat               cieluv_x;
  Pfloat               cieluv_y;
  Pfloat           cieluv_y_lum;
} Pcieluv;
```

Pclip_ind

```
typedef enum {
  PIND_NO_CLIP,
  PIND_CLIP
} Pclip_ind;
```

Pcolr_avail

```
typedef enum {
  PAVAIL_MONOCHR,
  PAVAIL_COLR
} Pcolr_avail;
```

Pcolr_facs

```
typedef struct {
  Pint                  num_colrs;
  Pcolr_avail          colr_avail;
  Pint              num_pred_inds;
  Pcieluv           prim_colrs[3];
} Pcolr_facs;
```

Pcolr_rep

```
typedef union {
  Prgb                  rgb;
  Pcieluv               cieluv;
  Phls                  hls;
  Phsv                  hsv;
  Pdata                 unsupp;
} Pcolr_rep;
```

Pcompose_type

```
typedef enum {
  PTYPE_PRECONCAT,
  PTYPE_POSTCONCAT,
  PTYPE_REPLACE
} Pcompose_type;
```

Pconf_res

```
typedef enum {
  PRES_MAINTAIN,
  PRES_ABANDON,
  PRES_UPD
} Pconf_res;
```

Pctrl_flag

```
typedef enum {
  PFLAG_COND,
  PFLAG_ALWAYS
} Pctrl_flag;
```

D

Pdata

```
typedef struct {
  size_t              size;
  void                *data;
} Pdata;
```

Pdata_rec_list

```
typedef struct {
  Pint           num_data_recs;
  Pint                *lengths;
  char                *data;
} Pdata_rec_list;
```

Pdc_units

```
typedef enum {
  PDC_METRES,
  PDC_OTHER
} Pdc_units;
```

Pdefer_mode

```
typedef enum {
  PDEFER_ASAP,
  PDEFER_BNIG,
  PDEFER_BNIL,
  PDEFER_ASTI,
  PDEFER_WAIT
} Pdefer_mode;
```

Pdisp_space_size

```
typedef struct {
  Pdc_units           dc_units;
  Pfloat_size         size_dc;
  Pint_size         size_raster;
} Pdisp_space_size;
```

Pdisp_space_size3

```
typedef struct {
  Pdc_units           dc_units;
  Pfloat_size3        size_dc;
  Pint_size3        size_raster;
} Pdisp_space_size3;
```

Pdisp_surf_empty

```
typedef enum {
  PSURF_NOT_EMPTY,
  PSURF_EMPTY
} Pdisp_surf_empty;
```

Pdyn_mod

```
typedef enum {
  PDYN_IRG,
  PDYN_IMM,
  PDYN_CBS
} Pdyn_mod;
```

Pdyns_structs

```
typedef struct {
  Pdyn_mod              content;
  Pdyn_mod              post;
  Pdyn_mod              unpost;
  Pdyn_mod              del;
  Pdyn_mod              ref;
} Pdyns_structs;
```

Pdyns_ws_attrs

```
typedef struct {
  Pdyn_mod            line_bundle;
  Pdyn_mod          marker_bundle;
  Pdyn_mod            text_bundle;
  Pdyn_mod             int_bundle;
  Pdyn_mod            edge_bundle;
  Pdyn_mod                pat_rep;
  Pdyn_mod               colr_rep;
  Pdyn_mod               view_rep;
  Pdyn_mod                ws_tran;
  Pdyn_mod           highl_filter;
  Pdyn_mod           invis_filter;
  Pdyn_mod             hlhsr_mode;
} Pdyns_ws_attrs;
```

E

Pecho_switch

```
typedef enum {
  PSWITCH_NO_ECHO,
  PSWITCH_ECHO
} Pecho_switch;
```

Pedge_attrs

```
typedef struct {
  Pasf                  flag_asf;
  Pasf                  type_asf;
```

```
    Pasf                  width_asf;
    Pasf              colr_ind_asf;
    Pint                  ind;
    Pedge_bundle          bundle;
  } Pedge_attrs;
```

Pedge_bundle

```
  typedef struct {
    Pedge_flag            flag;
    Pint                  type;
    Pfloat                width;
    Pint                  colr_ind;
  } Pedge_bundle;
```

Pedge_facs

```
  typedef struct {
    Pint_list             types;
    Pint                num_widths;
    Pfloat                nom_width;
    Pfloat                min_width;
    Pfloat                max_width;
    Pint              num_pred_inds;
  } Pedge_facs;
```

Pedge_flag

```
  typedef enum {
    PEDGE_OFF,
    PEDGE_ON
  } Pedge_flag;
```

Pedit_mode

```
  typedef enum {
    PEDIT_INSERT,
    PEDIT_REPLACE
  } Pedit_mode;
```

Pelem_data

```
  typedef union {
    Pint                  int_data;
    Pfloat              float_data;
    Ppoint_list3       point_list3;
    Ppoint_list         point_list;
    Ppoint_list_list3
                  point_list_list3;
    Ppoint_list_list
                   point_list_list;
    struct Pelem_text3 {
      Ppoint3             pos;
      Pvec3               dir[2];
      char               *char_string;
    } text3;
    struct Pelem_text {
      Ppoint              pos;
      char               *char_string;
    } text;
    struct Pelem_anno_text_rel3 {
      Ppoint3             ref_point;
      Pvec3               offset;
      char               *char_string;
    } anno_text_rel3;
    struct Pelem_anno_text_rel {
      Ppoint              ref_point;
      Pvec                offset;
      char               *char_string;
    } anno_text_rel;
    struct Pelem_cell_array3 {
      Pparal              paral;
      Ppat_rep            colr_array;
    } cell_array3;
    struct Pelem_cell_array {
      Prect               rect;
      Ppat_rep            colr_array;
    } cell_array;
    struct Pelem_gdp3 {
      Pint                id;
      Ppoint_list3        point_list;
      Pgdp_data3          data;
    } gdp3;
    struct Pelem_gdp {
      Pint                id;
      Ppoint_list         point_list;
      Pgdp_data           data;
    } gdp;
    Ptext_prec            text_prec;
    Pvec                char_up_vec;
    Ptext_path            text_path;
    Ptext_align           text_align;
    Pint_style            int_style;
    Pedge_flag            edge_flag;
    Ppoint            pat_ref_point;
    Pfloat_size           pat_size;
    struct Pelem_pat_ref_point_vecs
{
      Ppoint3             ref_point;
      Pvec3               ref_vec[2];
    } pat_ref_point_vecs;
    Pint_list             names;
    struct Pelem_asf {
```

```
    Paspect                id;
    Pasf                   source;
  } asf;
  struct Pelem_local_tran3 {
    Pcompose_type    compose_type;
    Pmatrix3               matrix;
  } local_tran3;
  struct Pelem_local_tran {
    Pcompose_type    compose_type;
    Pmatrix                matrix;
  } local_tran;
  Pmatrix3           global_tran3;
  Pmatrix             global_tran;
  struct Pelem_model_clip3 {
    Pint                   op;
    Phalf_space_list3 half_spaces;
  } model_clip3;
  struct Pelem_model_clip {
    Pint                   op;
    Phalf_space_list  half_spaces;
  } model_clip;
  Pclip_ind              clip_ind;
  Pdata                  appl_data;
  struct Pelem_gse {
    Pint                   id;
    Pgse_data              data;
  } gse;
} Pelem_data;
```

Pelem_ref

```
typedef struct {
  Pint                   struct_id;
  Pint                   elem_pos;
} Pelem_ref;
```

Pelem_ref_list

```
typedef struct {
  Pint               num_elem_refs;
  Pelem_ref             *elem_refs;
} Pelem_ref_list;
```

Pelem_ref_list_list

```
typedef struct {
  Pint           num_elem_ref_lists;
  Pelem_ref_list  *elem_ref_lists;
} Pelem_ref_list_list;
```

Pelem_type_list

```
typedef struct {
  Pint              num_elem_types;
  Pelem_type           *elem_types;
} Pelem_type_list;
```

Perr_mode

```
typedef enum {
  PERR_OFF,
  PERR_ON
} Perr_mode;
```

Pescape_in_data

```
typedef union {
  struct Pescape_in_r1 {
  ... /* registration dependent */
  } escape_in_r1;
  ... /* implemetation defined */
} Pescape_in_data;
```

Pescape_out_data

```
typedef union {
  struct Pescape_out_r1 {
  ... /* registration dependent */
  } escape_out_r1;
  ... /* implemetation defined */
} Pescape_out_data;
```

F

Pfilter

```
typedef struct {
  Pint_list              incl_set;
  Pint_list              excl_set;
} Pfilter;
```

Pfilter_list

```
typedef struct {
  Pint                num_filters;
  Pfilter               *filters;
} Pfilter_list;
```

Pfloat
```
typedef float   Pfloat;
```

Pfloat_list
```
typedef struct {
  Pint                    num_floats;
  Pfloat                   *floats;
} Pfloat_list;
```

Pfloat_size
```
typedef struct {
  Pfloat                   size_x;
  Pfloat                   size_y;
} Pfloat_size;
```

Pfloat_size3
```
typedef struct {
  Pfloat                   size_x;
  Pfloat                   size_y;
  Pfloat                   size_z;
} Pfloat_size3;
```

G

Pgdp_data
```
typedef union {
  struct Pgdp_r1 {
  ... /* registration dependent */
  } gdp_r1;
  Pdata unsupp;/*unsupported GDP*/
  ... /* implemetation defined */
} Pgdp_data;
```

Pgdp_data3
```
typedef union {
  struct Pgdp3_r1 {
  ... /* registration dependent */
  } gdp3_r1;
  Pdata unsupp;/*unsupported GDP*/
  ... /* implemetation defined */
} Pgdp3_data3;
```

Pgse_data
```
typedef union {
  struct Pgse_r1 {
  ... /* registration dependent */
  } gse_r1;
  Pdata unsupp;/*unsupported GSE*/
  ... /* implemetation defined */
} Pgse_data;
```

Pgse_id_dep
```
typedef struct {
  Pint                    id;
  Pws_dep_ind             ind;
} Pgse_id_dep;
```

Pgse_id_dep_list
```
typedef struct {
  Pint                 num_id_facs;
  Pgse_id_dep            *id_facs;
} Pgse_id_dep_list;
```

H

Phalf_space
```
typedef struct {
  Ppoint                  point;
  Pvec                    norm;
} Phalf_space;
```

Phalf_space3
```
typedef struct {
  Ppoint3                 point;
  Pvec3                   norm;
} Phalf_space3;
```

Phalf_space_list
```
typedef struct {
  Pint             num_half_spaces;
  Phalf_space         *half_spaces;
} Phalf_space_list;
```

Phalf_space_list3
```
typedef struct {
  Pint             num_half_spaces;
  Phalf_space3        *half_spaces;
} Phalf_space_list3;
```

Phls
```
typedef struct {
```

```
    Pfloat              hue;
    Pfloat              lightness;
    Pfloat              satur;
  } Phls;
```

Phor_text_align

```
  typedef enum {
    PHOR_NORM,
    PHOR_LEFT,
    PHOR_CTR,
    PHOR_RIGHT
  } Phor_text_align;
```

Phsv

```
  typedef struct {
    Pfloat              hue;
    Pfloat              satur;
    Pfloat              value;
  } Phsv;
```

I

Pin_class

```
  typedef enum {
    PIN_NONE,
    PIN_LOC,
    PIN_STROKE,
    PIN_VAL,
    PIN_CHOICE,
    PIN_PICK,
    PIN_STRING
  } Pin_class;
```

Pin_status

```
  typedef enum {
    PIN_STATUS_NONE,
    PIN_STATUS_OK,
    PIN_STATUS_NO_IN
  } Pin_status;
```

Pinq_type

```
  typedef enum {
    PINQ_SET,
    PINQ_REALIZED
  } Pinq_type;
```

Pint

```
  typedef int              Pint;
```

Pint_attrs

```
  typedef struct {
    Pasf                   style_asf;
    Pasf                   style_ind_asf;
    Pasf                   colr_ind_asf;
    Pint                   ind;
    Pint_bundle            bundle;
  } Pint_attrs;
```

Pint_bundle

```
  typedef struct {
    Pint_style             style;
    Pint                   style_ind;
    Pint                   colr_ind;
  } Pint_bundle;
```

Pint_facs

```
  typedef struct {
    Pint                   num_int_styles;
    Pint_style             int_styles[5];
    Pint_list              hatch_styles;
    Pint                   num_pred_inds;
  } Pint_facs;
```

Pint_list

```
  typedef struct {
    Pint                   num_ints;
    Pint                   *ints;
  } Pint_list;
```

Pint_size

```
  typedef struct {
    Pint                   size_x;
    Pint                   size_y;
  } Pint_size;
```

Pint_size3

```
  typedef struct {
    Pint                   size_x;
    Pint                   size_y;
    Pint                   size_z;
  } Pint_size3;
```

Pint_style

```
typedef enum {
  PSTYLE_HOLLOW,
  PSTYLE_SOLID,
  PSTYLE_PAT,
  PSTYLE_HATCH,
  PSTYLE_EMPTY
} Pint_style;
```

Pitem_data

```
typedef union {
  ... /* metafile records */
  Pdata unsupp;
} Pitem_data;
```

L

Plimit

```
typedef struct {
  Pfloat              x_min;
  Pfloat              x_max;
  Pfloat              y_min;
  Pfloat              y_max;
} Plimit;
```

Plimit3

```
typedef struct {
  Pfloat              x_min;
  Pfloat              x_max;
  Pfloat              y_min;
  Pfloat              y_max;
  Pfloat              z_min;
  Pfloat              z_max;
} Plimit3;
```

Pline_attrs

```
typedef struct {
  Pasf                type_asf;
  Pasf                width_asf;
  Pasf                colr_ind_asf;
  Pint                ind;
  Pline_bundle        bundle;
} Pline_attrs;
```

Pline_bundle

```
typedef struct {
  Pint                type;
  Pfloat              width;
  Pint                colr_ind;
} Pline_bundle;
```

Pline_facs

```
typedef struct {
  Pint_list           types;
  Pint                num_widths;
  Pfloat              nom_width;
  Pfloat              min_width;
  Pfloat              max_width;
  Pint                num_pred_inds;
} Pline_facs;
```

Pline_fill_ctrl_flag

```
typedef enum {
  PFLAG_LINE,
  PFLAG_FILL,
  PFLAG_FILL_SET
} Pline_fill_ctrl_flag;
```

Ploc_data

```
typedef struct {
  union Ploc_pets {
    struct Ploc_pet_r1 {
    .../* implementation dep. */
    } pet_r1;
    struct Ploc_pet_r2 {
    .../* implementation dep. */
    } pet_r2;
    struct Ploc_pet_r3 {
    .../* implementation dep. */
    } pet_r3;
    struct Ploc_pet_r4 {
      Pline_attrs     line_attrs;
    .../* implementation dep. */
    } pet_r4;
    struct Ploc_pet_r5 {
      Pline_fill_ctrl_flag
              line_fill_ctrl_flag;
      union Ploc_attrs {
        Pline_attrs    line_attrs;
        Pint_attrs      int_attrs;
        struct Ploc_fill_set {
          Pint_attrs    int_attrs;
          Pedge_attrs  edge_attrs;
        } fill_set;
      } attrs;
      .../* implementation dep. */
```

```
    } pet_r5;
    struct Ploc_pet_r6 {
    .../* implementation dep. */
    } pet_r6;
    .../* implem. defined PET's */
  } pets;
} Ploc_data;
```

Ploc_data3

```
typedef struct {
  union Ploc3_pets {
    struct Ploc3_pet_r1 {
    .../* implementation dep. */
    } pet_r1;
    struct Ploc3_pet_r2 {
    .../* implementation dep. */
    } pet_r2;
    struct Ploc3_pet_r3 {
    .../* implementation dep. */
    } pet_r3;
    struct Ploc3_pet_r4 {
      Pline_attrs      line_attrs;
    .../* implementation dep. */
    } pet_r4;
    struct Ploc3_pet_r5 {
      Pline_fill_ctrl_flag
              line_fill_ctrl_flag;
      union Ploc3_attrs {
        Pline_attrs    line_attrs;
        Pint_attrs      int_attrs;
        struct Ploc3_fill_set {
          Pint_attrs    int_attrs;
          Pedge_attrs  edge_attrs;
        } fill_set;
      } attrs;
    .../* implementation dep. */
    } pet_r5;
    struct Ploc3_pet_r6 {
    .../* implementation dep. */
    } pet_r6;
    .../* implem. defined PET's */
  } pets;
} Ploc_data3;
```

M

Pmarker_attrs

```
typedef struct {
  Pasf                  type_asf;
  Pasf                  size_asf;
  Pasf              colr_ind_asf;
  Pint                  ind;
  Pmarker_bundle        bundle;
} Pmarker_attrs;
```

Pmarker_bundle

```
typedef struct {
  Pint                  type;
  Pfloat                size;
  Pint                  colr_ind;
} Pmarker_bundle;
```

Pmarker_facs

```
typedef struct {
  Pint_list             types;
  Pint                  num_sizes;
  Pfloat                nom_size;
  Pfloat                min_size;
  Pfloat                max_size;
  Pint              num_pred_inds;
} Pmarker_facs;
```

Pmatrix

```
typedef Pfloat      Pmatrix[3][3];
```

Pmatrix3

```
typedef Pfloat     Pmatrix3[4][4];
```

Pmod_mode

```
typedef enum {
  PMODE_NIVE,
  PMODE_UWOR,
  PMODE_UQUM
```

```
} Pmod_mode;
```

Pmore_simult_events

```
typedef enum {
    PSIMULT_NO_MORE,
    PSIMULT_MORE
} Pmore_simult_events;
```

N

Pnum_in

```
typedef struct {
    Pint                    loc;
    Pint                    stroke;
    Pint                    val;
    Pint                    choice;
    Pint                    pick;
    Pint                    string;
} Pnum_in;
```

O

Pop_mode

```
typedef enum {
    POP_REQ,
    POP_SAMPLE,
    POP_EVENT
} Pop_mode;
```

Popen_struct_status

```
typedef enum {
    PSTRUCT_NONE,
    PSTRUCT_OPEN
} Popen_struct_status;
```

P

Pparal

```
typedef struct {
    Ppoint3                 p;
    Ppoint3                 q;
    Ppoint3                 r;
} Pparal;
```

Ppat_rep

```
typedef struct {
    Pint_size               dims;
    Pint                   *colr_array;
} Ppat_rep;
```

Ppath_order

```
typedef enum {
    PORDER_TOP_FIRST,
    PORDER_BOTTOM_FIRST
} Ppath_order;
```

Ppick_data

```
typedef struct {
    union Ppick_pets {
        struct Ppick_pet_r1 {
        .../* implementation dep. */
        } pet_r1;
        .../* implem. defined PET's */
    } pets;
} Ppick_data;
```

Ppick_data3

```
typedef struct {
    union Ppick3_pets {
        struct Ppick3_pet_r1 {
        .../* implementation dep. */
        } pet_r1;
        .../* implem. defined PET's */
    } pets;
} Ppick_data3;
```

Ppick_path

```
typedef struct {
    Pint                    depth;
    Ppick_path_elem        *path_list;
} Ppick_path;
```

Ppick_path_elem

```
typedef struct {
    Pint                    struct_id;
    Pint                    pick_id;
    Pint                    elem_pos;
} Ppick_path_elem;
```

Ppoint

```
typedef struct {
  Pfloat          x;
  Pfloat          y;
} Ppoint;
```

Ppoint3

```
typedef struct {
  Pfloat          x;
  Pfloat          y;
  Pfloat          z;
} Ppoint3;
```

Ppoint_list

```
typedef struct {
  Pint            num_points;
  Ppoint          *points;
} Ppoint_list;
```

Ppoint_list3

```
typedef struct {
  Pint            num_points;
  Ppoint3         *points;
} Ppoint_list3;
```

Ppoint_list_list

```
typedef struct {
  Pint            num_point_lists;
  Ppoint_list     *point_lists;
} Ppoint_list_list;
```

Ppoint_list_list3

```
typedef struct {
  Pint            num_point_lists;
  Ppoint_list3    *point_lists;
} Ppoint_list_list3;
```

Pposted_struct

```
typedef struct {
  Pint            id;
  Pfloat          disp_pri;
} Pposted_struct;
```

Pposted_struct_list

```
typedef struct {
  Pint            num_postings;
  Pposted_struct  *postings;
} Pposted_struct_list;
```

Ppr_switch

```
typedef enum {
  PPR_OFF,
  PPR_ON
} Ppr_switch;
```

Pproj_type

```
typedef enum {
  PTYPE_PARAL,
  PTYPE_PERSPECT
} Pproj_type;
```

R

Prect

```
typedef struct {
  Ppoint          p;
  Ppoint          q;
} Prect;
```

Pref_flag

```
typedef enum {
  PFLAG_DEL,
  PFLAG_KEEP
} Pref_flag;
```

Pregen_flag

```
typedef enum {
  PFLAG_POSTPONE,
  PFLAG_PERFORM
} Pregen_flag;
```

Prel_pri

```
typedef enum {
  PPRI_HIGHER,
  PPRI_LOWER
} Prel_pri;
```

Prgb

```
typedef struct {
  Pfloat          red;
  Pfloat          green;
```

```
   Pfloat                blue;
} Prgb;
```

S

Psearch_dir

```
typedef enum {
   PDIR_BACKWARD,
   PDIR_FORWARD
} Psearch_dir;
```

Psearch_status

```
typedef enum {
   PSEARCH_STATUS_FAILURE,
   PSEARCH_STATUS_SUCCESS
} Psearch_status;
```

Pstore

```
typedef void    *Pstore;
```

Pstring_data

```
typedef struct {
   Pint                 in_buf_size;
   Pint                    init_pos;
   union Pstring_pets {
      struct Pstring_pet_r1 {
      .../* implementation dep. */
      } pet_r1;
      .../* implem. defined PET's */
   } pets;
} Pstring_data;
```

Pstring_data3

```
typedef struct {
   Pint                 in_buf_size;
   Pint                   init_pos;
   union Pstring3_pets {
      struct Pstring3_pet_r1 {
      .../* implementation dep. */
      } pet_r1;
      .../* implem. defined PET's */
   } pets;
} Pstring_data3;
```

Pstroke_data

```
typedef struct {
   Pint                  in_buf_size;
   Pint                     init_pos;
   Pfloat                 x_interval;
   Pfloat                 y_interval;
   Pfloat              time_interval;
   union Pstroke_pets {
      struct Pstroke_pet_r1 {
      .../* implementation dep. */
      } pet_r1;
      struct Pstroke_pet_r2 {
      .../* implementation dep. */
      } pet_r2;
      struct Pstroke_pet_r3 {
         Pmarker_attrs  marker_attrs;
         .../* implementation dep. */
      } pet_r3;
      struct Pstroke_pet_r4 {
         Pline_attrs      line_attrs;
         .../* implementation dep. */
      } pet_r4;
      .../* implem. defined PET's */
   } pets;
} Pstroke_data;
```

Pstroke_data3

```
typedef struct {
   Pint                  in_buf_size;
   Pint                     init_pos;
   Pfloat                 x_interval;
   Pfloat                 y_interval;
   Pfloat                 z_interval;
   Pfloat              time_interval;
   union Pstroke3_pets {
      struct Pstroke3_pet_r1 {
      .../* implementation dep. */
      } pet_r1;
      struct Pstroke3_pet_r2 {
      .../* implementation dep. */
      } pet_r2;
      struct Pstroke3_pet_r3 {
         Pmarker_attrs  marker_attrs;
         .../* implementation dep. */
      } pet_r3;
      struct Pstroke3_pet_r4 {
         Pline_attrs      line_attrs;
```

```
      .../* implementation dep. */
    } pet_r4;
    .../* implem. defined PET's */
  } pets;
} Pstroke_data3;
```

Pstruct_net_source

```
typedef enum {
  PNET_CSS,
  PNET_AR
} Pstruct_net_source;
```

Pstruct_st

```
typedef enum {
  PSTRUCT_ST_STCL,
  PSTRUCT_ST_STOP
} Pstruct_st;
```

Pstruct_status

```
typedef enum {
  PSTRUCT_STATUS_NON_EXISTENT,
  PSTRUCT_STATUS_EMPTY,
  PSTRUCT_STATUS_NOT_EMPTY
} Pstruct_status;
```

Psys_st

```
typedef enum {
  PSYS_ST_PHCL,
  PSYS_ST_PHOP
} Psys_st;
```

T

Ptext_align

```
typedef struct {
  Phor_text_align      hor;
  Pvert_text_align     vert;
} Ptext_align;
```

Ptext_bundle

```
typedef struct {
  Pint                 font;
  Ptext_prec           prec;
  Pfloat               char_expan;
  Pfloat               char_space;
  Pint                 colr_ind;
} Ptext_bundle;
```

Ptext_facs

```
typedef struct {
  Pint                 num_font_precs;
  Ptext_font_prec      *font_precs;
  Pint                 num_char_hts;
  Pfloat               min_char_ht;
  Pfloat               max_char_ht;
  Pint                 num_char_expans;
  Pfloat               min_char_expan;
  Pfloat               max_char_expan;
  Pint                 num_pred_inds;
} Ptext_facs;
```

Ptext_font_prec

```
typedef struct {
  Pint                 font;
  Ptext_prec           prec;
} Ptext_font_prec;
```

Ptext_path

```
typedef enum {
  PPATH_RIGHT,
  PPATH_LEFT,
  PPATH_UP,
  PPATH_DOWN
} Ptext_path;
```

Ptext_prec

```
typedef enum {
  PPREC_STRING,
  PPREC_CHAR,
  PPREC_STROKE
} Ptext_prec;
```

U

Pupd_st

```
typedef enum {
  PUPD_NOT_PEND,
```

```
  PUPD_PEND
} Pupd_st;
```

V

Pval_data

```
typedef struct {
  Pfloat                low_value;
  Pfloat               high_value;
  union Pval_pets {
    struct Pval_pet_r1 {
    .../* implementation dep. */
    } pet_r1;
    .../* implem. defined PET's */
  } pets;
} Pval_data;
```

Pval_data3

```
typedef struct {
  Pfloat              low_value;
  Pfloat             high_value;
  union Pval3_pets {
    struct Pval3_pet_r1 {
    .../* implementation dep. */
    } pet_r1;
    .../* implem. defined PET's */
  } pets;
} Pval_data3;
```

Pvec

```
typedef struct {
  Pfloat                delta_x;
  Pfloat                delta_y;
} Pvec;
```

Pvec3

```
typedef struct {
  Pfloat                delta_x;
  Pfloat                delta_y;
  Pfloat                delta_z;
} Pvec3;
```

Pvert_text_align

```
typedef enum {
  PVERT_NORM,
  PVERT_TOP,
  PVERT_CAP,
  PVERT_HALF,
  PVERT_BASE,
  PVERT_BOTTOM
} Pvert_text_align;
```

Pview_map

```
typedef struct {
  Plimit                      win;
  Plimit                  proj_vp;
} Pview_map;
```

Pview_map3

```
typedef struct {
  Plimit                      win;
  Plimit3                 proj_vp;
  Pproj_type            proj_type;
  Ppoint3          proj_ref_point;
  Pfloat               view_plane;
  Pfloat               back_plane;
  Pfloat              front_plane;
} Pview_map3;
```

Pview_rep

```
typedef struct {
  Pmatrix              ori_matrix;
  Pmatrix              map_matrix;
  Plimit               clip_limit;
  Pclip_ind               xy_clip;
} Pview_rep;
```

Pview_rep3

```
typedef struct {
  Pmatrix3             ori_matrix;
  Pmatrix3             map_matrix;
  Plimit3              clip_limit;
  Pclip_ind               xy_clip;
  Pclip_ind             back_clip;
  Pclip_ind            front_clip;
} Pview_rep3;
```

Pvisual_st

```
typedef enum {
  PVISUAL_ST_CORRECT,
  PVISUAL_ST_DEFER,
  PVISUAL_ST_SIMULATED
} Pvisual_st;
```

W

Pws_cat

```
typedef enum {
  PCAT_OUT,
  PCAT_IN,
  PCAT_OUTIN,
  PCAT_MO,
  PCAT_MI
} Pws_cat;
```

Pws_class

```
typedef enum {
  PCLASS_VEC,
  PCLASS_RASTER,
  PCLASS_OTHER
} Pws_class;
```

Pws_dep_ind

```
typedef enum {
  PWS_INDEP,
  PWS_DEP
} Pws_dep_ind;
```

Pws_st

```
typedef enum {
  PWS_ST_WSCL,
  PWS_ST_WSOP
} Pws_st;
```

Pws_st_tables

```
typedef struct {
  Pint                  line_bundles;
  Pint                  mark_bundles;
  Pint                  text_bundles;
  Pint                   int_bundles;
  Pint                  edge_bundles;
  Pint                      pat_reps;
  Pint                     colr_reps;
  Pint                     view_reps;
} Pws_st_tables;
```

Bibliography

The Standards Documents

This manual was based on the following standards documents. See the Preface for more information on these documents.

International Standard for Information Processing Systems—Computer Graphics—Programmer's Hierarchical Interactive Graphics System (PHIGS), American National Standard ISO/IEC 9592–1, X3.144–1988.

International Standard for Information Processing Systems—Computer Graphics—Programmer's Hierarchical Interactive Graphics System (PHIGS), Part 4 Plus Lumiere und Surfaces, PHIGS PLUS ISO/IEC 9592–4:1992(E).

International Standard for Information Systems Computer Graphics—Programmer's Hierarchical Interactive Graphics System (PHIGS) FORTRAN Binding, ISO/IEC 9593–1:1989(E).

International Standard for Information Systems Computer Graphics—Programmer's Hierarchical Interactive Graphics System (PHIGS) C Binding, ISO/IEC 9593–4:1991(E).

Computer Graphics Metafile for the Storage and Transfer of Picture Description Information, ANSI Document X3.122–1986.

PHIGS Books

Refer to the *Preface* for more information on these books.

Howard, T., Hewitt, W, Hubbold, R, Wyrwas, K. (1991). *A Practical Introduction to PHIGS and PHIGS PLUS*, Reading, MA: Addison–Wesley.

Gaskins, T. (1992). *PHIGS Programming Manual*, Sebastopol, CA: O'Reilly and Associates.

Kosko, L. (1992). *PHIGS Reference Manual*, Sebastopol, CA: O'Reilly and Associates.

Computer Graphics Documentation

Newman W.F., and Sproull, R.F. (1979). *Principles of Interactive Computer Graphics*, 2nd ed., New York, NY: McGraw–Hill.

Foley, J. D., and Van Dam, A. (1990). *Computer Graphics: Principles and Practices*, 2nd ed., Reading, MA: Addison–Wesley.

Rogers, D. F., and Alan, J. A. (1976). *Mathematical Elements for Computer Graphics*, New York, NY: McGraw–Hill.

Rogers, D. F., (1985). *Procedural Elements for Computer Graphics*, New York, NY: McGraw–Hill.

Patterson, M. A., and Patterson, R. R. (1986). *Projective Geometry and its Applications*, Englewood Cliffs, NJ: Prentice–Hall.

Gouraud, H., (1971). *Computer Display of Curved Surfaces*, Pd.D thesis, University of Utah.

X Windows Documentation

Jones, O. *Introduction to the X Window System*, Englewood Cliffs, NJ: Prentice Hall.

Asente, P. J., and Swick, R.R. *The X Window System Toolkit*, Bedford, MA: Digital Press.

The Definitive Guides to the X Window System, Volumes 0 – 5, Sebastopol, CA: O'Reilly and Associates.

PEX Documentation

The following are the available PEX standard documents:

- *PEX Protocol Specification Version 5.0*, September 1990, MIT X Consortium, Cambridge, MA.
- *PEX Protocol Encoding Version 5.0*, September 1990, MIT X Consortium, Cambridge, MA.
- *PEX Protocol Specification Version 5.1P* (public review draft), May 5, 1992, Paula Womack, ed., MIT X Consortium, Cambridge Mass.
- *PEX Protocol Encoding Version 5.1P*, (public review draft) May 5, 1992, Paula Womack, ed., MIT X Consortium, Cambridge, MA.

For more information about PEX, see the following articles:

- Rost, R., Friedberg, J., and Nishimoto, P. (1989). "PEX: a Network–Transparent 3D Graphics System." *IEEE Computer Graphics and Applications,* July, p. 14.
- Hess, M. (1990). "Flexing PEX." *SunTech Journal,* Winter, p. 71.
- Rost, R. (1990). *Understanding the PEX Rendering Pipeline*, Randy J. Rost, 1990, Bedford, MA: Digital Equipment Corporation.
- Clifford, McConnell, Friedberg, (1988). "The Development of PEX, A Three Dimensional Graphics Extension to X11." *Proc. Eurographics 88.*

Index

A

D

E

F

G

Q

R

S

T

U

V

W

X

Z

PHIGS Routines

PHIGS Routines (continued)

PHIGS Routines (continued)

PHIGS Routines (continued)

PHIGS Routines (continued)

PHIGS Routines (continued)

PHIGS Routines (continued)